The Moral Resonance of Arab Media

HARVARD MIDDLE EASTERN MONOGRAPHS
XXXVIII

The Moral Resonance of Arab Media

Audiocassette Poetry and Culture in Yemen

Flagg Miller

DISTRIBUTED FOR THE
CENTER FOR MIDDLE EASTERN STUDIES
OF HARVARD UNIVERSITY BY
HARVARD UNIVERSITY PRESS
CAMBRIDGE, MASSACHUSETTS
LONDON, ENGLAND

ISBN-13: 978-0-932885-32-6
ISBN-10: 0-932885-32-2
Printed in the United States of America

Library of Congress Cataloging-in-Publication Data

Miller, Flagg.
The moral resonance of Arab media : audiocassette poetry and culture in Yemen / Flagg Miller. — 1st ed.
p. cm. — (Harvard Middle Eastern monograph series ; 38)
Includes bibliographical references and index.
ISBN 978-0-932885-32-6 (paper back)
1. Arabic poetry—Yemen—History and criticism. 2. Arabic poetry—21st century—History and criticism. 3. Audiobooks—Yemen. I. Title. II. Series.

PJ8007.2.M53 2007
892.7′17—dc22

2007026282

To the teachers in my life, especially my parents, my brother, and my companion in song, Gina Bloom

LETTER TO A CORPSE *(RISĀLAH ILĀ MAĪT)*

Khaledi said: How much yearning and hope?
  Aching, ache upon ache, has availed me nothing.
Craving and yearning empty, they have no meaning.
  I cannot recall my heart or hopes . . . such deceit. . . .
Never forgive that maligned era that misled and separated us,
  Separating those in the group from their own,
How my companions were lost, and we became lost ourselves
    after them—
  Each crossing a mountain, one to the left and another
    right. . . .

Where is our family, our beloved? Where have they gone?
  Where is the accompanying friend? Where am I to him?
Where are those whom I used to see with my own right eye?
  Our obliged prayers and our laws went with them.
Where are those spliced from the world ahead of me,
  Those to whom the world was so wretched?
Where are those who were with us, wherever we went?
  What do we say or tell those who ask about them?

No one has come from the cemetery to tell us.
  Are they in fire or in heaven?
Not a letter from the corpse allays our concerns
  About his health. How is he beneath that grave?
That the radio might tell him about us!
  Why, my heart can bring him not a single word, visible or
    hidden.
Or that a wireless telegraph could lead us there!
  Why, I would speak to the blessed corpse, to his ear.
I would explain to him how my gaunt heart suffers
  And how, after him, the tears of my eyes flow as streams
    upon my cheeks.
And yet I can seek consolation from nothing but empty loss. . . .

  How I was comfortable at his side with his poetic craft!
Yes, I taught him craft until he excelled and savored it.
  And a thousand of my verses were found in his song.

I have no other task but the path of poetry and singing
And the plucking of strings, the pursuit and delight of my comrade.
Remember his beauty, the winking of his fair eyes,
And the good words that flowed from his tongue? . . .

Never forgive death, which has brutalized us with such violence.
(Or shall I call with a voice of solace and peace? . . .)
Yet if cursing death were possible, I would curse, if only for the health of my own house!
I would curse death this very moment, a hundred curses. . . .

But from fate to fate we surrender,
Rebuking not death, from which there is no absolution.

—Shayef al-Khaledi (1932–98), from Alone and Wound-Struck (Waḥdah wa Min Qarḥin Yaqraḥ) (1980)

Contents

List of Maps and Figures

Acknowledgments

I express gratitude to the poet ʿAbdallah ʿAlī Jibrān al-Manāʿ, whose thoughtfulness enabled me to conduct my research in Yafiʿ and to endure hardships with some of the finest companionship I have known. I also thank his entire family, whose appreciation of music and poetry was limitless. Their assistance with interpreting poems contributed significantly to the insights of this book. I also am indebted to the poet Muhammad al-Wardī, whose kindness and extraordinary generosity were inspiring. Without his active promotion of my research in Yafiʿ, I would have accomplished far less than I did. I also thank his family for their hospitality.

Over the course of several years of research in Yemen, many others offered invaluable assistance and understanding, and I regret being able to mention only a few of them. To Shayef al-Khāledī, much of this book is devoted. Although my twenty-one visits with Khaledi were never long enough, his poetry has provided me with memories that are continually renewed as I have grown older. I also thank ʿAli ʿAbdallah al-Ghulābī, who first introduced me to Yafiʿ; Qasem al-Maḥbashī, with his intuitive insights into popular culture; ʿAli ʿAbdu Sālem and the associates of the "Ḥambalah" Archival Center in Aden, for their ongoing collaborative efforts; and the versatile poet Ahmad al-ʿAwāḍī. I also thank the president of Sanaa University, ʿAbd al-ʿAziz al-

Maqāliḥ, for his ongoing support of my work and ʿAbdallah al-Baraddūnī, Ahmad Bu Mahdī, Khaled Sūrī, and Nazar Ghānem for their profound insights into poetry and song. Of particular help in navigating through the labyrinthine world of cassette poetry were cassette-shop employees and fans. Foremost among them is ʿAli Muḥammad al-Ḥāj "Abu Jināḥ" and his son ʿAbd al-Majid, who endured my barrage of questions and tolerated repeated visits to their shop with gracious hospitality, but I also single out Qahtan al-Khalīfī, ʿAbdallah Ṣāleḥ al-Kawmānī, Ahmad al-Kibsī, Saleh al-Maṭarī, and ʿAli Muḥammad Qaḥṭānī.

While in Yafiʿ, literally or in spirit, I sat with thousands of others during afternoon *qāt*-chewing sessions, an important setting for chatting and taking notes. Some of my most stimulating discussions about regional culture and history were held with Yafiʿi scholars and intellectuals Zain Muḥammad al-Quʿaīṭī, Muhammad Jarḥūm, Mahmud al-Sālemī, Muhsen Dayyān, Muhammad Muḥsen al-ʿAmrī, Ahmad Zīr, Masʿud Ṭāleb, Khaled al-Rashīdī, Fadl Muḥsen, and Ahmad al-Wattāḥī. I also particularly valued my acquaintances with Yafiʿi Americans in Dearborn and Chicago, including Muhammad ʿAbd al-Rabb Munaṣṣer, Shaikh ʿAbd al-Qader Harharah, Jalal Harharah, ʿAbdallah Jaʿmūm, Saleh Nājī, ʿAli Sālem al-Ḥaṭībī, and Ahmad Ṣulṭān. For poetry, the most rewarding sources were usually the poets themselves. I particularly thank Muhammad Sālem al-Kuhālī, Naser Aḥmad al-Kaʿbī, Ahmad Ḥusaīn Bin ʿAskar, Yahya ʿAlī al-Sulaīmānī, Zaid Ḥusaīn al-Sulaīmānī, Khaled al-Khāledī, and ʿAli al-Ṭōlaqī. I also relished the opportunity to talk with some of the region's cassette singers, notably among them the older masters Haithem Qāsem and Salem Saʿīd al-Bāraʿī, as well as ʿAli Bin Jāber al-Yazīdī and ʿAli Ṣāleḥ Bin Jarḥūm. No small amount of thanks also goes to the employees of the Cooperative Bank in Labʿūs, especially Fadl Bin Yahyā and Saleh ʿAissā, who provided me with lodging and friendship during my first three months in the region. And finally, I am deeply appreciative of the assistance of regional leaders Salah al-ʿAbbādī, Qasem Thābit al-ʿAissāʾī, Shaikh ʿAbd al-Rabb, Shaikh ʿAbd al-Quwī, Shaikh

Faḍl al-Naqīb, Shaikh ʿAbdallah Bin ʿAtīq, Shaikh Husain al-ʿAṭṭāf, and Saleh ʿUbādī, as well as many others who have continued to demonstrate public support for my work.

Fieldwork research was made possible through the generous support of the Fulbright-Hays Program, the Social Science Research Council (IDRF), the Academy for Educational Development (NSEP-1995) (whose eight-month service requirement I met by teaching anthropology and literature), and the American Institute for Yemeni Studies. For research guidance and technical support while in Yemen, I relied on a host of extraordinary directors of the American Institute for Yemeni Studies, including Marta Colburn, Chris Edens, and Noha Sadek. I also thank the staff at the Yemeni Centre for Research and Studies in Sanaa and the German consulate for lodging accommodations.

When I began working on this project, I also received support from the University of Michigan and from a number of colleagues there. In particular, I thank Brinkley Messick, whose rigorous attention to textuality and discourse helped me understand how audiocassette culture could be a fruitful research topic. I am also indebted to Alexander Knysh, whose friendship and insights into Muslim moral inquiry helped me approach Arabic poetry with greater humility, and to Bruce Mannheim. While at the University of Michigan, two invaluable years of financial support were covered by the Institute for the Humanities and the Horace Rackham School.

I also had the good fortune of being able to conduct research under the sponsorship of several other universities. In 1993 and 1994, I spent eight months at Oxford University's Institute for Social and Cultural Anthropology. While at Oxford, I found no greater intellectual stimulus than from Michael Gilsenan, whose tutorials on social theory later became foundational, and also from Paul Dresch, who helped me to navigate a bewildering mass of field data. I am appreciative, too, for assistance from Peter Rivière and Institute administrator Isabella Birkin. From 2001 to 2003, I spent two years at the University of Chicago, rarely a day passing without an engaging discussion. In particular, I am indebted to the Franke Institute for the Humanities, where I received a postdoctoral fellowship, and give special thanks to Robert von Hallberg and Matthias Regan. It was during that year that I wrote much of chapter 5, a version of which was published in 2005 in volume 32 of the *American Ethnologist.* Thanks are due to the journal's meticulous staff and readers. My second year at the University of Chicago was spent with the department of anthropology, and I am deeply grateful to the vigorous support of Michael Silverstein and the participants in the 2002–2003 communication and politics workshop. During those years, I also benefited from helpful comments and encouragement from Paul Friedrich, Greg Urban, Asif Agha, Steven Feld, Susan Gal, Danilyn Rutherford, Martin Stokes, Victor Friedman, Philip Schuyler, Eric Skjon, and my fellow "Kepketarians" Robert Moore and Jan Blommaert.

The final revisions of this book were conducted in 2004 to 2006 at Lawrence University, whose faculty and library staff provided great support, and also at the University of Wisconsin at Madison, where I benefited from several write-up grants from the Graduate Research Fellowship program and the Institute for the Humanities. Special thanks are due to my generous colleagues in Madison, especially in the anthropology, religious studies, and Middle East studies programs. Most esteemed, at the end of the road, are also those at Harvard University Press who helped shepherd this project along smoothly. I would especially like to acknowledge the readers who offered trenchant comments on matters large and small that made this a much better book. Thanks is due, additionally, to the British Library for assistance with sources.

Friends and colleagues throughout the years have helped me persevere through bouts of intellectual pandemonium. To Steve Caton, fellow intellectual traveler and mentor, I cannot offer enough thanks. From the earliest stages of my work, his acumen in research guidance was matched only by his ardor for independent thinking. For reading comments and discussion, I am especially grateful to Jonathan Schofer and also to Shelagh Weir,

Isaac Hollander, Andrew Shryock, Alaina Lemon, Margot Badran, Mikhail Rodionov, Lucine Taminian, Dan Varisco, Najwa Adra, and Chris Butler. I struggle to express my appreciation for those who have been closest to this project. These include my parents, Tooey and Ann, and also my brother, Frazier, who have taught me to imagine with open eyes. They also include Gina Bloom, whom I thank for her no-nonsense advice on intellectual priorities, her meticulous readings of my chapters, and her unending personal encouragement. Finally, I am most grateful to the American Field Service cultural-exchange program and my Tunisian hosts, the Majdoub family, who, during a post–high-school year, introduced me to the Arab world and to the majesties of vernacular Arabic.

Orthography and Translation

Transliterating Arabic into English, especially vernacular Arabic, always involves difficult decisions between loyalty to the original text and accessibility for the reader. As a general standard, I rely on the transliteration format used by the *International Journal of Middle East Studies*. Some of the characters in this format will be unfamiliar to non-Arabic speakers:

VOWELS

[a] as in *but* or the [a] in *abut*
[ā] as in *bat* or *odd*
[i] as in *bit*
[ī] as in *beet*
[u] as in *put* or the [o] in *corner*
[ū] as in *boot*
[ō] as in *boat*
[ē] as in *bait*

CONSONANTS

[ṣ] an [s] that is pronounced with a more open dental cavity
[dh] pronounced like the middle consonant in the word *bother*
[ẓ] pronounced as a [dh] that is more hollow-sounding and velarized (or "emphatic")

[ṭ] a [t] that is similarly velarized
[kh] a grating, breathy fricative pronounced in the back of thethroat, like the Hebrew sound in *lachaim* ("to life")
[gh] a similar sound, though voiced
[q] pronounced deeper in the epiglottis than the English [q] and with a slight burst of air
[ʿ] pronounced through a constriction of the epiglottis, usually just before vowels
[ḥ] a breathy [h] sound that emanates from approximately the same area of the throat
[ʾ] the *hamzah,* a glottal stop that differs from the character [ʿ] in being reversed

Additionally, vernacular southern Yemeni Arabic features the nonstandard pronunciation of several other vowels and consonants.[1] Diphthongs such as [aw] and [aī] are typically converted in daily talk and casual recitation to long vowels [ō] and [ē]; however, they are not uncommonly maintained in song and more formal recitation. The letter [ḍ], pronounced in classical Arabic as a velarized dental stop, becomes a fricative, pronounced identical to the letter [ẓ] (see above). The letter [j] is pronounced as a hard velar [g] as in *game,* although a bit more fronted. In fact, to assist readers in pronunciation, I have substituted most [j] for [g] consonants in vernacular Yafiʿi texts. In this particular case, the only exceptions are certain older names, older verbal formulas, and words that have retained their associations with literate registers of Arabic, such as *jiwāb*. Finally, the *hamzah* [ʾ] is written when it is pronounced in song or where it is essential to clarifying a word. Otherwise, the *hamzah* becomes a [y], as in *bahāyim,* since this typically occurs in vernacular pronunciation.

To further assist with the translation of vernacular Yemeni, I have adopted a number of transcriptive modifications that accord with dialectal pronunciation. Occasionally, the definite article before nouns, either *al-* or its equivalent but with a consonant that matches the first consonant of its parent, becomes *am-*

or *um-,* a substitution that occurs in a variety of regions in Yemen. When cited independently, plural nouns tend to be kept in their singular form with an added [s] rather than being rendered as complex plurals. To distinguish words ending in the Arabic *tā marbūṭah* from words ending in long or broken vowels, I write *tā marbūṭah* consonants with an [h], as in *ʿarabiyyah*. The vowels of verbs are especially tricky. In most cases, the initial vowel of imperfect verbs is pronounced [i], as in *tibdhil* and *nirtagī.* When followed by an emphatic or uvular consonant, the vowel frequently becomes [a], as in *naḥkum, yaṣlaḥ,* and *yaqarrib.* Furthermore, when the initial vowel in verbs is [u], the middle vowel is frequently pronounced in kind, as in *tuḥruq* or *yuflut.*

Poetry and some verbal expressions receive special treatment. To convey the original sound of utterances as they are pronounced in Arabic, I convert definite articles on words beginning with "sun letters" to their equivalents (for example, *al-shaʿb* becomes *ash-shaʿb*). Since most of the poetry I examine in this book is sung, I also adopt certain transcriptions to reflect the rhythms of sung verse, which are different than recited verse.[2] Thus, I group syllabic clusters together, sometimes eliding vowels, to convey the sound of verses when sung: *min al-awṣār* becomes *min l-awṣār,* for example. Alternatively, a [y] is sometimes added where rhythmically suitable: *aṭ-ṭay[i]bī* rather than *aṭ-ṭaībī.* And consonants, usually [a] or [i], are added in brackets, as in the change just cited, to indicate that such vowels are not usually pronounced during vernacular speech.

When mentioning proper names that are not in transcriptions of poetry, I have drastically simplified the transliteration system in efforts to avoid imposing an orthographic "other" on people discussed in this book. First names are written without transliteration, except for the [ʿ] and [ʾ]: *Ahmad, ʿAwad, Fathiyyah.* Individuals' titles, such as *Abu* and *Bu,* and also *Qur'an* and *Allah* are written without transliteration. I transliterate individuals' middle and last names only when they are first mentioned in the main text of every chapter. I have also elided the definite article before last names (after their first mention). Furthermore, to prevent mispronunciations I have changed the final [i] in many cases to [e], as in Khaledi and Malek. As for place names, I generally present them in transliteration, except for better-known places that appear in such newspapers as the *New York Times,* as well as Yafiʿ. Finally, I capitalize the titles of Arabic source material, as I do other source material. It seems to me that computerized transcriptive fonts preclude the need to reference Arabic sources in lowercase letters.

Finally, all translations of Qurʾanic verse are adapted from ʿAbdullah Yusuf ʿAli's beautifully revised rendition.[3] Historical dates divided into two sets of numbers indicate Gregorian and Muslim *hijrī* standards.

NOTES

1. For a general introduction to Yafiʿi dialectal features, see Martine Vanhove, "Notes on the Arabic Dialectal Area of Yafiʿ, (Yemen)," *Proceedings of the Seminar for Arabian Studies* 25 (1995): 141–52.
2. For a fuller discussion of variations between sung and recited verse in Yemen, see Carlo Landberg, *Études sur les dialectes de l'Arabie méridionale: Haḍramoût,* (Leiden: E. J. Brill, 1901), 1:205–06.
3. *The Holy Quran: Text, Translation, and Commentary* (New Delhi: Kitab Bhavan, 2004).

The Moral Resonance of Arab Media

Introduction

THE MORAL AUTHORITY OF MEDIA APPERCEPTION IN THE ARAB WORLD

The global proliferation of media technologies in recent decades has spelled some distress for the study of verbal culture in the Arab world. As researchers detail the popularity of these visual technologies—including print media, radio, audiocassettes, network and satellite-broadcast television, home videos, and the Internet—evidence seems to suggest that Arabic audiences are increasingly speaking the same language. Not only are vocabularies being standardized and discourses homogenized, but audiences' communal identities are being made uniformly public. As privatized media networks encroach on the senescent programming of state-run media, diverse audiences affiliate with the roles, lifestyles, and dreams of consumers. Given the momentum of such collective mediation, a study of the political implications of Yemeni audiences' verbal habits of interchange and reflexivity may strike some as merely corroborative. Many accounts of Arab political formations have given up listening to what Arabs have to say and subordinate matters of persuasion—so central to political rhetoric in the Arab world—to the totalizing effects of ideology. In the wake of the terrorist attacks in the United

States on September 11, 2001, new books have emerged offering readings of purportedly core cultural texts, especially those available to Western audiences through translations. Amid token nods to institutional anchoring, recourse is often made to popular suspicions of unchanging civilizational essences.

This book offers a more responsible approach to the Arab political imagination by focusing on culture. Its point of embarkation is the struggle of poets to craft moral authority in Yemen. Attention is given, in particular, to how poets have used media technologies, especially audiocassettes, to promote and preserve their relevance for contemporary audiences. Arab poets have long composed verse without the assistance of writing, and oral traditions, often accompanied by musical performance, lie at the center of this book. Poets in Yemen have also long used writing in conjunction with some of the Arabian Peninsula's most venerable institutions of administration, law, and literary activity. Since writing has been instrumental to Islam and a range of moral discourses, material signs of writing—pages, pens, ink, script, alphabetic letters, and so forth—readily invoke a metaphysics of written inscription, knowledge, and authority that can be deployed toward moral and political ends. Audio-recording technologies, notably the audiocassette, have contributed a new set of physical and metaphysical variables to the demands of versification.

As I consider poets' work to explore continuities and changes in moral knowledge, I examine the relations between these various forms of oral, written, and audio-recording media. Although each medium favors certain competences in organizing, replicating, and selectively transmitting knowledge, media become salient sites of moral inquiry for Yemenis through culturally specific ways of knowing. By no means unified, these patterns of knowledge are multiple and hierarchized by age, gender, status, ethnicity, and other categories of social identity and are best approached through the lives and works of specific communities and individuals. I devote considerable attention, particularly in latter chapters, to the poet Shayef Muḥammad al-

Khāledī, whose imaginative engagements with media have guided many Yemenis in matters small and large. In examining his and other artists' efforts to cope with a revitalization of state-sponsored discourses of tribalism, especially since the country's unification in 1990, I argue that Yemenis are creating new ways to contextualize tribal identity in metropolitan and cosmopolitan spheres of public activism.

If traditional and modern forms of media are instrumental in contemporary moral debates, they become so within specific contexts of usage. In his study of Muslim knowledge and spirit possession on the island of Mayotte in the Indian Ocean, anthropologist Michael Lambek suggests that "If knowledge provides a means to the acquisition of power, morality speaks to its use. Morality has to do with evaluating and directing the uses to which knowledge is put, attempting to constrain the power of those who have it and rendering them accountable for their actions."[1] Such an approach invites us to remain wary of theoretical models of media influence and social authority and reasserts the value of the ethnographic study of everyday media practices. Media culture, whether elaborated locally or globally, is assembled contextually (or "pragmatically") by reflecting and engaged human beings.

Many of the book's basic analytic frameworks are guided by linguistic anthropology's interests in the social embedding of language. Media acquire meaning through verbal acts that are shaped by habits both in and beyond language in sequences of discursive and nondiscursive signs (or "texts"),[2] and those verbal acts define how knowledge can be acquired, condensed, and ultimately made to bear authority. Approaching media culture through textual practice grants us critical insights into persistent older paradigms, and foremost among them is what I call the objective fallacy of much new-media theory: the tendency to treat media forms as culturally neutral, independent variables.[3] When new media—typically identified as the radically decentralized technologies of the late twentieth century, such as the audiocassette, the telephone, the fax machine, the Internet, desktop publishing, and so forth—are presumed to be completely different from the earlier, clunkier, more centralized old media, uniform cross-cultural shifts in social imagination can be traced. Such an approach sidelines one of the most generative contributions of the concept of modernity to social theory—namely, the idea that categories of modern innovation are discursive and aesthetic and can be highly contested and variable over time. Such an approach also typically recurs to Western modernization paradigms that associate literacy, orality, and authorship with stages of social maturation.

In challenging such assumptions, this book argues that media forms are highly contested in the politics of representation in the Arab world. In fact, I suggest that historically elaborated reflections on media circulation constitute the moral validity and bearing of much authoritative political language. To consider how this is so, I privilege ethnography, studying how concepts of media are informed by a single community's efforts to manage its resources and collective identity.[4] Integral to this ethnographic project are the community's imaginative techniques for associating media with more general processes of moral formation. These techniques are explored, most explicitly, through Yemenis' efforts to assemble text artifacts, including poems, songs, cassettes, letters, and written and oral narratives.

The setting of this study is Yafiʿ, a region of southern Yemen defined by two interdependent social congeries: a mountainous homeland population that approaches 175,000 inhabitants and a smaller diasporic community that resides elsewhere in Yemen, especially in Aden, and also abroad. The people in Yafiʿ are typical of many Yemenis in relying on seasonal rains to irrigate highland terraces. Like many Yemenis, they also engage in trade and commerce to help substantiate their means of living. Modern conveniences are scarce. When I first arrived in the Yafiʿi highlands in 1995, paved roads were not widespread, and the first centralized electric power station had just been built, although Yafiʿis showed tremendous ingenuity in securing resources from beyond the region. In Yafiʿ, media technologies have long provided an important means for accessing information and wider contacts and for standardizing the region's legal, administrative, and economic systems.

Nevertheless, for the Yafiʿi poets, singers, and audiences who are the focus of this study, as for Yemenis generally, media forms are not transparent but opaque—as well as shiny, fragrant, wet, sticky, noisy, and decomposable. The sensory qualities of media, which are foregrounded through a heightened attention to language and sound, disrupt claims to impartial "information" that might be made by authoritative media channels, whether written, printed, audiovisual, electronic, spoken, or sung. When words become substantively moody, their usual associations erode into an entanglement of complex sensations with objectual forms—with things that can move in the world and become quantified (heavy or light, short or long, enumerable, metrically apportioned). Such experiential synesthesia constitutes the power of poetry. But such reflections on the material accretions of language are also general products of the human imagination, which we might understand as "the processes with which the unique individual puts together his knowledge, perceptions, and emotions."[5] Lingering imaginatively on the language-laden cargo of media, as Yemeni cassette poets, singers, and audiences invite us to do, allows us to reassess some general categories of expressive form and the conventions of social and political practice that sustain them. From this linguistic and phenomenological perspective, I argue that media provide users with moral leverage in calling public attention both to imbalances in systems of social authority and to ways to rectify those imbalances.

The moral credibility of media forms can be partly assessed by breaking them down into their sensory components, and Yemenis prioritize the qualities of these components in culturally specific ways. Culture, I suggest, lies in transmitted ways of knowing how to clothe society's needs in imaginative form. Although a culture can perpetuate ways of knowing and imagining that are harmful as well as beneficial, here I explore how debates over the nature and effects of media have positive cultural effects by providing signposts for those who seek creative solutions to social problems. Such an approach requires careful attention to be paid to the ethnographic particularities of social and political life and also to broader distinctions of morality, ethics, and aesthetics.

A few clarifications are in order. While I consider *morality* primarily through rules of social propriety and obligation that are formulated in discourses about authority and knowledge, I explore *ethics* in more contingent and pragmatic terms as conduct or behavior that establishes practical standards for healthy social interaction. Moral ideals are typically expressed in relation to society's key symbols, while ethical ideals foreground actions designed to achieve results. *Aesthetics* highlight the valuation of symbols, actions, and other orienting phenomena in the world. In their sensory unfolding, aesthetic values convey ideals of being that lend a playful, dynamic potentiality to notions of selfhood. Insofar as they provide frontiers of recognition, aesthetics are especially important to understanding historical shifts in moral and ethical norms and ultimately prove instrumental for Yemenis who seek to identify and redress enduring hierarchies in modern norms of public discourse. By incorporating such moral, ethical, and aesthetic considerations into a study of media, I aim to expand our vocabulary for assessing the complex power of the imagination in political life. Even as I focus on poetry and language to understand the cultural aspects of media usage, I find attending to such matters of moral philosophy helpful to understanding how social justice is addressed at cognitive, psychological, behavioral, and material levels.

As a first step toward understanding Yemenis' resourceful imaginations, I devote considerable attention in this book to a general outline of the signifying logic, or "semiotics," of media apperception. In much public life, some of the most reliable forms of knowledge are conveyed through vision in graphic signs. A proverb familiar to generations of Yafi'is as well as Muslims worldwide, for example, relates that "The gap between good and evil is only four fingers wide" *(bēn al-khēr wa-sh-sharr arbaʿ banān)*.[6] If the palm of the hand is placed on the cheek, only four fingers separate the eye (the keenest sensor of good) from the ear and its temptations to hearing evil. The power of graphic signs to convey commonsense truths about the world is reinforced by Yemenis in numerous idioms, poetic tropes, and argumentative turns. Indeed, the normative equation of visible things with shared knowledge and ethical orientations is documented in studies of Indo-European linguistic communities,[7] Buddhist phenomenology,[8] global nonmarket-exchange practices,[9] and popular traditions of Islam.[10] Things that are seen can be identified, fixed, and controlled.

Graphic things also circulate well. As publicly recognized signs, visible objects can serve as forms of currency that can be passed around to affirm collective ties and obligations. Much talk and poetry about media circulation in Yemen recurs to graphic aesthetics. Accessibility also brings with it a ripe potential for dissent. When diverse viewers can all claim to see and some allege the ability to do so exceptionally well, graphic aesthetics can become a populist resource. For marginalized communities whose access to revered sources of learning and power is restricted, such signs offer a valuable communicative currency. Disadvantaged by norms of public affiliation and identity, those who build consensus over graphic truths in the world—the beauty of a person, the delight of an object, the darkness of injustice—can affirm their own evaluative norms and establish bonds that are otherwise difficult to assert.

As a medium of apperception, graphic signs provide only the first stage of knowledge. The proverb about the eye and ear also hints at more complex hermeneutics: where the moral faculties of seeing and hearing are only four fingers apart, each implicates the other and undermines its unique association with good or evil. Since good seeing is almost malignant, and evil hearing almost beneficial, reliable knowledge must be sought in more imaginative recesses beyond the faculties of sight or sound alone. Although graphic aesthetics can provide immediate signs of moral order, they become more generative as portals to more culturally attuned ways of knowing. Throughout the book, highland Yafiʿis are shown as cultivating such indigenous knowledge by juxtaposing constructs of, on the one hand, an ecumenical world of pluralism, production, literacy, progress, giddy affect, alienation, and risk that is frequently coded as metropolitan and, on the other hand, a world of more particular, chthonic, tribal, traditional, embodied, coherent, and recuperative inclinations that is coded as rural. As Yemeni nationalism spread in stride with an expanding recording industry, metropolitan and rural identities were polarized in discourses of national culture, often by foregrounding their graphic and sonorous aesthetics, respectively. Nevertheless, diverse affiliations with metropolitan and rural life continue to inform and reflect one other within specific contexts of political action. Indeed, their qualities become even more interlocked as growing numbers of rural inhabitants find metropolitan competences both necessary and morally questionable.

The figure of written script has been an especially fertile resource for assigning graphic mediation a social content and for reappraising its commonsense authority. Although a graphic and visible medium itself, script is also explicitly associated with everyday human language, textual tradition, and communicative intent. The semiotics of script provides Yemenis with an extraordinary grammar for linking what is seen and known to a complex political economy of knowledge. Some Yemeni social groups have long been recognized for learning, scholarship, and mastery of the written word, while other groups have been known as their clients. At one level, script confirms this hierarchy of authoritative knowledge by fixing it graphically with ink, paper, and other physical marks. Signs of writing affirm the durability of such textual hierarchies and underscore authorial powers over the technical habits, dispositions, and bodies of human beings.

The resourcefulness of script also lies in its potential duplicity, however. Script is not just a graphic sign to be circulated before any number of potential viewers; script is also "seen." As an object of apperception, script can invite reflection on the nature and authority of perceivers, whomever they may be. Such authority is nowhere more evident than when attention is called to the transience, disappearance, and possible alienation of graphic things. In the front matter of this book, a poem called a *qaṣīdah* (pl. *qaṣāyid*) illustrates how such scriptive reflection works. In the second and third sections of the poem, script channels sentiments of bereavement and alienation—from graphic uncertainty about common social orders ("Where is our family," "Where are those") to meditations on deeply personal, embodied loss ("No one," "Not a letter from the corpse"). As the poet confronts the abrogation of social bonds, customs, and institutions that usually bring solace and security to humans, the written letter (*risālah*, pl. *risāyil*) and more precisely, its painful absence, reveals the true object of the poet's grief: the death of a beloved friend.

But script does not just signal alienation from all that is good. It brings relief. The writer of this poem opens a channel of communication in subsequent verses that is amplified by the "radio" and the "telegraph." Script enables the poet to rediscover his own moral bearing through an imagined dialogue with his comrade, much of which involves their joint composition of poetry, song, and music. The *qaṣīdah*, published in a collection of poems by the cassette poet Shayef al-Khaledi, illustrates the value of scriptive reflection in addressing urgent personal and social concerns. Potentially moral, risky, and socially redeployable, script provides a natural pathway for linking the presumed certainties of common knowledge to more familiar, intimate, and particular ways of knowing. Foremost among these alternative, knowing "ways" is orality, a potentially universal medium so often conceived as script's authoritative counterpart. Especially important in the refinement of ethical sensibilities is hearing, a keen register that, while susceptible to distraction, offers a rich apprehension of authoritative truths that lie beyond the dazzle and clamor of the *hoi palloi*. Political poets make creative use of the semiotics of speaking and hearing as they tailor traditions of written *qaṣīdah* composition to the moral demands of a growing community of audiocassette producers and consumers.

Where debates over moral authority often hinge on the credible elicitation of texts, attention to the sensory qualities of mediated texts provides valuable analytic leverage. Texts are not unchanging objects in the world whose value is delimited by their concrete physical qualities: oral textual tradition, for example, is not the necessary sign of oral recitation. Texts are apperceived amid the situated negotiations of authority. By considering how traditions of texts are identified by Yemenis through a deft interweaving of senses within specific contexts, we can approach texts through a "natural history" of cultural forms of knowledge.[11]

In general, texts are defined for participants as much through a metaphysics of perception—often a highly restless, oscillating, and imaginative kind of perception—as through their physical reality. Using an analogy that is historical and material, we might think of a given text artifact as a segment of warped polyester recording tape that is registered more or less smoothly by different tape players. At times, the tape engages the listener fully in its sonic depth, and at other times, especially on cheaper and overused players such as are common in developing societies, the tape produces static and other noise. A study of text assemblage requires documenting practices of composition, transmission, reception, and circulation, and these practices are central to this book. But determining the quality of texts is itself a process of discovering loci of moral discrimination and agency. To study transformations in the meaning of mediated texts for a particular community of Yemenis, I have tried to employ a method that is similarly oscillating and reflexive—considering how texts serve as conduits for regularized concentrations of social power and political authority while also assessing such conduits as projections of moral subjectivity. For Yemenis, mediated texts contain assertions about particular ways of interacting with the world's established orders.

PERCEPTUAL ECOLOGIES OF MUSLIM MORAL INQUIRY

Agents of textual apperception emerge from historical engagements with prevailing attitudes about moral authority. Providing an account of such moral claimants requires developing a methodology that can situate people's reflections in an ecology of textual practices, both within Yemen and farther afield. In broadest terms, speculations over textual form and fixity in the Middle East have long been informed by the technical competences of historically restricted cadres of religious and state notables whose talents in reading and writing secured their influence among diverse populations. Indeed, although the first ideographic writing systems emerged from the dynastic houses of ancient Mesopotamia and Egypt around 3300 B.C., the advantage of the pen remained the privilege of select, often urban families until nationalist movements instituted educational reforms and literacy campaigns in the mid- to late twentieth century. During the 1940s in southern Yemen, for example, a literacy rate of 17 percent was recorded for the populace in Aden, where formal education was most accessible, although an estimated 63.8 percent of the country's populace had become literate by 1973, and rates increased by the 1980s. Literacy rates in the northern governorates, by contrast, have always remained considerably lower, and figures in 1994 estimated that approximately 44 percent of all Yemenis were literate. Although these statistics inadequately account for regular variations in the distribution of literacy among men, urban populations, and groups of higher socioreligious status or economic standing, they illustrate the general remove of the practices and privileges of written culture from the daily communicative life of large numbers of even modern Middle Eastern inhabitants.

Despite the historical restrictions of writing technologies and literacy, however, peoples of the Middle East have long appreciated the power of writing to affix signs of the world into an ordered and durable template. The possibility of immanent script has been an especially valued resource for those who have sought to secure authority beyond the transmitted oral heritage of venerable ancestors and the occasional otherworldly voice made incarnate. Most often, claims to such authority have recurred to the rhetorics of established religious orders, mercantile networks, and state administrations. Where written characters could index the power of those who accumulate and administer written texts, such characters might also provide signs of moral integrity that could legitimate pecuniary and transactional investments. In the ancient world, moreover, concepts of heavenly books could also be wielded by the dispossessed. During the several centuries before the Christian era, immanent scriptive letters began to appear in the creative iconography of prophetic sermons delivered by "messengers" who sought to revitalize transcendent truths for human listeners in the world.[12] Ideas of fixed and world-abstracted texts had long found germination at the explosive intersections of material accumulation and truth and were not solely epiphenomena of actual practices of writing. Such considerations can help us move beyond the technological constraints of "restricted literacy"[13] to explore how salient media forms are ontologically constituted in processes of social upheaval, textual adaptation, and moral inquiry.

Common among monotheistic religions is belief in a God who delivers a singular and typically unified message to believers. For Muslims, such a message is fundamentally oral. *Qur'an* literally means "recitation," and while the Qur'anic message is believed to have been delivered in a series of revelations by the Prophet Muhammad, the Prophet's words were representative of God's own. Arabic is held by Muslims to be the divine tongue, a fact that has ensured an exceptional role for Arabic in Islam ever since and has made the translation of the Qur'an a far more contentious affair than has been the case with the Bible in Judaism or Christianity. To recite the Qur'an is thus to invoke the aural presence of the divine and to endow even the least-understood enunciations with moral quality. According to a saying *(ḥadīth)* attributed to the Prophet Muhammad, God has said: "Whoever is so absorbed in reciting the Qur'an that he is distracted from praying to Me and asking [things] of Me, him I shall give the best reward [that is granted to] those who are grateful."[14] Divinely inspired words, when spoken in reverential Arabic, have a special power to summon truth.[15]

The immediacy of the divine in oral articulation makes the mediation of scripture, of the book, important to the moral order. Where contact between the sacred and the mundane is so proximate, a hierarchy must be established between the two different registers of truth and a medium produced to distinguish the causal forces of unique authorship from the functions of mere transmission. Thus, throughout the Muslim world one finds an exceptional attention being paid to calligraphy, to the aesthetics of the book, to symbols of writing, and more broadly to a metaphysics of inscription in much Qur'anic verse.[16] As William Graham has argued through comparisons with other world religions, Islam is especially emphatic in remaining at once preeminently oral *and* scriptural.[17] Such a dialectic of concrete articulation and abstracted text grants Muslims notable advantages in proselytizing. Individuals who learn to recite can access the divine word despite vastly different ranges of literacy and Arabic competence, and yet rearticulation of the divine message, no matter how materially variable, can index, within the framework of concerted Muslim devotion, the same fixed text.

The holy book is not the only "book concept," however, as noted by other scholars of the Muslim thought.[18] Other morally salient text concepts have helped give meaning and relevance to the Qur'an and other key Islamic texts, although their cultural elaborations have received scant attention. These associated textual traditions have proved to be instrumental moral resources insofar as they help situate inimitable divine words in relation to more conventional forms of human understanding. The Arabic *qaṣīdah* remains one of the most important of such concepts and is the focus of this book. Were the *qaṣīdah* tradition not already well established in the Arabian Peninsula by the time of the Prophet's lifetime, would the 6,236 "verses" *(āyahs)* of the

Prophet's message and his urgent invitation to recognize its unique authorship have resonated with such acclaim for Arab audiences at the time? How did the concept of the Qur'anic text intersect with dominant text concepts in other regions, and how have these relations undergone steady change? Such questions lie well beyond the scope of this book. Nevertheless, by developing a richer set of perspectives on the "entextualization"[19] of moral inquiry amid multiple and contending regimes of inscription, I aim to ask a broader range of questions about how truth and authoritative knowledge are meaningful to people not solely by virtue of timeless norms of value. I am interested in historicizing moral authority, and I propose to do so by exploring how authoritative texts come to be differently mediated over time.

Such a project can fruitfully begin by considering the work of those who grapple with pressing moral issues through what *they* recognize to be the discursive forms (linguistic registers, expressive genres, poetic tropes, and performance styles) that mediate and instantiate textual authority in the world. Part of the groundwork for my study of discourse and authoritative knowledge was initially established by Michel Foucault.[20] Discursive order and modes of classification are historically specific ways of knowing and also are informed by the institutional processes (legal, administrative, medical, ethical, and pedagogical) that define the practical boundaries of what can and cannot be known. To avoid viewing discourse as an instrument of predetermined structures of power, however, I approach discourse as a culturally conditioned interplay between patterns of everyday talk and ideology.[21] Moreover, in locating discourses of moral discrimination in culturally situated acts of entextualization, I aim to avoid Foucault's tendency to distill epistemology into realms of abstracted, unified power that reside largely in the subconscious and remain resistant to practical reconfiguration.[22] By attending closely to the work of poets and singers in specific political engagements, I approach the construction of knowledge and authority both as a pragmatic task of attuning texts to contexts and also, and perhaps even more important, as a matter of recognized contingency. Much of the ethical credibility of such artists lies in their conveying true words through accredited texts and through reflection on makeshift epistemological postulates that are adopted as authority is tailored to present interaction and conduct. In this respect, I share the aim of cultural-studies scholars who seek to understand how an experience of the "real" is acquired through an often prearticulated sense of difference from normative understandings of the world.[23] Special attention to matters of rhyme, melody, and affect will help identify some of the nondiscursive resources that Yemenis use as they engage in such critical ethics.

My interest in how poets, singers, and their audiences navigate through the demands of often quotidian textual forms distinguishes my approach from the methods of many earlier scholars of more conventional forms of state and legal textual authority in Yemen.[24] By focusing on informal epistolary exchanges and cassette tapes, I attend to the moral aspects of a broad range of textual practices. Moreover, in exploring how these textual habits are informed by and, in turn, reshape daily sociolinguistic practices, I seek to construct a capacious model of moral authority that can provide critical leverage against what are often seen to be overly insulated domains of state, Islamic, and tribal law. As Antonio Gramsci has suggested, the moral foundations of human action cannot be reduced to predetermined categories of material and intellectual production. Rather, moral tenets operate in fragmented and episodic ways precisely because individuals are members of many social groups simultaneously.[25] Since moral subjects are constituted through "traces" of common sense that cycle in and out of recognition, Gramsci suggests that we develop a better methodology for identifying the ethics of political action. What is needed, he ventures, is a "monographic history" that provides insight into wider latitudes of moral knowledge and agency than predetermined categories of identity typically allow.[26]

Throughout this book, I locate the culture of moral apperception in Yemenis' practical engagements with a specific genre of poetry. Known by its fans as *bidʿ wa jiwāb,* "initiation and response" poetry, this genre is one of the most popular forms of political verse in southern Yemen. *Bidʿ wa jiwāb* poetry consists of one "initiator" who composes a *qaṣīdah,* widely recognized to be the oldest and most prestigious genre of poetry in the Arab world, and sends it to a second poet, who then responds with a second *qaṣīdah* that matches the former in meter, rhyme, and thematic organization. Today, such poems are recorded back to back on audiocassettes and circulate to great acclaim among audiences young and old, wealthy and poor, male and female. Poets, singers, and audiences who participate in such exchanges consider themselves part of a community of debate that has an especially important role in public political culture. As I suggest, however, the moral fabric of such a community is founded on a hybrid and dynamic history of poetic exchange that stretches back at least 250 years in rural Yafiʿ and whose mediation requires a full consideration of cultural, political, and technological changes that have accompanied such poetry and helped imbue it with persuasive power.

To account for such power, we can consider, at one level, the kind of poetic subjectivity or "self" that is explored in *bidʿ wa jiwāb qaṣīdahs.* A study of the *qaṣīdah* invites delving into a vast literature on what is one of the world's great forms of human expression. For generations of poets and critics, the brilliance of the *qaṣīdah* lies in its capacity to invoke a historical reservoir of rigid poetic forms that can be used to meditate on life's many cycles of transformation. A single *qaṣīdah* composition typically confronts moral breaches and repairs, departures and returns from given social settings, and temporal journeys backward and forward, all managed through the poetics of theme, mood, figure, prosodic sequence, and intertextual parallelism. Suzanne Stetkevych has generatively suggested that such cycles be considered a "rite of passage,"[27] and her work has been helpful to me in linking the subjective nuances of *bidʿ wa jiwāb* poetry to specific structural and performative regularities. With the aim of bringing her insights to the embattled turf of political practice, I consider how such regularities enable the *qaṣīdah's* wide dissemination as common poetic forms are dispatched to diverse audiences and also encourage reflection on the demands that such circulation makes on participants. Where poets consider surpluses and shortcomings of textual form—often through metaphors of tailoring, measurement, and commerce in which the poem itself becomes a certain quantifiable medium—they urge audiences to assess the utility of their composition's discursive and nondiscursive elements as standards of exchange. As a result, the performance or reception of one group's *qaṣīdah* by another creates the experience of a common journey toward moral authority that is polyvocal, hybrid, and charged with difference.

Genre has typically been studied as a set of prescribed formal conventions that individuals can vary as needed. Arab poetry has had no shortage of studies detailing rules of composition that define specific genres, and the *qaṣīdah* has been the most celebrated among them. In recent decades, a formal approach to genre has been deployed by anthropologists in studies of performance and ritual. Most notable among them is Steven Caton, whose ethnography of tribal self-representation in the *qaṣīdah, zāmil,* and *bālah* genres remains a watershed study of the politics of performed Yemeni verse.[28] My interest in generic form is directed toward a related but different approach to political subjectivity that aims to understand selfhood as a materially informed historical experience. As an exercise in what might be called a "historical poetics," this monograph underscores the importance of situating generic trends not only in the changing economic and social circumstances of highland Yemen but also in textual instantiations that constantly change as people address social conflicts with imaginative insights.

Part of this ethnography is thus devoted to the flexible resourcefulness of *bidʿ wa jiwāb* poetry for Yemenis. My focus on this single genre offers a number of advantages to the development of a culturally attuned theory of media activism, despite its apparently restricted application. One of the principal advantages of studying *bidʿ wa jiwāb* poetry is that it has not been formally codified to the same extent as other genres of poetry or prose, either in scholastic circles or in popular practice. Such poetry thus lends itself to being easily redeployed. Indeed, although constituted by formal *qaṣīdahs,* "initiation and response" pairs can be conceived as a dyadic and interactional method of authorial knowledge. Accordingly, *bidʿ wa jiwāb* verse draws from a vast ethics of social responsibility, even as it enables participants to foreground their creative management of practical, everyday human engagements. At one level, for example, *bidʿ wa jiwāb* poetry can be considered the historical legacy of literate religious notables who originally exchanged *qaṣīdahs* through written correspondence, documentation for which extends back over two and a half centuries in Yafiʿ. Even though such poetry was commended by religious scholars as an important component of personal and professional training, however, *bidʿ wa jiwāb* exchanges were also aesthetically distinct from most of their other occupational engagements. While working with the textual parameters of the Qurʾan, moral custom *(sunna),* and Islamic jurisprudence *(fiqh),* such scholars swapped *qaṣīdahs* to build political alliances with one another and exchange news through unofficial channels. This account of the moral import of *bidʿ wa jiwāb* verse for correspondents requires that a consideration of the genre's textual embedding in complex social practices that both incorporate and extend beyond whatever formal criteria might be assigned them by virtue of their historical significance as notable literary correspondence.

A second advantage of studying the *bidʿ wa jiwāb* genre is its currency among multiple communities of text users, a phenomenon that has probably contributed to its resistance to formal codification. One unexpected aspect of such poetic exchanges, for example, is that not all correspondents were religious notables. Some poets were tribal shaikhs who had acquired rudimentary writing skills to assist them in communal politics. Indeed, shaikhs occasionally used poems to send written missives across battle lines that were otherwise impenetrable. The performance settings of *bid' wa jiwāb* poetry tended to reinforce such intercommunal dynamism: poems were generally recited in especially public venues where highlands tribal rhetoric—exemplified in distinct poetic genres, oral performance routines, expressive aesthetics, and moral values—was the dominant mode of political discourse. As a result, correspondents faced the task of having to appeal to the political authority of both a literate community of religious intellectuals and a popular tribal community whose hallmark expressive mode was oral declamation performed out of doors. The unique political functions of *bid' wa jiwāb* poetry make it distinctly cross-textual *(dia-textual)* and require an approach that can locate its moral power at the intersection of different aesthetics of textual mediation.

A third factor that distinguishes *bid' wa jiwāb qaṣīdahs* as a distinctly socialized textuality is the temporal and spatial distance that usually separates composers and that offers rich possibilities for considering the physical and metaphysical conditions of mediation. In the past as well as today, *qaṣīdahs* are not infrequently exchanged between those who migrate (typically to Saudi Arabia, other Gulf regions, India, Great Britain, or the United States) and those who remain in the homeland. On other occasions, correspondents live in neighboring villages or regions. Although distances of time and space are often portrayed by poets in imaginative terms, typically through the mediation of script-bearing birds, genies, radio waves, and so forth, such distances also make practical and often ad hoc demands on poets as they seek common foundations of moral authority. The uncertain sociality of *bid' wa jiwāb* exchanges makes the genre especially conducive to debates among resident and diasporic poets, who find a somewhat conflicted aesthetics of mediation helpful in interrogating and reasserting their own ideas about communities in transition.

My focus on the *bid' wa jiwāb* genre considers two final factors that are often overlooked in studies of modern media but are indispensable to a fuller consideration of aesthetics in the Arab Islamic world. These factors are song and musical composition. In southern Arabia, which has known centralized kingdoms and statelets for over 3,200 years, a culture of song and musical performance emerged that was more sophisticated than the culture elsewhere on the Peninsula. During the heyday of Yemen's Rasulid dynasty, founded between the thirteenth and fifteenth centuries, an enduring tradition of poetry arose in conjunction with courtly song and musical entertainment. Known as *ḥumaīnī* verse, this poetry became elaborated with love and spiritual themes that are laced with social and political commentary.[29] As musical instruments and courtly melodies filtered out to Yemen's remoter sultanates and fiefdoms, other genres of political verse were also set to song and rudimentary musical accompaniment. Vernacular *qaṣīdahs,* especially those featuring themes of love and wisdom, were especially conducive to such adaptations and flourished beside genres of political poetry that were identified apart from affiliations with "song" *(ghinā'),* as it is defined by Yemenis in registers of recitation and chanting.[30] *Bid'wa jiwāb* poetry offers extraordinary insights into these various traditions because it accommodates all of them in varying degrees. Its oscillating themes and performance structures, in fact, draw attention to relations between multiple currents of song and music. Whether sung to the accompaniment of a simple rhythmic drum (*ṭār* or *tanak*), ornamented more elaborately with the help of a stringed instrument, read aloud to whomever was gathered, or heard on audiocassette, each performance invites audiences to affiliate with a plurality of moral registers and with the practical and creative competences of its producers.

In exploring Yemenis' own categories of moral authority, I consider genre to be an important "horizon of expectation."[31] My focus on cassette poets, singers, and audiences lends to a discovery that the genre proves especially useful for Yemenis in times of uncertainty, when multiple compositional structures and text concepts are in play. Genre provides helpful analytic leverage, moreover, since it is both a topic of explicit discourse and also a "metadiscursive" device—that is, a way to talk about organizing talk, poetry, and habits of aesthetic attunement broadly. Ultimately, however, genre remains an overly general tool for understanding the finer points of ethical discrimination that lie at the center of this study. The relations of conventional expressive categories to emergent forms of apperception are explored by Yemenis through a repertoire of nuanced linguistic registers, figures, themes, and tropes that appear regularly in poetry and in talk about poetry and that become objects of lively debate. This repertoire, which is elaborated in tropes of community, place, region, character, personality, and history, draws the bulk of my attention throughout the book. By focusing on how Yemenis employ and develop this repertoire through their imaginative use of media technologies, I aim to understand how the sensory qualities of media help mobilize prominent idioms of identity toward new scenarios of credible moral action and, in the process, how they help refurbish older texts and genres for modern political engagement.

THE CIRCULATION AND RESONANCE OF MEDIATED SONG

Given the importance of the audio-recording industry to the present study, a brief review of the development of this industry and its implications for *bidʿ wa jiwāb* poets will help refine this work's approach to Yemenis' moral apperceptions of media. The recording industry, so exciting to audiences by virtue of its charismatic metropolitan song brokers, introduces new forces of entextualization into Yemen political life. On the one hand, the industry's solicitations to identify with new forms of mechanically reproduced sound are intimately connected to nationalist discourses that have emerged in stride with the industry. At the same time, new strains of musical panache, especially those channeled through decentralized audiocassettes, offer rural Yemenis distinct opportunities to revisit the moral entailments of authoritative inscription.

The Yemeni recording industry first got underway in Aden in the years after World War II and within a decade had grown to become the second largest in the Middle East after Cairo. In its initial phase, the industry developed through a felicitous coupling of disc technologies and radios, the latter of which had begun to reach popular audiences by the mid-1950s. Reflecting the ecumenical diversity of Aden's populace of Indians, Pakistanis, Somalis, British, Greeks, Italians, Armenians, as well as indigenous Jews, the industry was from its outset cosmopolitan. Indeed, early recording virtuosos, most of them from elite urban families, were largely non-Yemeni Arabs who resided elsewhere. Although well known in Egypt and other countries of the Middle East and North Africa, they were unfamiliar to Yemenis.

As the industry's production capacities grew and an indigenous radio station was established in 1954, recording companies increasingly promoted a growing supply of local artists. Throughout Yemen, listeners were gaining access to a more regular flow of song and music than had ever before been available. Along with this burgeoning "sound industry,"[32] moreover, Yemen's most progressive nationalist movements developed, informing and being informed by the industry's dynamic cultural horizons. Attuned to broader political currents, recording stars gained authority as cultural and political luminaries, especially when they tailored their songs to genres, styles, and discourses that were more familiar to Yemen's vast rural populace. Indigenous recording companies, too, began offering consumers a greater diversity of recorded song, much of it tailored to the dialects and expressive registers of regional audiences. Amid such polyphony, political perspectives on Yemen's colonial status could be heard, and they were more dissonant than those heard on state-managed media networks.

Technological advances in this sound industry were instrumental to Yemenis' broader participation in exciting trends further afield. Audiocassette technologies—first open-reel recorders in the 1950s, then eight-track tapes, and in the late 1960s the standard Philips cassette—provided a diverse range of audiences with an increasingly affordable, transportable, and user-friendly means to access recorded song. The most important contribution of cassettes, however, lay in their facility not as transmitting but as recording devices. As major state institutions and private companies supervised a lucrative commercial recording industry, far more decentralized cassette-recording initiatives emerged alongside it. Although considered marginal by those in the commercial recording business, the participants in such an alternative industry had a different view. For many tribal highlanders who had long disdained the use of political verse for profit, their own recordings were valued in inverse relation to commercial gain. Poetry and political song were ideally meant for spiritual refinement, honor, or communal health and were not to be used as mere tools for material advancement.

Cultural and political transformations facilitated by cassette media were accompanied by debates among producers and audiences over the moral and political value of a decentralized sound industry. In some respects, Yemenis resisted implications that new media technologies were changing traditional forms of expression and moral inquiry. Categories of genre, especially the time-worn *qaṣīdah,* often provided useful frameworks for defending the general continuities of expressive culture against corrosion. According to such views, media technologies were neutral conduits for disseminating authentic local letters or messages *(risāyil)* to broader audiences. In other respects, however, Yemenis found advantages and a certain delight in considering how media technologies could facilitate particular transformations. Rural singers, musicians, and poets who were linked with urban recording entrepreneurs were often most willing to acknowledge the influence of a wider range of regional and often metropolitan styles on their performances. Those attuned to nationalist movements, moreover, readily understood the advantages of media for mobilizing audiences toward larger arenas of political engagement and for revitalizing what many saw as stultified customs at home.

Such debates inevitably landed on the matter of communal identity. To what extent did the sound industry and its advocates enable or harm community integrity and its moral coherence? It is this question that reflection on media addresses most productively. The sounds, scripts, images, and sensory qualities of media provide aesthetic cues for understanding the foundations of such integrity. To help develop an approach to the hermeneutic resourcefulness of media, whether in the sound industry or in more general contexts of media culture, I propose differentiating between two kinds of aesthetics. I call these the aesthetic of "circulation" and the aesthetic of "resonance."[33] The former aesthetic enables reflection on abstract objects—types of things recognized to circulate in the world, whether representational habits, conventions of behavior, or symbols. Since such objects are held to travel through formal systems of value whose durability over time can be conceptualized, they can be easily repeated and reiterated. The aesthetic of resonance, by contrast, enables reflections on the emergence of such objects from the sensate, dynamic, and therefore partly metaphysical qualities of media. Although both aesthetics are integral to each other and work in a dialectic relation, it is through the aesthetic of resonance, I suggest, that moral inquiry can best meet the demands of creative change. The relations of the two aesthetics of circulation and resonance are explored by poets, singers, and audiences through talk about community, place, character, personality, and history.[34]

An introduction to the terms of such a metadiscourse is provided by one of Yemen's most beloved singers, Muhammad Murshed Nājī, in a small collection of essays on sung Yemeni folk poetry that he published in 1959. Naji was a pioneer in the audio-recording industry and one of the first singers in Yemen to bring nationalism to popular audiences through radio, records, and later cassettes. In his small paperback volume, Naji describes the importance of song to Arab society:

> The successful popular song is a weapon, and the resonant folk song is a force that can function in the same respect. The song is a faithful envoy that can carry a true and comprehensive portrait to all sections of our society, a portrait of simply a slice of life and its

> toils, as well as of life's traditions, customs, and character, its morals, goals, and templates, its environment and the influence exerted on its constitution, progression, and development. All of this is conveyed in an advanced and orderly register that is but one portion of the language of our Arab society. If this register is not comprehensible via the dictionary, then it will be understood through sensation, as it is a genuine emotional stirring as well as an expression of human discernment. Although this register may differ in details, it unites, at its source, the purely humane.
>
> Through the spread of song, the language of song spreads. Moreover, a linguistic similarity between our society's segments is the most effective aspect of our battle for social unity. This similarity, if achieved through the medium of circulating song, would produce a real blend between the resonant forms of our society's segments. It would create the opportunity for linguistic contact between our popular dialects, as each dialect takes from the other, each social sphere repeats the expressions of the other social sphere. It is possible that this will lead to the clarification of our numerous popular dialects. It may help to bring them closer and blend them, so that a comprehensive popular vernacular is created that is at once understandable in every sphere and yet proximate to the usage of each segment of our society.[35]

Muhammad Naji, a luminary of nationalist song for many southern Yemeni, chooses the analogy of language to express his sense of the power of song in effectuating social and political change. Song is "an advanced and orderly register that is but one portion of the language of our Arab society." His discourse model of song, however, hinges on a delicate interplay between "circulating song" and an expression that is deeply reflective and resonant. It is worth unpacking his model before continuing to consider its implications for emerging forms of textual authority and subjectivity in Yemen.

Naji begins his narrative by invoking a distinction between "successful popular song" and "resonant folk song," two genres that were becoming topics of much discussion in Yemen in the 1950s. Articulated most poignantly by men of the socialist vanguard, some of whom were beginning to receive state educational training in Moscow, these two song styles demonstrate a difference between a standardized and contemporary vernacular that is spoken by the general populace and a customary vernacular spoken by the "folk."[36] For Naji, who by 1959 was joining the ranks of Yemen's most famous local boys made good, success is a measure of fame, influence, and sales. His opening assertion clearly establishes the political value of such popular authority. In the same breath, however, he hastens to assure his audience of the commensurate political value of folk song, which he describes as "resonant" *(mu'abbirah)*. The semantics of the verbal base *'abara* evoke a rich poetics of water imagery and nature, both of which foreground the more unfolding and contingent qualities of circulation and thereby initiate a dialectic with circulation, a pattern that is observed in repeated forms throughout this book.[37] The combination of both forms of song is glossed by Naji as a "faithful envoy" and is said to carry a powerful message to Yemen's polyglot community. Naji's vision of the transformative effects of an audible "envoy" would have likely been attractive to many readers given developments in audio-recording technologies in the late 1950s. Records, radio, and increasingly audiocassettes were becoming instrumental for Yemeni nationalists as media that could circulate identical audio copies to many thousands of listeners and also engage the imaginative responses of those listeners.

The integrity of Naji's ideal society lies in the perfect communicative act or at least an act that he feels can be constructed as such. The agent for this act, for this "faithful envoy," is the singer himself. By sending a "true and comprehensive" song into the world, the singer can produce an "advanced and orderly register" that unites listeners of diverse dialectal "segments" into a single *sensus communis*. Note that in describing the principal vehicle for this common register, Naji employs a poetic figure, or "trope," likening song to a "portrait" *(ṣūrah)*, a graphic medium with decidedly metropolitan associations for most Yemenis. By means of a visual currency that is ostensibly available to all, a linguistic message is produced, circulated, and mobilized toward political ends. This act is a challenging one for media theory, however, for attunement between interlocutors is enabled less by language and more by "sensations." Indeed, sensations must first be stimulated through song, which leads to the spread of language ("linguistic contact") and ultimately, through the repetition of vernacular expressions, to a blend of "social spheres." The sensory experience of song, in fact, *creates* language that can circulate in the world as a set of iterable "dictionary" units. Through the subtle cues of sonorous emotion, linguistic units become standards for a new social populace. As Naji concludes, "A comprehensive popular vernacular is created that is at once understandable in every sphere and yet proximate to the usage of each segment of our society." With poetic imagination, Naji's sonorous "portrait," construed in a critically metropolitan register, becomes the authentic expression of a truly vernacular discourse community and is not merely a tool for refining sensibilities. Sound, through vision, has produced true speech.

The concept of resonance may be a fitting one for this dialectic between the physical and metaphysical aspects of sound. Georg Hegel suggested in his work *The Philosophy of Nature* that "resonance" *(erzittern)* expresses a special relation between two oscillating substances.[38] As each substance pulses in syncopation with the other, friction gives way to a single polyphonic vibration, and noise turns to sound. In the presence of such sonic unity, however, lie the seeds for moral reflection on a new kind of difference, as he proposed was true in the case of song in particular. When vibrating human vocal chords encounter the sonic world outside, song enables both an experience of shared being and a sudden sense of the difference between them—and thus a sense of a sort of spiritual independence in the singing subject. Resonance is an experience through time that is recurrently jarring and true.

For Naji and for the others I consider in this book, such resonance is not just sonic and aural. Poets, singers, and audiences who seek to identify their own relations to networks of social prestige and power find tropes of graphic mediation especially germane to moral inquiry. Debates over visual media introduce opportunities to explore contestations of selfhood that are foreclosed by Hegel's philosophical bent. In Naji's introduction above, this graphic ("portrait") and increasingly scriptive ("dictionary") impulse is instrumental to the circulation success of song and is conveyed in a form that, while capable of disseminating sound faithfully, also seems to acquire a willful independence of its own. The heady tendencies of this scriptographic messenger are illustrated by Naji in a sequence of tightly stitched triads that describe the particular "slices" of life that will be conveyed by the portrait to its diverse audiences: "traditions, customs, and character," "morals, goals, and templates," and "constitution, progression, and development." Note that the single elements of each triad are stitched together in what strikes me as a remarkable mythopoetic narrative that moves from durable foundations to dynamic and practical continuities and ultimately to self-maturation. Indeed, the structural elegance of this narrative encompasses the arrangement of the three triads themselves as well. The complex aesthetics of Naji's living "portrait" anticipate several key observations that are pursued in this book. First, scriptographic media prove instrumental for Yemenis in securing oral and sonic vitality amid social and technological transformation. Second, and more important, such media help Yemenis organize a complex set of aesthetic experiences into a vision of political agency that can be refined in dialogue with others.

Naji's narrative of song is nationalist and, like many other narratives of twentieth-century nationalist reformers, presents an optimistic scenario of the civic functions that media can perform in public life. The poets and singers who lie at the center of this book lack Naji's prominence as a national performer and intellectual and are disposed to express somewhat more critical attitudes toward the effects of media on Yemenis. Lacking access to records and radio, they have used cassettes to convey their views of the world. Although such individuals are often as passionate as Naji is about Yemen's collective horizons, they are more engaged than he is with local political concerns and the interregional histories of mostly rural highlands Yemeni communities that comprise the bulk of their audiences. The advantage of considering politics and mediation from such a perspective lies in being able to reexamine nationalism not only from its "margins"[39] but also from its embedding in the ethical life worlds of a diverse Yemeni populace. Such an approach, I suggest, helps us move beyond older moral essentialisms, most notably those that categorize social affiliations by alternate orders of "tribes" and "states." Instead, we become positioned to consider how an enduring ethics of exchange, managed through poetry and discourse, helps Yemenis address changing relations of inequality that continuously threaten the well-being of interlocutors and their communities.

THE POLITICS OF POETRY AND INSCRIBED SUBJECTS

Persuasion remains central to this study of political discourse. As master wordsmiths, poets (*shāʿirs*, pl. *shuʿarāʾ*) are exemplary politicians in this regard and are the focus of this book.[40] I also attend closely to the work of amateur and semiprofessional singers who work with poets in publicizing their verses. While singers have long contributed to Yemenis' appreciation of political poetry, they have gained prestige and leverage in recent decades through the recording industry. Their adaptations of poetry provide important insights into the changing requirements of political verse in Yemen. Audiences, too, receive sustained treatment throughout the book as crucial participants in acts of persuasion and in media culture generally, despite their relatively scant treatment in other studies of Yemeni poetry. In addition to examining audience responses to three folk-poetry cassettes in chapter 1, I consider interchanges between listeners and cassette-shop managers in chapter 3 and provide regular notes on interviews with audiences throughout the other chapters. A study of media aesthetics invites special attention to the construction of audiences as "addressees," and I also examine the ways in which both artists and audiences collaborate in crafting new witnessing subjects whose ratification underscores new forms of collectivity. Choices of words, genres, melodies, musical arrangements, participant structures, and means of dissemination all become cues to the efficacy of new social claims and the nature of their claimants. Indeed, as collaboration between poets, singers, and audiences becomes more necessary with the development of the cassette industry, I argue that discussions about such choices occur more regularly in composition events and that, as a consequence, Yemenis are reflecting more on their own roles in shaping ideas about social collectivity.

Some of the most compelling efforts to link new forms of addresseeship to emergent forms of political collaboration and engagement have been formulated by theorists of the "public sphere," a concept originally elaborated by political philosopher Jürgen Habermas.[41] According to Habermas, a distinct kind of "public" discourse emerged in eighteenth-century Europe when a tradition of private letter writing, practiced largely by bourgeois men, was brought under the auspices of state postal authority, and a host of literary circles concomitantly began flourishing in coffee houses, salons, and literary clubs. As citizens discussed an increasing variety of literary and philosophical texts, many of them cheaply printed and disseminated in burgeoning consumer markets, they began to grow aware of their own identities as entitled, "private" individuals and to see these identities as integrally linked with those of many other similar addressees. Amid debates over private rights and duties, a sense of shared "public" legitimacy emerged that was viewed as separate from and indeed morally superior to the legitimizing claims of states and markets.[42]

Such an account of the subjective entailments of new, media-assisted discourses contributes to the study at hand. As regimes of inscription enabled by writing and later audio-recording technologies have become decentralized and made available to increasingly diverse participants, new conditions of public discourse are developing to sustain the claims of ostensibly liberated and rational authors. The easy reproduction of amateur cassette recordings by tens and hundreds of thousands of copies has facilitated these claims insofar as cassettes are less directly censorable than state-controlled media such as the television and print media. Indeed, as other media theorists have shown, cassettes are helping to create expressive domains that, being somewhat autonomous of state control, foster the articulation of alternative forms of public opinion.[43]

However, the capacity of such media to enable transformations in notions of public affiliation must be measured against socioeconomic factors that are historically informed and that continue to constrain actors' abilities to stake public claims. The power to address and be addressed is always qualified and is subject to perceived hierarchies of authorship that ratify some participants over others. In Yemen, the economic foundation for Habermas's "public sphere"—namely, state-sponsored ownership of property by bourgeois men of letters—only roughly coincides with the economic and legal entitlements of most Yemenis, not least of them members of the "cassette public" who are the focus of this ethnography. Where communal rights and obligations in Yemen have long been situated at the intersection of state authority with semiautonomous Islamic legal institutions and where both state and Islamic law have further been correlated with tribal law, claims over individuals' status as subjects under the law have arguably been more polyphonic than they were in mid-eighteenth-century Europe and America. Moreover, the centrality of public oratory and poetry to political life in Yemen requires expanding our notions of textual culture beyond the kind of literate, formally educated domains typically foregrounded in studies of public culture. In short, our analysis of public identity must begin with finer considerations of the social resources (status, gender, ethnicity, regional background, competence, and other registers of social value) that inform verbal communication.

Some of the most generative accounts of the use of verbal resources in performance were developed in the 1960s by sociolinguists who later became identified as pioneers of the "ethnography of speaking." I consider their insights instrumental to my own. Critical of the universal presuppositions of formal language models that were developed by Leonard Bloomfield and Noam Chomsky, these scholars argued that speaking is a socially and culturally constructed activity whose linguistic resources are apportioned through a hierarchized division of labor.[44] Sociologists later used their work to refurbish political theory. Most notable among them was Pierre Bourdieu, who proposed that verbal competence should be considered a form of "linguistic capital" whose value is determined competitively in a "linguistic marketplace."[45] Bourdieu's writings on linguistic capital, along with his work on structures of capital that are "social" and "cultural" as well as economic, proved to be a beacon for many scholars who sought to refurbish the study of expressive culture with broader attention to political economy and history. As a new generation of studies focused on the intersections of language and power, Michel Foucault's approach to "discourse" as an institutionalized regime of order and knowledge provided much guidance.[46] However, Bourdieu's more nuanced structural recursivity, much of it expressed in terms of game theory, continued to supply especially dialectical frameworks for those who wanted to keep discursive life from being abstracted into an historical moment of power.

In accounting for cassette poetry as an especially contested public space, I too focus on how people negotiate communicative interactions by trying to grant new values to discursive forms. Words are continuously being reappraised by individuals within specific contexts; indeed, such assessments are highly political. However, a study of media culture allows us to integrate sociolinguists' interests in value with broader understandings of texts and aesthetics. Given the salience of writing to the Arab Islamic world's morally esteemed text concepts, the inscriptive aspects of media deserve special attention. A focus on inscription enables us to explore the moral significance of conventional scribal practices and to examine how users compare script to other forms of knowledge fixation and accumulation, including print, audio recording, photographs, photocopying, television, films, and even song and music. In short, an "ethnography of speaking" is supplemented with an ethnography of inscription.

A final word on the dynamics of inscription will help clarify some of the challenges that are involved in such a project.[47] First and foremost, inscription is meaningful to people by virtue of analogy. A script or mark is significant as a force that fixes or "inscribes" something in the fashion of a more authoritative force or object. The relations between fashioned script and the analogous fashioner are complex. We might note, for example, that an inscription can be symbolic (as in conventionalized representation), proximal (as in a copy), or imitative (as in mimesis). However construed, the pair of scriptive elements becomes socially and morally charged for people insofar as they each partly draw on the other for their power. In Yemeni moral discourse, this relationship is explored through both the aesthetics of circulation, which highlights a sense of maximal difference between each element, and resonance, which highlights a sense of their similarity and mutual interdependence.

In its circulatory aspect, for example, inscription helps Yemenis consider certain abstractive forces in the world as one medium comes to be perceived, essentialized, and represented in the form of another. In Naji's trope cited above, multiple kinds of song are distilled into a single "portrait." Circulation is the principal means for achieving this transformation, and although Naji does so in explicit discursive terms, preferred forms of power can be circulated in more subtle, metadiscursive ways as people negotiate the conditions by which language will be used. According to this aesthetic, some thing—a discrete and transportable form—is understood to move through the world depositing its mark on other things, people, and events but nevertheless retaining its particular value. Although the circulating object can certainly be converted into other equivalent forms, it nevertheless retains its abstract value as an expression of some general equivalent and can be accumulated as such. Otherwise, it would be seen as something else and would exit the set of recognizable equivalents by which a given circuit exists. According to this logic, an audiocassette would retain the mark of a "cassette" even if it accommodated songs, letters, or the aspirations of a beleaguered people. The ideological work to invest such a medium with power of this sort is by no means simple and, as I aim to demonstrate in this book, incorporates a range of variables.

Another aspect of inscription, however, emphasizes something less fungible and abstractive. This "resonant" aesthetic highlights the power of the script to share something of the inscriber's force and to reflect this back, if obliquely, on its dominant orders. This aesthetic is more inchoate and resistant to general forms of representation and draws attention instead to its own formative process. Equivalences and conversions of circulating forms become less important than their ontological fitness in a given context. One might feel right in speaking of a "cassette poet" in the elegy of a famous nationalist and tribesman (as was done for the first time at the funeral commemoration of Shayef al-Khāledī in 1999), just as the written style of a *qaṣīdah* might evoke a sense of present authorship that seems singularly appropriate for a given moment.

This sensate dialectic of inscription and its deployment toward persuasive ends in political poetry ultimately provides some of the surest insights into how media aesthetics are deployed in acts of "performativity," which might be defined, following Friedrich Nietzsche, as the recognition of being behind practice.[48] My ethnographic focus considers modern subjectivity less through the formalist concerns of speech-act theory, however, than through a phenomenology of media that emerges from the situated aims of poets, singers, and their audiences. Although discursive grammars centrally inform the subjective experience of versification, I explore how the sensory qualities of media help create fissures between discursive units that can unsettle routine interpretive habits, elicit creative strategies for mobilizing action, incite new understandings of one's capacities as an agent in the world, and even, if conventionalized, provide a weft for new kinds of accumulation. As is shown in chapter 1, genre provides Yemenis with a culturally specific aesthetic framework for collating the materiality of textual reproduction with a sense of accumulating moral subjectivity. Other orienting frameworks, such as poetic tropes, do so with more particular elegance.

The audiocassette remains the primary site for exploring how Yemenis manage textual and aesthetic convergences. As a user-friendly technology for recording the human voice, among other sounds, the cassette can situate the human subject at the convergences of local sonic culture and translocal sound industries that are associated with mass production and commercial profit. An ethnographic approach informs the core postulates of my argument. For the rural Yemenis whom I interviewed, the cassette was only one minimal tool in a vibrant, frustrating, and changing repertoire of political options that were available to them under impossible circumstances. Nevertheless, the phenomenon of cassette poetry also provided them with a unique resource that has continued to attract attention, especially among the southern highlanders from Yafiʿ. Inheritors of a particular legacy of Muslim learning, political organization, and global economic change, Yafiʿis have valued cassettes for their simultaneous risks and potential benefits to conventions of moral authority. The twin advantage of cassettes in this regard have been explored, above all, through poetic tropes. Through imaginatively reworking commonsense discourse, tropes turn the cassette and its ordering norms into a medium of inscription that defers to accumulated forms of knowledge and power, even as it questions the justice of their inflexible perpetuation. While circulating as a graphic mark, the cassette also projects the strange vision of a circulating sound, inciting new conditions of knowledge, action, and voice. In the postunification era in Yemen, when discourses of tribalism have gained controversial currency in southern governorates, this sound has offered special solace.

By attending to moments of concerted poetic action, I hope to substitute the rush to identify social imaginaries with a more capacious understanding of the role of the imagination in progressive political formations. Such a delay might win a moment's reprieve from overdetermined teleologies of modernity and instead plunge us into the ebullient, kinetic, and sometimes silent surpluses of the experience of mediated verbal performance. Such an approach might help us better understand how the social self is cultivated through the dialogics of discursive and poetic form as much as through history's totalizing narratives. Common experiences of difference might then be found even as the "impact" of media on human subjectivity is addressed head on.

YĀFIʿ: THE PLACE OF FIELDWORK

A brief introduction to Yafiʿi social and political history will help prepare the way for a consideration of the moral and political significance of cassette poems and media aesthetics generally for Yemenis. Spanning the governorates of Lahej and Abyan, Yafiʿ contains the second densest population in southern Yemen outside of Aden (175,000 out of a total population of over 18 million). Yafiʿi communal identity has been shaped by a particular history of social and economic interactions, religious organization, and state development. In what follows, I give special attention to the roles played by writing and media in facilitating the articulation of communal identity.

Yafiʿ's political organization and cultural life stem from its location in the borderlands. Both mountainous and coastal, tribal and stately, isolated and mercantile, defiant of colonial penetration and zealous in its own orderly initiatives, Yafiʿis have long taken pride in their community's adaptive proficiency. Narratives recounting the region's integrity sometimes begin with ge-

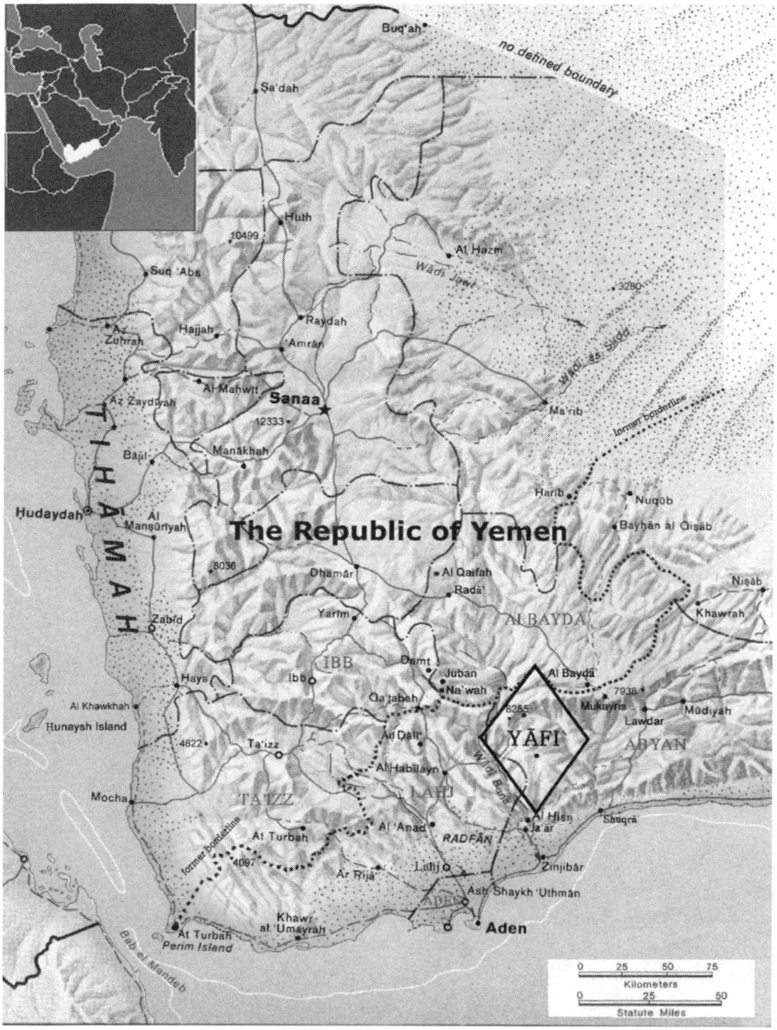

Map A. The Republic of Yemen

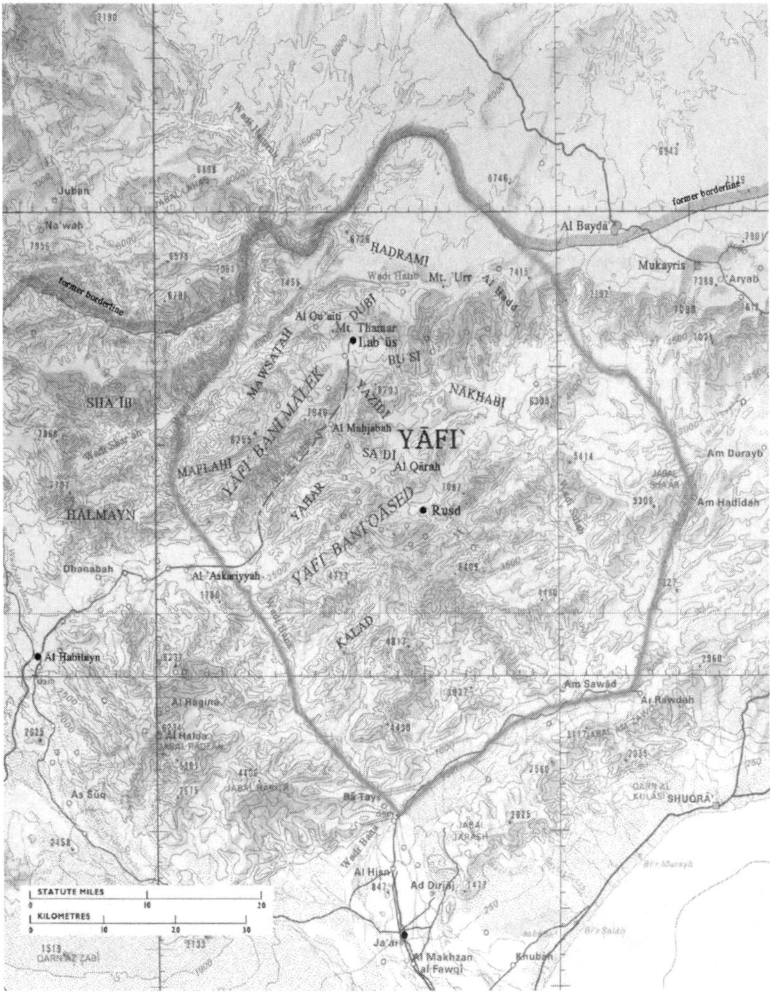

Map B. Yafi': Approximate Postindependence Boundaries

nealogical descent in a manner often heard throughout the Arab world. The eponymous ancestor of the Yafiʿi people is identified as the father of a long line of sons (sing. *bin* or *ibn*)—Yafiʿ Bin Qāwil Bin Zaīd Bin Nāʿtah Bin Sharḥabīl Bin al-Ḥārith Dhū Ruʿaīn al-Aṣghar Bin Zaīd Bin Yarīm Dhū Ruʿaīn al-Akbar, a descendant of Qaḥṭān, the earliest shared ancestor of all southern Arabs. Subnarratives linking this genealogy to specific lineages in the region or geographical places, however, are neither consistent nor rigorously maintained. Particularly obscure are the origins of the two major moieties that have long informed the political geography of the region: the people of Yafiʿ Bani Mālek ("Yafiʿ, from the sons of Mālek"), who are located in the northernmost highlands in an area that was designated as "Upper Yafiʿ" by the British, and the people of Yafiʿ Bani Qāsed ("Yafiʿ, from the sons of Qāsed"), erstwhile "Lower Yafiʿ," who are located along an escarpment that gradually descends southward toward the plains. Where genealogical origins are obscure, most historical narratives of regional identity begin with more general points of commonalty: Yafiʿ has long proven home to a consolidated group of tribes (*qabāyil;* sing. *qabīlah*). Tribal historians, both professional and amateur, frequently describe Yafiʿ as one of the largest tribal confederations on the Arabian Peninsula, preceded in Yemen only by northern Ḥāshed and Bakīl populations.[49]

In more quotidian accounts of Yafiʿ by its inhabitants, narratives of genealogical descent and tribal solidarity are secondary to descriptions of Yafiʿ's ecological terrain. The region's arid mountains and valleys (many of whose names have not changed since at least the tenth-century historian al-Hasan al-Ḥamdānī's account of the region) provide the coordinates for describing a highlands community that has survived through farming and pastoralism for several millennia. Oral historical narratives frequently begin with descriptions of Yafiʿ as *sarwu ḥimyar,* translated from ancient sources as the "mountain-refuge of the Ḥimyar." Although these narratives partly draw attention to the region's rugged isolation, they also recollect Yafiʿ's prominence as the second-century B.C. homeland for a population of farmers, herdsmen, and warriors whose leadership would help found one of South Arabia's most powerful kingdoms.[50] Such an early experience with centralized authority was possible only by virtue of Yafiʿ's precipitous slopes, some of which, at 8,200 feet, define Yemen's highest southern peaks. Providing a natural catch basin for moist air moving inland from the Arabian Sea, the region's mountains enabled a network of agricultural and mercantile enterprises to develop as early as the second millennium B.C., when Yafiʿ became one of the three largest producers of frankincense in South Arabia and Africa after Dhufar and Somalia.[51] The region's prosperity waned after the spread of Christianity led to the banning of incense-burning rituals in pagan temples throughout the ancient world and the demand for frankincense dwindled. However, the rise of sea trade during the first to third centuries C.E. and later the coffee industry in Yemen ensured the region's importance as a global supplier. In the late seventeenth and eighteenth centuries, revenues poured into Yafiʿ as its leading families consolidated their roles as exporters of coffee to Europe, as leading dyers and textile producers in Yemen, and as succorers to the often besieged port of Aden, approximately fifty miles southwest of Yafiʿ.

As Yafiʿis enjoyed intermittent periods of agricultural and commercial development, regional religious and administrative structures gradually grew consolidated, and with them developed new systems of textual authority. By the ninth century, some of the first compounds *(rubāṭs)* for religious instruction (mostly Shafiʿi) became established by Muslim notables *(sayyids)* whose descent through ʿAli from the Prophet Muḥammad made them valued intermediaries in tribal disputes. Some visiting delegates acquired a reputation for aggressive proselytizing. In the early tenth century, a firebrand social reformer of the Qarmatian sect, ʿAli Bin Faḍl, briefly secured Yafiʿ's cooperation in a sizeable military campaign that struck northward and then fizzled.[52] Over the following centuries, however, a more peaceable coterie of reformers established a network of religious compounds to provide rural Yafiʿis with valuable community services, including the drafting and storing of written legal documents and land titles and basic religious teaching and counsel. Rudimentary classes in reading and writing were offered at such compounds and, as I discuss in chapter 2, helped contribute to the expansion of a community of literate rural notables, many of who corresponded with one another through poetry.

But the spread of literacy was also important for larger administrative ends. In the mid- to late seventeenth century, a series of military campaigns was mounted against Yafiʿ by the Zaidi imams Qasem Bin Muḥammad Ḥamīd al-Dīn and his sons, who sought to extend suzerainty over huge tracts of northern territory as well as many southern regions. As Yafiʿi tribal shaikhs redoubled their efforts to recruit men to fight the imamate army, a need for scribes arose to keep accounts of volunteers, weapons, numbers of wounded and killed during battles, and taxes for maintaining an adequate political infrastructure. Tribalism began to express a more polished *esprit de corps.*

Two leading juridico-religious families led the way in organizing such activity and in establishing longer-term regional consolidation. The first of these was the ʿAfīfī family, who resided in the towering fortress town al-Qārah in Yafiʿ Bani Qāsed. Their religious authority was traced to ʿAbdallah Bin ʾAsʿad "ʿAfīf al-Dīn" (d. 1366/768), a fourteenth-century scholar of the religious sciences and chief counsel *(quṭb)* of Mecca.[53] The ʿAfifis, who had long been recognized for their martial leadership, coadministered with a second prominent religious leadership, the Harharah family, which resided in Maḥjabah in Yafiʿ Bani Mālek. Their authority attached to a spiritual leader from Hadramawt (eastern Yemen), Shaikh ʿAli Bin Abu Bakr Bin Sālem (d. 1594/992).[54] From 1654 until late 1695, when the Qasemids finally retreated into the northern highlands, both families established treaties with the imamate, which recognized their authority as "sultans."[55] More important, they helped organize Yafiʿ into ten administrative districts whose coordinates continue to define sociopolitical space in Yafiʿ even today: five districts in Yafiʿ Bani Qāsed (Yihar, Kalad, Nakhabī, Saʿdī, and Yazīdī) and five districts in Yāfiʿ Bani Mālek (Mawsaṭah, Maflaḥī, Buʿsī, Ḍubī, and Ḥaḍramī) (see Map B). The affairs of each district were entrusted to a shaikhly family or more often several shaikhly families whose political authority rested on the allegiances of constituent subsections (sing. *rubʿ, khamīs, sadīs*) and their leaders *(ʿārifs)*. But the whole network of districts was nominally subject to the authority of the sultans, to whose treasury *(bait al-māl)* subjects contributed annual tithes in crops and animals. The administrative responsibilities of the districts were expressed in their being named *maktabs* (pl. *makātib*), literally "places of writing," a term that remains the most prominent nomenclature for regional administration today. Documents referring to the establishment of such inscriptive spaces in the seventeenth century should not mislead us into overestimating the role of literacy in political life at the time: writing and reading were extremely restricted. Nevertheless, the creation and naming of such a districting system suggests a commitment to new forms of literate textual authority, as Yafiʿi tribesmen sought to anchor themselves within rather than beyond the civil compass of states.

The reach of Yafiʿi political life beyond the region's precipitous isolation was enabled by sustained outmigration. Drought and limited arable land had long factored into the mobilization of Yafiʿis, usually young men, who traveled in search of a better livelihoods elsewhere. Before the late nineteenth century, Yafiʿi migrants typically relocated either within Yemen or in East Africa, India, or Southeast Asia. By the 1890s, Aden became an especially attractive and more proximate source of work, and through Aden a host of world ports, including Cardiff, Tyneside, Marseilles, and New York, became available. But beginning as early as the first decades of the sixteenth century, Yafiʿi migration was also fueled by more orchestrated movements of men. In 1519, the first of three sizeable Yafiʿi campaigns into Hadramawt began as various factions recruited Yafiʿi support in regional conflicts.[56] Over the next two and a half centuries, Yafiʿis would prove especially valuable to Hadrami allies because they commanded an exceptional supply of firearms acquired through Aden and Yafiʿi links abroad. In the nineteenth century, the founding of the Quʿaīṭi state in Hadramawt by ʿAwad Bin ʿUmar, a migrant of Yafiʿi descent whose father had acquired the rank of chief commander under the *niẓām* of Hyderabad, India, provided Yafiʿis with a secure base for accelerated migration, settlement, and sociopolitical consolidation in the region.[57]

Over the course of three centuries of sustained contact with regional systems of commerce and cultural exchange, the legal and administrative system in Yafiʿ matured. A nuanced codex of orally maintained tribal customary law *(ʿurf)* and the increasingly institutionalized practice of Islamic law *(sharīʿah)* became articulated in relation to administrative reforms whose language and structures drew impetus from abroad. Learned notables and community leaders as well as merchants harnessed such textual authority to wider patronage networks and contacts with state institutions, bringing home wealth, weapons, and technologies, all of which provided infrastructure for new hierarchies of knowledge and power. As I detail in chapter 2, however, along with the arrivals and departures of resources and people were handwritten letters composed as *bidʿ wa jiwāb qaṣīdahs,* which, along with the Qurʾan, had long provided the master loom for a poetic koiné in the oral expressive culture and moral life of Yemenis. Typically exchanged as "initiations" and "responses" between those who sought to bridge spatial and sociopolitical divides (many of them migrants writing home), such *qaṣīdah* letters were crafted less to display the ornamented output of the literati than they were to situate their correspondents in worlds of highland political discourse and action. Deployable toward this end, as I will show, were a variety of poetic registers, topoi, and themes, each associated with different social and moral affiliations. The craft of such letters provided correspondents and audiences with a unique template for situating political events practically in the thick of social interchange and also imaginatively in spatial and temporal frameworks elicited in sporadic efforts to conceptualize broader social horizons through writing. Indeed, the problem of mediated social distances becomes central to such poems and provides a flexible grammar for models of community. By addressing disjunctions of place and time through the parlance of poems, correspondents contributed an especially persuasive set of reflexive resources to common initiatives for societal reform.

Over the course of the twentieth century as state consolidation in southern Yemen expanded under British colonial administration, the practical and imaginative spaces of community underwent more accelerated changes, many of them directed from farther afield. The Federation of Arab Emirates of the South was established in the 1950s, and out of twenty-five rural statelets in southern Yemen, only Yafiʿ Bani Mālek (then Upper Yafiʿ) and Dathīnah (farther east) refused to join. For many Yafiʿis whose ancestors had won an historical prominence among South Arabian regional players as well as foreign powers, signing what seemed euphemistically labeled an "advisory treaty" was outright submissive, especially when contracted with a non-Muslim European intruder.[58]

The costs of remaining outside the emerging British-led federation were high, however. From the 1940s until independence, Yafiʿ's political infrastructure deteriorated severely. The eroding of traditional tribal and sultanate authority could be traced, in part, to Britain's colonial methods, which are pointed out by many Yemenis today. Cash payments, political titles, development projects, educational opportunities, and so forth were used with some effect to set one party against another. More direct coercion also occurred as air-bombing sorties were led against the villages of uncooperative rural leaders. But the most devastating blows to traditional methods of maintaining law and order came from broader economic transformations. The growth in the supply of guns definitively ruptured older tribal arrangements concerning the protection and management of trade routes. Commodity markets fueled through the port of Aden threatened the traditional livelihoods of Yafiʿi weavers, dyers, exporters of madder and aloe, and silversmiths. And as job opportunities grew in the cities, many young men sought work in Aden or other provincial markets, where they benefited from new commercial ties and systems of patronage. In the wake of such economic changes and shifts in loyalty, Yafiʿ was immersed into a maelstrom of fierce conflicts. An atmosphere of bitter deceit and self-recrimination led many to search for new models of communal viability that could help end internecine bloodshed that had become so endemic to tribal life.

Nationalist sentiment had begun to percolate in communal debates from as early as the 1930s, when a host of literary clubs based in Mukallā (Hadramawt) and Aden began to assemble broader currents of pan-Arab, socialist, and religious discourse into a set of indigenous demands for reform *(iṣlāḥ)*. By the early 1950s, Yafiʿ joined a plethora of other cultural and political organizations by forming its own Yafiʿi Youth Club Union *(Ittiḥād Nādī Shabāb Yāfiʿ)*. In 1963, a broad-based organization with more explicit political aims was formed in Labʿūs, Yafiʿ, and was called the Yafiʿi Reform Front *(Jabhat al-Iṣlāḥ al-Yāfiʿī)*.[59] Devoted to ending tribal conflict, members of the Front helped negotiate peace between feuding families and assisted several prominent shaikhs in drafting constitutions *(dastūrs)* that forbade blood revenge *(thār)*.[60] But the Front also worked toward more comprehensive goals, building underground political cells, coordinating resistance with urban-based political directors, and eventually joining the Front for the Liberation of Occupied Yemen (FLOSY) and the National Liberation Front (NLF) in an armed struggle that would lead the country to independence on November 30, 1967.

In the years following independence, nationalism radically transformed tribal ethos *(qabyalah)* in South Yemen. The customary role of tribalism in Yemen has long figured prominently in highland political life, and other anthropological studies provide a more detailed analysis of a wide range of legal, procedural, and ethical norms than I can cover in this book.[61] Many of these studies, conducted in North Yemen from the 1960s to the 1990s, focus on codes of honor and shame that define tribalism in many societies. In Yemen, tribal values of honor *(sharaf)*, dignity *(nāmūs)*, self-esteem *(ʿizz)*, courage *(shajāʿah)*, generosity *(karāmah)*, autonomy, and manliness *(marjalah)* provide a distinctive vocabulary for managing social order and regulating the exchange of goods and services.[62] Such values continue to figure centrally in Yemenis' world views in the twenty-first century. Nevertheless, during the early 1970s, as I discuss below and in other chapters, political changes in South Yemen inaugurated the most radical transformation of tribal discourses that the two Yemens had known. My attention to these southern contexts of tribal reform and their implications for Yemenis generally provide the book's insights into the ongoing relevance of tribalism to debates about moral authority and the role of media in public life. As other studies have suggested, tribalism gains significance only in relation to other discourses of corporate identity.[63] In highlighting changes in tribal discourse over time and especially in postindependence periods, my own interests lie in understanding the moral fabric of a popular tradition of epistolary practice and also in showing how tribalism helps Yemenis seek accountability from regimes of commerce, accumulation, and metropolitan authorship that operate at national and global levels.

Just two years after independence, the critical leverage of tribalism became invested with a new set of countermodern associations. After a "corrective move" orchestrated by the South Yemeni leadership in June 1969, one of the most radical leftist regimes in the Middle East came to power under President Salem Rubaīʿ ʿAlī. After renaming the nation the People's Democratic Republic of Yemen (PDRY), President ʿAli promoted a new language of state in which Arab nationalism was brought into line with more international socialist discourses. Donning a worker's uniform, the president drew ranks with Yemen's communist party and pledged the nation's loyalty to the spirit of Mao Zedong's Green Revolution. Within months, almost all foreign economic institutions were nationalized, popular youth leagues were organized, and a sweeping agrarian reform law was passed. In the rural countryside, a spate of popular uprisings ensued against landowners, whose "feudalist" *(iqṭāʿī)* practices would no longer be tolerated by the working "proletariat" *(brūlitāriyyah)*. The future status of traditional shaikhly and sultanate families, all of whom had become categorized as feudalists, had been foreshadowed in the Tribal Reconciliation Decree passed immediately after independence.[64] By the early 1970s, the brutal side of the ideological fervor that was rallied against the tribes became apparent. A growing number of tribal organizations were banned, and their representatives were sentenced to prison or executed.[65] The language of "tribalism" *(qabaliyyah)* or "sectarianism" *(ʿashāʾiriyyah)*, as it became known among party leadership, would form no part of public political discourse at any level.

In the wake of such changes, *bidʿ wa jiwāb qaṣīdahs* were stigmatized by official parties as regressive vestiges of tribal life that had no place in the expressive repertoire of true revolutionaries. Poets and singers were encouraged to perform musically didactic nationalist songs or anthems *(nashīds)* that citizens could chant while marching or free-verse poetry that featured themes of love, national loyalty, and sacrifice. Where such genres favored a knowledge of formal Arabic as well as neoclassical and modern Arab poetry, rural inhabitants were at a disadvantage. The early 1970s were thus a lean period for those poets and singers who were not equipped to adapt to the urgent demands of metropolitan political culture.

At a period in which traditional tribal idioms were disparaged, major social reforms across South Yemen helped make public political expression more accessible to a wider spectrum of people and set the stage for the return of more populist forms of tribalism in the mid-1980s and especially after unification. In addition to aggressive land redistribution efforts that benefited impoverished rural laborers, literacy campaigns launched throughout rural areas helped bring illiteracy down from 90 percent before independence (74 percent in cities) to roughly 40 percent by 1973 (38 percent in cities).[66] Women were special beneficiaries of these campaigns, and they increasingly entered the country's work force as clerks, secretaries, lawyers, judges, soldiers, and public singers and poets.[67] In 1974, moreover, some of the most progressive family law legislation in the Arab world was passed, legalizing support for equal relations within the household and empowering married women in matters of inheritance and divorce.[68] For the general populace, moreover, the ideals of the socialist revolution were positively realized in dramatic improvements in health care and life expectancy, subsidized foodstuffs and housing, greater access to primary and secondary school education, liberalizing press reforms, and growing levels of political enfranchisement.

By the late 1970s, the spread of literacy worked with the standardization and mass production of newspapers, political pamphlets, educational manuals, and books to secure for writing a range of public affiliations that was wider than the medium had had before independence. As I show in chapter 6, marks of history were theoretically the property of all citizens, although some were more equipped to claim their authority than others. Simultaneously, however, the accelerated production of audio and audiovisual media supplemented the standard claims of citizenship with an increasingly eclectic range of authoritative public texts (as explored in chapters 3 and 4). Diverse radio programs brought audiences innovative song genres and styles. By the mid-1980s, television stations were broadcasting regular evening news programs and marvelous pictures of the country's diverse cultural and natural wonders to a considerable segment of the Yemeni populace. Audiocassettes continued to supply audiences with an increasingly polyphonous range of material, much of it produced by amateurs and addressed to regional audiences.

Through the formative years of both the Yemens' national trajectories, an increasingly variegated media culture provided Yemenis with critical signposts by which to assess the merits and shortcomings of modernity for its subjects. In *bidʿ wa jiwāb* poetry, conversions between registers of stentorian oral performance, quiescent literary embellishment, whispered prattle, imagistic chimeras, tasteful greetings, sordid material commerce, and so forth all signaled nuances of social revaluation that could be alternately true and risky depending on their combination. By and large, certain registers preserved their conventional social associations despite influence from other medial transformations. Tribalism, for example, continued to be expressed through certain modes of strident oral performance, and the melodies of national anthems continued to tout revolutionary socialism for many audiences long after South Yemen's radical socialist rhetoric had faded. Stereotypical expressions remained political resources for some, especially in the bitter acrimony of political debate, when "residual" marks of identity could underscore enduring forms of difference or defiance. Nevertheless, confronted with some of the most radical swings in political orientation in the Arab world, Yemenis looked to the transvaluation of such medial associations as a moral bellwether in periods of dramatic change. Where tribalism remained a source of moral revindication for those who felt marginalized by nationalist promises of universal equality and inclusion, a resilient set of oral and aural resources supplied listeners with a means to reflect on the limits and legacies of truth as it had come from the mouths of their tribal forebears. In public debate over the politics of social allegiance, the audiocassette's capacity for vocal duplication would prove especially resonant for audiences seeking to understand the relevance of Yemen's modern tribal identity.

The relations between tribalism and civil political life gained renewed import for southern Yemenis when the PDRY and the Yemen Arab Republic (YAR) formally declared unification on May 22, 1990, a consolidation approximated only by the Qasemid imamate some 350 years earlier. In the incipient years of the new Republic of Yemen (ROY), northern tribal leaders who had never confronted open state animosity to tribal politics figured centrally in public political discussion.[69] Southern leaders observed new power relations emerging in Sanaa and began adopting some of the paradigmatic markers of tribal discourse. Although southern-style socialism provided a viable alternative in the first few years of unification, the Yemeni War of 1994 erased its legitimacy for most Yemenis. In ensuing years, the victorious administration pursued national reconstruction with little regard for the traditional interests of many southern leaders. With the additional burden of supporting some 800,000 Yemeni workers who had been expelled from Saudi Arabia and the Gulf states during the Gulf War of 1990, the result of Yemen's neutrality toward American- and British-led Operation Desert Storm, the administration's ability to provide law and order in the many rural governorates became severely strained. As a result of these events, southerners have increasingly turned to tribal law to procure more efficient and lasting settlements to pressing local conflicts. Although tribalism for many Yafiʿis and Yemenis remains a second-rate moral discourse for managing such transformations, tribal identity also invokes localities of social interaction, place, personhood, and event making that ensure its ongoing relevance to Yemenis, especially in an era of mass media.

THE PLAN OF THIS BOOK

Cassettes in Yemen, even those produced by vernacular poets and singers who use inexpensive home-recording machines and distribute their work to cassette shops free of charge, are disseminated at an astonishingly rapid rate and scale.[70] Within two weeks, tens of thousands of listeners hear the contents of some cassettes. Where releases are especially "topical" *(mawḍūʿ)*, as Yemenis say, and address current events in periods of political tension, the verses of such cassettes become referenced, cited verbatim, and reiterated in new poems by a wide range of audiences of young and old, rural and urban, and men and sometimes women. The two longest-running series of folk-poetry cassettes in Yemen have been produced by Yafi'i singers Husain 'Abd al-Nāṣer and 'Ali Ṣāleḥ and provide the principal material for this book. The 'Abd al-Naser series began in the late 1970s and reached cassette 105 by 1996, averaging one new cassette of the latest political verse every three months for over two decades. As the reputation of this series has expanded, over sixty-four poets from across the country have contributed to it. In recent years, 'Ali Saleh's production has surpassed that of 'Abd al-Naser, and their cassettes have been reaching hundreds of thousands of listeners.

To provide a general introduction to this remarkable cassette industry, I devote chapter 1 to the interactive phenomenon of cassette poetry and its salience in political discourse. After describing the contexts of my arrival in Yafi' and initial research observations, I explore how Yemenis distinguish folk-poetry cassettes from other major categories of the Yemeni cassette industry. I then consider the use of cassettes in political life. I focus on three cassettes that helped resolve disputes in Yafi' between 1995 and 1997 and on a composition event in which a group of poets and listeners designed a cassette in response to an attack by Islamic Jihad in Aden in 1997. In each case, I show how genre provides producers and audiences with a discourse for tailoring the aesthetic qualities of poetry and song to the political demands of audience reception. While distinctions of genre enable participants to assemble broad textual forms interactively, they also supply producers with a metadiscourse for assessing the social benefits and costs of cassettes for traditional practices of political entextualization. My concept of "discursive community" helps foreground the conflicted nature of the newly mediated consensus sought by poets and their audiences. The concept invokes, for speakers as well as listeners, a community of shared discourse users. It also signals the active construction of such a community through talk and through a mediated aesthetics of talk in which a range of sensory registers (patterns of rhyme, meter, tonal sequence, interactional behavior, and so forth) are hierarchically organized to the advantage of some participants over others.

Chapter 2 provides a more encompassing historical framework for considering the social aesthetics of inscriptive media. Although *bidʿ wa jiwāb* poetry has attracted politically engaged cassette audiences, the genre has emerged from a much older tradition of written epistolary exchanges between rural highland notables. In the initial sections of the chapter, I outline previous scholarly approaches to orality and literacy, both Western and Yemeni, and consider their contributions to a media aesthetics in Yafiʿ that unfolds over centuries of Muslim education, learning, and legal practice. In subsequent sections, I explore the legacy of this aesthetics in contemporary moral and political life by conducting a detailed analysis of two *bidʿ wa jiwāb qaṣīdahs* composed by Yafiʿi poets in the 1950s. Drawing on the methods of structural poetics and microhistory, I argue that poets' power as moral agents emerges through expressive styles that juxtapose two circulatory registers: a literate metropolitan register that is understood to circulate words effectively and a more resonant tribal register whose features are linked to practices of public oral performance. Although each register presupposes distinct orders of sociality and authority, their oscillation together in *bidʿ wa jiwāb* poetry expresses a culturally attuned reflexive practice that provides a powerful means to address communal conflicts with moral sensibility.

Chapter 3 focuses on changes in textual production and consumption that accompany the development of the sound industry in Aden and its hinterlands. As recording companies proliferate in stride with indigenous nationalist movements, new styles of metropolitan music and song express exciting possibilities for inclusive forms of national identity as elite Adeni singers and musicians gain performance privileges. The radical changes in political discourse that followed the two Yemens' independence, however, and an increasingly decentralized audiocassette market have led to a metropolitanism that has proved to be an effective aesthetic template for registering the ambitions and disappointments of growing numbers of Yemenis. Within discourses of metropolitanism, a general shift is noted from graphic aesthetics in performance and in poetic imagery to more populist, scriptive aesthetics and to a wider range of authoritative oral aesthetics. Such cues serve primarily as signposts for considering the growing cultural and political influence of two groups of song brokers: rural cassette singers and cassette-shop managers. Both groups are instrumental in tailoring the particular textual features of folk poetry to more general habits of social affiliation and moral reflection and thus in mediating between "our song" and a more diverse, transregional song industry. By attending closely to their work throughout the chapter, I show how the cassette technology *(sharīṭ)* becomes invested with a particular set of social associations and suggest that its value as a moral resource comes to inhere in a "scratch" or "obligation" *(sharṭ)*. Even as cassettes facilitate regional song markets and enable older forms of discursive authority, the singer and the song's virtuous listeners are granted greater agency in the politics of aesthetic discrimination.

Having identified the social, economic, and technological conditions that have informed the work of poets, singers, and cassette-shop managers, I return in chapter 4 to strategies of poetic composition and cassette production. The cassette industry has accommodated more diverse groups of rural Yemenis since the 1960s, and poets' and singers' roles as arbiters of knowledge have become more intertwined. Writing again proves instrumental to their collaboration. As a sign of metropolitan authorship, writing also becomes a critical resource that can be mastered and then performatively disowned when poems are designed for acoustic reception by cassette audiences. As I weave narratively between career trajectories and their various compositional strategies, I suggest that both poets and singers build moral credibility and political leverage by polarizing their roles as brokers of rural and metropolitan culture. Poets' verses are stylized with rustic oratory, folksy wisdom, and disruptive violence and represent unchanging rural tradition. Singers foreground visible signs of financial success in the market, providing poets with an urbane circulatory agency. Both roles remain performative acts that allow audiences to consider the emergent agency of the "cassette poet," a more complex and vibrant nexus of textual habits. Toward the end of the chapter, I suggest that the ethical leverage of such performance lies in growing concerns over authorship. Even as poets and singers seek greater control over written texts and cassette production, the uncertainty of authorship in a poorly regulated recording market allows both groups of artists to signal their estrangement from concentrations of metropolitan culture and political power and to propose their own alternative visions of moral authority.

Chapters 5 and 6 examine how poets have used tropes of character *(ṭibāʿah),* personality *(shakhṣiyyah),* and history *(tārīkh)* to situate their political verse within commonsense norms of identity without jeopardizing their credibility as critical moral spokespersons. All of these tropes are, to varying degrees, graphic and scriptive, though they also invite tentative speculations on the authority of the sensory self. The poetry and life of Shayef al-Khaledi provides an anchor for both chapters, although other poets are also discussed. Chapter 5 suggests that the trope of character has long been used by Arab poets and wordsmiths to explore a problematic of authorial subjects who are caught between contending traditions of textual authority. As contemporary Yemeni cassette producers consider the benefits and costs of an audio-recording industry for the integrities of political speakers, a graphic alienation inherent to a trope of character is used to articulate moral ambivalences over and expressive possibilities of authorial iteration. While providing insight into Yemeni poets' own modern expressive challenges, the chapter also offers a comparative analytic framework for considering the moral entailments of circulation in a variety of cultural settings.

The death of al-Khaledi in 1998 and the discussions of his life and work by Yemeni Americans provide the context for examining tropes of personality and history in the final chapter. Much of the chapter focuses on Khaledi's collaborations with the singer Husain ʿAbd al-Naser and with sixty-two other poets in producing Yemen's longest series of political poetry. Observations of poets' *bidʿ wa jiwāb* debates are accompanied by analyses of broader trends in national politics, historiography, and tribalism that unfolded in southern Yemen over the latter half of the twentieth century. Special consideration is given to a trope of "news" *(akhbār)*. While evocative of traditional oral narratives of social events, *akhbār* also associates such narratives with the deceptive graphics of mainstream audiovisual news and in so doing invites listeners' attention to the recorded oral pronouncements of cassette personalities. If personality is finally shown to be an icon of history's fraudulent comprehensive logic, the chapter also suggests that Yemenis employ tropes of history and personality together, defining their relations of complementarity and opposition in specific debates over place, event, responsibility, and collective memory.

The conclusion reviews the book's arguments with special attention given to the importance of culture and the imagination to studies of public activism and public sphere theory.

NOTES

1. Michael Lambek, *Knowledge and Practice in Mayotte: Local Discourses of Islam, Sorcery, and Spirit Possession* (Toronto: University of Toronto Press, 1993), 7.
2. The notion of the text as a signifying practice has a long history in poststructural theory. To differentiate the semiotics of textuality from mediation in this book, I approach the text (when I am not discussing actual, material text artifacts) primarily in terms of iteration and representational authority, whereas I approach media in terms of textual aesthetics. My study of media thus becomes a way to consider how the finicky residues of textual iteration become socially valued through, as Clifford Geertz has said, a "model for" producer-consumer interchange and concomitantly for new forms of social affiliation. Clifford Geertz, "Religion as a Cultural Sys-

tem," in *The Interpretation of Cultures* (New York: Basic Books, 1973), 93–94.

3. Even otherwise exemplary media studies that acknowledge diverse practices of reception, reproduction, and knowledge can overdetermine the social content of given media forms by rendering them as functions of discrete "societies" rather than as culturally contingent sites of social articulation. See, for example, Terry Flew, *New Media: An Introduction* (Oxford: Oxford University Press, 2002), 10. The legacy of mass-media theorist Marshall McLuhan looms behind many such claims, especially Marshall McLuhan, *Understanding Media: The Extensions of Man* (New York: McGraw Hill, 1964), and Marshall McLuhan and Eric McLuhan, *Laws of Media: The New Science* (Toronto: University of Toronto Press, 1988). Although I share McLuhan's interest in how given technologies are perceived to have specific social functions, I find his presumptions about the collective experience of given technologies (by which a given "medium" can be given a constancy of form or "message") not only too dismissive of established habits of cultural interpretation (genre, for example) but also too conducive to methodological leapfrogging.
4. First defined by Frenchman George Depping in 1812, the term *ethnography* originally described the study of how ethnic groups differently exhibit indolence and industry, as noted by Timothy Mitchell, *Colonizing Egypt* (Berkeley: University of California Press, 1988), 106–07. My interest in Yemenis' use of writing and media technologies to categorize different communities, especially in graphic distinctions of metropolitan productivity and their counterparts, reflects the aims of a neo-Boasian anthropology that can better accommodate comparative studies of the native ethnographer. Matti Bunzl, "Boas, Foucault, and the 'Native Anthropologist': Notes toward a Neo-Boasian Anthropology," *American Anthropologist* 106, no. 3 (2004): 441. Yemenis, too, use scriptive practice to categorize people as members of communities informed by different orders of production and iteration. By attending more to the coexistence and relationality of such orders than to stages of racial development, however, Yemenis exhibit an ethnographic sensibility that is more contextually refined or pragmatic than we tend to think possible.
5. Paul Friedrich, "Poetic Language and the Imagination: A Refor-

mulation of the Sapir-Whorf Hypothesis," in *Language, Context, and the Imagination* (Stanford: Stanford University Press, 1979), 446.

6. This proverb is widely known through oral tradition in Yafiʿ. I also found it recorded in a tenth-century compendium of the sayings attributed to Imam ʿAli Bin Abī Ṭālib (d. 661), the fourth caliph of Islam. *Nahj al-Balāghah (Peak of Eloquence)*, 2d ed. (Bombay: Islamic Seminary for World Shia Muslim Organisation, 1978), 265.
7. Stephen Tyler, *The Unspeakable: Discourse, Dialogue and Rhetoric in the Postmodern World* (Madison: University of Wisconsin Press, 1987); Benjamin Whorf, "The Relation of Habitual Thought and Behavior to Language," in *High Points in Anthropology,* ed. P. Bohannan and M. Glazer, 149–71 (New York: Knopf, 1988 [1939]).
8. Robert Desjarlais, *Sensory Biographies: Lives and Deaths among Nepal's Yolmo Buddhists* (Berkeley: University of California Press, 2003).
9. David Graeber, *Toward an Anthropological Theory of Value: The False Coin of Our Own Dreams* (New York: Palgrave, 2001); Nancy Munn, "Gawan Kula: Spatiotemporal Control and the Symbolism of Influence," in *The Kula: New Perspectives on Massim Exchange,* ed. J. Leach and E. Leach, 277–308 (Cambridge: Cambridge University Press, 1983).
10. Michael Gilsenan, *Recognizing Islam: Religion and Society in the Modern Arab World* (London: I. B. Tauris, 1990 [1982]); el-Sayed el-Aswad, *Religion and Folk Cosmology: Scenarios of the Visible and Invisible in Egypt* (New York: Praeger, 2002); Gregory Starrett, "Violence and the Rhetoric of Images," *Cultural Anthropology* 18, no. 3 (2003): 398–428.
11. Michael Silverstein and Greg Urban, *Natural Histories of Discourse* (Chicago: University of Chicago Press, 1996).
12. In the third century C.E., for example, the Persian mystic Mani alleged that God's revelation had been delivered to him in the form of an imminent scripture and that his sermons thus signaled a truth more ultimate than the orally transmitted claims to scriptural insight that had distinguished the authority of the Jews.
13. Jack Goody, "Introduction," in *Literacy in Traditional Societies,* ed. Jack Goody (New York: Cambridge University Press, 1968), 11–19.

14. Cited in William A. Graham, *Beyond the Written Word: Oral Aspects of Scripture in the History of Religion* (Cambridge: Cambridge University Press, 1987), 79.
15. The immanence of text becomes especially secure when it can command a distinctive orality by which it might be distinguished from everyday locution even as it enacts the authoritative moral tenets of community. Thus, the historical value of (1) mellifluous styles of Qur'anic recitation, (2) a transregional poetic koiné as the foundation of the Qur'an's eloquence, and (3) listeners' associations of Qur'anic diction with a nonurban, tribal (specifically Quraīsh) dialect. At the risk of generalization, I would suggest that all elements seem to invest the holy text with a sense of honored and removed acoustic difference. The divine speaks with an inscrutable lilt. Later in the book, I discuss the value of parochial vernacular idioms and diction for cassette singers and poets who craft more progressive forms of metropolitan textual authority.
16. God's first revelation to the Prophet Muḥammad begins: "Recite! In the name of your Lord and Cherisher, who created / Created man out of a [mere] clot of congealed blood. / Recite! And your Lord is Most Bountiful. / He Who taught (the use of the) pen / Taught man that which he knew not. / Nay, but man does trangress all bounds" (96:1–4). For a comprehensive analysis of the semantics of authoritative inscription in the Qur'an, see Daniel Madigan, *The Qur'an's Self-Image: Writing and Authority in Islam's Scripture* (Princeton: Princeton University Press, 2001).
17. Graham, *Beyond the Written Word,* 80.
18. A special appeal to studies of alternative "book concepts" is made by Graham, *Beyond the Written Word,* 52. Muslim scholars of exegesis and theology who urge similar attention include Mohammed Arkoun, "The Concept of Authority in Islamic Thought," in *Islam: State and Society,* ed. K. Ferdinand and M. Mozaffari (London: Curzon Press, 1988), 60–62; and Nāṣer Ḥāmid Abū Zayd, *Mafhūm al-Naṣṣ: Dirāsah fī 'Ulūm al-Qur'ān* (Cairo: al-Hay'at al-Miṣriyyat al-'Āmah li-l-Kitāb, 1990), 120. Anthropological studies include Michael Gilsenan, "Sacred Words," in *The Diversity of the Muslim Community,* ed. A. al-Shahi (London: Ithaca Press, 1987), 92–98; Brinkley Messick, "Kissing Hands and Knees: Hegemony and Hierarchy in Sharī'a Discourse," *Law and Society Review* 22 (1988): 637–59; and John R. Bowen, "On Scriptural Essentialism

and Ritual Variation: Muslim Sacrifice in Sumatra and Morocco," *American Ethnologist* 19, no. 4 (1992): 656–71.

19. Richard Bauman and Charles L. Briggs, "Poetics and Performance as Critical Perspectives on Language and Social Life," *Annual Reviews of Anthropology* 19 (1990): 73–74.
20. Michel Foucault, *The Archaeology of Knowledge and the Discourse on Language* (New York: Pantheon Books, 1972); Foucault, *Madness and Civilization: A History of Insanity in the Age of Reason* (London: Tavistock, 1967).
21. Such an approach is familiar to linguistic anthropology and is described concisely by Joel Sherzer: "Discourse is the locus of the expression of ideology and especially of the playing out and the working out of conflicts, tensions, and changes inherent in ideological systems. . . . Related to ideology is a historical perspective in conjunction with the influences of the world economic and political system, both of which can be shown to be perceived by and interpreted by interactants and performers in concrete instances of discourse." Joel Sherzer, *Verbal Art in San Blas* (New York: Cambridge University Press, 1990), 7. I privilege poetry as the principal expressive domain through which discourse and ideology are explored.
22. Politics becomes a struggle to structure discourse or performance in relation to previous texts and to entextualize authoritatively with the aim of achieving social justice for one's community. Such an approach has been carefully delineated by Silverstein and Urban, *Natural Histories of Discourse.*
23. For theories of the real, Michel de Certeau deserves special mention. See Tom Conley's introduction in Michel de Certeau, *The Writing of History* (New York: Columbia University Press, 1988), xviii. Raymond Williams continues to provide important groundwork for semiotic approaches to human apperception. Raymond Williams, *Marxism and Literature* (Oxford: Oxford University Press, 1977).
24. Brinkley Messick's work is exemplary in linking the articulations of modern subjectivity to the regimentation of legal textual practices as instituted primarily by the state. See especially Brinkley Messick, "Legal Documents and the Concept of Restricted Literacy," *International Journal of the Sociology of Language* 42 (1983): 41–52; Messick, "Kissing Hands and Knees"; Messick,

"Just Writing: Paradox and Political Economy in Yemeni Legal Discourse," *Cultural Anthropology* 4, no. 1 (1989): 26–50; and Messick, *The Calligraphic State: Textual Domination and History in a Muslim Society* (Berkeley: University of California Press, 1993). Other notable introductions to legal authority, both state and tribal, focus on northern Yemen and include Paul Dresch, *Tribes, Government, and History in Yemen* (New York: Oxford University Press, 1989); Martha Mundy, *Domestic Government: Kinship, Community, and Polity in North Yemen* (London: I. B. Tauris, 1995); Shelagh Weir, A Tribal Order: Politics and Law in the Mountains of Yemen (Austin: Texas University Press, 2006); Hassan A. al-Hubaishi, *Legal System and Basic Law in Yemen* (Worcester, UK: Billing and Sons, 1988); and Bernard Haykel, *Revival and Reform in Islam: The Legacy of Muhammad al-Shawkani* (Cambridge: Cambridge University Press, 2003).

25. Antonio Gramsci, *Selections from the Prison Notebooks* (New York: International, 2003 [1971]), 54–55, 355.
26. Ibid., 55, 328.
27. Suzanne Pinckney Stetkevych, *The Mute Immortals Speak: Pre-Islamic Poetry and the Poetics of Ritual, Myth and Poetics* (Ithaca: Cornell University Press, 1993), 6–8.
28. Steven Caton, *Peaks of Yemen I Summon: Poetry as Cultural Practice in a North Yemeni Tribe* (Berkeley: University of California Press, 1990).
29. Several of the finest introductions to *ḥumaīnī* verse include Muḥammad ʿAbduh Ghānem, *Shiʿr al-Ghināʾ al-Sanʿānī* (Damascus: Dār al-ʿAwdah, 1987); Robert Serjeant, *Prose and Poetry from Hadhramawt* (London: Taylor's Foreign Press, 1951); and Jaʿfar S. Ḍafārī, "Humaini Poetry in South Arabia," Doctoral thesis, University of London, 1966.
30. Examples of genres that were recited and chanted rather than sung include rousing tribal verses *(zāmils)* and poetic satire *(hijāʾ)* that expressed a kind of martial vigor better accompanied by war drums and clanging metal tambourines than by the delicate strains of "song," as well as some *qaṣīdah* genres that were best read aloud in the oratorical fashion of loquacious public speakers. Most of these genres were typically shorter and less embellished with transportable notions of authorship than were *ḥumaīnī* verse

and *bid' wa jiwāb* poetry. I focus on the formal distinctions of *bid' wa jiwāb* poetry in chapter 2.

31. M. M. Bakhtin, *The Dialogic Imagination* (Austin: University of Texas Press, 1994 [1975]), 428.
32. I thank Steven Caton for suggesting this term.
33. In Muslim jurisprudence and language theory, the dialectic between circulation and resonance is best expressed as the semiotic relation between conceptualization and judgment. As linguist Mohamed Ali notes: "Signification is commonly defined as 'the fact of something being in a state where the cognition of it necessarily implies the cognition of something else' *(kawnu l-shay'i bi-ḥālatin yalzamu mina l-'ilmi bi-hi l-'ilmu bi-shay'in ākhar)*. The word *'ilm* in this definition is frequently regarded as synonymous with *idrāk* (cognition), which covers both *taṣawwur* (conceptualisation or non-propositional apprehension) and *taṣdīq* (judgement or propositional apprehension)." Mohamed M. Ali, *Medieval Islamic Pragmatics: Sunni Legal Theories' Models of Textual Communication* (Richmond, Eng.: Curzon Press, 2000), 141.
34. Circulation and resonance are sometimes explicitly discussed by Yemenis (as seen in the Nājī excerpt below and throughout the book). More often they are reflexive ways of knowing that are explored in tropic juxtapositions. Insofar as they help channel fundamental indexicalities of discourse toward broader representational patterns, they can be considered metadiscourses.
35. Muḥammad Murshed Nājī, *Aghānīnā al-Sha'biyyah* (Aden: Dār al-Jamāhīr, 1959), 140–41. Here is the text in full: "Al-ughniyyat al-'āmat al-nājiḥah hiyā hadhā al-silāḥ, al-ughniyyat al-sha'biyyat al-mu'abbirah hiyā hadhā al-quwah allatī tastaṭī' an taqūm bi-hadhā al-dawr. . . . Hiyā al-rasūl al-ṣādiq alladhī yastaṭī' an yunqul li-ajzā' mujtama' ṣūrah ḥaqīqiyyah kāmilah min fahm juz' min ajzā'ihi li-l-ḥayāh wa li-l-mashākil, min taqālīdihi wa 'ādātihi wa ṭibā'ihi, min akhlāqihi w-ahdāfihi wa muthulihi, min bī'atihi w-atharihi fī takwīnihi wa sīrihi wa taqaddumihi, wa hiyā tunqul kulla hadhā fī lughah hadhā al-juz' min ajzā' mujtama'nā al-'arabī lughah mutaqaddimah munasiqah, in lam tafham qāmūsiyyan fa-hiyā sa-tafham shu'ūriyyan, sa-tuḥiss li-annahā infi'āl ṣādiq, wa li-annahā ta'bīr 'an shu'ūr insānī in ikhtalaf fī tafāṣīlihi fa-huwa yataḥadd fī manba'ihi al-insānī al-ṣāfī.

"Wa bi-l-intishār al-ughniyyah tunshir lughat al-ughniyyah, wa-l-taqārub al-lughawī baīn ajzā' mujtama'nā huwa akhṭar juz' fī ma'rakatinā fī sabīl al-waḥdat al-ijtimā'iyyah. . . . Wa hadhā al-taqārub in tamm bi-wāsaṭat al-ughniyyah al-sayyārah yuḥaqqaq mazajan ḥaqīqiyyan baīn al-qawālib al-ta'bīriyyah li-ajzā' mujtama'nā, wa yatīḥ furṣah li-l-iḥtikāk al-lughawī baīn lahjātinā al-'āmiyyah fa-tā'kudh kulla min-hā min al-ukhrā wa turaddid kullu bī'ah ijtimā'iyyah ta'bīrāt al-bī'ah al-ijtimā'iyyat al-ukhrā, wa la'alla hadhā yu'addī ilā taṣfiyyah lahjātinā al-'āmiyyat al-muta'addidah wa yusā'id 'alā taqārubihā wa mazajihā wa khalq lahjāt 'āmiyyah 'āmah mafhūmah fī kulli bī'ah, qarībah ilā isti'māl kulla juz' min ajzā' mujtama'nā."

36. Marxist literary critic and socialist party leader 'Umar al-Jāwī, for example, reports that this distinction began being drawn by Arab intellectuals and Yemenis in the early 1950s. To summarize this position, he cites the fifth edition of a *Soviet Literary Encyclopedia,* published in 1962, to differentiate between "folk" *(sha'bī)* poetry (which is oral, collective, anonymous, and inherited and typically addresses "traditional popular" matters relating to labor and social life) and "popular" *('āmī)* poetry (which has been influenced by contemporary Arabic as disseminated through television and the radio, and which is promoted more vigorously by the intelligentsia). 'Umar al-Jāwī, "Kayfa Nafham al-Shi'r al-Sha'bī?," *al-Turāth,* no. 4 (1992 [1980]): 70–79.

37. The ethics of "resonance" that I discuss in this book is better expressed through the semantics of *'abara* than it is through a variety of onomatopoeic Arabic words for sonic reverberation, such as *ranīn, jaljalah,* or *mula'la'.* The verbal declensions of *'abara* include (cvcvcv): to wade across, to shed tears (both of which suggest moving through a liquidous interstitial zone); (cvccvcv): to interpret (especially dreams), consider, weigh; and (ictvcvcv): to reflect upon, learn a lesson, hold in esteem. In the Yemeni vernacular, the noun *'ubar* refers to a water channel, and related words suggest a similar kind of liquidity that lingers and unfolds: a bridge or ferry *(mi'bar),* perfume *('abīr),* and the quality of being transient *('ābir),* such as I often heard referring to clouds. All such associations seem to contemplate an ephemeral or metaphysical distance amid full sensory contact. In early Muslim spirituality, *'ibrah* was a term for deep gnostic insight and advice, as noted by Kamāl al-Dīn 'Abd

al-Razzāq, *Kitāb al-Istilāḥāt al-Ṣūfiyyah,* 2d ed., ed. A. Sprenger (Lahore: al-Irshād, 1974 [1845]), 123–124. Arab exegetical scholars have long referred to the study of noncanonical texts to confirm or clarify the revealed word as "resonant reflection" *(iʿtibār).*

38. Georg Wilhelm Hegel, *Hegel's Philosophy of Nature* (New York: Allen and Unwin, 1970), 69–74.

39. On nationalism as a form of textual and social affiliation from global margins, see Homi Bhabha, "Dessimi-Nation: Time, Narrative, and the Margins of the Modern Nation," in *Nations and Narration,* 291–322 (New York: Routledge, 1990).

40. In approaching politics through persuasion, I contribute to a panoply of studies of Yemeni political poetry. Analyses of the use of poetry in tribal dispute negotiations include Caton, *Peaks of Yemen,* 1990; Ṣāleḥ Hārethī, *al-Zāmil fī al-Ḥarb w-al-Munāsabāt* (Damascus: al-Kātib al-ʿArabī, 1990); W. Flagg Miller, "Public Words and Body Politics: Reflections on the Strategies of Women Poets in Rural Yemen," *Journal of Women's History* 14, no. 1 (2002): 94–122; and ʿAbdallah al-Baraddūnī, *Riḥlat fī-l-Shiʿr al-Yamanī Qadīmihi wa Ḥadīthihi,* 5th ed. (Damascus: Dār al-Fikr, 1995 [1972]). Other scholars have focused on stately verse and oratory, including Lucine Taminian, "Persuading the Monarchs: Poetry and Politics in Yemen, 1920–1950," in *Le Yémen Contemporain,* ed. R. Leveau, F. Mermier, and U. Steinbach, 203–19 (Paris: Éditions Karthala, 1999); and Robert Serjeant, "The Yemeni Poet al-Zubayri and His Polemic against the Zaydi Imams," *Arabian Studies* 5 (1979): 87–130. Several important studies of the use of poetry in daily social networking include Mikhail Rodionov, "Poetry and Power in Hadramawt," *New Arabian Studies* 3 (1996): 118–33; and Steven Caton, "Salām Taḥīya: Greetings from Highland Yemen," *American Ethnologist* 13 (1986): 290–308. Finally, I note a fine article on prisoners' efforts to seek clemency by H. E. Aḥmad Shāmī, "Yemeni Literature in Ḥajjah Prisons," *Arabian Studies* 2 (1975): 43–60.

41. Jürgen Habermas, *The Structural Transformation of the Public Sphere,* trans. T. Burger (Oxford: Polity Press, 1992 [1962]).

42. Habermas's insights on addresseeship have been developed most generatively by Michael Warner. Michael Warner, *The Letters of the Republic: Publication and the Public Sphere in Eighteenth-*

Century America (Cambridge, Mass.: Harvard University Press, 1990), 39–41; and Warner, "Publics and Counterpublics," *Public Culture* 14, no. 1 (2002): 77–78. Warner suggests that acts of reading by those engaged in the public sphere cultivate a kind of "stranger-sociability" in which one addresses unrecognized and potentially limitless others from one's own vernacular social contexts. I bring Warner's insights to my own analysis of culturally situated media aesthetics in chapters 5 and 6, especially.

43. Annabelle Sreberny-Mohammadi and Ali Mohammadi, *Small Media, Big Revolution: Communication, Culture, and the Iranian Revolution* (Minneapolis: University of Minnesota Press, 1994), 21; Peter Manuel, *Cassette-Culture: Popular Music and Technology in North India* (Chicago: University of Chicago Press, 1993), 3; Asghar Fathi, "The Role of the Islamic Pulpit," *Journal of Communication* 29, no. 3 (1979): 102–06; and Chris Cutler, "Necessity and Choice in Musical Forms: Concerning Musical and Technical Means and Political Needs," in *Cassette Mythos,* ed. R. James, 160–64 (Brooklyn: Autonomedia, 1992).
44. Dell Hymes, "The Ethnography of Speaking," in *Anthropology and Human Behavior,* ed. T. Gladwin and W. C. Sturtevant, 13–53 (Washington, D.C.: Anthropological Society of Washington, 1962); Dell Hymes, "Toward Ethnographies of Communication: The Analysis of Communicative Events," in *Language and Social Context,* ed. P. P. Giglioli, 21–44 (Baltimore: Penguin Books, 1972 [1964]); John Gumperz and Dell Hymes, *The Ethnography of Communication* (Washington, D.C.: American Anthropological Association, 1964); and Hilary Putnam, "The Meaning of 'Meaning'," in *Mind, Language and Reality* (Cambridge: Cambridge University Press, 1975).
45. Pierre Bourdieu, "The Economics of Linguistic Exchanges," *Social Science Information* 16, no. 6 (1977): 645–68; Bourdieu, *Language and Symbolic Power,* 3d ed. (Cambridge, Mass.: Harvard University Press, 1994 [1982]). See also Ferruccio Rossi-Landi, *Language as Work and Trade: A Semiotic Homology for Linguistics and Economics* (South Hadley, Mass.: Bergin and Garvey, 1983).
46. Michel Foucault, *Discipline and Punish* (New York: Vintage Books, 1979 [1975]).
47. My approach to inscription draws from the earlier creative writ-

ings of French poststructuralists, notably Jacques Derrida and Roland Barthes. See, especially, Jacques Derrida, "The Double Session," in *A Derrida Reader: Between the Blinds* (New York: Columbia University Press, 1991 [1972]); and Roland Barthes, "The Death of the Author," in *Image-Music-Text,* 142–48 (New York: Hill and Wang, 1977). Chapter 5 presents an especially strong argument for why their positions need revision.

48. This definition follows Judith Butler, whose concept of performativity, outlined in *Gender Trouble* (1990), draws from Friedrich Nietzsche's assertion that "there is no 'being' behind doing, acting, becoming; 'the doer' is merely a fiction imposed on the doing—the doing itself is everything." Friedrich Nietzche, *On the Genealogy of Morals,* trans. D. Smith (New York: Oxford University Press, 1996), 29.
49. Among the tribal highlands in Yemen, Yafiʿ is distinguished for its especially pronounced emphasis on regional integrity over time. Tenth-century Yemeni historian al-Hasan al-Ḥamdani mentions the two largest "houses" *(baīts)* that are still recognized today, the Bani Mālek and the Bani Qāsed, as well as several of the region's other largest *maktabs.* al-Ḥasan Bin Aḥmad al-Hamdānī, *Kitāb Ṣifah Jazīrat al-ʿArab,* ed. M. al-Najdi (Cairo: Maṭbaʿat al-Saʿādah, 1953). As I discuss later in the introduction, such integrity has been a product of the region's historic agricultural and military prowess, its sultanate authority, and its early development of enclaves for religious learning.
50. Klaus Schippmann, *Ancient South Arabia: From the Queen of Sheba to the Advent of Islam* (Princeton, N.J.: Markus Wiener Publishers, 2001), 57–58.
51. R. J. Gavin, *Aden under British Rule, 1839–1967* (New York: Barnes & Noble Books, 1975), 3–5.
52. The Qarmatians were an offshoot Ismaʿili (Shiʿite) movement that began in a revolt against the entrenched ʿAbbasid elite in Baghdad in the late ninth century. Their movement later spread across the Middle East. ʿAli Bin Fadl, whose origins and affiliations are the stuff of wild legend, is reported to have begun recruiting Yafiʿis in 903–04/291–92. After establishing headquarters in Madhaīkhirah, Abyan, he successfully rallied local tribes in aggressive campaigns into northern Yemen, until his troops met defeat some eigh-

teen years later at Wadi al-Dawar, near Ibb. ʿUmārah Bin ʿAlī al-Ḥakamī, *Taʾrīkh al-Yaman* (Cairo, 1957), 168–69.

53. Biographical details of ʾAsʿad are recorded in ʿAbdallah Muḥammad al-Ḥibshī, *Ḥayāt al-Adab al-Yamanī fī ʿAṣr Banī Rasūl,* 2d ed. (Sanaa: Ministry of Information and Culture, 1980), 227–29.
54. Shaikh Abu Bakr Bin Salem, of the famed Bā ʿAlawī line in Yemen, enjoyed an especially strong fealty among Yafiʿis who had migrated to Hadramawt. Exchanges between Yafiʿ and Hadramawt have been documented by W. Flagg Miller, "Yafiʿ Has Only One Name: Shared Histories and Cultural Linkages between Yafiʿ and Hadramawt," in *Cultural Anthropology of Southern Arabia: Hadramawt Revisited* (St. Petersburg: Museum of Anthropology and Ethnography (1999), 68–69; and Robert Serjeant, "Yāfiʿ, the Zaidīs, Āl-Bū Bakr b. Sālim and Others: Tribes and Sayyids," in *On Both Sides of the al-Mandab: Ethiopian, South-Arabic and Islamic Studies Presented to Oscar Lofgren,* 83–05 (Stockholm: Svenska Forskningsinstituteti Istanbul, 1989). One of the earliest members of the Harharah family, ʿAli Bin Aḥmad Harharah, studied under the hand of Shaikh Bin Salem at his residence in ʿĪnāt. Just before the shaikh's death in 1592, Harharah was given writ to serve as a conciliator *(muṣliḥ)* and religious guide *(murshid dīnī)* for all of Yafiʿ. Naṣer Sabʿah, *Min Yanābīʿ Taʾrīkhinā al-Yamanī* (Damascus: al-Kātib al-ʿArabī, 1994), 58; Serjeant, "Yāfiʿ, the Zaidīs," 85; see also ʿAbd al-Qāder ʿĀṭaf Harharah, *Taʾrīkh al-Usrah al-Harharah* (Dearborn, Mich.: Discovery Marketing, 1998).
55. Oral narratives and scholarship in Yafiʿ feature lively debates over the exact dates and terms of each sultan's "appointment." In general, it can be said that the ʿAfifi sultanate became firmly established during Maʿwdah Bin Muḥammad's lifetime in the late seventeenth century and especially during his son Qahtan's lifetime. The Harharah sultanate was established at roughly the same time by Saleh Bin Aḥmad Bin ʿAlī Harharah, as noted by Aḥmad al-ʿAbdalī, *Hadiyyat al-Zaman fī Akhbār Mulūk Laḥaj wa ʿAdan* (Beirut: Dār al-ʿAwdah, 1980 [1930]), 109; and Ḥamzah Luqmān, *Taʾrīkh al-Qabāʾil al-Yamaniyyah* (Sanaa: Dār al-Kalimah, 1985), 174. The appointment of "sultans" was a strategy employed by the imamate to end war with regional power players and to win favorable concessions, usually involving taxation of some sort.

Whatever legal arrangements were obtained, a much celebrated narrative in Yafiʿ recounts the marriage of Nur Bint ʿAfīf (d. 1092), a gun-slinging warrior *shaīkhah,* into the Harharah lineage and the subsequent easing of relations between the two sultanates.

56. Miller, "Yafiʿ Has Only One Name," 66–71.
57. Among Hadramis, Yafiʿis became designated by the simple term "soldiers" *(ʿasākir),* a label that glossed over the thousands of Yafiʿis who, after conflict had calmed, established residence and took up farming and family life.
58. In chapter 2, I focus on two *qaṣīdahs* that express the reluctance of many Yafiʿis to collaborate with the British. For discussion of another pair of anticolonialist *qaṣīdahs* in Yemen, see W. Flagg Miller and Ulrike Freitag, "Three Poems on British Involvement in Yemen, from the Yemeni Press 1937," in *The Modern Middle East: A Sourcebook for History,* ed. C. M. Amin, B. C. Fortna, and E. Frierson, 492–500 (Oxford: Oxford University Press, 2005).
59. A history of the Front has been written by Sālem ʿAbd Rabbuh and Mundaʿī Dayyān, *Jabhat al-Iṣlāḥ al-Yāfiʿiyyah* (Aden: Mu'assasat 14 Uktūbir, 1990).
60. The new nationalist terms of the Front were expressed unequivocally in Resolution 11 of the Front's first meeting on April 13, 1963: "Shaikhs and tribal leaders *(ʿāqils)* must listen and comply. Their word will be heard if it adheres to the interests of the nation *(waṭan).* But if it differs from them, we must not accept it; indeed, we must refuse it decisively." Resolution 6 declares that the Front's own constitution *(dastūr)* is the Qur'an and its legal premise Islamic law. In a holiday festival that directly followed this meeting, a banner was carried that read "No tribalism. . . . No clannishness. . . . We are all an Arab people" *(lā qabaliyyah. . . . lā ʿaṣabiyyah. . . . kullunā ummah ʿarabiyyah).* Ibid., 80–82.
61. The English literature on tribal life in Yemen is extensive. Paul Dresch's landmark study remains the finest introduction. Dresch, *Tribes, Government, and History.* Najwa Adra's provides an especially sensitive account of tribal ethos. Najwa Adra, "Qabyala: The Tribal Concept in the Central Highlands, the Yemen Arab Republic," Doctoral thesis, Temple University, Philadelphia, 1982. Other suggested introductions include Tomas Gerholm, *Market, Mosque, and Mafraj: Social Inequality in a Yemeni Town* (Stockholm: Stockholm University Press, 1977); Paul Dresch, "Tribal Re-

lations and Political History in Upper Yemen," in *Contemporary Yemen: Politics and Historical Background,* ed. B. R. Pridham, 154–74 (London: Croom Helm, 1984); Dresch, "The Position of Shaykhs among the Northern Tribes of Yemen," *Man* 19, no. 1 (1984): 31–49; Dresch, "Imams and Tribes: The Writing and Acting of History in Upper Yemen," in *Tribes and State Formation in the Middle East,* ed. P. D. Khoury and J. Kostiner, 252–87 (Berkeley: University of California Press, 1990); Steven Caton, "Icons of the Person: Lacan's 'Imago' in the Yemeni Male's Tribal Wedding," *Asian Folklore Studies* 52 (1993): 359–81; Caton, *Yemen Chronicle: An Anthropology of War and Mediation* (New York: Hill and Wang, 2005); and Weir, *A Tribal Order.*

62. For ethnographic discussion of these terms in Yemen, see Caton, *Peaks of Yemen,* 26–35; Adra, "Qabyala," 129–58; and Dresch, *Tribes, Government, and History in Yemen,* 38–74.
63. My own work on this topic focuses on language ideology and media in southern Yemen. W. Flagg Miller, "Metaphors of Commerce: Trans-valuing Tribalism in Yemeni Audiocassette Poetry," *International Journal of Middle East Studies* 34, no. 1 (2002): 29–57; also see Paul Dresch and Bernard Haykel, "Islamists and Tribesfolk in Yemen: A Study of Styles and Stereotypes," *International Journal of Middle East Studies* 27 (1995): 405–31; Najwa Adra, "Dance and Glance: Visualizing Tribal Identity in Highland Yemen," *Visual Anthropology* 11 (1998): 55–102; and Isa Blumi, "Looking beyond the Tribe: Abandoning Paradigms to Write Social History in Yemen during World War I," *New Perspectives on Turkey* 22 (2000): 117–43.
64. Helen Lackner, *P.D.R. Yemen: Outpost of Socialist Development in Arabia* (London: Ithaca Press, 1985), 110–11.
65. In 1971, twenty-one members of former Yafiʿi tribal families, including one of most celebrated early rebels against the British, Muhammad Bin ʿAīdrūs al-ʿAfīfī, were ambushed and killed in a motorcade returning to Yafiʿ after their release from prison.
66. Karāma Muḥammad Sulaīmān, *al-Tarbiyyah wa-l-Taʿlīm fī al-Shaṭr al-Janūbī min al-Yaman* (Sanaa: Markaz li-l-Dirāsāt wa-l-Buḥūh al-Yamanī, 1994), 1:238, 2:76.
67. The role of literacy campaigns in changing women's relation to public culture and poetry in southern Yemen is discussed by Miller, "Public Words."

68. Lackner, *P.D.R. Yemen,* 116–18.
69. At first, northern Yemeni political leaders, notably among them the speaker of parliament and paramount shaikh of the Ḥāshed tribe, ʿAbdallah Bin Ḥusaīn al-Aḥmar, initiated the republic's open support of tribalism through a series of pantribal conferences held in 1991 and 1992. Paul Dresch, "The Tribal Factor in the Yemeni Crisis," in *The Yemeni War of 1994: Causes and Consequences* (London: Saqi Books, 1995), 46–55. In the second conference, a declaration was released that "The weapon composes an integral part of the Yemeni person." Abu Bakr Saqqaf, "Problèmes de L'Unité Yéménite," *La Révue du Monde Musulman et de la Méditerranée* 67 (1993): 99. This statement, while not exceptional for northern Yemenis, represented a radical departure from the public rhetoric that had been familiar to the southern populace.
70. A simple tape recorder cost 2,500 YR. All prices quoted in this book have been calculated at 2006 exchange rates (roughly 185 YR per U.S. dollar).

• ONE •

Folk-Poetry Cassettes: Between Community and Conflict

Poetry is the public register of the Arab people: by its means, genealogies are remembered, and glorious deeds are made known.

—Tenth-century grammarian Ahmad Ibn Fāris[1]

There are three ranks of folk-poetry interpreters. Number 1 is a son of the homeland. Number 2 lives in the city. Number 3 is a migrant abroad.

—Employee of a cassette shop for Yafiʿi folk poetry

ARRIVAL AT THE FIELDSITE AND INITIAL OBSERVATIONS

Yafiʿ remains a place of sublime isolation only on old roadless maps or in much-recounted histories of mountain refuges. As a place of acoustic innovation and industry, Yafiʿ is close to the experiences of many Yemenis, especially those living in Aden and its precincts. I first heard Yafiʿi song in the summer of 1995 when walking through "Crater," the name that Yemenis give to downtown Aden, which is located in an ancient volcanic cone that once glowed with molten lava. Barely into my first year of fieldwork, I did not understand much of the vernacular Yemeni that blared from a local cassette shop's loudspeakers. Had I been able to grasp the lyrics, I may well have heard the following verses, which employed the metaphor of an illegal satellite-television decoder *(sāriq al-dīsh)* to express a poet's frustration with injustices in Yemen. Operated by someone else, the decoder weakened the sounds and images of the poet's own television, leading to his frustration:

Yahya ʿAlī said: May the wind take you, satellite-dish pirate!
Every time I came to a program, you stole the channel.
You steal the sound and the picture and cause such static.
How I wish that [Yahya] Abu Ḥāfeẓ retained some authority.

The advantages of potentially universal televisual images for those who could listen to satellite television and watch its programs were undermining the poet's own authority *(sulṭah)*.

In Aden's Office of Cultural Affairs a few days later, several employees spoke with me about the style of such cassettes. Composed by poets mostly from Yafiʿ, these cassette-recorded poems featured head-to-head debates *(musājalāt)* over the latest political events in the country and in the world at large. The most famous of these exchanges were between the northern poet Aḥmad al-Ṣunbaḥī and Shayef al-Khāledī from Yafiʿ, both of whom had collaborated with one singer to produce nearly a hundred cassettes over the last several decades. "In Yafiʿ, you'll find many of the finest folk poets of anywhere in this part of the country—true rural folk composing in the traditional style." Many of them, I was told, did not read or write.

The singer who had collaborated with the two poets was Husain ʿAbd al-Nāṣer, whose cassettes I later devoted much of my work to studying. Several days later, after taking a four-wheel-drive Toyota, loaded with passengers, up a precipitous eight-thousand-foot ascent, I arrived in Labʿūs, the region's main settled plateau, where I had been told ʿAbd al-Naser and a number of cassette poets could be found. One of my first surprises was to learn that none of these celebrated artists resided locally. Since the gathering point in Labʿūs was a market center inhabited largely by temporary residents, the regular social networks of domestic life were mostly to be found in villages that clung to the plateau's numerous ridges and canyons (see figure 1.1). I would need transportation to access them: After several day-long visits to find the artists in situ, I discovered another complication: they were highly mobile individuals, though not of the pastoral nomadic vein I might have imagined at the time. ʿAbd al-Naser and other leading cassette singers of the region were wage-earning migrants in Qaṭar and Saudi Arabia for much if not all of the year. One of the villages best known for its poets, moreover, had some seventy-five of its members living part- or full-time in New York City (see figure 1.2 for a photograph over the village of Falasān). But migrants were not the only ones accustomed to living in multiple locations. Most resident Yemeni artists had two homes, often one in Aden and one in the highlands, and moved between them depending on seasonal labor opportunities. All of them also traveled during summer months to a multitude of weddings and social gatherings where their verses and opinions were in high demand.

Although I settled in the commercial hub of Labʿūs, the only place where strangers could find temporary residence, fieldwork held other surprises that cautioned me against assuming folk poetry to be a largely provincial phenomenon.[2] The Office of Cultural Affairs employees had been right about the reverence with which Yafiʿis held their older, nonliterate poets. Once I found the means to spend time with poets and singers who were prolific cassette producers, however, I quickly learned that they were not illiterate but were avid readers and writers of a wide array of material. The poets had reams of handwritten poems, many of them photocopies, as well as tattered volumes of regional or Arab poetry, often printed and bound by small publishing houses in Aden or Beirut. The most prolific among them displayed their poetic competences by reading aloud from sturdy notebooks in which they had copied their best verse rather than by reciting their verses by rote. Singers, especially the younger men, preferred to read from such written texts while they performed.[3] Sadly, the famous Arabian rhapsode *(rāwī)*, in whose memory was preserved the collective oral archives of countless generations, rarely appeared in the daily gatherings I attended.[4] As I discuss later in this chapter (as well as in chapters 3 and 4), poets and singers alike found written copies useful memory aids for live performance and poetic composition, for textual collaboration and cassette planning, and even for the marketing and sales of cassettes.

Figure 1.1. The village-lined ridges of Yafiʿ, 1995.

As a general introduction to this study of poets' and singers' navigation among various forms of media, I begin by considering three fields of cultural production and consumption that inform Yemenis' assessments of the cassette industry.[5] These fields are commercial popular song *(fann)*, Islamic cassettes *(al-ashriṭāh al-islāmiyyah)*, and folk poetry *(al-shiʿr al-shaʿbī)*. In

Figure 1.2. The houses and coffee fields of Falasān, 1997. Surveyed by poet and informant ʿAbdallah ʿAlī Jibrān, the village is known for its poets and migrants in the United States.

sketching the outlines of what is a continuously varying set of native orientations toward audio recordings, I rely on general signs of what a nonspecialist observer (such as myself) often sees when first walking into a cassette shop. As I suggest in chapter 3, my decision to begin with a shop customer's viewpoint is not as arbitrary as it may seem, given the cassette shop's importance as an institutional locus for coordinating textual production among the industry's various participants. In the following sections of this chapter, I consider how Yafiʿis used folk-poetry cassettes during three separate conflicts that occurred in and around Yafiʿ between 1995 and 1997. By attending to how cassettes helped people talk and compose poetry about pressing issues of locality, communal solidarity, and action, I explore how cassette-oriented discourse contributes to defining participation hierarchies that constitute what I term "discursive community."[6]

Resurgent discourses of tribalism, which were especially controversial throughout southern Yemen at the time I was doing fieldwork (see introduction), prove especially important in helping Yemenis consider the expressive repertoires of this community.

THE POLYGLOT FIELDS OF THE CASSETTE INDUSTRY

In the business of attracting new clientele, cassette shops usually solicit passers-by with visual cues that help identify the kinds of products that are available for sale. Shops that specialize in popular songs advertise their commercial viability: large, bright signs and production-company fliers cover their exteriors, and their capacious interiors are festooned with photographs of Yemeni pop stars. The window fronts of Islamic cassette shops suggest a more discreet sensibility: while featuring large signs with such shop names as "Recordings of Faith" and "The Veneration Center," customers also see Qur'anic sayings written in calligraphy, and the shop interiors are generally smaller. The cassette shops with the least visual adornment are often devoted to folk poetry. Servicing a largely rural clientele, these shops are typically located either in regional towns or in larger urban hubs where rural inhabitants frequently gather: in traditional commercial quarters, in outdoor markets, and next to bus and taxi stations where rural inhabitants might make a few last-minute purchases before continuing their journeys. These shops usually rely on their own rudimentary copying machines and distributional networks to circulate their products.

The visual hallmarks of cassette shops are conduits to more complex social and cultural orientations. By far the largest and most profitable of the three fields is that of "popular song" *(fann)*,[7] which features the releases of the most acclaimed Yemeni and Arab singers and musicians. Yemeni customers who seek such cassettes typically ask for releases by the name of their principal artists, or if interested in something new, they request songs *(aghānī)*, cultural-heritage songs *(aghānī turāthiyyah)*, varieties *(munawa'āt)*, or a "cocktail" *(kūktēl)* of different performers and song genres. To a greater extent than cassettes in the folk-poetry and Islamic fields, popular-song cassettes are distinguished for their polished execution: they are the product of multiple stages of engineering by professional studio technicians. Such songs are typically arranged beforehand, orchestrated for performance by multiple participants, edited and rerecorded through the assistance multiple recording tracks, and tailored closely to the popular tastes of specific target audiences. They are also sold in sleek, custom-designed cassette jackets that display a picture of the featured artist and tend to be wrapped in a tight encasing of plastic that promises consumers the quality of an original copy *(nuskhah aṣliyyah)* that has not been cheaply manufactured or pirated. Ultimately, the relations between performers and consumers are striated by a network of vertical and horizontal levels of production, marketing, distribution, and sales.

Most singers and musicians in the pop-song field are Yemeni. Given the tremendous diversity of regionally specific musical styles in Yemen, regional audiences tend to have their own favorites.[8] The stars are both men and women, and while most reside and work inside Yemen, a handful live abroad where they have better access to the Arab world's finest recording technologies. The classical and popular Arab superstars from outside Yemen are also popular,[9] but Yemeni audiences are loyal to indigenous song and music traditions, and the most celebrated performers tend to be Yemeni.

The second-largest cassette-recording field is comprised of "Islamic cassettes," as they are often labeled by their audiences, although these cassettes vary in content and style and overlap with the other fields. A random sampling of Islamic cassettes reveals an amalgam of live oratories, studio-recorded sermons on religious, spiritual, and political topics, scripted dialogues, conference discussions, religious anthems *(anāshīd dīniyyah)* and songs in praise of the Prophet *(madā'iḥ nabawiyyah)*, and genres of popular and tribal songs that are inflected with religious themes. Islamic cassettes are produced by both Yemeni and foreign Muslim preachers *(dāʿiyyahs)* and clerics (*ʿālims*, pl. *ʿulamāʾ*). Among the most successful of the Yemeni cassette preachers is ʿAbd al-Majid al-Zindānī, who rose through the ranks of the Muslim Brotherhood during the 1960s and 1970s. Having received an education in Egypt and become secretary general of the Institute for the Scientific Inimitability of the Qurʾan and *Sunnah* in Saudi Arabia, Zindani has used cassettes with great success in Yemen for over two decades. Many of his top releases focus on the compatibility of the latest scientific discoveries with Islamic scripture. After becoming the leading religious guide of Yemen's largest political Islamist organization, the Yemeni Reform Congregation *(al-Tajammʿ al-Yamanī li-l-Iṣlāḥ)*, in 1990, Zindani accelerated his release of more overtly political cassettes. Other Yemeni clerics—including the leaders of conservative Islamist movements such as Muhammad al-Ānisī, Hazzāʿ al-Maswarī, ʿAbdallah Saʿṭar, and the Reform Congregation's former Minister of Justice ʿAbd al-Wahhab al-Daīlamī—enjoy a wide circulation of cassettes as well. Given the political oratory of such preachers, audiences have varied over the past few decades with the changing tides of national politics.

After the first Gulf War in 1990 and increasingly in the first decade of the new millennium, foreign Muslim clerics have also grown popular and have contributed to the growing conservatism of Islamist discourses in Yemen. The cassettes of Egyptian cleric ʿAbd al-Ḥamīd Kishk are widely disseminated, as are those of the Saudi shaikhs ʿAli al-Qarnī, ʿAʾid al-Qarnī, and Salman al-ʿAwḍah as well as the Kuwaiti cleric Ahmad al-Qaṭṭān. A smaller audience is devoted to the cassettes of the Saudi cleric Ahmad al-Mawraʿī, a figure whose impassioned sermons, often riven with bouts of sobbing, make him somewhat controversial. The distance of such clerics from the embroilments of local party politics and their focus instead on religious and spiritual topics as well as on global political conflicts have made them appealing to many audiences.

Islamic cassettes are popular in the cities, particularly in quarters whose populations have swelled with rural migrants in recent years, but they are especially widespread in rural areas where illiteracy rates are highest. In recent years, the Reform Congregation has met with considerable success in expanding its influence among large sectors of the rural populace in the middle and lower regions of Yemen by embroidering its messages with popular song melodies and genres of poetry. Traditional songs in praise of the Prophet, for instance, are set to melodies by such popular singers as Ayyub Ṭārish and ʿAli al-Anisī; tribal *ẓāmil* chants from the middle regions are employed on cassettes designed for populations in those areas. While the group's adaptations of traditional Islamic song have helped popularize Islamist discourses in Yemen, they have also exposed the group to accusations of "reprehensible innovation" *(bidʿah)* from other ultraconservative groups. Some leaders of the *salafī* movement, for example, have accused the Reform Congregation of perverting Islam for popular entertainment. In response, the group defends its adaptations as necessary for reaching an increasingly secularized youth. As various Islamist movements compete for adherents through the dissemination of cassettes, major debates about Islam and the moral fiber of the Islamic community are being waged in terms of oral performance and musical style.[10] Where Islamist cassettes have the potential to play a significant role in popular cultural orientation and in political transformation,[11] these debates are far from peripheral.

The third field to be recognized by Yemeni cassette fans is that of folk poetry *(al-shiʿr al-shaʿbī)*, the principal focus of the rest of this section. On a continuum of economic profit, this field is the least commercialized, a distinction that remains highly salient for many of its stoutest devotees.[12] These cassettes typically feature the work of singers and poets who have no formal arrangements with studios or production and distribution centers. In many cases, they receive little or no financial compensation for their work. The cassette shop serves as the central institutional locus for bringing the industry's diverse participants into collaboration. An introductory overview of this peculiar institution will help lay the groundwork for subsequent discussion of the textual, aesthetic, and moral associations of folk-poetry cassettes for listeners.

Folk-poetry cassette shops are almost invariably small, family-run operations. Although managers possess operation licenses that are purchased from the Ministry of Culture and are renewed every few years, they tend to lack formal agreements with production studios and distribution companies. Rather than being regularly supplied with large quantities of new releases, managers acquire cassettes through informal networks. When a singer or a poet produces a new folk-poetry cassette, he or she brings it to the shop personally and either gives the cassette to the store or requests a small fee (generally from 1,000 to 6,000 YR).[13] Cassettes that are not brought directly to the shop can be obtained by shop managers through networks of personal friends and acquaintances who have access to local distributors or through contact with other shops or itinerant sales representatives. After a cassette is received, advertising occurs in one of two ways: by word of mouth, or by a shop's loudspeakers. Given the lack of vertical and horizontal institutional structuring in the field, the profits from each sold cassette go directly to the shop. As a result, the prices of folk-poetry cassettes are low. Although a pop song or Islamic cassette can cost 130 to 200 YR and up to 260 YR for a top-of-the-line cassette imported from distributors in the Gulf, most folk-poetry cassettes can be purchased for between 80 to 130 YR. The low production costs and nonexistent marketing costs are also reflected in packaging: folk-poetry cassettes typically lack any screen printing and are sold either without cases or occasionally in unmarked clear plastic cases.

Rather than servicing large national and transnational audiences, folk-poetry cassette shops are typically geared to specific regional audiences. Decisions about sales, marketing, and product design are not linked to broad institutional networks that are managed by production offices, distributors, corporate affiliates, and government institutions such as the Ministry of Culture. Shop managers therefore can court more focused, local audiences with appropriate material, as I discuss in chapter 3. Central to such audience design is a close relationship among shop managers, producers, and consumers. Local poets and singers, for example, can often be found sitting inside the shops chatting with managers, sometimes discussing procedural plans and stylistic issues with the managers before or after releasing a cassette. Recording is occasionally done in makeshift studios in a shop and also in the homes of shop managers. Consumers also have more direct and influential access to local forms of production. When purchasing cassettes or just passing time, customers enjoy long discussions with managers about the state of the field, the latest poets and their poems, possibilities for new cassette releases, and politics in general. Through such discussions, their preferences are registered and are ultimately relayed, in however modified a form, to producers. Finally, collaboration between shop managers and folk-poetry producers and consumers is facilitated by managers' intimate knowledge of the particular genres of poetry sold at the shop. In most cases, shops manager-owners originate from the regional homelands of the poetry featured at the shop, and they tend to be avid patrons of poetic verse, poets, and singers. Many such managers assert that the rewards of business are as much social as they are economic. By providing a valuable service to some of the region's most popular wordsmiths and by supplying recordings to tens and even hundreds of thousands of listeners, they expand personal and professional contacts. They also keep in touch with the latest events and news in the community and acquire a degree of social status linked to their own regional reputations.

The small and personalized operations of the folk-poetry cassette shop provide an extraordinary forum for tailoring associated textual habits and generic orientations toward a particular cassette product. Crucially, as is shown in chapter 3, the product is as much a merging of clients' interests, concerns, and desires as it is a cartridge-bound spool of tape. In cultivating customer loyalty, cassette-shop owners and managers have developed a variety of recording formats. These range from the least inscriptively mediated formats (such as live recordings) to formats with a great deal of inscriptive lamination (such as written *qaṣīdahs* that are introduced and sung by participants through multiple stages of recording). In general, the inscriptive complexity of recordings corresponds with greater price. In later chapters, I develop a set of tools for understanding how such formats provide listeners with aesthetic criteria for assessing political action and its participants.[14] For now, I consider four formats of recording that are typically identified by producers and consumers as they confront a selective sample of the world's sounds packaged for audio reproduction and circulation.

At one end of a continuum of recording formats are cassettes called "live" *(ḥayy)* by store managers and others who are familiar with technical audio production. These cassettes generally feature performances of music and song at weddings, celebrations, and other festive occasions. The primary audience for such performances is typically the one gathered at the event. Indeed, audience participation may be central to listeners' enjoyment of these recordings, and in the more homey productions, children, car horns, excerpts of side conversations, and other "backchannel" noises can be heard. The principal material featured on such cassettes is typically either professional musical troupes or soloists or amateur groups of men or women who perform sung poetry at weddings and other major events.

The improvisational and often outdoor settings for such recordings generally result in poor sound quality. Nevertheless, this format offers audiences certain advantages compared with other recording formats. Most important, such cassettes feature rare and relatively unedited recordings of favorite local groups that may have distinct dialectal features, genre preferences, performance routines, musical arrangements, and modes of instrumentation.[15] Typically, such recordings are purchased by listeners who want to hear an event that they could not attend or who wish to recollect their own experiences sometimes many years after the event. Not infrequently, such recordings may supply participants at celebrations with primary musical entertainment if the fee for a live professional band (some $50 U.S. or 9,200 YR) is too high.[16] Devoid of time- and event-specific cues, such recordings can help listeners feel as if they have transcended gaps in recording space and are experiencing something immediate.

A second format of recorded folk poetry features poems read aloud and unaccompanied by music. This format is called "prose poetry" *(al-shiʿr al-natharī)* by popular Yemeni audiences for whom poetry without song lacks readily recognizable meter *(wazn)*.[17] The prose-poem format appeals to its fans for different reasons. For some poets, a spoken recitation may simply be most expedient. Production may be executed more quickly when audience demand is urgent or when singers are occupied or altogether inaccessible. Alternately, poets who prefer certain formal meters and diction find folk song ill-suited to their verse. Receivers, on the other hand, may prefer poetry to be read aloud rather than sung since singers and instrumentation can obscure the words. Some feel the strident messages of political verse to be better conveyed through no-nonsense oratory.

Related to the prose-poem format are cassettes of oral narrative and read-aloud prose, which often are shelved with folk-poetry cassettes in most cassette shops. Such cassettes are sometimes labeled "speeches" *(mukhāṭibāt)* and include excerpts of famous political oratory by Yemeni heads of state and erstwhile Arab nationalist leaders (such as Gamal ʿAbd al-Nāṣer, Muʿammar Qadhdhāfī, and Saddam Ḥusaīn). Selections of broadcasted radio reports and televised speeches *(idhāʿah)* can also sometimes be found. In addition to formal speeches and official material, cassettes that feature comedians and pundits abound.[18] The preferred rhetorical mode of such cassettes, whether in vernacular or standard Arabic, is generally more suited to official or public settings than those heard on other formats. The address of such formats identifies listeners accordingly, albeit through a variety of alignments or "footings" that situate listeners as ratified addressees, bystanders, or overhearers.[19]

A fourth recording format is the most popular: sung and musically accompanied folk poetry that is produced primarily for recording purposes. Chapter 4 is devoted to the textual features of this format. These cassettes are generally recorded in private settings with fairly rudimentary recording equipment, though they exhibit a greater measure of inscriptive planning and musical arrangement than the "live" recording format. Actual performance events are more formally organized around the act of recording so that artists have direct access to microphones and can enunciate their words clearly. Poetic genres chosen for performance typically reflect more formal methods of composition and performance (such as the *muwashshaḥ* and *qaṣīdah* genres); only rarely are listeners treated to extemporaneous competitions of the sort found on "live" cassettes. This format is generally what most Yemenis think of when asked about cassette-recorded "folk poetry" since for many it best captures the defining elements that differentiate poetry *(shiʿr)* (as a socially and politically charged reflexive practice that can accommodate discomfiture) from the moving and more pleasurable experiences of song *(aghānī)* or pop-song *(fann)*.[20] Indeed, the verse content of poems usually assigns musical instrumentation to secondary accompaniment. Rather than an assemblage of traditional instruments, the Middle Eastern lute *(ʿūd)* and vocals—a classic combination in formal Yemeni and Arab performance—are the instruments of choice. If additional instruments are included, they are often selected to achieve a more metropolitan effect, such as might be conveyed by the bongo drums *(īqāʿ)*, the double-reed flute *(mizmār)*, and the violin *(kamān)*, their combinations varying according to aesthetic aims and regional customs. As I show through analysis of a composition event in the final section of this chapter, the collaboration required to produce cassettes requires heightened attention to the varying textual orientations of participants and also to the regimenting demands of audio-recorded inscription. As negotiations occur over audience design strategies, metropolitan stylization, nuances of affect, hierarchies of status specific to the cassette industry, and so forth, distinctive marks of recording become a means to reflect on the opportunities and challenges of the task at hand.

In introducing folk-poetry cassettes through the categorical distinctions of a recording industry for its participants, one challenging task is understanding how cassette-recorded verse functions as a distinct domain of practical action and moral inquiry. To begin addressing this question, I focus in the rest of this chapter on three major political events that occurred during and shortly before my fieldwork. By examining how poets and audiences use folk-poetry cassettes to mobilize public opinion toward resolving urgent conflicts, I show how cassettes help redefine the hallmark tokens of discursive community. In all three events, cassettes are considered authoritative by audiences as markers of a nationally relevant "imagined community"[21] shared by all listeners but first and foremost as instantiations of a tradition of entextualized poetic talk and interaction that is socially hierarchized and technologically mediated.

SHAIKHS IN EVERY HOUSEHOLD? CASSETTE CIRCULATION AND DISCURSIVE COMMUNITY

Several weeks after the end of Ramadan, when Muslims fast for an entire month as one of the annual Islamic pillars of faith, the inhabitants of Yafiʿ, Shaʿīb, Ḥālmīn, and neighboring regions gather at the natural thermal spring of Nuʿmah, nestled in a deep canyon, to celebrate and socialize. Toward the beginning of my fieldwork, I received marvelous descriptions of the annual visit to the spring. "Like the ancient fair of ʿUkāẓ!" exclaimed one regular visitor, who remembered lively assemblies in his boyhood by both Muslims and Jews and compared the event to a legendary gathering in the Hijaz (today a part of Saudi Arabia) where pre-Islamic poets had frequently sparred. Although few Jews are left in Yemen, Muslim families still gather for two to three weeks annually to catch up with old acquaintances, enjoy separate men's and women's hot baths, and feast on sheep and goats brought to the local market. At the approach of dusk, the traditional *bāl* performance featured male and female poets who competed with one another in producing extemporaneous verse while two lines of women sang the final verses of each poet to the accompaniment of a gentle, rocking dance.[22] It was an occasion, I was told, that I could not miss.

I first visited the spring with several Yafiʿi friends in early March 1996, a half year into my fieldwork. After a long morning's journey down the slopes of a massive valley, we arrived in a jeep loaded with our bedding, food, and other supplies in a tiny village that clung to rocky ledges above a few, recently built concrete bathhouses. As I was to discover, the spring was not quite the oasis that I had been led to imagine. In the three days that I spent at the spring, no *bāl* performances or other collective celebrations were organized. "The poets have yet to come," I was told by some. Others lamented that *bāl* performances and traditional poetic competitions had withered in recent years under criticism from conservative Islamist groups that condemned the mixed dancing and late-night revelry in such events. Ravenous biting insects proliferated after dark and left us writhing under hot blankets every night.

Despite the absence of collectively performed poetry, the gathering at the spring proved to be a festive occasion that was enjoyed by hundreds of visitors of all ages. In the shuffle of bathhouse camaraderie, poets did appear, and lively dialogue ensued in everyday performance settings. Inside rudimentary cinderblock shelters built around the baths, *qaṣīdahs* were read aloud from handwritten or printed copies, and shorter poems and riddles were recited from memory. During the performances and conversations that I witnessed during my visit, a consensus began to be formed about several cassettes that had been released in the previous month by Yafiʿi cassette poets. The cassettes addressed a serious regional event.

On Sunday, January 7, 1996, a violent clash erupted between

members of the Saʿdī tribe near Ruṣd, Yafiʿ Bani Qāsed, and government forces. By the end of a confrontation outside the village of Falasān, twenty-one soldiers had been killed and ten injured.[23] There were no Saʿdī casualties. Within a week, a tank battalion and some five thousand government troops surrounded the entire region of Yafiʿ Bani Qāsed, blocking all roads from exit or entry. The putative issue that led to the clash was the government's confiscation of illegal weapons. Local politics were more complex. At the core of the problem was a strong-arm appointment of district governor Muhammad al-Kassādī in Ruṣd, the administrative center of Yafiʿ Bani Qāsed. Once a supporter of the former People's Democratic Republic of Yemen president, ʿAli Nāṣer Muḥammad, Kassadi had made new allies after unification in 1990, especially with the northern-based Islamist group, the Reform Congregation. The governor aimed to use his newly acquired political weight to pressure two Ṣāʿdī men to relinquish several Chekov antiaircraft guns that they had acquired after the Yemeni War of 1994. After the Saʿdī men balked, battle lines were drawn.[24] When Kassadi preempted diplomatic negotiations by calling in the second armored division from Zinjibār and advanced to take the men from their homes by force, Saʿdī men responded decisively. In a canyon just outside the village, Kassadi, his son, and scores of others were killed in a barrage of gunfire, resulting in the worst bloodshed the region had known since the late 1960s.

In the aftermath of the killings, leaders throughout Yafiʿ made an extraordinary show of solidarity with Saʿdī by sending delegations from every tribal *maktab* (the traditional seat of sultanate and tribal authority) to dispute mediations locally and in Sanaa. Ensuing negotiations lasted for over a month and were conducted according to what Yafiʿi observers (who had been used to the legal language of a socialist state), found to be a bizarre amalgam of state, Islamic, and tribal laws. A vocabulary of tribal dispute negotiations that had not been seen since independence reappeared as weapons were taken as ransom *(wabah)*, bulls were slaughtered *(ʿaqīrah)*, and blood-debt settlements *(diyyah)* were stipulated. These proceedings were personally monitored by none other than the paramount shaikh of the northern Ḥāshed tribe, ʿAbdallah Bin Ḥusaīn al-Aḥmar, who had stood with Kassadi during his visit to the region just one month earlier (see Figure 1.5). Al-Ahmar's exceptional qualifications as mediator stemmed not only from his tribal leadership or even from his position as speaker of parliament but also from his post as chair of the Reform Congregation, whose leverage the slain governor had tried to exploit.

Popular uncertainty about the tribal tone of the proceedings was revealed to me in discussions that I had with young men at the time of the negotiations. For some, the event was an ominous sign of the extent to which northern Yemen's tribal customs had swept vengefully into southern governorates after unity and the Yemeni War in 1994. These men spoke wistfully of earlier era in which worker's unions rather than tribal lineages set the tenor of political activism. For others, the Saʿdī affair was a hopeful sign that Yafiʿ maintained its regional prowess. They insisted that the event dispelled suspicions fomented after the war that Yafiʿ's leadership was factionalized. The people of Yafiʿ could stand together against the illegitimate use of force by outside powers.

During the negotiations following the Saʿdī affair, two cassettes were released on the market, each featuring a different recording format. The first cassette, appearing approximately one week after the clash, contained a collection of sung poems released by Yafiʿi singer and *ʿūd*-player ʿAli Bin Jāber with a small troupe of instrumentalists. The six featured poems, most by well-known Yafiʿi cassette poets, were arranged and recorded in the weeks before the Saʿdī affair and did not directly address the event. They treated broader issues of national mismanagement, rampant corruption, poverty, and possibilities for Yafiʿi leadership. Several of the leading *qaṣīdahs* focused on "the Ḥunaīsh affair," another national scandal that had erupted one month earlier when Ethiopia's seizure of a cluster of desolate islands in the Red Sea had created an imbroglio for the Yemeni administration. Nevertheless, the timing and regional focus of the "Ḥunaīsh cassette" provided ample kindling for widespread grievances against government incompetence in both national and international arenas. The cassette's catchy melodies and rhythmic accompaniment ensured its national success. Sales of the Ḥunaīsh cassette were record-breaking. ʿAli Bin Jaber told me that cassette sales surpassed fifteen hundred in the first week, an amount confirmed informally by shop managers in Aden, who stated that the cassette was one of the best-selling cassettes they had ever known. In Sanaa, where sales of cassettes by southern poets are predictably lower than in Aden, one shop manager insisted that he had sold a whopping two hundred to three hundred cassettes per day for approximately two months.[25] Within several months of the cassette's release, tens of thousands of copies were sold throughout Yemen, not counting those duplicated on home-recording machines. The publicity generated by this cassette prompted administrative officials to respond with exceptional though not unprecedented severity: the poet responsible for the most popular *qaṣīdah* on the cassette, ʿAskar ʿAlī, was jailed for a week.[26]

In early February, approximately two weeks after the Hunaīsh cassette, a second cassette appeared, produced this time by Yahya ʿAlī al-Sulaīmānī, a poet from the Saʿdī village of Falasān where the massacre took place. The poems on this cassette were read aloud by the poet himself rather than sung, a style of oratory that many felt suited the searing political verses that directly addressed the Saʿdī events. Capitalizing on the Ḥunaīsh cassette, the first *qaṣīdah* on side A featured an unflinching refrain: "Ḥunaīsh is in the Red Sea. It is not in Yafiʿ." Why had the military mobilized against Yemen's own people, the poet asked, when national territory was falling to Ethiopian "vultures"? What kind of priorities was the administration setting? Who would set things right? Other *qaṣīdahs* recontextualized the broader national and international themes of the earlier Ḥunaīsh cassette within local frameworks, ensuring the cassette's instant local appeal. Moreover, Sulaimani's aggressive style of declamatory recitation drew on a rich vein of conventional political and tribal performance in the highlands, which contributed to the cassette's circulation among audiences in Yafiʿ. The tape's lack of song and music, however, inhibited it from achieving the national fame that the melodious Hunaīsh release had obtained and ultimately diminished its longevity even among audiences in Yafiʿ.

For several weeks after their release, these two cassettes could be heard in a variety of settings throughout Yafiʿ. In densely settled areas like Labʿūs, where young men ride trucks and rural taxis to and from the market every few days, the cassettes could be heard blaring from car stereos by passengers and passers-by who might catch a refrain and learn that a new set of poems had been released. The cassettes could be heard in stores and cassette shops, despite the occasional complaints from those who disapproved. In domestic settings, audiences listened to the cassettes with sustained attention, often flipping from side A to side B without interruption. Relatives and close friends gathered to listen in private family rooms, on front steps (where children played and sometimes danced to the cassette songs as they learned their refrains by heart), or in kitchens (a markedly female domain in Yemen where women have principal control over cassette recorders). Large groups of listeners gathered in the *mabraz* (*mafraj* in northern regions), literally "a place of visible distinction," which is a long, upper-story room lined with floor mats and colorful cushions. The *mabraz* accommodates a household's most public activities, such as same-sex socializing among friends and visitors for what is one of Yemen's most celebrated social institutions, the daily afternoon *qāt* chew, when the leaves of an indigenous herbal stimulant provide a means for hours of sitting, conversation, laughter, and listening (see Figure 1.3). In *mabraz* rooms, the cassettes were heard by groups of up to twenty listeners. Among such large audiences, whose numbers could surpass fifty or sixty during major social events, or in the presence of prominent guests, the cassettes were generally heard only in segments and were secondary to obligations of social networking and discussion.

Figure 1.3. A Yafiʿi shaikh plays the latest folk-poetry cassette as guests chew *qāt,* smoke the water-pipe, and listen, 1996.

Before the era of cassette recording, poems of great import to the community would have been recited aloud by noted village poets, rhapsodes, and those who could read from written manuscripts. Poetry dealing with more everyday affairs was also performed in a range of settings from intimate encounters to larger social events, and Yemenis' competences in memorizing entire *qaṣīdahs* were acute. In contemporary contexts, opportunities for hearing poetry still abound. Nevertheless, since rhapsodes with powerful memories are scant, cassettes provide valuable services to audiences who wish to listen to poetry collectively with others. Hosts of large *mabraz* gatherings, for example, can entertain guests with topical poems without having to decipher a photocopy of a handwritten poem and then put their grammatical competences to test in public. Cassette lyrics are often quickly incorporated into group conversations and social activities, despite having been recorded in other times and places. Even as a cassette tape is rolling, participants regularly comment on lyrics, explode in laughter, or even preempt cassette singers' end-strophe rhyme words. After recording machines are turned off, listeners often discuss the significance of poems in great detail. These discussions unfold procedurally. First, broad topics are introduced that implicitly link cassette poems to more general concerns, and those with the most political savvy or historical knowledge tend to hold the floor. Since the poetry has cued linked events with specific verses, however, other participants, some of them with less established status or authority, begin weighing in with charged performances of poetic competence and moral insight. Some participants with strong memories may cite specific verses verbatim. Others may paraphrase sections of poems, draw analogies with verses heard in other poems, or elaborate on contextual information, such as details about the poets involved, the contexts of production, and so forth. By linking ongoing events to the significance of cassette texts, participants signal their own access to a valued register of vernacular knowledge and show others that they are, as the manager of one cassette shop explained to me, "number one" sons of the homeland.

The frequency with which topical verses were exchanged at large gatherings was demonstrated to me during my stay at the Nuʿmah thermal springs. Although I had arrived a full two months after the Ḥunaīsh cassette had been released, I noted four separate incidences over two and a half days at the springs at which the cassette's verses were alluded to or cited verbatim in conversations. I also heard several verses recycled from the Sulaimani cassette by both men and women. In discussions of politics, culture, history, and daily affairs, the only other literary text that was cited as frequently that week was the Qurʾan.

Folk-poetry cassettes are clearly authoritative for audiences. Their authority derives less from invoking general discourses that are available to everyone, however, than to instantiating a certain kind of poetic discourse or cassette-mediated koiné. Sociolinguists have long employed the concept of a "speech community" to refer to a group of people whose shared patterns of verbal practice reflect and reinforce common underlying social norms.[27] As studies of community have been refined to account for the ongoing mobilities of people and things, language theorists have increasingly viewed the circulation of linguistic forms as central to notions of community.[28] Speakers, listeners, overhearers, witnesses, and others who receive discourse can maintain and reproduce notions of a single, discursively mediated community. Under such conditions of communicative exchange, media technologies can assume instrumental roles in lending language routines a cross-context "detachability" that can enable and channel talk about the community.[29]

We might think of cassettes as a useful medium for circulating a set of "insider" texts that could help define a given vernacular speech community. Nevertheless, when such texts become embedded in broader conversational routines and recycled in modified forms, their associations with specific, original media channels can be weakened. In a moment ripe with social possibilities, texts that are produced on cassette are also recognized to be emblems of conventional public discourse and moral reflection. The circulation of inside texts now becomes the currency of a general community, which now acquires a responsive resonance with the habits and orientations of participants. This exploration of the use of cassettes in consensus building and the formation of communal identity attends closely to how cassette texts are held to oscillate from "inside" to "outside" and back again. Citations of cassette poems always venture across this uncertain reflexive terrain, becoming authoritative precisely where they manage such oscillation persuasively for audiences.

The emergence of cassette authority from acts of socially situated performances was evident to me in afternoon *qāt* chews at the hot springs where the presence of men from diverse regions, many of them new associates, introduced a greater uncertainty to conventions of discussion participation. On one afternoon, I was sitting with a group of over a dozen men in one of the houses clustered around the springs. Although quiet conversations were occurring between pairs, a broad topic of common interest had not yet been identified, causing increasing awkwardness as time passed. On some occasions, I would be asked by someone in the group to speak about my research interests and impressions of Yemen, at which point a general discussion ensued about broad topics of concern. More frequently, prominent participatory roles would be initially seized by others who were able to fill them. This afternoon, doubts lingered about who should initiate group talk.

Finally, an older man suggested that he could read aloud his "response" *(jiwāb) qaṣīdah* to one of the poets featured on the Ḥunaīsh cassette. His proposal was welcomed by the others with relief. As he took out a tattered folder of written poems, one of the young men in the room urged him to delay reading until a cassette recorder could be brought from a nearby house. When the machine arrived and was set to record, the poet introduced his composition: "This is to the *qaṣīdah* that was set forth by ʿAskar ʿAli, the one sung by al-Jaberī about Ḥunaīsh—Ḥunaīsh, who has so roiled the Yemeni people." Although ʿAskar ʿAli had not sent him a direct "initiation," the poet had interpreted his poem as a general call to arms and had taken the opportunity to respond. By clearly identifying his addressee as the poet ʿAskar ʿAli and by mentioning the singer who performed his poem on cassette (although he mispronounces his name), the poet was establishing his own relation to his region's important political voices. He then read his *qaṣīdah,* which closely paralleled the meter, rhyme scheme, distinctive phrases, and symbolic terms of ʿAskar ʿAli's original *qaṣīdah*. During his recitation, others in the room who were familiar with the conventions of *bidʿ wa jiwāb* verse collaborated by audibly announcing his final rhyme words, sometimes even before the poet himself, and repeating key phrases with him as he read them aloud a second time for emphasis. After finishing his poem, much of which reiterated criticism of the nation's military leadership, the poet was encouraged to recite other *bidʿ wa jiwāb qaṣīdahs* that he had written recently about other major events: an initiation to a state dignitary and northern Yemeni shaikh who had just visited the region and a response to a poet who had lambasted Yafi'i poet Shayef al-Khaledi on a cassette released approximately a year earlier. Each *qaṣīdah* was preserved on the young man's cassette recorder for later review and possible dissemination.

The poet could have begun by simply reading compositions that were unaddressed to anyone in specific. His choice to address his first poem to a well-known cassette poet featured on a popular recent cassette was pragmatically tailored to ratify his role as an initiator of group conversation. Neither a politician nor a man of intellectual accolades, he could nevertheless claim the authority to speak about pressing political events. Crucially, the condition of his authority lay in his ability to tailor his performance to the textual and specifically cassette textual parameters of *bid' wa jiwāb* poetry. By demonstrating his competence in a well-known genre of highlands epistolary poetry and more important in the reproduction of a specific sequence of mediated textual practices (namely, his written and now cassette-recorded "response" to the release of a specifically authored *qaṣīdah* a few months earlier by a specific cassette singer), the poet performed his audio-inscriptive relevance to key figures engaged with the resolution of major events.

In my other days at the springs as well as throughout my fieldwork, I found local poets and audiences using the textual links in *bid' wa jiwāb* poetry to connect themselves to broader "outside" events in precisely this ratifying way. When poets replicated the poetic form of other correspondents who were well known in the region or when audiences performed in ways that displayed their familiarity with cassette poems to underscore important topics in everyday discussion, cassette poems acquired political and moral force akin to what Brinkley Messick has called "genealogies of the text."[30] At the most basic level, *bid' wa jiwāb* exchanges are conceptualized by listeners as conjugal couplets between identified authors, such that the meaning of any one poem is incomplete without the other. The contingency of *bidʿ wa jiwāb* poems on one another was evident to me when approaching single poems with Yemenis, for whom interpreting a poem without its partner was a project doomed to aesthetic mediocrity. But dyadic exchanges are themselves embedded in longer chains of initiations, responses, and further responses. Indeed, these genealogical histories are topics of tremendous interest for audiences, who memorize and relate serially the particular terms used by various authors. Some listeners know only the prominent exchanges of the major poets. Avid fans may expound on the details of *bidʿ wa jiwāb* sequences that have continued for years and sometimes decades. The most authoritative genealogies include the region's most famous cassette poets, men known for their political savvy and fiery wit.

The particularly decentralized productive capacities of the cassette industry have helped turn such poetic exchanges into a currency that, while mass produced, is also regionally reticulated and thus fairly accessible to most people. Through the widespread availability and marginal cost of cassettes, diverse groups of listeners have firsthand access to poems that are seen to provide valued perspectives. Poets perform an added service to such listeners by using inclusive terms of audience address. While continuing to direct their verse to specific addressees in the traditional epistolary fashion, poets also deploy a wide range of pronominal terms so that practically any listener or aspiring poet could be included. One fan described this practice as a clever "trick" *(munāwarah)*.[31] As evident in the "response" formulated at the thermal springs, listener-poets of diverse backgrounds and competences are able to employ the head-to-head, dialogic format of *bidʿ wa jiwāb* poetry to attach themselves to the textual genealogies of the most famous cassette stars. As similar individuals in other locations compose, recite, and correspond with one another and as audiences contribute through listening, competing with end rhymes, and discussing, a transregional collective of grassroots participants is instantiated. Its members are defined in degrees of proximity to the potential publicity that a cassette release might bring.

On another afternoon at the springs, I sat with two men, one a poet from Yafiʿ and the other from neighboring Shaʿīb, who began talking about recent poems, cassettes, and their friendship together. As they spoke about the candor and righteous political criticism that had recently been recorded by Yafiʿi cassette poets, the Shaʿībi told his friend: "Things are going to change, by God. These cassettes are the harbingers *(bawādir)* of a new age. . . . They are important means. A man like me in Shaʿīb can listen to new releases and can learn how a Yafiʿi feels . . . and in that way adopt a single perspective *(rāy wāḥid)*." His sense of the importance of cassettes to building translocal solidarities and to achieving civil justice conveys the extent to which cassette audiences consider themselves one of a community of like-minded listeners. In heralding a transition to a "new age" of shared feeling and political unity, the speaker's statement recalls Benedict Anderson's account of the role of vernacular print technologies in inculcating new kinds of collective self-awareness that define nationalism's early "imagined community."[32] As in Anderson's account, the speaker views his fellow interlocutor and their nascent community as mediated by a common inscriptive medium *(wasīlah)*, though in this instance audiocassettes, along with a single, graphic perspective *(rāy)*, rather than vernacular print technologies. According to the speaker, cassettes bring together audiences' diverse spational (regional) and temporal (a "new age") orientations. In the fashion of Anderson's widely read print media, cassettes produce a homogenizing effect that is the hallmark of nationalism.

Although the social value of given media forms for their users might be sought in overarching nationalist narratives, communal associations are assembled by interlocutors in the gritty work of specific textual encounters. In his study of eighteenth-century American print subjectivity, Michael Warner shows how notions of public identity are produced through ongoing struggles for textual clarification.[33] While taking us a good way toward entextualizing Anderson's notion of the "imagined community," Warner's restricted focus on print media and its role in cultivating a subject of republican letters begs a fuller account of how routine acts of interpretation employ an eclectic range of social affiliations. Since audiocassette users recur to a diverse set of textual practices, their work invites us to develop finer tools for evaluating technological influences on social life.

Yafi'i uncertainty over authoritative structures was evident in the aftermath of the Sa'dī violence during debates about the respective merits of tribal or state laws in resolving the conflict. As Yafi'is recurred to genealogies of cassette texts to help clarify orders of moral legitimacy, different kinds of social abstraction were produced, not all of which conveyed the "empty, homogenous" commensuration that Anderson identifies as intrinsic to nationalism. On the afternoon of poetry recitation that I discussed earlier, one young man summed up his view of the authority established by the poet Yahya al-Sulaimani through the recent release of his cassette to countless possible respondents across the region: "There's our shaikh of Yafi', distributed in every household!" Although conveying a radically populist and even reproducible authority, the cassette also bore traces of a social investiture that had long informed the organization of political power in the Yemeni highlands. For the listener, these traces signaled a sense of return to something whose authority was more proximate. The effect of the cassette lay partly in its reiteration of traditional tribal oratory, this time through a read-aloud format that contrasted with cassette poems that were sung to metropolitan rhythms and melodies.

Cassette-recording formats and performance styles provide producers and audiences with a rich vocabulary for redeploying older models of authority in new contexts. For the young man who appreciated the Sulaimani cassette, a read-aloud style best expressed a tribal prowess that he felt was conducive to the cassette's circulatory success. But tribal aesthetics and traditional models of community are also being reworked as new political contexts demand new responses. In what follows, I examine another major regional conflict in which models of discursive community are formulated in attempts to address uncertain contexts of "locality."[34] As I suggest, genre provides a way to discuss the organization of talk and poetry—a "metadiscursive" framework—as poets and singers build consensus over the kind of community that is best able to address the needs at hand. In examining how producers combine multiple genres and recording formats in a single performance, the cassette medium is shown to be a distinct resource for tailoring a diverse set of audience expectations toward the moral and medial orders of a particular set of competences.

THE SHOWDOWN AT MT. ʿURR: ORDERING GENRES AND CONTEXTS OF LOCALITY

Many fans of folk poetry throughout Yafiʿ know the story of how ʿAli Saleh's cassette 25 ended the showdown at Mt. ʿUrr. Cassette singers and poets had political leverage and could use their authority to "solve problems" *(yaʿālaj al-mashākil).* On July 7, 1994, a seventy-day war between government forces commanded by the Republic of Yemen's president, General ʿAli ʿAbdallah Saleh, and a separatist army fighting in the name of the Yemeni Socialist Party (YSP), came to a fiery end as resistance to a several-week siege of Aden collapsed and a painful period of reconciliation began. In the immediate aftermath of the war, a network of military outposts was established in Aden and its hinterlands to prevent retaliatory activities. One of the outposts was positioned on top of Mt. ʿUrr, over which the main access road passed into Yafiʿ from the northeast. Many of Yafiʿi regional leaders had demonstrated support for the administration during its campaign against separatists and were infuriated by the government's poor faith. The placement of the outpost was especially provocative. Mt. ʿUrr had long been a symbol of regional pride and autonomy, as expressed in a well-known local proverb: "If ʿUrr remains, Yafiʿ is alive and well" *(ʿUrr bāqī wa*

Yafiʿ bi-l-wujūd). In a political climate of postwar tensions, the military's presence on Mt. ʿUrr struck many as blatant intimidation.

Soon after the military outpost on Mt. ʿUrr was set up, popular discussions throughout Yafiʿ about the best ways to launch peaceable protests. Some proposed coordinating high-level negotiations with press releases in national newspapers accompanied by a series of popular demonstrations. At the same time, leading cassette poets, who were aware of the restricted circulation of print media in rural areas and among partially literate audiences, began organizing efforts to release a folk-poetry cassette that could canvass support among a broader public. A meeting was held with three poets who represented Yafiʿ's largest administrative *maktabs,* and contact was made with Yafiʿi singer ʿAli Saleh, who was living in Saudi Arabia at the time. A fourth poet, from another of the region's historically prominent *maktabs,* was also telephoned at his residence in Qatar. A collaboration in recording poems began.

This assembly of poets from four principal *maktabs* in Yafiʿ was an indication of the challenge at hand: to mobilize a sense of locality that could justify taking action in response to this particular incident. A wide repertoire of contextual frameworks for identifying what was "local" meant that the relationship between the troops on Mt. ʿUrr and local identity could have various interpretations, some of which could have dissolved Yafiʿi particularities into more diffuse theaters of compliance. A plan of political action had to present an account of locality that emphasized the moral grounds for regional opposition to the military outpost. Given state, military, and national support for postwar security measures, the challenges presented by such contextualization were acute. Particular details of place, time, social custom, accountability, and collective responsibility had to be narrated for both Yafiʿis and those in Sanaa who could redeploy the troops.

In addressing audiences not only locally but nationally, the producers faced certain determining contexts over which they had little control. One of the most dominant of these was expressed in a discourse of separatism *(infiṣāliyyah)* that the Republic of Yemen administration, as well as diverse political groups, had launched against the southern Yemeni Socialist Party leaders and those who supported them. Within the terms of this discourse, Yafiʿ figured ambiguously: regional leaders had not thrown their weight behind the southern-based dissidents, but neither had they demonstrated much support for the military campaign that eventually achieved victory and sacked Aden. Confronting a context of separatist accusations, ʿUrr cassette producers had to walk a fine line. To draw on socialist rhetoric, in however distilled a form, could prove inflammatory to audiences at a national level who viewed the socialist cause as irrevocably discredited by its leaders' perfidy. However, to acquiesce to the political will of the administration in Sanaa was equally risky given widespread misgivings throughout southern Yemen about the bad turn that unification plans had taken in recent years. Between a local discursive context in which the troops on Mt. ʿUrr were described as "occupiers" and a state-sponsored context in which the troops were designated as "precautionary measures," resentment on all sides threatened to explode any effort to narrate a resolution.

Presented with a restricted latitude for expression, the producers saw distinct advantages in using the cassette medium to disseminate and craft their message. Most notable, they explained to me, was the opportunity that cassettes afforded to reach larger audiences than might otherwise be accessed. After all, as one of the poets stated at the outset of an interview, "Our first objective was to ensure that our poems would be widely disseminated and received by listeners."[35] Where access to state-monitored media such as newspapers, radio, or television was difficult to acquire, the cassette proved an amenable conduit for reaching audiences both within Yemen and abroad among Yemeni diasporic communities that often relished topical cassettes from the homelands. The sheer availability of the cassette medium to producers and audiences also comprised its principal weakness: cassettes could be poorly executed. Cassettes could be made too entertaining, as when an overly creative singer or musician blunted the impact of political verses by turning poets' compositions into mere popular ditties. Alternately, cassettes could be boring, especially where a poet's read-aloud verses failed to mobilize listeners' energies toward demanding tangible action. The challenge for producers was to use the cassette competently. Through a balance of song and word, the cassette had to convey a context of locality whose novel craft engaged the passions of listeners while also securing the political force of reasserted traditions of moral authority.

A choice of genre was the first decision to be collectively taken by the producers, according to one of the poets whom I interviewed. In light of recent events, all agreed that a stern warning had to be issued to those who would intimidate regional authorities. "For this task, we selected the *zāmil* genre—one without a midverse rhyme scheme and that lacked opening and concluding supplications to God." Generally four to eight verses in length, *zāmils* (pl. *zawāmil*) are concise, hortatory poems that are chanted outdoors by large groups of participants at weddings, holiday festivals, collective social events, and other public occasions.[36] *Zāmil* poems are also widely recognized throughout Yemen to be distinctly tribal. Indeed, they are typically shouted out with daggers drawn and weapons slung over shoulders and are often performed as participants circle and twirl synchronously in a classic tribal dance called the *bar'ah*. A year later, I witnessed an especially large assembly of village delegations perform *zāmil* poetry when Yafi' received a visit from government dignitaries (see figures 1.4 and 1.5). Among the guests on that occasion were two of the most prominent representatives of northern Yemen's Ḥāshed tribal confederation, Shaikh Mujahid Abu Shawārib and Shaikh 'Abdallah Bin Husain al-Ahmar, the latter of whom had played a prominent role in overseeing military campaigns during the 1994 war.

The cassette begins not with the standard strains of the *'ūd*, as listeners of 'Ali Saleh's cassettes have come to expect, but with

Figure 1.4. Highland Yafiʿis greet visiting government officials with tribal *barʿah* dance and *zāmil* poetry, 1995.

the sound of tribal drums (the *ṭāṣah* and *tabal*), which are the hallmark instruments that accompany *zāmil* performances. After several seconds of drumming, the first two verses of the initial contributing poet are heard shouted in a high pitch:

> I will ask the poets and the people of insight,
> Those who understand the depths of politics and administration.
> They said that the borders of separation were cancelled,
> Yet they continue to post soldiers and guards along them.[37]

A chorus of men then repeats these verses three times in the fashion of a group of marching *zāmil* performers who might be heard on a "live" recording. The next two verses of the poet's *qaṣīdah* are then announced in the same way:

> They made the plateaus of ʿUrr a military checkpoint,
> [While] the people are observing and watching with interest.

Figure 1.5. Government dignitaries stand with Yafiʿi leaders in Ruṣd, 1995. From left to right: Shaikh Mujahid Abu Shawārib, Shaikh ʿAbdallah Bin Ḥusaīn al-Aḥmar, District Governor Muhammad al-Kassādī, and perhaps his son.

Is their aim to make the nation a set of nations,
Or is it to drive us backward seventy years?[38]

After the chorus repeats these verses three times, ʿAli Saleh moves to the second poet's composition and performs his opening verses in the same manner, followed by the chorus's uptake. By successively presenting the first four verses of every eighteen- to twenty-two-verse composition in the standard fashion of a *zāmil* performance, the performers provide a pointed commentary on the nature of the event that took place on Mt. ʿUrr. Establishing a military outpost at the region's border is a matter of communal honor and tribal standing as much as of administrative miscalculation.

The choice of the *zāmil* genre was not simply an act of local contextualization or a transparent bid for traditional tribalism.

In light of recent southern Yemeni political experiences, the genre evoked a pan-Yemeni contextual framework that was well suited to postwar reconciliation. Although the *zāmil* genre had been practiced in Yafiʿ since before independence, the genre was not markedly southern. For many years, in fact, southern leaders had discouraged the use of such tribal genres in public political life and had instead espoused a range of classic nationalist genres, including anthems *(nāshīds),* metropolitan "sentimental" songs *(al-aghānī al-ʿāṭifiyyah),* love poetry inspired by neoclassical Arab poetry *(al-shiʿr al-ghazalī),* and free-verse poetry *(al-shiʿr al-ḥurr).* By contrast, the *zāmil* genre selected by the Mt. ʿUrr cassette producers reflected an affiliation with the new terms of public rhetoric that were being broadcast from Sanaa. The public dissemination of tribal *zāmil* poetry via cassettes was an entirely new phenomenon for former inhabitants of the People's Democratic Republic of Yemen and signaled certain rapprochements with a pan-Yemeni highland culture in which tribalism had long been a constitutive political discourse.

The producers of the Mt. ʿUrr cassette were caught between a powerful context of postwar national identity (in which distance from southern socialist rhetoric could signal proximity to a northern-led Republic of Yemen administration) and a local context of regional autonomy (in which *zāmil* poems reconnected Yafiʿi listeners with a preindependence history of tribalism that was at once honorable and problematic). They resolved to deploy a tactics of style that used multiple genres to help Yafiʿi audiences situate the Mt. ʿUrr military outpost. These generic frameworks were expressed most clearly in an interview I had with one of the other contributing poets. He explained to me that while the *zāmil* genre had been discussed, he and the others had agreed beforehand to adopt an innovative compositional tack: "We decided that instead of composing short *zāmil* poems to be performed at scattered rallies, we would each compose a *qaṣīdah* and yet write it in the *zāmil* style *(namaṭ).*"[39] According to this poet, the *qaṣīdah* was considered by composers to be a prioritized generic framework to which the *zāmil* added a certain preliminary salvo.[40]

The producers' own metapoetic analysis suggests that they were involved in crafting a "dialogue of genres."[41] In the process of creatively reworking verbal tradition according to current demands, the producers relied on genre to signal their adherence to tradition even as they created new terms by which traditional verses would be defined. In this case, genre also signaled something new. "Our cassette offered the first sung *zāmil* that audiences had ever heard," explained one of the poets to me. The other producers also felt that the cassette they assembled marked a divergence from tradition; they felt a certain pride in bringing what one of them called "renewal" *(tagdīd)* to Yafiʿi folk poetry. As a medium, the cassette was clearly instrumental to achieving such renewal and actually enabled talk about renewal. Genre, however, provided the accepted vocabulary through which the exciting new text object could be considered abstractly as a thing for independent circulation. Whether expressed in terms of audience, composition, context, or locality, genre supplied producers with a metadiscourse on the social entailments of cassettes.

The resourcefulness of genre derived from participants' experiences with performance and a conventional "horizon of expectation"[42] by which moving political verse had long had effect in the highlands. *Zāmil* poetry, for example, drew from a wide range of oral performance and dance customs that were featured in dispute negotiation and other major social events and that frequently defined tribal politics. *Qaṣīdahs* privileged an even broader range of expressive associations—from the soulful lyrics of singers who had become vanguards of metropolitan transformations in music and political verse (see chapter 4) to the sage counsel of preindependence notables, many of them religious men, whose carefully composed verses and literary themes reflected their privileged access to the written word. Other genres were certainly used by Yemenis, and each of them could be further broken down into minor genres and variations associated with innumerable aspects of daily life.

Genre also provided "rules of formation" for directing participants' primary discursive and nondiscursive experiences toward more formalized, secondary relations.[43] The sheer accessibility of genre as a system of categorization for audiences in Yemen and throughout much of the Arab world underscores the extent to which the ordered relations of genre, codified by Arab linguists and religious scholars in a voluminous system of formal poetics since the eighth century, had become part of the cultural vocabulary for citizens. Discriminations of genre became especially widespread during aggressive educational and literacy programs that were launched by nationalist reformers in the decades of the People's Democratic Republic of Yemen (see chapter 6). In those years, generic distinctions were conventionalized, objectified, and circulated among Yemenis as hallmarks of moral form and communal affiliation. The *zāmil* was the genre of retributive tribes, the *mawwāl* of gainful seafarers, the *bāl* of fateful pastoral nomads and farmers, and so forth. Such equivalences of poetic and social form provided Yemenis with a ready set of analogies for considering the entailments of cassette circulation. The moral and political resourcefulness of the new medium lay in determining which genres would be deployed, how they would be ordered sequentially, and how they might be reassembled in hybrid combinations.

The novel force of the Mt. ʿUrr cassette becomes especially salient after a shift in genre, recording format, and instrumental arrangement after the initial eight-minute sequence of *zāmil* poems. Gradually, the drums and high-pitched chants segue to the playful, improvisatory strumming of an *ʿūd,* the criterion of metropolitan finesse in sung *qaṣīdah* poetry. As the vociferous orality of quick-stepping tribesmen is followed by the string work of a musical aficionado, a sentiment of modern cultural civility is evoked. Shortly later, this transition is given more defined cultural locality: a contemporary drum rhythm *(īqāʿ)* is heard, its pattern heralding from the deltas of Lahej, a region of palm trees and fruit plantations between Yafiʿ and Aden that is often romanticized by Yemenis as a place of amorous rural charm. In yet another lamination of rich musical texture, the *ʿūd* player ʿAli Saleh begins singing a Yafiʿi melody that has been adapted elegantly to the *zāmil* meter. These broad frameworks of genre allow the feeling of a unique performance, to take hold through a sequence of sonic registers. As the entirety of each poem is sung in turn, poets' contributions are identified as *qaṣīdahs* through the performance of music and song more than they are through the poets' own words. Ultimately, as the *qaṣīdah* performances approximate styles of metropolitan recorded song, their sonorous laminations evoke particular contexts that situate broad discursive communities within regionalized habits of musical pleasure, affect, and ethical comportment. By the time listeners hear poets' stern tribal admonitions that the "bats of darkness" that are atop Mt. ʿUrr had best decamp before compensation is sought in "skulls and souls," a set of emotive filters have been assembled to situate a resolute and defiant Yafiʿi locality beside generalized contexts of cultural and political expression. Poets announce unequivocal support for established goals of national unity and the correct application of Islamic law *(sharīʿah)*. So, too, as one of the poets remarks, they urged "renewal." Although in accordance with older habits of discursive juxtaposition (as is shown in chapter 2), listeners are invited to consider the novel authority of metropolitan tribalism.[44]

Many Yemenis praise the use of folk poetry for "solving problems" in the community. Like medical doctors, I was told, poets could "reveal the truth" *(yikshif al-ḥaqīqah)*. On countless occasions, I was treated to blow-by-blow descriptions of how folk poets had used their intimate knowledge of local affairs, histories, and actors to alleviate dangerous tensions. In many ways, cassette poets are also seen as truth tellers and problem solvers. I was told by listeners on multiple occasions, for example, that shortly after ʿAli Saleh's cassette 25 was circulated, the military withdrew from its outpost on Mt. ʿUrr. Cassette poets were seen to resolve conflicts through persuasive means in the age-old fashion of the most skilled political wordsmiths.

Cassette poets and singers are also widely praised as spokespersons who can bring local issues to those outside the community. They can help solve problems that may not be locally resolvable. Cassettes are "means of broadcasting" *(wasāyil al-iʿlām)* or "letters" *(risāyil)* that can send strong messages to those in circles of national or even international power.[45] The role played by cassettes in communicating local perspectives to outsiders is especially valued in a modern world in which folk poets vie for audiences with other media channels, mostly to their own disadvantage. One older man commended cassettes for disseminating regional news *(akhbār)*. "All the news on television is about you foreigners!" he joked with me. "We get tired with this kind of news after a while. With these cassettes, we can at last listen to someone speaking about our own circumstances." For this man, cassette poets and singers were valued community members who had access to public political spheres and centers of administrative power beyond his community. But they were especially appreciated as local news readers who could relay—in spoken words rather than projected televisual images—his own "circumstances" *(aḥwāl)*.[46] These circumstances were significant because they were newsworthy and could be made commensurate *(taḥwīl)* with a broader realm of public narratives and events. As one fan claimed in a discussion about ʿAskar ʿAli, the poet made famous by the Ḥunaīsh cassette, "His voice is my voice, . . . and through his verses, I can learn how people like myself are suffering too." For such listeners, the rhetorical frameworks employed by the cassette poets are persuasive because as they engage with politics at large. Cassette poets show how the "local" is an expression of relative locality that emerges between and within grander contexts in relation to similar members of other communities who attune themselves to national and even global circuits of discourse.

A RESPONSE TO ISLAMIC JIHĀD

Activists' plans for addressing communal strife focus on the nature of a conflict, ways to resolve it, and matters of media publicity. Cassette poets and their audiences seek consensus on these matters by devoting special attention to genre. Indeed, through discussions about genre, the roots of social turmoil and the leverage of given media technologies for raising public awareness are explored together. At one event, five poets, including the celebrated cassette poet Shayef al-Khaledi, gathered with onlookers to compose a set of poems for cassette release.[47] The poets addressed an event that had taken place outside their region on the previous night, July 28, 1997. A bomb had exploded on a bus carrying boys and girls near the University of Aden. The poets did not know the identity of the perpetrators and had to tread carefully in assigning blame. When suspects were arrested a month later, the evidence of previous bombings in Aden and of the growth of attacks in recent years by radicalized "Afghan Arabs" pointed to the group called Islamic Jihad.[48] An immediate response condemning the attack was needed, however, and the cassette medium could reach the broad national audiences who were interested in the tragedy. The cassette was also useful for redressing anger closer to home. Sitting among the dozen students in the bus was a young boy from a nearby village who died in the blast.

As the five poets collaborated in deciding how to react to this event, they confronted the competing contexts that inform their work. Like the Mt. ʿUrr cassette producers, they had to make decisions about poetic genre to situate the event within a set of discursive conventions and communal affiliations that are both local and translocal. A closer analysis of compositional negotiation can answer important questions about how genre is actually used in political practice: To what extent are the discursive hierarchies of genre replicated by users? How do users interpolate genre according to diverse orientations and talents? How do the inscriptive capacities of the audiocassette medium contribute to a general and prioritized set of intergeneric competences in invoking discursive community and in facilitating political intervention? In the interests of conveying some of the uncertainty and excitement of the composition event, I defer most of my analysis of the event and its poetry to later sections.

Situating Verbal Action

In the summer of 1997, I was sitting with a group of men in the *mabraz* of a private house in Yafiʿ, chewing *qāt* throughout the evening on the third day of a wedding. That day and the previous had been filled with activity, including a trip to the bride's village down the valley and several late-night poetry competitions. Conversations were subdued, and everyone was relaxed.

After a snack and coffee, the host of the wedding, a poet, spoke up: "O.K., guys. Guys, I thought we could put a few verses together. Each of us will compose something, and then we'll assemble our compositions into a single whole. I'll start. Then we can move around." He gestured to the other poets in the room.

After about five minutes, the host announced that he was ready. I quickly fetched my tape recorder and asked permission to record his verses, which he granted. Another man brought his own tape recorder, at the host's request, and pressed Play:

> I will ask the poets and the people of insight
>   About our present situation and what worries we have.
> We said: A sheep has left, and after him comes a chicken.
>   But in truth, the Day of Judgment will come after him.
> The blood debt remains, and troubles abound.
>   The Interior Ministry does not perform its obligations.
> As for the security and police, we see them silent
>   Despite their supply of troops and gun trucks.[49]

After he finished reciting, the tape recorders were turned off. The other poets looked at their own verses and began to refine them. The metrical structure of the poem might have been announced before my arrival, but it was now obvious: a *rajaz* meter, common to the *zāmil* genre and useful for rapid improvisation.

One of the poets in the room objected to the rhyme scheme: the poem included three final rhyme endings. "Shouldn't it have only two?" he asked. The host read aloud his poem a second time, and the objection was found to concern the first strophe of the second verse. Although the rhyme endings in the other verses were consistent (-uh/-ūm), this strophe ended differently: *qulnā kharag ghānim wa gā baʿduh farag* (lit. "We said: Left a sheep, and (in) came after him a chicken"). The poet's observation pinpointed a larger generic ambiguity that he appeared to want resolved. If they were composing in the rhyme scheme of the typical popular folk *qaṣīdah,* in which each verse contains two end rhymes, one at the end of each strophe (ab/ab/ab/ab), then the host's verse was flawed. If they were composing in the manner of much *zāmil* poetry, then the first strophe of each verse need not be rhymed (-b/-b/-b/-b). The questioner, a migrant who was well known for his singable *qaṣīdahs,* seemed to suggest that the rhyme scheme of the *qaṣīdah* was preferable.

At this point, the others who were chewing *qāt* in the room, most of whom were not poets, protested the poet's objection. Although the host's line could have been rewritten, its symbolism and homophones could not go unappreciated. The ridiculous pun on the Minister of Finance's name, Faraj Bin Ghānem—"A sheep (*ghanam* in standard Arabic) has left, and after him comes a chicken *(farag)*"—was irresistible. Moreover, the crude resonance between the first and last words of the poet's quip, *kharag* and *farag,* produced a rich proverbial interplay and was hilarious. The audience gave scattered assurances that the host's line had delighted their puckish sensibilities and was accepted.

At that point, one poet asked me for a piece of paper from my notebook. After I handed him a few sheets and a pen, he passed one of the pages to a poet beside him. Another poet tore the cover off his cigarette box and began scrawling a few words on the back. Another was deep in thought, his lips occasionally fluttering as he mouthed out verses. The host added: "Let's focus on the issue in Aden."

Although I had not yet heard about the bus bombing, the poets seemed to know what was meant and were busy composing. The others in the room continued chewing *qāt* and looked on.

After about twenty minutes, the host asked the group a question about arranging their verses: "We have two possible approaches. Each of us could compose a short piece of five or seven lines or so, and we could then put them together back to back. Or we could put one line after the other to make it like *ragzah* poetry."

In Yafiʿ, *ragzah* poetry was a recent adaptation of the *bāl* genre (described earlier in this chapter) and featured extemporaneous competitions between poets who delivered verses orally between two lines of chanting and clapping men (see figure 1.6).[50] With the *ragzah* competitions perhaps still in his mind from previous nights of the wedding, the host suggested that the first line be taken from each poet's composition and then assembled serially with the first lines of other poets (and so for the second line, etc.) to produce a composite of separate contributions.

"Yes, like the *dān* in Hadramawt," said one of the men at the far end of the room. He was referring to a somewhat slower-paced, more songful poetic competition that was practiced some 250 miles to the east of Yafiʿ. *Dān* features poets who extemporaneously produce verses to a common meter and rhyme and a singer who chants each verse as it is produced. *This* poetry had been popularized in recent decades through television programs organized by the Ministry of Culture and Tourism. His suggestion struck me as extraordinary at the time, especially since I did not know the poets were hoping to release their verses on cassette. Since *dān* poetry was rarely performed in Yafiʿ, who would assemble such an event?

The host modified the man's suggestion: "Well, perhaps more like *zāmil* poems."

Figure 1.6. Poet Shayef al-Khāledī recites extemporaneous verse at a *ragzah* competition during a wedding near his home, 1998.

One of the contributing poets agreed with the host: "Yes, we've got to produce them as *zāmil* poems. Maybe in the sound of the *bāl.*" The softer, rhythmic melodies of the *bāl* event had been popularized in the media in recent decades by singers from the lower, desertic areas of Abyan and Shabwah, geographically between the mountains of Yafiʿ and Hadramawt. Although not traditionally associated with the *zāmil,* the *bāl* had long included women participants and was popular among listeners of all ages, providing an interesting alternative to the more aggressive, tribal chants of *zāmil* poetry. Others in the room voiced their approval of his somewhat novel idea.

Imagining the performance of such poetry, the host then added that the poets' verses could be divided into clusters to facilitate the accompaniment of the *ʿūd* and also the *mizmār,* a double-reed flute that was also common in Abyan and Hadramawt but, like the *dān* and *bāl,* was no longer found in Yafiʿ.

As poets and onlookers contemplated the many possibilities of composition and performance, the best-known poet in the room, Shayef al-Khāledī, cleared his throat and read his verses aloud in accordance with the rhyme and meter schemes that had been selected:

To him who asked of us, wanting our news:
  Get the news straight. As long as it continues circulating, by God,
Chaos [reigns] from bottom to top.
  Censure for whom? And you: who will you blame?
The catastrophe for which we wait is now arriving.
  After the first one covered every inch of the land,
There is no substitute for you. Those with me are witnesses.
  The sorceress left, but in came Mother Ṣarūm.[51]

"Ṣarūm!" was boomed out in chorus by several listeners who liked the poet's ending. In popular legends, Mother Ṣarūm was a demon who lurked around tombs and craved human flesh. The poet's allusion and anteceding verses framed the Aden bus bombing as a metonym of the country's chaotic state, originally caused by the Yemeni War of 1994 (the "first" catastrophe) and exacerbated by a succession of inept leaders.

The third poet in the group, the young man who had proposed the idea of the *bāl* melody, then read his poem. It drew on the more romantic, classical imagery of stars that could be appreciated by the audiences who enjoyed the *bāl* melodies promoted in the pop-song industry:

O Aḥmad ʿAlī, the air that your eye sees:
  [How its] currents stir while the sky is all clouds.

All astronomers grasp their foreheads.
  Not one is able to divine the changing of stars.
The Mother still discriminates between them. In her head,
  She favors one even after she has delivered twins.
Pray and fast now for we are in charge,
  While those who should be fasting have begun eating dinner.[52]

Addressing his poem to the host and group leader that evening, the poet had drafted a response that similarly problematized the succession of leaders and luminaries who had not achieved justice for Yemenis. Agreeing with the previous poet, he suggests that the "Mother" is partial and gluttonous.

After a few minutes of silence, the host spoke: "We should produce verses that try to resolve this issue." Perhaps he had sensed that the poets' verses were becoming too diffuse and sought to steer everyone back toward forming an explicit consensus about the bus bombing. Although the next poet in the circle had just leaned forward and was sitting on his heels to recite, he sat back down to review his poem again.

At this point, another poet attempted to take the floor. Calling out to the host, he declared that he was ready to recite. There was a tense silence in the room as participants looked down and fidgeted. I knew this man to be a fine poet. However, the reactions of the others, who had previous popular cassette releases and more prominent reputations, revealed a participation structure that had remained tacit until then. The poet looked around for a signal from someone.

The host tried to clarify the situation: "This involves blood debt in a particular case." The poet assured the host that he understood and proceeded with his reading:

[With] our vision, I'll see the seasons still coming.
  We'll ask him who is an astronomer of stars.

Immediately, objections were muttered by several younger members in the room who seemed unconvinced that this man should be allowed a turn. Nevertheless, with signals from the host, he was allowed to finish:

> The Pleiades in the sky have still not [yet] dipped.
> What destruction! How it has left the world flooded.
> The watering is in the hands of God on high.
> How long will we wait through time, O sorrows?
> The first didn't care for me, and the successor has shown no compassion.
> [How the] snakes of the forest pour forth [their] venom.[53]

The poet's verses continued the theme of astronomy and stars, embodying them eloquently in an extended series of watering motifs. His verses were still somewhat obliquely related to the bus bombing in Aden, however, and an awkward silence ensued.

The last poet, a younger man whose verses had not yet established his reputation beyond Yafiʿ, then recited the following lines:

> To you who began the talk: accept no excuses.
> From the citadel, distribute the cases [of ammunition] and serial numbers.
> Whatever he said about beginning with driving,
> Since long ago he's had a general driver's license.
> He has controlled the road after pledging us his confidence.
> [So] after today, who but the stallion will be blamed?
> [Only] blame shelters Saʿd on the day of blame.
> I smell the powder of bombs and gun trucks.[54]

Speaking pointedly about bringing parties to justice, the poet responded to the host's initial verses, telling him that the one with the "driver's license" had a long record of authoritarianism. His reference to a "stallion," the symbol of the General People's Congress party to which the president belonged, suggested in no uncertain terms who the poet felt to be responsible. But the threat conveyed in the final verse went overboard. After the poet finished reading it, the others in the room exploded in laughter and shook their heads. "Choose something else! Anything but bombs and gun trucks!"

Imaginative Collusions, Entextualized Collisions

A community of folk-poetry fans is assembled through subtle evaluative adjustments that participants make as they negotiate between conventions of genre and inchoate experiences of poetry that slowly acquire textual form. Between "our present situation" *(waḍʿnā al-ḥālī),* given a generic impress at the outset of the first poem, and each participant's "worries" *(humūm),* which might inspire heartfelt poems, lies the production of a certain moral authority.

One level of moral activity in the composition event can be explored in the topical crafting the poets' verses. In drafting their compositions about the Aden bus bombing, the five poets at the wedding party addressed a pivotal issue: how can we establish a discursive community whose oral versifiers can act persuasively and ethically even as they confront real challenges to their authority? As the poets addressed this question, they employed sensory registers to help evaluate the relative moral standing of influential agents and events in the world. Among these senses, oral speech indexes poets' relative command of political authority while vision provides access to commonsense evidence of just and unjust behavior. In the first poem, the oral advice of "poets and people of insight" is solicited and received in attempts to decide how to address the wrongdoings of Yemen's security forces, whose silence about the Aden bus bombing is literally seen. The next poet, Khaledi, urges his listeners to visually rectify or "get the news straight" as long as it continues circulating among people, and in a sweeping assessment, he indicts the current administration, whose handling of the Yemeni "catastrophe" in 1994 had covered "every inch of the land." The third poet awards oral activists a more explicit role in leadership by declaring that "we are in charge," an assertion that acquires special urgency since visual observations of "air" and its "currents" may not be reliable sources of knowledge. In an interesting twist, oral activism consists, in this case, of abstaining from oral production or "fasting," an act whose ethical and religious merit is contrasted with the gluttony of immoral leaders. The fourth poet provides the bleakest assessment of the power of poetry to create positive change by offering a painful and personal lament about the imbalance of the world's liquidous oral forces. The final poem, composed by a young poet, ventures a different opinion. Beginning "To you who began the talk: accept no excuses," the poet urges his colleagues to take decisive action precisely because the state's authority, backed by scriptive documentation of a "driver's license," is deeply corrupt. His final bid to privilege violent action over measured oral discourse receives a collective rebuke, however, as others with more experience urge him to develop a more credible formula for public action.

Together the five poets' verses build successively on each other, assembling questions and cautious assessments about available means of redress. While poets strive to found a discursive community that can resolve pressing conflicts, they also emphasize faculties of sensory apperception, such as speaking, seeing, hearing, and scriptive observation. In noting and prioritizing sensory signs of the world, poets help each other build moral consensus and call attention to the obstacles before them and to the need to redouble their efforts. In the rest of the book, I focus on epistolary "initiation and response" *(bidʿ wa jiwāb) qaṣīdahs,* a lengthy and elaborate genre of poetry, and I devote special consideration to how poets, singers, and audiences invoke sensory aesthetics of media technologies, particularly to help craft political verse. In this fuller study, the audiocassette's capacities to reproduce sound are shown to provide Yemenis with a distinct set of resources. The compositional event at the wedding anticipates some of the directions of this argument. Although the cassette technology is nowhere explicitly mentioned, either in the poems or in talk about the poems, I suggest that the force of the cassette is conveyed in a set of interactive presuppositions among participants that are all the more powerful in remaining oblique and inferential. The political power of the cassette medium lies in its *use* in organizing moral discourse and poetry. An analysis of the initial sequences of the event might illuminate the nature of a presuppositional ordering through which collaboration was begun and plans for action formulated. Those who initiate authoritative public dialogue convene as representatives that they might not otherwise have been. As they engage in tentative and imaginative interactions, they create new horizons of talk and political action and identify the new competences that are required to reach them.

Consider the first poet's convocation of the event. He called for collaboration between an ambiguously inclusive "we," designated himself as the initiating poet, and subtly nodded to selected addressees around the room. The poet clearly held some authority, though whether this capacity derived from his role as household host, village elder, relative of the deceased, migrant with valuable contacts, or some other agent remains unclear. Consider, then, the poet's first verse: "I will ask the poets and the people of insight / About our present situation and what worries we have." For those familiar with ʿAli Saleh's famous "Mt. ʿUrr" cassette 25, which probably included all those in the room, the initial strophe may have resonated with the same strophe that had been used by the poet three years earlier at the beginning of the cassette: "I will ask the poets and the people of insight / Those who understand the depths of politics and administration." Certainly three other poets in the room, who were featured on that cassette, would have understood the reference. Consider, finally, that on the same cassette released earlier, the poet's contribution had also initiated the collection of *zāmil* poems that had been recorded. Indeed, the textual evidence suggests that the collaborators on that older cassette had probably initially met in this household, just as they were doing again to help resolve another serious conflict.

Before recurring to the general terms of genre, a restricted group of participants, "the poets and the people of insight," employed textual and practical cues that defined the terms by which collaborative success would likely be achieved. These cues were mediated by the audiocassette, though again the technology was never explicitly mentioned. The implications of such mediation for poetic form, participation, and interactive orientation, moreover, were elaborated not in a single instant of media "impact" but were instrumented over time tentatively as the event progressed, each cassette-relative cue being perceived in different ways by participants. Indeed, some of the individuals sitting in the room probably never learned exactly which event the orchestrated cassette was meant to address. As the host had told the fourth aspiring cassette poet, the matter of concern was a "particular" or "private" *(khāṣ)* case, and no explicit discussion of the details surrounding the Aden bus bombing ever ensued. In the interests of expedient political action, the fewer uninitiated contributions the better, and poetry supplied an exquisite "restricted code" for managing access to sensitive information and its various forms of mediation.[55]

Genre provided one of the most important frameworks for defining the larger social entailments (and, in turn, participatory structures) of textual form. After the poets heard the first poem and located pens and writing surfaces, one of them asked for clarification about the rhyme scheme, a fundamental distinction for most Yafi'is between the formal structures of the *zāmil* and other genres of poetry such as the *qaṣīdah*. At this early stage, larger vehicles of poetic form needed grounding in the basic qualities of good sound, and the *zāmil* rhyme scheme proved most appropriate. Generic orientations became more explicitly addressed by the host poet after twenty minutes passed without an uptake.[56] In proposing a choice between five- to seven-verse miniature *qaṣīdahs* (*zāmil* poems are rarely over two verses in Yafi') and a more competitive *ragzah* genre in which poets' shorter contributions are sequentially arranged in the style of a live competition, the host set out two different models of social engagement through which the group's verses could be transmitted to audiences. The *qaṣīdah* is typically the product of individual poets who compose and reflect in isolation, and its performance would foreground a more independently authored set of compositions. When condensed in length and combined as segments in a chain, such *qaṣīdahs* would resound with the longer traditions of epistolary *bidʿ wa jiwāb* exchange that had been tailored to Yafiʿi cassette song in recent years and performed with a certain metropolitan moral civility (see chapter 2). The *ragzah* genre, by contrast, was rarely recorded or written and emphasized a competitive style suited to more celebratory, oral performance settings in rural areas. The genre thus bespoke a community of participants from a wider range of educational backgrounds, literate competencies, and status groups. Subsequent genres proposed by participants each lent their own horizons of social affiliation to the task at hand—the pan-southern community of Ḥaḍramī *dān* listeners that was popularized through television, tribal *zāmil* poems, and a geographically more proximate community of *bāl* audiences of both men and women, especially of pastoral nomadic background. With the host's concluding remarks on the use of the double-reed flute and *ʿūd* (two instruments never used for martial *zāmil* poems), the group's consensus on the *bāl* genre seemed final.

The flurry of generic possibilities discussed by participants underscores the extent to which cassette mediation, though unacknowledged, remained central to the production of verses and possible textual outcomes. At other folk-poetry composition occasions I had attended where performance settings and audiences were explicitly known, genre was rarely a topic of debate. When the cassette offered possibilities for reaching communities with a variety of plausible effects, genre became instrumental in helping poets craft a successful cassette product. The power of genre in organizing talk, however, and its metadiscursive advantage lay in supplying participants with a set of "secondary relations" for organizing a fundamental, nondiscursive as well as discursive "primary" set of relations that emerged through subtle clarifications of poetic organization, musical performance, and participation structure. The potentially radical nature of these primary relations is evident in the final genre that was selected. After participants raced through a full gamut of generic possibilities, imagining the future contributions of other producers and receivers (including singers, musicians, listeners, and people of political influence), they finally settled on *bāl* poetry. To some extent, *bāl* poetry was an aesthetic stretch given the genre's disappearance from Yafiʿ since the early 1990s under pressure from conservative Islamists, who disapproved of coparticipation by men and women in the genre's song and dance traditions (see the discussion earlier in this chapter). Nevertheless, the *bāl's* fitness for participants expressed their political savvy in deploying cassettes. The *bāl* genre was a sure hit in the pop-song industry because its easy rhythms were reminiscent of camel caravans and of a romanticized rural life that metropolitan audiences found appealing. Since the Aden bus bombing was not the matter of regional prowess that the 1994 military installation on Mt. ʿUrr had been, *bāl* poetry conveyed relatively more modest ridicule of the administration's failure to secure law and order. Finally, the choice of *bāl* poetry sent a subtle message to radical ideologues who would use violence to destroy expressive traditions involving both women and men.[57]

The singular fitness of the *bāl* genre among many possible genres was the result of collaborative effort. This work was required of participants because the cassette medium accommodates a wide spectrum of rhetorical repertoires, recording formats, performance styles, and audiences. Although a show of traditional tribalism through *zāmil* poetry had been proposed and might have been adopted without qualification, the experiences of cassette poets with singers, cassette-shop managers, and other agents in the recording industry nudged them toward a product more in keeping with a commercial pop-song field that was patronized by a wider range of audiences. The poets' collective censoring of the last participant's final verse ("I smell the powder of bombs and gun trucks") marked the consensus that had been reached. Just as the Mt. ʿUrr cassette's initial tribal vigor had segued into a more metropolitan sung *qaṣīdah,* the release being planned needed to stylize a strong Yafiʿi response with a sentiment more attuned to the contemporary political culture of a broader populace. Tribalism had again found renewed relevance to public political discourse, but it was infused with new inscriptive demands, imaginative possibilities, and genres of recorded song.

CONCLUSION

In exploring the formation of community in folk-poetry cassette practice, I have given special attention to the role of everyday talk in helping Yemenis assemble texts. By attending to discussions about poetry and performance, I have shown how participants reflect on the formal components of their verse and the criteria by which such forms should be prioritized. Discussion about poetry is not merely instrumental but is necessary to the political efficacy of cassettes. Yet where the expressive means for resolving major political conflicts lie beyond the reach of most citizens, many Yemenis feel that everyday talk alone is often insufficient. Poetry thus continues to serve as an important conduit for popular political opinion, especially when it is disseminated widely on cassettes.

By integrating my analysis of community formation with attention to technologically mediated reflexive practice, I have initiated a dialogue with studies of media performativity and especially the public sphere. I have suggested that cassette media enables a reflexive difference. We might be tempted to think of the cassette as a straightforward reflexive resource. The plastic cassette cartridge contains a roughly predictable range of contents, is assembled by producers through a fairly routine set of procedures, and is consumed, circulated, and perhaps pondered by listeners in the same manner anywhere in the world. This chapter has suggested some of the problems that arise with such assumptions. Insofar as the productive relations of a folk-poetry field are engaged by individuals through specific acts of political text making, the resources of the cassette are contingent on producers' and consumers' habits, competences, needs, and desires. In practice, the cassette medium is often not even an explicitly formulated destination or effect. More typically, its presence is instrumented through unacknowledged shifts in aesthetic apperception and practical sense.

I have approached the aesthetics of community in terms of the formulation, in using cassettes, of a certain abstract "object": a single, united, "discursive" community that has its own independent existence. I have given special particular attention to the roles of text genealogy, audience address, and genre in allowing individuals to consider their own relation to such an object. New patterns of communal recognition also direct participants to a more hybrid community, however, especially when collaboration occurs between poets, audiences, and singers in organizing cassette production. The resourcefulness of the cassette for users emerges from its immediate connection with major events and event makers that lie just beyond direct access.

In the collaborative resonance of the final composition event that was conjoined by the five poets at the wedding party, medial differences revealed shared interactional competences that could deftly manage both outside and inside associations and could decide hierarchies in emerging social norms. The dissonance of such norms was nowhere more jarring than for the fourth poet and those who tried to silence him. Although the poet had anticipated that his own competence in writing and versification was adequate for his participation, the presence of another inscriptive medium introduced a range of social and symbolic qualifications that left him handicapped. Unlike most of the others, the poet had never had his verses recorded on cassette by the region's top singers, nor did he have contacts with urban cassette producers. He also lacked a broader reputation for political verse that might help attract listeners. Suddenly, the participants' reactions heralded a set of technical demands and hierarchies that expressed new challenges to his own social inclusion. Although preference had been signaled for an opening tribal genre *(zāmil)* that was ideally performed orally by participants of equal social footing, tribal orality had become mediated by new forces of vocal alienation. Even the ostensibly participatory civil genres of *qaṣīdah* poetry and metropolitan pop song had failed to intervene to his advantage.

In this chapter, I focus on the role that folk-poetry cassettes play in political discourse and action. In latter sections, I attend to how the cassette medium is registered by participants as a specific set of inscriptive demands. However, formal as well as historical means are needed to consider such reflexive inquiry in its fuller moral sense. The next chapter presents a project in historical poetics that is designed to situate cassette poetry within a hierarchized inscriptive culture that has developed over several centuries. Genre has been shown to provide one of the principal frameworks for identifying, through an aesthetics of circulating form and resonant particularity, the moral substance of political affiliation. I next examine poetic oscillations within and across genre that are deployed toward similar ends.

NOTES

1. Cited in ʿAbd al-Raḥman Suyūṭī, *al-Muzhir fī ʿUlūm al-Lughah w-Anwāʿihī* (Cairo: Dār Iḥyāʾ al-Kutub al-ʿArabiyyah, 1971), 470.
2. I spent eight months in a rented house in Labʿūs in upper Yafiʿ. I also frequently conducted interviews in the areas between al-Qudmah and al-Qārah, two historical headquarters of tribal administration in upper and lower Yafiʿ. My research also led me to other areas within Yafiʿ and in surrounding regions, especially Aden.
3. Jean Lambert notes the same trend of reading singers. Jean Lambert, "Musiques régionales et identité nationale," *Révue du Monde Musulman et de la Méditerranée* 67 (1993):177. See chapter 4 for a full discussion.
4. During my several years in Yafiʿ, I heard long *qaṣīdahs* (of twenty or more verses) recited in their entirety only three times, all by elderly men. I found this to be a general trend across Yemen. It is difficult not to conclude that television, audiocassettes, radio, mobile phones, and faxes as well as massive labor migration and in-

creased mobility are major factors contributing to the demise of the traditional rhapsode.

5. As originally articulated by sociologist Pierre Bourdieu, the concept of a "field" of cultural production foregrounds native acts of recognition. Pierre Bourdieu, *The Field of Cultural Production* (New York: Columbia University Press, 1993). Although I'm not sure Yemenis would begin by categorizing the recording industry in the same way, these fields do correlate with native terms and moral frameworks that are employed in discussions of cassettes. Although Bourdieu's theory of the field has justly been criticized as overly materialist, I find his methodological approach helpful insofar as it foregrounds the relation of material values to a culturally attuned system of "belief" (164). The nature of a given field is mediated by individuals' dispositions toward socialized patterns of aesthetic recognition, or "symbolic capital."
6. In lieu of the term "speech" community, I foreground "discourse" to emphasize the ongoing importance of state-managed regimes of knowledge to ethnolinguistic identity. The book's attention to the public entailments of media culture and nationalism provides the most important insights into the state's ongoing relevance to tropes of identity. Jan Blommaert submits an especially compelling argument for making stratified and polycentric matters of "discourse" more integral to analyses of speech and language communities. Jan Blommaert, *Discourse: A Critical Introduction* (Cambridge: Cambridge University Press, 2005), 216–17.
7. The term "popular song" has several drawbacks. Where popular song is often contrasted to an elite variety of "classical song," a mistaken impression is conveyed that popular folk song in Yemen has been categorically separated from a classical musical tradition. In practice, the boundaries between folk and classical song are difficult to maintain. The term "popular" can also overemphasize links between song and the mass media. Not only has much popular song long been transmitted orally, but in comparison with many Western countries, Saudi Arabia, and the Gulf, Yemen's song and music industry is less centralized, and its scales of profit are more modest.
8. The most celebrated stars include Ayyub Ṭārish, Faisal ʿAlawī, and Ahmad Fatḥī from the Taʿizz governorate; Ahmad Sunaīdār, al-Ānisī, and Fu'ad al-Kibsī from near Sanaa; Najibah ʿAbdallah from

Dhamār; Abu Bakr Bā Sharhabīl and Muhammad Murshid Nājī from Aden; and Muhammad Jumʿah Khān and Abu Bakr Bā al-Faqīh from Hadramawt. But any such list shortchanges the diversity of popular performers who have become nationally known in this field.

9. These include Umm Kalthūm, Farid al-Aṭrāsh, and ʿAbd al-Halim Ḥāfeẓ from Egypt; Majed al-Rūmī and Diana Ḥaddād from Lebanon; Samirah Tawfīq from Syria; Kadhem al-Sāhir from Iraq; Wardah from Algeria; and Khaled ʿAbd al-Raḥman from Saudi Arabia, among others.
10. W. Flagg Miller, "Invention (Ibtidāʿ) or Convention (Ittibāʿ)? Islamist Audiocassettes and Tradition in Yemen," paper delivered at the American Anthropological Association Meeting, San Francisco, November 2000.
11. For Egypt's Islamic revival, see Charles Hirschkind, *The Ethical Soundscape: Cassette Sermons and Islamic Counterpublics* (New York: Columbia University Press, 2006). For an account of how cassettes were used in the Iranian revolution, see Annabelle Sreberny-Mohammadi and Ali Mohammadi, *Small Media, Big Revolution: Communication, Culture, and the Iranian Revolution* (Minneapolis: University of Minnesota Press, 1994).
12. Given artists' primary interests in influencing public opinion and building a reputation among popular audiences, economic profit for cassettes is generally disdained or is collected inconspicuously. Political poets and singers are especially cautious about receiving money or gifts for their verses.
13. All prices quoted in this book have been calculated at 2006 exchange rates (roughly 185 YR per U.S. dollar).
14. My term "recording formats" is drawn from Erving Goffman's notion of footings, which he also terms "production formats." Erving Goffman, "Footing," in *Forms of Talk,* ed. I Goffman, 124–59 (Philadelphia: University of Pennsylvania Press, 1981). In my case, the four formats provide an approach to the kinds of discursive subjects that are inculcated through the act of listening to specific recording formats. I am primarily interested in how recording formats are productive as modes of recorded or inscribed subjectivity.
15. In the southern highlands, such traditional instruments include the *shawbābah,* the *ṭār* (a round-framed tambourine without bells that

often is used for softer songs like the *muwashshaḥ*), the *tanak* (a makeshift tin pan), the *ṭāsah* (a large round drum hung from the neck), and the *ṭabal* (a long drum hung horizontally from the neck). The manager of a small cassette shop in Labʿūs told me that such live cassettes of local events were given to him to sell every three to four months, on average.

16. Women are increasingly purchasing cassettes for these purposes since the growth of religious conservatism in recent years has dissuaded many from sitting in the same room with male singers and musicians.
17. See chapter 4 for a discussion of song meter in composition.
18. The city of Dhamār is noted across Yemen for its traditions of joke telling and comic skits, much of them infused with social and political parody. I also found cassettes of comedians from other regions, including Saʿdah, Taʿizz, Hadramawt, and Saudi Arabia.
19. Goffman, "Footing," 132.
20. The formal distinctions between this final format of sung and recorded folk poetry and commercially recorded popular song *(fann)* are, in many cases, narrow. Where discourses of authenticity and modernity are salient, Yemenis' distinctions between folk poetry and popular song may hinge as much on moral and social discriminations as on commonly recognized formal criteria.
21. Benedict Anderson, *Imagined Community: Reflections on the Origin and Spread of Nationalism* (New York: Verso, 1983).
22. An extraordinary documentary featuring a *bāl* event in Yafiʿ is featured on the film *Communists since the Year 1000,* directed by G. Troeller and C. Deffarge, First Run/Icarus Films, 1973. In northern regions, versions of the *bāl* are often called *bālah.*
23. *Al-Ayyām* and *al-Ḥayāt* newspapers reported sixteen killed and thirty injured (January 10); the socialist paper *Al-Thawrī* reported twenty-four killed and forty injured (January 11).
24. According to my sources, Saʿdī leaders secured an agreement by which the first gun would be handed over in exchange for the construction of a road to their principal village, and the second gun would be delivered on completion of the road. However, after two Saʿdī men appeared to present the first gun, the mayor in Ruṣd imprisoned them and demanded the second be brought as well.
25. Interview with the manager of Stereo *Alḥān al-Khulūd,* February 14, 1998.

26. *Yemen Times,* 1996, v. 6.
27. John Gumperz defines a "speech community" as "any human aggregate characterized by regular and frequent interaction by means of a shared body of verbal signs and set off from similar aggregates by significant differences in language usage." John Gumperz, "The Speech Community," in *Language and Social Context,* ed. P. P. Giglioli (Baltimore: Penguin Books, 1972 [1968]), 219. See also Dell Hymes, "Toward Ethnographies of Communication: The Analysis of Communicative Events," in *Language and Social Context* ed. P. P. Giglioli (Baltimore: Penguin Books, 1972 [1968]), 28–29.
28. Accounts of the sociolinguistic aspects of circulation include Pierre Bourdieu, *Language and Symbolic Power,* 3d ed. (Cambridge: Harvard University Press, 1994 [1982]); William F. Hanks, *Language and Communicative Practices* (Chicago: Westview Press, 1996); and Greg Urban, *Metaphysical Community: The Interplay of the Senses and the Intellect* (Austin: University of Texas Press, 1996).
29. The concept of detachability is discussed by Debra Spitulnik, "The Social Circulation of Media Discourse and the Mediation of Communities," *Journal of Linguistic Anthropology* 6, no. 2 (1996):161–87.
30. Brinkley Messick, *The Calligraphic State: Textual Domination and History in a Muslim Society* (Berkeley: University of California Press, 1993), 15–16.
31. See chapter 4.
32. Anderson, *Imagined Communities.*
33. Michael Warner, *The Letters of the Republic: Publication and the Public Sphere in Eighteenth-Century America* (Cambridge, Mass.: Harvard University Press, 1990).
34. Arjun Appadurai, *Modernity at Large: Cultural Dimensions of Globalization* (Minneapolis: University of Minnesota Press, 1996), 178.
35. This and subsequent comments by poets are taken from separate interviews I held in December 1995.
36. For exceptionally informative readings on the *zāmil* genre, see Steven Caton, *Peaks of Yemen I Summon: Poetry as Cultural Practice in a North Yemeni Tribe* (Berkeley: University of California Press,

1990), 127–54; and Ṣāleḥ Hārethī, *al-Zāmil fī al-Ḥarb w-al-Munāsabāt* (Damascus: al-Kātib al-ʿArabī, 1990).

37. The transcriptions here and in the rest of this chapter do not reflect the regular metrics that are elicited through song performance since they are chanted (as *zāmil* poems) or read aloud:

bā-atkhabbar ash-shuʿār[a] w-ahl il-maʿrifah	dhī yaʿrifū baḥr is-siyāsah wa-n-niẓām
qālū ḥudūd il-infiṣāl ittkansalat	w-in ʿādahum sawū bi-hā ʿaskar wa zām

38.

radū safūḥ al-ʿUrr[a] mawqiʿ ʿaskarī	wa-n-nās[a] titraqqab wa tunẓur b-ihtimām
hal qaṣdahum bā tirgaʿ ad-dōlah duwal	aw qaṣdahum nirgaʿ warā sabʿaīn[a] ʿām

39. Interview with Muhammad ʿAlī al-Sulaīmānī, November 21, 1995.

40. Their *qaṣīdah* compositions contain a number of formal criteria that differentiate them from typical *zāmil* poems. These include, most notably, length and syntax. Poems extend eighteen to twenty-two lines, much longer than *zāmil* poems. They are composed in a journalistic and narrative style (rather than a concise style) that parallels the syntactic form of many popular political *qaṣīdahs* that are written for diverse audiences. Enjambment is a paradigmatic feature of such syntax.

41. Richard Bauman, "Contextualization, "Tradition and the Dialogue of Genres: Icelandic Legends of the Kraftaskāld," in *Rethinking Context,* ed. C. Goodwin and A. Duranti, 125–45 (Cambridge: Campridge University Press, 1992)." 1992.

42. M. M. Bakhtin, *The Dialogic Imagination* (Austin: University of Texas Press, 1994 [1975]), 428.

43. Michel Foucault, *The Archaeology of Knowledge and the Discourse on Language,* trans. A. Smith (New York: Pantheon Books, 1972), 41.

44. The combination of genres creates a juxtaposition between an oral register (through the *zāmil*) and metropolitan scriptive register (through the *qaṣīdah*) that creates an effect of diatextual authority long achieved in *bidʿ wa jiwāb* poetry, as I show in the next chapter. In *bidʿ wa jiwāb* verse composed before independence, however, metadiscourses of genre and their abstracted social totalities were not as yet available to most rural Yemenis.

45. The regional and national influences of cassette poets are sometimes considerable. In 1994, for example, folk poets featured on a cassette released by Yafiʿi singer Husain ʿAbd al-Naser were invited to Aden to discuss politics with the president's regional representative. In less prominent cases, poets' cassettes earn them reputations for political savvy among regional leaders and can lead to important contacts and expanded influence. For example, some cassette poets and singers receive gifts from supportive migrants in the Gulf, Great Britain, and the United States and occasional invitations to perform abroad.
46. See chapter 6 for a fuller discussion of the moral and political coding of "news" *(akhbār)*.
47. Although the poets designed their verses for cassette release, their poems were never recorded on tape. Given the controversy I observed during the composition event, I have omitted or changed the names of the most active participants to preserve their anonymity. Khaledi's name is preserved because he played a less prominent role in the controversy.
48. Islamic Jihad and an affiliate organization, the Aden-Abyan Islamic Army, were responsible for bombings in Aden in 1992, 2000, and 2001. Islamic Jihad began its activities in Yemen after the Soviets withdrew from Afghanistan in 1989 and launched its first attack in Aden three years later with the assistance of Osamah Bin Lāden. The Aden bus bombing in 1997 followed tense elections in the spring of the same year, and state officials immediately blamed the event on southern socialist opposition parties that were said to be trying to "tarnish Yemen's reputation" ("Yemeni President Confers with Oppositiion as It Steps Up Campaign against Detention of Activists," *Mideast Mirror,* August 19, 1997). When the perpetrators were brought to justice in court a year later, the sponsoring organization for the bombings was unnamed, although these terrorist activities were said to have been financed by "a foreign government" ("Leader of Armed Gang Sentenced to Death, Other Members Jailed," Republic of Yemen Television, via *BBC Summary of World Broadcasts,* October 23, 1998). By fall 1997, President Ṣāleḥ had taken a more aggressive stance against Islamic Jihad and the "Afghan Arabs" in the south, shutting down their camps and deporting many of them (Donna Abu-Nasr, "Islamic

Groups Benefitted from Loyalty in Civil War," *Associated Press,* October 28, 2000).

49.

bā-atkhabbar ash-shuʿār w-ahl il-maʿrifah	ʿan waḍ ʿnā al-ḥālī wa mā buh min humūm
qulnā kharag ghānim wa gī baʿduh farag	w-in al-qiyāmah ʿād[a]hā baʿduh taqūm
ath-thār bāqī wa-l-mashākil wāgidah	wa-d-dākhiliyyah mā bi-wāgibhā taqūm
wa-l-amn wa-sh-shurṭah narāhum sākitah	raghm al-ʿasākir dhī maʿhā wa-ṭ-ṭuqūm [meter rough]

50. I was told by one informant that the word *ragzah* was not indigenous to the region but had been borrowed from regions near Mukaīras in Abyan after traditional *bāl* events began to disappear under criticism from conservative Islamists after the Gulf War. His account confirms Carlo de Landberg's early observations of a genre in Abyan, Shabwah, and Hadramawt that was called the *margūzah* (of similar etymological derivation), which was similar to the *zāmil* in performance style but quicker in pace. Carlo de Landberg, *Études sur les dialectes de l'Arabie méridionale: Haḍramoût* (Leiden: E. J. Brill, 1901), 143–44.

51.

yā dhī takhabbarnā yabī min-nā khabar	ṣaff al-khabar ṭōl w-Allah mā dāmah tadūm
ḥashwah min sāshā lā rāshā [rough meter]	ʿitāb ʿalā min w-inta min dhī bā talūm
al-kārithah dhī nantaẓarhā wāṣilah	wa-l-awwalah qad ʿammat as-sāḥah ʿumūm
mā fī badīl lak dhā amāmī shāhidāt	as-sāḥirah rāḥat wa gāt Umm aṣ-Ṣarūm

52.

yā Aḥmad ʿAlī al-gaw dhī ʿaīnik tarā [rough meter]	l-aryāḥ taʿṣif wa-s-samā kulluh ghuyūm
w-ahl il-falak kullan mask fī ṣābirah	mā ḥad qadar yuḍbuṭ mukhālifat in-nugūm
al-Umm ʿādat tifriquh fī rāshā	ba-tiḥibb wāḥid baʿdamā gābat taʾūm [rough meter]
ṣalī wa ṣāmah ḥēn w-iḥnā saʿf[a]hā	w-aṣbaḥa tākul ʿashāʾ dhī bā yaṣūm [rough meter]

53.

raʿnā ba-shūf ʿād al-mawāsim muqbilah	bā nisʾaluh dhī huwa mufallak bi-n-nugūm

ʿāduh thurayyā bi-s-samā mā sariba [rough meter]
ar-rāy bi-yad Allah dhī huw muʿtalī
lā l-awwal ashfaq bī wa lā tālī raḥam

yā kharibah yā khallāhā ad-dunyā dahūm [rough meter]
kam bā naḍallī ṭūl waqtī yā humūm
ḥayyāt bi-l-ghābah tisqīnī sumūm

54. yā dhī bidēt al-qawl mā taqbil hugag
mahmā yaqūl annuh badā bi-d-darwalah
wa-l-khaṭṭ sēdah baʿdamā awlēnā ath-thiqqah
al-lōm ya'wī Saʿd yōm al-lāyimah

min qaṣr tawzīʿ al-ḥaqāyib wa-r-raqūm
mundhu zaman ʿinduh bi-hā lāysan ʿumūm
li-l-khēl baʿd al-yōm min ʿāduh yalōm
b-ashumm bārūt al-qanābil wa-ṭ-ṭuqūm

55. Basil Bernstein, "Classes, Modalities, and the Process of Cultural Reproduction: A Model," *Language in Society* 10 (1981):330–33. The use of poetry for debating sensitive political matters in public was repeatedly illustrated for me in afternoon discussions when tremendously complex issues would be negotiated through verse without my slightest awareness of what was going on. Yemenis assured me that this function of poetry had long been one of its principal advantages for political leaders, such that until recently, any skilled politician in Yemen had to have mastered the poetic craft.

56. Given that most poets can compose four rhymed verses fairly quickly, I suspect that the poets were tactfully deferring to the authority of Khaledi, who was known to be slower than the others in extemporaneous verse and had not yet weighed in. After the cassette poet had finally delivered his verses, a third poet skilled at extemporaneous verse immediately supplied his poem, and others followed.

57. See chapter 4 for a discussion of women poets and performance challenges in recent decades.

· TWO ·

"*Metropolitan Tribalism*" *in the* bidʿ wa jiwāb qaṣīdah: *A Social History of Media Aesthetics*

The *qaṣīdah* tends to be the ambassador in any survey of poetry in the Arab world. In Yemen, fans of political verse give special regard to a genre of *qaṣīdahs* called "initiation and response" *(bidʿ wa jiwāb)* poetry, in which two poets exchange sometimes heated verses over the latest events both great and small. Cassette audiences are among the most avid devotees of this profoundly dialogic form of poetry. The mediation of *bidʿ wa jiwāb* dialogue between poets has not been achieved solely through oral recitation, song, and more recently polyester recording tape, all of which have been instrumental in coordinating poets' own meditations with those of listeners. Writing has also helped poets constitute and reflect on the sociality of dialogue. I propose that the moral and political value of *bidʿ wa jiwāb* poetry cannot be understood without considering it as a textual practice that is aesthetically rendered amid the events of history, both oral and written.[1]

The solicitations of orality and writing are explored in this chapter through a microhistory of the spread of literacy in the Yafiʿi highlands. As rural notables established compounds for religious education and legal services in the fifteenth century, their embellished literary language increasingly evoked piety, as elaborated in the Qur'an and moral custom *(sunna)*. The diction of notables also expressed the *social* valences of piety as secured through the authority of a growing community of religious scholars whose intellectual and cultural accomplishments spread from village- and town-based centers of training and scholarship. In narrating the expansion of this community of estimable Yafi'i writers, I maintain a constant interest in practices of writing and literacy. However, I also consider such technological competences to be informed by a more general metaphysical entity: the *idea* of a written text as it becomes elaborated socially and morally.[2] In specific, I explore how the "text concept" of the *qaṣīdah* invests practices of writing and orality with ontological and symbolic import and, in the process, encodes both written and oral utterances as socially significant forms of media.[3] To link this argument to the concerns of specific poets, I focus in the latter half of the chapter on two *bidʿ wa jiwāb qaṣīdahs*. Through close readings of these poems, I suggest that while the ideal fixity of the text concept is conveyed through reflection on writing, written marks also bear an unstable materiality that requires that they be embodied in comparatively more stable tokens of spoken oral mediation. While such oscillation between styles of written and oral mediation is notable in other major text concepts in the Arab world, I show how its particular elaboration in *bidʿ wa jiwāb* epistolary verse both shapes and reflects an affiliation that I call "metropolitan tribalism."[4]

To avoid associating what may appear to be a new form of social subjectivity with underlying, culturally essential communicative modes, I begin with a hermeneutic question: how have orality and literacy been approached as specific styles of apperception and knowledge? A review of several currents of scholarship on verbal culture provides a starting point and considers how studies of oral performance and writing by both Western and Yemeni scholars have privileged certain genres and epistemological assumptions.

A STYLISTIC APPROACH TO MORAL AUTHORITY

Distinctions between oral performance and written composition have long informed the sociological study of texts. In the early to mid-twentieth century, linguistic anthropologists focused on identifying universal formal features that could help distinguish authentic, oral "texts" from those that might have been imported from elsewhere. Franz Boas, one of the earliest anthropologists to devote serious study to documenting the narratives of nonliterate peoples, suggested in the 1920s that one of the key marks of such indigenous oral texts is repetition.[5] Other scholars argued that the most important organizing principle in oral literature is "parallelism," a type of repetition in which one element (often a stretch of syntax) is kept constant while analogous elements are slightly modified.[6] One of the most generative approaches to the "oral" component of verbal art has been developed in studies of verbal formulas that abound in much extemporaneously composed narrative and verse.[7] These observations on repetition, parallelism, and oral formulas have greatly advanced our understandings of the power of oral performance and are all drawn on in this chapter.

As methodologies of documentation and comparative material have accumulated, efforts to establish universal distinctions between "oral" and "written" features of verbal art have largely been abandoned.[8] Instead, previous observations are being incorporated into more socially responsive, context-sensitive approaches that can account for the cultural salience of oral and written forms without glossing over the complexities of textual practice. As Ruth Finnegan notes of the study of poets, scholars might be best served by thinking of oral and written forms as "stylistic possibilities that provide both constraints and opportunities for clothing the human imagination in what are recognized as beautiful and appropriate poetic forms. Any poet operates with a set of agreed local conventions within which he can operate, communicate with his audience, and even, on occasion, innovate."[9] I take Finnegan to suggest that oral and written differentiations are as much matters of subjective and aesthetic apperception as they are historically rigid codes of social affiliation.

I define *style* as a convention of verbal practice whose difference from normative patterns of verbal expression is recognized by users as socially significant.[10] To stylize verse is to signal affiliation with one social group while preserving ties to another. In this study of media aesthetics, attention to style allows a consideration of how *bidʿ wa jiwāb* poets have routinely sought a measure of literate and, I argue, metropolitan distinction even while remaining firmly committed to oral, vernacular poetry. This argument requires that Yemenis' own formal distinctions between oral and written features be approached as conventionalized social "markers," or stereotypes, that prove to be effective resources for affiliating with specific discursive communities. Equally important, however, is the need to locate the meaning of such markers within historically elaborated frameworks of imaginative apperception. Where both layers of meaning cohere together in socially significant regularities of sound, grammar, symbolism, affect, and so forth, their moral value can be spoken of as "texts," or sequences of repeated signs that instantiate conventions apperception and interpretation. By attending to the stylistic tensions within and between these layers of meaning, however, I also explore how orality and writing are defined in relation to each other, as *text differences* that can jar listeners into considering new conditions of moral authority.

A STYLE OF VERNACULAR LITERACY: THE VALUE OF APPROACHING YEMENI POETRY THROUGH SOCIAL AESTHETICS

Before investigating matters of style and aesthetics, I introduce several principle genres of Yemeni poetry and their conventional associations for Yemenis and Western scholars. The relation of *bidʿ wa jiwāb* poetry to these genres and to a broader set of verbal exchange routines helps identify how a *bidʿ wa jiwāb* discursive community is situated ideologically amid a variety of expressive practices. A general appreciation for the usual social valences of *bid' wa jiwāb* poetry for Yemenis can help explain the historical foundations of such associations in practices of highlands epistolary exchange. Only then will the styliziation of poetic forms in acts of moral reflection be available for examination.

Contemporary Yemeni scholars have developed a set of generic classifications for Yemeni poetry that are as formally detailed as they are embroidered with degrees of social prestige. At the most general level, poetry is arranged into two major genres, defined formally through language variety and meter. These genres are called *ḥakamī* and *ḥumaīnī.* The former, *ḥakamī* verse, composed in near classical Arabic and in classical meters, represents the quintessence of poetry for most educated Yemenis. By contrast, *ḥumaīnī* poetry is a more popular, parochial genre that is composed largely by urban Yemeni elites in upper-level vernacular Arabic and in meters suited to folk song.[11] In recent decades of Yemeni scholarship, much excellent work has been devoted to delineating further subgenres: variations of *ḥumaīnī* (the sung *mubayyit* and *muwashshaḥ* genres), chanted tribal poetry, sea chanteys, and other styles of folk poetry composed in vernacular varieties.[12] Although formally elaborated through centuries of scholarship, genre classification also inevitably wends toward dominant discursive alignments (as noted in chapter 1). One frequently encounters attempts to identify specific genres with particular tribes, regions, or national communities.

The genre most exquisitely documented by recent generations of Yemeni intellectuals is *ḥumaīnī.* Celebrated by Yemenis for its historical connections to Andalusian Spain as well as to the fourteenth-century courtly cultures of Ta'izz and, several centuries later, Sanaa, *ḥumaīnī* has been formally codified in line with standards of eloquence *(balāghah)* that were developed as early as the ninth-century by Arab grammarians and literary scholars.

Studies of more vernacular genres of poetry, by contrast, have begun to be produced only in the last few decades, and many of these have focused on the work of elite folk poets and singers.[13] Where such studies often draw from Western and Soviet folklore paradigms, they tend to replicate certain romantic views of rural culture by focusing almost exclusively on oral poetics (especially genres of tribal poetry) and song traditions.[14] With few exceptions, little attention has been given to the intersection of such traditions with historically durable textual traditions that might nuance stereotypes of "folk" poetry as a purely oral, traditional, collective, and authentic expression of rural inhabitants.[15]

For Western scholars of poetry on the Arabian Peninsula, orally performed texts from the most remote, nonliterate Arabian tribes long proved integral to a larger philological project whose measures of linguistic purity were commensurate with certain Western romantic notions of the authentic "Orient." Partly due to such methodological biases, Western Arabists made sound contributions to studies of Arabian poetry by documenting traditions of oral versification from the early decades of the twentieth century.[16] With advances in textual theory that were enabled by structuralist studies in the mid- to latter decades of the century, Western anthropologists and folklorists eventually formulated useful critiques of analytic models that had represented texts as fixed forms that are passed down intact over time, impervious to individual manipulation. Attention to the situated performance of texts and to ethnographies of speaking during the 1960s and 1970s produced a new generation of scholars who were better equipped to document and contextualize oral poetry. In light of these advances, Western-trained scholars have produced benchmark ethnographic studies of Yemeni and Arabian poetry and song.[17] However, as a result of the emphasis on oral poetics and performance, such ethnographies have devoted little attention to the intersections between vernacular poetry and writing. This is especially the case for rural expressive cultures, which are typically essentialized in terms of a purer orality that confirms stereotypes of generic tribalism.[18] As a result, the comingling of oral and written textual forms is a possibility allowed almost exclusively to cities.

In the rest of this chapter, I present what might be called an "historical poetics" of written *bid' wa jiwāb* verse with the aim of developing a better discursive approach to the nuances of textual form and practice in Yemen and to models of social identity generally. Highland poets have been extremely versatile in crafting their verse to different discursive communities, each associated with distinctive forms of talk and poetry. Let us begin exploring this panoply of social orders by considering a variegated field of *bid' wa jiwāb* genres and then focus on the historical ethnography of one specific community of *bid' wa jiwāb* poets in Yafiʿ.

COMMUNITIES OF REPARTEE

In Yemen, verbal dexterity in social encounters is highly valued. Proverbs amply illustrate the just return of spoken words: "He who pronounces a word does not return empty-handed" *(min qāl kalimah mā raga' min dūnahā),* as well as the merit of guarding words carefully: "If my word slips out [in speech], it governs me. But if I keep it to myself, I remain its governor" *(in faltat kalimatī malakatnī w-in 'ādhā malikthā).* From daily greetings that require the appropriate exchange of formulaic sequences, to public challenges and ripostes between contestants, the well-applied phrase helps demonstrate men's and women's capacity as social actors. Indeed, a properly managed verbal challenge, a response, or a silent rebuff signals a turbulent political world and constructs a relationship between participants that is mediated by degrees of honor, as has been noted in other studies of expressive culture in the Middle East and North Africa.[19]

To situate *bid' wa jiwāb* verse within the practical conventions of verbal dialogue and exchange, we should begin by acknowledging that there are multiple genres of "initiation and response" routines and that each is associated with different discursive communities. On one level, tribal poets in the Arabian Peninsula have long practiced specific forms of dyadic oral sparring, which has been brilliantly illustrated by the poems of pre-Islamic and early Umayyid poets who exchanged *qaṣīdahs* that have become known as *naqāʾiḍ* (sing. *naqīḍah*) poems. These *qaṣīdahs*—sometimes vitriolic, at other times cordial, nearly always agonistic—became opportunities for tribal poets to express their own views about politics and interpersonal relations with the aim of swaying public opinion.[20] In a pioneering monograph of vernacular poetry in northern Yemen, Steven Caton examines a version of such verbal parleying called the *daʿwah w-ijābah* "challenge and counterchallenge"[21] and demonstrates its centrality to notions of honor that sustain tribal identity and personhood.[22]

Initiation and response routines are not exclusively tribal or oral, however. They are equally central to more literate traditions of literature and legal practice. The technique of "questions and answers" *(masāʾil wa-ajwibah)* has long influenced numerous genres of Arabic writing, especially scientific presentations and inquiries into the philological and textual problems of the Qurʾan.[23] In earlier Islamic periods, theological and juridical disputation known as *munāẓarah* was conducted through questions and answers between Muslims and non-Muslims before large audiences.[24] This practice was replicated in literary genres in the form of debates between living or inanimate beings over points of merit and was also instrumental to centuries of theological as well as juridical literature. As Brinkley Messick notes in his study of judicial process in the northern Yemeni highlands, the format of question and answer has traditionally been central to the practice of *muwājahah* (from *wajh* meaning "face"), in which judges sit in public spaces and address plaintiffs.[25] But debates over law, religion, and practically every other subject have also been waged by Yemeni religious and legal scholars through poetic verse.[26] The nineteenth-century Yemeni Islamic scholar and jurist Muhammad al-Shawkānī (1760–1834), one of the most influential jurisprudists in Yemeni history and widely read by Zaidis and Shafiʿis, explains the importance of composing poetry and eloquent prose to religious scholars. The following passage, written by Shawkani as a veritable textbook for practicing legal scholars, underscores the need to refine scholarly and practical competence through written exchanges of "questions" and "answers" conducted through poetry. I quote the excerpt at length for its exceptional clarity:

> What adds to the aims of this high level, raising and benefiting the strength of perception and soundness of comprehension, are two mental methods: examining the poetry and the works of the finest poets, the most famous among them, with the aims of extracting their most brilliant meanings and delightful witticisms and, additionally, of acquiring facility with composition and the use of its various aspects. Indeed, the scholar *(ʿālim)* needs to be able to compose a response to well-framed questions that he receives or to prolific observations directed to him by the scholarly community. And sometimes he will need to compose poetry in one of its varieties toward one of its more proper aims. If he who attains such a high position of learning cannot compose poetry, it is a mar on his fine faculties and a fault in his completeness. For this reason, there is a prolific production of verse by the most eloquent composers, who are famous for their excellence and beneficence and who exhibit the most eloquent diction and clearest exposition in both their letters and writings. Such competences serve them well when they need to compose a letter or respond to an acquaintance or write to a friend. One's words must be commensurate with one's learning. Indeed, the language of those who do not practice good composition of poetry and prose will be considered deficient by those who are eloquent. Knowledge is a tree, and its fruits are articulations. How vulgar it is when the scholar, proficient in every art, should make light of them by composing poetry and prose that is not equivalent to the other arts. He will be the laughingstock of those who have the basest knowledge of adequate language and clear composition. One must have recourse to an appropriate maturity, matching one's status with one's metrical composition and prosody.[27]

For Shawkani, the importance of answering "well-framed questions" through poetry "in one of its varieties" is put in no uncertain terms: those who cannot match "one's status with one's metrical composition and prosody" risk being ridiculed by far less competent men. The exchange of poetry through written letters was the scholar's means to preserve and indeed to demonstrate his reputation, status, and honor.

In examining the practice of *bidʿ wa jiwāb* epistolary exchanges and working toward an understanding of style, it is important to keep in mind the existence of multiple genres of initiation and response routines that correspondents can use in practice. Indeed, these genres continually leak, and their distinctive formal components and interpretive frames constantly overlap as they circulate in and out of different communities. The stylistic possibilities inherent in *bidʿ wa jiwāb* compositions make them especially exciting for listeners, who often debate after the conclusion of a poem about what was signified, which community of interpreters addressed, or what the poet sought to express about his own position. The dynamism of style in rural Yafiʿi poetry can be better understood through a consideration of the practices and forms of *bidʿ wa jiwāb* poetry within a specific ethnographic context. Since stylistic choice is a matter of both literary form and moral distinction, I attend especially closely to associations of learning and status that rural religious scholars and other elites enjoyed and to the ways that such distinctions become elaborated with the spread of writing in Yafiʿ.

DISTINCTIONS OF EPISTOLARY PRACTICE

Practices of writing in Yafiʿ, despite its rural isolation, have considerable historical depth. Local records suggest that the first schools to be established in Yafiʿ were introduced by religious authorities who migrated to the region in the ninth century. Many of these men were from the leading religious houses of Hadramawt (eastern Yemen). One of the first protected enclaves *(rubāṭ),* located in what is today the district of Labʿūs, is recorded to have established ʿAbdallah Bin ʿUmar al-Qadīm (d. 1403/806), of the Bā ʿAbbād family in al-Ghurfah (Hadramawt). In exchange for seasonal tithes, he served as a mediator between warring parties, provided basic religious services and counsel to the surrounding communities, and taught young children rudimentary reading skills as part of their religious training. Over the next few centuries, the Bā ʿAbbād would establish numerous similar enclaves throughout Yafiʿ.[28] The largest influx of religious authorities began arriving in Yafiʿ between the late sixteenth to seventeenth centuries.[29] Some of these men came to Yafiʿ in recognition of services that the Yafiʿis had provided to their allies during military campaigns in Hadramawt.[30] Others were invited to the region by the Imam Hasan Bin Qāsem and his representatives, who managed to secure temporary control over the region after 1654–55/1065. The first of these appointees *(nāʾib al-ḥafāʾiẓ)* established his headquarters at Yafiʿ's earliest place of worship, the Mosque of Light *(Masjid al-Nūr),* in 1670/1081. In addition to directing administrative tasks, mosque appointees provided basic religious training—including how to read, write, and employ basic mathematics skills—to both boys and girls.[31]

While the number of students who learned to write at these small religious schools, called *maʿlāmāt* (sing. *maʿlāmah*),[32] is difficult to estimate, it is not unlikely that by the mid-eighteenth century dozens of students in every tribal district were being taught the rudiments of writing and reading every year. In many cases, education at the *maʿlāmah* was not sufficient for producing competent readers and writers, especially in remote areas where resources were limited.[33] Nevertheless, literacy skills could be refined through a growing culture of home instruction and lessons at the mosque. Moreover, an increasing number of Yafiʿis who acquired several years of basic education at the local *maʿlāmah* and perhaps initial training at the local mosque ventured farther afield to acquire higher-level education.[34] While the proportion of literate and semiliterate people was still far surpassed by the nonliterate population, these centuries witnessed an increasingly steady exchange of written poetry among the men of letters in rural Yafiʿ.[35]

In the twentieth century, literacy and writing competences finally became available to thousands of inhabitants throughout the rural highlands. In the 1930s, several primary schools *(madrasahs)* opened in urban centers around Yafiʿ, offering up to three years of education to young men of shaikhly and *sayyid* families.[36] A decade later, administrative, legal, and educational reforms supervised by the British colonial government enabled the spread of such schools throughout many of the protectorates, especially Lahej and the ʿAwdhali, Dathīnah, and Faḍli territories.[37] Illiteracy rates remained high: surveys of Aden's urban population in 1946 revealed that approximately 72.6 percent of men and 94.5 percent women remained illiterate, though approximately a decade later this ratio had dropped to 58 percent and 90 percent, respectively.[38] Moreover, the inhabitants of Yafiʿ Bani Qāsed and especially Yafiʿ Bani Mālek began to fall significantly behind the other protectorate regions during the 1940s and 1950s, largely because its leadership resisted conciliations to British colonial authority.[39] Nevertheless, with corresponding improvements in the *maʿlāmah* institutions in the rural areas and with growing opportunities for rural children to access urban primary schools during the decades before independence, literacy and the ability to write were becoming less novel than they had been. Such transformations are considered in greater detail at the end of this chapter.

Setting the stylistic contexts for *bidʿ wa jiwāb* poetry requires more than an inquiry into the spread of writing and educational opportunities. For even as literacy spread, it spread unequally among Yemenis. Like any technology, writing was subject to hierarchies of power. Those best positioned to access and wield its power were religious elites, and foremost among them were the *sayyids,* descendants of the Prophet who were widely recognized for their high status. But other families of religious judges *(qāḍīs)* as well as those educated in Islamic jurisprudence *(fa-*

qīhs) also had considerable status. Although these religious elites espoused equality between all believers in the Muslim community *(ummah),* they also maintained that society was divided into two general categories of individuals: the scholar who has knowledge *(ʿilm),* called the *ʿālim* (pl. *ʿulamāʾ*), and the individual without knowledge, called the *jāhil,* or "ignorant person."[40] Where writing was a technology, the mastery and deployment of which were restricted to circles of elite and educated men, its tools, methods, and styles were a means to distinction.[41] Hierarchies of competence were maintained in daily performances of literate knowledge: through interpretive authority, technical know-how, manners of reading, usage of upper Arabic language varieties, and so forth. As Messick notes, "The ideology of literacy was a component of the overall ideology of social differentiation."[42] Such competences opened doors to social honors, prestigious occupations, an endogamous upper stratum, and wealth. A demonstration of literary competence signaled the symbolic capital of learned tradition, and a certain *style* was communicated in the daily expressive routines (both oral and written) of these men. Those religious scholars who wrote poetry to one another in the form of epistolary exchanges drew from an elaborate stylistics meant in part to convey their proximity to this literate domain. This stylistics in *bidʿ wa jiwāb* poetry is examined below.

Although such correspondents were men of literate authority, they were also thoroughly engaged in a world of tribal politics. The most prominent of these men were the sultans themselves, who originally were both spiritual and the military leaders—men in whom religious and tribal domains were incorporated in one figure.[43] Other religious scholars, such as the *sayyids* and *qāḍīs,* also had to integrate such domains in their capacities as negotiators between tribes, as is noted in ethnographic studies of tribal dispute settlements in northern Yemen.[44] And as literacy spread, a number of nonreligious elites learned to write, too. Most notable among these were tribal shaikhs who understood the value of writing and could use their prestigious family connections to acquire rudimentary training in reading and writing.[45] Inasmuch as all of these literate cohorts used writing within practical political contexts, they were keenly attuned to styles of tribal oratory that might be leveraged in a variety of communicative modes, including writing as well as oral performance. An oral style, especially when inflected with tribal political discourse, was not of "low" value in a communicative economy that favored "high" varieties of learned, classical Arabic.[46] Rather, such an oral style was a powerful and persuasive medium among popular audiences, even though and, in some contexts, precisely *because* it contended with the literate authority of the educated elites. Through the proper usage of poetic forms and stylistic devices of certain genres of tribal poetics, *bidʿ wa jiwāb* poets could demonstrate their affiliation with the social and moral spaces of tribal politics, spaces that any political leader in the highlands would have been foolhardy to ignore.

In examining several *qaṣīdah* compositions below, we must keep in mind that the discursive contours of *bidʿ wa jiwāb* poetry were a product of the composite styles of a heterogeneous community of leading notables composed of tribal leaders as well as Muslim scholars and literati. For this reason, *bidʿ wa jiwāb* poems were not simply opportunities for elites to swap literary verses for enjoyment and aesthetic pleasure, as were other genres of poetic correspondence *(al-murāsalāt al-shiʿriyyah)* in other parts of the Arabian Peninsula.[47] Rather, their themes tended to be more explicitly political and practical. I argue, nevertheless, that part of the political pragmatism of such men involves the demonstration of a refined moral sensibility. In what follows, I show how the moral aspects of *bidʿ wa jiwāb* poetry can be articulated most clearly by exploring how correspondents attend to the mediation of their verses to help them solidify alliances across an instable political landscape of shifting alliances and uncertain rumor. In reflecting on the risky temporal and spatial distances that are detonated by written marks or on the need to impress oral articulation onto the bodies of carefully instructed messengers, correspondents willfully linger on potential ruptures to communicative action and its social foundations in general. Amid such uncertainty, however, correspondents each work, in their own style, to assert a set of claims whose circulation can underscore the common resources of discursive community.

To ground my analysis, I examine a specific poetic exchange that occurred between two Yafiʿi poets in the mid-1950s. The initiator is a blacksmith, Husain ʿUbaīd al-Ḥaddād, and the respondent is a tribal leader, Shaikh Rageh Haīthem Bin Sabʿah. In exploring how both poets invoke styles of written and oral discourse that reference different communities, I attend closely to modes of written and oral performance. My observations on style will ultimately show how *bidʿ wa jiwāb* poets seek to develop a metropolitan "text concept" that signals their translocal attachments to circuits of metropolitan culture even while they tailor these attachments to a highlands community in which conventions of oral, tribal poetics predominate.

BIDʿ: INITIATION

The first *qaṣīdah* is by Husain ʿUbaid al-Haddad, a poet from a family of blacksmiths who practiced their trade in Yihar, the largest tribal district in Yafiʿ.[48] Although not a religious scholar, Haddad had learned to write at his local *maʿlāmah,* where he had acquired a rudimentary religious education. Due perhaps to the orientation of the local teacher, his education had also been influenced by a group known in Yafiʿ as the "People of the Truth" *(Ahl al-Ḥaqīqah),* a minority community of spiritual practitioners with gnostic orientations.[49]

Haddad composed during a decade in which Yafiʿis were witnessing some of the worst internal violence that they had experienced for as long as anyone could remember. Over the preceding two decades, the port city of Aden, a British colonial outpost with a population of over 140,000, had trebled in size to become the busiest harbor in the world after New York City.[50] While facilitating massive new labor flows and, for some, extraordinary profits, the heyday of commercial activity in Aden had done little to alleviate poverty in the rural hinterlands. British colonial administrators worked to ensure such imbalance. The protectorate policy in the hinterlands beyond the city hung on an arrangement of treaties that were designed to supply traditional leaders with cash, guns, and ammunition in exchange for noninterference with Aden port activities and other matters of vital colonial interest. When leaders became unruly, the British generally circumvented problems by appointing pliable sultans and emirs. In the years following World War II, however, occasional recalcitrance had begun to be met by air-bombing campaigns. In 1957, thousand-pound bombs had begun to be dropped on villages just over the ridge from Haddad. When children heard the planes approaching low over the horizon, they would run, yelling, "Big Mr. Ragab is coming!" Mr. Ragab was a local resident and the largest man in the district.

Haddad used his rudimentary writing skills to compose a *qaṣīdah* and send it as a letter to the shaikh of his tribal section and his friend Shaikh Rageh Haithem Bin Sabʿah (who died in the late 1950s). His aim was to discuss the events of the day and domestic unrest and to voice his support for Bin Sabʿah's election to sultan of Yafiʿ Bani Qāsed. Yafiʿ was in need of leadership. In the past several years, a few tribal leaders had broken league with the Yafiʿi community and had signed agreements with the British. A particularly bloody incident had occurred in 1953 when Shaikh Ahmad Bu Bak al-Naqīb, leader of the largest *maktab* in Yafiʿ Bani Mālek, was assassinated in the stairwell of his house by his cousin. Fueled by the influx of arms and bribes from interested parties, conflict had broken out between many sections in Yafiʿ, and there was no signs of its abating.[51] At the same time, the blacksmith Haddad noticed that he was receiving fewer customers every year, a trend that Yafiʿi dyers, silversmiths, seamstresses, leather workers, and other small-scale crafts workers were experiencing with some concern. Imports from Aden and the disruption of traditional trade patterns had begun constraining rural sources of livelihood. As a result of these worrying changes, Haddad sought to express his hopes for a restitution of a tribal order that might return unity and prosperity to Yafiʿ.

In the following translation, I seek to preserve the rhyme scheme by foregrounding alliteration where appropriate and maintaining as much of the word order in final rhyme words as possible (see appendix A for a full transliteration). Punctuation is added both for clarity and to foreground what I sense to be the performance potentials of the composition. To appreciate some of the moving prosody that is achieved in Arabic, the poem is best read aloud at a slow pace:

In the name of God, I seek refuge with the Lord of daybreak 1
With words that from the heart of stones have burst forth,
[Protected] from all that He despises and from the mischief that He formed 2
Through created talk as well as talk that is not created.
Glory to Him who molded the universe from an existence that gushed 3
Favored [human] forms, from [between] the spine and thorax, gushing.
Pray to the one whose light first became resplendent among them [i.e., Muhammad]. 4
Even before Adam, the flower of [his] light split forth illumination
From which [God] created [the light] that circles the seven heavens. 5
How [each] angel encircled them, reaching [harmonious] cohesion.
The loving believers, they loved the light of lights that shon in radiance 6
Following the Prophet of lights, from his cheeks radiated.
May You be satisfied with his companions, Bā Bakr the trustworthy 7
And his people and his friends who are in faith believing.
May You be satisfied with ʿAli, who has in his hand an eliminating sword. 8
[He] routed armies of the infidels when they attacked.

Their dwellings razed, incinerated, and destroyed. 9
  Their idols smashed and all else destruction.
The young man Brother Hādī says: People are oppressed! 10
  From tyranny and decrees, the government has become constrained!
Now, O traveler who overcomes all impediments 11
  From the precipitous nests where the bird has screeched,
Deliver my script before dawn's twilight. 12
  Travel to the shaikh's enclave, [and] heed his intentions.
Perform the opening chapter [of the Qur'an] at the saint's tomb, the sagacious ancestor, 13
  And at the house of diplomacy, insight, and perspicacity.
Five tribal sections, one discourse in plight: 14
  At night, they hold council before confronting the fury.
Your path is through Yihar. As [sons of] Sheba's monarchy, they hold council in a circle. 15
  Their customs have been raiding and counsel.
Reach Ḥamūmah, and spend a day there for the vista 16
  Over the coffee trees and strongholds splendid.
Go settle in the home of insight; its oath is trusted 17
  With Shaikh Rageh, whose pacts are trustworthy.
My greetings to Bin Haithem and those in accord with him 18
  Among brothers and his sons and consenting friends,
With flower water, its origin from the deep-lineaged Ḥāshemī [i.e., Muhammad] 19
  And with perfume, the kind in the packaged vial.
And if he should ask you, do not speak of ignominy and conflict, 20
  Of the news from Yafiʿ, of fission and confliction.
They have a day calling them to avarice and bloodletting, 21
  They want fission, or else they want bloodshed.
Tell him to see what is meant from where it shrieks. 22
  The truck drivers destroy their [own] roads!
He is still on the lands of Abyan, [such] an outrage broke out there yesterday, 23
  And [yet] today the "officer" has no [desire to] prosecute.
Bin ʿAṭiyyah stole money and pillaged Abyan, 24
  And in the lands of the Quʿaīṭi, what theft!
For gluttony, they eliminated the leaders of Yafiʿ, 25

Trailing the four who hunger for government.
Why has the state of al-Qārah become paralyzed with Mt. Baraq? 26
[And] he who was under its banner: [why has he] kept silent about Abyan?
Three [things] are occurring in front of you, and they are not the just path, 27
Else the world will remain in ashes, obliterated:
We do not accept cash crops or biding time on the edge of plowed rows 28
Or giving up daggers or fine-painted carbines as bond.
If they appointed Rageh as sultan, we would have a purpose in talk. 29
He deserves our tenth [i.e., tithes], such a well-coiled turban.
How many of our people's leaders would follow to where he advanced 30
With his fire, no concessions by way of depravity or masquerade?
In Yafiʿ, tribal sections are visible; they have split in divisions. 31
Those who devise [such a] folk-broken time are blood kin.
For truly, from Banā to ʿAqwar, its terraces are cramped. 32
Tortuous, torturous, the heights are entrapped.
Intractable, its roads fractured for [all] means of passage. 33
Its folk in refuge, at dark they are beasts.
An island at which no anchors are thrown, ever, 34
Nor do trucks pass across it [by] land, ever.
O Shaikh, forgive me for straying, no harm intended. 35
We implore forgiveness from God for injurious words.
I ask you a riddle about a camel that with a camel consented. 36
Along with [the] two camels is a compliant creature.
He asked for a she-camel from them, and each one of them spoke, 37
And the words [are] in the Qur'an, [which is so] clearly articulated.
Pray to the one whose light first became resplendent among them. 38
Even before Adam, the flower of [his] light split forth illumination.

Before discussing the details of this beautiful *qaṣīdah,* a word is needed about the genre form itself. The *qaṣīdah* (pl. *qaṣāyid*) is one of the oldest and most familiar genres of poetry to listeners throughout the Arab Islamic world.[52] As a form that is central to the cultural life of diverse communities, its composition and performance are strongly managed by verbal, thematic, and aesthetic conventions. One of the most durable structures of the *qaṣīdah* has been the division of each line *(shaṭr)* into two to four strophes *(baīts)* that, when arranged layer on layer, appear as columns *(āʿmidahs)* on the page. Rhyming schemes can be relatively basic (as in the single end-line rhyme of many classical Arabic *qaṣīdahs*) or more elaborate (such as the rhyme schemes of much folk poetry in which each strophe has its own rhyme). Most *qaṣīdahs* are composed of between fifteen to sixty lines. Although it is not unusual to find *qaṣīdahs* that are longer, such a length enables them to be recited, sung, or read in a relatively short timeframe. Such terseness facilitates their easy insertion into larger speech events, conversations, and other occasions of varying formality.

A PROSODY OF ORAL CONTACT

On several occasions, I heard this *qaṣīdah* recited both in Yemen and in the United States by Yemeni Americans who discovered this *bidʿ wa jiwāb* exchange in my folder of poems. Among Yafiʿis, it is a well-known exchange though not because of its distribution on cassette. To my knowledge, it has never been recorded by regional singers, for reasons I explore below. Still, Yafiʿi listeners told me that Haddad's initiation *qaṣīdah,* once heard, left an impression that could never be forgotten.

The power of oral articulation had long been acknowledged by Yemenis, no more so than for highland political poets for whom tribal discourses provided the defining idioms of public address. The tribesman's honor is ideally proclaimed through his voice, which is frequently depicted in poetry as echoing from the highest peaks. Greetings must similarly resound publicly and are often likened to bursts of gunfire or deafening thunder. The volume of the tribesman's voice also signals his moral constitution: "As the trees bear fruit, so the tribesman holds to his word" *(al-ashjār tathmar wa-l-qabīlī min kalimatuh)*. A capacity for powerful speech is considered to be a sign of personhood and of social life itself. According to these terms, orality has ontological primacy. To call someone by the epithet "Mr. Prattle" *(Abū Hadarah)* can be a heavy charge in Yemen.

Haddad's poem conveys his competence in highland oral performance.[53] Some of his verses even reproduce verbal formulas that are distinct to tribal dispute-mediation poems *(zāmils)*, as I discuss in my later analysis of the poem's principal themes. And yet Haddad's verses also resonate within, as if their oral intonations could not circulate freely through the regular channels of tribal discourse and instead met resistance to public conversion. Several of the listeners whom I spoke with about Haddad's initiation to Shaikh Bin Sabʿah confided that they had been overcome with a restlessness, a feeling of shaking (*taqayyid* or *tashannug*) that poets experience when on the verge of deep inspiration or else madness. In pressing for the source of such a feeling, I found listeners recurring to Haddad's membership among the "People of the Truth" *(Ahl al-Ḥaqīqah)*, although further details about his gnostic insights or its evidence in the poem were left unelaborated.

Wherein lies the power of Haddad's *qaṣīdah* to exert such a reverberating bodily effect? To avoid equating orality with a kind of unmediated "presence" in the manner of some schools of Western philosophy, I consider the basic phonic structure of Haddad's composition with the aim of understanding how oral articulation is mediated by larger textual patterns and made into an object of authority. At the poem's acoustic foundation lays its rhyme scheme, the most salient pattern of which is embedded in the words at the end of each strophe (ab/ab), a format typical of highlands *qaṣīdahs* in particular. In this case, the first strophe ends with a constricting, uvular consonant [-q], while the second strophe morphologically parallels the first, with the addition of a plosive suffix [-qah]:

```
^  -  -    \ ^   -   -   -     \ ^   -    -   \ ^  -    ^  -
wa bis-mill- \ lāh at- ʿw- wadh- \ t[-] min rab- \ bi dhīl-fa-laq      1
bi-kal-mā- \ t[i] min ṣumm il- \ ḥi- gā- rah \ ta-fal-la-qah
```

The regularity of the end rhymes contributes to the rhythmical structure of the poem, which follows a *ṭawīl* meter. Such regimented rhyme and metrical schemes clearly identify the poem as a certain conventional type: in this case, a political *qaṣīdah*.[54] Such prosodic regularities can also link the poem with more specific types of poetic form: where particular combinations of end rhymes could signal affiliation with other poems that feature the same scheme, listeners are able to appreciate intertextual references that expand the poem's referential and emotive connections. In short, the oral structures of the composition engage broad generic and textual patterns that are familiar to Yemeni audiences. As a verbal product of a recognizable type, the composition can be circulated as a unit associated with other equivalent units.

While the more conventional aspects of rhyme secure the poem's ready circulation, however, a more complex weave of rhyming patterns foregrounds the individuality of the composition and demands that attention be paid to the poet's unique craft. Crucial toward this end is the punning, or paronomasia, achieved through rhymes. Almost without exception, the first of the two strophic end rhymes follows the pattern FvMvL (for (F)irst, (M)iddle, and (L)ast root consonants, interwoven with other consonants (C) and vowels (v)), as in *falaq, khalaq, dafaq, fataq,* and *ṭabaq*. The second rhyme is patterned in one of two ways:

Cv-FvM-Mv-Lah *(tafallaqah, mukhallaqah, -ri fattaqah)*[55]

or

Cv-Fvv -Mv-Lah *(muṭābiqah, muḥādhaqah, -bi dāfaqah).*

Notice that the first end rhyme cuts sound short by constriction in the throat (as in *falaq*), while the second opens and releases the sound by appending an extra, open syllable [-ah]. Additionally, in the second end rhyme, a long vowel or consonant is inserted in the middle of the word to draw out its articulation and extend its vocal brilliance. The result of such verbal interplay draws attention to the complementarity of each strophe: given the constriction of the first end rhyme, the second end rhyme not only produces a feeling of release and completion at the end of each strophe but wondrously extends the meanings of both rhyme words as they take definition from each other. In the first strophe, for example, the noun modifying "Lord" in the expression "Lord of daybreak" (*rabb[i] dhī-l-falaq,* literally *Lord possessor-the-daybreak*) is followed in the second end rhyme with a verbal root of the noun that signals the reflexive qualities and potentiality of "daybreak," which I have rendered "have burst forth" *(tafallaqah)*). In juxtaposition to the noun's decisive finality, the verb conveys the kinetic power of God's unfolding nature. A similar poetics emerges in the next line. In the first end rhyme, God's causal finality is conveyed in a verb ("He formed" *(khalaq)*), while creation becomes more dynamic and immanent in the second end rhyme through through its adjectival rendition ("created talk as well as talk that is not created" *(qawlah mukhallaqah wa ghēr[a] mukhallaqah)*). Having once, in his omnipotence, created mischief that might test believers' faith, God's "talk" continues to inform the expressive worlds of men. Where the poet's own use of words is subject to potential mischief, the supplication assumes special importance.[56]

The miniature cycles of constraint and release that are achieved through the poem's rhyming paronomasia create an impression of ordered volatility that anticipates tumultuous events discussed subsequently in the poem. Although formalized as a general circulating type, the poem also clings to the unprocessed here and now, its authority remaining attached to its performance in a specific time and place. The power of the rhyme scheme to achieve effects through its own accord is conveyed semantically through rhymed puns and symbolically in the composition's larger aesthetic of domesticity. Throughout Yemeni poetry, the task of assembling verses is often metaphorically described as building a house.[57] Many of the conventional terms for poetic form are taken from well-known architectural concepts: *baīt* can mean both a poetic "verse" and a "house"; *miṣrāʿ* is a strophe as well as a section of a door; *bāb* signifies both the beginning of an intellectual or poetic theme as well as a "door"; *taqfīl,* or "locking," is the term used for the summarizing or concluding sections of poems; and *ʿamūd* is a "column" of either a poem or a house. In this case, where the constraining rhyme is located on the "inside" end rhyme of every *baīt* (verse/house), the poet's composition iconically replicates the constriction that he declares to be afflicting the "houses" in Yafiʿ. Correspondingly, the open-vowel rhyme scheme on the "outside" of every *baīt* releases vocal articulation, offering hope for escape from irreconcilable conflict.

In my discussion of the poem's contents, I show how themes of constraint and release found in the poem's sound symbolism are replicated more explicitly in both *qaṣīdahs.* Such tightly woven parallelisms in rhyme underscore the composition's integrity as a unique and well-wrought whole. By drawing listeners' attention from generic regularities and intertextual similarities to equivalences that are specific to the poem itself, the composition performs something of its own power, as does the poet.

As I have suggested, however, the rhyme scheme does not only affirm structures of authority, whether socially regularized or contextually specific. The sound of the poem also creates profound dissonance as experienced by listeners whose bodies shook uncontrollably on hearing the poem. Such dissonance is achieved through poetic tension between intrastrophe rhyming patterns, through the poet's use of phonetic, morphological, and syntactic parallelism, and also through repetition. One of the most explosive moments of the poem, for example, occurs in verses 32 to 34 in a section that discusses the gridlock of tribal "blood kin" *(riḥm)* in Yafiʿ:

wa Yāfiʿ makātib bayyanuh qasamū firaq 31
  riḥm dhī tiḥzir ḥill[a] mā an-nās[a] farraq[ah]
li-qaṭ min Bannā lā ʿAqwar ashʿāb[a]hā ḥazaq 32
  wa ʿawgā ʿagiyyah wa-sh-shawāmikh muḥazliqah
ʿagiyyah wa ṭurūqhā mushaqqah ʿalā aṭ-ṭuruq 33
  kinān ahl[i]hā wa-l-lēl[a] hum min ṭawāraqah
gazīrah fa-lā yalqūn[a] marsā bi-hā ṭalaq 34
  wa lā mashū l-bābūr[a] luh arḍ[a] maṭlaqah

In Yafiʿ, tribal sections are visible; they have split in divisions. 31
  Those who devise [such a] folk-broken time are blood kin.
For truly, from Banā to ʿAqwar, its terraces are cramped. 32
  Tortuous, torturous, the heights are entrapped.
Intractable, its roads fractured for [all] means of passage. 33
  Its folk in refuge, at dark they are beasts.
An island at which no anchors are thrown, ever, 34
  Nor do trucks pass across it [by] land, ever.

The tight succession of [q] and [g] consonants, achieved through alliteration of lexical units, produces a weave of overlapping morphemes and, by destabilizing the independence of individual words, weakens their conventional linkages to specific concepts. English poet Gerard Manley Hopkins has called such tension "instress," a force that creates through the use of rhythmic compression, inversion, and paradox an emotional response in which all contraries are fused into a sense of unfolding immediacy.[58] In line 33 above, for example, the word *ṭuruq* indicates "means of passage," its conventional concept. Through its rhyming consonant [q], *ṭuruq* also references adjacent words that contain the same sound:

ḥazaq, "cramped" (line 32, 1st strophe end rhyme)

muḥazliqah, "entrapped" (line 32, 2d-strophe end rhyme)

ṭurūqhā, "its roads" (line 33, 1st strophe)
mushaqqah, "fractured" (line 33, 1st strophe)

As the above verses are read aloud, phonologic equivalences accumulate successively and underscore disturbing ruptures in the world's customary orders. The impassability of roads normally used for unrestricted travel becomes iconically reproduced in a language where the word for "means of passage" comes to evoke such antonyms as "cramped," "entrapped," and "fractured" and, in the verse that immediately follows, with such dangerous entities as "beasts" (line 33). Most concerning of all is the primary social locus of such conflict: the tribe's "bloodkin" or, more accurately, "womb" *(riḥm)* (line 31), humanity's creative origin.

Through a density of overlapping sounds and words, Haddad's poem actively severs its links with normative expectations of linguistic pattern and meaning. Hearing this and similar sections of Haddad's poem becomes a disturbing experience that compels listeners to confront deep connections between language and the immediate, inchoate presence of performance. When poets experience this radical form of detached authority in bouts of passionate shaking, they say they are visited by the *ḥalīlah,* one of two poetic muses. Unlike the *ḥājis,* a male-gendered muse that is known for enabling poets to contextualize wild emotion appropriately and to produce political verse well suited to public occasions, the female *ḥalīlah* produces brilliant if fleeting verse, the stuff of raw energy.[59] Yemeni listeners who admitted being moved to shaking may have been recovering from their encounter with the forceful *ḥalīlah.*

Oral performance clearly draws its power from multiple currents of phonic authority—from the more regularized and conventional patterns of genre and textual pattern to the more irregular patterns of embodied articulation in the present. A full account of the textual condensations of oral articulation allows us to acknowledge the variability of orality as a moral resource that can direct listeners not only to different horizons of discursive community—whether "tribal," "People of the Truth," or yet some more specific group of participants—but to tones of inner "voice" that are more or less social. In the case of Haddad's poem, an especially dense weave of phonic patterns lingers with listeners, and this residue of wild energy is not fully channeled by neat textual orders.

Even so, Haddad did not leave his audiences in the tempests of aural vulnerability. As attested by listeners, Haddad communicated an essential "truth" that was difficult to hear. I suggest that this truth was conveyed by channeling orality toward a sense of reiterable fixity that lay beyond sound alone. Something unheard and immanent secured sound with its more rarified aesthetic medium. In a highlands society in which literacy was at once morally valued and highly uncommon, I suggest that this medium is writing.

The significance of writing has long been evident, in part, through performances of *bidʿ wa jiwāb* poems. Exchanges between poets have almost always been read aloud from the page rather than recited in full from memory. To be sure, poets and audiences occasionally memorize full *qaṣīdahs*. Indeed, an earlier generation of skilled reciters, or rhapsodes *(rāwīs)*, could readily recite hundreds of poems by rote. Nevertheless, the specific interpersonal and event-specific content of *bidʿ wa jiwāb* poems has typically discouraged audiences from committing them fully to memory. Other *qaṣīdahs* that contain more general reflections on spiritual or political matters can better survive a diversity of performance contexts and reward efforts at memorization. For similar reasons, *bidʿ wa jiwāb* poems have not traditionally been sung, though exceptions might be made for especially fine compositions. Indeed, as I explain in later chapters, performances of *bidʿ wa jiwāb qaṣīdahs* that are sung and musically embellished become innovative stylistic variations that provide poets and audiences with a means to reflect on larger social and moral changes introduced by the audiocassette. We might note, in this regard, that the rhyme scheme of Haddad's *qaṣīdah,* with its dense weave of uvular consonants and rhyme endings, explicitly discourages sung performance. His poem is markedly not a genre of sung *ḥumaīnī* verse common to urban elites in which open final vowels are drawn out in melodious vocal ornamentation. Rather, his poem is the hallmark of the rural highland tribesman and mystic whose spoken word—especially when enabled through writing—is his mettle.

The read-aloud salience of *bidʿ wa jiwāb* poems has been ensured, finally, by the fact that poets have not typically commissioned rhapsodes to carry their poems to correspondents. Geographical distances often have been prohibitive, especially in times of drought, famine, or war.[60] More important are stigmas traditionally attached to poetic professionalism in Yafiʿ. Unlike in other regions in Yemen, where rhapsodes have sometimes been paid to carry messages and to recite in front of recipient audiences, customs of praise poetry and professionalism have long conflicted with a strong tribal ideology of egalitarianism and with meager systems of patronage. Before the 1960s, the only rhapsodes who sought money through their verses were of servant status (the *shāḥidh* or *khādim*), and *bidʿ wa jiwāb* correspondents were reluctant to allow such lower-status go-betweens to perform their own poetic words. (As is shown later, the "messenger" described in a messenger journey section in poems is always envisioned as a trusted companion, and suggestions of status differences continue to be avoided.) For these practical purposes, writing is thus a necessary medium.

Although *bidʿ wa jiwāb* exchanges are political statements to be overheard by audiences and related, in part or in full, to others in the community, these poems are also performed from the pages of written letters. I argue, however, that the writing-mediated difference of such poems is not solely a matter of performance constraints. In what follows, I suggest that the *idea* of writing proves even more important than actual written evidence. The moral value of this peculiar medium, at once physical and metaphysical, can be found in a stylistics that references written authority without visually displaying it.

A POETICS OF RARIFIED METROPOLITAN STYLE

In a highlands political culture in which practices of writing were long restricted to groups of religious and political elites, poets have not been indifferent to the distinctive practical and symbolic value of writing. Nevertheless, writing remains a potentially risky medium. As other scholars of textual authority in the Middle East have shown, the written word has often been perceived as instable in traditions in which orality is a text-constitutive practice.[61] Several of the most important of these traditions are the Qur'an and the texts recording the Prophet's sayings *(ḥadīths)*. Although the written inscription of these texts proved fundamental to their standardization in the early centuries of Islamic expansion and have been indispensable to subsequent Islamic thought and legal practice, their *oral* preservation and circulation have continued to inform Islamic learning and pedagogical practices. The primacy of orality to Islamic legal practice in Yemen is treated elegantly by Brinkley Messick, who suggests that the privileging of the spoken word in Muslim scholarship relates to traditional concerns over authorship. Where writing was viewed to circulate the text away from the author, "the general misreadability of the medium was dangerously extended by the open potentiality of the texts themselves."[62] Insofar as the author's voice and thus the truth of a given message remains secured through oral vocalization, recitation proves central to written textual practice in many institutional settings in Muslim societies.

In chapter 5, I discuss notions of authorship and alienation more explicitly in my analysis of cassette-poetry exchanges. Here I confirm the centrality of oral recitation to the authorial foundations of the *bidʿ wa jiwāb* written tradition as well. In a rural society in which tribal discourses portray oral articulation as a medium of human vitality, writing proves to be an instrument of questionable substance. During my fieldwork, popular concerns with the instability of written poems were related to me during interviews that I conducted with contemporary cassette poets and singers who told me stories about how written verses, when circulated, became mispronounced by singers and how their meanings were misinterpreted with sometimes serious consequences.[63] Given these narratives and noting comparable concerns in traditions of Muslim learning, I suggest that earlier *bidʿ wa jiwāb* correspondents were especially concerned with the stability of their messages sent to one another across distances. Accordingly, a thematic sequence emerged in poems to help redress popular anxieties over the corruptibility of material texts.

In what follows, I show how poets have stylized their verse to manage the material risks of the written word. This stylization helps create a distinct "text concept" that is crucially founded in the oral vitality of highland tribal political culture and that also abstracts moral authority into forms of literate authority. Insofar as the institutions, technologies, and practical competences of literacy have centered in towns throughout Yemen, I suggest that poets' stylistic attunements convey a distinct *metropolitanism* to their audiences.[64] This metropolitan style is communicated through traditional marks of writing that define the highland epistolary *bidʿ wa jiwāb qaṣīdahs* at five formal levels:

- Scarcity of verbal formulas
- Overall compositional unity
- Length
- Seven-part thematic sequence, especially supplications and a topographically detailed messenger journey
- Dense intertextuality in the response poem

Let us begin with verbal formulas, the first mark of written style. As initially defined by the folklorist Albert Lord in his work on Yugoslav oral epics, formulas are regular sequences of verbal material, usually only several words in length, that help poets and singers recall metrically regular segments of verse for quick deployment in performance.[65] Although formulas abound in much South Arabian song and in extemporaneous oral poetry, they are relatively infrequent in *bidʿ wa jiwāb* compositions that are written for specific occasions and are not designed to be widely disseminated through song or recitation.[66] Written *bidʿ wa jiwāb* compositions do contain formulas, especially when a composition is crafted hastily and the poets must rely on a memorized store of verbal material. Such formulas are particularly common in certain sections of *bidʿ wa jiwāb* compositions that are stylized toward oral tribal poetics, as I discuss below. However, since most *bidʿ wa jiwāb* compositions are produced in multiple stages of meticulous composition and since as a result they become inflected with an especially written style, formulas tend to be expurgated.[67]

Given the *qaṣīdah's* prestige among genres of formal Arabic poetry, the work of composing a *qaṣīdah* can take many hours, days, and sometimes weeks and typically involves multiple stages of writing and revision. *Bidʿ wa jiwāb* poems, even though composed in the vernacular and set to traditional meters, are generally produced in the same manner. In addition to the paucity of formulas, such poems also demonstrate an overall compositional unity that distinguishes them as the product of written practice.[68] Other scholars have noted the tendency of written Arabic *qaṣīdahs* to exhibit a dense synthesis of grammatical detail.[69] The complexities of compositional practice require case-by-case analyses. Indeed, as I show in later chapters, many poets who compose poetry for the audiocassette re-tailor written stylistics in the effort to adapt their verses for song and wider dissemination. Nevertheless, these authors' observations corroborate a stylistic trend in many written *bidʿ wa jiwāb qaṣīdahs* toward a lengthier[70] and more synthetic development of tropes, motifs, and themes.

Haddad's composition serves as an excellent example. Motifs of constraint and release unite the entire *qaṣīdah* from initial to final verses. In the supplication (lines 1–9), Haddad implores protection from God, the "Lord of daybreak," who can break the most implacable "stones" with his words. Metaphors of opening and freedom are carried through subsequent supplications to the Prophet Muhammad, whose radiance, like a flower, "split forth illumination" even "before Adam" (4–6). After turning to the dangerous moral and political "constraint" that grips Yafiʿ in line 10, the poet once again invokes release through the imagery of a "traveler" who "overcomes all impediments" like the sound of a bird that has screeched from "nests" (11). In following lines, the turmoil of war is described in images of circular "council" (15), of "fission and confliction" (20), of "entrapped" mountain Yafiʿis (32), and of roads, islands, and trucks whose passages are "intractable" and "fractured" (33–34). With optimism, the poem concludes by returning to a description of the Prophet, who, as a flower, "split forth illumination" (38). Through the entire poem, the recurring motifs of constraint and release, delivered powerfully through carefully crafted metaphors, give the composition a sense of balance and wholeness. Other motifs, such as hurling censure at infidels and the British in particular (lines 8–10, 22, 25–28, 30), unify the composition in the much same manner.

In addition to such unifying motifs, one of the most enduring compositional matrices of *bidʿ wa jiwāb* poetry is the thematic sequence. Over centuries of *qaṣīdah* scholarship, no topic has engaged critics more than themes or "intentions" (*gharaḍs*, pl. *aghrāḍ*).[71] In efforts to identify fundamental expressive functions of *qaṣīdah* poetry, recent scholars have proposed that thematic sections help listeners explore mythopoetic rites of passage,[72] assess conflicts over political action,[73] consider underlying cultural binaries,[74] and reflect on remembrance through chains of symbols.[75] Although these observations illuminate some aspects of the *bidʿ wa jiwāb qaṣīdah,* I suggest that the genre's conventional thematic sequence is an aspect of a distinctly written style. The sequence is linked to the communicative aims of rural notables who, at once connected both to centers of metropolitan literate tradition *and* to the oral performance settings of tribal poetics, sought parlay with one another through writing.

In what follows, I delineate seven of the most prominent thematic sections or "intentions" in *bidʿ wa jiwāb* poetry: opening supplication, prelude, messenger journey, greetings, main message, riddle, and concluding supplication. While these sections continue to feature in most contemporary compositions, they are especially common in poems written before independence in South Yemen in 1967, when the pace of socioeconomic, political, and cultural change accelerates considerably.[76] To foreground the metacommunicative aspects of this thematic sequence, I call particular attention to several textual devices that inform and organize the sections. First, these sections are arranged in "frames," defined as socially relevant metamessages that inform language users about how to identify and interpret a given text.[77] The notion of frame requires attention to the *sequence* of sections and the ways that some sections may be embedded within the frames of others. I suggest that the written style of opening and concluding supplications can frame the entire composition as written. Second, I also attend to what I would suggest is a stylistic "oscillation" between oral and written styles. Where dialogue brings different voices into relation where they modify and can become modified by one other, stylistic oscillation takes the form of a recurring sequence of dialogic moments. In this way, I suggest that the sections of the *bidʿ wa jiwāb* poem can be organized according to theme and also to stylistic marks that are arranged in the following way: *written* (opening supplication), *oral* (prelude), *written* (messenger journey), *oral* (greetings), *indefinite* (main message), *oral* (riddle), and *written* (concluding supplication).[78]

The Supplication, or duʿāʾ (Markedly Written)

Most *bidʿ wa jiwāb qaṣīdahs* begin with a section devoted to praising God and the Prophet Muhammad, asking for mercy and forgiveness and sometimes invoking the blessings of other early prophets and holy men. Typically, poets who are more religious or who wish to demonstrate their connection to learned Muslim traditions extend their supplication beyond three to four lines, occasionally to as much as half of the composition. Haddad begins his poem with seven verses that signal his knowledge of the Qur'an in both content and form. His first two verses draw close syntactic parallels with a passage in the Qur'an: "I seek refuge with the Lord of daybreak / From the mischief of things created" (*sūrah* 113:1–2). Verses 3 to 4 continue to praise God as the Creator by invoking the Qur'an's revelation that human beings are formed out of sperm, or "gushing water" *(mā'in dāfiqin)* that originates between the lower spine and thorax (*sūrah* 86:6–7). The supplication then moves to a description of the Prophet Muhammad, whom Haddad describes as "the one whose light first became resplendent amid them." Haddad refers here to a description of Muhammad as a source of divine light that appeared "before Adam" or any of the other pre-Islamic prophets and that then became diffused among the seven heavenly spheres, each of which is shepherded by an angel. Haddad then mentions the Prophet's companion Abu Bakr al-Siddīq and also ʿAli Bin Abī Ṭālib, the Prophet's cousin, who is held in venerable regard by Sufis and Alid groups. A description of his powerful capacity for violence against infidels moves Haddad from supplications to more political issues to be addressed.

Supplication sections are a regular component of many genres of Arabic *qaṣīdah* in oral as well as written traditions. Despite their variety of forms, however, I suggest that the regular presence of the supplication in the *bidʿ wa jiwāb* genre is traceable in part to the genre's development as an epistolary practice among religious scholars.[79] Not uncommonly, the supplication sections composed by poets of other literate groups such as tribal shaikhs or lower-status praise poets *(maddāḥs)* tend to be shorter and are not infrequently skipped altogether to make room for lengthier political or love themes. As Steven Caton remarks, such elisions have become common among contemporary urban poets who, seeking to convey bold, political messages to audiences, find awkward the formulaic protocol of the supplication.[80] For religious scholars and other rural notables who committed their poems to writing, however, the supplication was an important opportunity to communicate their affiliation with realms of learned authority.

The Prelude (Markedly Oral)

Either within or after the supplication, poets compose a prelude *(barāʿat al-istihlāl)* consisting of one or several verses that indicate the main theme of the message to follow.[81] In the above *qaṣīdah,* the prelude begins with a formulaic cue that clearly establishes the authorship of the composition: "The young man Brother Hādī says" (line 10). In this formula, the poet typically identifies himself in the third person using one of a selection of epithets. Teknonymns of the form "father of" *(Abū/Bū),* "son of" *(Bin),* or "brother of" *(Akhū),* followed by the name of the appropriate patrilineal relative, are especially popular. Other possibilities include "the young man" *(al-fatā),* as in the above verse, "the initiator" *(al-biddāʿ),* and "the composer" *(al-muṣannif).* But authorship is denoted not solely in terms of poetic intention (initiator, composer, young man) or corporate affiliation (often the descent group) but also through orality. The verb *qāl,* "he said," is used with invariable consistency and highlights the primacy of oral authorship, even as the poet writes a letter. Where the supplication indicates affiliation with a tradition of Muslim learning that was distinctly associated, for rural Yemeni, with realms of literacy, the prelude locates this tradition within a domain of socially charged oral recitation.

The Messenger Journey (Markedly Written)

Before commencing the main section, the poet asks a messenger to supervise his poem's delivery to the recipient. In the beginning of this section, the messenger is typically addressed as a sprightly agent whose primal, nonhuman attributes are salient. Poets typically describe this agent as a bird *(ṭaīr),* pigeon *(ʿīlah),* poetic muse *(ḥājis),* traveler *(sayyār),* messenger *(rasūl),* caretaker *(muʿannā),* or willful one *(ʿāzim).* The missive entrusted to the agent is described explicitly as a form of writing, whether the poet's script *(khaṭṭ),* writing *(kitāb),* or letter *(risālah).* Setting aside the prelude's conceit of pure oral recitation, the messenger journey section signals the poet's hesitancy to relinquish written competences entirely.[82]

Certainly, given conventional communicative mores, to acknowledge the written medium of exchange is to risk undermining its integrity and efficacy. The prelude is clearly a gesture toward securing the written word within practices of spoken poetry and affirmed authorship. In the resonant messenger journey section, however, the written word begins to acquire its most stable form through both corporeal embodiment and through topography. I discuss the former of these narrative devices first.

The "letter" that is to be delivered to the recipient is not simply sent directly and received. Rather, the distance between correspondents must be bridged by a messenger whose primal, nonhuman attributes make the written letter a more responsive medium for intuitive forces of the world. In the poet's *qaṣīdah,* the "traveler" is said to originate "from the precipitous nests where the bird has screeched" (11) and is told to "deliver my script before dawn's twilight" (12). This messenger, in other words, emerges from a realm that lies beyond sight in a dark, pregraphic world whose natural origins are marked by sensual, if clarion, orality. In delivering the poet's script, the messenger acquires knowledge of the world by relying on common forms of sensory apperception, first reciting the Qur'an (13) and then visually observing the beauty of the landscape and the customs of its inhabitants (16). Indeed, as in many poems, the messenger's physical, sensory presence is foregrounded through the entire course of the narrated journey. The role of a "document witness" in preindependence Yemen has been detailed by Brinkley Messick, who notes that judges customarily appointed such witnesses *(shāhids)* to deliver important documents across the countryside.[83] Since written documents were popularly considered "loose" texts that could be forged, modified, mistakenly transcribed, and so forth, a live witness could personally accompany the text from its producer to its receiver, vouchsafing its authenticity and authorship to those who were concerned.[84] I suggest that the messenger figure works toward a similar end in *bidʿ wa jiwāb* poetry, physically accompanying the written word with an embodied presence. Here, such presence is allotted to a remarkably naturalized agent whose estimable powers might be claimed by any sentient human.

In moving between producer and receiver, the messenger figure secures the written communicative channel by bearing special witness to the topography that lies between correspondents. On route to the correspondent's residence, the messenger observes mountain ridges, wadis, wells, sahel plains, caravan routes, and tribal districts that lie along the way. These topographic points are not randomly evoked but chart the most efficient path that a messenger would actually take to deliver the poet's *qaṣīdah*. Communicative exchange is secured through medial embodiment and through the messenger's socially relevant spatialization. The messenger journey section in Haddad's *qaṣīdah* (lines 11–17) serves as a fine illustration of such an effect. To reach the house of Shaikh Bin Sabʿah, who lives approximately four miles across mountainous territory from Haddad, the messenger is instructed first to pass through a protected enclave *(rubāṭ)*. Here the poet tells the messenger to read Qurʾanic verses at the local saint's tomb. The first stop along the messenger's route evokes a realm of piety that, like the opening supplication, frames the task at hand and invites listeners to affiliate with a communally sanctioned moral space. Moreover, given that religious authorities mediated disputes between tribes, the location of the messenger's first visit is especially significant as a social nexus. In subsequent lines, Haddad tells the messenger to follow a similar protocol at the local "house of diplomacy, insight, and perspicacity" (13) and mentions the single "discourse" *(shawr)* of the five tribal divisions of Yafiʿ Bani Qāsed (14). Finally, special praise is reserved for the courageous warriors of Yihar, the tribal district over which Shaikh Bin Sabʿah presided at the time (15). The warriors of Yihar are described as sons of the queen of Sheba's early South Arabian monarchy (Sabā), and they are commended for skills in "raiding" and "counsel." Specific reference is made, in the next line, to the valley in which Bin Sabʿah's house was located, Wadi Ḥamūmah, whose spectacular views give perspective on a thriving social world of "coffee trees, and strongholds splendid" (16). The journey section concludes when the messenger arrives at the Bin Sabʿah's residence, a "home of insight, its oath is trusted" (17). In short, Haddad's narrative of the messenger journey draws Bin Sabʿah with him into a topography of piety and political will that is, above all, socially grounded.

The journey section has long been one of the most distinctive and stable sections in the *bidʿ wa jiwāb qaṣīdah*. Some journey sections may comprise two-thirds of the *qaṣīdah* and detail routes that stretch hundreds of miles across Yemen and abroad as well. The description of the messenger's journey differs from the journey section *(raḥīl)* featured in other traditions of Arabic poetry in which the poet imagines *himself* traveling across a landscape. Such sections tend to foreground more introspective and nostalgic themes that are closely linked to the poet's own yearnings for his beloved or for youth, his admiration for his mount, and his memory of former hunting expeditions. The journey section in *bidʿ wa jiwāb* poetry focuses instead on a third party's journey between two correspondents, investing the narrative with what I would suggest is a more dialogic, social function: to affirm a relationship between two correspondents who are separated from one another by distance.[85] In this respect, the messenger's journey is especially useful in *written* exchanges.[86] Where writing in the Yemeni highlands was seen as an inherently instable medium, the messenger journey could be employed and extended toward the particular end of allaying recipients' concerns about the mutability of messages that were alienated from authors, conveyed across long distances, and subject to the vagaries of risky communicative channels.[87]

Greetings (Markedly Oral)

When the messenger arrives at the recipient's house, he is told by the poet to give greetings to the recipient and friends. The messenger delivers the greetings not by simply handing over a letter. After the written word has made the risky journey between correspondents, the greetings section resounds with an oral flourish that, much like the prelude before the outset of the journey, assures recipients of the exuberant human sociality of the written message.

A distinct orality is foregrounded in this section through classic formulas of hortatory tribal poetics. The grammatical structures of *zāmil* poetry, recognized by other scholars as the hallmark genre of tribal expressive culture, are specifically replicated here.[88] The *zāmil* is a concise poem, typically between two to eight verses, that is used in dispute mediation, at major social occasions, during visits by dignitaries, at political rallies, and so forth to express the opinion of a group in a trenchant and persuasive format. Although the *zāmil* is usually composed by a single author, it is recited collectively by large gatherings of men and sometimes women, who shout its verses out loudly as they walk, brandishing weapons and performing the tribal *barʿah* dance (see figure 1.4). *Zāmil* performances are some of the most spectacular expressions of tribal identity in Yemen.

The close parallels between the verbal formula of the greetings section and the tribal *zāmil* are shown below, where selected verses in *bidʿ wa jiwāb qaṣīdahs* (BJ) are compared with *zāmil* verses (Z) that I collected. The opening line of the first comparison is drawn from Haddad's *qaṣīdah:*

> My greetings to Bin Haithem and those in accord with him. (BJ)
> *Greetings to the village and those who reside there.* (Z)

My greetings to you as much as the pelting of rain. (BJ)
From me greetings as much as the rain made fertile. (Z)
Two billion greetings, numerous in numbers, / As much as the weight of rain when the surplus overflows. (BJ)
Greetings from me repeated, as much as the Javanese have built, / As much as the weight of Mt. Thamar and ʿUrr in ambergris and perfume. (Z)
My greetings as the flash of lightning in Shalālah / And as the rain brought bounteous honor. (BJ)
Greetings as much as the flood washes over the fields. (BJ)
Greetings as the thunder and as the rain that pounds. (Z)
Greetings as the darkening from the edges of rain clouds. (Z)

In paralleling the *zāmil,* the formulaic greetings in the *bidʿ wa jiwāb* brandish an oral, tribal poetics by which the authorship and integrity of the written message are ensured.

Securing the written word within the context of oral communication is achieved both in grammatical terms and symbolically as well. One of the most recurrent themes in the greetings section involves the distribution of various salubrious liquids. Descriptions of rain *(maṭar),* thunderclouds *(muzan),* thunder *(raʿd),* and floods *(sēls)* caused by rain showers feature centrally and can be said to evoke a long tradition of fertility and life symbolism that runs through much Arabic folk poetry.[89] After the messenger finishes greeting the recipient's group, the poet often instructs him to distribute *(rashsh)* perfume *(ʿiṭr),* musk *(misk),* scented water *(mā wardī),* and powerfully fragrant plants and incense to his hosts. In the *qaṣīdah* cited above, Haddad's messenger is told to give greetings "With flower water, its origin from the deep-lineaged Ḥāshemī [i.e., Muhammad], / And with perfume, the kind in the packaged vial" (19).[90] Here are other excerpts from selected greetings sections that illustrate such commands to distribute liquidous bounty:

Tell him first my greetings to you, how it covers
With perfume, still packaged from the lands of Rome.
Shower on Khaledi and the guest and cousin

And whoever has attended our *shaqr* herb and give them
hamhūm.

—Abu Badr al-Naʿwī, cassette 37 in the Husain ʿAbd al-Nāṣer series

Return my heartfelt greetings and my many thanks,
Twice as much as Bu Badr sent to me with a marked thing.
Tell him it arrived. Thanks, may he be in peace.
As for me, my greetings are with the scent of jasmine and
mashmūm.
In *shamaṭrī,* its fragrance and scent gladdens you.
And its perfume is still from the factory. It arrived guaranteed.
Especially Bin Qasem and among the family, let it be distributed
And the people of Naʿwah and whoever came as a guest or
invitee.

—Khaledi, cassette 37 in the ʿAbd al-Naser series

Give praise to him who expounded its verses
To me and to whomever is sitting at his residence.
Give one thousand greetings to him, as heavy as its peaks
With a green branch whose scent gladdens
And authentic ambergris, whose value is dear,
Greetings that cannot be reckoned by accountants.
Give a welcome that fills its valleys
With loyal words that have eager receivers.

—al-Shaikh Muhammad al-Naqīb, mid-twentieth century

Greetings as the flood strikes the bank
And revives branches that were flaccid,
With authentic perfume and ambergris most select
For him in particular and for those who have come to him
and who stay.
His script arrived to us. Tell him it is an obligation.
By my eye and honor, I see that he understands.

—Unknown, mid-twentieth century

The messenger's performance of liquidous distribution in *bidʿ wa jiwāb* poetry is especially interesting given its contravention of other kinds of greetings rituals. In the *qaṣīdah* traditions of largely nonliterate communities, including pre-Islamic *qaṣīdahs,* the messenger's greetings may be described as rain showers, floods, mist, and so forth, but rarely is the messenger instructed to distribute *his own* liquid onto the bodies of the hosts. The messenger's ritual distribution in this respect is somewhat distinctive in *bidʿ wa jiwāb* poetry. It is particularly distinctive given its difference from normative practice. When guests arrive at others' homes in Yemen, it is customary for *hosts* to offer *them* perfume or scented water, sometimes after their arrival but especially after lunch and before *qāt* is chewed in the afternoon. The fragrant liquids refresh the guest and dissipate odors that might linger after a meal. Such ritual performance by the messenger—the guest in the recipient's home—is remarkably odd and suggests that something more than sheer hospitality (and the hope of fertility) is being communicated.

I would suggest that the imagery of liquidous distribution has a metadiscursive role in representing the secure delivery of the written message from producer to receiver. The use of water as a symbolic catalyst in written textual practices has been noted by other scholars of Islamic expressive cultures. Jack Goody discusses how "drinking the word" in Ghanan traditional medicine enables written Qurʾanic verses to penetrate orally the bodies of recipients.[91] Brinkley Messick notes that this practice is common in Yemen as well as throughout the Middle East and North Africa generally.[92] And in his study of Rwala Bedouin oral narratives, Michael Meeker describes how Bedouin poets deploy images of wells and drinking to signify effective speech.[93] In *bidʿwa jiwāb* poetry, too, poets can invest their written style with an oral "guarantee" by using such liquidous imagery to convey the integrity of the written message as it is delivered across distances between correspondents. Through such a strategy, the messenger and medium of communication itself, more than the poet, become the agents of their own successful journey, assuring listeners with their soundness. The high proportion of [r] and also

[l] phonemes (what Western linguists call phonetic "liquids") in the keywords and phrases of this section may well help convey a material substrate that gives resonant fitness to symbolic form.

Main Message (Indefinitely Marked)

After supplications have been made, journeys negotiated, greetings proffered, and the arrival of the written word orally secured, the main message of the *qaṣīdah* is set forth in what is typically the largest section of the poem. This section contains the most explicit articulation of the poet's ideas about social and political issues, historical events, friendships, spiritual issues, and so forth. Haddad cues the initiation of this section with a formulaic device "If he should ask" and then identifies, albeit with heaviness, the primary issues at hand: ignominy, conflict, avarice, and bloodshed (lines 20–21). The cause of the bloodletting, he continues, is specific and observable:

> Tell him to see what is meant from where it shrieks. 22
> The truck drivers destroy their [own] roads!
> He is still on the lands of Abyan. [Such] an outrage broke out there yesterday. 23
> And [yet] today the "officer" has no [desire to] prosecute.

The source of turmoil is the political and commercial exploitation of Yafiʿis by "truck drivers" as well as the British colonial "officer" (*al-sirkāl,* from the Hindi *sarkār*). Both parties are complicit in developing southern Yemen's most lucrative cotton project, located in Abyan.[94] In the wake of the project, traders and small-scale farmers encountered considerable losses through the disruption of traditional trade relations and markets and through massive settlements that took place on Yafiʿi land that was sold to tens of thousands of laborers who migrated to the area. The first to gain were the regional elites,[95] perhaps "the truck drivers" to whom Haddad refers. They are mentioned more explicitly in subsequent lines, beginning with the Kaladī shaikh "Bin ʿAtiyyah" in Yafiʿ Bani Qāsed, who a few years earlier broke rank with other Yafiʿi leaders and claimed the title of sultan through British recognition. In exchange, he signed a treaty with the British enabling them to extend the Abyan cotton project into his territory (line 24). Haddad then mentions the Quʿaīṭi sultan, of Yafiʿi descent, who had established one of South Yemen's largest states in Hadramawt (eastern Yemen) and who was in recent years cooperating with the British. Like four other unspecified sultans, such men "hunger for government" (25), despite the best interests of their people. He then decries the complacency of the local ʿAfīfī sultan of Yafiʿ Bani Qāsed, who is accused of turning his head to traditional tribal obligations and refusing to help the tribes of Mt. Baraq, in Abyan, drive out the British (26). Ultimately, Haddad summarizes his criticism against the British in lines 27 and 28, in which he refuses cash crops *(shaklah),* which deprive farmers of their traditional livelihoods, "biding time" as their fields are being exploited by others, and relinquishing any form of tribal power. Yafiʿ will solve disputes immediately without having to enter into lengthy negotiations in which weapons are given as bond to mediators. He concludes the main message section by asking for Bin Sabʿah's leadership and by vividly depicting the depths of conflict and fission to which Yafiʿ had fallen (29–35).

Riddle (Markedly Oral)

The concluding riddle is a common feature in *bidʿ wa jiwāb* poetry and is often one of the most engaging components for receivers. In this section, the initiator poses a riddle to the correspondent, and the correspondent must then respond with the answer or a riddle of his own that can set off another round of poetic exchange. The riddle genre has its own distinct oral tradition that often is performed extemporaneously in afternoon *qāt* chews when poets pose riddles to audiences as a form of entertainment and a demonstration of wit. In more recent decades, construction workers in the Yafiʿi highlands have become well known for exchanging riddles on the job, confirming the suitability of the genre to oral performance. The riddle in southern Yemen, usually from two to six verses, begins with a standard expression "I ask you of" *(aḥzīk/maḥzātik min),* which is then followed by a grammatically gendered clue word—typically either a male camel *(bāzil)* or a young female camel *(bakrah)*—that indicates the corresponding gender of the answer word. Haddad's riddle involves two answers, both male:

I ask you a riddle about a camel that with a camel consented. 36
Along with [the] two camels is a compliant creature.
He asked for a she-camel from them, and each one of them spoke, 37
And the words [are] in the Qur'an, [which is so] clearly articulated.

The answer to this riddle is provided after Bin Sab'ah's response below. Even without knowing the answer, however, the main themes of the riddle—consent between two male "camels," dialogue, and pious oral legitimacy—serve as an especially germane commentary on the poetic exchange that Haddad hopes to initiate with Bin Sab'ah, and as a clever transition to the conclusion.

Concluding Supplication (Markedly Written)

A pious conclusion is required in *bid' wa jiwāb* compositions. Praising the Prophet Muhammad, the messenger of God who delivered the Qur'an to the world, is the most important component of the conclusion, and some poets add names of other Islamic prophets as well. Haddad's decision to repeat a verse already mentioned in the *qaṣīdah* (line 7) is not unusual in folk poetry and is not generally considered a flaw in composition. In producing a formal parallel with the opening supplication, the conclusion contrasts with the more oral style of the riddle section. In concluding the poem, the supplication frames the entire composition in terms of a literate, learned tradition of rural notables.

JIWĀB: RESPONSE

The response *(jiwāb)* to an initiation *qaṣīdah (bid')* is appraised carefully by listeners. As a "response," the *qaṣīdah* should address most or all of the major points raised by the first poet, whether critiquing, reframing, or supporting them. The more completely a poet covers the issues raised by the initiating poet, the more eloquent and authoritative the response becomes. But the response must also model itself closely on the form and content of the initiation *qaṣīdah*. The finest responses are those that can replicate the aesthetic nuances of the initiation *qaṣīdah* while extending their import and meaning. Ultimately, the authorial voice of the composition, so important to the *bid' wa jiwāb* genre, is asserted through dialogue rather than through independent authorship. It is the relation of the author's voice to another, as noted by Mikhail Bakhtin, that makes it distinctive.[96] In discussing Bin Sab'ah's response to Haddad's initiation *qaṣīdah* that follows, I devote special attention to its intertextual dialogism with the initiation *qaṣīdah*. I suggest that Bin Sab'ah's own stylistic difference from Haddad's composition—one modeled on a more oral, tribal style—comprises an important aspect of its distinct authorship.

Shaikh Bin Sab'ah, one of the prominent shaikhs in Yafi' during his time, was known for his fierce resistance to British colonialism. His father had cooperated with the Ottoman sultan Sa'id Pāshā during World War I to repell British advances and subsequently worked with Imams Yahya and Ahmad to counter British influence in the southern hinterlands. While carrying the mantle of a fighter and poet, Bin Sab'ah was famous for his humility and judicious ways. When sitting in counsel, he disdained the title of shaikh, insisting on equality between tribesmen, and in refusing to use his authority to accumulate land, he died poorer than many of his companions. For many Yafi'is today, he represents the shaikh of the preindependence era, a legacy that is confirmed through the many written poems that remained after his death (see appendix A for a full transliteration):

I entrusted myself to you, O God, Breaker of the lock. 1
You commission all measurements and have opened blocked doors.
O Guardian, preserve every Muslim from sinking, 2
And drive God's enemy into the sea and sink him.
You delivered us from the work of treachery and duplicity 3
And from the business of the devil and people of hypocrisy.
By invocation to [the Prophet] Muhammad who split open his chest, dividing 4
And unleashed the camel, bound for sacrifice, releasing him,
The son of Haithem said: Whoever builds [a house] governs the windows, 5
And should a stone be crooked, he breaks them with a hammer.
Those who fail to measure ruin the house. Perverted, 6
The cornerstones go akimbo, off-kilter, perverse.
I have a mighty shoulder. By the strength of its forearm, it shoves, 7
And following me, Yihar, at the hour of convening [they go] for the knock-out.
If conflict draws out, there is no loss of appetite. 8
Not a single one of the tribal *maktabs* becomes sated.
I say: Hail to all! As much as the cascading and showering 9
And as the thunderclouds roil and the mists drizzle,
Speech has arrived from him who knows truth and ire 10
And the path of the riding camel, with so many whips.
Brother Hādī, renowned for arranging his words, 11
At any moment, he plunges into the onerous sea.
When some Arabs carry, they drag only on one side. 12
Breaking the well's pulley and severing the bucket,
Whoever carries will know about loading and calibrating. 13
If the ends fall short, he extends it in equilibrium,
For if the shoulder should tip what is set aright in the harness, 14
He would discover only that his charge is forsaken.
His breastwork [by contrast] is the one that did not discharge, 15
Instead setting down his load with dripping spittle.
Yafiʿ is a land of free-traveling fighters from wherever lightning flashes. 16

No one has ever said Yafiʿ forsook its rifles.
How many a serpent injects venom when it bites. 17
The most honorable of tribes, with fine-pointed blades,
Whoever approaches the flame gets scorched by its fire. 18
Yafiʿ is an inferno. To belittle it is to burn.
The height of perdition: they who take too large a morsel choke. 19
Exhaustion in swallowing it, they'll never pass stool.
They forbid eating fetus, yet they drink of its broth. 20
Whoever eats among [such] people of the house are later indignant.
Such [people] do not cross under the cliff face or step too close to the scree. 21
The friend at one's side cannot be undermined.
For me, God has prescribed bounty from where he bestows, 22
And so [I am] patient, content with God and his providence.
And in Bu Ḥāshem, too, I have confidence, who with his dagger stabbed. 23
Seager extended his hand to shake it, but his arteries were sliced.
And Davey approached, even as that old wooden rifle clapped, 24
And Ibn ʿAwās said: Receive its clapping,
For amid the patching and amid the trimming 25
The hems extend and the belts are clipped.
From you came astringent honey, and from me comes bitter honey. 26
[I will] not forego reimbursement, through trickery or flustery:
From the age of our lord Sulaiman, who preceded [us], 27
He who sought Bilqis (Queen of Sheba), in a moment of passion,
Said he who is endowed with knowledge and eloquence 28
That we should come to her now, appearing as a nascent flame.
And the Efreet responded before he could blink. 29
Then the fringes of her eyes descended, veiling her pupils.
By invocation to [the Prophet] Muhammad who split open his chest, dividing 30
And unleashed the camel, bound for sacrifice, releasing him.

While Bin Sabʿah's *qaṣīdah* is clearly a political statement that outlines the direction of his leadership and his own solution to Haddad's concerns about conflict, his *qaṣīdah* is, in equal measure, an expression of personal intimacy in the fashion of much *bidʿ wa jiwāb* poetry. The terms of Bin Sabʿah's friendship with Haddad are portrayed in the long-greetings section (lines 9–15) in which he praises his correspondent's knowledge of "loading and calibrating" and especially in the riddle and concluding supplication. In these latter sections, Bin Sabʿah explains that he will not forgo "reimbursement," implying that he will respond to Haddad's riddle without "trickery or flustery" (26). By beginning his answer to the riddle with the contextual framework "From the age of our lord Sulaiman, who preceded [us]" (27), he signals listeners to the Qur'anic passage (27, 29–31) referred to by Haddad in his cryptic scene of two "camels": the encounter between King Sulaiman and the Queen of Sheba, known in Yemen as "Bilqis" of Sabā, that involves what is probably the most famous epistolary exchange in the Arab world.[97] Not content merely to demonstrate his knowledge, however, Bin Sabʿah extends Haddad's reference by describing the amorous scene of an encounter between King Sulaiman and Queen Bilqis that is enabled with the help of an Efreet. The description, which ends with the queen's eyelids closing rapturously, replicates Haddad's themes of solidarity and unity with an original twist. The concluding supplication (30), although a repetition of an earlier verse (4), becomes laden with meaning. Its themes of release offer poignant commentary on the lovers' tryst and on the correspondence relationship between poets.

In keeping with *bidʿ wa jiwāb* generic conventions, Bin Sabʿah demonstrates his affinity with Haddad on more formal and stylistic levels as well. To begin with, his prosody matches Haddad's in its metrical structure, rhyme scheme, alliteration, assonance, and parallelism. Like Haddad's *qaṣīdah,* a dense weave of uvular consonants, concentrated at the end of each strophe, invites listeners to reflect on the poetic message itself and on the emotive parallels between sounds of conflict and release and a political world in turmoil. The compositional unity of Bin Sabʿah's *qaṣīdah* also matches Haddad's in its tight sectional structuring (all seven sections are replicated) and in its thematic content. Themes of constraint and release, for example, are replicated in Bin Sabʿah's own metaphorical terms in fairly equivalent positions to those of Haddad's poem:

HADDAD'S VERSES:

In the name of God, I seek refuge with the Lord of daybreak 1
With words that from the heart of stones have burst forth. . . .
Pray to the one whose light first became resplendent among them. 4
Even before Adam, the flower of [his] light split forth illumination.

BIN SABʿAH'S VERSES:

I entrusted myself to you, O God, Breaker of the lock. 1
You commission all measurements and have opened blocked doors. . . .
By invocation to [the Prophet] Muhammad who split open his chest, dividing 4
And unleashed the camel, bound for sacrifice, releasing him.

Bin Sabʿah's verses parallel those of Haddad with remarkable precision. In the opening strophe, for example, Bin Sabʿah's reference to God as the "Breaker of the lock" parallels Haddad's reference to the "Lord of daybreak." In the following strophe, the image of the opened doors parallels that of burst heart of stone. In the fourth line of each poem, an initial strophe offers a prayer to the Prophet Muhammad, and a second strophe describes the Prophet being physically laid open to God's majesty (whether as a flower or as a man whose chest is opened). Themes of constraint and release continue in fairly equivalent positions, moreover, throughout Bin Sabʿah's *qaṣīdah* (compare Bin Sabʿah's lines 1, 4, 12–16, 19, 25, 30 with Haddad's lines 1,

4, 10–11, 15, 20, 32–34, 38), as do themes of apostasy and the British (compare Bin Sabʿah's lines 2, 3, 20, 23–25 with Haddad's lines 8–10, 22, 25–28, 30).

Such verse-for-verse, section-for-section intertextual pairing is standard in most *bidʿ wa jiwāb* poetry. I suggest that such pairing is the distinct product of written practice. Shaikh Bin Sabʿah was a terrific oral poet, and he was renowned for witty and at times searing poems produced extemporaneously in social events. However, his *jiwāb* compositions were composed in a different manner. Aside from its compositional unity and length, the extremely tight match of his *qaṣīdah* to Haddad's is one of the surest signs that he worked with Haddad's written text at his side. I suggest that such intertextuality was itself a sign and not merely the happenstance result of epistolary communication. It was one of the distinctive marks of a written style that was meant to signal Bin Sabʿah's affiliation with a tradition of learning practiced by rural notables. Compositions were meant to be compared with one another, carefully examined, read over and again (or at least compared with someone's memorized version), passed around, and preserved together in pairs. Indeed, with a growing attention to the archiving of historical poems in Yemen in recent decades, the significance of such textual doubling for informants seems to have increased and was made apparent to me when interpreting poems with Yemeni colleagues, who would regularly acknowledge the difficulty of interpreting a single *qaṣīdah* without its partner.[98] The exceptional intertextuality of *bidʿ wa jiwāb qaṣīdahs* was a mark of their formality as written compositions invested with the capital of notable writers.

Even as Bin Sabʿah uses the compositional style of a literate tradition, however, he also draws more explicitly than Haddad from an oral style of tribal rhetoric that is distinctive in both content and form. The orality of this style is mediated less by gnostic insight, with its demands that discursive conventions be dislodged, than by common terms of highland political discourse that assure listeners of established social custom. Tribal idioms of honor, manliness, and the just application of violence feature prominently in Bin Sabʿah's poem and invoke a vein of political oratory in which he was known to excel. Accordingly, his metaphor of house construction signals the poetic task at hand and also the competence of a shaikhly leader: the word *baīt* "house" can commonly refer not only to the family unit but to the patriline and the tribe in particular. Featured in the opening supplication (line 1), in the prelude (5–6), and in the main message (20), house construction becomes a recurring motif that speaks to the importance of resolving internecine conflicts that have erupted in Yafiʿ. The metaphor represents the tribes and their shaikhs as political actors—"Whoever builds [a house] governs the windows" (*min banā ḥakam aṭ-ṭawaq,* line 5)—who can reestablish tribal administration *(ḥukūmah)* and successfully manage Yafiʿ's internal and external affairs. The power of tribes is evoked repeatedly in other ways throughout Bin Sabʿah's *qaṣīdah.* Where Haddad speaks of tremendous constraint, Bin Sabʿah reassures him in the main message section that Yafiʿis are "free-traveling fighters" who pay no road tolls.[99] Yafiʿis are compared to serpents, flames, and tested mountaineers (16–18, 21), while their enemies are portrayed as hypocrites,[100] gluttons, and men whose bowels are clogged (19–20). In one of the most dramatic sections of the *qaṣīdah,* Bin Sabʿah describes how the British will be prevented from sowing further discord in Yafiʿ. While expressing faith in God's providence (22), he reminds listeners of the tribesman's vengeful nature:

> And in Bu Ḥāshem, too, I have confidence, who with his dagger stabbed. 23
> Seager extended his hand to shake it, but his arteries were sliced.
> And Davey approached, even as that old wooden rifle clapped, 24
> And Ibn ʿAwās said: Receive its clapping,

The gory vignette describes an event that occurred a winter earlier in 1950 when Major Basil Seager, one of the most influential men of Aden's post–World War II colonial office and chief architect of the Western Aden Protectorate, was attacked by a tribesman. As Seager was walking in countryside with his wife, just outside of the town of al-Ḍāliʿ, north of Yafiʿ, he was attacked by a man who was nicknamed, as Bin Sabʿah recalls, "Bu Ḥāshem." While Seager barely escaped death, British political officer Peter Davey had not been so lucky, falling victim to an assault three years earlier.[101] With steely resolve, Bin Sabʿah's verses suggest that the British presence would not long be tolerated and that tribal justice and solidarity—evoked shortly afterward in motifs of terms of measurement and liquidous equivalence (25–26)—would be returned.

Formally, Bin Sabʿah's composition is also marked as tribal through devices of an oral style common in highland poetry. Certain characteristic formulas used in much orally recited tribal poetry are employed at key junctures. Hallmark *zāmil* formulas are used in the greetings section, and a motley series of tribal epithets (lines 16–20) are used just before the scene of murderous revenge in the main message section ("land of free-fighting travelers" *(bilād agbār)* with "fine-pointed blades" *(haṣīn al-murannaqah)* who strike "from wherever lightning flashes" *(min ḥayth[a]mā baraq)* and who "inject venom when they bite" *(lā qad lasaʿ bi-l-ḥummah zaraq)*.[102] Through such formulaic epithets, conventional performance settings of tribal poetry are evoked and given ready circulation in an aural, tribal soundscape.

The marks of an oral style and its tribal inflections are also formally conveyed through the arrangement of sections in the *qaṣīdah*. Overall more concise than Haddad, Bin Sabʿah signals his compositional straight talk by greatly condensing the opening supplication and by focusing immediately on the "treachery and duplicity" of "God's enemy" (lines 2–3). By line 5, Bin Sabʿah has begun his prelude with the formulaic assertion of authorship "The son of Haithem said," here emphasizing patrilineal descent rather than siblinghood. The prelude then continues with descriptions of his own competence as a tribal leader who "governs the windows" (5) and who commands strength: "I have a mighty shoulder. By the strength of its forearm it shoves" (7). Following the prelude, the messenger journey—which typically serves to acknowledge written mediation—is almost entirely edited. The poet only briefly mentions his reception of an oral message: "Speech has arrived" along "the path of the riding camel, with so many whips" (10). The greetings section immediately ensues with a formulaic oral cue "I say: Hail to all!" (*bā-aqūl ḥayyā,* line 9) in which Bin Sabʿah employs the conventional imagery of thundershowers and fertility. The orality of the *bidʿ wa jiwāb* exchange and the underplaying of its written mediation are further underscored in subsequent verses in which Haddad, rather than the messenger, performs liquidous distribution (lines 11–14). It is Haddad who "plunges into the onerous sea" (11) and who knows about "loading and calibrating" (13) to avoid "breaking the well's pulley and severing the bucket" (12). By the end of the greetings section, it is ultimately Haddad who, through his proper arranging *(nasaq)* of poetic words (11), can achieve balanced equilibrium as a poet and tribesman: just as water ascends upward from Haddad's bucket, his camel's spittle drips downward, counterbalancing the flow of liquid and poetic words (15). Through such an exceptionally long greetings section, Bin Sabʿah not only pays the highest tribute to Haddad's generosity.[103] He also secures the written medium of the epistolary exchange within the framework of oral communication. Where the messenger journey focused explicit attention on the mediation of the written word, if only to represent it as safe, an extended greetings section could achieve similar ends with less acknowledgment to the problematic of writing. Insofar as tribal poets could distinguish themselves from learned, scholarly tradition through certain discursive and performance conventions, Bin Sabʿah evokes customs of face-to-face, oral exchange that stylize his poem as the work of a distinctly "tribal" shaikh.

A TRIBAL METROPOLITANISM? ACCOUNTING FOR THE MULTIPLE DISCURSIVE LEVELS OF STYLE

I have argued that, in a community of *bidʿ wa jiwāb* poets that existed in southern Yemen through the 1950s, a metropolitan difference is communicated as a socially marked, written style that is distinguished from domains of orally performed poetics that predominated in the highlands. This argument has been made in the following terms. First, writing is a form of literary distinction that was circulated primarily among restricted groups of notables in the highlands and that, increasingly through the nineteenth and twentieth centuries, was associated with metropolitan areas. Second, marks of writing are communicated through salient textual features (scarcity of verbal formulas, compositional unity, length, thematic sequence, intertextuality), and these features can be emphasized or deemphasized depending on poets' narrative aims. Third, when marks of written text are performed orally, they become signs of fixed inscription rather than actual physical inscriptions, and as such they create a resonant stylistic difference from the normative units of oral currency that define traditional oral performance. Fourth, as inscriptive forms of orality, as instantiations of gnostic and tribal "text concepts," these metaphysical utterances are more likely to be aestheticized as inscribed objects, especially given the embedding of orally marked themes in "written" supplications at the beginning and end of poems. Finally, the ultimate product is situated discursively amid broader patterns of talk that are at once expressions of normative social hierarchies in the highlands while also being similarly aestheticized forms of script-relative truth. Given my focus in this book on prominent political discourses and the resurgence in southern Yemen of tribalism, the implications of such media aesthetics for tribal identity should be emphasized. Tribalism becomes especially oral, while new possibilities are also illuminated for its assembly into more complex sign systems that are informed by new social hierarchies. As is discussed later in the contexts of the audio-recording industry, tribalism continues to be expressed by Yemenis through quintessential registers of oral performance, although its modern exemplars now emerge by juxtaposing orality to new regimes of inscription, especially audio recording.

Before continuing in the following chapters to explore the transformations of these stylistic elements in *bidʿ wa jiwāb* cassette poetry, I want to review the implications of my argument for contemporary anthropological theories of folk poetry and tribalism in the Middle East. I also want to assess more generally how the approach to style that I have outlined in this chapter might help explain other discourses, inscriptive practices, and social formations.

To begin with, *bidʿ wa jiwāb* poems are not the purely oral compositions of essentialized tribal poets who have practiced an unvarying *qaṣīdah* tradition for centuries. Rather, such poetry is subject to tremendous dialogic tension between aesthetics of verbal form that express the authority of different discursive communities. I have argued that an "oral" style is the currency of nonliterate poets whose oratory has featured centrally in a tribal political sphere in which acts of verbal persuasion are instrumental to political success. By contrast, a "written" style is the principal currency of literate notables who have had access or could claim access to learned written traditions. Crucially, however, while the value of these two currencies is derived from their respective abstract discursive communities (one "tribal" and the other "metropolitan"), neither of these communities has been conceptually stable over time. These communities are ongoing objects of affiliation that are rearticulated in each dialogic encounter. Thus, although the poets Haddad and Bin Sabʿah each drew on slightly different social backgrounds, competences, and moral allegiances—the former skilled in a regional version of gnostic poetry and the latter in the public oratory of tribal politics—both worked from their primarily oral currencies toward a common difference of metropolitan written authority. The ultimate effect was their coproduction of a shared vision of community, one that nevertheless resonated with their initial, orally mediated communities to different effects, as listeners of Haddad's initiation *qaṣīdah* could attest by virtue of the tremendous shaking that they experienced in the wake of his poem in particular.

The failure of much scholarship to account for the stylistic heterogeneity of tribal discourses is a product, to some extent, of broader cultural prejudices. As explained earlier, dichotomies between the "tribes" and "sedentary" populations have been remarkably durable in both Arab and Western scholarship. Where "tribal culture" continues to be essentialized as fundamentally "oral," inquiries into the nuances of textual hybridity and the aesthetics of textual form are subordinated to grander narratives addressing the "segmentary logic" of tribal history, tribal sociopolitical models, and unchanging tribal values.[104] A fundamental misstep in such scholarship is the tendency to confuse style with stereotype. Stereotypes of tribalism as purely oral are prevalent in Yemen and, as with all stereotypes, ring true in some respects. Oral tradition has been central to the discursive contours of tribal history, ideology, and performance. Nowhere is this more clearly the case than in comparison with the defining discursive mechanisms of sedentary populations and the state. Moreover, these stereotypes are significant for language users, as we have noted in *bidʿ wa jiwāb* poetry.

However, style is significant for users at multiple discursive levels, as noted by Deborah Tannen in her early study of orality and literacy.[105] As a salient text difference, style is signaled through grammatical form and also through aesthetics of discourse that operate at discursive as well as nondiscursive levels of behavior, apperception, interpretation, affect, and imagination. The meaning of textual form requires us to ask such questions as, How do the inflections of style at one level of discourse modify or become modified by the stylistic levels at another? How do patterns of stylization become prioritized by specific regimes of signification, these structured by hierarchized material and symbolic practices? Finally, how do these priorities then reinvest normative symbolic domains with "resonance"? In trying to address these questions in this chapter, I have suggested that we view *bid' wa jiwāb* poetry as a typical example of a stylized genre of oral poetry, compelling to users precisely because it facilitates dialogue between and about rather different discursive communities. To capture a sense of the dialogic and imaginative potentials of *bid' wa jiwāb* style, I have described the generic history of *bid' wa jiwāb* poetry as one of "tribal metropolitanism."

POST-1950S: THE SPREAD OF LITERACY AND ACCELERATED TRANSFORMATION OF METROPOLITAN CULTURE

During the 1950s, the pace of political, cultural, and conceptual transformation in the rural southern highlands accelerated considerably.[106] With economic growth and migration came expanded educational opportunities for highland populations. At first, education was accessible largely to elites only. By the late 1950s, however, a heightened awareness of the need for education and literacy had spread, and new schools were being opened in rural towns. As I discuss in the next chapter, demands for education and for distinctive metropolitan competences were invested with an especially popular, pan-Arab sentiment through new forms of media that spread throughout the rural south in the 1950s: record players and, more important, the radio. By the mid-1950s, highland inhabitants were avid fans of the Egyptian radio program *The Voice of the Arabs,* which couched its opposition to British colonial interests within an exciting array of rousing nationalist anthems, love songs, and distinctly urban genres of poetry. Signs of metropolitan distinction were becoming communicated through an increasing range of popular music and song texts as much as through marks of writing.

After South Yemen's independence from the British in 1967, the conventional generic contours of *bid' wa jiwāb* poetry became contested in more sustained ways as metropolitan culture was further transformed and popularized. The expansion and consolidation of state authority throughout the south was accompanied by an aggressive socialist cultural policy that aimed at educating the populace through a massive media initiatives. Through newspapers, cultural journals, radio programs, television broadcasting, folk festivals, and conferences, new genres of poetry were promoted, and the columnar *qaṣīdah* composition became branded by some as retrogressive "reactionary" *(ragʕī)*. As part of the promulgation of an active national consciousness *(al-waʕī al-qawmī)*, the state also undertook one of the most progressive literacy campaigns known in the Middle East. Although literacy had been expanding before independence, by the mid-1970s large numbers of men and women of all ages had acquired basic literate competences and with them access to new forms of cultural prestige.

The *bidʿ wa jiwāb* exchanges endured, particularly in the rural areas where more traditional genres of poetry and performance events lingered quietly, despite the consternation of more radical socialist party members. But the defining marks of discursive authority were undergoing fundamental changes. Such changes were induced by state-sponsored purges of traditional tribal elites, campaigns against tribalism by the radical left, and the party's successes in divesting rural religious elites of all traditional contractual and administrative powers—all definitive blows to extant models of discursive community. Even so, such changes were largely induced by new aesthetic orientations that enabled and were instantiated by new regimes of discourse and media practice. Written and oral styles continued to be dichotomized and stereotyped by highland poets and audiences as different forms of moral authority. But where the institutions and exemplars of writing became far more diversified—among popular audiences, state educational institutions, and modernist ideologues—and where oral poetics became flushed with a rich variety of metropolitan musical and poetic forms, the difference of the "written" from the "oral" became reconfigured. The relations between signs of writing and a popular oral poetics were still meaningful though as expressions of new circulatory communities. The audio-recording industry provided Yemenis with an especially persuasive context for considering the moral challenges of modern communal life.

NOTES

1. In developing this argument, I join other anthropologists and literary scholars in showing both how distinctions of "oral" and "written" styles can be formally defined and how these distinctions are socially and historically variable. Niko Besnier, "The Linguistic Relationships of Spoken and Written Nukulaelae Registers," *Language* 64, no. 4 (1988): 708; Benjamin Lee, "Textuality, Mediation, and Public Discourse," in *Habermas and the Public Sphere,* ed. Craig Calhoun (Cambridge, Mass.: MIT Press, 1992); Ann Banfield, "Where Epistemology, Style, and Grammar Meet Literary History: The Development of Represented Speech and Thought," In *Reflexive Language: Reported Speech and Metapragmatics,* ed. J. Lucy, 341–64 (Cambridge: Cambridge University Press, 1993); Ruth Finnegan, *Oral Poetry: Its Nature, Significance and Social Context* (Bloomington: Indiana University Press, 1992).
2. To help clarify my distinction between the text idea and the text artifact, I use the term "written style" to foreground the moral authority of the idea of an ontologically prescriptural, fixed text, while my scattered references to a "literate style" emphasize the embellished rhetorical performance of highland notables.
3. See introduction, pp. 13–21.
4. By considering generic and stylistic form as a product of this particularly heterogeneous group of notables, I seek to dislodge studies of Arab verbal culture from polarities of "the tribe" *(al-qabīlah)* and "sedentary life" *(al-ḥaḍārah)* that, as noted by Dale Eickelman, have defined the parameters of both Arab and Western social history since ʿAbd al-Rahman Ibn Khaldūn's influential magnum opus "An Introduction" *(Muqaddimah)* in the fourteenth century. Dale F. Eickelman, *The Middle East: An Anthropological Approach* (Englewood Cliffs, N.J.: Prentice-Hall, 1981), 127–30. One of the unfortunate consequences of such a legacy is the tendency to locate the ideal tribesman in a world of oral poetry and narrative that is unencumbered by the written

practices of towns and cities. In a recent monograph of tribalism in Jordan, the purest expressions of tribal identity reside in what are called resolutely "antitextual" inclinations. Andrew Shryock, *Nationalism and the Genealogical Imagination: Oral History and Textual Authority in Tribal Jordan* (Berkeley: University of California Press, 1997), 34.

To be sure, such a model can be justified as a dominant ideology of linguistic community in the Middle East and North Africa. Tribal expression is stereotypically defined in oral volubility for Arabs, and this iconic association between a social group and a specific form of media becomes a useful "metapragmatic" resource for signaling social affiliation in more conventional ways, as I show in this chapter. Such stereotypical associations might even be shown to provide marginalized groups with a means to narrate identity in a more favorable light amid pressures from centralized state authorities to dictate identity in terms of official, written historiography, as explored in more helpful ways by Andrew Shryock (ibid.). Nevertheless, the more contextually variable, "pragmatic" habits of speech community can entextualize stereotypes in ways that are coded altogether differently than they tend to be in normative language communities. Such differences are elegantly explored, for example, by Steven Caton, "Diglossia in North Yemen: A Case of Competing Linguistic Communities," *Southwestern Journal of Linguistics* 10, no. 1 (1991): 214–34. As I suggest in this chapter, poets who have engaged centrally with tribal politics in the Yemeni highlands have long drawn from both oral and written aesthetics as they situate their verse in relation to multiple modes of textual authority.

5. Franz Boas, "The Stylistic Aspects of Primitive Literature," *Journal of American Folk-lore* 38, no. 149 (1925): 329.
6. W. Whallon, *Formula, Character, and Context: Studies in Homeric, Old English, and Old Testament Poetry* (Cambridge, Mass.: Harvard University Press, 1969); and D. Buchan, *The Ballad and the Folk* (London: Routledge and Kegan Paul, 1972).
7. These studies draw on the pioneering work of Albert Lord, *The Singer of Tales*, 4th ed. (Cambridge, Mass.: Harvard University Press, 1960). Studies of Arabic poetry have focused on pre-Islamic and early Islamic periods and include James Monroe, "Oral Composition in Pre-Islamic Poetry," *Journal of Arabic Lit-*

erature 3 (1972); M. V. McDonald, "Orally Transmitted Poetry in Pre-Islamic Arabia and Other Pre-Literate Societies," *Journal of Arabic Literature* 9 (1978); and Michael Zwettler, *The Oral Tradition of Classical Arabic Poetry: Its Character and Implications* (Columbus: Ohio State University Press, 1978).

8. Finnegan, *Oral Poetry,* 130.
9. Ibid., 133.
10. My approach to style is inspired by sociolinguistic anthropology and cultural studies, especially Dell Hymes, "Phonological Aspects of Style: Some English Sonnets," in *Style in Language,* ed. T. Sebeok (Cambridge, Mass.: MIT Press, 1960); and Dick Hebdige, *Subculture: The Meaning of Style* (New York: Methuen, 1979). As a semiotic practice, style inheres in the meaning of grammatical form as it is produced within socially situated communicative acts, settings, and ideological frameworks.
11. In its most general definition, as often employed by nonspecialists, the *ḥumaīnī* genre includes any sung poetry that is divided into strophes or sections with consistent end rhymes that lack case endings (that is, each rhyme ends in a *sukūn*). More restrictive formal accounts of *ḥumaīnī* are developed by Jaʿfar Ḍafārī, "Humaini Poetry in South Arabia," Doctoral thesis, University of London, 1966, 301–76; and Muhammad Ghānem, *Shiʿr al-Ghināʾ al-Sanʿānī* (Damascus: Dār al-ʿAwdah, 1987), 92–138. Both authors identify principle meters (especially *basīṭ, sarīʿ,* and *rajaz*) as well as rhyme schemes, the latter of which include (1) "first *mubayyat*" [aaaa bbba ccca ddda . . .]; (2) "second *mubayyat,*" the most popular of the three schemes [abababab cdcdcdab efefefab . . .]; and (3) either first or second *mubayyat,* regularly interspersed with short interluding verses (called *tawshīḥ* and *taqfīl* sections). In studies of the genre that are less formalist, criteria of content, performance style, and setting are emphasized. Typically, *ḥumaīnī* is associated more with courtly or metropolitan entertainment than with traditions of agonistic polemic, an orientation that is reflected in themes of love, spirituality, and eroticism.
12. Landmark studies include ʿAbdallah al-Baraddūnī, *Riḥlat fī-l-Shiʿr al-Yamanī Qadīmihi wa Ḥadīthihi,* 5th ed. (Damascus: Dār al-Fikr, 1995 [1972]); Baraddūnī, *al-Thaqāfah wa-l-Thawrah fī-l-Yaman,* 4th ed. (Damascus: Dār al-Fikr, 1998); Ghānim, *Shiʿr*

al-Ghinā'; Ṣāleḥ Hārethī, *al-Zāmil fī al-Ḥarb w-al-Munāsabāt* (Damascus: al-Kātib al-ʿArabī, 1990); and ʿAbd al-ʿAzīz al-Maqāliḥ, *Shiʿr al-ʿAmiyyah fī-l-Yaman* (Beirut: Dār al-ʿAwdah, 1978).

13. These include Saʿd Ṣaḥlūl, Ahmad Bin Faḍl al-ʿAbdalī, and ʿAbdallah Hādī Subaīt. I should note that despite the lag in scholarly study of vernacular poetry, popular interest in vernacular genres is reflected in coverage by Yemeni newspapers and local publications.
14. A paper delivered by southern intellectual and socialist party leader ʿUmar al-Jāwī in May 1980 reveals the extent to which many Yemeni literary critics borrowed from Western folklore studies. After reviewing Western folkloric theory, Jawi devotes most of the paper to advocating the study of Yemeni poetry in six respects: (1) traditionalism and popularity, (2) orality, (3) heritage, (4) anonymous authorship, (5) collective expression, and (6) attachments to work and social issues. ʿUmar al-Jāwī, "Kayfa Nafham al-Shiʿr al-Shaʿbī?," *al-Turāth,* no. 4 (1992): 72. Socialist intellectuals such as Jawi were especially interested in identifying rural poetry in contradistinction with "literary" *(adabī)* and "modern" *(ḥadīth)* genres.
15. One of the central aims of ʿAbdallah al-Baraddūnī's *al-Thaqāfah wa-l-Thawrah* is to provide perspective on the contributions of institutions and technologies of inscription (writing, print media, recording, and broadcasting technologies) to cultural and political development in Yemen. al-Baraddūnī, *al-Thaqāfah wa-l-Thawrah.* His analysis is admirably extensive and includes one of the few considerations of *bidʿ wa jiwāb* poetry (identified in more literary terms as *musājalah* and *muʿāraḍah* poetry) that I have found in Yemeni scholarship (ibid., 132–38). He devotes particularly fine attention to the interdependencies of written and oral texts in his discussion of "praise poetry" *(shiʿr al-madā'iḥ)* (ibid., 140–41).
16. Carlo de Landberg, *Études sur les dialectes de l'Arabie méridionale: Haḍramoût,* 2 vols. (Leiden: E. J. Brill, 1901); Landberg, *Études sur les dialectes de l'Arabie méridionale: Daṯînah,* vol. 1 (Leiden: E. J. Brill, 1905); Landberg, *Glossaire datînois* (Leiden: E. J. Brill, 1920); Landberg, *La langue arabe et ses dialectes. Communication faite au XIVe Congrès interna-*

tional des orientalistes à Alger (Leiden: E. J. Brill, 1905); Albert Socin, *Diwan aus Centralarabien* (Leipzig: B. G. Teubner, 1901); and Alois Musil, *The Manners and Customs of the Rwala Bedouins,* ed. J. K. Wright (New York: American Geographical Society, 1928).

17. Robert Serjeant, *Prose and Poetry from Hadhramawt* (London: Taylor's Foreign Press, 1951); Michael E. Meeker, *Literature and Violence in North Arabia* (Cambridge: Cambridge University Press, 1979); Jean Lambert, "Aspects de la poésie dialectale au Yémen," Master's thesis, University of Paris, 1982; Saad Sowayan, *Nabati Poetry: The Oral Poetry of Arabia* (Berkeley: University of California Press, 1985); Steven Caton, *Peaks of Yemen I Summon: Poetry as Cultural Practice in a North Yemeni Tribe* (Berkeley: University of California Press, 1990); Philip Schuyler, "Music and Tradition in Yemen," *Asian Music* 22, no. 1 (1990–91): 51–71; and Clinton Bailey, *Bedouin Poetry from Sinai and the Negev: Mirror of a Culture* (Oxford: Clarendon Press, 1991).

18. A review of the anthropological literature on Yemeni poetry is indicative. Jean Lambert's work on urban Sanaani song and its relation to other song genres, while an outstanding contribution to ethnomusicology and *ḥumaīnī* scholarship in Yemen, resorts to a geography of rural illiteracy: "Popular and village songs are transmitted through purely oral means and do not accommodate formal apprenticeship: they are learned through practice. By contrast, urban sung poetry is transmitted through writing, in manuscripts carefully preserved by families, either amateur or highly educated" (author's translation). Jean Lambert, *La médecine de l'âme: Le chant de Sanaa dans la société yéménite* (Nanterre: Société d'ethnologie, 1997), 34. Steven Caton is attentive to the transformation of scriptural cultures but also shows reluctance in attributing traditions of written poetry to rural areas in Khawlān: "I would contend that the role writing has played in the structuring of the tribal *qaṣīdah* has only become important since the 1962 revolution, when education began to spread to the tribes." Caton, *Peaks of Yemen,* 187. Robert Serjeant, one of the earliest scholars of Yemeni poetry, attends with admirable skill to the overlapping between the oral, song traditions of rural areas and the carefully meditated, written practices—notably *ḥumaīnī*—of

the urban elites. Serjeant, *Prose and Poetry,* 7, 57. In discussing his collection of vernacular *maqāmah* poems, he explains that many of his finest examples were "not written by men of learning, but by shaikhs and tribesmen" (ibid., 52). Nevertheless, his interest in origins leads him ultimately to designate the written *maqāmah* genre as a poetry of the town, "where it could be committed to writing" (ibid., 53).

19. Such dialogic constructions of honor have been explored fruitfully by Pierre Bourdieu, *Algeria, 1960: The Disenchantment of the World* (New York: Cambridge University Press, 1963 [1960]), 99–117; Raymond Jamous, *Honneur et Baraka: Les structures sociales traditionelles dans le Rif* (New York: Cambridge University Press, 1981), 69–71; Meeker, *Literature and Violence;* and Caton, *Peaks of Yemen,* 27–28.
20. Charles Pellat, "Hidjā'," in *Encyclopedia of Islam* (Leiden: E. J. Brill, 1971), 3:354.
21. Caton, *Peaks of Yemen,* 28.
22. I encountered a similar expression, *da'wah w-istijābah,* used by a young intellectual to describe obligations of moral reciprocity. Throughout southern Yemen, however, the term *bid' wa jiwāb* is far more common. It seems to me that the pairing of the marked vernacular word *bid',* which in standard Arabic *(bad'ah)* lacks the final uvular consonant, with the standard word *jiwāb* captures the essential dialogic spirit of the genre. In his book on Yafi'i culture and history, Muhsen Dayyān begins a detailed discussion of Yafi'i poetry by focusing on this genre: "And among the long *qaṣīdahs* is the *al-bid' w-al-jiwāb* in particular." Muhsen Dayyān, *Yāfi': Bayn al-Aṣālah wa-l-Mu'āṣirah al-Yamaniyyah* (Damascus: al-Kātib al-'Arabī, 1995), 328. Mikhail Rodionov discusses the use of the genre in Hadramawt. Mikhail Rodionov, *Poetry and Power in Hadramawt* (St. Petersburg: St. Petersburg University Press, 1992). Moshe Piamenta also notes the wider use of the expression. Moshe Piamenta, *Dictionary of Post-classical Yemeni Arabic* (New York: Brill, 1990), 1:22. For brevity's sake, I use a version of this expression that lacks the definite articles.
23. H. Daiber, "Masā'il wa Adjwiba" in *Encyclopedia of Islam,* 636–39 (Leiden: E. J. Brill, 1954).

24. E. Wagner, "Munāẓara," in *Encyclopedia of Islam* (Leiden: E. J. Brill, 1993 [1954]), 7:565.
25. Brinkley Messick, *The Calligraphic State: Textual Domination and History in a Muslim Society* (Berkeley: University of California Press, 1993), 168–71.
26. Ibid., 268.
27. Muḥammad Bin ʿAlī al-Shawkānī, *Adab al-Ṭalab wa Mashhā al-Adab,* ed. A. Y. al-Surayhi (Sanaa: Maktabat al-Irshād, 1998 [1834]), 206–07.
28. The main sites were Ḥawfar (Maktab Yazīdī), Bīr al-ʿArūs (Maktab Yihar), Shibr (in al-Ḥadd), and Lakamat al-ʿAbbādī (Maktab al-Mawsaṭah). ʿAbdallah al-Qadīm's son, ʿAbd al-Ghaffar, was buried in a tomb that is still standing near the main road in Labʿūs. His nickname was "the bull" *(al-thōr),* an appellation that has been incorporated into a popular local tale that the tomb was built for his cow, who, as it perished one day in the field, miraculously bid his owner farewell. The Bā ʿAbbād line adhered to the Aḥmadī branch *(ṭarīqah)* of Sufism.
29. These included, foremost, the shaikhly descendants of Shaikh Abi Bakr Bin Sālem al-Saqqāf (d. 1584/992), of the Bā ʿAlawī lineage, who was the Yafiʿi spiritual leader in Hadramawt. The first of this family to visit Yafiʿ was Shaikh Husain Bin Sālem (d. 1634/1044). He came to Yafiʿ for two years and built a mosque in ʿAntar and purchased lands for its religious endowment *(waqf).* After his departure in 1584, Shaikh Husain appointed ʿAli Bin Aḥmad Harharah as religious authority in Yafiʿ Bani Mālek. Ḥamzah Luqmān, *Taʾrīkh al-Qabāʾil al-Yamaniyyah* (Sanaa: Dār al-Kalimah, 1985), 173. Other prominent religious families (not all of them *sayyids*) included the Miḥḍār, who were also descendants of Shaikh Abu Bakr Bin Salem; the Ḥaddād family, originally from Qaīdūn in Hadramawt; the Tayyār of the Sufi Bin ʿAlwān lineage; the ʿIzz al-Dīn family of *faqīhs* who became the archivists of Yafiʿ Bani Mālek; and the Harīrī *qāḍīs* who were of the Jaīlānī Sufi order and served the Harharah sultanate.
30. Several major military campaigns by Yafiʿis into Hadramawt during these centuries provided bases for cooperation between regional religious and political authorities. In 1519/925, over five thousand Yafiʿis succored the Kathīri Imam Badr Bin ʿAbdallah

"Bu Ṭwaīraq" in his campaign against rivals in inner Hadramawt. A second and even larger campaign was launched in 1704/1116 under the banner of the spiritual leader *(manṣab)* of Yafi'is in 'Īnāt, Hadramawt, Shaikh 'Ali Bin Aḥmad Bu Bakr. Aḥmad al-'Abdalī, *Hadiyyat al-Zaman fī Akhbār Mulūk Laḥaj wa 'Adan* (Beirut: Dār al-'Awdah, 1980 [1930]), 111. Many Yafi'is remained in Hadhramawt to farm lands seized as booty after the campaign ended.

31. Ṣalāḥ al-Bakrī, *Fī Sharq al-Yaman* (Beirut, 1955), 31–32.
32. In other places in the south, these schools are also known as *kuttāb*.
33. Brinkley Messick notes that in the town of Ibb, general literacy skills of a fairly low level were attainable after a couple of years' study. Brinkley Messick, "Legal Documents and the Concept of Restricted Literacy," *International Journal of the Sociology of Language* 42 (1983): 45. Topics of instruction varied. A comprehensive review of the development of educational institutions in the south, published by the Yemeni Center for Research and Study, reports that, in the early part of the twentieth century, the *ma'lāmah* typically provided students with rudimentary competences in the following areas: writing and reading skills, mathematics, religious practices and obligations, Islamic history, the histories of important social customs, geography, and health issues. Karāma Sulaīmān, *al-Tarbiyyah wa-l-Ta'līm fī al-Shaṭr al-Janūbī min al-Yaman* (Sanaa: Markaz li-l-Dirāsāt wa-l-Buḥūh al-Yamanī, 1994), 1:89.
34. Early primary destinations for Yafi'is were various religious lodges *(zāwiyyahs)* located in 'Īnāt, al-Ṭariyyah (Abyan), Zabīd, Saḥfah (Ibb), and Maṣn'at Sīr (Ibb). Some Yafi'i students also occasionally studied further afield, such as in Shahārah and Maswarah, in upper Yemen. Later, during the nineteenth and twentieth centuries, Yafi'is also began to study in Aden, Tarīm, Ghayl Bā Wazīr, Rubāṭ Bā 'Ashān (in Wādī Do'ān), and Rubāṭ al-Ḥaddād (al-Baīḍa').
35. A few sources point to the presence of a lively exchange of written *naqā'iḍ* poems in Aden as early as the thirteenth century. One scholar notes that during the mid-thirteenth century, the Zuraī' emirate in Aden sponsored a veritable cultural renaissance in which written poetic competitions—of the *naqā'iḍ* genre—were

prominent. Aḥmad Ṣāleḥ Rābiḍah, "Shuʿarāʾ ʿAdan fī ʿAṣr Banī Zurayʿ," *al-Turāth,* no. 4 (1992): 49–69. Poets who participated in these courtly exchanges were from Aden as well as from the hinterlands. Some of this poetry criticized the Ismaʿili doctrines of the Fatimid state and some praised its patrons, who distributed lavish rewards. One distinguished poet was Abu Bakr al-Yafiʿi (1097–1157/490–552), who would serve for part of his life as the leading judge *(qāḍī)* of Upper Yemen. In light of such written poetic activity in the urban areas, I would also point out that in the premodern era, Yafiʿ Bani Mālek was only a four-and-a-half-day walk from Aden.

36. One of the first of such schools was founded by Imam Yahya in Qaʿṭabah, a small town lying on the border between North Yemen and the protectorate areas. Designed to win the allegiance of southerners just across the border who were oscillating between loyalties to the British or the imamate, the *madrasah* provided primary education to some sixty students annually. Toward similar aims, the British established their own *madrasah* for an annual class of forty students on Jabal Ḥadīd, Aden, in 1935, and the Sultan of Lahej founded a similar school in Lahej around the same time. Sulaīmān, *al-Tarbiyyah wa-l-Taʿlīm,* 1:134–38.
37. Reports from the 1946–1947 academic year revealed that there were 4,410 students (out of some 600,000 inhabitants) attending *madrasahs* in the protectorate areas and 5,540 students in Aden (with a population over 80,000). Ibid., 150, 191.
38. Ibid., 158, 238.
39. Whereas *madrasahs* opened in the late 1940s in the neighboring regional capitals of Ḍāliʿ, al-Kawr, and Zinjibār, Yafiʿ's first *madrasah* opened only in 1963. In the mid-1990s, Yafiʿ's illiteracy rate was estimated at 42.6 percent.
40. Messick, *Calligraphic State,* 153.
41. Pierre Bourdieu, *Distinction: A Social Critique of the Judgment of Taste* (Cambridge, Mass.: Harvard University Press, 1984).
42. Messick, "Legal Documents," 51.
43. The third ʿAfīfī sultan of Yafiʿ Bani Qāsed, Sultan Saif Bin Qaḥṭān, nicknamed "The Believer" *(Ḥanīf al-Dīn),* was a renowned poet. The nineteenth-century Harharah sultan of Yafiʿ Bani Mālek, nicknamed "Bin Zāmil," was also an accomplished poet and composed written verse.

44. Paul Dresch, "Imams and Tribes: The Writing and Acting of History in Upper Yemen" in *Tribes and State Formation in the Middle East,* ed. P. S. Khoury and J. Kostiner, 252–87 (Berkeley: University of California Press, 1990), 271.
45. One of the earliest poetic exchanges I found to have occurred between a shaikh and several tribesmen dates to the wars between the Qasemid Imamate and Yafiʿ in the mid-seventeenth century. This exchange was reproduced on a cassette in the early 1990s and was accompanied by an interesting story describing its written composition. Over the course of one of the Imam's campaigns, the Yafiʿi poet Zaid al-Ḥuraībī sent a poem to a certain Bakīlī tribesman, ʿAli Bin Nājī, in the imam's army. After receiving a response *qaṣīdah,* the Yafiʿi poet began another counter-response, but before he had completed his *qaṣīdah,* he was killed in battle. When his incomplete "initiation" *qaṣīdah* was found among his garments by his comrades, Yafiʿi Shaikh ʿAbd al-Rabb Bu Bakr al-Daʿfalī took up his poem, completed it, and sent it off to the Bakīlī, writing "I'll tell your leader to settle down and not to hasten. / Neither vaunting nor tilting, / He who rants at Yafiʿ writes *(yukātib)* to all the tribes. / His hand will encounter a state of distress" *(Ha-aqul li-sayyidik yirtazī lā yaʿjal // lā yahtarī lā yamīl // Min haraj Yāfiʿ yukātib lā gamīʿ al-qabāyil // wa yaduh ba-tilqī al-maḍīl).* That these individuals were exchanging furious words of tribal poetry through correspondences smuggled across battlefronts conveys a quite different image of poetic practice than descriptions of orally performed war poetry (such as the *zāmil*) convey and suggests that practices of writing were becoming somewhat familiar not only to leading sultans and shaikhs but to rank-and-file tribesmen as well.
46. Such blanket demotion of vernacular Arabic is asserted by Jack Goody, "Alternative Paths to Knowledge in Oral and Literate Cultures," in *Spoken and Written Language: Exploring Orality and Literacy,* ed. D. Tannen (Norwood, N.J.: Ablex, 1982), 212.
47. Saʿd Sowayan discusses such correspondences between tribal elites in northern Arabia. Sowayan, *Nabati Poetry.* He notes that most poems, however, are characterized more by their entertainment value than by the need to communicate specific, practical information: "The poems we are discussing now seem to have no

apparent motive aside from the literary exercise and aesthetic pleasure derived from composing and reading them" (180). Ibrahim ʿAwaḍaīn, too, discusses this more classical genre of poetic correspondences and suggests that it emerged in earnest with such poets as Abī Tammām in the Abbasid era. Ibrahim ʿAwaḍaīn, *al-Muʿāraḍah fī-l-Adab al-ʿArabī* (Cairo: Maṭbaʿat al-Saʿādah, 1980), 114–17.

48. While some members of the Ḥaddād family in Yemen have belonged to well-known religious households of Bā ʿAlawī descent, Husain ʿUbaid was among the many members of the family who have held professions in other fields, such as blacksmithing (*ḥidādah* in Arabic).
49. The *Ahl al-Ḥaqīqah* order suffered persecution during the years of the People's Democratic Republic of Yemen and during conservative backlashes against Sufis during the 1990s and 2000s. I found no one who would acknowledge membership. Their intellectual foundations are generally a matter of speculation by Yemenis. Many attribute their interests in social justice and the use of reason *(ʿaql)* in spiritual practice to links with the tenth-century Qarmatian movement that arose in Yafiʿ. More credible sources told me that the group had close relations with the Bā ʿAlawī order of Hadramawt and that the book *The Sun of Grand Insights and the Subtleties of Insights,* by thirteenth-century numerologist and clairvoyant Shaikh Ahmad Bin ʿAlī al-Būnī, has been important for members.
50. R. J. Gavin, *Aden under British Rule, 1839–1967* (New York: Barnes & Noble Books, 1975), 319.
51. It was during this conflict that Shayef al-Khaledi first earned a reputation for powerful political verse. When Shaikh Bu Bak's wife traveled to his district to ask for support, Khaledi wrote a *qaṣīdah* that won him the gift of a new rifle (see chapter 4).
52. The *qaṣīdah's* remarkably durable couplet structure and conventional themes have ensured the genre's proliferation in North Africa, Turkey, Central Asia, India, Indonesia, and Malaysia. Additionally, the influence of Arabic *qaṣīdahs* on European lyric poetry has been explored by scholars of Spanish troubador *kharjas* and later European traditions of romantic ode. Stephen Reckert, *Beyond Chrysanthemums: Perspectives on Poetry East*

and West (Oxford: Clarendon Press, 1993); and Jaroslav Stetkevych, "The Arabic Lyrical Phenomenon in Context," *Journal of Arabic Literature* 6 (1975): 57–77.

53. The significance of Haddad's poetry as an oral medium had struck me when watching a video of the elderly Haddad, blind after an eye infection in the last years of his life. In the recorded event, he was reciting his verse to a crowded *mabraz* in Yafiʿ in the early 1990s shortly before he died. Varying his delivery from whispered insinuations, to plaintive exhortations, to stormy admonishments accompanied by the dramatic flailing of arms, Haddad commanded his audience's attention through tremendous talents in oratory. His was not poetry to be read silently.
54. As noted by Serjeant, Yemeni political verse frequently employs the *ṭawīl* meter. Serjeant, *Prose and Poetry,* 78.
55. This rhyme pattern is frequently based on verbal declensions (forms II and V) of feminine subjects. Although such verbs typically end in a final [-at], this phoneme is frequently modified in vernacular poetry to [-ah].
56. The poem's first Qurʿanic reference, invoked in the syntax of the first two verses, comes from a chapter entitled Daybreak *(al-Falaq)* (113:1–2) and was originally associated with delivery from curses caused by blowing on knots to bind people metaphysically. *The Holy Qurʿan,* trans. A. Y. ʿAlī, 6th ed. (Lahore: Muslim Converts' Association of Singapore, 2004 [1946]), 1808.
57. See lines 5 and 6 of the response *qaṣīdah* by Shaikh Bin Sabʿah, where he too evokes the metaphor of house building to describe poetic construction.
58. Catherine Phillips, *Gerard Manly Hopkins: The Major Works* (Oxford: Oxford University Press, 2002), xx.
59. I discuss these muses in fuller detail in chapter 4.
60. During the 1940s to 1960s, when literacy was expanding in the countrysides and *bidʿ wa jiwāb* exchanges were becoming more frequent, intertribal conflict in Yafiʿ grew especially nasty; Haddad's verses (32–34) above suggest the difficulty of traveling even short distances during such periods.
61. Messick, *Calligraphic State,* 25–26; Meeker, *Literature and Violence Arabia,* 81–82; and Shryock, *Nationalism,* 95–110.
62. Messick, *Calligraphic State,* 25–26.
63. I was told by one informant that the verses of one of his relatives,

a well-known cassette poet, had been mispronounced when performed by a singer and that the error had caused one of the poet's colleagues living abroad to divorce his wife back home. The misunderstanding occurred when the word *ginn[a]* "a genie" was pronounced as *gannah* "paradise," which happened to be the name of the migrant's spouse. Although the incident seems farfetched, this informant's report suggests the real concerns that some poets have with the corruptibility of written words that travel.

64. For earlier reading on the symbolic importance of the city to early Islam, see Janet Abu-Lughod, "The Islamic City: Historic Myth, Islamic Essence and Contemporary Relevance," *International Journal of Middle East Studies* 19 (1987): 155–76. Like Abu-Lughod, I consider metropolitan identity as an historically variable and textually conditioned imaginative practice. Since I approach metropolitanism through a broader range of textual hermeneutics, however, I also explore how Yemenis, especially highland rural populations, regularly identify its aesthetics in circulatory terms that can be contrasted, positively or negatively, with more emergent forms of sensate recognition. Whether metropolitan circulation is conceptualized by Yemenis through signs of written authority (as in this chapter) or through music and song (as discussed in chapters 3 and 4), I propose that its resourcefulness is expressed in a "rarefied" graphic aesthetic that asserts commonsense norms of authoritative knowledge while also inviting speculation on their moral credibility (see the introduction).
65. Lord, *Singer of Tales.*
66. Orally transmitted love poems *(ghazal),* for example, have a rich supply of stock formulas describing the beauty of the beloved: the lover has "red eyes" *(w-aʿyānuh ḥamrāʾ),* a "nose like a blade" *(w-al-anf[ah] kā-s-sēf),* a "neck like a gazelle" *(wa-l-ʿunq[ah] kā-ḍ-ḍabī),* a smile "like the lightning of dusk" *(mithl[i]mā barq al-ghulūs),* breasts like a garden growing "quince and pomegranates" *(safargil wa rumān),* saliva like "Jirdān honey" *(ʿasal Jirdān),* and so forth.
67. In following chapters, I show how *bidʿ wa jiwāb* compositions become more orally stylized (with mnemonic devices) when tailored for musical song on cassettes. During and after independ-

ence, the song *(ughniyyah)* becomes highly politicized, and *bid' wa jiwāb* poets become more disposed to making their political lyrics musically resonant.

68. In my earlier discussion of the oral prosody of *bid' wa jiwāb qaṣīdahs,* I identified tightly wrought parallelisms in rhyme, especially noted in end-strophe paronomasia, as indicative of compositional integrity. Ultimately, such integrity underscores the textual objectification of the entire composition, thus contributing to listeners' sense of the performance's inscriptive durability and its displacement to a domain of more rarified written and metropolitan authority.
69. Monroe, "Oral Composition," 43; Meeker, *Literature and Violence,* 120; and Renate Jacobi, "The Origins of the Qasidah Form," In *Qasida Poetry in Islamic Asia and Africa,* ed. S. Sperl and C. Shackle (New York: E. J. Brill, 1996), 26.
70. I found concision of poetic composition to be a popular topic of discussion among Yemeni fans of folk poetry. On many occasions, informants traced lengthier compositions to inscriptive technologies: earlier 45 r.p.m. records, for example, require shorter compositions, while sixty-minute cassettes encourage poets to compose longer poems. Although it is difficult to surmise the meaning of length for earlier generations of Yemenis, I suggest that length has likely been one of the salient markers of inscriptive practice and should not be excluded as one of the marks of a literate style for earlier *bid' wa jiwāb* poets and audiences. Most *bid' wa jiwāb* compositions that I collected from both recent and earlier periods are regularly longer than orally composed compositions: such poems usually have sixteen to sixty verses, contrasting with an average of twelve to twenty verses for most sung *qaṣīdahs* composed without the assistance of writing. I have found a general lengthening of written compositions to be verified in the folk *qaṣīdah*s that other authors have gathered from rural Yemen and Saudi Arabia.
71. The derivation of *qaṣīdah* from the verb *qaṣada,* meaning "to aim for" or "intend," has supplied critics with ample incentive to consider the genre's terrific performative resources. A conventional typology, based on the work of ninth-century scholar Abu Muhammad Bin Qutaībah, often includes themes of divine supplication *(du'ā'),* amatory suffering *(nasīb),* travel *(raḥīl),* praise

(madīh), eulogy *(rithā')*, love *(ghazal)*, and satire *(hijā')*. Although *qaṣīdahs* can be tailored to private settings and feature esoteric or erotic themes, they are typically delivered in more public settings in which the performer's own creative sensibility emerges in dialogue with moral and political responsibilities.

72. Suzanne Stetkevych, "Structuralist Interpretations of Pre-Islamic Poetry: Critique and New Directions," *Journal of Near Eastern Studies* 42 (1983): 85–107.
73. Meeker, *Literature and Violence.*
74. Kemal Abu-Deeb, "Towards a Structural Analysis of Pre-Islamic Poetry," *International Journal of Middle Eastern Studies* 6 (1975): 148–84.
75. Michael Sells, "The Qasidah and the West: Self-Reflective Stereotype and Critical Encounter," *Al-Arabiyyah* 20 (1987): 307–57.
76. Although *bid' wa jiwāb* compositions often lack one or several of these distinctive sections (especially the short prelude section and occasionally the supplication), the thematic sequence is generally one of the surest indications of the written epistolary format of the genre before independence. Indeed, the stability of this thematic sequence in other *bid' wa jiwāb* genres throughout the Arabian Peninsula suggests that the sections I identify in this chapter serve important metacommunicative ends for a broad selection of Arab correspondents who exchange poetry through writing. I provide the following comparative notes on similar compositions documented by other scholars. In observing correlations of thematic sequence, I do not mean to suggest that all of these compositions can be considered "*bid' wa jiwāb*" genres. Each genre has its own distinctive features and orientations and must be considered within its own sociocultural settings. Nevertheless, the correspondences of thematic sequence are striking and suggest that rural poets exchanging poems over some distance have resorted to similar metacommunicative strategies to secure the instabilities of the mobile word (either written or oral).

    Caton's analysis of the vernacular *bid' wa jiwāb qaṣīdah* is the most comprehensive non-Arabic account of the genre before my own. Caton, *Peaks of Yemen,* 188–196, 223–48. Although he describes only five of six sections, the prelude can be located in the compositions he examines. Serjeant's collection features several versions of *bid' qaṣīdahs*. Serjeant, *Prose and Poetry,* 54–58. The first poem, sent to a Hadrami by a migrant in Java in the early part of the twentieth century, lacks a supplication and contains an extremely prolonged prelude section that serves just as well as the main message section. The messenger trope (lines 65–66), greetings section (lines 67–68), and conclusion (lines 74–77) follow in sequence. The second poem (ibid., 62–65), though probably not sent as a *bidʿ qaṣīdah,* is labeled a "route-poem," and all sections can be identified as long as the "main message" section is understood to be the journey itself. Landberg's only *bidʿ qaṣīdah,* composed over two centuries earlier by the poet Yahya ʿUmar and heavily wrought with love themes, contains all sections except the prelude. Landberg, *Études sur les dialectes,* 1:64–101. Further afield, Clinton Bailey discusses a Sinai Bedouin tradition of *bidʿ wa jiwāb* that is largely, though not exclusively, oral performance. Clinton Bailey, *Bedouin Poetry from Sinai and the Negev: Mirror of a Culture* (Oxford: Clarendon Press, 1991), 72. Although these *qaṣīdahs,* much shorter in length, tend to lack supplications and conclusions, they typically contain a subtle prelude, a messenger journey that often features descriptions of the mount, and greetings and main messages sections. Alois Musil considers a fine example of a forty-seven-verse *bidʿ qaṣīdah.* Musil, *Manners and Customs,* 292–300. Though it parallels Bailey's Bedouin *qaṣīdahs* in lacking a supplication and conclusion, the poem displays the other sections in full. Sowayan examines "poetic correspondence" *(al-murāsalāt al-shiʿriyyah),* a slightly more literate, classical Arabic version of the genre that has long existed throughout the Arab world. Sowayan, *Nabati Poetry,* 181. Although he does not mention the prelude, he delineates five characteristic sections of the genre that are nearly identical to those I have outlined above. ʿAwaḍaīn, too, mentions the genre and gives examples, suggesting that the genre began in earnest with such poets as Abī Tammām in the Abbasid era. ʿAwaḍaīn, *al-Muʿāraḍah,* 114–17.

77. The concept of frames is developed by Erving Goffman, *Frame Analysis: An Essay on the Organization of Experience,* (New York: Harper & Row, 1974); and Gregory Bateson, "A Theory of Fantasy and Play," in *Steps to an Ecology of the Mind,* 177–93 (San Francisco: Chandler, 1972).

78. I suggest that the oscillation between literate and oral styles is a

constitutive textual device not only for *bidʿ wa jiwāb* poetry but for other genres of Arabic poetry and narrative where inscription is problematized as means of translocal circulation. For example, the narrative describing the Prophet Muhammad's first inspiration follows a similar oscillation between oral and literate coding. Although God's word is orally delivered to Muhammad and is subsequently conveyed to listeners through Muhammad's oral recitations, the word is secured both by the "embodied messengers" (see below) of either the Archangel Gabriel or Muhammad himself, as well as by the Archangel's command to Muhammad to "Recite!" as if he were reading from a "book" of God's eternal and incorruptible spoken words. Although not all of the Prophet's subsequent revelations were mediated by the Archangel, most of them were. Moreover, the "bookish" stylistics of Muhammad's recitations increased dramatically in the latter years of the Prophet's life, in Medina, when he came to be perceived as a more scriptural prophet whose style was altogether unlike the performance styles of oral poets. *Pace* the rich vein of historiographical scholarship that has treated the Prophet's revelations, I would suggest that such narratives confirm my own observations. Oscillation between oral and literate codes becomes more salient precisely as the inscription of spoken word gains public, social consequence and risks of circulatory reauthorship become acute. My thanks to Andrew Shryock and Alexander Knysh for helping me with these observations.

79. With an eye toward the developmental history of the Hadrami *qaṣīdah,* Robert Serjeant asserts that the supplication and conclusion "are unquestionably an Islamic addition," a point that I see no reason to dispute. Serjeant, *Prose and Poetry,* 6.
80. Caton, *Peaks of Yemen,* 324.
81. The term *barāʿat al-istihlāl* is discussed by fourteenth-century social historian ʿAbd al-Rahman Ibn Khaldūn. ʿAbd al-Raḥman Ibn Khaldūn, *Les Prolégomènes d'Ibn Khaldoun,* trans. M. d. Slane (Paris: Imprimerie Impériale, 1868), 3:452. Note that in Yemeni performance traditions, the *barʿah* is the classic tribal dance that accompanies *zāmil* poems, and is typically executed at the forefront of armed, marching delegations as major political and social proceedings get underway.
82. Poets could simply disregard the written medium of the ex-

change. Indeed, in cassette poetry, as I discuss in chapter 4, they work with singers to portray cassette-mediated *bid' wa jiwāb* exchanges as imaginably face to face. Nevertheless, the fact that most poets have traditionally acknowledged the written format suggests that writing itself has been significant and meaningful to poets. I suggest that written media and practices are forms of symbolic capital whose value derives from their circulation among restricted circles of rural notables.

83. Messick, *Calligraphic State,* 210–12.
84. Messick writes: "Mobile witnesses, who travel with the text (and whose probity must be so manifest, so little context-dependent, as to be apparent even in districts where they are not known), are the ultimate conveyers of truth. Such traveling witnesses also figure in another type of writing, a judge's appointment letter from the imam. When the imam writes to the appointee, two witnesses must witness the letter *(kitāb)* and then 'go out with him to the district.' An ordinary, unaccompanied letter is specifically ruled out" (ibid., 210).
85. The function of the messenger journey section in this respect (by no means its only function) is evident in its comparatively high frequency and elaboration in amicable exchanges between correspondents separated by distance—many of them migrants. In more agonistic exchanges, where poets seek to isolate one another, this section tends to be greatly reduced, if not eliminated altogether.
86. The messenger journey is featured in the poetry of nonliterate Arabian communities, as documented by previous scholars, including Landberg, *Études sur les dialectes,* 1:64–101; Musil, *Manners and Customs,* 292–300; and Bailey, *Bedouin Poetry,* 72. I would suggest that the section probably performs a similar mediating function, evoking an empirically observable topography that links poets. Nevertheless, I have found that the messenger-journey sections in such oral poetry tend to be neither as central nor as elaborate as those in *bid' wa jiwāb* exchanges. In cassette poetry, as I discuss in the next chapter, the messenger journey is greatly curtailed in *bid' wa jiwāb* poetry due, in part, to the fact that the oral/aural nature of the communicative channel is less problematic than the written medium was for earlier poets.

87. In many *bidʿ wa jiwāb* exchanges, the messenger journey in the initiation poem is more elaborate than its equivalent in the response. This discrepancy underscores the fact that the elaboration of the messenger journey is a matter of securing a viable communicative channel between poets. Where initiation *qaṣīdahs* usually commence dialogue that is new or has been neglected for weeks if not years, special care seems to be taken to ensure the success of the opening "turn," especially since it is achieved through the instable form of writing. Since the response poem is usually composed and sent within a week, it is likely that less attention is given to securing phatic connections. As always, a range of social distances and intimacies can be conveyed by varying such conventions.
88. The *zāmil*'s tribal coding is discussed by Najwa Adra, "Qabyala: The Tribal Concept in the Central Highlands, the Yemen Arab Republic," Doctoral thesis, Temple University, Philadelphia, 1982, 274–75; Najwa Adra, "Dance and Glance: Visualizing Tribal Identity in Highland Yemen," *Visual Anthropology* 11 (1998): 55–102; and Hārethī, *al-Zāmil fī al-Ḥarb.*
89. The symbolism of water as generosity is one of the most consistent features of *qaṣīdahs* throughout the Arabic-speaking world. Symbolic patterns are regionalized, as noted by Stefan Sperl and Christopher Shackle, "Introduction," in *Qasida Poetry in Islamic Asia and Africa,* ed. S. Sperl and C. Shackle (New York: E. J. Brill, 1996), 43–44. Serjeant attends to the heavy use of water and rain symbolism in the poetry of southwestern Yemen. Serjeant, *Prose and Poetry,* 56. Suzanne Stetkevych has argued convincingly that such symbolism is drawn from a long Near Eastern tradition of equating rain and sweet water with male fertility. Stetkevych, "Structuralist Interpretations," 104–05. She observes that such symbols of water and fertility are especially common in the final stage of a "rite of passage" that is central to the structural form of the pre-Islamic *qaṣīdah* (ibid., 105). Her model suggests that references to the abundance of rain showers and sweet waters are particularly appropriate in the greetings section of *bidʿ wa jiwāb* poetry, when the messenger's liminal journey has been completed and social life reestablished. I suggest, however, that these symbols of fertility are refracted in a particular form

through the metacommunicative ideologies and practical concerns of highland rural notables who exchange poetry through written letters.

90. Although Haddad does not explicitly address the messenger in this verse, most of the initial strophes in surrounding verses (11–13, 15–17, 20, 22) begin with explicit imperatives. Such emphatics suggest that the poet is instructing the messenger throughout this entire section.
91. Jack Goody, "Restricted Literacy in Northern Ghana," In *Literacy in Traditional Societies,* ed. J. Goody (New York: Cambridge University Press, 1968), 230–31.
92. Messick, "Legal Documents," 49.
93. Meeker, *Literature and Violence,* 37.
94. Begun in 1947 with the intention of replicating the gains of the al-Jazīrah project in the Sudan, the Abyan project became the cornerstone of a cotton production industry that would supply more than half of the protectorate's export earnings by the late 1950s. Robert W. Stookey, *South Yemen: A Marxist Republic in Arabia* (Boulder: Westview Press, 1982), 78–79. For certain sectors of the South Yemeni population, the project was by all measures a success: a long conflict over water rights between the Faḍlī and Yafiʿi peoples was essentially quelled, thousands of workers from across South Yemen gained employment as tenants and sharecroppers, development brought gravel roads, housing, water, and electricity to regional capitals, and the supply of fresh fruits and vegetables increased in Aden. For others, however, the tremendous profits generated by cotton, planted on over 60 percent of Abyan project land, were leading to great stress in traditional systems of law and order in the countrysides. Similar, smaller cotton projects were established soon after in Lahej, Dathīnah, and Mayfaʿ as well as the ʿAwdhalī, Lower ʿAwlaqī, and ʿAqrabī territories. During the late 1950s and 1960s, cotton came to account for more than half the protectorate's export earnings (ibid., 79).
95. The class-based distributional networks of British colonialism are discussed by Stookey (ibid., 80).
96. Bakhtin's complex agent is described as a "will" of independent but recombined voices. Mikhail Bakhtin, "The Problem of the Text in Linguistics, Philology, and the Human Sciences: An Ex-

periment in Philosophical Analysis," in *Speech Genres and Other Essays* (Austin: University of Texas Press, 1986), 21.

97. The correspondence and encounter between King Sulaiman and the Queen of Sheba are described in detail in the Qur'an (27:20–44). Medieval historian Aḥmad Thaʿlabī gives several popular accounts of this exchange that feature a whole series of clever riddles that each posed to the other to test their mettle. Aḥmad Bin Muḥammad al-Thaʿlabī, *ʿArāʾis al-Majālis* (Beirut, n.d.). Haddad's original riddle to Bin Sabʿah can be deciphered as follows. When King Sulaiman (one of Haddad's "camels") learns from a hoopoe bird (the "compliant creature") of a fabulously wealthy queen (the "female camel") who reigns over an empire to the south, he sends a letter to her asking her to acknowledge God and convert. After receiving his letter, the Queen of Sheba crafts a response and sets out to visit Sulaiman's palace in person. Learning of her impinging visit, Sulaiman asks an Efreet (Haddad's second "camel") for something to help him persuade her to convert when she arrives. The Efreet concedes, and the queen's throne is transported to Sulaiman "before he could blink" (some say with the intervention of an angel). After discovering the throne, along with a brilliantly polished floor, the queen submits to Islam's divine summons.

98. While it is useful to think of a certain kind of tight intertextuality as a mark of a literate style, generalizations are difficult given historical transformations in written and oral compositional practices and in interpretive expectations. It is my impression that in earlier periods, before the mid-twentieth century, poets were not in the habit of preserving poems that they received or even of making copies of their own *bidʿ* or *jiwāb* poems sent to correspondents. *Qaṣīdahs* would be read aloud on their own and then compared to verses of the pair *qaṣīdah* that the poet or others had memorized by rote. This practice is confirmed for me by the collections of pre-mid-century poetry possessed by Yafiʿis today, most of which contain either *bidʿ* or *jiwāb qaṣīdahs* but usually not both. As the century progressed, however, intertextual pairing may have gained salience as the preservation and documentation of poems has become more common. As explained in the next chapter, the cassette medium has lent a particular salience to intertextuality between *qaṣīdahs* since *bidʿ* and *jiwāb* poems are

generally recited head to head. But this intertextuality is largely an aural one: where cassette poems are more quickly composed and less synthetically structured than *bidʿ wa jiwāb* poems used to be, their intertextuality has actually diminished at a compositional level.

99. Yafiʿi traders and travelers were permitted to travel without paying tolls to local authorities in recompense for their regular provision of mediators and occasionally men and weapons during conflicts.
100. With sarcasm, Bin Sabʿah compares regional leaders to traditional religious *sayyids,* "people of the house." The regional leaders are far from pious: although they pretend to comply with religious interdictions against eating an animal's fetus, they violate them by "drinking of its broth," to the rage of those who later discover the infraction.
101. James D. Lunt, *The Barren Rocks of Aden* (London: Jenkins, 1966), 61.
102. Such a serial assortment of motley images, many of them drawn from popular oral tradition of proverbs and adages, may seem awkward to readers unfamiliar with Arabic poetry but has long been a valued aesthetic element in tribal poetry. Ḍafārī, "Humaini Poetry," 277.
103. Bailey notes a similar tendency in Sinai Bedouin poetry to describe beneficent persons as perennial wells that never run dry. Bailey, *Bedouin Poetry,* 93.
104. This tribal-sedentary dichotomy can also be traced to traditional disciplinary boundaries that have polarized realms of linguistic expertise. Where scholars of Arabic texts draw from philological methods, they remain generally unprepared to consider the pragmatic value of textual features within specific sociocultural settings. Sociolinguists, on the other hand, have typically lacked the knowledge of historically based textual and generic practices that routinely inform communicative encounters. Cultural anthropologists, meanwhile, have often lacked the linguistic skills required to synthesize theories of textual and linguistic form.
105. Deborah Tannen, "The Oral/Literate Continuum in Discourse," in *Spoken and Written Language: Exploring Orality and Literacy,* ed. D. Tannen (Norwood, N.J.: Ablex, 1982), 13–14.
106. Between 1946 and 1952, Aden became the world's premier ship

bunkering port. It experienced an economic boom that drew unprecedented numbers of rural inhabitants to the city in search of work. Although capital remained largely concentrated within the city, rural workers regularly returned home with cash and supplies, effecting dramatic changes in the highlands. Growing labor migration to the Gulf countries, especially during the 1950s to 1970s, added to the pace of change. From 1946 to 1963, the population of the protectorate areas swelled six times, from 6,500 to 35,000. Abdallah S. Bujra, "Urban Elites and Colonialism: The Nationalist Elites of Aden and South Arabia," *Middle East Studies* 6, no. 2 (1970): 193.

· THREE ·

"Cars of All Styles and Colorful Ways": The Emergence of the Recording Industry and Its Denizens of Song

Yahya ʿUmar said: Oh eye of mine, why remain awake this night?
If you have seen something in your path and were pleased, then take it!
If you are unaccustomed, knowing naught of such port traffic (bandar),
Then say "In the name of God" whenever you enter the metropole (madīnah).
Pursue your fancy for the white, woo the blackish-green,
Get intimate with the brown, while you leave aside the typical red.
The blackish-green is a vase filled with the scent of ambergris,
While the white is suited to late-night revelry and good words.
Have a nightcap with the white. How much the room is sweetened.
How the candle would burn in seeing its likeness in splendor.
This, this, and this—their love robs all sleep.
Whoever knows their passion is deserted by his reason.

—From a love poem by Yahya ʿUmar, a Yafiʿi singer reputed to have lived in the early eighteenth century

A change in tempo can bring about a gradation of semantic significance, tempo can express the emotional coloration of meaning.

—Czech linguist Jan Mukarovsky, "The Sound Aspect of Poetic Language" (1976)[1]

Folk singer and cassette-shop owner ʿAbdallah al-Kawmānī estimated that poets in his community took approximately one decade to adjust their traditional melodies *(alḥān)* to the demands of the cassette industry:

> When I first began recording songs in the 1970s, I had to do a lot of editing. Poets came to me with [written] poems composed in dense parochial verse unsuitable for the melodies I wanted to sing. So I had to adapt some of their words. By the mid-1980s, though, things had changed, and it was new instrumentation that made the difference. . . . When poets began to hear *qaṣīdahs* being sung and recorded to the accompaniment of the *ʿūd,* an instrument that had not traditionally been part of their musical repertoire, . . . it was then that they learned to compose in melodies that suited my recording aims. That was when I was really able to step up production.[2]

Working with rural poets near Dhamār in northern Yemen, Kawmani sketches a period of time that probably occurred at least a decade later than in southern Yemen, where rural poets were listening to records of indigenous singers as early as the 1950s. Nevertheless, his estimate underscores the extent of the challenge that highland poets faced in writing verse at the onset of a new era of oral inscription. Audiocassettes introduced marks of metropolitan style that were no longer predominantly written or even sung to urban melodies and rhythms but were above all musical and disseminated in identical copies that could be heard in the same way everywhere. Meeting the demands of the new industry did not occur overnight.

In the following chapters, I explore the ways that poets, singers, and audiences consider the audiocassette as a medium of inscription, the moral and political advantages of such an assessment, and the discursive and aesthetic resources that are employed in crafting new kinds of authority through cassettes. In this chapter, I examine audio recording as an inscriptive medium: Why do Yemenis perceive audio recordings as having a regimenting, causal effect on their lives and culture? If, as I argue in chapter 2, written script is aesthetically wrought as a circulating form that is both alienating and true—that is, both a medium of physical departure from a relatively more inherent oral vitality and yet also a medium of metaphysical immanence that strengthens the language user's relationship with authoritative knowledge—then in what respects do poets, singers, and audiences come to view audio recording as similarly alienating and immanent? Part of the answer to this question requires situating recording technologies historically in an expanding industry of song and poetry that has developed in Aden and its hinterlands over nearly a century. The audiocassette and its technological predecessors have not been neutral conduits for relaying the content of Yemenis' experience but are adaptive cultural constructions. They have been useful and influential for Yemenis because they can store, disseminate, and entextualize knowledge, fixing it into particular authoritative sequences that can be deployed politically and reflected on.

I approach these changing patterns of knowledge and recognition by focusing on how cassettes are invested with authority through the intervention of two influential groups of song brokers: rural singers and cassette-shop managers. Both groups are instrumental in tailoring folk-poetry texts to more general habits of social affiliation and moral reflection and thus in making "our song" part of a more diverse, transregional song industry. Each group also brings distinct social competences to its work. Singers have traditionally foregrounded their own moral and cultural sensibilities by modeling their songs after the rarified musical strains of early elite singers or metropolitan Arab virtuosos, whose hits grew popular in Aden after the 1940s. Since singers who took advantage of the decentralized audiocassette industry tended to be from lower-status families whose stigmatization in preindependence years had encouraged their members to migrate to large cities or other countries, they have gained a special status as innovative brokers of metropolitan culture or even as national luminaries. Among home audiences, their recordings are especially influential because they accommodate local dialects, tastes, and interests. Where their performances of metropolitan song can be perceived as the entextualization and reproduction of "our song," such singers offer audiences opportunities to consider the benefits and costs of domesticating what seemed most strange. Cassette-shop managers have brokered a different set of metropolitan translations. Neither stigmatized traditionally nor celebrated as bearers of authentic national culture, shop managers can tailor recorded songs to local discourses with comparatively greater freedom. By using a whole range of recording, marketing, and sales techniques, these unsung middlemen provide listeners with the invaluable service of making metropolitan songs and their interpretive frameworks seem truly homegrown. The second half of this chapter is devoted to their work.

Throughout this chapter, nationalism remains a principal amplifier of the recording industry's texts. In few corners of the Arab world, nationalism and the efflorescence of an indigenous recording industry matured more integrally than it did in southern Yemen. For many audiences, midcentury recording stars were true emblems of their country's national culture. Given material and cultural disparities between British-occupied Aden and the hinterlands, however, nationalist song initially seemed foreign and strange for many Yemenis. Such song was a curiously mediated experience that singers tried to alleviate by foregrounding Adeni vernacular Arabic, even as they continued to perform with classical instrumental ensembles. Marks of indigenous moral "orality" began to change from their identification, in a literate epistolary culture, with tribalism or gnostic spirituality to their expression of a nationalist essence or at least set of essences. When contrasted with nationalism's singular, unified, and often anticolonial aesthetics—whether conveyed sonically in the model of the influential nationalist radio program broadcast from Cairo, *The Voice of the Arabs*, or graphically through new techniques of seeing, observing, or writing promoted by the expanding state—orality acquires a polyphonic localism that offers Yemenis the chance for their own voices to be heard by the whole.

The relations of vocal particularism to more generalized national aesthetics gain salience as Yemeni nationalists pitch their messages to the rural hinterlands and as Aden's own demographic composition changes dramatically during the 1950s and 1960s with the vast influx of rural wage laborers. Toward the latter part of the chapter, I consider how new concepts of regionalism help mediate the demands of local discursive practice on national integrity. By considering the lives and work of several Yafiʿi cassette singers and cassette-shop managers, I show how regional frameworks prioritize the logic of a new social imaginary that is nationalist in its circulatory power, is predisposed toward trendy genres of metropolitan music and song, and also permits claims to be made on national culture from local hierarchies of discursive authority. The ethical value of the cassette *(sharīṭ)* lies in the reflexive nature of its "scratch" or "obligation" *(sharṭ)*. Even as cassettes facilitate regional song markets and enable older forms of discursive authority, the singer and song's virtuous listeners are granted greater agency in the politics of aesthetic discrimination.

THE MORAL CREDITS OF SONG, MUSIC, AND DISCOURSE

In the Yemeni highlands, song has long accompanied the performance of tasks both mundane and extraordinary. Agricultural songs have provided farmers with an easy rhythm to help them plant and harvest crops, work songs have enabled builders and water carriers to toil long hours, religious and spiritual songs have provided moral inspiration during celebrations and rites of passage, and love songs have created opportunities for relaxation and entertainment at the end of the day. Although the daily performance of song has diminished in recent decades with the arrival of television and the spread of conservative religious

Figure 3.1. A singer and musicians perform live as they are videotaped at a cultural club in Aden, 2005.

attitudes toward public singing, Yemenis still consider song central to cultural life and enjoy listening to their favorite singers in a variety of settings (see figures 3.1 and 3.2).

Yemeni song has also long benefited from traditions of musical accompaniment. Since musical instruments are valuable and have been restricted to certain social groups and networks of material distribution, instrumentalized song has become regionalized over time. Throughout Yemeni history, the most prestigious instruments have typically belonged to urban residents, whether from small towns such as Kawkabān and Tarīm or from the large cities' great houses, such as the Rasulid palaces of thirteenth-century Taʿizz, Zabīd, Aden, or Sanaa, the latter of which is heir to the oldest tradition of continuous song on the Arabian Peninsula.[3] The instrument of choice for these singers *(mughannīs)* has long been the stringed lute: the four-string *qanbūs* or *ṭurbī* initially and later the five-string *ʿūd,* which was introduced into Yemen from North Africa or Turkey after the

Figure 3.2. The pleasures of song and *qāt*. A folk-singer *(muṭrib)* entertains audiences with Yafiʿi verse while enjoying an afternoon chew, 2005.

1930s. Although northern Zaidi imams occasionally banned song and music during various campaigns for moral reform, singers and audiences nevertheless continued to find performance venues. Indeed, most of the finest performers were themselves descendants of the Prophet Muhammad *(sayyids)* or religious judges *(qāḍīs)* who showed a special relish for *ḥumaīnī* verse that featured both secular and religious themes. In rural areas of southern Yemen, some of these singers were from sultanate families that presided over rich agricultural valleys and trade routes. In the Yafiʿi highlands before independence, these families were the Harharah sultanate of Yafiʿ Bani Mālek and the ʿAfīfī sultanate of Yafiʿ Bani Qāsed, both of whose members had long been distinguished for their proficiency with the *qanbūs*.[4] Musical talent was not uncommon in other sultanate families throughout southern Yemen.[5]

As entertainers of a certain refinement, such singers were occasionally known as *muṭribs* (from the noun *ṭarab*, meaning a special "musical pleasure"), and this designation gained fashion among singers and other musicians during the recording era. The quintessential musical genre for *muṭribs* was the Sanaani concerto *(qawmah)*, whose arrhythmic vocal melisma, interverse pauses, and instrumental interludes allowed meditation on the cyclicality of moods and spiritual progression.[6] Such arrangements created an effect of "detemporalization" common in traditions of *ṭarab* in other parts of the Arab world[7] and conveyed the sense of an enduring moral order whose moving and emotional components were secured by the immanence of natural grace. Transcending the logic of script and oral words, such *muṭribs* possessed a competence of musical interpretation sometimes described as "envisioning meanings" *(taṣwīr al-maʿānī)*. Although they traveled widely in their capacities as legal and administrative officiates and sometimes as paramount sultans of tribes, this competence provided the evidence of authority beyond the business of professional service, however glorified. As custom had it, they embodied all that was right in the world.

Song and music signified quite different competences for other social groups, however, especially when connected to the necessity of making a living. Among sultanate entourages were a variety of semiprofessional singers, some of them guardsmen slaves *(ʿabds)* who, despite the perceived circumstances of their birth, enjoyed a certain license in entertaining courtly elites and visitors. Beneath this class of performers were the servants *(shāḥidhs)*, who held song to be a matter of survival. Bound to specific districts although categorically landless, these lower-status men and women held occupations of small public esteem, such as leather workers, slaughterers, and barbers.[8] Rather than spiritual wholeness and contemplation, *shāḥidhs* offered boisterous, frolicking dance music that was best suited to moving people across social boundaries. They were called on, for example, to orchestrate *zāmil* poems that accompanied groups of disputants toward mediation grounds or bridal parties, and they also performed poems suited to religious celebrations, festivals, and other events. The tools of their trade had no strings, and instead they played a variety of percussion and wind instruments designed for outdoor performance, including a variety of drums *(ṭāṣah, ṭabal, tanak),* the metal fife *(shawbābah),* the double-reed flute *(mizmār),* and occasionally the cane flute *(nāy).*[9]

However socially managed, song and music remained especially pliable forms of media, and the powerful emotions that they could invoke caused them to be continuously monitored by the enforcers of conservative codes of moral discourse and textual authority. In the light of public politics, the poet's words, whether recited orally or read aloud from the page, garnished the esteem that their musical rendition did not. Some of the finest singers made regular recourse to song-text "preservers" *(ḥāfiẓs)* to assure audiences of their loyalty to transmitted tradition.[10] As I show in my analysis of poetic composition in the next two chapters, such concerns for authorial deference continue to inform the work of performers, even as poets and singers develop new strategies for accommodating the growing moral leverage of singing politicos.

First, however, we need to explore how the recording industry introduced substantial changes to the traditional status hierarchies of singers and to norms of public expression that monitored them. Although the initial years of the industry promoted the celebrity of elite urban singers, the increasing availability of identical audio copies helped demonstrate the authority to entextualize songs. Where the integrity of metropolitan song no longer depended on the physical presence of traveling sultans or slaves but could travel in the company of new technological objects whose fidelity was ensured by industrial standardization, new kinds of credit devolved to more diverse groups of producers. As middle-class singers increasingly won professional contracts during the heyday of the recording industry, from the 1950s to 1970s, the political leverage of elite metropolitan singers grew ephemeral in several respects. Not only was urbane metropolitan song becoming commercialized and thus less transparently "graceful," but under the expansive cast of new nationalist discourses, metropolitan song also failed to represent the increasing diversity of Yemenis. In this chapter's consideration of the gradual decentralization of the recording industry, I show how singers from a wider range of backgrounds become key representatives of metropolitan song. Indeed, in this setting the audiocassette becomes a generative register for expressing and qualifying new nationalist discourses. Where the human voice proves a fertile nationalist symbol (a tool that, in contrast to musical song, could be produced by each and every member of the nation's people), the cassette promises a more technicolored set of vocalities, some of which are more adept than others in representing the nation. Coming to full force in Yemen during pivotal years of nationalist populism and especially in a tumultuous postindependence era, the cassette offers Yemenis both a means to reflect on the estrangement of the identically reproduced voices and an aesthetic and technological platform from which to draw producers closer to home.

ESTRANGED WORDS: INDIGENOUS RESPONSES TO ADEN'S COSMOPOLITAN NATIONALIST SONG

In the years before World War II, Aden hosted the initiatives of several multinational companies that offered customers the latest in sound-recording technologies.[11] The city's well-established networks of international commerce, its high number of foreign-born residents, and its reserves of capital that far exceeded anything in the rest of the country made Aden Yemen's strongest consumer market. One of the first of recording companies to open its doors to customers was German-owned Parlophone, which began operations in 1938. Its customers were largely prosperous merchants, hotel owners, and foreign residents who were able to afford the company's imported 7.5-inch records as well as its hand-cranked phonographs. For these pioneers in acoustic duplication, Sanaani *ḥumaīnī* song was initially the genre of choice. Poets and singers were generally of wealthy urban families, and a considerable proportion came from religious houses.[12]

In an expanding recording industry that monitored its customers' tastes, however, the vogue for Sanaani song did not long remain uncontested. As retail prices for records and phonographs gradually diminished over the 1940s, Sanaani song grew more popular and could be heard at middle-class weddings, soirées, and afternoon *qāt* sessions throughout the city. Wealthy customers turned to other registers of metropolitan refinement,[13] and a new relish emerged for foreign song and music, recordings of which became available for purchase and could soon be heard broadcasted for several hours each day on Adeni radio. With sounds of the London Philharmonic Orchestra and the Boston Pops drifting through Aden's neighborhoods, audio recording conveyed a sense of something that was different than whatever Yemenis had heard before. Arab and Indian classical music also gained audiences, and while song lyrics in classical varieties of Arabic were poorly understood by most Yemenis, these musical alternatives provided a somewhat more familiar supply of new material.[14] Through the 1940s, the popularity of such music grew with the success of political nationalism in contesting colonial rule in India and parts of the Arab world. By the middle of the decade, Parlophone was offering a ready supply of songs by such Arab recording stars as Umm Kulthūm, Farid al-Aṭrāsh, ʿAbd al-Halim Ḥāfeẓ, and Sayyid Darwīsh from Egypt, Salamah Ḥijāzī from Saudi Arabia, Fairuz from Lebanon, and singers from Kuwait, all of whom expressed broad affinities with Yemen's own expanding cultural, social, and political frontiers.

Indigenous recording stars began securing contracts at roughly the same time. As early as the late 1930s, Parlophone produced recordings of Yemeni singers in both vernacular and classical Arabic. At about the same time, Odeon, another German-owned company, also began operations in Aden and quickly began realizing profits from a wealthy diasporic community of Yemeni merchants and migrants who traveled between Hadramawt (eastern Yemen) and Indonesia.[15] Aden's golden age of recording, however, was launched in the late 1940s, when a host of studios and outlets owned by Yemenis emerged to accelerate the commercial production of recorded Yemeni song. Jaʿfarphone was one of the earliest and largest of such recording ventures. Run by an Indian merchant known as "Mister Ḥamūd," the company's catalog featured the recordings of "The Nightingale of the Land" ʿAli ʿAwaḍ al-Jarrāsh, "The Adeni Semite" ʿUmar Maḥfūẓ Ghābah, and "The Man with the Mellow Voice" Muhammad Manṣūr.[16] Jaʿfarphone's commercial success provided a template for other entrepreneurs, many of whom named their shops after themselves (Ṭaḥāphone, owned by Hamud's son, as well as Shabībphone, Sālemphone, and Ṣāleḥphone), while others chose nationalist trade names such as Aden Crown and the Arabian South *(al-Janūb al-ʿArabī)*. By the 1950s, Aden was awash with graphite-record celebrities and had become the second-largest recording center in the Middle East after Cairo.

The growing polyphony of indigenous recordings dismayed some of those who sought to preserve the authenticity of modern Yemeni song. An Adeni musical movement soon began to craft a more authentic brand of metropolitanism. The Adeni Music Club *(Nadwat al-Mūsīqā al-ʿAdaniyyah)* was founded in 1947 and quickly became a vanguard of tasteful musical innovation.[17] The club helped popularize the works of a new generation of urban poets who renovated the well-worn themes of traditional love songs with the emotional life of a new bourgeois urbanite. Lyrics about the pleasures of strolling on the beach, eating ice cream, and sporting fashionable clothes were all performed live for audiences in handsome public auditoriums or broadcast through the recordings of Kāyāphone, a company that favored the club's members.[18] Although composed in varieties of classical or standard Arabic, such lyrics also became embellished with oral Adeni colloquialisms that were never heard on earlier recordings. Even as singers indulged listeners with themes of upper-class sentiments, they enacted a curious kind of discursive performance. Everyday oral discourse was offered to listeners as a potential index of metropolitan sentiment and yet only as a form of orality that was valued reflexively through urban acculturation.

Through the mid-1950s, as southern Yemeni nationalist leaders negotiated plans for self-governance with British authorities, the cultural and linguistic purism of Adeni song expressed the hopes and fears of the city's populace as dramatic political changes grew imminent. When a constitution was drafted and Aden was slated to join scores of other southern shaikhdoms and sultanates into a single pan-southern federation, the slogan "Aden for the Adenis" proved a rallying cry for those committed to preserving Aden's autonomy from its impoverished hinterlands. As singers and poets won opportunities to compose and record nationalist songs, conflicts between Adenis over the future of the country were expressed in lyrics that sought to reconcile populist sensibilities with the aesthetics of the city. In 1956, the Adeni Trade Unions Congress (ATUC) was formed under the leadership of Idris Ḥanbalah, an English teacher and prolific poet, and during the 1960s, the ATUC would become the most radical and militant workers' union the Middle East had ever known.[19] Keen to channel the rallying cries of the ATUC's foot soldiers, many of whom were from rural areas, Hanbalah released a short poem just after independence in 1967 that expressed the mood that Aden's cosmopolitan nationalists had crafted:

Form pleases me, without exception:
  Spirit of life, the elegance of things,
The refinement of bodies in their sentiments
  Of love, ecstasy, and lavishings.
Color in the form of bodies is a feast
  Of the charms of lights and enticements,
And the incandescent smile in its curls,
  Life's meanings in their radiant light
Traversing distances deep within us
  As the light, rather than as the voice in [its] ramblings.[20]

Foregrounding a socialist aesthetics of "form" *(shakl),* "spirit" *(rūḥ),* "things" *(ashyā'),* and "bodies" *(ajsām),* Hanbalah foresees rewarding possibilities in modernism for the sentient life of human beings. The liberating pleasures of visual apperception are given special attention, with romantic descriptions of the "color" *(lawn)* and "lights" of the human body (line 3). Indeed, "life's meanings" are equally available to all, capable of "traversing distances deep within us" so long as they are graphic (4–5). In the final strophe, Hanbalah asserts, in no uncertain terms, that the medium of the "voice in [its] ramblings" *(ṣawt fī-l-izjā')* is least disposed to inculcating modern subjectivity.

Singers who performed Hanbalah's lyrics became mouthpieces for progressive nationalist movements that foresaw the inclusion of all citizens in their solution to the country's colonial past. And yet even as recording stars helped chart the metropolitan orientations of Aden's national leadership, they also confronted dramatic changes in the nature of metropolitan life during the 1950s. Such changes would place a wider, more regionalized set of demands on exemplary nationalist singers. A review of some of these changes can help identify how the mediation of recorded song became especially important as an ideally generalized currency for a diverse set of producers and consumers and as a means to reflect on metropolitan difference. Graphic signs conveyed in song could certainly travel and convey a potentially universal moral sensibility, but they could also be appropriated by those who viewed them, especially when stylized by more "clamorous" reproductive media. After considering the uptake of nationalist discourses by a wider array of producers and consumers across Yemen, I assess the growing significance of a decentralized cassette industry for listeners.

Aden's demographic composition changed dramatically through the 1940s and 1950s as large numbers of rural inhabitants sought work at port facilities, at a newly opened oil refinery, and in expanding service and construction sectors. The population of Yemenis from the rural protectorates swelled six times after World War II from 6,500 in 1946 to 35,000 in 1963.[21] Northern Yemenis were even more numerous and came to Aden from al-Ḥujariyyah, al-Baīḍā', and Qa'ṭabah. By 1950, over 40 percent of the Adeni populace was composed of rural émigrés.[22]

At the same time that rural inhabitants came to the city to work, they also returned to their villages with goods, money, and new experiences and tales to share. From June to October, many workers regularly returned home to help tend crops, and others stayed home for longer stints of several years. Such sustained contact between Aden and rural areas enabled a healthy cross-fertilization of attitudes and lifestyles as rural inhabitants became familiar with metropolitan customs and vice-versa. But the economic disparities between Aden and the rest of the country quickly outpaced any hopes of achieving parity. While Aden's profits soared and with them the fortunes of its closest patrons, workers' incomes remained unchanged from 1914 through the 1940s.[23] Concomitantly, the sluggish implementation of British rural-development schemes and the outright isolation of Aden's elites ensured a chronic neglect of rural areas. What little of Aden's surpluses trickled into the hands of a rural populace whetted desire and resentment. Despite modest material gains and cultural cross-pollination throughout the south, ideological boundaries between the countryside and the city grew more pronounced than they had ever been.

Nationalist movements found ample sustenance in the federation's faltering promises. By the mid-1940s, the Free Yemeni Movement assembled in Aden to translate wider pan-Arab nationalist sentiment into demands for independence at home.[24] A panoply of other political groups, the Adeni Trade Unions Congress foremost among them, emerged in subsequent years, and each group promoted its own program for better distributing the wealth and authority that was being amassed in urban centers. In the decade of the 1960s, nationalist authority shifted dramatically toward rural Yemenis, who composed the vast majority of South Yemen's population. When the National Liberation Front (NLF) was founded through the consolidation of a handful of militant, rural-based political organizations, the rural hinterlands became mobilized toward achieving independence at all costs. By the morning of November 29, 1967, the last British warship loosed its moorings from 128 years of colonial enterprise.

Through the tumultuous years of struggle, Yemen's national political culture incorporated the countryside, and Aden's recording stars drew increasingly from the vernacular song traditions and poetic genres of rural Yemenis. In a book published in 1959 entitled *Our Folk Songs,* Muhammad Murshed Nājī, a preeminent singer at the time, excoriates his elite Adeni associates for promoting foreign and especially Egyptian song at the expense of Yemen's rural "cultural heritage" *(turāth):* "Get out of your enclave! Get rid of your tunnel vision and look. Look for inspiration in the place where you live. Practice *(mārisū)*! Practice the experiences of your people and brothers. On that alone, you [must] speak resonantly about what befits us and our conditions."[25] Employing a graphic aesthetic privileged in the mores of his metropolitan colleagues, Naji tells them to retrain their vision on the practical experiences *(tajārib)* that lie closest at hand and then invokes the kind of discourse community of song cited in the introduction to this book, urging them to "speak resonantly" *(tu'abbirūn).* To illustrate the new practice that he feels Yemeni singers should adopt, Naji cites the verses of a monologue *(mūnūlūg),* a new genre of song that was being popularized on radio programs across the Arab world and that he would soon help introduce to Yemen:[26]

Cars of all styles and colorful ways,
Yet I'm in love with the latest phase:
  "Your cash advanced, with a tally-ho!"
  Saying: "Coffee-man, here. Now take it and go!"
  With bondsman, you're off to his shop that you know.
While grinding away, he cuts to the chase:
  "It'll last two months. It's a real deal,
  As long as the driver holds firm to the wheel."

In the third month—well, how strange I feel,
When the engine meets its final days.[27]

Naji commends the *mūnūlūg* for its vernacular style and in particular its approach to work-a-day "economic life" through a distinctly popular style of criticism, parody, and humor. In this poem, the vignette of a coffeehouse server making a deal on a used car evokes a poignant contrast between Yemen's traditional role as a world coffee supplier and its new role as an underequipped consumer of new global imports. Despite Naji's hopes that the *mūnūlūg* might provide a new means of expression for Yemen's populace, however, the genre could foster no more than a bourgeois fantasy for most rural Yemenis because it was composed of innovative meters, rhyme schemes, and performance formats that were best suited to an *ʿūd* and a fuller ensemble of musicians. Naji's passion for "colorful ways" had a decidedly metropolitan slant. Nevertheless, Naji's summons to his fellow artists reflected the desire of growing numbers of song producers at the time to ground progressive sentiments in accessible patterns of talk and moral reflection.

Other recording singers and poets, especially those raised outside of Aden, agreed with the tone of Naji's indictment and had been developing somewhat more successful adaptations of metropolitan song to rural political verse. Beginning in the 1930s, one of the most influential schools *(madrasahs)* of alternative metropolitan song arose in Lahej under the tutelage of the political poet, musical patron, and brother to the Sultan of Lahej, Ahmad Bin Faḍl al-ʿAbdalī (d. 1943), nicknamed "The Commander" *(al-Qumandān)*. Although Qumandan composed some verse in classical Arabic and favored the *ʿūd* over the traditional lute *(qanbūs)*, he became primarily known for bringing the traditional, gentle rhythm of a well-known Laheji dance (the *sharḥ*) to classical song.[28] Through Qumandan's influence, a generation of rural poets and singers had already begun to tailor aggressive political verse to "styles and colorful ways" that indexed their non-Adeni and oral heritage, even while attesting to their competences in metropolitan melodies that not uncommonly were arranged through written notation.[29] Decentralized media technologies, especially the audiocassette, would provide this generation with a host of further opportunities to shape modern political expression.

RURAL MEDIA MARKETS AND PRODUCTIVE DECENTRALIZATION

The capital-intensive nature of recording ensured centralization in the industry throughout the 1950s. Until the recording industry could make its products accessible to the huge population of Yemenis who lived in the rural protectorate areas, metropolitan song and its increasingly nationalist message would largely remain the privilege of urban consumers. This situation began to change with several technical and industrial developments that occurred during the 1950s and 1960s.

To begin with, the recording industry itself underwent structural adjustments as costs of production diminished, competition for consumers grew, and marketing grew more sophisticated. With the proliferation of recording companies and studios in downtown Aden by the mid-1950s, enterprising merchants actively developed clientele among lower-income rural populations both in the city and in the southern highlands. Accordingly, studio managers invited a wider variety of well-known rural singers, many of them from lower socioeconomic backgrounds, to record specific styles of regional song.[30] Record labels and catalogs accordingly mentioned the regional provenances of the featured musicians and did not categorize their songs as either "Adeni" or "Sanaani" as was done earlier.

The radio delivered a hybrid metropolitan national song to mass audiences with a sense of unprecedented immediacy.[31] By the late 1950s, most large rural villages had at least one radio, and it usually was found in the house of a shaikhly family. For much of the decade, however, the only radio emissions available were those broadcast by Egyptian radio, notably *The Voice of Cairo (Ṣawt al-Qāhirah)* and the even more popular program *The Voice of the Arabs (Ṣawt al-ʿArab)*.[32] Although broadcast times were limited to several hours in the evening, these two programs brought many Yemenis their first exposure to classical Arab song. Toward the end of the decade, airtime increased and diversified as transmissions from Yemen's own radio station, the South Arabian Broadcasting Service, known as "Radio Aden" *(Idhāʿah ʿAdan)*, began reaching those beyond Aden's immediate vicinity.[33] Indigenous metropolitan songs therefore were reaching rural audiences by the 1960s.[34]

The mass dissemination of recorded song by radio enabled a diverse listenership to draw on a common reservoir of sung political poetry, and soon a certain "imagined community" emerged[35] with new discursive and aesthetic priorities. In one of its monthly program guides in 1961, Radio Aden expressed the nationalist tenor of such a community as a matter of new utilitarian aims: "Folk poems occupy a distinguished place in the programming, but we believe that now the words of poems must have a goal and foundation that bring benefit to all of our listeners. For this reason, the station, from hence forward, will broadcast only what it feels will avail the sons of the south and the poetry and prose that they will benefit from. If we devote an effort to the production of our programs in a way that wins the satisfaction of all, then we hope to obtain ample cooperation from poets and speakers in developing a consciousness *(waʿī)* in the south, thereby raising the current nation higher and higher."[36] The discursive and especially vernacular foundations of Radio Aden's imagined community are foregrounded explicitly in the program's emphasis on folk poetry *(al-shiʿr al-shaʿbī)* rather than on song. In particular, the "words of poems" will avail listeners with meaning, and "poets and speakers" are charged with raising the consciousness of diverse audiences. Through the medium of radio, vernacular orality gains moral value as a certain political utterance and mode of knowledge rather than as a style of audio-recorded cultural authenticity. Nevertheless, radio's diction is still governed by a command economy of sound. Radio Aden's station managers reserved a new supervisory role in deciding which poems "have a goal and foundation," and production facilities were still intimately linked to the recording industry.

Radio and records went a long way toward popularizing the consumption of metropolitan song and providing listeners with access to important cultural, emotional, and political transformations that were underway in cities across the Arab world. However, as long as electronic mass media remained controlled by the state and the recording industry remained closely integrated with state interests and tightly regulated by major transnational producers, metropolitan song would remain the koiné of urban classical artists. The vast majority of rural musicians and poets remained ineligible for the distinctions that such media offered.

This began to change with the spread of cassette technologies. The first machine to arrive in Yemen was the open-reel recorder, a bulky device that, like the film projector, operated from two large tape spools. Invented in the 1930s for broadcasting purposes, this machine began to become generally available to higher-end socioeconomic groups in the early 1950s.[37] At approximately the same time, however, the eight-track cassette cartridge appeared on the market, providing users with an affordable, durable, and transportable cassette technology.[38] By the late 1950s, the open-reel and eight-track cassette technologies were replacing the record player; indeed, within a few more years, they were household items in most rural areas. The most transformative cassette technology, however, reached audiences in the late 1960s: the audiocassette technology that is popular today.[39] By the mid-1970s, this cheap, portable, and easy-to-use cassette technology was fueling a cassette industry in Yemen that was reaching full maturity at a pace that matched that of other Arab countries at the time.

As a means of disseminating and popularizing metropolitan

song, cassette technologies were far more effective than records had been. The low production costs of cassettes enabled a greater number of small-scale producers to provide customers with relatively affordable access to their favorite radio and record stars. The vitality of a grassroots production and distribution industry was seen throughout the 1970s in the appearance of cassette shops in regional capitals and provincial towns across Yemen. Such decentralization ensured that the interests of regional consumer audiences became increasingly reflected in the products available for sale. The most revolutionary aspect of the cassette medium, however, lay not in its capacity to disseminate prerecorded song but in its function as a user-friendly recording device. For the first time, amateur and semiprofessional rural singers who had no contacts with major recording companies began to produce recordings of their own. In a prerecording era, such singers had been able to reach audiences only through live performances at weddings, at religious festivals, or in private homes. However, as early as the late 1950s, open-reel and eight-track recorders allowed such individuals to produce and disseminate their songs and musical performances to local audiences as well as to a broader translocal "public" of anonymous listeners.

The advent of such grassroots recording figured centrally in a growing variety of publicly performed metropolitan songs in Yemen. Moreover, through the ostensibly innocuous medium of song, cassettes gradually contributed to the pluralizing of public political discourse. As a decentralized recording medium that was less subject to the apparatuses of state censorship that monitored national radio stations and centralized recording facilities and that was equally liberated from the scales of profit that were required to sustain a capital-intensive record industry, cassettes enabled producers to publicize a greater spectrum of political vocabularies, not all of them consistent with the state's own. To consider the alternative political discourses that were aired by rural cassette producers and to assess how such discourses helped to foster a greater plurality of nationalist perspectives, I consider the work of several early Yafiʿi cassette pioneers.

SINGERS' ROLES AS RURAL CASSETTE CELEBRITIES AND AS MODELS FOR REGIONAL "COLOR" *(LAWN)*

Singers' access to cassettes did not automatically change their styles or enhance their expressive repertoires, nor did such access necessarily make them more influential public voices. Cassettes were largely a tool for use in accordance with given social and cultural practices. In the earliest years of the cassette industry, most rural singers who began to use cassettes had already established reputations among local audiences. Often members of notable religious families, they performed without fees and typically used cassettes as a means of distribution to audiences who could not always hear live performances. Sometimes these recordings were made by the request of listeners who brought their own machines, and other times these recordings were made by the artists themselves.

The recording styles of these early singers were invariably conservative, especially when planning cassettes for general distribution. Singers saw little value in prearranging pieces for recording or in recreating studio conditions for the sake of audiences who were absent from original performance settings. Indeed, they always performed in front of live audiences. Their recordings thus convey an intimate setting that contrasted, perhaps not altogether unintentionally, with the polished sounds and standard nationalist discourses of the commercially recorded stars. Their material also tended to be cautious. Rather than attempting variations on the Egyptian, Indian, or Kuwaiti songs that were popular in Aden, they preferred vernacular *qaṣīdahs* composed by Yafiʿi poets who were mostly were either living at the time or who had recently died. In reviewing forty-one poems that were recorded on eight cassettes by early Yafiʿi singers, I found two thirds (66 percent) of all *qaṣīdahs* to be *bidʿ wa jiwāb* exchanges between Yafiʿi poets, many of them between tribal shaikhs.[40] Although their poems did speak of contemporary political faultlines involving the British or the Zaidi imamate in the north, rarely did their songs mention nationalist watchwords such as "the people" *(al-shaʿb)*, "the revolution" *(al-thawrah)*, "progressivism" *(taqaddumiyyah)*, or "reactionaryism" *(ragʿiyyah)* that were circulating in Aden and other centers at the time.[41] Their recordings were less symbols of their own metropolitan distinction than they were symbols of their deference to a public highland political order that accommodated a broad spectrum of rural Yafiʿi audiences. Cassettes and singers were not yet conduits to entextualizing discourses of metropolitan song as the radio might have been.

Although the performance styles, genres, and discourses of these early rural singers evoked a domain of highland politics altogether distinct from that of Aden, their musical variations were not entirely parochial. Their instrument of choice was the Mediterranean *ʿūd* rather than the traditional lutes and drums that their predecessors would have played. Even more telling, fashionably Western applause from the live audience follows the conclusion of each song. Cassette producers were trying to create the effects of metropolitan style, even as they drew from rural song genres and political discourses that were familiar to their listeners.

Other highland Yafiʿi singers were somewhat better positioned or more inclined to develop a metropolitan style. The growth of outmigration that occurred from the 1950s to the 1970s was especially instrumental in familiarizing rural singers with metropolitan song culture. Beginning in the 1950s, an increasing number of landowning tribesmen who were also part-time migrants began performing in private gatherings and stylizing themselves as amateur singers *(hāwīs)*.[42] In many cases, such amateurs became semiprofessional artists *(fannāns)*, although traditional stigmas against using song for financial gain required a discreet management of revenues. In Yafiʿ and surrounding regions, two men in particular became household names during the late 1950s and early 1960s: Haithem Qāsem and Salem Saʿīd al-Bāraʿī. A third singer, Husain ʿAbd al-Nāṣer, would gain comparable fame in the 1970s. These singers never achieved the stardom that many of Yemen's most celebrated stars have enjoyed and do not appear in histories of national song as personalities of note. Nevertheless, I provide brief biographical sketches of these three artists with the aim of exploring the kinds of transformations that a decentralized audio-cassette industry enabled in the status of singers and in their roles as national artists. As we prepare to consider the cassette as a particular moral resource, these sketches will demonstrate how Yafiʿi cassette-recorded song acquired a social content for audiences that its graphic mediation would help express and problematize.

Haithem Qasem is known to his listeners as a sensitive and an elegant *ʿūd*-player who has had a special affinity for the easy, rocking rhythms of Hadrami song. Of the three singers, Qasem had achieved the widest reputation in Yemen and the Gulf, while his listenership in Yafiʿ remained smaller. His musical success is remarkable given the challenges he overcame in gaining a foothold in the recording industry, though he is no different than the other two singers in this regard. Born into a family of tribal farmers whose mountain terraces abutted an arid coastal desert, Qasem left Yafiʿ as an adolescent to find work as a soldier of the Quʿaiṭi state in Hadramawt, approximately 250 miles to the east.[43] While serving in Hadramawt, he acquired an *ʿūd* and during his occasional off-duty breaks attracted the attention and tutelage of the recording star Muhammad Jumʿah Khān. After independence, Qasem followed the path of many Yemenis to Saudi Arabia, where a flourishing oil economy was contributing to the development of a vital entertainment industry.[44] In Riyadh, he obtained regular opportunities to perform at private parties, landed a contract with a recording company, and was eventually invited to perform on national television. In such an atmosphere, Qasem became far more willing than those singers who remained in Yafiʿ to experiment with a broader range of metropolitan songs and genres of poetry. Ultimately, however, his long years abroad and devotion to a translocal recording industry inhibited his reputation and influence at home.

Migration and international recording interests were not necessarily deleterious to singers' popularity in the homeland, however. Although Salem al-Baraʿi was also a migrant, his plaintive melodies, laced with throaty crescendos and diminuendos, drew lavish praise from audiences in Yafiʿ even as he introduced a range of metropolitan innovations to his song.[45] Born in Hadramawt, Baraʿi was a first-generation migrant who grew up learning about Yafiʿ from his father and grandfather, both of whom performed songs by poets whom they had known during their own youths in the Yafiʿi highlands. Yafiʿ became imbued with a certain nostalgia that would fill his songs with passionate yearning throughout his life. As a young man who, like Qasem, faced chronic unemployment in his village in the 1950s, Baraʿi moved westward toward his homeland instead of east, finding work as a stevedore in the port of Aden. When at last he found the opportunity to visit Yafiʿ for the first time in his twenties, he renewed his efforts to learn the traditional song of a community that he had long considered his natural home.

As Baraʿi's appreciation of rural Yafiʿi song developed, his continued residence in Aden ensured that his style would remain attuned to city tastes. His innovative embellishments of Yafiʿi dance rhythms with the more contemplative rhythmic sequences of the Sanaani concert *(qawmah)*, his performances of songs to two shortened melodies rather than only one, and his experiments with bongo-drum *(īqāʿ)* accompaniment were eagerly promoted by several Saudi-based cassette producers. By the late 1950s, he had signed contracts to market his songs both in Yemen and abroad. During the next several decades, over 160 cassettes of his live performances, often recorded in Aden and at village weddings, became available to Yemenis across the south as well as to listeners in Saudi Arabia and the Arabian Gulf emirates. Many of his songs reflect the popular metropolitan orientations of these transnational Arab audiences with romantic depictions of Yemen as a beautiful and resourceful homeland, descriptions of the migrant's yearnings for home, conventional narratives of love and the pangs of separation from the beloved, and diplomatic commentary about political conditions.[46] Nevertheless, unlike Qasem, such exposure did not ultimately alienate him from rural Yafiʿi audiences. On the contrary, he managed to maintain his original passion for Yafiʿi song, while stylizing it rhythmically and melodically for transregional and even foreign audiences. Moreover, he continued to sing the aggressive political discourses of highland tribal poets, as is attested by a substantial number of *bidʿ wa jiwāb* poems (18 percent of twelve cassettes reviewed) that feature on his cassettes. As Baraʿi explained to me, "They suited the popular agitation *(taḥrīḍ)* of the day." His success in maintaining the traditional sounds and political registers of highlands audiences became evident in the high demand for his cassettes in ʿAsīr and Najrān, regions lying along the borders between Saudi Arabia and Yemen where tribal song and poetry as well as Yemeni politics have been especially familiar to audiences.

The last of these early singers is a generation younger than either Qasem or Baraʿi and has been the least disposed to metropolitan innovations. Born in the early 1950s, Husain ʿAbd al-Naser became the largest producer of Yafiʿi folk-poetry cassettes until the late 1990s. Since the poetry I discuss in the next three chapters is drawn mostly from his cassette series, some discussion of his life and work is especially relevant.[47] ʿAbd al-Naser was one of seven children from a family of farmers and herdsmen who resided in one of the many rugged canyons in the Saʿdī district of Yafiʿ. Given the inadequacy of the family terraces for supporting the entire family, he and his brothers grew accustomed in their youth to looking for work wherever it could be found. The family ox, a valuable animal that few Yafiʿis could afford, was the most reliable source of extra income. During the winter months when crops are typically plowed and sown, ʿAbd al-Naser, his brothers and father tilled neighbors' plots. When he was not working, ʿAbd al-Naser obtained rudimentary reading and writing skills at his local religious school *(maʿlāmah).*

In 1973, barely twenty years old, ʿAbd al-Naser received a work permit from the embassy of Qatar. With the promise of better employment abroad, ʿAbd al-Naser set off by truck across the vast desert known as "the Empty Quarter" of the Peninsula. In Doha, the capital of Qatar, he obtained a position in the civil service that paid extremely well compared to what he could earn at home. He eventually saved enough money to rent an apartment, marry a cousin from his village in Yafiʿ, and begin to raise a family. As the years passed, he sent money home and occasionally returned to visit, but he was unable to bring the rest of his family to Qatar and gradually became accustomed to long absences from Yafiʿ and Yemen.

ʿAbd al-Naser has maintained contact with people at home through a sizeable Yafiʿi migrant community in Doha, Qatar. Frequent visits by friends and extended family from his home village have also kept him supplied with news. It is through song, however, that ʿAbd al-Naser has been able to position himself as a leading cultural and political presence in Yafiʿ. Shortly after his arrival in Doha in 1973, his friends heard his sonorous voice and collected contributions to present him with an *ʿūd* and a small drum *(darbūkah)* to encourage his musical talent. Although he listened to the radio, records, and cassettes of leading Yemeni artists to learn songs, he developed a special passion for the traditional musical styles and folk poetry that he had learned as a youth in Yafiʿ.

When groups of friends and acquaintances in Doha gathered together in the afternoons and evenings, ʿAbd al-Naser began treating them to songs from home. On occasion, he tailored his verse to metropolitan instrumentation, most notably through collaboration with other musicians who played the bongo drum *(īqāʿ),* double-reed flute *(mizmār),* and violin *(kamān)* and with amateur choruses composed of male and sometimes female singers. He developed a conservative performance style during these early years that appealed to audiences back in the highlands.

Most of his cassettes, for example, feature the traditional combination of *ʿūd* and solo voice. His musical arrangements adhere to a single melody and do not weave together several melodies in the fashion of younger recording artists. His simple musical ornamentation is placed at the service of poets' verse rather than vice-versa, which is evident in the sheer length of most of his songs.[48] Ultimately, such a performance style is fully consonant with his predilection for *bidʿ wa jiwāb qaṣīdahs,* which are featured on over 70 percent of his cassettes. From his earliest years of performance in Qatar, such poems were popular among audiences at home and also among the diasporic community of nostalgic Yemenis who lived with him abroad. Drawing from vernacular textual traditions that would have been accessible, in varying degrees, to anyone who had grown up in Yemen, *bidʿ wa jiwāb* poems relayed the perspectives of fellow migrants and travelers who similarly hunger for news, long for home, recollect familiar landscapes, and have concerns for friends and social relations. These poems were especially popular among migrant audiences insofar as they tended to focus on contemporary highland political issues and their relations to longstanding moral orientations, foremost among them tribalism. A considerable number of migrants in Qatar, as in other diasporic communities, were members of leading tribal families that had been exiled by socialist ideologues in the years following independence. Given the ongoing campaigns by exiles to create political change in Yemen, such poems provided listeners with rich symbolic vocabularies for discussing how social justice might be promoted at home in keeping with the finer aspects of tribal custom.

ʿAbd al-Naser's personal interest in *bidʿ wa jiwāb* poetry gradually matured within the specific sociocultural and political environment of his migrant community in Qatar. Such a genre had long been part of a politically charged migrant experience and was especially interesting to those in Saudi Arabia and the Gulf who were experiencing the vigorous promotion of cultural and tribal heritage *(turāth)* by the state at the time.[49] Within a few years of performing, ʿAbd al-Naser began to receive invitations to perform in front of wider groups of migrant Yemenis in Qatar as well as Saudi Arabia. He sang at weddings, cultural events, holiday parties, and other special occasions hosted by migrant community associations. In a Gulf culture that was benefiting from a thriving oil industry, opportunities for performance and magnanimous patrons were far greater than at home.

When ʿAbd al-Naser grew comfortable performing in public gatherings, he began trying to reach wider audiences through his own release of cassettes. Typically, he recorded songs in private settings, at his home or the residence of a friend, and then sent his cassettes to cassette shops that specialized in Yemeni folk song. In his early years, these shops included Jeddah-based Stereo Shamsān, who was named after the mountain that overlooks Aden, and later Valley Recordings (Tasjīlāt al-Wādī) in Doha, which was owned by one of his acquaintances. Beginning in the 1980s, ʿAbd al-Naser began sending his cassettes further afield to shops in Aden, Sanaa, Taʿizz, and Abu Dhabi.[50] These shops then established regular distribution arrangements with small-scale outlets in rural areas that serviced many of his most eager audiences. Over the years, he became a household name for fans of political cassette poetry in southwestern Yemen and Yafiʿ, a reputation consolidated by his steady and prolific production. By 1996, he had released 105 cassettes, an average production rate of one cassette every two months for approximately two decades. Such a rate of new releases has made him one of the most prolific amateur singers in Yemen.[51] Some of his most popular cassettes were reaching hundreds of thousands of listeners. I discuss the phenomenon of his cassette series, which has featured more than sixty-five Yemeni poets, in chapter 6.

In some respects, the recording careers of Baraʿi, Qasem, and ʿAbd al-Naser represent different professional trajectories. Although all three singers are from poor tribal families, each has used recording technologies and networks to cultivate a distinct role as a public singer. Even as Baraʿi and Qasem have become regional celebrities, they have also reached broader national and international audiences with the assistance of multiyear recording contracts and occasional performances on the radio or on television. ʿAbd al-Naser remains less professionalized, though his adherence to traditional highlands song and poetry ensures his greater popularity among fans of political poetry and Yafiʿi heritage *(turāth).*

Despite their differences, however, each of these singers has also contributed centrally to dissolving the disparities between metropolitan song, as a formerly elitist register, and traditional Yafiʿi highlands verse, notably *bidʿ wa jiwāb* poetry. In the process, they have helped create a new register of regional song that can engage highland and migrant listeners more centrally in national politics and culture. As influential representatives of public discourse in the early years of the southern republic, such singers popularized poetic genres as well as political vocabularies that had rarely been heard on state-sponsored media channels. ʿAbd al-Naser's role in this regard is especially notable. During years of radical political transformation, especially in southern Yemen, ʿAbd al-Naser's tribalist folk songs—particularly *bidʿ wa jiwāb qaṣīdahs*—provided audiences with a rural symbolic framework that bridged a variety of moral, ideological, and spatial fault lines. As is discussed further in chapter 6, the *bidʿ wa jiwāb* poetry on his series has continued to prove instrumental in linking narratives of tribal history and regional identity to public discourse, providing an alternative perspective that was valued in the years following independence in 1967 when references to tribalism and regionalism were officially banned.

As aesthetic innovators, these singers have contributed to a distinct Yafiʿi "color" *(lawn),* as it became known in national culture after independence. According to a standard account of Yemeni song first articulated by cultural reformers, this color exists alongside at least four others: Sanaani, Laheji, Adeni, and Hadrami.[52] The political utility of identifying five regions of song that were discrete, although equally commensurate with each other, has been noted by ethnomusicologist Jean Lambert, who suggests that the postindependence "coloring" of song helped alleviate certain regional imbalances in South Yemeni politics by extending a common cultural heritage to Aden's growing rural labor force, many of whom originated from the somewhat removed southern highlands, especially Yafiʿ.[53] According to this model of national song, the terms of which developed just as cassettes were becoming household items for many Yemenis, the contributions of the three Yafiʿi singers took place on an even, national tableau.

As a trope of metropolitan acculturation, however, the tableau's particular moral value for Yemenis may lie less in its graphic than its nongraphic aspects. In discussions I had with Yemenis, the pigmentation of regional varieties of *lawn* was never mentioned. Indeed, to do so would likely have introduced questions of differentiation and hierarchy—which regions were represented by given colors, comparisons of lightness and darkness, the symbolic content of colors, and so forth—all of which would have been contrary to the inclusive drift of our conversations. In recalling how such song colors were invoked, it seems to me that the very absence of visual pigmentation enabled a tacit recognition that the stable graphics of regional song were less important than the contents of its unfolding sounds. Much as English speakers talk about a song's "color" to suggest the mood that it invokes, *lawn* was a sign of something more subjective than objective, more representative than actual, a creative "model for" some orderly grammar in the world, rather than a precise "model of" it.[54] *Lawn* sometimes means a "type" or "kind," suggesting that it denotes a conventional part of a more abstract whole. Situated between visible and nonvisible worlds, however, the trope also connotes the power of other modes of knowledge, entextualization, and apperception that inform what appears to be common sense. National identity, in short, might be constituted by multiple and contending metropolitan sensibilities.

The moral leverage of this tropic model for song, moreover, depends centrally on a recognition among Yemenis of the importance of media in shaping ideas about nationalism. The power of media to influence ideals about national song was nowhere more salient and controversial than in the case of the Yafiʿi *lawn*. Yafiʿi informants cited much evidence of the historical dissemination of Yafiʿi song without the use of modern media technologies. Some told narratives of their own personal experience with Yafiʿi songs relayed across Yemen by word of mouth, while others invoked accounts of wide-ranging Yafiʿi migrants and sailors such as the legendary Yahya ʿUmar, one of the most influential singers in South Arabia before the 1940s.[55] Nevertheless, as Yafiʿis confront a broader consensus over regionally marked colors of Yemeni song, they also routinely find that their own contributions are framed as largely a media phenomenon that lacks the historical depth of the others.[56] Southern nationalist singer Muhammad Naji credits Odeon records with first introducing Yafiʿi song to audiences outside of the region in the years before World War II.[57] Others cite the contributions of prominent urban recording stars from Yemen or the Gulf to popularizing Yafiʿi song in Yemen and abroad.[58] And for those attuned to political folk poetry, cassettes are widely recognized to have played an important role in disseminating Yafiʿi song in recent decades. Yafiʿis have no reason to doubt that their songs are rooted in longstanding indigenous practices of customary dance, poetry, and performance. Nevertheless, the translation of such songs into the public register of *lawn* is frequently accompanied by speculation about the politics of technological mediation and the role of the media in shaping an authentic Yafiʿi identity.

THE YAFIʿI CASSETTE SHOP: *A PIECE OF MY LAND* AND *THAMŪD EXHIBITION*

As a small-scale, decentralized site for producing and marketing vernacular song, the cassette shop is a crucial link between broader circuits of commercialized song and the social, economic, and interpretive inclinations of local producers and consumers. Shops that specialize in Yafiʿi folk poetry are not impersonal consumer outlets; they are places for communal interaction, patronage, camaraderie, and news for both producers and consumers. A short ethnographic study of several cassette shops demonstrates how the regional "coloring" of song is a process and not merely the by-product of an unchanging nationalist palette. Shop managers' talents in orchestrating the production and release of cassettes prove especially important in translating the metropolitan aesthetics of a commercial recording industry into more familiar discursive and textual habits that define moral authority in the highlands. As active brokers of song, however, managers also subtly recontextualize customers' views of authoritative verse. By encouraging customers to situate highland oral tradition and epistolary exchange in relation to more encompassing frameworks of state history, nationalism, and popular musical trends, managers promote the entextualizing authority of singers and shop managers and also help conditionalize the cassette as a powerful force of verbal inscription.

The earliest cassette shops in Yafiʿ opened for business in the mid-1970s. They appeared in the region's largest commercial centers (several in Labʿūs and one in Ruṣd) and sold eight-track cassette tapes to a small but growing pool of consumers. As cassette technologies became more affordable, other shops opened for business in remoter areas. Today, there are approximately a dozen cassette shops in the region (several of which specialize in Islamic cassettes), as well as a number of dry-goods stores that stock small selections of cassettes on an irregular basis. Although the low number of shops might suggest a relatively limited consumer base, several factors weigh against such a conclusion. Most important, a single purchased cassette is rarely enjoyed by a single listener alone but is played repeatedly among family members and large gatherings. Often, such a cassette is quickly passed around to different households and eventually given away to friends and acquaintances, especially if it features poetry that deals with recent events. Additionally, the duplication or "piracy" of cassettes on home recording machines is extremely common, especially in rural areas where budgets are tight and transportation to shops is limited.[59] Single cassettes purchased in a shop are often reduplicated in multiple copies for friends. Finally, this number represents only the rural Yafiʿi cassette shops. Some of the most vigorous sales of Yafiʿi cassettes occur at two shops in Aden, the city where tens of thousands of Yafiʿis live in permanent or part-time residence and where rural Yafiʿis frequently visit to conduct personal or business affairs. Both of these shops are located in downtown Aden and are called A Piece of My Land *(Qiṭʿah Min Baladī)* and Thamūd Exhibition *(Maʿriḍ Thamūd)*. These two shops are the principal suppliers of Yafiʿi cassettes to other cassette shops in Yafiʿ and elsewhere in Yemen, especially Sanaa.

A Piece of My Land is without a doubt the oldest and most active Yafiʿi cassette shop and has become legendary among fans of Yafiʿi song and poetry both in Yemen and abroad. An introduction to the shop and its owner-manager provides a glimpse of the Yafiʿi cassette shop as an extraordinary locus of social mediation (see figure 3.3). A Piece of My Land was opened by ʿAli Muḥammad al-Ḥāj in 1968, a year after the south achieved independence. Haj was the son of a leading judge *(qāḍī)* in Mawsaṭah, Yafiʿ Bani Mālek, a man who had received extensive training in Muslim jurisprudence in Tarīm, Hadramawt, and later Cairo. Earlier that year, however, a sharp leftist swing initiated by members of the National Liberation Front in the highlands swept up his father and family in a wave of hostility directed against families of tribal shaikhs, sultans, and traditional learned notables. His father was stripped of his rank, and a decree was passed that nullified any legal contract or document that he had ever signed. With his father's career in ruins and resentment brewing, Haj struck out for Aden in search of better opportunities to earn a living. Unable to pursue his father's path as a man of letters, Haj looked for innovative ways to continue his family's long commitment to knowledge and community service.

Lacking the capital to buy even the smallest apartment, Haj sold an inheritance, a small plot of family land, to his brother,

Figure 3.3. Cassette fans gather outside A Piece of My Land cassette shop, in downtown Aden, 2006. The author is on the left.

who had remained in Yafiʿ. He then established his cassette shop in a small room that opened onto a busy Aden square where urban and rural passers-by still gather to board buses and taxis. He named his shop *Qiṭʿah Min Baladī*, A Piece of My Land, a name that commemorated the inheritance that he had been forced to sacrifice to start his business and captured the postin-

Figure 3.4. Shop owner ʿAli Bal Ḥāj and his nephew inside A Piece of My Land, 1997. Photographs of Yafiʿi singers and personalities hang above them.

dependence mood of the day. Downtown Aden also had shops named A Piece of Paris, A Piece of New York, and A Piece of London, but Haj's business expressed a new nationalist sentiment whose iconography was decidedly local (see figure 3.4).

Walking through the front door of A Piece of My Land, the customer sees a large poster of New York City's Roosevelt

Bridge, which sometimes is used as a studio backdrop for traditionally clad Yafiʿi musicians, poets, and dignitaries who want to be photographed with an emblem of a highly esteemed world metropolis. Other poster backdrops feature fanciful Indian landscapes. Across the walls hang old photographs of Indian film actresses, famous Gulf singers, and even the father of Arab nationalism, former Egyptian president Gamal ʿAbd al-Nāṣer. Most eclectic of all are the cassette cases that climb from floor to ceiling in little wooden shelves, sprawl across tabletops, and lurk beneath glass counters. This vast stock of sound recordings merely hints at the extraordinarily diverse tastes that Aden's customers have cultivated over a half century. They seek early Adeni recording stars, Tihāman *mawwāl* troupes, Hadrami wits, Yemeni Jewish singers, Egyptian prima donnas, Somali bands and itinerant musicians, Laheji and Abyani tribal dance music, tribal songs from northern areas such as Dhamār, Khawlān, Sanaa, and Mā'rib, nationalist anthems from the days of the People's Democratic Republic of Yemen, radio programs and news from major periods of southern Yemeni history, classical *takht* performances from television, Saudi stars, Jordanian folk songs, B. B. King, the Beejees, Qur'anic recitations, religious sermons, live recordings of weddings, and *bāl* events from every corner of southern Yemen. A customer confronted with such a recording archive might well conclude that the "piece of land" to which the shop gave access was anything but provincial.

Yafiʿi cassettes of folk song and poetry are the shop's largest source of revenue, a regional predilection that is sometimes readily apparent to visitors. When one customer dropped in to inquire about the kinds of cassettes that were for sale, Haj's quick reply "Yafiʿi!" signaled clearly the products and services that have become privileged. Although this customer left the shop when hearing Haj's response, most customers who come to A Piece of My Land are interested in Yafiʿi cassettes, which are stocked in large quantities on the nearest shelves and arranged for accessibility on the front counter. Many copies of the politically charged cassettes of singers Husain ʿAbd al-Naser, ʿAli Ṣāleḥ, and ʿAli Bin Jāber are visible. Indeed, popular demand for such recordings has increased notably in recent years. After the easing of restrictions on political expression that followed unification in 1990 and especially after the civil turbulence unleashed by the Yemeni War of 1994, many Yafiʿi folk poets and singers have become famous for using cassettes as podiums for political reform (see chapter 1). And their cassettes stimulate a broader interest in Yafiʿi song in general. In 1998, approximately 90 percent of the cassettes sold at A Piece of My Land featured Yafiʿi poets and singers.[60]

Haj explained to me that Yafiʿi cassettes have sold well in recent years but that his shop had specialized in sung Yafiʿi folk poetry from its initial establishment. In many ways, A Piece of My Land reflected his own passion for his homeland and for Yafiʿi poetry and song. A poet himself, Haj had grown up chanting poems for friends and select audiences while he tapped a simple mettle drum *(tanak)*. His father, the judge, had also been a poet and had taught him to distinguish good verse from poor. When I visited the shop, Haj sometimes wanted to share poems with me and would drag a dusty folder from his shelves, becoming so absorbed in the poems that customers wandered in and out of his shop unattended. "I have always been a fan of eloquent language *(kalām faṣīh)*, especially exchanged *qaṣīdahs,*" he told me. "I love to hear a strong initiation and then wait in suspense for the response. How will the poet possibly respond to such an assault?" The finest poets were those who could not only respond aggressively, if needed, but could also keep their compositions respectful *(sharīf)*, not vilifying their opponents through rank insult or vulgarity. "The best poems are those that people can learn something from." Poems could teach moral lessons or "wisdom" *(ḥikmah)*. But poems could also teach people about history and its bearing on the present: "People who want to understand relations of power today look to relations of power in the past for explanations, and poetry can help people return to the past." When I asked Haj about the role of cassettes in enabling such a use of poetry, he replied, "Well, cassettes are in many ways preferable to written poems. When handwriting is poor, for example, written poems are sometimes difficult to read. Moreover, paper becomes torn and worn out over time. For these reasons, cassettes make poetry more receivable."

Supplied with his cassette shop and knowledge of his region and its folk traditions, Haj has become known as a patron of Yafiʿi cultural heritage *(turāth)*. One of his most influential roles has been as a collaborator with singers. Haj encourages singers to record their material and send their cassettes to him, informs them about what has been selling well, makes recommendations about themes to emphasize and possible musical arrangements, and often steers poems and poets to them. His collaboration with poets is also considerable and sometimes involves recording interviews on cassettes that he subsequently sells from his shop. By remaining open to a diverse community of producers, Haj attracts lesser known amateur singers and poets to his shop and often sells their home-recorded cassettes free of commission. In fact, Haj is convinced that cassettes have contributed to a general improvement in cultural life that has stimulated the practice of folk poetry in Yemen: "There is more production of poetry than there used to be before the revolution. Compared with those days, there is more prosperity now."

The sense of communal vitality is readily apparent in the camaraderie that characterizes business at the shop. In the late morning or early evening, the shop's front door is usually wedged with customers who are listening to samples of requested songs played on the shop's speakers, and crowds often assemble outside to hear cassettes that have just been released. On many occasions, commerce takes a back seat to socializing between acquaintances, migrants who have returned home to visit, elders with stories from the countryside, younger singers, and poets. Celebrated cassette poets regularly visit the shop and receive special welcome with an old metal stool that is produced for them to sit on. Since such poets provide the political substance to what is ultimately sung, crowds frequently gather to chat with them, gather their perspective on events, and occasionally listen to their live recitations of recent poems, which they read aloud from their notebooks. A Piece of My Land has become a revered destination for countless Yafiʿis as well as other fans of Yemen's expressive heritage, regardless of birthplace, class, or gender. As Haj told a non-Yafiʿi customer who entered the shop one morning: "There's no difference between one place and another. This is about Yemen."

A Piece of My Land is not the only cassette shop in Aden that specializes in Yafiʿi song and folk poetry. A second shop, Thamūd Exhibition, is located on the same street. Thamūd is a larger shop that offers more varied products, including Indonesian waistcloths *(fūṭahs),* turbans *(mushaddahs),* and shirts. Its clientele is more diverse than that of A Piece of My Land and includes a higher proportion of young men and women who seek popular music cassettes produced by major recording companies in Yemen and the Gulf. The shop's up-market appeal is reflected in its location in Aden's busiest merchandising blocks and in the large numbers of customers who regularly drift in and out.

The owner of the shop, Saʿid al-Khalīfī, is not from Yafiʿ but from Shabwah (some 120 miles northeast of Yafiʿ). He was drawn to Yafiʿi folk music when he lived in Jeddah, Saudi Arabia, and worked as an employee at the cassette shop named Stereo al-Aṭlāl (later Stereo Shamsān). The shop there catered to Yemeni migrants and, like A Piece of My Land, specialized in folk song. Using his savings and his experiences with the cassette industry in Jeddah, Khalifi has been able to undertake more professional recording ventures than Haj. He marketed some of Salem al-Baraʿi's first cassettes, for example, which he recorded himself during trips to Yemen and Yafiʿ specifically. In 1976, he returned to Aden to open Thamūd Exhibition and began offering Yafiʿi consumers high-quality recordings of their favorite folk singers. Today, Thamūd Exhibition is managed by several of Khalifi's sons, who share their father's expert knowledge of Yafiʿi and Yemeni heritage. As in A Piece of My Land, lively discussions frequently are held in Thamūd Exhibition. Customers talk about recent releases, the events associated with them, singers, poets, and other affairs related to the general community of cassette fans.

Despite the overlapping interests and aims of ʿAli al-Haj and Saʿid al-Khalifi, their business relations remain close. If a new Yafiʿi cassette arrives at one of the shops, it will quickly be passed to the other, and a similar cooperation is demonstrated when one shop runs out of a given cassette. Thamūd Exhibition may have slightly closer links with some of the migrant producers, singers, and poets in the Gulf, given Khalifi's personal contacts, but A Piece of My Land maintains a loyal customer base among Yafiʿis throughout Yemen.

SOCIALIZING WITH CASSETTES

In a radically decentralized recording market where cassette duplication is rampant and fans are constantly wooed by large commercial production companies, both Haj and the Khalifis understand the benefits of working together to build a community of loyal customers. Such a task requires keeping in touch with the concerns, needs, and preferences of the Yafiʿi community and providing a unique set of services. To understand the operations of folk-poetry cassette shops, I spent twenty-two hours in A Piece of My Land and additional hours in Exhibition Thamūd and other cassette shops in Yafiʿ and Sanaa, observing interactions between managers and clients.[61] I found that each shop's business aims are achieved through small acts repeated constantly throughout the day and through a pursuit of grander visions.

The most important service to customers is providing access to a regular supply of topical and finely crafted vernacular poetry sung by the most popular Yafiʿi singers. Such service requires shop managers to be intimately familiar with regional issues and events and competent in selecting and promoting the kinds of verses that customers prefer. Haj is most capable in these respects, given that he is native to Yafiʿ and also a prominent social leader there. In fact, Haj provides members of his district with legal expertise, which he learned from his father. He has also served as a mediator in legal disputes and assistant to his young nephew, who was appointed shaikh in the district after unity in 1990. Returning to his village, sometimes for several weeks, to assist the shaikh and attend to the social and political affairs of his district, Haj has been able to keep abreast of pressing issues throughout Yafiʿ. Such knowledge translates directly into his work in the cassette shop when choices must be made about cassettes to market, singers to promote, poems to send to singers, and so forth. The Khalifis are less well connected with people and events in Yafiʿ, although their frequent visits home to Shabwah give them special insights into the concerns of rural Yemenis in general. Nevertheless, they too manage to keep informed through contact with Yafiʿi acquaintances and customers in Aden and as well as with old friends in Jeddah.

One of the most direct benefits of keeping in touch with the Yafiʿi community in Yemen and abroad is the cultivation of relations with the region's top singers, the suppliers who can make or break each shop's business. Both Haj and the Khalifis maintain regular contact with singers to keep abreast of upcoming releases, arrange deliveries of cassettes, and inform them about audiences' preferred poets, topics, genres, musical styles, and so forth. Singers often recognize the patronage of each shop at the beginning of their cassettes. Shop managers also occasionally arrange recording sessions, which can take place in private residences in Aden or at major holiday festivals, celebrations, weddings, or dispute-settlement events in Yafiʿ. Alternatively, they may assemble "greatest-hit" medleys that feature given singers' renditions of fiery *qaṣīdah* exchanges between the most popular poets or else retrospective medleys of *qaṣīdahs* composed forty to two hundred years ago. Given that some of the most prolific producers of Yafiʿi song specialize in political lyrics and, as a result, do not ask for much payment for their cassettes, cultivating relations of patronage with prominent singers is an especially important task.

To promote folk-poetry sales among diverse audiences, shop managers use their extensive experience and knowledge to "improve" the cassettes they receive with adjustments of their own. Thamūd Exhibition has developed a basic cassette jacket with the shop's name and a calligraphic stamp that advertises the releases of "The artist *(fannān)* Husain ʿAbd al-Naser." A Piece of My Land's cassettes are sold without jackets, but Haj has become proficient in recording his own vocal tags at the beginning of cassettes ("Khāledī's head is still held high! A Piece of My Land recordings, Aden, Crater, if you please!") and in adding more elaborate clarifications when needed. On one cassette, for example, when a singer confides that he does not know the name of the poet whose work he is about to sing, Haj cuts in with a recorded excerpt of his own in which he announces the name of the poet and his origins. On other cassettes, Haj occasionally adds lengthier commentaries about featured poets and their families and backgrounds, brief synopses of events discussed in given poems, and his own opinions and plugs for exceptional poems. Since the density of expression and parochial referential frameworks of some poems can obstruct comprehension by even native Yafiʿis and Yemenis, Haj's clarifications render poems more understandable. And since many people purchase Yafiʿi cassettes for their poignant political commentary as much as for their entertainment value, Haj's modifications make the cassettes released by A Piece of My Land especially popular.

Shop managers' expertise in regional culture and politics is reflected both in product design and in archival service: each shop contains huge collections of specialized recordings that cannot be found elsewhere.[62] Not infrequently, customers come to their shops looking for specific poems, some of them composed decades or more earlier. Even more challenging, their only references to poems may be the name of the poet and a single strophe or verse. Thus, in asking for a *bidʿ wa jiwāb* exchange that occurred in the mid-1980s, one customer asked: "Can you sell me the Ṣunbaḥī-Khaledi exchange? You know, the one with the riddle about the television and the watch?" Haj's and the Khalifis' vast knowledge of southern Yemeni folk poetry and their familiarity with the contents of their collections enable them to address even the more arcane requests with exceptional acumen.

Customer service is a function of having contacts, experience, and archival expertise and also of addressing customers' needs. When sitting in the shops, I was often amazed at how much effort managers devoted to making a single sale to customers who had specific requests and also to those who were uncertain about what they wanted. In the following exchange, a customer demanded the manager's full attention as he tried to decide between a variety of recordings:

Customer: Anything new of Khaledi?
Manager: No.
Customer: Thabit 'Awaḍ? *(The manager places the cassette featuring this Yafiʿī poet into the machine and plays an excerpt. The customer listens to several verses, then asks:)* Is there a response? *(The manager shakes his head.)* What about the Ḥajjājī [poet]. Qutannā's latest? *(The manager takes a cassette from the shelf and plays it on the machine.)* There's not a more recent one? *(The manager again shakes his head. The customer pauses and then says:)* And Bin Ṭwaīreq? *(The manager again finds a selection of the older Yafiʿī singer and plays it. The customer immediately frowns:)* No, no. *(The manager then stops the cassette and replaces it with a release by Husain 'Abd al-Naser that was several years old. After a minute, the customer asks:)* Is there a response to this? *(The manager nods this time, so the customer continues listening. He then asks:)* Is this Khaledi?
A second customer in the shop: No. this is ʿUlafī.
The friend of the first customer: Hold on a second, let me listen. *(After the next set of verses, the customer becomes satisfied, and a sale is made.)*

As this series of turns illustrates, customers' requests can be complex when they are looking for specific poets or singers and even particular themes or verses. Here it was not enough that a cassette featured recent poems, political lyrics, the *bid' wa jiwāb* genre, or verses of a specific singer: a cassette had to feature all of these before the customer was willing to make a purchase. Some customers spend up to an hour lingering in the shop to listen to selections of songs and find a rare old poem that speaks to a matter of concern. But since Haj and the Khalifis have built their reputations on archival expertise, they have become accustomed to working closely with customers to address their individual needs.

When a new cassette is released, individual sales become less labor-intensive, although satisfying popular demand becomes exhausting in other ways. As dozens of customers squeeze in and out of the shop, each shouting requests and passing money over the heads of those in front, managers are faced with a barrage of tasks that includes making change, answering questions, playing samples on one and sometimes two cassette players simultaneously, searching the shelves for cassettes, making extra copies on the copy machine in back, writing down numbers on cassettes to distinguish them, and varying the songs played on the sidewalk speakers to attract new customers. Business hours extend six to seven hours a day, six days a week. In the summer, when temperatures in Aden climb to 90 degrees Fahrenheit with high humidity, the task of satisfying customers becomes grueling. Nevertheless, the business of maintaining a loyal clientele is important when people look for diversions to help them get through their days.

Despite the rigors of maintaining levels of production and sales, one of the keys to securing customer satisfaction and building a larger client base is to ensure that customers affiliate with the shop and its products. A customer should feel welcomed when he or she enters the store, and special friends and regular customers receive the sincerest greetings, usually accompanied with chat, news and jokes, and sometimes considerable discounts: cassette prices can be reduced by a quarter to a third of their regular prices or given away free of charge. Ideally, all customers should be made to feel personally invested in the products that the shop has to offer.

A large part of cultivating a clientele involves persuading customers that their interests are addressed in a unique way by the products available in the store. A survey of customer requests that I conducted suggests the nature of interests that shop managers must address. Most remarkable is the priority that customers give to poets over singers. In 114 initial requests by customers that I documented, thirty-one began with the mention of a specific poet's name (28 percent of total), and twelve of these were for the Yafiʿi poet Shayef al-Khaledi (11 percent of total) in particular. By contrast, eighteen requests were made for specific Yafiʿi singers (16 percent of total).[63] The discursive content of cassettes, in other words, is considered more important than song virtuosity by a ratio of nearly two to one. This preference is evident in the conversation between the customer and the manager cited above. After initially asking for Khaledi, the customer pursues more recent releases by other leading political poets from Yafiʿ and beyond (the Hajjaji poet is from Damt, northern Yemen). In his indecision about what to purchase, the customer requests a specific singer known for his early tribal verse. However, he again asks about poets, eventually abandons his quest for the latest releases, and settles on an exchange between two famous poets released several years earlier that may yet speak to his interest in current affairs.

Customers' tendency to privilege poets over singers reflects broader hierarchies of moral authority that continue to define public politics in the highlands, as discussed earlier in the chapter. Such hierarchies are coded textually in *bidʿ wa jiwāb* verse and in the genre's social embedding in the ongoing transformations of highlands political life, as is explored in chapter 2. Within such a conventional order, singers have long had to pursue their craft with delicacy, especially when performing in public and lacking the social credentials of religious notability. Nevertheless, in recent decades singers have also become vested with new kinds of public authority. As their contributions became increasingly ratified by nationalism and cultural reforms during the revolution and especially after independence in 1967, they became representatives of the metropolitan competences, aspirations, and harmonious "colors" of Yemen's diverse citizenry. Moreover, their currency of moral value remains more aural than oral: they offer products that are to be heard rather than memorized and reiterated in like acoustic measure. Indeed, as I suggest in the next chapter, their products require that their own authorship be downplayed to preserve the moral integrity of poets, whose discursive authority remains paramount. Even as singers draw audiences to cassette shops with the promise of an enjoyable metropolitan aesthetic, their authority is best delivered morally intact. It is precisely this challenge that shop managers face in winning customer loyalty: how to carefully bracket singers' newfound public agency even while marketing their sonorous invitations to new, more generalized aural subjects.

The tact with which cassette-shop managers handle such attunement is particularly evident when managers lack credentials in the traditional order of highland political discourse, as in the following exchange that took place in Thamūd Exhibition. In this exchange, the manager (whose home governorate Shabwah lies between Yafiʿ and Hadramawt) builds solidarity with a Yafiʿi consumer through the equivalence of regionalized cultural heritage to which he too can lay claim:

Customer: What do you have of Khaledi's latest? 1

Manager: A cassette released a week ago. He [Khaledi] is from 2 Quʿaīṭi, right?

Customer: Yes, I know him well. He used to come by my uncle's once in a while and smoke the Hadrami water pipe. 3

Manager: They started the Quʿaīṭi state in Hadramawt with the Kathīri, or have you read up? 4

Customer: Yes, I have! I have a *whole* notebook at home stuffed with information about the Quʿaīṭi and Kathīri days. 5

In the first conversational turn, the customer begins with a fairly predictable request. In responding to the customer (line 2), the manager suspects that he is from Yafiʿ and frames a question that is tactfully designed to defer to the customer's authority in regional knowledge. The manager knows where Khaledi is from, but by asking for the customer's opinion, the manager invites a counterresponse in which the customer might share "inside" information derived from his familiarity with Yafiʿi poets and their origins. The manager's bid proves successful: not only does the customer know about Quʿaīṭi, but he has personally sat with Khaledi at his uncle's house. Again, the manager's next turn is similarly designed as a question, though it contains a subtle challenge to the customer concerning his knowledge of pan-southern history.[64] The customer responds (line 5) affirmatively by declaiming his long-time passion for Yafiʿi history and his understanding of Yemeni history. Note that the manager's opening frame of Quʿaīṭi history, established in line 2, predisposes the conversation to move from the authority of provincial highland poets to that of states and particularly toward Yemeni national heritage as documented in the written media of "a whole notebook."

Such conversational routines are instrumental in building solidarity between managers and customers. Part of what makes such routines especially successful is the ease with which they can be applied to typical requests made by customers. As noted earlier in my survey of opening requests, customers' initiations are predictable, which allows managers to recycle such routines easily, expanding questions about the particular origins of given poets or singers into broader conversations about shared backgrounds, experiences, histories, affiliations, and so forth.

Most important, such routines encourage customers to perform their loyalty to the particular "package" that a shop sells to affiliate with discursive communities that share a particular aesthetic coherence. Although references to a customer's origins begin such routines, the customer's broader discursive attunements—practical, textual, informational—become their primary tokens of identity. Thus, as illustrated in the conversation cited above, the customer's competence in history, acquired through word of mouth and also by reading and researching, becomes the particular grounds on which his identity as a Yafiʿi is tested. And where discursive attunement rather than origin can become constitutive of identity, membership in the "community" becomes more achieved than ascribed. As the case of Thamūd Exhibition's Khalifi family suggests, individuals from multiple regional backgrounds can quickly become incorporated within a Yafiʿi history that is inclusive but not altogether rid of its own hierarchies. Despite differences in competence, the performance of achieved identity in such routines underscores a common will to discern the public virtues of cassette poetry. Enjoying sung cassette poems requires audiences to refine their particular discursive habits with an appreciation for broader circuits of national song. Not incidentally, customers show themselves to be competent speakers and good listeners as well.

Even as conversational routines directed by managers can help expand the bounds of discursive community for diverse customers, such routines are also constrained both by the communal identities emphasized in particular shops and by sales. In running shops that operate on margins of profit, however small, sales managers actively incline customers toward communal affiliations that are espoused by the majority of the shop's clients. Horizons of public identity, such as those of national heritage and history, are thus always delineated through ongoing patterns of social interaction that are informed by economic and material activity. At the same time that customers are steered toward more generalized virtues of apperception and listening, however, these virtues also become continuously reembedded in resolute processes of technically mediated social practice. In the interplay between production values and consumption, the moral authority of cassette song is constantly changing and always linked to listeners' evolving dispositions.

Again, managers' sales techniques are central to accomplishing such attunement. In the following case, a customer makes a specific request but is presented with additional options that leave him uncertain and in need of guidance:

Customer: Do you have the latest of Khaledi and Sunbahi? 1

Manager: Sure. We have a recent release with both poets on 2
one cassette. *(The manager takes the cassette off the shelf. As he returns, he adds a caveat:)*

The only thing is, Sunbahi's exchange is with a Khawlāni poet 3
[near Sanaa]. And Khaledi has his own, separate *qaṣīdah*. *(The customer hesitates, appearing uncertain. Seeing his indecision, the manager makes a suggestion:)*

What about the latest ʿAli Saleh cassette, with Khaledi and 4
Ḥunaīsh? It's sweet. You might really like it. *(The customer takes his advice and purchases the ʿAli Saleh cassette.)*

When he hears the customer's request for Khaledi followed by the name of the northern Yemeni poet Ahmad al-Sunbahi, the manager responds affirmatively (line 2) and fetches a cassette. However, suspecting that the customer might be seeking a *bidʿ wa jiwāb* exchange between the two poets, who are widely known for their fiery exchanges about Yafiʿi regional prowess, the manager adds a caveat (turn 3): the *bidʿ wa jiwāb* on the cassette is between Sunbahi and another northern Yemeni poet and not with Khaledi. Seeing the customer's uncertainty, the manager suspects that he is looking for poems that foreground Yafiʿi or southern communal identity and recommends a second cassette that deals with a recent armed conflict in Yafiʿ and a foreign-affairs imbroglio that had been a source of public embarrassment for the Yemeni administration.[65]

In this exchange, the manager convinces the customer to forgo his original request for a *bidʿ wa jiwāb* exchange between the Sunbahi and Khaledi, the two poets who had become the uncontested verbal heavyweights of the ʿAbd al-Naser series. Instead, the manager steers the customer toward a release by the top-selling singer ʿAli Saleh, whose cassette featured a set of

Yafiʿi *qaṣīdahs* that directly criticized the government's capabilities without recurring to the interregional equivalences of highland poetic debate. ʿAli Saleh's cassettes were tremendously popular for their metropolitan musical style. As a migrant in his mid-thirties living in Jeddah, ʿAli Saleh had become more proficient than ʿAbd al-Naser in his use of creative melodic variations, diverse instrumentation, and the Laheji dance rhythms that were enjoyed in the pop-song industry. Most indicative are the proportionally fewer number of *bidʿ wa jiwāb* poems on his cassettes, compared with those of ʿAbd al-Naser: 28 percent of total poems from 1992 to 1998, as opposed to 71 percent over roughly two decades for ʿAbd al-Naser. ʿAli Saleh, however, remained devoted to vernacular political *qaṣīdahs,* especially in periods of political turmoil during which *bidʿ wa jiwāb* exchanges climb to 80 percent of his recorded poems.[66] Moreover, many of his most famous releases featured the poets who had become known through the ʿAbd al-Naser series. Nevertheless, ʿAli Saleh's more musical, metropolitan style ensured his ascendance as the most frequently requested Yafiʿi recording artist by the mid-1990s, and his community of listeners increasingly dictated the terms for national and public affiliation.

CONCLUSION: THE OBLIGATION OF THE CASSETTE

Although they appreciate internationally renowned pop singers from across the Arab world, Yemenis are passionate about their own homegrown celebrities. Yemenis' patronage of local pop singers is due partly to the country's distinct traditions of song and music and its regional dialects. Indigenous song is also enjoyed because it reminds listeners of the not-so-distant past. In a country that has experienced tremendous social and economic change since its two wars of national independence, Yemeni singers remind listeners of their cultural heritage and its ongoing relevance to contemporary issues. Such customer loyalty ensures the vitality of a decentralized recording industry.

Nostalgia undoubtedly helps explain some of the attraction of Yemeni song for Yemenis. The nostalgic aspects of songs may be especially enjoyed by migrants, many of whom feel distanced from their home communities. But nostalgia does not seem to be the primary motivation for customers who visit folk-poetry cassette shops. For most customers, Yemen's rural past is a mixed record of tragic loss, failure, and stark poverty as well as of honorable achievement and dignity. For southern Yemenis, ambivalence about their rural heritage is closely intertwined with negative ideas about tribalism, a result of the state's efforts to champion its own efforts by contrasting them with the violent and backward tendencies of tribal life. Customers who flock to folk-poetry shops when a new cassette is released likely do so to experience a medial difference from nostalgia and the tribal past. Recorded on cassettes are poets and singers whose voices are still evocative of former times but reverberate with something new from their metropolitan medium.

As a moral resource, cassettes provide sonic analogues that can link the familiar patterns of the human voice to multiple discursive communities and multiple forms of media circulation. For some listeners, such as the customer who sat with Khaledi at his uncle's house, the lyrics of a sung *bidʿ wa jiwāb* poem keep him abreast of the latest perspectives of someone in his own network of oral interaction. For others, especially the non-Yafiʿi shop manager, the lyrics of the same poem affirm the salience of written national history to daily life. Still others hear a vein of political dissent in *bidʿ wa jiwāb* poetry and are led to identify its common register in new styles of musical, metropolitan song that contest normative national claims with reasserted links to highland traditions of agonistic poetry exchange. Whatever the primary social referent of listeners' analogues, this chapter has demonstrated that these analogues resonate together, even within the same listener, and that they are routinely prioritized according to, first, the ongoing demands of social interaction and, second, their relation to a large recording industry that privileges metropolitan song.

The complexity of cassette users' social affiliations presents enormous challenges to any effort to correlate specific forms of media with associated models of modern political identity. Daunted by the sheer creativity of listeners' decoding strategies, I have sought to recur less to the presumptions of "imagined community" invoked by nationalism or even to regionalism's "colors" and more to the interpretive competences that engage listeners as they work together in decoding larger frameworks of identity. In theory, such competences can be achieved by anyone. In actuality, some producers are recognized to have advantages over others by virtue of their affiliations with a metropolitan cassette industry (as was noted in the wedding-party composition event discussed in chapter 1).

In this chapter, I have attended to the shifting technological, material, and social conditions that have informed Yemenis' metropolitan affiliations over a half century. The aesthetics of various forms of media have provided us with signals for Yemenis' expressive tactics over this period. Where signs of restricted writing, music, and song were originally best suited to metropolitan sentiments, orality conveyed dynamic tribal or gnostic intonations. When an expanding sound industry lent audio-recording technologies a new prestige, orality was evaluated according to a wider range of entextualizing practices. Given recording stars' preference for classical or standard varieties of Arabic, the vernacular Arabic spoken by most Yemenis became tarnished as a register of public metropolitan discourse. Nationalist reformers conveyed somewhat more positive views of the potential role of vernacular registers in modern life, especially where such registers could represent, preferably in graphic aesthetics, the "monologue" of a collective popular voice. Most of this chapter has considered the rural redeployment of such metropolitan frameworks, however. Two trends justify this approach: the migration of rural workers to Aden and other major Yemeni cities and the decentralization of the recording industry with the advent of the cassette technologies. Amid such changes, the aesthetics of metropolitanism moved from graphic to more populist scriptive terms. Beside reasserted traditions of writing, written documentation, and metaphysical reflections on the social associations of script, a wider range of authoritative oral vocalities has emerged.

Any overview of changing expressive conditions can lose its moral bearing without firmly connecting to human needs for social engagement, interpretation, and action. My ongoing ethnographic attention to the audiocassette and some of its principal brokers has helped me bring observations on changing historical conditions back to socially mediated practices of entextualization. Many Yemenis appreciate cassettes for accommodating local traditions of song, music, and moral authority, but singers and especially shop managers frequently privilege more general frameworks of state history, nationalism, and popular music as they design and sell cassettes to customers. In the next chapter, such industrial conditioning is shown to become a reflexive resource for Yemenis who seek to preserve and improve the moral and political force of sung cassette poetry.

NOTES

1. Jan Mukarovsky, "The Sound Aspect of Poetic Language," in *On Poetic Language* (Lisse: Peter de Ridder Press, 1976), 34.
2. Interview, June 18, 1998.
3. Jean Lambert, "Musiques régionales et identité nationale," *Révue du Monde Musulman et de la Méditerranée* 67 (1993): 174.
4. Sultan Bin Ṣāleḥ Bin Shaikh ʿAlī Harharah (d. 1900/1286), of the Yafiʿ Bani Mālek moiety, became one of the first *ʿūd*-playing singers in Hadramawt during the late nineteenth century. Khāled al-Qāsimī and Nazār Ghānem, *Judhūr al-Ughniyyah al-Yamaniyyah fī Iʿmāq al-Khalīj,* 2d ed. (Beirut: Dār al-Ḥadāthah, 1993), 106. His songs were spread throughout Hadramawt and were carried by sailors to India and Kuwait. Muḥammad Nājī, *al-Ghinā' al-Yamanī al-Qadīm wa Mashāhīruh* (Kuwait: al-Ṭalīʿah, 1983), 103–04.
5. In the twentieth century, the southern Yemeni amirs Muhsen Bin Aḥmad and Saleh Mahdī were among the most famous of these

singers. Muḥammad Nājī, *Aghānīnā al-Shaʿbiyyah* (Aden: Dār al-Jamāhīr, 1959), 196. The renowned founder of the "Laheji color of song," ʿAbdalī prince Ahmad Bin Faḍl "al-Qumandān," appears not to have sung himself, though he sponsored many virtuoso singers in what would become Yemen's Musical Club of the South.

6. On the Sanaani concerto, see Jean Lambert, *La médecine de l'âme: Le chant de Sanaa dans la société yéménite* (Nanterre: Société d'ethnologie, 1997), 109–115.
7. Jonathan H. Shannon, "Emotion, Performance, and Temporality in Arab Music: Reflections on *Tarab*," *Cultural Anthropology* 18, no. 1 (2003): 87–88.
8. Although *ṣhāḥidh* status is largely a function of genealogical descent, such designations were known to vary in sociopolitical practice. In Yafiʿ, several *shāḥidh* families were known to have held tribal status until they had committed some serious infraction some time before independence. Traditionally, *shāḥidhs* were fairly itinerant, traveling short distances from permanent hamlets where they were guaranteed legal protection by host tribes. See Paul Dresch, *Tribes, Government, and History in Yemen* (New York: Oxford University Press, 1989), 118–20; Robert Serjeant, "Société et gouvernement en Arabie du Sud," *Arabica* 14, no. 3 (1967): 284–97; and Carlo de Landberg, *Études sur les dialectes de l'Arabie méridionale: Haḍramoût* (Leiden: E. J. Brill, 1901), 1:145.
9. The *ṭāsah* and *ṭabal* drums are used especially for the tribal *barʿah* dance and *zāmil* performances. The former is a round, deep drum, and the latter is a long drum that is held horizontally and struck on both ends. The *tanak* is a crude metal tambourine that is typically used to accompany the recitation of longer *qaṣīdahs*.
10. Lambert, *La médecine,* 49.
11. Jihad Racy, whose dissertation remains one of the most insightful analyses of the early recording industry in the Middle East, observes that records first reached customers in the Middle East in 1904. Ali Jihad Racy, "Record Industry and Egyptian Traditional Music: 1904–1932," *Ethnomusicology* 20, no. 1 (1976): 25. Cairo saw the quickest proliferation of recording companies, most of them British-owned. By the end of World War I, such companies were offering a large selection of Egyptian music as well as music

from Syria, Lebanon, Turkey, and Europe. During the 1930s, the industry's consolidation led to the intensified promotion of popular celebrities throughout the Arab world. See ibid.; and Salwa C. El-Shawan, "Some Aspects of the Cassette Industry in Egypt," *The World of Music* 24, no. 2 (1987): 33.

12. The virtuoso of this genre was ʿAli Abu Bakr Bā Sharāḥīl, who regularly recorded for Odeon, but others like Muhammad and Ibrahim al-Mās, Ahmad ʿAwaḍ al-Jarrāsh, and his pupil Muhammad ʿAbd al-Rahman al-Makkāwī were also popular. The poets who composed Sanaani songs were mostly from elite religious families and included Muhammad Sharaf al-Dīn, ʿAbd al-Rahman al-Ānisī, and ʿAli al-Khafanjī, all of whom composed written *ḥumaīnī* verse.
13. Muḥammad Ghānem, *Shiʿr al-Ghinā' al-Sanʿānī* (Damascus: Dār al-ʿAwdah, 1987), 36.
14. Classical Arab and India music made inroads into southern Yemen quite early through Indian cinema entrepreneurs. As early as 1919, ʿAbd al-ʿAziz Khān converted a tool shed in Aden's Tawāḥī district into Yemen's first cinema, and other cinemas followed elsewhere in Aden and in Mukallā. *al-Thaqāfat al-Yamaniyyah: Rūʾiyyah Mustaqbiliyyah* (Sanaa: Ministry of Culture and Tourism, 1991), 261–67. Yemeni singers of middle-class backgrounds were able to afford tickets, and by the 1940s, Ahmad al-Qaʿṭabī and Yusef ʿAbd al-Ghanī had become known for adapting Egyptian and Indian film melodies to popular Yemeni songs.
15. The most popular singer recorded for Odeon was Muhammad al-Bār, who was from a sayyid family in Wādī Doʿān, Hadramawt. He recorded from his home in Indonesia, often to the accompaniment of a full orchestra. Robert Serjeant, *Prose and Poetry from Hadhramawt* (London: Taylor's Foreign Press, 1951), 51. Songs of Yahya ʿUmar, one of the most famous of South Arabian singers and a Yafiʿi of Hadrami birth, were also frequently recorded by Odeon, as were those of a number of other leading Yemeni folk musicians, including Ibrahim and Muhammad al-Mās, ʿAli Bu Bakr Bā Sharāḥīl, and Husain al-Sūrī.
16. Singers were paid substantial sums of up to 100 rupees per recording session. Recordings were pressed in England and released on either Gold or Purple labels, depending on price.
17. Founded by young musicians of middle- and upper-class families,

such as Khalil Muḥammad Khalīl, ʿAli Amān, Yahya Makkī, and Jamil ʿUthmān Ghānem, all of whom had formally studied music in either Cairo or Baghdad, the club trained young musicians in the fine arts, organized events and parties where they could perform, and helped negotiate contracts.

18. Kāyāphone's influence is documented by Taha Farʿa, *Lamaḥāt min Ta'rīkh al-Ughniyyah al-Yamaniyyah al-Ḥadīthah* (Aden: Dār al-Hamdānī, 1985), 21. Three years after the Adeni Music Club was started, the Adeni Musical Union *(al-Rābiṭat al-Mūsīqiyyat al-ʿAdaniyyah)* was founded by Muhammad ʿAbduh Ghānem and became another center for musical innovation and training. Khāled al-Qāsemī and Nazār Ghānem, *al-Ughniyyah al-Yamaniyyah al-Khalījiyyah* (al-Sharqah: Dār al-Thaqāfah al-ʿArabiyyah, 1993), 161–62. Like the club, the union was patronized by its own recording company, the Arabian South Company *(Shārikat al-Janūb al-ʿArabī)*.
19. Fred Halliday, *Arabia without Sultans: A Political Survey of Instability in the Arab World* (New York: Penguin, 1975), 192–93.
20. Idrīs Hanbalah, *Al-Majmūʿat al-Kāmilah* (Aden: Mu'assasat 14 Uktūbir, n.d.), 271.
21. Abdallah Bujra, "Urban Elites and Colonialism: The Nationalist Elites of Aden and South Arabia." *Middle East Studies* 6, no. 2 (1970): 193.
22. Calculations based on Bujra (ibid., 211).
23. Aḥmad al-Qaṣīr, *al-Yaman: al-Hijrah wa-l-Tanmiyyah* (Cairo: Dār al-Thaqāfah al-Jadīdah, 1985), 76.
24. The decade of the 1950s witnessed the most dramatic nationalist successes across the Middle East. In Egypt, the British withdrew in 1952, and four years later the Suez Canal was nationalized. In Algeria, the war of independence against France began in 1954 and would conclude seven years later. In 1958, the United Arab Republic between Egypt, Syria, and Yemen was formed.
25. Nājī, *Aghānīnā al-Shaʿbiyyah,* 167.
26. Farʿa, *Lamaḥāt min Ta'rīkh,* 69.
27. Cited in Nājī, *Aghānīnā al-Shaʿbiyyah,* 161. These verses were originally composed and sung by ʿUmar Maḥfūẓ Ghābah. I have translated them very liberally, trying to maintain their playful end-verse rhyme sequence (aa/bbb/a/ccc/a) in an effort to capture a sense of the vernacular *joi de vivre* that the *mūnūlūj* poem fre-

quently conveyed. In homage to the ironic spirit of the "monologue," I offer the original text to those who wish to propose a better translation:

mawātir ashkāl w-alwān	wa lakin agwā' b-ākhir az-zamān
tuwdī rās mālik kulluh	taqūl yā qahwāgī shalluh
tagīb luh ḍamīn lammā maḥalluh	yaqūl lak wa fī bi-l-gīrān
shahraīn min-uh tiksib	law mā ad-draīwal yil'ab
thālith shahr at'aggib	'ind al-agnīr qaduh khirbān

28. On *sharḥ* dance, see Lambert, "Musiques régionales," 178.
29. In verses made famous over several decades of north-south tension, 'Abdalī emphasizes the political merit of a distinct southern orality over a more rarified vein of northern metropolitan song, which he equates with an apricot syrup *('uqyān)* drunk by Sanaani Jews on holidays: "Sing the anthem of the nation's people, O shepherd. / Sing the voice of *dān* [poetry]. / We want nothing of Yemen's Sanaani song, / A branch of apricot syrup."
30. When record companies had trouble locating well-known itinerant rural musicians, they turned to younger urban men who originated from selected regions or who were at least versant with certain dialects and could reach rural audiences. Saleh 'Antarī, Hamed al-Qāḍī, Yusef 'Abd al-Ghanī, and Ahmad al-Qa'ṭabī were all such musicians who became known for singing Yafi'i song to the accompaniment of the *'ūd.*
31. During the late 1950s, the importation of radios into Aden grew over 1,000 percent at the following rate: 1956: 13,645; 1957: 14,963; 1958: 18,215; 1959: 46,572; 1960: 86,701; 1961: 137,509. Approximately 10 percent of radios imported during 1956 were shipped to rural protectorate areas. R. J. Gavin, *Aden under British Rule, 1839–1967* (New York: Barnes & Noble Books, 1975), 439–40 note 44.
32. Begun in 1952, *The Voice of the Arabs* probably became, for most rural Yemenis in the 1950s, the single most important source of information about pan-Arab ideology and anti-imperialist sentiment. Abdallah Bujra, "Political Conflict and Stratification in Hadramaut," *Middle Eastern Studies* 3–4 (1966–1967): 355–75; Douglas A. Boyd, *Egyptian Radio: Tool of Political and National Development* (Lexington, Ky.: Association for Education in Journalism, 1977). Indeed, this and other Naserist radio stations ap-

pear to have played key roles in the initial resistance that many South Yemeni sultans expressed to Britain's plans for a federation. Bujra, "Political Conflict," 192. For colonial documents describing Britain's consternation over the influence of Egyptian radio, see Doreen Ingrams, *Records of Yemen* (Chippenham: Archive Editions, 1993), 15:602, 622–23, 701–06.

33. Ḥusaīn Bā Salīm, *Idhā'at 'Adan: 42 'Āman fī Khidmat al-Mustami'* (Aden: 14 Uktūbir, 1996), 14.
34. A survey of monthly program guides from the years 1959 to 1961 provides a sample of the station's output. Approximately half of the programming features classical songs by the Arab world's major stars as well as Western classical music. The rest of the programming features Yemeni singers, both older recording stars as well as rising talent. Prominent among these are male singers such as Abu Bakr Sālem Bā al-Faqīh and Muhammed Naji, both of whom were especially successful in addressing the metropolitan aspirations of rural audiences, and also some of the recording industry's first female singers, including Umm al-Khair al-'Ajamī, Fathiyyah al-Ṣaghīrah, and Sabah Munaṣṣer, all of whom were from upper-class urban backgrounds.
35. Benedict Anderson, *Imagined Communities: Reflections on the Origin and Spread of Nationalism* (New York: Verso, 1983).
36. *Hunā 'Adan* (Aden: South Arabian Broadcasting Service, May 1961).
37. Sumanta Banerjee, *Audiocassettes: The User Medium* (Paris: UNESCO, 1977). The world-renowned Philips machine was the earliest open-reel model, but locally manufactured alternatives quickly reached the market. A variety of epithets were invented for the machines as they spread across the country: the *Sīrah* model, named after a neighborhood in Aden, "the box" *(al-ṣundūq)*, "the pick-up" *(al-bikup)*, the "hasty-one" *(al-'ajal)*, "Mr. Spin" *(Abu Liff)*, and, most commonly, "the reel" *(al-raīl)*. As a recording machine, the open-reel technology became more affordable for non-professional producers after 1960, when low-cost transistor circuits replaced the vacuum-tube amplifier (ibid., 20).
38. Some audiences were still using the eight-track cartridge as late as the mid-1970s.
39. The first cassettes of this generation were made by the Netherlands-based company Philips. To ensure standardization of the

cassette format, Philips gave up the manufacturing rights to anyone wanting to produce cassettes, provided they use Philips specifications. The result today is complete standardization and interchangeability of any cassette in any part of the world (Banerjee, *Audiocassettes,* 20). By 1970, Japanese companies had geared for the mass production of cassettes and cassette-recording equipment and were spearheading the popular use of cassettes worldwide. Peter Manuel, *Cassette-Culture: Popular Music and Technology in North India* (Chicago: University of Chicago Press, 1993), 28.

40. These cassettes were produced by three of the most popular rural Yafiʿi singers during the 1940s to 1970s: Muhammad al-Miḥḍār, of a *sayyid* family (six cassettes: 68 percent *bidʿ wa jiwāb*); ʿAli Bin Ṭwaīreq (one cassette: 80 percent *bidʿ wa jiwāb*); and ʿAli Bin Ṭawq, whose religious background is unknown, though he was known to have been one of the ʿAfīfī sultanate's favorite singers (one cassette: 40 percent *bidʿ wa jiwāb*). Note the inverse correlation between religious-political prestige and the *bidʿ wa jiwāb* genre, a trend that suggests that the tribal associations of such poetry were becoming marked. My limited sample of such recordings is due to their scarcity by the 1990s.

41. Adeni intellectual ʿAbdallah Bā Dhīb, who was one of the most influential of early socialist ideologues in South Yemen, was writing articles in Adeni newspapers about these four terms as early as 1955. ʿAbdallah Bā Dhīb, *ʿAbdallah Bā Dhīb: Kitābāt Mukhtārah,* vol. 1 (Beirut: Dār al-Farābī, 1978).

42. On the substantial cultural influence of such amateur singers, see Jean Lambert, "Du 'chanteur' à 'l'artiste': vers un nouveau statut du musicien," *Peuples Méditerranéans* 46 (1989): 61; and H. Yammine, "Correspondence entre la musique tribale et la musique citadine (Sanaʿa) dans la région des hauts plateaux yéménites," in *Le chant arabo-andalou* (Paris: L'Harmattan, 1995), 126.

43. This biographical material was collected over the course of two interviews I held with Qasem, on December 3, 1995, and July 20, 1998.

44 The commercial recording scene in Aden shrank considerably in the years following independence in South Yemen as Indian and foreign merchants moved away or had their businesses seized by the state. The few recording studios that remained were regulated

by the Ministry of Culture and Tourism. By contrast, recording companies in Saudi Arabia and the Gulf were booming by the early 1970s, and state officials there were less hostile than their South Yemeni colleagues to traditional rural music, including the performance of customary tribal dances and songs. Note that privately owned studios in North Yemen fared somewhat better during the 1970s and 1980s.

45. This biographical material was collected from an interview I held with Baraʿi on February 26, 1996.
46. My own review of twelve Baraʿi cassettes suggests the extent to which his songs differed from those of rural singers who didn't migrate: 18 percent of seventy-six poems examined are of the *bidʿ wa jiwāb* genre (compared to 66 percent of the poems sung by the nonmigrant musicians mentioned earlier). Moreover, 17 percent of his songs were composed by Yemenis outside of Yafiʿ, most of them from southern regions. On several cassettes, a majority if not all of his songs are composed by Yemeni poets that Baraʿi had met during his visits to Saudi Arabia and the Gulf.
47. Despite my attempts to contact ʿAbd al-Naser, I never had the opportunity to interview him. When I asked his friends in Yemen why he never responded to my faxes, they replied that after his daughter died in 1992, he had withdrawn somewhat from public life. His diminished rate of cassette production after 1992 seemed to confirm their remarks. My information about ʿAbd al-Naser's person and life is drawn from interviews with his associates in Yafiʿ.
48. One index of ʿAbd al-Naser's attention to the "text utterance" is the average length of his poems. Where commercially recorded singers generally restrict themselves to fifteen- to thirty-verse poems that can accommodate preludes, chorus repetition, and instrumental sections, ʿAbd al-Naser frequently sings poems of fifty to eighty verses. In a highlands tradition in which sung poetry has long been as much a source of information as entertainment, the performance of such poems is by no means uncommon.
49. Tribal heritage was especially promoted by Saudi Arabia and the Gulf during the 1970s, quite unlike in South Yemen. One Yafiʿi migrant explained to me that in Jeddah, the Saudi Ministry of Culture actively encouraged performances of tribal dancing, poems, and song during major festivals and that Yafiʿi cultural clubs had

helped organize such public performances. Thus, tribal rhetoric probably had a more positive valence for ʿAbd al-Naser than it would have had for singers performing at home.

50. These shops included A Piece of My Land and Thamūd Exhibition in Aden, Studio Anghām al-ʿĀsimah in Sanaa (in front of the old-city gate "Bāb al-Yaman"), Stereo 13 Yūnyū in Taʿizz, and Studio al-Barāghah in Abu Dhabi. ʿAbd al-Naser's distribution efforts were facilitated by his co-ownership of the cassette shop Valley Recordings (Tasjīlāt al-Wādī) in Doha, Qatar. Although he left this business in the mid-1980s, he cofounded another shop, The Voice of Yemen (Stereo Ṣawt al-Yaman), in 1988. However, after the severe dwindling of Yemeni migrants in the region following the Gulf War, this shop was eventually sold.
51. Professional singers involved in the commercial recording industry produce in excess of this average. For amateur or semiprofessionals like ʿAbd al-Naser, however, such production levels are rare. I found one series of exchanges between two poets from near Dhamār, ʿAbd al-ʿAziz al-Qaʿshemi and Muhammad Ḥusaīn al-Ḥarūjī to have surpassed ninety cassettes. As of 1999, Yafiʿi singer ʿAli Saleh is the only singer I know to have surpassed his record, averaging one cassette every month since 1994.
52. al-Qāsemī and Ghānem, *Judhūr al-Ughniyyah,* 101–17; Khāled Ṣūrī, *Khalīl Muḥammad Khalīl* (Adan: Dār al-Hamdānī, 1984), 33; and Lambert, "Musiques régionales."
53. Lambert, "Musiques régionales," 181–82.
54. The contrast between models "of" and "for" reality has been insightfully developed by Clifford Geertz in an essay on ritual. Clifford Geertz, "Religion as a Cultural System," in *The Interpretation of Cultures* (New York: Basic Books, 1973), 93–94.
55. Serjeant, *Prose and Poetry,* 64; also see ʿAlī al-Ghulābī, Aḥmad Bū Mahdī, et al., eds. *Ghināʾiyyāt Yaḥyā ʿUmar* (Damascus: al-Kātib al-ʿArabī, 1993), 11–30.
56. Such positions are taken by al-Qāsemī and Ghānem, *Judhūr al-Ughniyyah,* 95–142; and Muḥammad Nājī, "Fann al-Ghināʾ wa-l-Mūsīqā fī al-Yaman," in *al-Thaqāfat al-Yamaniyyah: Rūʾiyyah Mustaqbaliyyah* (Sanaa: Ministry of Culture and Tourism, 1991), 202–03.
57. Naji states: "There wasn't the opportunity to learn about [song] in such . . . regions due to their isolation at that time, other than

through the disc recordings made by Odeon, which was established in Aden in 1938. Many tunes from such regions were recorded on their records by their own hired musicians. As for Yafiʿ, I haven't heard of a professional singer there, but its tunes were recorded by this company from Adeni musicians, who learned them from itinerant musicians who came to Aden from time to time." *al-Thaqāfat al-Yamaniyyah*, 202–03.

58. Khāled al-Qāsemī, *al-Awāṣir al-Ghināʾiyyah: Bayn al-Yaman wa-l-Khalīj* (al-Sharqah: Dār al-Thaqāfah al-ʿArabiyyah, 1988), 55–59; al-Qāsemī and Ghānem, *Judhūr al-Ughniyyah*, 116–17. Urban musicians most known for performing Yafiʿi song on early recordings include "Bin Nāṣer," Muhammad Saʿd ʿAbdallah, Saleh al-ʿAntarī, Hamed al-Qāḍī, Yusef ʿAbd al-Ghanī, and Ahmad al-Qaʿṭabī. Gulf singers include Muḥammad ʿAbduh and ʿAwad Dūkhī.
59. A simple cassette-recording machine could be purchased for 4,200 YR (about $23) in 2006.
60. This estimate is based on over twenty-two hours of observing sales trends in the shop. See note 63 for details.
61. In addition to A Piece of My Land and Thamūd Exhibition, the other shops that I visited include Stereo Thamar in Labʿūs, Stereo al-Kawmāni in Dhamār, and five cassette shops in Sanaa: Stereo al-Maṭari, al-Dunyā al-Saʿādah, Stereo Alḥān al-Khulūd, Stereo Anghām al-Āṣimah, and Ṣawt al-Yaman. I held extensive interviews with managers or owners at each of these locations.
62. I would estimate that A Piece of My Land regularly carries over 3,200 cassettes. Thamūd Exhibition has a somewhat more limited selection of cassettes. Whatever is lacking in the shop can often be fetched from additional archives that the owners keep at home.
63. My methods of documentation at A Piece of My Land were as follows. After obtaining permission from the shop owner, ʿAli al-Haj, I took handwritten notes on the shop's contents and on the managers' interactions with customers. Of 114 initial customer requests, I found that 102 (90 percent of the total) were for Yafiʿi folk poetry, mostly using a variant of "What's the latest?", implying the most recent cassette from one of several singers' series. The remaining requests were specifically for Laheji, Hadrami, and Adeni song. Of the requests for Yafiʿi songs, twenty-three (20 percent of the total) were for cassettes by the singer ʿAli Saleh (including re-

quests for poets featured on his cassettes). By 1998, when I conducted this research, Husain ʿAbd al-Naser's production rate had dwindled, and customers were largely asking for the poets on his series. Finally of note were seven event-centered requests (such as "Do you have something about Ḥunaīsh?") (6 percent of the total), and three requests by women customers.

64. The Quʿaīṭi state was established through a series of campaigns in Hadramawt in the 1850s by a migrant from Khaledi's district in Yafiʿ, ʿAwad Bin ʿUmar Bin ʿAwaḍ. Sultan ʿAwad had originally acquired his power through membership in an elite corps of Arab soldiers in Hyderabad, India. The principal contender for state authority in Hadramawt was the Kathīri confederation. Both groups acquired statehood through agreements with the British colonial authority in Aden.
65. This cassette was released by ʿAli Saleh. Like the two cassettes that I discuss in chapter 1, released a few weeks earlier by ʿAli Bin Jaber's and Yahya al-Sulaīmānī, this cassette also addressed the Saʿdī conflict and the seizure of Yemen's Ḥunaīsh Island by Ethiopia in late 1995.
66. The low overall percentage of *bidʿ wa jiwāb* poems in ʿAli Saleh's series is due to his early penchant for love poems, especially suitable to the peaceful years that immediately followed Yemeni unification in 1990. Since the 1994 Yemeni War, his cassettes have regularly featured more aggressive political verse. From mid-1995 to 1996, 80 percent of his songs were *bidʿ wa jiwāb* poems, and from 1996 to 1998, this average fell only to 70 percent. The demand for *bidʿ wa jiwāb* verse has clearly fluctuated according to political tensions in Yemen.

· FOUR ·

From Pen to Polyester and Back

I consider the name Thabit 'Awaḍ to have begun with the release of my first cassette in 1972.

—Interview with the poet Thabit 'Awad, 1998

Poet: All right, I am thinking of something now.
Clairvoyant: It is long. [pause] It is something that revolves. [pause] It has two sides. [pause] It's a cassette.

—Exchange between a Yemeni poet and a famous clairvoyant. Radā'a, Yemen, 1995

Four decades of centralized state authority, increased urban economic opportunities, and waning traditional agricultural practices have contributed to Yemen's growing need for metropolitan textual competences. Cassettes have provided consumers and producers of folk poetry with an important means of demonstrating such metropolitan know-how. They are inexpensive, portable, and easily copied, and the primary producers of this user-friendly recording technology are based in urban areas. Cassettes have enabled rural poets and singers to establish closer working relations with recording agents in the city. Yet cassettes are famously double-sided. Even as they enable users to affix older textual forms to newer urban affiliations, they reference rural lifestyles that are valued for their distance from the city. Cassettes are lettered side A and side B.

Having devoted previous chapters to considering some of the broad contextualizing forces with which cassette poets and singers grapple, I attend in this chapter to poets' and singers' strategies for song composition and cassette production. Understanding how Yemenis turn cassettes into rich moral resources for marking as well as unmarking metropolitan affiliations requires a clear perspective on textual practice. Toward this end, I explore the "noetic" habits of cassette producers; that is, the set of processes—particular to cassette culture—by which knowledge is shaped, stored, retrieved, and communicated.[1] By using cassettes to encode knowledge in new and more useful ways, poets and singers highlight a "necessity" in cassette-mediated discourse that comprises, as Antonio Gramsci argues, a "healthy nucleus that exists in 'common sense'."[2] Choices of meter, rhyme, linguistic register, theme, genre, and so forth all become interpretive cues for understanding how political lyrics can best be circulated to influence audiences' opinions about political problems and their solutions. The cassette is instrumental for putting knowledge to critical use. It also is an imaginative resource for assessing the ethical costs of tailoring verse to broader public audiences. As the cassette industry accommodated more diverse groups of rural Yemenis after the 1960s, poets and singers increasingly sought to preserve the ethical leverage of cassettes by calling attention to the different roles that each of them has played in an industry marked as metropolitan. Poets have become stylized as rural stalwarts, singers as brokers of metropolitan culture, and the political voice of cassette poetry as a kind of comparatively unmediated highland verse. Such performances belie the fact that poets' and singers' roles as arbiters of knowledge are intertwined in the cassette industry. Indeed, I argue that in the interests of political activism, Yemenis confront this apparent contradiction in the concept of authorship. Although discourses of authorship typically benefit those with higher education and metropolitan literary accolades, cassette producers find leverage in such discourses where they foreground an aesthetics of writing and inscription that has long enabled reflection on hierarchy and alienation. Amid a commercialized and poorly regulated audiocassette industry that is rife with debates over textual authenticity, a trope of cassette-mediated authorship emerges in the figure of a wry, poet-singer hybrid that I call the "general singing tribesman." Ultimately, I suggest, this trope coaches Yemenis in how to balance their attachments to multiple discursive communities, their multiple political objectives, and their critical judgment.

My account of poets and singers' new textual competences begins with an introduction to the life and work of one poet who was born during the early twilight of the recording industry. Yafiʿi poet Shayef al-Khāledī found cassettes useful in exchanging *bidʿ wa jiwāb* verse with poets across Yemen when the borders between North and South Yemen were closed and open dialogue in state-controlled media channels was especially difficult. Khaledi found cassettes especially helpful in attempting to relate the ongoing vitality of rural highland verse and tribal discourses to southern Yemeni nationalism. A self-stylized cassette-poet humor allowed him to accommodate his verses to metropolitan cassette song, but Khaledi also was able to cue listeners to a truer poetic self that resided in a tribal ruralism that was nationalist in its commitment to public dialogue and moral reflexivity. Writing again proves central to his and other poets' discursive strategies. Written texts not only enable collaboration with singers but also signal a metropolitan authorship that could be mastered and then transcriptively disowned as poems are designed for the ears of cassette audiences. In the second part of the chapter, I show how such transcriptive dissonance is managed by singers, whose textual interventions complement but also vary from poets' own. I propose that while both groups of performers find collaboration necessary to produce successful cassette texts, collaboration is also an interpretive framework that acknowledges tensions in a larger and increasingly technologized culture of *qaṣīdah* authorship. Toward the end of the chapter, I suggest that the supposed untenability of authorship through the sonic pandemonium of a cassette-recording market provides just the leverage that performers need to signal their estrangement from metropolitan regimes of power and capital and to propose their own alternative visions of moral authority.

A BIOGRAPHY OF SHAYEF AL-KHALEDI

Widely recognized as one of the finest poets in Yafiʿ, Shayef al-Khaledi acquired a national reputation in no small way through his use of cassettes. Born in 1932 in Jāh, a remote hamlet of two houses, Khaledi was the son of an extended farming family whose rocky, terraced fields were barely sufficient for supporting its thirteen members. The closest market was Lamm, a village of twenty-four houses about a half mile's distance from his home where large tribal meetings were held, trade managed, and religious affairs conducted under the auspices of the region's largest mosque. His skill in composing poetry was developed at an early age through opportunities presented to him at social gatherings in Lamm or at extemporaneous poetry competitions *(ragzah)* at weddings. As a youth, he excelled at composing short two- to four-verse poems *(zāmils)* for such occasions. After receiving rudimentary training in reading and writing at the local two-year Qurʿanic school *(maʿlāmah),* he also began to write *qaṣīdahs* with sentimental themes and meditations on love, friendship, ethical conduct, and spirituality. One of the first *qaṣīdahs* to secure his reputation as a poet drew on a combination of such themes. Written on behalf of a neighbor whose husband had migrated to England sixteen years earlier, his *qaṣīdah* spoke so eloquently about her isolation and abandonment that, it is said, her husband returned in the same year. After several years of refining his poetic talents, Khaledi began exchanging *qaṣīdahs* with other poets in neighboring villages. As his confidence grew, he was soon composing aggressive poems about local politics, colonialism, and the affairs of shaikhs, sultans, and other leaders throughout southern Yemen.

Khaledi's success as a poet depended on a detailed knowledge of local history and broad changes in relations of power. His perspective on such changes was sharpened by his experiences as a worker in the British colonial port of Aden, about a four-day walk (over 100 land miles) from his home. His first trip to Aden was in 1947 at the age of fifteen. Since high-paying jobs were reserved for elite families from Aden and the protectorates, most rural inhabitants found it difficult to obtain employment there. Khaledi had no connections, but after several weeks he found irregular work as one of Aden's fifteen thousand Yemeni housekeepers. A few years later, he was employed at the docks, where the pay was better but the jobs lasted only two or three days at most. Occasionally, Khaledi went an entire week without work, which meant missing daily meals.

In 1950, Khaledi abandoned day labor at the docks to take up more secure employment as a herdsman in Abyan, a barren desert expanse stretching east of the city: "I was convinced that I would be able to scratch together a living from the livestock owners and their sheep, camels, and cattle." He remained working there for twelve years: "My mother was with me and two sisters and their husbands. But I never earned much. I regretted those years. Life was very hard. We didn't even have enough to return home to Yafiʿ. We relied on ourselves." Despite his hardships, he continued to write and exchange verses with poets from the neighboring governorates of Abyan and Shabwah. The knowledge that he acquired of the poetic forms, melodies, and accents of poets throughout these areas would later help him adjust his poetry to more diverse audiences, establishing his reputation throughout the south.

At the age of thirty, after having spent a third of his life earning a meager living as a migrant in foreign pastures, Khaledi returned to Aden to work in the port again for seven months and married in 1963. As he began to settle down with his new family, a feud broke out in his homeland after Shaikh Ahmad Bu

Bak, the paramount shaikh of his tribe, al-Mawsaṭah, was assassinated. When a poet from a neighboring tribe ridiculed al-Mawsaṭah for its inability to resolve disputes more peaceably, Khaledi defended his tribe to great acclaim by demonstrating an impressive knowledge of local history that simultaneously placed events in perspective and put his opponent and his tribe to shame. In exchange for his poem, a leading Mawsaṭah shaikh awarded Khaledi a brand-new Kennedy rifle. With his weapon and a growing reputation as "the poet of response" *(shāʿir al-jiwāb),* Khaledi soon set out on the longest journey he had ever undertaken. He traveled northward to Sanaa to fight with republican forces, which had just begun a sustained campaign to overthrow the entrenched Mutawakkilite imamate. Along with many thousands of other Yemenis from the southern regions who volunteered to fight, over the next four years he became acquainted with many areas of the north. His experiences strengthened his sense of patriotism and his understanding of national politics.

During these years, Khaledi began exchanging poems with other northern poets. Swapping opinions on the ebb and flow of politics, economic ills and cures, and general concerns of the nation would become a lifelong pursuit for which he would gain a national reputation: "I exchanged poetry with northerners, and we always had respect for one another. Even though our *qaṣīdahs* were sometimes delivered in a sharp tone, we still respected one another when we met. The injuries in words didn't go inside." It is estimated that by the time that the two Yemens achieved independence in 1967, Khaledi had written over one thousand *qaṣīdahs* and was fast becoming a recognizable voice across Yemen's southwestern governorates.

In many ways, Khaledi's trajectory as a political poet matched that of many other mid-twentieth-century Yemeni poets who sought to contribute to broader nationalist debates. While drawing from discourses of moral authority that had been familiar to him from his rural experiences as a tested political mediator, he had also learned to read and write and to use his literary competences to reach wider groups of readers, whether through photocopies of his own handwritten poems, through newspapers, or (beginning in 1990) through paperback collections of his verse. However, his role as a political poet also underwent new modifications as a result of his use of cassettes. Cassettes allowed him to disseminate his poetry to vastly larger audiences, especially in the rural areas, and they also influenced the content of his verse, allowing him to discuss nationalism with northern Yemeni poets during several decades in which relations between North and South Yemen were severely strained and travel between the two countries was restricted.[3]

On one occasion, I asked Khaledi about how he was able to continue exchanging with poets from the northern regions over these years: "Did you maintain contact with them by devising ways to travel there or through written letters, or did they come here?"

He responded: "No, no. We exchanged cassettes. After independence [in 1967], they would listen to what was said between me and another poet or a couple of others. When I would criticize some peoples' ways, they would hear my poems on cassette. They would then decide to write and sent me their poems. Then I would respond."

A burgeoning cassette industry, in other words, fueled by a growing number of local singers, provided the means for his transnational *bidʿ wa jiwāb* exchange and for his growing reputation as a poet who could speak to all Yemenis. I subsequently asked Khaledi about the content of poems he exchanged in those early years, and his reply confirmed a concern for national issues: "The northerners would take a side attacking the south, and I would take my side attacking the north. They would accuse us of communism and apostasy, and I would accuse them of spreading propaganda, leading the country astray, and being agents [for foreign interests]. It was powerful poetry." To reassure me that he stood with unity between the two Yemens, he then added: "Even today, and especially after the conflict in 1994, some people consider me secessionist. They send *qaṣīdahs* to me and accuse me of secessionism and of apostasy and of being against unity, despite the fact that I am entirely for unity and was long before it occurred. Since President [ʻAbdullah] Sallāl's time [in the late 1960s], I have written about my hopes for unity."

In chapter 6, I examine the history of unfolding debates between cassette poets that were orchestrated by Khaledi, Husain ʻAbd al-Nāṣer, and several other singers. In exploring Yemenis' efforts to maintain traditions of transregional dialogue, I argue that cassettes provided a unique forum for considering the costs of nationalism, the dangers of tribal violence, and the obligations of poetry fans to consider more pliant templates for moral discourse. At present, I want only to note that cassettes enabled Khaledi to conduct nationalist debates with his correspondents that underscored new possibilities for demanding public accountability from Yemen's leadership. The tenor of these demands differed in at least two respects from that typically found in state-managed channels of mass media. First, such poetry featured aggressive political rhetoric whose vernacular and pointedly tribal registers were usually censored from state media. Such registers were partly suitable because they were embedded in epistolary traditions of *bidʻ wa jiwāb* verse that were well suited to conveying notable moral sentiments across vast distances, though as I discuss in the following chapter, such registers also enabled a criticism of elitist and nationalist discourses that was valued by listeners. Second, such vernacular tribal discourse had to be tailored to larger and more diverse audiences by cultivating various levels of anonymity.[4] More and more contributing cassette poets and singers were corresponding with performers they had never met. Poets and singers also had to design their verses for imagined audiences rather than for small groups of listeners or even readers (as discussed in chapter 1). A third and even more radical level of anonymity involved constructing a new kind of setting for such performances and performers. Poets and singers who designed verses for cassette reception grew more skilled at imagining a final product in which their work was integrated in body and intent into one, sixty-minute metropolitan sound space. As is discussed later in this chapter, these conditions of cassette-medium anonymity would be negotiated through a specific transcriptive techniques and tropes, all of which would help construct the somewhat vexed position of a "general singing tribesman." For now, I simply note that Khaledi's use of cassettes favored a performative collapsing of national, spatial, and temporal differences between poets, even as the content of their political verse continued, in the tradition of highland verbal sparring, to foreground these differences.

When Khaledi returned to the south after participating in the 1962 revolution against the imamate in Sanaa, he had several jobs as a state employee that drew him more centrally into unfolding nationalist movements in the south. First, he obtained a post with the general security police in Aden. He worked for the police for four years, living in cramped quarters and continuing to write poetry. He intermittently traveled home to his family in Yafiʿ but returned to the city to maintain his post. In the mid-1970s, however, his poetic talents landed him a more advantageous sinecure. He was offered a job at the Ministry of Culture and Information, where he worked until retirement in the late 1980s. His job with the ministry would not be the most prestigious he would acquire, however. In 1983, he won election to a three-year appointment on the Local People's Council, the seat of regional administration in Yafiʿ. His reputation as a poet and political leader was opening doors to prominent contacts and influence. His success at state levels did not interfere with his work as a poet, however. Between 1971 and 1985, his critical verse landed him in regional jails seven times, "none of which stopped me from writing," he told me: "I wrote poems about economic duress and poverty, and the party kept a very tight surveillance over everything we did." By 1990, his reputation among migrant Yemenis and Yafiʿis in particular had reached such levels that he made a trip to the United States, where he recited poetry before avid audiences in New York City, Buffalo, and Chicago.[5] He also received invitations to Qatar, Saudi Arabia, and the Gulf emirates, where migrant audiences were especially passionate about his cassette poems. In short, by the late 1950s, Khaledi had converted his poetry into a success known only to a handful of vernacular folk poets in Yemen.

Khaledi would never become iconized by such visual media as newspapers, magazines, or television. Audiences were often astonished to learn that the old man sitting on the stool in one of their favorite Adeni cassette shops was the legendary poet himself. The fame he acquired through cassette sales won him the specific epithet of "Bu Khulād," a nickname that means, roughly, "Father of Eternity," but among fans, his image acquired its richest hues from the privileged seats he occupied at regional celebrations, the many invitations he received to prominent weddings and private events, and the verses and stories of his life that circulated in daily gatherings.

"CASSETTE POET" COMPETENCES

Khaledi's success as a folk poet was attributable largely to his poetic talents, to his ability to address complex political issues with skill and clarity, and to a prolific production that lasted over a half century. But his success was also amplified by his use of the audiocassette. Such media celebrity was not acquired by all poets. Other folk poets in Yafiʿ and throughout Yemen were as talented and as prolific as Khaledi. How, then, did Khaledi make such a name for himself? What distinguishes his success as a "cassette poet" from that of other poets?

The category of a cassette poet, as distinct from a noncassette poet, has few equivalents in the traditional interpretive repertoires of Yemenis or anyone else, for that matter. In a paperback volume of recollections assembled by Khaledi's closest friends after his death in 1998, I was struck by the first published attempt I had found to designate the role of "the poet who uses (the cassette) to disseminate his poetry" *(al-shāʿir alladhī yustakhdim (al-kāsēt) fī nashr shiʿruh).* Coined by one of the region's leading politicians, this description is inserted seamlessly into a section that praises Khaledi's early leadership in defeating the British—fighting fire with fire, as it were—and in later helping to establish Yemen's first nationalist movements.[6] Nevertheless, while the politician clearly sees the cassette *(kāsēt)* as a force of national integration that was an outgrowth of the poet's overall political life, he still feels obliged to mark off the loan word with parentheses, as if to secure its significance from influencing the overall assessment of the poet's identity.

It would seem simple enough to begin with the general assumption that the cassette poet, by definition, needs access to a cassette. As explained in the previous chapter, however, poets do not usually sing their own verses and instead leave the task of performing and recording poetry to amateur and semiprofessional singers. Many cassette poets rarely use a cassette recorder for recording purposes. To understand the roles and orientations of the cassette poet, we need to look beyond purely technical cassette competences to discursive domains that are engaged through acts of composition and performance. Since my aim in this chapter is to explore the growing authority of singers in public discourse, it might be helpful to investigate how successful cassette poets adapt their verses to the interests of popular cassette singers through a specific set of skills, competences, orientations, and dispositions. As Michael Warner has suggested in his illuminating analysis of colonial American political discourse, print technologies did not in themselves found the basis of a republic of letters.[7] What enabled developments in printing and distribution to become instrumental to the efflorescence of republican public sphere was the simultaneous emergence of a political discourse that allowed readers and correspondents to recognize their own, individual acts as socially significant: each discourse participant was one among a republic of like-minded, reasonable participants. Yemeni cassette poets, like American colonial men of letters, also invest textual acts of reading and composition with social significance. In this case, the community invoked by poets is heavily indebted to the contributions of singers.

In approaching the discursive domains that inform poets' views of social community, we can begin with the general observation that cassette technologies were exceptionally democratic media or that they appeared as such to many poets who began using them during the 1950s. In an era of restricted literacy that had defined much public verse prior to those decades, poets who composed the most prestigious genres of popular poetry, foremost among them the *qaṣīdah,* were largely from upper-status groups. Members of families of religious scholars, tribal leaders, and sultans were especially well positioned in this respect. As established leaders, they had enjoyed regular access to the most prominent performance settings and audiences. Poets of lesser status also became well known, on occasion, by force of their strong verse and charismatic personalities; some slaves *(ʿabds)* in Yafiʿ were exceptional poets and were widely known for their persuasive poems. Nevertheless, poets of higher-status families were more likely to have access to the public limelight, whether through personal connections or through their prominent roles in religious events, dispute mediations, weddings, and other major social events.

As media technologies grew cheaper and the recording industry became more decentralized, poets' access to such audiences was exponentially eased by records as early as the 1940s, by open-reel recorders and eight-track tapes in subsequent decades, and—for poets who could compose in more urban genres of *ḥumaīnī*—by nationally sponsored radio stations, newspapers, and amateur literary journals. It was the cheap, transportable, and user-friendly cassette, however, that provided the widest range of rural poets with access to large audiences. Technically, any poet working with any singer could borrow a cassette recorder and successfully distribute his or her verses, especially by the 1970s. In this respect, the audiocassette became instrumental in fostering a genuine political "public" of folk-poetry production and consumption.

However, the democratic potentials of cassettes, as with previous audio-recording technologies, have been somewhat less open-ended than they have appeared. Here lies the problem with attaching the label "cassette poet" to anyone whose verses are recorded on cassette. While the cassette might offer its user possibilities for reaching diverse audiences (as seen in the composition event described in chapter 1), the actual practices of cassette production and reception have still been subject to hierarchies of textual knowledge, performance skill, social connection, personal disposition, and gender. It is one thing to release a cassette of recited vernacular poetry for a small circle of friends; it is quite another to attract thousands of listeners and develop a national reputation. Success as a cassette poet has been neither easily obtainable nor equally accessible to all.

What kinds of discursive competence have cassette poets had to cultivate in their efforts to compose persuasive verse? To begin with, a cassette poet needs to be able to compose verses that can be understood by the kinds of popular audiences that enjoy cassettes. In a country where, before the 1970s, entire dialects could sometimes be confined to individual village units, securing the interests of multifarious listeners has required versatility in tailoring poems to different speech communities and their frames of reference. As I discuss below, the best cassette poets become masters in designing verses for a wide range of audiences. Although rural texts and poetic forms continue to be privileged, successful cassette poets also demonstrate fluency in navigating between specific dialects, linguistic registers, genres, musical variations, symbolic frameworks, and so forth.

Becoming fluent is easier for some than for others. In cities that have long been hubs for acquiring information, translocal skills, competences, and technologies of communication, migrant cassette poets have become positioned even more centrally as the brokers of cultural capital. Metropolitan centers both within Yemen and abroad (such as Aden, Taʿizz, Sanaa, Manāmah in Bahrain, Jeddah, Riyadh, and Doha) have provided havens for some of the most successful cassette poets, who are largely from rural backgrounds but have been able to take advantage of economic and cultural opportunities that are not available at home.[8] Wage-earning jobs have been one of the most important ways to access the material, social, and cultural benefits of metropoles. Many cassette poets, like people from other sectors of the rural populace, have worked as unskilled laborers throughout the Gulf during decades of growth in commercial, construction, and service industries.

Aside from wages, mobility also provides many migrant cassette poets with opportunities that are rarely available to other poets. After arriving in Yafiʿ for my first interviews, I found the most highly regarded cassette poets difficult to locate since many of them either frequently traveled throughout the region to maintain social contacts or resided part- or full-time in Aden or abroad (see chapter 1). Such mobility has certain rewards for poets who seek to understand and communicate with broader audiences. One young cassette poet explained the benefits of mobility to poetic composition in this way: "The best poets acquire some of their keenest skills through traveling far and wide. In traveling, poets experience the world and learn to enhance their powers of perception *(idrāk)*. By developing an ability to appreciate the most minute things, they find ways to produce more creative utterances *(alfāẓ)* and to introduce an advancement *(taṭawwur)* to the traditional columnar *qaṣīdah* used by their forebears."[9] In general, the young man asserted, mobility introduces poets to the wondrous complexities of the world and teaches them to observe what is closest at hand. Such powers of perception are especially important for the cassette poet, who must understand the relations of metropolitan and cosmopolitan culture to local experience in order to summon the creativity felt necessary to reach broader audiences. Whether travel, in fact, sharpens perceptions, the young man's comments confirmed a view shared by many Yemenis that mobility is important to a poet's broad discursive competence and his or her appreciation by diverse audiences.

But mobility also brings more tangible returns in the form of valuable contacts with singers and cassette producers. As explained in the previous chapter, singers in the rural highlands have been few in number, and those who finally become recording stars overcome tremendous challenges in learning to play the instruments and styles that are in demand by urban recording producers. Typically, such singers must live in urban areas to maintain their contacts and participate in regular recording sessions. Poets are likewise advantaged. Although poetic talent and reputation are still of fundamental importance, poets who get to know leading cassette singers and who can regularly supply them with their work enjoy strategic advantage over those who remain isolated in the highlands.

Translocal knowledge, experience, mobility, social contacts, and income all provide important means for rural poets to gain competence in the cassette industry. A final set of factors, no less important than the others, derives from poets' access to literacy and education. In fact, literacy remains, in many ways, one of the most important means to gain access to the kinds of metropolitan and cosmopolitan discourses that are common among diverse popular audiences. Many cassette poets I interviewed, both young and old, emphasized the contributions made by reading to their perspectives on life and to their work as poets.[10] Almost all poets I spoke with regularly read national Yemeni newspapers to keep in touch with the latest political events and current affairs. In addition to reading, most poets regularly watch evening television news programs and international satellite broadcasts.

While some poets are advantaged by these new domains of knowledge and discourse and can find new opportunities to circumvent traditional hierarchies of economic and symbolic capital, other poets find such domains more exclusive than those that existed before. Older poets, many of whom are no longer as mobile and socially active as they once were, have much greater difficulty keeping in touch with urban cassette producers than do younger poets, especially those who are migrants abroad. And if age is a constraining factor for some, gender is even more so. Women poets in the highlands have faced especially severe obstacles in getting their verses recorded or sung on cassette. Much of the problem stems from conservative attitudes toward women's authorship. From the earliest decades of the recording industry through the 1970s, gains were made by women singers, who were able to secure professional contracts in Aden and Ta'izz and who regularly performed live in public concerts. However, such women were almost entirely confined to singing either men's poetry or anonymous traditional songs *(aghānī turāthiyyah)*. Moreover, the growth of conservative Islamic attitudes toward women's public performances during the 1980s, partly a result of growing rapprochement between Saudi Arabia and northern Yemeni tribal shaikhs, led to the steady disappearance of women singers from the public eye, further removing rural women's poetry from public audiences.[11] A decade of post-unity domination by a conservative northern government has been especially hard on women activists from southern Yemen who, after independence, had succeeded in securing a place for women's voices in a public sphere that was at once state-sponsored and Islamic.[12]

In sum, poets' competences in regional dialects, customs, social histories, village-level politics, genealogical connections, and other sources of "local knowledge" are still key to the cassette poet's success. Few of the folk-poetry cassettes that I discuss in this chapter are listened to by non-Yemenis; indeed, most of the cassettes cater to regional audiences. However, in a cassette market whose audiences are steadily expanding, cassette poets must also gain metropolitan competences in standardized Arabic varieties, musical styles, genres, and symbolic frameworks.

COMPOSING BY PEN: METROPOLITAN STYLE AND TRANSCRIPTIVE DISSONANCE

Cassette poets who want to reach listeners while accommodating a range of discursive communities must walk a fine line. To be understood by national and transnational Yemeni audiences, they must adopt the conventions of metropolitan popular song, much of which is heavily informed by state-controlled institutions and media channels. To maintain the interests of rural highland audiences who are accustomed to more traditional genres of folk poetry, song, and music, however, they must also continue to produce verse that is popular precisely for its difference from metropolitan discourses. The challenge of bridging these ideological divides is not difficult to appreciate. Migrant Yemenis who live abroad are in especially delicate positions, since they must retain their skills in vernacular poetry and song, sometimes by extolling their competences as rural farmers and tribesmen, even as they become removed ever more permanently from traditional rural lifestyles at home.

To engage the moral sentiments of diverse audiences, cassette poets learn to "stylize" their verse,[13] signaling affiliation with metropolitan producers while reasserting ties to their rural backgrounds. In this section, I explore how style is conveyed through transcriptive competences that indicate poets' attunements to metropolitan song culture. With the genuine popularization of cassettes during the 1960s, transcription becomes increasingly central to the production of poetic texts; that is, poets have grown more adept at designing verses to travel across different media channels, especially manuscripts and audiocassettes. In part, transcription contains its own objectifying power insofar as it is aimed at producing a cassette text that transcends the contributions of individual participants and reflects a more general collaborative product. However, poets work with singers in calling attention to the costs of cassette-text collaboration to traditional political discourse. Where transcriptive routines are invested with critical dissonance, a stage is set for identifying the problems with metropolitan conventions of authorship.

To assess the transcriptive strategies of cassette poets, a brief introduction to poetic composition is needed. In Arabic, the word "poetry" *(shiʿr)* is closely related to "feelings" *(shuʿūr)*, suggesting poetry's foundation in bodily emotions and sentiments. But where do these feelings begin? According to the late ʿAbdallah al-Baraddūnī, one of Yemen's foremost national poets, the impetus toward composing a *qaṣīdah* starts with "the desire to say poetry from within" *(al-raghbah an yaqūl al-shiʿr min dākhil)*.[14] *Qaṣīdah* verses, then, emerge from a particular yearning to give inward "feelings" vocal expression. Such a desire, he continued, is founded in a poet's reaction to something: an event, a piece of news, a poem received from another poet, a community issue. Poets describe this experience of responsive desire as an acoustic, aural agitation that is untranslatable in the language of humankind. Poets hear an indecipherable "whispering" *(waswasah)* or "babble" *(haraj)* from unknown realms. As Baraddūnī told me, one hears what lies "beyond the language of ordinary talk and is driven to decipher its intended meanings." At this stage, poets suffer from bitter feelings in the heart *(qalb)* and the liver *(kibd)*; typically, they experience restlessness, loss of appetite, insomnia, and, in extreme cases, violent shaking and sweating. To prevent these whisperings from leading to psychological stress, madness, or even death, poets must use their faculties of reason *(ʿaql)* and cleverness *(shaṭārah)*—usually located in the head *(rās)*—to translate such raw, prearticulated energy into poetic form.[15]

In the depths of emotional experience, poets become compelled to translate the language beyond "ordinary talk"—to "say poetry" through the medium of poetic muses. These muses are known as the *ḥājis* and the *ḥalīlah*. Each muse enhances a somewhat different set of poetical skills. The *ḥājis*, akin to poetical savvy, enables the poet to tailor emotional murmurings to social language and to produce powerful verses that creatively express the crux of an issue, a situation, or an event. By granting exceptional percipience, the *ḥājis* allows the poet to produce meanings that endure beyond their place and time and that move, as one student told me, from the sensory to the rarefied *(min al-shuʿūr ilā lā shuʿūr)*. The *ḥājis* is thus an objectifying, circulatory force. Because the *ḥājis* guides poets in seamlessly linking language with social reality *(al-wāqiʿ)*, this muse is especially important to poets who compose in the more prominent political genres of poetry such as the *qaṣīdah*. The second, more volatile muse is the *ḥalīlah*.[16] The *ḥalīlah* grants access to aesthetic brilliance, enabling poets to produce immediate, ad-hoc verses that may be eloquent, penetrating, and at times verbally dazzling but may not have the broader social meaning that can be summoned up by the *ḥājis*.[17]

In the period of inspiration, when a flood of disjuncted sounds, words, and half-formed ideas demands inscription, the poet must initiate composition by first selecting a metrical structure *(wazn)*. In some cases, the melodic structure is determined by generic constraints: a poet responding with a *jiwāb* to another, for example, must replicate the meter of the initiator's poem. Whatever formal conventions may exist, however, a poet's choice of meter is crucial for the structure and meaning of the *qaṣīdah*. Other scholars of south Arabian folk poetry have noted the customary practice by which folk poets identify meter through song and melodious recitation.[18] I found few poets versant with classical poetic meters, although poets could use basic parsing techniques to identify given syllabic structures. Nevertheless, only by setting *qaṣīdahs* to familiar rural melodies can poets and interpreters of poetry identify given compositions in relation to familiar styles of vernacular performance. Poems that do not adhere to such melodies cannot be recited easily or circulated in recognizable form. Assistants who worked with me generally considered such poems to be imbalanced, calling them "prosaic" *(natharī)* or flawed by connections with the lettered constraints of urban *ḥumaīnī* verse. The vernacular *qaṣīdah*, even if committed to pen, had to resonate inextricably with musical sound.

With a metrical structure to guide words into recognizable generic patterns, a poet then begins assembling the broader sonic contours of the composition with the poem's discursive content. A rhyme scheme is chosen to embroider prominent themes: short, clipped consonants suit a more aggressive declamatory poem; open vowels better express spiritual reflection or sentiments of love; a specific combination of sounds may foreground an intertextual reference to another poem; and so forth. Once the metrical structure and rhyme have been established, verses are individually composed, more or less in keeping with conventional thematic sections, depending on the poet's generic parameters and personal aims. Verses often come haphazardly and must be arranged, broken down, recombined, and revised until, gradually, the contours of a *qaṣīdah* take shape.

The process of writing down verses that are first heard and imagined by the poet can vary considerably between individuals. Some of the finest poets, especially those skilled in extempore poetic genres, can quickly combine a repertoire of verbal formulas and conventional idioms with their own unique message and style. Others compose more slowly and laboriously. As one poet explained to me, they must work to iron smooth *(yakwī)* the rougher seams of their text. Such composers are occasionally known as compilers *(muṣannifs)* rather than true poets *(shāʿirs)*. The process of composing, writing, and editing typically involves several drafts, even if scribbled messily on the back and front of a single sheet of paper. Finally, most poets test their verses out on friends, revising them where necessary before publicly releasing them.[19]

All poetic composition involves the structuring of sound into durable textual patterns—"objects" in the world that lend sustained patterns of meaning and recognition to nondiscursive life worlds. This process can elicit varying degrees of resonance with the moral forces of the world. A traditional Yafiʿi gnome compares the experiences of skilled poets' with the two inspirational muses, both of them risky if life giving, to the deadening work of the struggling amateur: the *ḥalīlah* is like flower pruning, the *ḥājis* is like sea diving, and the compiler is like throat stabbing *(al-halīlah qaṭf az-zuhūr, al-ḥājis ghāriq al-buḥūr, al-muṣannif ta'n an-nuḥūr)*. The question is: when does a salubrious poetic act become dangerous? Part of the answer to this question, I suggest, lies in exploring how certain forms of knowledge are conceptualized as becoming alienated from the sensual experience of poets or other language users and also in assessing the extent to which this alienation is held to be harmful. Does producing poetry require severing a gorgeous blossom if only to preserve the vitality of a larger bush? In this case, the *ḥalīlah,* as a kind of "flower pruning," would prove most helpful. Or is poetry a more adventurous feat that requires submersion into the poetic unconscious, often called the "sea" *(baḥr),* and possibly the loss of the poetic self? Under these conditions, the *ḥājis* seems more suitable. Or is poetry the work of an amateur compiler whose artificial and incoherent categorizations *(aṣnāf)* present a threat to the producer's moral being?

The cassette technology figures centrally in dramatizing these traditional concerns in relation to new forces of production, consumption, and circulation. The cassette's technical conditioning, whether helpful, risky, or deadening, is interesting to Yemenis because it is socially relevant and thus has everything to do with political life and the moral evaluations of its members. As we seek to appreciate the technology's leverage as a critical moral resource, it is important to understand that the cassette's relation to written, more than oral, tradition initially most concerns activists. Audio-recording technologies have been called a form of "secondary orality" insofar as they enable a more deliberate, self-conscious orality that is crafted through the use of writing and print.[20] And yet if the advantage of cassettes in challenging onerous moral convention lies in their power to inscribe discourse with authority, the cassette might be better understood as a form of "secondary inscription" that is equally reflexive by virtue of its emergence from oral craftsmanship. As is shown below, the critical leverage of poets' transcriptive styles draws primarily from notions of cassette lyrics as written, and the dramatic oral rendition of inscription gives poetry its performative edge.

Much of the leverage of cassette inscription derives from the fact that written text artifacts are useful for cassette producers. The written text provides poets and singers with essential documents for collaboration. For poets, who are often separated from singers by considerable distances, a written transcript provides the easiest and most inexpensive means to deliver their work into the hands of singers. In an earlier era, before the advent of audio recording, poets might have considered conveying their own verses through live performance.[21] With new performance standards that have come to define recorded song, however, poets have come to feel that their own voices pale in comparison to those of well-known amateur or semiprofessional cassette singers and are almost universally dissuaded from singing their own work.[22] As a result, poets devote considerable attention to preparing written copies of their work. As a proxy for the poet's voice, the final transcript should be well executed, especially when the poet has not established a close, working relationship with the singer.

Good writing instruments must be selected accordingly. A fresh sheet of paper that is clean along the edges, perhaps slightly tinted, and without preprinted lines is the choicest medium, although poets often write on three-hole sheets or pages carefully extracted from notebooks. A poet is also best served by a quality pen and an ability to produce a decent script.[23] Poets who cannot write or those who wish to make a finer transcript of their verse often employ someone skilled in the art of calligraphy, a not uncommon talent even in the rural south. For formal occasions and perhaps a more modern effect, a poet may make use of a typewriter or, on rare occasions, a computer. Singers appreciate written copies of poems, which spare them the trouble of transcribing cassette-recorded texts or memorizing poems delivered to them orally through an intermediary. In a cassette industry geared to the rapid production and circulation of new songs, a clean written text is a valued document that can be read, studied, edited, and consulted at every stage of its journey to listeners. Writing is thus constitutive of the audio-recorded *qaṣīdah* genre and also of many recorded genres of poetry and prose.

The written aesthetics of cassettes are valued for more than their utility, however. They are also appreciated as a reflexive template that can draw attention to standards of authorship, hierarchies of textual authority, and active contests over inscriptive distinction. Poets are best able to convey their evaluation of written norms through transcriptive strategies as they design verses to travel toward singers and ultimately cassette audiences. Even as they write, verses are tailored to multiple moments of text reception, not all of them equally loyal to established conventions of literary recognition (as we began to explore in the composition event, described in chapter 1). The subtlety with which poets could invest their written work with transcriptive "dissonance" was illustrated to me poignantly by one cassette fan's comments on the signature that concluded every poem by Khaledi (see figure 4.1). Known by poetry enthusiasts throughout Yafiʿ from copies of written poems that circulated widely, Khaledi's signature was one of the most formally elaborate that I had seen among poets. Nevertheless, the signature also conveyed something beyond mere literary panache. The signature was creative to a degree exceeding the bounds of decorum, the fan told me, and to him, it had always looked like "an armored tank" *(dabbābah)*. In the aesthetics of penmanship lurked an explosive twist.

By and large, cassette poets have continued to foreground the kind of written stylistics that had long characterized *bidʿ wa jiwāb* verse. As detailed in chapter 2, prominent features (such as overall compositional unity, length, a seven-part thematic sequence, and dense intertextuality in the response poem) signal deference to an esteemed tradition of highland epistolary verse.

Figure 4.1. The signature of Shayef Muḥammad al-Khāledī.

In addition, poets have employed fairly eloquent varieties of Arabic, following conventions of poetic embellishment that have developed over time and can be understood by poetry aficionados in many parts of the Arab world.[24] Although poets regularly employed vernacular words, their diction varied from that typically heard in everyday conversation, as affirmed to me by some young Yemenis who were not conversant with poetry and admitted difficulty in understanding cassette poets' verses. The tendency of established poets to ornament their verse with more rarefied vocabulary, sometimes drawn from classical Arabic, was partly a result of their efforts to reach poetry fans of diverse backgrounds, including those living in urban centers and foreign diasporic communities. The privileging of such literary language for these reasons was illustrated to me by one well-known cassette poet, Thabit ʿAwad, in an especially poignant way.

Writing a *qaṣīdah* for cassette release in 1979, ʿAwad decided to compare the instability of South Yemeni political appointments to the succession of leaders that had marked national struggles in the Sudan and in Libya. Living in Saudi Arabia at the time, ʿAwad had been keen to link Yemeni affairs to events in the Arab Islamic world that were more germane to migrant communities abroad than to villagers in the highlands at home. After some thought, he composed the following verses:

gā Jaʿfar an-Numaīrī wa daff Ismāʿīl min ʿālā raṣīf
wa-l-Lībī muʿammar qadhaf b-Idrīs as-Sanūsī qadhīf

[Along] came Jaʿfar al-Numaīrī, [who] nudged Ismāʿīl from the highest platform
While the antiquated Libyan gave Idris al-Sanūsī a mighty boot.

Just as the Sudanese premiere Jaʿfar al-Numairi had overthrown the government of Prime Minister Ismaʿil al-Azharī in 1969, so had Libya's Muʿammar Qadhdhāfī replaced the King of Libya, Idris al-Sanusi, in the same year. The pun on Qadhdhafi's name endowed the poet's comparison with special humor: in the opening section of the second strophe, the name "Muʿammar" is used as a modifying adjective meaning "antiquated," and in the second part, Qadhdhafi becomes *qadhaf*. In classical Arabic, *qadhaf* comes from the verb "to evict," "to hurl," or, as I have rendered to preserve the sense of fun, "to give a boot."[25] The message was readily familiar to wider cosmopolitan audiences abroad.

As ʿAwad explained, *qadhaf* has a quite different meaning in the Yafiʿi dialect: "to vomit." As a result, such a verse was bound to be almost nonsensical for audiences in his native homeland. ʿAwad explained to me that his dilemma was vexing since to craft his verse for one audience meant sacrificing its meaning for another. Ultimately, however, he decided that producing a ripe pun for cosmopolitan audiences outweighed the costs of its misunderstanding at home. The verbal wordplay was kept, and ʿAwad received explicit criticism from Yafiʿi residents at home when he returned to visit several months later. Transcription for cassette release had alienated local audiences by compelling ʿAwad to privilege an especially literary language variety that had few admirers at home.

As poets use written stylistics and classical Arabic, however, they have also taken advantage of the cassette medium to convey a transcriptive dissonance that signals their estrangement from norms of epistolary decorum. As we have seen in the composition event described in chapter 1, the cassette is considered a medium of rarefied prestige by rural poets who wish to reach broader audiences. While perhaps lacking the public cachet of more influential media channels, the cassette nevertheless offers imaginative possibilities that are more finely attuned to the concerns, needs, and moral dilemmas of a discursive community that includes a variety of rural as well as urban listeners. Indeed, where writing has become a far more accessible competence for most Yemenis than a voice worthy of recorded song, the cassette proves host to a set of inscriptive competences that demonstrate new kinds of metropolitan virtue. In this respect, leading cassette poets are celebrated less for their attachments to traditional families of religious notables or to the epistemological frameworks of state education than for their savvy world view as rural migrants who have made good in the big city. With some irony, however, performing in a metropolitan style is not a matter of disclaiming rural heritage but of demonstrating that self-awareness of the metropolitan "frame" of bumpkin can make possible a resolute difference from metropolitan identity.[26] In this sense, poets *perform* metropolitan competence rather than merely demonstrate it and in the process reassert a generalized rural sensibility.

A range of techniques can be identified to help us understand how poets reassert rural identity amid the metropolitan demands of inscriptive media. One method is to inflect standardized verse with marked dialect words that signal the poet's partial deference to the speech communities of intended audiences. Although all Yemenis are Arabic speakers, numerous dialects are scattered across Yemen's peaks and valleys and are sometimes specific to individual clusters of villages. Although such linguistic differentiation has waned since the 1960s with the growth of labor migration, mobility, standardized education, and print and audiovisual media, poets still take pride in their abilities to tailor poems to specific dialect groups, especially when communicating with one another across considerable distances. One successful Yafiʿi cassette poet explained the practical importance of such accommodation: "Although I compose in a popular language *(lughah ʿāmah)* that is accessible to everyone, I sometimes adopt the dialect *(lahjah)* of my correspondent. This way, he can enjoy my poem when hearing it, understand it quickly, and circulate it among his friends more rapidly." One can speculate about the degree of success with which poets tailor verses to the nuanced language codes of speech communities other than their own. Nevertheless, the poet's statement indicates the value that Yemenis place on poems that defer to the linguistic habits of audiences. At the very least, unusual dialect words suggest to listeners that a given poem might be circulating well among a community of speakers other than one's own.

In addition to choices of dialect and language variety, poets can address audiences in ways that emphasize rural familiarity, even while pitching verses to broad audiences. Instead of addressing specific individuals at the outset of *qaṣīdahs,* cassette poets demonstrate a special talent in generalizing pronominal references with rural flair in order to address multiple potential addressees. Poets compose verses to the "People of al-Baīḍāʾ," for example, rather than to a specific poet from al-Baīḍāʾ and often use place names to stand in synecdocally for a single poet or social group. One fan of cassette poetry in Yafiʿ remarked that Shayef al-Khaledi became highly skilled at composing *jiwāb qaṣīdahs* that invited responses from any listener. Indeed, in one *qaṣīdah* that spoke broadly of Yafiʿi and Yemeni history and was released on cassette a few months earlier, Khaledi's addressee was no more specific than "those who sought me." Although such broad addresseeship had existed in earlier poetry, it was unusual in a poem of *bidʿ wa jiwāb* style, which was noticed by this fan and remarked on, not altogether disapprovingly, as a clever "trick" *(munāwarah).* Switching deftly from collective third-person to direct first-person address, Khaledi had turned a custom of narrow epistolary address into a populist summons that spoke to every listener, irrespective of qualifications or accolades.

In the interests of pitching their work to broader audiences, including listeners who are less familiar with highland verse, poets have also excelled in a conversational, even journalistic style of narration that enables their *qaṣīdahs* to be more easily consumed.[27] Such chattiness frequently results in compositions that are exceedingly prolix, sometimes extending to eighty verses and occupying most of the side of a single cassette.[28] Although the length of poems was traditionally associated with a written stylistics (as discussed in chapter 2), such associations have become modified as compositions are rendered less grammatically dense, partly the result of an increasing tolerance for verbal formulas that can foreground a sense of everyday rustic traditionalism. In general, longer compositions have provided nonspecialist listeners with a fuller range of cues for understanding latent meanings and may well be helping cassette poets find a niche for folk poetry in a competitive media industry that is increasingly geared to supply audiences with relevant news and information. Longer cassette poems have become popular, however, as sources of witty entertainment. While many poets continue to be celebrated for measured words and stentorian oral vocality, cassette poets take a certain relish in double meanings, corny humor, self-parody, and feisty claptrap that is designed to expose the seams of a powerful metropolitan frame that defines their rural identities only incompletely. As is shown in the following two chapters, few poets have mastered this style with more finesse than those on the cassette series produced by Yafiʿi singer Husain ʿAbd al-Naser. Such poets have provided Yemeni audiences with a key resource for maintaining and reworking traditions of rural political activism in southern Yemen and with an important framework for resolving disputes during years in which the discursive authority of rural highlanders was challenged by state authorities.

The tenor of such modifications has lent poets' compositions a sense of unbridled political oratory that conveys an impression of dialogue occurring face to face. Indeed, opening supplications to God and the Prophet, conventionally a mark of eloquent written style (as I explain in chapter 2), are not uncommonly elided altogether, a practice that is rare in conventional *bidʿ wa jiwāb* verse but finds parallel in traditions of more aggressive, orally performed political satire in Yemen. By recalling earlier traditions of highland tribal invective, cassette poets have thus created a more generalized tribal voice that might be disseminated and reinvoked by diverse groups of people. And yet this general tribalism is a curious one. Even while stylized in relation to written epistolary verse, in the updated fashion of "metropolitan tribalism" that I discuss in chapter 2, it is given songful foundations in meter and rhyme schemes that are heavily indebted to a popular recording industry. Although poets continue to use longer meters that have expressed the refined literary stylistic of epistolary *bidʿ wa jiwāb* poetry (such as *baṣīṭ, ṭawīl,* and *hazaj*), some also regularly employ shorter meters that are suited to traditional highland chanting and dance. These include the *rajaz* as well as *mutaḍārik* meters, the latter of which conveys a somewhat novel, upbeat tempo that has become popular among fans of metropolitan pop song. Rhyme schemes that end in open vowels are employed to suit singers' tastes for vocal melisma at the end of each verse. In recent years, such performances have reinvigorated popular tastes for the end-verse sonority of a plaintive genre of southern rural song called *dān*. In short, poets' renditions of epistolary verse, while fashioned in the witty discourse of vociferous tribal firebrands, have also been rendered with rustic oral songfulness at the most elemental levels of heard poetry.

Insofar as poets stylize their verse to distance themselves from the civility of traditional epistolary decorum and regimes of writing, their work might be described as contributing to a critical "counterpublic."[29] Such collective resistance to norms of public identity is especially pronounced when poets employ marked colloquialisms, unbridled chattiness, peripheral topicality, irreverent humor, and other signs of estrangement from rational political discourse. Yet poets' attention to the latest trends in recorded song and their transcriptive attunement to the popular interests of cassette audiences also cue listeners to the challenges that poets face as activists who wish to reach broad audiences. Metropolitan sentiments are not easily shed, just as rural affiliations are not lightly acquired. While recorded song invites Yemenis to cultivate attractive and, in some ways, necessary metropolitan competences, its performance skills, instruments, and institutions have become less accessible to most people than those of orality and writing. To a greater extent than other media, audio recordings require collaboration, and successful releases are very much the product of people other than poets themselves. In tailoring their work for well-known cassette singers, poets cue audiences to the benefits as well as the costs of orchestrating political action through a recording industry. Collaboration with metropolitan song producers is necessary, but inscriptive regimes continue to risk alienating Yemenis from more accessible channels of political discourse, further depriving them of their traditional means to resolve communal problems.

The costs of poets' transcriptive accommodations are expressed graphically on a cassette jacket that Yafiʿi singer Husain ʿAbd al-Naser designed in the late 1980s. For many years, an enlarged copy of this jacket hung at the entrance of the Adeni cassette shop Thamūd Exhibition for display to visiting customers (see figure 4.2).[30] In some respects, the cassette jacket borrows from designs produced by Yemeni commercial recording companies for their pop-song stars. These jackets typically feature studio photographs of the singers, usually shown from the waist up and dressed in modern attire: men in a sport coat or light sweater and women in a dress with a throw or sometimes a veil *(ḥigāb)* draped over the uppermost part of the head. Photographs typically occupy at least half of the jacket cover, and rarely are stars shown holding musical instruments. The names of artists, album titles, and trade logos are arranged on the cover, and the overleaf contains song titles as well as studio contact information. 'Abd al-Naser's own cassette jacket reproduces many of these features. He is positioned centrally on the cover without his instrument. His studio trade symbol is located at the left margin, and his contact information is included on a ribbon design that wraps across the overleaf. His association with pop-star metropolitanism is awarded special salience at the ribbon's center, which displays the name of his Doha-based cassette shop and studio: "The Voice of Yemen Recordings for Video and Audiocassette" *(Tasjīlāt Ṣawt al-Yaman li-l-Fīdyū wa-l-Kāsēt)*. Drawing on the early twentieth-century designation of audio-recording technologies as "voice recordings" *(tasjīlāt sawṭiyyah)*, the label clearly announces that the studio's aim is to record Yemen's voice for graphic and then audio display. 'Abd al-Naser is positioned, above all, as a doyenne of visual media, a fitting role given that his shop offered customers cassettes and videos, most of which would have featured films from Egypt, Lebanon, India,

Figure 4.2. Cassette-jacket of Yafi'i folk-singer Husain 'Abd al-Nāṣer, with the former sultanate village of Lower Yafi' in the horizon.

and Southeast Asia. Few videos would have featured films from Yemen, given its lack of an indigenous film industry.

ʿAbd al-Naser's jacket design also differs from those of other pop-song cassettes, however. Although I was unable to interview him about his aims, the jacket's carefully arranged graphics suggest that a performance of a modern metropolitan identity is underway that is designed to signal its own artifice and construction. Indeed, I'd like to suggest that the singer works beside the poet, cuing audiences to the dilemmas of metropolitanism and signaling the resources available to political activists who are engaged in critical discourse. To begin with, the jacket's most salient image is not ʿAbd al-Naser himself, whose photograph occupies only a small portion of the cover, but his backdrop: a hilltop village in a vast landscape. The village pictured is al-Qārah, the preindependence capital of lower Yafiʿ and the revered headquarters of the former ʿAfīfī sultanate. In photographs of other Yafiʿi singers, such as those pictures hanging in the Adeni cassette shop A Piece of My Land, artists typically stand in front of studio backdrops that feature decidedly nonlocal settings, such as idealized rural landscapes, courtly gardens, and ultramodern foreign sites such as the Roosevelt Bridge in New York City. By contrast, ʿAbd al-Naser's backdrop presents a distinctive regional landmark for Yafiʿis, identified for nonlocals at the upper right corner by a sprouting coffee plant whose miraculous blossom reads "Yafiʿ al-Qārah." More pointedly, the former ʿAfifi sultanate is not simply a vision of timeless rural charm. For nearly three centuries, the sultanate capitals of lower Yafiʿ and upper Yafiʿ had represented the quintessence of indigenous metropolitan culture for Yafiʿis. Nowhere in Yafiʿ had stately decorum and authority been more prominently correlated with tribal politics than in the sitting room *(maglis)* of the reigning ʿAfifi sultan. There the sultan's legal counsels advised litigants on reconciling tribal and Islamic law,[31] his slaves distributed the sultan's wisdom and largesse to visiting delegates, his resident singers and musicians entertained guests with poems from near and far, and the sultan himself occasionally indulged friends and dignitaries with his own vocal performances accompaniment by his lute. There above all, the paramount tribal chief, who was the head of five tribal districts *(maktabs),* exemplified the coordination of metropolitan and tribal tact and preserved the moral order, in part through sung poetry and music. The force of the ʿAfifi musical imperium was captured in legends about a massive copper war drum that when hauled before enemy troops and struck summoned forth ten thousand genies *(ginn)* for the sultan's army. In modern nationalist contexts, the political power of musical sultans was inherited by the young singer and political activist Muhammad Bin ʿAīdrūs al-ʿAfīfī, who led a resistance movement against British colonial interests in the cotton-growing areas of Lahej and Abyan. A raid led by Muhammad in 1957 won a counterresponse from the Royal Air Force: the village of al-Qārah was decimated in a saturation bombing campaign from 1957 to 1962. Subsequent purgings of sultanate and tribal leaders by socialist officials after independence ensured the final demise of the ʿAfifi house.

ʿAbd al-Naser's cassette jacket is less a portrait of himself or his own authority in conveying pop song than it is a portrait of history and the moral standing of a certain culture of politics and song as it unfolded in a particular place. His carefully crafted vision invites the viewer to consider how metropolitan identity changes over time and has multiple registers, each continually struggling against the others in hopes of supremacy. The photograph of ʿAbd al-Naser captures this struggle as a tension between two different styles of metropolitan dress, expressed in his turban and tie. Surmounting his head is a traditional Yafiʿi turban that was made in India of a fine cotton fabric and that was once in vogue among preindependence sultanate elites but would have been viewed by more contemporary audiences as a heritage item. The association of the turban with an older world order is captured in its diagonal coils, which naturally parallel the slopes of the cliffs supporting al-Qārah above. The necktie and its accompanying suit are adornments that only Yemeni diplomats, international businessmen, or television personalities would wear even in modern Yemen, and their associations with such metropolitan culture seem confirmed by their pedestal: ʿAbd al-Naser's business card, which advertises his shop's audio-cassette, videocassette, telephone, and fax services. Between turban and tie, ʿAbd al-Naser's face suggests the glimmer of a subtle, playful smile. Which piece of clothing represents the real singer? A small black strip, placed carefully under the bust of the singer, partially covers his tie, as if someone were trying to suggest the answer "The traditional me!" but could only do so half-heartedly. A performance of two styles is underway, even if it seems amateur. Its collage invites viewers to consider how backgrounds, costumes, cover-ups, and transcriptions work together in conveying something that may be ultimately poorly suited to visual display.

Given what is known of consumers' interests as expressed in their requests at Adeni cassette shops (see chapter 3), one of the most glaring omissions from the jacket is the poet. The absence of poets is certainly common to other pop-song jackets; indeed, poets rarely appear at all. Here, however, the small size of the photo of the singer provides a striking contrast with other jackets, and it turns him into a figurehead for something of greater permanence and authority. With his own agency downplayed, the presence of others becomes foregrounded, whether they inhabit the village of al-Qārah, the highlands of Yafiʿ, or the verses of his song. Whatever their communal origins, much of the force of *bidʿ wa jiwāb* verse for listeners resides with the poets, and their authority hovers in the jacket's background as an invisible assembly whose reticence to appear in public might offer a final resolution between competing metropolitan images.

If ʿAbd al-Naser's jacket is considered as a trope—a poetic figure that conveys two layers of meaning, one accessible and the other more covert—then his work signals two different expressive forms: a metropolitan pop song that can circulate in cassette markets far and wide, and a subtler product by composers whose indigenous loyalties present no risk to the vitality of local communities. The poet is clearly missing, and yet as the inward moral anchor of a "general singing tribesman," the poet is also present as the singer's concealed twin, a collaborator whose discreet power lies in graphic negativity.

What kind of critical advantage could this stage-shy tribal songster possible offer to modern listeners? In the final sections of this chapter, I address this question by exploring the leverage that poets gain from the notion of a collaborative and scriptive author that is fundamentally split between two orders of being. Spoken words, I suggest, gain credibility when they are fashioned with inscriptive force in an altogether different register than the much-handled commerce of celebrated metropolitan producers. Before examining poets' authority under such tropic devices, however, I consider singers' own transcriptive work as they select, prepare, and adapt poets' compositions for audio recording.

THE CASSETTE SINGER'S TRANSCRIPTIONS: THE DIFFERENCE THAT DRAMA MAKES

In many ways, singers' own interventions parallel and amplify those of poets. Like poets, singers emphasize rural discourses that inform given poems and that unite correspondents in a shared moral universe. Nevertheless, I also attend to the ways in which singers' transcriptive strategies differ from those of poets. As producers who are more keenly attuned to the metropolitan tastes of urban audiences, singers dramatize a nationalist agonism between poets and also render poets' tribal associations more violent. By promoting a different set of representations of poets and their work than is usually conveyed in epistolary verse, singers ultimately provide both poets and audiences with the means to justify a more independent set of ethical claims.

Selecting, Preparing, Performing

When a singer receives a poem, several options are at hand. The poem can be discarded, a likely possibility if it is a poor composition or if its subject matter fails to engage the singer's interest. On the other hand, a good poem will likely be considered among other poems that a singer has in mind for an upcoming cassette. Some well-known singers receive dozens of poems each month, and others must solicit poems from acquaintances whose work they appreciate and would like to perform. Not uncommonly, a singer's decision about poems depends partly on advice from friends, on events that suddenly cast poems in new contexts, on poets' reputations, and on previous collaborations that have proven successful.

Once a singer decides to perform a given set of poems, written texts must be collected and prepared. Although things were different in the recent past, it is unlikely today that the singer will memorize the entirety of any given poem by rote and then perform it, especially where poems are over fifteen to twenty verses (as most cassette poems are nowadays), where topics covered are especially personal and event-specific, and where demands for rapid production favor a quick, no-frills recitation. This is particularly the case for recently authored poems that have not become part of the popular, orally circulated repertoire of folk songs. For this reason, a singer's first task is to produce texts that can be read carefully, parsed, mentally digested, and portions memorized. Usually, a singer can begin with a written or typed text that is supplied by the poet.

To give sound to the inscribed word of a given poem and ultimately to produce a metrically performable text, a singer must initially select a melody *(laḥn)*. Choosing an appropriate melody for a poem is not straightforward, since in Arabic poetry, written verse can be parsed in multiple ways. The art of tailoring word to song is one of great nuance.[32] In the transcriptive journey from poet to audience, a singer's selection of melody is an essential first step: an evocative melody that complements the thematics of a poem can deeply sway listeners, whereas a poor melodic choice can ruin even the finest composition. The complexity of adapting a text to melodic performance was illustrated for me by 'Ali Bin Jāber, a cassette singer who is widely considered to be one of the most creative music producers in Yafiʿ today (he released the record-breaking Ḥunaīsh cassette, discussed in chapter 1). Jaber explained to me that one of the challenges of performing Yafiʿi highland *qaṣīdahs* for popular audiences is the adaptation of traditional poetic texts to interesting new melodies. "Most poets who send me *qaṣīdahs* use a restricted set of traditional meters," he told me, "and each of these meters can be sung to perhaps five or six melodies only. These conservative techniques—which come from the isolation of the region from other regions—prevent me from introducing creative adaptations to Yafiʿi song." To enhance a poem's appeal for popular audiences, Jaber uses a variety of compositional techniques to adapt vernacular texts for broader audiences. These techniques, which are employed by many Yemeni popular singers, include tailoring traditional melodies to new rhythms *(īqāʿs),* introducing melodies with preludes that are adapted from widely recognized, pan-Arab song genres,[33] changing melodies midtext for longer compositions, recruiting amateur choruses to help sing selected refrains, and using a broader arrangement of instruments not traditionally used in the highlands, such as bongo drums, violins, double-reed flutes, and occasionally electric keyboards. In a conservative highlands musical culture, such adaptations have not been without controversy. Although they have helped render highland vernacular texts more performable and appealing to broader audiences, they also open Jaber to criticism from traditionalists at home that he panders to a mass market in the interests of fame and fortune.

Aside from choices of melody, instrumentation, and performance style, one of the most effective means for underscoring the thrust of a poet's verse is repetition. Typically, a singer performs three to six verses in succession and then adds a brief instrumental riff. On resuming the lyrics, the last one or two verses of the previous verse cluster are sung again. This technique ensures that the most meaningful verses of the poem, at least from the singer's perspective, are underscored twice, both through elaborated instrumentation and through repetition. A different technique, used to similar effect, is to employ an amateur chorus (usually male friends, though women choruses can be heard on some cassettes that were recorded in the early 1980s) to chant out a refrain at the end of every verse cluster. This refrain may be the first verse of the poem or, on occasion, another verse that a singer feels to be important and wishes to emphasize. Aside from repetition, more direct textual interventions can be made. A singer can emphasize the distinctive dialectal markers of a given poet, for example, to foreground his regional origins. Through such conventions of performance, all of which are widely accepted by poets and audiences, a singer can foreground particular interpretations of poems without accusations of textual meddling.

Editing Texts

To examine the nature of cassette singers' textual modifications, I conducted a word-for-word comparison between a set of original, handwritten poems that I gathered from poets in Yafiʿ and their sung renditions as performed by two well-known Yafiʿi singers, Husain ʿAbd al-Naser and ʿAli Ṣāleḥ.[34] I then discussed my observations with Yemenis to assure myself that I understood the implications of some of the finer attunements. My aim was to understand better the demands that were being made on poets and audiences who looked to cassette poems as examples of authoritative public verse. To what extent did singers' modification differ from those of corresponding *bidʿ wa jiwāb* poets? To what extent did such differences identify the cassette medium as a distinct instrument of transcription and reproduction?

Out of sixteen cassette poems examined on the ʿAbd al-Naser series, all but one contained notable departures from the original handwritten texts (aside from expected mispronunciations, vocal extensions for song performance, repeated verses and choruses, and so forth). Some *qaṣīdahs* had as little as two notable modifications; one especially popular twenty-seven-verse *qaṣīd-*

ah contained eleven modifications (Šunbaḥī's *qaṣīdah* on cassette 99; see chapter 6). Many of the changes were not simply instances of leveling toward transregional linguistic and poetic standards, as I had imagined might be the case. Changes also involved rendering poems even more vernacular and, more generally, translating unfamiliar extraregional and extranational references for local audiences. Singers were, in some respects, amplifying the vernacular, rustic tenor of poets' verse even as they were pitching their work to more diverse metropolitan audiences.

To begin with, most modifications by both ʻAbd al-Naser and Saleh involve furthering poets' own aims of rendering poems more conducive to song and more digestible by nonspecialist highland audiences. Words with pinched fronted vowels and consonants, for example, are replaced with synonyms that contain open rounded vowels and pharyngeal consonants *(yaglis → yabqā, qaṣar → faṣal, antum → antū, fī rabʿhā → min ḥawlihā)*. Such changes are often made for melodic purposes and can involve more complete revisions of syntax and aspect. Thus, in a verse that is set to a *rajaz* meter (- - ^-/ - - ^-), the phrase "You need not follow" is changed to "You need not have followed" *(mā wāgib annak tatbaʿ → mā kān*[a] *wāgib tatbaʿ)* so that a long note can be drawn out with the appropriate word *(wāgib)*. Despite a change in verbal aspect, in this extreme case, singers make such revisions to achieve a more melodious interpretation that can be better enjoyed by listeners.

Sometimes grammatical changes are made less for musical reasons than to avoid monotony. Occasionally, a word repeated twice in succession may be replaced with a synonym. More often, a singer can modify a verse when singing it more than once (at a refrain, for example). Thus, the verse "Even if he went to the Prophet's place" becomes, in the second singing, "Even if he made a pilgrimage and visited the Prophet," and in one case the verse "There is no dignity when we are in conflict, such deadly combat" is rephrased "There is no dignity when we are *always* in such deadly conflict" to imply a more permanent, ongoing struggle. Such adaptations are akin to the lexical substitutions that poets make in oral improvisation. Here, however, more premeditation is involved as the singer makes written transcriptive notes on the text ahead of time, cuing himself to alter verses later in performance.

Aside from grammatical substitutions, singers can subtly tailor poems to more diverse audiences by altering poetic conventions as well. Such modifications tend to foreground oral parallelism over dense written composition, and where these oral conventions reinforce traditional patterns of social interaction, they help underscore the traditional rural roots of poets' discursive communities. Rendering a verse more proverbial is one of the most common ways to accomplish such oral effects. In these cases, a verse is changed slightly to focus on a single word whose reiteration in an altogether different context provides grounds for a commonsense moral judgment. In one case, a singer reworks the phrase "Is that justice, or is fear absent?" with a more proverbial ring: "Is that justice, or is justice absent?" Embedded in such lexical parallelism is the kind of self-correcting retribution that is found in the proverb "Whoever stones his guard dog is stoned by people" *(min ragam kalbuh ragamūh an-nās)*. A slightly different modification toward oral parlance also involves lexical parallelism, but this time it concentrates on the rhyme words at the end of each strophe in a couplet. In the verse "They are supporters with me, and the house needs supporters / Who persevere and demand protection and repairing" *(hum murādim maʿī wa-d-dār yishtī murādim / dhī taṣummuh wa yataṭallab ṣiyānah wa rammām)*, the final rhyme word "repairing" *(rammām)* is changed, with the substitution of a single consonant, to the word "supporting" *(radām)* to establish a more pronounced lexical parallelism with the preceding strophe. Since such a change conforms to a oratorical punning structure found frequently in traditional highland *qaṣīdahs*, the verse becomes more easily accessible to audiences, sometimes allowing the most competent listeners to guess the final rhyme word ahead of time and shout it out with gusto (as illustrated in chapter 1).

Finally, orally marked themes in poems can also be foregrounded, as when one singer flipped two lines to consolidate verses that address the correspondent poet, even though an intervening verse of more general commentary had separated these lines in the poet's original text.[35] In all such cases, modifications serve to rework the "written style" of poets' epistolary verse toward an "oral style" that also happens to be sung, as if each poet was regaling the next with live performances of melodious letter poems. For a diverse range of listeners who are less familiar with the nuances of highland *bid' wa jiwāb* poetry, such adaptations help dramatize poets' verses by investing them with a heightened immediacy and also allow them to enjoy a fluid performance of poems without having to stop the cassette, rewind it, and listen a second time.

In many modifications, singers expurgate regionally circumscribed vocabulary to help audiences quickly appreciate poets' political messages (e.g., *rā'* → *shūf, yiglis* → *yabqā, talāṭim* → *taṣādim, luḥfatī* → *shiffatī*). Such changes are somewhat predictable, given 'Abd al-Naser and Saleh's residence abroad and experiences with a diversity of Arabic-speaking audiences. Nevertheless, an equivalent number of modifications do just the opposite, replacing standard words with vernacular alternatives. In many poems, for example, Husain 'Abd al-Naser replaces standard Arabic nominal articles *(al-)* with a vernacular article common to certain middle-highlands regions of Yemen *(um-)*. Given linguistic standardization by the 1970s and 1980s, such an article would nowhere have been heard in the public performances of artists in Yemen and would certainly have struck many listeners as rustic. Another substitution toward similar ends foregrounds vernacular syntax to convey a model of traditional rural authority that might provide both North and South Yemen with a common moral resource. In this instance, a Yafi'i poet describes the valor of his correspondent's allies from al-Qaīfah, an area in the northern highlands: "Shaikh al-Dhahab is in it, and in it are people of dignity and substance. / Since long ago and even now in Qaīfah, how many snakes and vipers" *(Shēkh adh-*

Dhahab fīhā wa fīhā ahl ash-shahāmah wa-sh-shiyyam / min qabl wa-s-sā'ah bi-Qēfah kam min il-ḥayyah wa-l-hām). The singer reworks the first phrase, using a vernacular expression that, while common in everyday speech, is rarely ever encountered in poetry, thus producing the following verse: "There is a man, Dhahab, a village leader *('āqal),* and in it are (also) people of dignity and substance" *(fī ḥad Dhahab 'āqal wa fīhā ahl ash-shahāmah wa-sh-shiyyam).* Even as the verse is rendered more vernacular, however, the content of the verse is made more accessible for southern Yemeni audiences who lack a knowledge of the northern Yemeni figure Shaikh al-Dhahab. My informants noted that the singer's generalizing strategy hinged on his modification of the term "shaikh." After decades of socialist reform in the People's Democratic Republic of Yemen in which tribes and tribal shaikhs had been labeled vestiges of the backward past, the term "shaikh" had acquired negative connotations for many southern audiences, implying a supercilious character or someone who might flaunt his money. The substituted word "village leader" *('āqil),* by contrast, had long been used by a southern populace in both preindependence days and afterward and thus averted implications of sarcasm that might have inflected the poet's words. Additionally, the singer's modification helped avoid a possible linguistic canard that resulted from the poet's term of address. When the title of "shaikh" modifies proper names, it requires an article *(ash-Shēkh adh-Dhahab).* Since the poet had elided the article, probably for metrical purposes, the resulting phrase could be misinterpreted pejoratively as "the shaikh of gold," since *dhahab* coincidentally means "gold" in Arabic. With deft transcription, the singer's version at once bracketed a politically touchy reference to tribalism, sidestepped potential hints of sarcasm, and ensured that southern listeners would receive a favorable view of the commonalities of village-based moral authority that were shared in both Yemens.

By foregrounding vernacular speech, oratory, and traditions of rural moral authority, singers helped emphasize a substrate of rural political discourse that informed poets' work and that helped underscore pan-regional commonalties that united the majority of Yemenis. As a Yafi'i colleague told me when referring to a recently released cassette of *bid' wa jiwāb* exchanges between two poets from northern governorates, "Such cassettes are important because they might serve as a stimulus to audiences in those regions to ask questions about scandals rather than sit idly by." *Bid' wa jiwāb* cassette poetry could provide a common language for political mobilization wherever it was disseminated.

Singers' transcriptive strategies also differed in important respects from those of poets. In the context of escalating tensions between the People's Democratic Republic of Yemen and the Yemen Arab Republic over the course of the 1970s and 1980s, cassette poetry provided a lively forum for agonistic debate over contending nationalist programs, and singers geared their modifications toward highlighting the stakes of political competition between the two countries. As is shown in chapter 6, discourses of tribalism grew increasingly central to debates between cassette poets, and singers again tailored poets' correspondences to wider audiences. While careful to avoid charges of tribal recidivism by those loyal to PDRY nationalist agendas, both singers' transcriptions suggest that they invoke armed versions of tribalism that underscore and dramatize poets' capacities to mete out stern justice during an age in which competing nationalisms have failed to alleviate social inequities.

Although singers' efforts to foreground vernacular Arabic emphasize shared discourses of rustic moral authority, so too can vernacular modification invoke rustic violence. After the Yemeni War of 1994, a singer modified one of Khaledi's most vitriolic openings to the northern poet Ahmad al-Sunbahi: "Death's poison is in my dagger. I'll slice into the jugular vein." The verse itself, while expressing the deeply bitter public mood that followed on the heels of the war, nevertheless preserved a literary elegance in selecting the classical Arabic word "my blade" *(ṣārimī)* to describe the poet's weapon of choice.[36] For this word, the singer substituted a rough equivalent "my dagger" *(khanjarī)* that is more readily understood by Yafi'is. The hallmark symbol of tribal honor has long been the curved dagger, although the weapon became disparaged by southern nationalist reformers during the 1970s and 1980s. Known as the *jambiyyah,* the dagger is typically displayed by men by being placed in a sheath that extends prominently upward from the belt line. The singer's modification invokes this tradition, suggesting that tribal mores of honor and self-protection were perhaps being invoked. Yet he does so with a vulgar twist: the *khanjar,* a much cruder variant of the *jambiyyah,* was historically the weapon of the lower status nontribesmen, thus signaling a capacity for violence without honor. The singer's revision invests the verse with a raw irreverence for the ideals of civil society or even northern discourses of high-minded tribalism and conveys something profoundly dangerous about the scrappy retribution that defeated rural southerners could employ to achieve justice.

In a second example, an equally subtle lexical substitution is made to dramatize the potential threat of a more Islamic and tribal system of governance in the former YAR against the socialist revolution in the PDRY. In the following verses, a northern poet questions a Yafi'i correspondent about upcoming negotiations over unity between the two Yemens and expresses his own opinion through a metaphor of marriage:

> And the caliphate, to whom? Tell me, if you haven't been impaired, 13
> Which of the uncle's children do you see having claim to the virgin?
> He who has the right is the one who governed the Quraīsh, the son of Ḥāshem.
> It is he who protects the house and the virgin, safeguarding the orphans.[37]

In invoking a potential union between a "virgin" and children of the (paternal) uncle *(awlād al-a'mām),* a link between parallel cross-cousins that is preferred throughout the Arab world, the northern poet recurs to a framework of patrilineal descent. In the second verse, the poet qualifies such descent in Islamic terms. Where the patrilineal group traces ancestry to the Prophet Muhammad's Quraīsh tribe, the poet implies that Yemen's leadership should be composed of religious *sayyids,* whose most powerful members in the north were historically Zaidi imams who "governed" (the poet uses the verb *sāda,* the cognate of *sayyid*) largely from Sanaa.[38] In the final strophe, verbs of tribal protection *(yakfil)* and safeguarding *(yaḍman)* suggest that the authority of tribal honor *(ʿirḍ)* is also central to Yemen's future Islamic state.

Although the poet's two verses clearly imply that Yemen should be governed by a northern leadership, ambiguity still lingers over exactly which "Yemen" is intended. As one interviewee pointed out, the word "house" in the final strophe is especially misleading as it suggests the possibility that "Quraīsh" governance might be restricted to the protection of its own ruling descent group and "virgin." Accordingly, in the sung version of the poem, the phrase "the house and the virgin" *(al-bēt wa-l-ʿadhrāʾ)* is replaced with one that sounds almost the same: "The daughter and family" *(al-bint wa-l-usrah).* Through subtle phonetic substitution, a pair of symbols well known in socialist slogans and political poetry engenders South Yemen's revolution as a "daughter" or "mother" and North Yemen's tribalism and religious conservatism in masculine terms. The singer's intervention leaves no doubt that the northern poet's hopes for tribal protection, extended now across the whole of both Yemens, are radical indeed.

Singers' efforts to embellish the vernacular, oral, and frequently agonistic tenor of poets' correspondences contribute to a final pattern that is regularly found in their modifications: an emphasis on nationalist violence. My Yafiʿi informants corroborated that, in a number of cases, singers inflected poets' nationalist descriptions with a greater martial and combative tenor. In one verse, a description of the poet's own dedicated, laboring "people" as comfortable *(murtāḥ)* is changed to staunch *(ṣāmid)* to avoid implying that good citizens are indolent. In other verses, "Here, the people will not submit" becomes an aggressive "You confront a people who will not submit!"; a playful expression "tigers slapping *(talāṭim)* with gnashes" becomes "tigers colliding *(taṣādim)* with gnashes"; the verb "we crossed" *(igtāznā)* becomes "we scorched" *(aḥraqnā)* in a battle narrative; a poet's past-tense insinuation of socialist party fanaticism—"You had advanced them *(qaddamt[a]hum)* in front of their banners"—becomes recast in the present: "Those who still remain" *(mā dāmat hum);* and so forth. For singers, nationalism becomes a violent enterprise that, like tribalism, highlights poets' raw rural verve, one situated at a critical angle to more civil traditions of metropolitan song and discourse.

In sum, the two singers' transcriptive strategies foreground poets' rural authority by calling greater attention to their competences as vernacular wordsmiths whose talents in oratory are demonstrated in proverbial wit, rhymed puns, hearty greetings, and colloquial diction. By contrast, singers downplay poets' competences as epistolary correspondents whose principal medium is writing. As a result, singers promote cassette poets' reputations as political wordsmiths who are adept in the finesse of metropolitan song but nevertheless retain a profound connection to traditions of rural discourse. Ultimately, singers' transcriptive interventions imbue such poets' orality with new social significance. Insofar as cassette poets become exemplars (or metonymns) of a traditional highland community of rural inhabitants whose conversancy with metropolitan letters and song is necessarily incomplete, their oratory also conveys more disturbing threats to established conventions of civil society. Whether through martial tribalism or aggressive nationalism, cassette poetry broadcasts a different set of competences than is typically evident in poets' own written letters. Dramatized strains of violence in poets' discourse represent rural political authority as potentially very nasty. Such representations enable cassette poets' political roles by promoting their ability to contest enduring forms of injustice that are perpetuated by state and global orders. Simultaneously, singers' interventions in cassette poetry provide poets and audiences with a reflexive template for considering the moral costs of political action through modern forms of media. I explore how Yemenis evaluate these costs further below and in the next chapter.

LETTERS, BULLETS, SANDWICHES, COCKTAILS: COLLABORATIVE AUTHORS AND THE MORAL LEVERAGE OF TROPES

In assessing the textual adjustments that poets and singers make as they craft political verse for cassette audiences, the strategies of both groups of artists parallel and complement each other in many ways. Poets tailor the form and content of their epistolary poems to suit the more metropolitan inclinations of singers and their audiences, while singers accommodate poets' interests in preserving their influence as political authorities with strong rural roots. Over the course of a half century of recording experience, both groups of artists have learned the importance of collaboration to producing popular cassettes, and they have modified their competences accordingly.

The transcriptive strategies of poets and singers, however, also reveal differences that distinguish their contributions. Whereas poets foreground their mastery of traditional themes in rural highland political discourse, singers inflect poets' verse with a more pronounced rustic veneer and, in doing so, underscore a violence in poets' rural tendencies that threatens to disrupt more civil traditions of metropolitan order and moral sentiment. To some extent, these alternate emphases accord with the traditional roles that poets and singers have played as critical activists. Since poets have been valued mediators in political disputes and continue to provide guidance in regional leadership, administration, and arbitration, an emphasis on their traditional, if restylized, political capacities suits their practical work. Professional singers, by contrast, are held to lack the necessary qualifications to undertake the serious business of dispute negotiation. Although they may be influential brokers of political culture, especially as public performers who enjoy special leeway in dramatizing underlying moral tensions, singers cannot match poets' reputations as credible proponents of traditional political action. In these respects, poets and singers' transcriptive strategies might be seen to serve moral functions for different, if overlapping, communities.

The dramatization of poets' rustic and potentially violent inclinations, however, underscores tensions that poets confront as they struggle to retain credible moral authority in the twenty-first century. By participating in the cassette-recording market, poets confront their own stereotyping not simply as countermetropolitan but, more troubling, as extrametropolitan—beyond the pale of civil orders and those who live in them. Such profound social exclusion, playful though it may be, risks eroding poets' already dwindling influence on political discourse in modern Yemen. Aside from the growing array of state services that have rendered poets' traditional verbal talents less integral to the conduct of daily political life, poets have also become far more dependent on an expansive range of producers and consumers for delivering their work to audiences. For many Yemenis, performances of clamorous tribal sparring that are so endemic to political cassette verse do little to retrieve the kind of gravitas and dignity that they expect of public voices.

In this context, the concepts of authorship through writing and of the leverage of graphic tropes become enabling resources for poets and their supporters. I first consider poets' attitudes toward authorship and conclude the chapter by exploring the advantages that graphic tropes present when addressing authorial dilemmas. Given cassette poets' competences in reading and writing and their commitments to education and literary knowledge, it is not surprising that poets take authorship seriously. While in Yemen, however, I was always struck by the tendency among poets to redouble their efforts to perform the conventional signs of authorship. When reciting their *qaṣīdahs* live in front of public audiences, cassette poets would always read aloud from their own notebooks of handwritten originals rather than recite their verse from memory (see figure 4.3). Such performances contrasted with the script-free recitations of an older generation of nonpublished poets, who had few stakes in debates over authorship, and with the tendency of established neoclassical poets who often took special delight in reciting at least a few verses by heart, perhaps to convince audiences of their connections with indigenous oral tradition. Cassette poets differed from these individuals, preferring large notebooks that they held prominently before them. Where their reputations had preceded them in registers of mellifluous chat, oral declamation, and barbed rustic wit, these icons of the homegrown recording industry took special pains to assure audiences that their compositions had sprung from original penned inscriptions and had not been transmitted blindly from the accumulated wisdom of oral tradition.

The association of writing and "authorship" *(tā'līf)* has a long history in the Arab world.[39] Attuned to this legacy, cassette poets carefully foreground their own production of original and authoritative written texts. Some poets hand out photocopies of

Figure 4.3. Shayef al-Khāledī recites his latest cassette poetry from a personal notebook, 1998.

their written work to audiences, while others who are better known distribute copies of their poems in newspapers or occasionally, if they gain a national reputation, assemble a small paperback volume of their verse. In the early 1990s, Khaledi had a small collection of his own *qaṣīdah* verse published, mostly featuring nationalist and love poems that had never been released on cassette.[40] Such have been the signs of the enfranchised, productive author.

To some extent, such obligations of authorship reflect conventions of genre. *Qaṣīdah* poetry, in particular, has long been one of the most prominent venues for authorial distinction in the Arab world, as is evident in early written records of *qaṣīdahs* from the Arabian Peninsula.[41] Studies of *qaṣīdah* composition by recent generations of scholars suggest that authorship of the *qaṣīdah's* "text utterance" remains a lively topic, as evidenced in listeners' debates over the circumstantial origins of given verses, even in traditions of oral *qaṣīdah* poetry among nonliterate Arab Bedouin.[42] Singers who perform *qaṣīdahs,* likewise, take far greater care in adhering to poets' texts than they do when performing other more improvisatory verbal genres, such sea-chantey *mawwāl* songs or epic narratives *(sīra)*.[43]

Over the last century in Yemen, the *qaṣīdah* genre has been integrated ever more centrally with notions of authorship through nationalist discourses. Where nationalism seeks historical moorings in notions of cultural authenticity, *qaṣīdah* composition has provided citizens with an extraordinary resource for identifying links between cultural heritage and the nation's progressive modern ambitions. Nationalist reformers have found special leverage in making such connections when using media technologies that invite audiences to reflect on how traditions of *qaṣīdah* poetry can be sustained and also modified under new social and technological conditions. Whether reprinted in early twentieth-century lithographs of handwritten manuscripts, published in socialist party pamphlets or newspapers, broadcast through the radio and audio-recording technologies, or performed on television during prime-time talk shows, *qaṣīdahs* have helped Yemenis consider how newly mediated forms of identity and selfhood might draw from collective expressive repertoires. Central to such initiatives are debates not solely about textual traditions and influential composers but also about the challenges of balancing creativity *(ibdāʿah)* and authenticity *(aṣālah)*. Even as artists are expected to produce new variations in the formal structures, themes, or moods of *qaṣīdah* poetry, so too they are expected to transmit something essential and unchanging, the true nature of which has inevitably remained obscure.[44] I devote more attention to cassette poets' reactions to these heavily nationalized discourses of authorship in the following chapter.

The impetus for cassette poets to demonstrate their authorial competences comes less from nationalist reformers or certified arbiters of intellectual creativity, however, than it does from their own prime audiences. Cassette listeners showed a special interest in monitoring poets' integrities as composers. Indeed, when I interviewed listeners, concerns over authorship seemed to be expressed with vehemence for reasons that were rather straightforward. First, such listeners felt greater connection to the textual and aesthetic repertoires of regional cassette producers than they did with more prominent producers of state-run media. Second, and more vexing, authorial claims on cassette poetry were easily manipulated given the industry's informal regulation, haphazard production practices, and decentralization. For these two sets of reasons, listeners felt that cassette poets occupied sensitive positions in larger debates over authorship. Some listeners, for example, expressed concern over the way the cassette industry's fast-paced production standards encouraged poets to disregard the integrity of original written texts. One informant explained that, in the interests of frequent and timely releases, cassette poets borrowed others poets' verses without acknowledgment and abandoned any effort to tailor words to a graceful melody *(laḥn)*. Such haste, he insisted, marked the inferior quality of cassette poetry in comparison with poetry composed and sung by prerecording-era masters. For other listeners, new styles of cheeky verbal sparring, satire, and rustic violence advertised the fundamental disingenuousness of poets, singers, and their fans. Poets' desire for fame *(shuhrah)* seemed to eclipse their sense of moral balance and was directly attributable to the access they had to the popular mouthpiece of the audiocassette. By securing contacts with well-known singers, poets untried in the broader waters of conventional authorship could leverage their "language of the market" *(lughat al-sūq)* onto popular cassettes, compelling even the finest poets to respond to them, if only to quash their slanderous doggerel. Cassette poets were different from their forebears, one critic suggested, insofar as they indulged in wild "exaggeration" *(mubālaghah)* designed to sustain a "media war" *(ḥarb iʿlāmī)* that prevented them from commenting on local conditions with "dignity and moral virtue" *(adab w-akhlāq)*. Again, fans of cassette poetry regularly celebrate poets' abilities to disseminate political verse widely to help redress urgent social and political tensions. But the same fans also lament the passing of an earlier era in which such tensions were addressed at more local levels with poems that, in one informant's words, were "measured" *(mawzūn)* and had "traces" *(āthār)*. Contributing to lively controversy over the role of cassettes in Yemeni moral life, such comments all revealed concerns that the noisy dissonance of cassettes might be somehow depreciating the value of public discourse.

The challenge for cassette poets in addressing such concerns is enormous. Especially tricky is the question of how to address such impugning of credibility within the cassette industry itself. Part of the trouble would seem to stem from the medium itself. Unlike books or written documents, whose aesthetic and functional benefits Yemenis have long esteemed, plastic cassette cartridges are not typically given much credit as potential vessels for communal knowledge and so are typically left in make-shift parts of the house, passed on to friends, or stuffed in plastic sacks rather than stored on shelves where they can be displayed to guests and visibly monitored. The recording capacities of cassettes present especially serious challenges to authorial standards. Cassettes flout authorial norms when, precisely because they are "user friendly," they can be used by those who would plagiarize and take credit for verses other than one's own. Audiences had all heard narratives about poets or singers who had unfairly gained recognition for work that had originally belonged to someone else. Most concerning of all, especially among poets, are unwarranted modifications of poems that are made by singers. In numerous interviews that I held with poets, I was told of a host of procedures that were usually taken to monitor verses as they passed through multiple stages of planning, editing, performance, and recording. These included, ideally, collaborating with singers when planning cassettes so that prior agreement could be reached about compositional aims, topics, and audiences.[45] More frequently, poets spoke of their efforts to advise singers on performance and cassette production only after their poems had been received. Such advice included clarifying the meaning and pronunciation of vernacular words or proposing appropriate melodies. The preferred mode of communication for such matters was face-to-face contact and regular phone calls with the singer, although poets also acknowledged spending time annotating their written texts with Arabic diacritical marks *(ḥarakāt)* that could cue singers on how to pronounce unfamiliar words.[46] Indeed, several of the most famous cassette poets whom I interviewed acknowledged that without such contact, poems could wither on the vine. Reflecting on a cassette that had recently been released, the poet Thabit ʿAwad (whose verses about Qadhdhāfī are discussed earlier) remarked: "The cassette didn't circulate too well. Basically, I didn't have adequate contact with the singer who performed it. The poem is all right, since people like my poems, but the whole thing didn't exactly happen as I would have liked." Even as highly valued technologies, cassettes remain fraught with authorial anxieties, no more so than for poets who grapple with the transcriptive demands of moving written texts from pen to polyester recording tape.

Poets and singers alike understand the need to channel popular attitudes about cassette-text manipulation toward a more stable authorial center. The question that confronts them is how to bring the cassette lyrics of metropolitan singers back to the valued customs of everyday speakers. It is precisely here, I suggest, that the trope of what I have called the "general singing tribesman" proves instrumental. As a hybrid product of collaboration between poets and singers, the trope offers Yemenis a way to reassert the authorial integrity of poets while also acknowledging the pressures of cultural and technological standardization that they face. In broadest terms, tropes work by making a single concept, such as a "cassette poet," into a function of two signifying orders, each of which correlates with the other to indicate how the concept can truly be known.[47] While one order takes a position of greater salience, identifying the concept by more commonly recognized features, another order cues interpreters to a subtler logic, one whose features are informed by forces of entextualization that can be appreciated only with more refined ways of knowing. This latter, more "resonant" moral authority winks at the interpreter, signaling that the priorities of normative ordering are only decoys. In the particular case at hand, the two "orders" of the general singing tribesman are attached to the respective roles of poets and singers, each of which is polarized from the other through association with different moral communities.[48] Despite relatively minor discrepancies between poets' and singers' transcriptive strategies, singers come to be identified as the primary instigators of metropolitan attunement that distinguishes cassette poetry from traditional highland verse. Graphic aesthetics are especially helpful in staging the difference of singers from poets, as is shown on the cassette jacket designed by Husain ʿAbd al-Naser. What is most evident and "seen," however, is also a function of commonsense ideas about what circulates well. Unlike singers, who are identified with personas, lyrics, and sequentially numbered cassettes that have a popular metropolitan cachet, poets become wordsmiths whose moral resources lie in what is latent, localized, and less visible.

Since poetic verse gains force, according to this trope, through its most oral and rustic articulations, poets would seem to benefit from their disassociation with writing and metropolitan norms of authorship. Such exile is never fully imposed, however, for the primary reason that poets' compositions, oral though they may be, are also inscribed onto cassette tape, where they are fixed and "written" in a new metropolitan register. Under such conditions, the force of their voice travels with the currency of recording singers while also remaining, by virtue of tropic difference, imaginably distinct. My own photograph of Khaledi, taken of him at an extemporaneous poetry competition *(ragzah)* in 1998, conveys something strange and resilient about poets' engagement with the world's demands for graphic mediation (see figure 1.6). In his gentle, always slightly formal way, Khaledi indulged me at the time, allowing me to try to capture him on film as a classic tribesman—orally declaiming, dagger at his waist, Kalashnikov on his knee. After the film had been developed later, however, I discovered, to my surprise, another form lingering at his side. Hugging the contours of his body, a holographic silhouette takes on a life of its own. The "real" tribesman has, perhaps, not been captured at all.

As we move ahead, in the following chapters, I suggest that this subtle force of the graphic double, preserved momentarily in a photograph, serve as a reminder of the tensions inherent in constructing an authentic voice through media. For fans of critical political verse, as we will learn, graphic tropes acquire special urgency as the potential guarantors of poets' moral integrity and the means by which their authority might be circulated in larger metropolitan markets. At the very least, such tropes provide imaginative lessons on how to engage with the world's generalizing orders while continuing to foreground the vitality of transmitted cultural practice. Much like the silhouette of Khaledi, the moral fabric of tradition can survive in global settings, as long as it accommodates more imaginative fanfarons.

In exploring the emerging identity of the cassette poet in this chapter, I have focused on a range of competences that poets and singers have had to cultivate when using cassettes. I have also drawn attention to the ethical liabilities involved in tailoring verse to diverse audiences. The tensions at play in this emerging and dynamic agent are expressed, in part, through the various labels that Yemenis give to the cassette technology. When addressed to state authorities, folk-poetry cassettes are often described as "letters" *(risāyil)*. Even as they demand acoustic reception, cassettes can retain their authoritative connection with traditions of writing. It remains unclear whether such literary distinction is due primarily to cassette poets' own competences in reading and writing or, more figuratively, to tropes of authorial inscription that gain force at a step removed from singers. Another label invokes a different strain of political activism. In discussions of *bidʿ wa jiwāb* exchanges among political activists, cassettes can also be described as "bullets" *(raṣṣāṣ)*. In this register, cassettes command a cruder and more direct locutionary force that is potentially disruptive to conventions of authorship, civil society, and state-managed discourses of authenticity. Much as tribesmen of old are said to have spoken through direct action, their words being compared to bullets that whiz from the projector's body with no delay, such cassettes are imaginably armed, dangerous, and back in command of a shattering voice.

Even as cassettes are labeled "letters" and "bullets" by those who would emphasize their unambiguous political leverage, they have acquired stranger appellations. Most common are English loan words that have been acquired from Aden's former colonial residents or from global news networks such as CNN. Aside from "cassette" *(kāsēt)*, a common vernacular word throughout the Arab world, I also heard Yemenis describe the cassette's tailored modern contents as a "sandwich" *(sān-*

wīsh) and its mélange of styles and genres as a "cocktail" *(kūktēl)*.[49] Where the vast majority of Yemenis associate sandwiches and cocktails only with Western contexts, as conveyed to them through global media channels, the two loan words construe the cassette's political capacities as oblique at best, though whether pleasurable, risky, morally reprobate, or a mixture of all these qualities it is difficult to tell. Whatever their benefits or costs, the latter two loan words certainly identify the cassette as an object of oral consumption rather than production. Although the orality of cassettes might continue to agitate the regimes of authorship, it is largely bound to them. In the following chapters, I explore further how such costs are explored and negotiated through tropes as poets struggle to preserve the moral and political relevance of their verse for audiences.

NOTES

1. This definition of *noetics* was outlined by the influential media theorist Walter Ong in the 1970s, as noted by Alton L. Becker, *Beyond Translation: Essays toward a Modern Philology* (Ann Arbor: University of Michigan Press, 1995), 318, 385. Becker's sensitive attention to the cultural embedding of noetics in acts of textual interpretation avoids Ong's reductive view of the impact of media systems on ways of thinking.
2. A. Gramsci, *Selections from the Prison Notebooks,* trans. Q. Hoare and G. N. Smith (New York: International, 2003 [1971]), 328.
3. Before Yemeni independence, the borders of North and South Yemen had been more porous, and goods and poetry flowed both ways. Paul Dresch, *A History of Modern Yemen* (Cambridge: Cambridge University Press, 2000), 74.
4. The cultivation of strangerhood is central to public-sphere theory. Michael Warner describes such public attunement as "stranger-sociability" that is achieved when a person addresses unrecognized and potentially limitless others from his or her own vernacular social contexts. Michael Warner, "Publics and Counterpublics," *Public Culture* 14, no. 1 (2002): 77–78.

5. During his visit to New York City in 1990, Khaledi greeted listeners with a poem that began with a barbed salute to the cities' lofty towers and their capitalizing owners:

   My greetings to expansive New York,
   Homeland of the bourgeoisie and landlords:
   As many greetings as the insurmountable floors [of the city's towers]
   [May they] fill up their walls, from top to bottom.
   May my greetings be heard by the vanguard generation,
   The sons of Yemen, men each and every one of them,
   The buttress of my people, their treasure, their custodian,
   Their ample store from one hour to the next.

6. "The Last of the Cavalry," by the former secretary general of the Yemeni Socialist Party and the People's Democratic Republic of Yemen's foreign minister, Salem Ṣāleḥ Muḥammad, published in *Turāth Shaʿbī Khālid: Shāʾif al-Khāledī* (Aden: University of Aden, 1999), 13–14.
7. Michael Warner, *The Letters of the Republic: Publication and the Public Sphere in Eighteenth-Century America* (Cambridge, Mass.: Harvard University Press, 1990), 62.
8. See chapter 6 for a discussion of poets' who are part- or full-time migrants.
9. Interview with Muhammad ʿAlī al-Sulaīmānī, November 21, 1995.
10. The preferred reading materials of poets vary. The younger cassette poet who spoke of the benefits of travel listed the following books in order of importance to his work: the Qur'an, collections of poetry such as the famed pre-Islamic "Golden Odes" *(al-Muʿallaqāt)* and early Islamic verse, history books that shed light on Yafiʿ's or Yemen's distinctive past, Arabic grammar books and encyclopedias, al-Hasan al-Ḥamdānī's *al-Iklīl* (an early exhaustive history of the tribes and cultures of the southern peninsula), more recent historical accounts of tribal history, and a variety of contemporary poets who composed in classical verse. Older cassette poets such as Shayef al-Khaledi tended to be less familiar with the latest history books and pre-Islamic poets and mentioned reading a higher proportion of books concerning the great oral narratives of Arab conquest, romance, and adventure: *Qais and Lailah, Mus-*

lim Victories in Northern Territories (Futūḥ al-Shām), One Thousand and One Arabian Nights, and the stories of such Arabian heroes as ʿAntar Bin Shaddād and Zir Sālem.

11. On women's public verse in Yemen, see W. Flagg Miller, "Public Words and Body Politics: Reflections on the Strategies of Women Poets in Rural Yemen," *Journal of Women's History* 14, no. 1 (2002): 94–122. There have been very occasional exceptions of rural women poets who are interviewed on television, especially during the 1980s in the former People's Democratic Republic of Yemen. A cassette released in the mid-1990s features a rural woman poet from the northern town of Ṣirwāḥ and indicates the obstacles that aspiring authors continue to confront. Although one poem lamenting her own forced marriage has gained widespread acclaim by both male and female audiences, the author remains known only by her pseudonym, "the girl from Ṣirwāḥ" *(fatāt Ṣirwāḥ).* Urban women poets have met with somewhat better success in reciting their verses on television and radio throughout Yemen, although their performances are still minimal compared to those of men.
12. On the history of feminist movements in Yemen, see Margot Badran, "Unifying Women: Feminist Pasts and Presents in Yemen," *Gender and History* 10, no. 3 (1998): 498–518.
13. See chapter 2, note 5.
14. Interview, August 29, 1995.
15. The experience of composing Arabic poetry has often been described by anthropologists as an episode in the classic struggle, reiterated in much literature on emotional and spiritual experience in Arab world, between feelings or emotions *(shuʿūr)* and the measured products of reason *(ʿaql).* See, for example, Steven Caton, *Peaks of Yemen I Summon: Poetry as Cultural Practice in a North Yemeni Tribe* (Berkeley: University of California Press, 1990), 37–38. For wider discussions, see Lawrence Rosen, *Bargaining for Reality: The Construction of Social Relations in a Muslim Community* (Chicago: University of Chicago Press, 1984), 31; and Dale F. Eickelman, *The Middle East: An Anthropological Approach* (Englewood Cliffs, N.J.: Prentice-Hall, 1981), 205–06. This perspective emphasizes the discipline required in tailoring emotions to linguistic and social forms that can be communicated effectively.

Lila Abu-Lughod, however, notes that the relations between the emotions and reason are viewed by Awlād ʿAli poets in Egypt less in agonistic than in complementary relations; indeed, the heart *(qalb)* and reason *(ʿagl)* are frequently used interchangeably. Lila Abu-Lughod, *Veiled Sentiments: Honor and Poetry in a Bedouin Society* (Berkeley: University of California Press, 1986), 181. I suggest that her careful observations apply to male as well as female poets, who are the focus of her study. Stories of warlike Yemeni tribesman who have little tolerance for emotional display do not do justice to the centrality of sentiments and emotions to men's public and private expressive modes, as Najwa Adra notes in her ethnography of northern Yemeni tribal life. Najwa Adra, "Qabyala: The Tribal Concept in the Central Highlands, the Yemen Arab Republic," Doctoral thesis, Temple University, Philadelphia, 1982, 232. A number of Yemeni cassette poets whom I interviewed emphasized the complementarity of the "heart" and the "head." According to Khaledi, the heart "speaks" and "whispers," while head produces strophes *(abyāt).*

16. I am uncertain about the root of this word. One informant explained that it originates from a vernacular word *ḥāl/yaḥwal,* meaning "to shake." Another pointed to similarities with *maḥlūl,* meaning "inhabited," as by unseen spirits *(ginn).* Other poets I spoke with objected to these etymological explanations, saying that their implications of a trancelike state inappropriately imply a lack of agency or control.
17. The personification of the *ḥājis* and *ḥalīlah* is common throughout Yemen, as noted by Mikhail Rodionov, "Poetry and Power in Hadramawt," *New Arabian Studies* 3 (1996): 118–33; and Caton, *Peaks of Yemen.* In the Hadramawt and al-Baīḍa', the *ḥājis* and *ḥalīlah* are sometimes rendered male and female, respectively, a patterning of supernatural gender binaries that was common in the ancient world and may be preserved in traditions of rationalist knowledge. Yafiʿi poets never explicitly mentioned such personification.
18. Carlo de Landberg, *Études sur les dialectes de l'Arabie méridionale: Haḍramoût* (Leiden: E. J. Brill, 1901), 101; Robert Serjeant, *Prose and Poetry from Hadhramawt* (London: Taylor's Foreign Press, 1951), 76.

19. As I explain in the introduction, I found the oral composition of the *qaṣīdah,* without the assistance of writing, to be rarely practiced any longer in Yemen.
20. Walter Ong, *Orality and Literacy: The Technologizing of the Word* (New York: Routledge, 1993 [1982]), 135–38.
21. See chapter 3.
22. On rare occasions, a poet records his own compositions by reading them aloud on a cassette and sends the cassette to a singer. However, as I explain later in the chapter, this method is less preferable because it requires the singer to transcribe the aural text into writing and then reperform it in song.
23. Penmanship is a venerable art in the Arab Islamic world and has acquired an elaborate repertoire of ornamented calligraphic scripts—from *nashkī,* the preferred script of contemporary schoolteachers in Yemen, to *diwānī,* a highly ornamented, Persian script occasionally used for classical poetry. Most poets compose in a basic scripts such as *ruqaʿ* or *thulth.*
24. Linguists have long noted the use of different levels of Arabic in daily communicative life in the Arab world. Many of the studies that have been conducted on Arabic linguistic registers focus on discussions of *diglossia,* a term defined by Charles Ferguson as "a relatively stable language situation in which, in addition to the primary dialects of the language (which may include a standard or regional standards), there is a very divergent, highly codified (often grammatically more complex) superposed variety, the vehicle of a large and respected body of written literature." Charles Ferguson, "Diglossia," *Word* 15 (1959): 336. Such a model calls attention to distinctions between standardized varieties of vernacular Arabic *(ʿāmmiyyah)* and eloquent Arabic *(fuṣḥā)* that are often used to signal formality and religious piety and are based on the classical language of the Qurʾan. On the Arabic koiné, see Charles Ferguson, "The Arabic Koiné," *Language: The Linguistic Society of America* 35 (1959): 616–30.
25. The cognate accusative construction in this strophe *(qadhaf . . . qadhīf)* is typically translated in this manner (interview, April 8, 1998).
26. On the concept of "frames," see Gregory Bateson, "A Theory of Fantasy and Play," in *Steps to an Ecology of the Mind,* 177–93

(San Francisco: Chandler Publishing Co., 1972). Further discussion is included in chapter 2.

27. Such trends toward rendering formal literary genres more journalistic have been noted in neoclassical Arabic poetry. Sasson Somekh, "The Neo-Classical Arabic Poets," in *Modern Arabic Literature: The Cambridge History of Literature,* ed. M. M. Badawi (Cambridge: Cambridge University Press, 1992), 60–61. Similar observations have been noted in Yemeni radio programs that explain complicated *fatwas* to popular audiences. Brinkley Messick, "Media Muftis: Radio Fatwas in Yemen," in *Islamic Legal Interpretations: Muftis and Their Fatwas,* ed. M. K. Masud, B. Messick, and D. S. Powers, 311–20 (Cambridge, Mass.: Harvard University Press, 1996).
28. Through numerous interviews I held with listeners during my fieldwork, I found fans of political commentary generally less likely to complain about length. The clairvoyant's statement in one of the epigraphs of this chapter, narrated to me by an informant, hints at the cassette technology's extraordinary aesthetic dynamics for activists: the cassette is "long," but it "revolves" and has "two sides." Overall, the cassette's capacity to record longer *qaṣīdahs* has been especially appreciated where other media venues have curtailed poets' compositions. Notable in this regard are the television and radio industries and commercial audio-recording standards, which were set in the 1930s by 7.5-inch records that permitted only fifteen minutes of recording.
29. Warner, "Publics and Counterpublics," 81–89.
30. This cassette jacket seems to be the only one ever produced by Husain ʿAbd al-Naser. The jacket appears to have gone out of use fairly quickly, perhaps partly for cost reasons. Most folk-poetry cassettes are sold without a cassette jacket, unlike pop-song cassettes.
31. The region's first Muslim courthouse, called an "appellate court" *(maḥkamat al-istiʾnāf)* by my informants, was established in the late sixteenth century by the judge *(qāḍī)* Taher al-Sulaīmānī, who was trained in ʿĪnāt, Haḍramawt, under Shaikh Abu Bakr Bin Sālem (d. 1584/992) of the Bā ʿAlawī lineage. The courthouse was located in Falasān, a village located a few miles from the bluff and known for its poets, rather than in al-Qārah itself, perhaps to help

maintain its independence from the sultanate's suzereignty. Litigants were fed and housed through the court's *waqf* treasury for a maximum of three days, after which all subsequent costs were born by litigants. The most important court documents and other written materials concerning the sultanate were stored at the top of the bluff in the region's oldest manuscript repository. Like many other repositories throughout the south, the building and its contents were burned after independence in 1967 by the socialist state to prevent the state's land-redistribution initiatives from being contested by earlier property deeds.

32. Key studies of Yemeni song performance include Jean Lambert, *La médecine de l'âme: Le chant de Sanaa dans la société yéménite* (Nanterre: Société d'ethnologie, 1997); Lambert, "Musiques régionales et identité nationale," *Révue du Monde Musulman et de la Méditerranée* 67 (1993): 171–86; Philip Schuyler, "Music and Tradition in Yemen," *Asian Music* 22, no. 1 (1990–91): 51–71; Muḥammad Ghānem, *Shiʿr al-Ghinā' al-Sanʿānī* (Damascus: Dār al-ʿAwdah, 1987); and Jaʿfar Ḍafārī, "Humaini Poetry in South Arabia," Doctoral thesis, University of London, 1966.
33. These genres include the *mawwāl*—an easy, seafarers' song genre traditionally alien to the highlands—and the *muwashshaḥ*, a short, rhythmic song genre especially suited to the love lyrics of urban poets.
34. I was unable to interview these two singers about their editing strategies.
35. Rearranging verses in this fashion is generally very rare and is considered by informants I questioned to involve too much interference by the singer.
36. Yafiʿi informants also explained to me that *ṣārim* can mean "will" or "intention" in vernacular Arabic, an interpretation that would have rendered the poet's violence figurative. Whatever the result, the singer's modification renders the verse much less ambiguous.
37. Verses by Ahmad al-Qaīfī, released in the late 1980s on Husain ʿAbd al-Naser's cassette 64.
38. In keeping with most public debate in Yemen, poets' references to historical tensions between Zaidi and Shafiʿi Islam are kept subtly masked. Indeed, listeners generally view Qaifi as a Shafiʿi Muslim, an affiliation he sometimes makes explicit (see chapter 6). In these verses, Qaifi alleges Zaidi loyalty to dramatize northern differenti-

ation from the south, an unusual move that several listeners acknowledged to be more a rhetorical ploy than an actual gesture of belief. Few listeners admitted to ever having met him (see the conclusion for an account of Qaifi's remarkable unveiling).

39. For an innovative recent study, see Abdelfattah Kilito, *The Author and His Doubles: Essays on Classical Arabic Culture,* trans. M. Cooperson (Syracuse, N.Y.: Syracuse University Press, 2002).
40. Shāyef al-Khāledī, *Waḥdah wa Min Qarḥin Yaqraḥ* (Aden: Dā'irat al-Ṣaḥāfah wa-l-Ṭibā'ah wa-l-Nashr, 1990). Most of the poems in this volume are composed in a more standardized modern Arabic; see the epigraph of the book.
41. Pre-Islamic Arabian *qaṣīdahs* are frequently set in the first person, although variations with second-person plural and other pronominal referents commonly lend rich social intimations to the poetic voice. Although authorial distinction reached a fine art only during the Abbasid period in the seventh to thirteenth centuries, traditions of early South Arabian kingship, writing, and poetry provide antique precedents for authorial declamation, including the use of first and second persons in daily records and letters. Klaus Schippmann, *Ancient South Arabia: From the Queen of Sheba to the Advent of Islam* (Princeton, N.J.: Markus Wiener, 2001), 20.
42. Caton, *Peaks of Yemen,* 218–19; and Alois Musil, *The Manners and Customs of the Rwala Bedouins,* ed. J. K. Wright (New York: American Geographical Society, 1928), 283.
43. On *sīra* performance in Egypt, see Dwight Fletcher Reynolds, *Heroic Poets, Poetic Heroes: The Ethnography of Performance in an Arabic Oral Epic Tradition* (Ithaca, N.Y.: Cornell University Press, 1995), 12. Before every poem is sung on cassette, Yemeni singers announce the author of the composition, sometimes adding a further comment about the author's national provenance or tribal affiliation. Singers also never fail to mention the names of a poem's specified recipients. Such clarifications help signal homage to original text producers. Of the two singers discussed in this chapter, the younger performer, 'Ali Saleh, makes comparatively fewer text modifications, suggesting that textual monitoring has increased in recent decades.
44. Yemen's earliest laws safeguarding intellectual and artistic property rights were established in Aden in the 1940s. During the 1950s and especially after independence, a host of state institu-

tions were set up to promote and regulate the business of national culture, including Radio Aden, the Democratic Yemeni Artists Union, the Writers and Intellectuals Union, and the Ministry of Culture and Tourism. A new law passed in 1994 entitled the Yemeni Law of Intellectual Rights updates earlier legislation through attention to wider array of textual variations. Exempted from protection are "Poetry, prose, and musical selections that are not regarded as creative. Copyright protection in this case covers the original authors of the selections only." Anwar Al-Sayyādī, "Yemen Comes to Grips with Intellectual Rights," pts. 1–2, *Yemen Times,* April 14–20, 21–27, 1997. While creativity continues to be the defining criterium of ownership, its parameters remain unspecified.

45. The influence of poets during singers' recording sessions is conveyed only too starkly on one widely available cassette in which a conversation is accidentally recorded at the outset of the first song. When a migrant singer who resides permanently abroad solicited suggestions from those in attendance about the ordering of poems to be recorded, a reply is immediately heard from an attending poet: "My *qaṣīdah* should go first!" The success of the poet's bid is evident enough in the ordering of poems on the first side. Such observations correlated with my interview with the former poet laureate of southern Yemen, Husain Abu Bakr al-Miḥḍār. In his comments about linguistic collaboration noted above, Mihdar confided that his ability to take regular trips to the Gulf enabled him to maintain a level of collaboration that might otherwise be impossible to sustain.

46. Thabit ʿAwad, who has become one of the best-known cassette poets in Yafiʿ, explained to me that in his youth he refused to let anyone sing or recite his poems on cassette for fear that they would mispronounce words and accidentally corrupt the meaning of his verses. Being a singer himself, he was also concerned that other singers would perform his verses poorly. On one occasion, he recalled, he did relent and let a fellow singer record his poems with his own choice of song and dialectal adaptations. Afterward, however, friends came to him acknowledging that his verses had not been performed well. Although friends urged him to send his poems to better-known Yafiʿi singers residing in the Gulf, he remained reluctant. Only when he became a migrant abroad and de-

veloped a collaborative relationship with a well-known singer did he begin allowing his verses to be regularly recorded (interview, April 8, 1998).

47. Asif Agha, "Tropic Aggression in the Clinton-Dole Presidential Debate," *Pragmatics* 7, no. 4 (1997): 461–97.
48. Symbolic anthropologists have explored how the perceived characteristics and functions of symbols can be polarized into contrasting moral categories during periods of ethical and social contestation. See Robert Hertz, "The Pre-eminence of the Right Hand: A Study in Religious Polarity," in *Death and the Right Hand,* 89–113 (Glencoe, Ill.: Free Press, 1960 [1909]); and Emiko Ohnuki-Tierney, "The Monkey as Self in Japanese Culture," in *Culture through Time: Anthropological Approaches,* ed. E. Ohnuki-Tierney, 128–53 (Stanford: Stanford University Press, 1990). Tropes can work in similar ways, although they invite closer attention to the role of discourse in prioritizing orders of knowledge and causality. Paul Friedrich explores how such polarizing tropes work through vertical analogies that contrast global and local relations. Paul Friedrich, "Polytropy," in *Beyond Metaphor: The Theory of Tropes in Anthropology,* ed. J. Fernandez (Stanford: Stanford University Press, 1991), 39–41.
49. The term *kūktēl* is occasionally found on jackets of pop-song cassettes that feature a mix of artists and genres and was used toward similar ends by my informants. The term *sānwīsh* was used in a pejorative and ironic sense by a rural cassette-shop manager whom I interviewed in Yafiʿ when he responded to my question about why contemporary cassette songs tend to be so much shorter than earlier, sometimes hour-long songs recorded by classical Arab singers before the 1970s. The manager had remarked by way of prelude only moments earlier, "Today, everything is ordered to go."

· FIVE ·

Signs and Songs of the Poet: Moral Character and the Resonance of Authorship

The poets are trailed (yatabbiʿ) by those who stray.
Do you not see (ā lam tarā) how they aimlessly rove in every valley,
Preaching what they never practice,
Except those who believe, work righteousness, engage much in the remembrance of God, and defend themselves only after they are unjustly attacked?
—The Qurʾan (26:224–27)

Discourse that possesses an author's name is not to be immediately consumed and forgotten; neither is it accorded the momentary attention given to ordinary, fleeting words. Rather, its status and its manner of reception are regulated by the culture in which it circulates.
—Michel Foucault, "What Is an Author?" (1977)[1]

In recent decades, poets who provide the Yemeni cassette industry with some of its most critical political verse have developed a special interest in the moral integrity of character *(ṭibāʿ)*. On one popular cassette, a poet known for his wry views of political events launches his poem by evoking a difference between the character of his correspondent, ʿAbdallah "Abu Qaīs" al-Ḥāshedī, and the character of the poet and his ally ("Saḥḥāgī"). After several opening verses, the poet dismisses his correspondent's earlier prediction that his own fortunes would change as a mere reflection of his timeworn fickleness:

> To [him] who said things would change: The thing that dazzles deceives.
> His character is the coward, selfish and ever superficial. 5
> He no longer weighs his words before he circulates them.
> [While] the gallant errs not, however much his opponent sallies forth, 6
> [The finest] incense exudes what it contains and displays.
> We won't rebuke the Hashedi and his family. We might even boast about him. 7
> [Now that] Sahhagi's words have left Abu Qais in a mad delirium
> From the age of the Queen of Sheba until now, [Abu Qais] has been bigoted. 8
> At night reactionary, he'll join whomever pulls together.[2]

Where the poet describes his correspondent's weak "character" as a perversion of the values of courage *(shagāʿah)*, generosity *(karāmah)*, and expressive dignity *(adab)*, he pays homage to classic registers of tribal honor that would be familiar to those acquainted with the standard moral bearings of highland political discourse in Yemen. Indeed, in contrasting these lines with the poet's subsequent theme of retrogressive state authority—expressed in his opponent's bigotry and "reactionary" *(ragʿī)* character, which appear to have remained unchanged since Yemen's early Sabaen (Sheban) monarchy—listeners might attribute the moral power of such verse to a variation on the rhetorics of tribes and states that previous anthropological scholarship has helped nuance and problematize.[3]

Yet the poet's keen attention to the appearance, weight, movement, and smell of words and things urges his audience to move beyond normative values and themes. These sensory aspects of circulation draws listeners into familiar realms of ethical bearing in the world. In this case, a trope of character prioritizes and assembles sensations into larger signifying clusters: graphic uncertainty is evoked in the first strophe, which is followed by a trope of character that indexes the moral constitution of his opponent, who is described as a "coward, selfish, and ever superficial." Such personification of graphic duplicity enables reflection on larger social costs, described in terms of circulatory credibility: "He no longer weighs his words before he circulates them *(yansharuh)*." By contrast, the character of "the gallant" retains his integrity, expressed through a fragrant, salubrious kind of circulation. As one who "errs not," the gallant is likened to the finest "incense" that "exudes what it contains and displays." Such steadfastness allows the gallant to disseminate a purer, original essence—a publicly perfused incense whose benefits might reaffirm his true character. Through the uncertainties and risks of circulating characters, moral credibility emerges.

In previous chapters, I consider the challenges that Yemeni cassette producers confront in addressing multiple discursive communities and the compositional strategies that they employ to maintain their authority as persuasive brokers of political verse. Chapter 4 focuses on how poets and singers collaborate in enhancing the political leverage of recorded poetry and shows how artists foreground stereotypical modes of public comportment that polarize their respective competences in addressing different audiences. On the one hand, where poets are stylized as chatty rural firebrands and singers as flashy metropolitan celebrities, a certain moral credibility accrues to poets who appear to engage in the hustle of a modern cassette market without jeopardizing their associations with traditional highland discursive authority. Such stylized performances, however, allow the competences of a hybrid "cassette poet" to underscore new repertoires for addressing urgent social and political issues, including the relations between tribalism and state governance, socialist legacies from the former People's Democratic Republic of Yemen and the Yemen Arab Republic, rural communities and cities, and migrant lifestyles and traditional customs. Throughout the chapter, we observed the utility of literacy and written texts in collaboration between poets and singers and the increasing importance of authorship in mediating artists' political objectives.

As aspiring authors, however, artists hold an ambivalent relation with conventions of authorship. Although competences in literacy are elemental to authorial claims, they are also given new symbolic laminations in cassette poetry, where they become downplayed as poets acquire rustic self-images whose credibility requires distance from metropolitan media circuits that are morally suspect.

To develop a finer appreciation of poets' moral repertoires, this chapter extends this study of conflicted authorship by focusing on "character" *(ṭibāʿ)*, a particular trope of selfhood. Like other tropes explored in this book, character invokes the graphic and scriptive aesthetics of an object. Character can move in the world, be stored and controlled, and also be alienated from their users. At the same time, however, as a variant of "temper" or "disposition" *(ṭabʿ)*, character embodies profound notions of nature and causality.[4] I consider the historical resourcefulness of this moral concept for a specific group of media users by focusing on the problematic of authorship.

In particular, the trope of character reflects an experience with physical and metaphysical iteration or, in a moral sense, with duplicity. I argue more broadly that the Yemeni trope of character helps articulate a problematic of duplicitous authorship (in standard Arabic, *taʾlīf*) that takes on a particular form in an extremely decentralized and commercially productive cassette industry.[5] For poets, I suggest, authorship is primarily a matter of persuasive agency, and poets' ability to be persuasive depends on two factors. First, an author must have "circulatory efficacy"—that is, the capacity to put verses into public circulation so that they will be consumed and passed on by others. Second, an author must also produce something original; an author has an identity that is defined apart from sheer dissemination. Character highlights the disparity between these two notions of authorship: poets who want to reach broader audiences with cassettes must betray something "original," something noncirculatory and close at hand. To have character is, paradoxically, to admit a certain necessity for duplicity.

The challenge for poets is to manage duplicitous authorship while remaining moral. I suggest that the resourcefulness of character *(ṭibāʿ)* in managing such a challenge lies in the trope's asserted graphic aspect. In general, the graphic aspect of character functions for poets as what Maurice Merleau-Ponty has called "a repeated index."[6] At one moment, a graphic symbol can index a publicly available concept that is more abstract and nonvisible ("His [graphic] character is the coward, selfish and ever superficial. / He no longer weighs his words before he circulates them"). In view of such symbolic things, the inner character of an opponent can be known objectively, and its permanent qualities can be identified even if they are invisible words. As the symbol image flutters, however, the conceit of its "dazzle" can also reveal something else: the power of its beholder. At the moment that graphic signs are better viewed by some than by others, the causal vector between the seen and unseen is reversed: seen things become the mere holograph of some more secretive, projecting knower. As a graphic trope that poets unfurl over time, character allows meditation on both alienation and permanence since graphic things visibly move in the world for all to see, and in becoming ephemeral they also induce a sense of enduring recognition, selfhood, and credibility ("My incense exudes what it contains and displays"). The complex aesthetic indices of character provide poets with a valuable tool for clarifying others' moral foundations amid heated political debate.

In a recent analysis of presidential politics in the United States, Jane Hill suggests that the framework of "character," as it is typically invoked in this country, evokes the moral compass of intentional actors who seek to establish credibility across diverse events and contexts.[7] To have character is to assert personal moral fiber. In an arena of high political stakes in which multiple discourses of truth and reference are leveraged toward persuasive advantage over an electorate, "true character" becomes a critical signpost by which politicians define themselves against their theatrical and poll-driven opponents. Ultimately,

Hill suggests, "character" coexists in dialogic tension with modes of performativity and referential instability, and understanding how character emerges at the intersection of alleged virtue and performance requires that attention be paid to "personalist language ideology."[8]

Although I am interested in ideology, I return again to aesthetic considerations to examine presumptions that a strictly ideological approach might make about coherent regimes of symbolic and material domination. The trope of character that I explore is certainly ideologically informed, but character also remains the product of situated habits of apperception that are cultivated in verbal practice and lyrical *qaṣīdah* poetry.[9] When hitched to technologies of inscription, the duplicity of visual signs is elaborated in relation to traditional habits and dispositions of authoritative mediation. Instruments of writing and script, which have long been integral to traditions of scholarship and state authority in the Arab Islamic world, supply poets with key images of public, graphic authority. More recently, however, an audio-recording industry has contributed new possibilities for building cultural and political authority and has ensured that the trope of character continues to feature in the work of cassette poets even as their principle medium of credit is inscribed sound. By reflecting on the alienations and moral demands of character, cassette poets are able to conceptualize new duplicities of sonic abstraction and new indexes of authorial integrity.

AN AESTHETIC OF CHARACTER

During my second visit to Yafiʿ for fieldwork, I occasionally confronted questions from those who didn't understand my research goals. Why are you asking about family genealogies when your research is about poetry? Why did you choose Yemen, of all places, for research? What does an American hope to get out of such work, and will it be used to influence the United States' foreign policy? Such questions were understandable, given decades of cold war tensions during which the United

States had been identified as an anchor of Western capitalism, imperialism, and moral decadence. Aware of the relevance of such questions, I spent many afternoon *qāt* sessions explaining my goals to audiences, meeting with regional leaders, and swapping ideas about global and domestic politics. By the end of my second round of fieldwork, I felt that I had made gains in building trust with the community, although doubters inevitably remained. When I asked my closest friend in the region how best to address suspicions, he told me a proverb about character: "Whoever walks across the marketplace [proves that] his hand is white" *(man khaṭar as-sūq yaduh bēḍā')*. The purity of my character would be demonstrated by visible action in the local market, the community's most public forum where the stakes of exposure were the highest.

Anthropologists have long appreciated the power of public social action to shape common ideas about individual identity. In Muslim legal settings, studies of intentionality *(niyyah)* have shown that notions of personal responsibility are, in many ways, inseparable from processes of deductive reasoning from inferences about social authority.[10] Some have even ventured that the Muslim individual can be only a *homo contextus* whose identity is traditionally determined through outer action and that no deeper, truer self is ever concealed.[11] Concepts of individual subjectivity, however, have long been closely intertwined with hierarchized registers of moral knowledge, each of which informs ideas about the "agent" *(sā'is)* through particular habits of talk, textual practice, and aesthetic representation.[12] My colleague didn't take me into the market himself to demonstrate the purity of my intentions; rather, he placed me in trust of a traditional proverb. Along with other narratives and hermeneutic frameworks, the proverb defined the compass of possible action that I might take to assert my character and employed the image of a white hand to encode my intentions as necessarily pure: even though I was a stranger in the community, Yemenis' previous familiarity with the proverb would define my appearance in the marketplace as a sign of my good character. Knowledge could define action rather than vice-versa. The text of the proverb and its aesthetics of character preceded and conditioned my action, although speculations about the proverb's transparency could certainly ensue.

Embedded within traditions of poetry are substantial resources for reflecting on the agentive and social "intentions" or "themes" *(aghrāḍ)* of character, and these resources are the focus of this chapter. Although the trope is deployed partly to assign responsibility and establish intentionality, character *(ṭibāʿ)* proves especially fertile for Yemenis insofar as it enables reflection on the multiplicity of subjectivities as informed by historically situated media regimes. Where studies of intentionality often explore how shared norms and social sensibilities are leveraged toward instantiations of public, visible agency, my analysis of character begins with a visual problematic of circulating things that is used by interlocutors to consider inward, invisible intentions and ultimately to manage them relationally and thereby build moral credibility. Character can thus work together productively with assignations of intentionality, although it is useful to distinguish them.

Claims of visible character, hidden sources of authority, and unique textual authorship have long been intertwined in Arabic poetry. As early as the ninth century, satirical debates were held between famous poets who treated listeners to lengthy, often excoriating descriptions of one another's characters. In the *qaṣīdah* in particular, authorial integrity was a vital issue, and many heated debates took place over charges of plagiarism *(sarqah)*.[13] Poets frequently attempted to clear themselves of such charges by alleging that poetic muses, rather than familiarity with other authors' work, had been their primary inspiration.

In twenty-first-century Yemen, the muses still bring authentic words directly from beyond. In a growing industry of publishing and audio recording, however, poets and audiences express increasing concerns about the powerful social and industrial intermediaries that may be informing the claims of individual authors. Such concerns are explored, I suggest, through attention to the difference between character and appearances of character.

In 1981, during tensions between former North and South Yemen, a poet from North Yemen released a *qaṣīdah* on cassette that ridicules his South Yemeni correspondent. His *qaṣīdah* treats listeners to an extended exposition on his correspondent's character. In opening verses, the correspondent is labeled "the sleeper" and is described as having a bad habit of mistaking dreams of national prowess for real visions:

> [The poet] Bu Zaid Aḥmad says: "If it were only so!
> [If only] dreams of sleeping people could be fulfilled!"
> The sleeper said: "I saw it!"
> He thinks that he saw the highest of heights
> Along with Yemen's plains and valleys,
> Which he would rob of interests and profits.
> He wishes that [Yemen]'s protection
> [Extended] from the tip of Najrān to the desert of Thamūd.
> I have sworn to him: "You did not envision it!
> [Such protection] is far, farther than the farthest distance!"[14]

Notice here the terms in which the poet's discourse on character is framed. Although putatively about Yemen's "protection," the more urgent matter is visibility—more precisely, visual uncertainty. This theme is introduced by the character of the sleeper but is developed in more explicit terms: "I saw it," "He thinks that he saw," "You did not envision," and so forth. Since the 1980s, such specular anxiety increasingly has engaged a trope of character in many of the most popular cassette poems.

The duplicity of sight occasioned by shifty characters is especially disturbing given how stable highlanders imagine sight to be. Commonsense idioms suggest that sight is the most reliable and the least morally suspect of the senses. A highland proverb neatly captures this sensibility: "The gap between good and evil is only four fingers wide" *(bēn al-khēr wa-sh-sharr arbaʿ banān).*

If the palm of the hand is placed on the cheek, only four fingers separate the eye—the keenest sensor of "good"—from the ear and its temptations to hearing "evil."

Insofar as character destabilizes a primary medium of apperception, I suggest that the trope invites consideration of a wider range of potentially moral media. The generative reflexivity of character in this respect is expressed in a broader set of philosophical ideas about selfhood and the relation of the self to the natural world. This perspective was outlined for me by Yemen's foremost poet laureate, ʿAbdallah al-Baraddūnī, when I visited him at his home in 1995. After being led into his public sitting room by a personal attendant, I noticed a replica of an oil painting hung prominently on the wall, the likes of which I'd never seen anywhere in Yemen. It was a sixteenth-century painting by Diego Velázquez showing the back side of a nude Venus who was gazing at the viewer through a mirror. After a moment, my surprise turned to appreciation for the poet's delight in paradox. Baradduni had been blind since birth.

In response to my initial question about the defining skills of the folk poet, Baradduni began by speaking about the trope of "character" *(ṭibāʿ)* and the "authenticity of self" *(aṣālah fī-l-nafs)*. Character, he ventured as his face wrinkled in thought, marks the difference between sentient humans and animals. It emerges from two sensory domains. The first domain is linked to basic bodily needs—eating, drinking, sleeping, and so forth. The second domain is more imaginative and is best expressed as poets reflect back on life experiences with poetic as well as religious insights. This second, more reflective domain *(ṭibāʿ thānī)*, Baradduni explained, is especially important to the development of character. The poet's observations here roughly map the model of authorship that I have proposed—a model that emphasizes reflection on something original and close at hand (like bodily needs) from a more distanced, abstracted, and as I ultimately suggest, circulatory vantage point.

The bifurcation of character between natural and symbolic

orders is to some extent reminiscent of early European moral philosophy, which national poets like Baradduni are familiar with. But this framework also draws from a metaphysics of human nature that has had considerable currency throughout Yemen and other parts of the Arab world. In discourses of Islamic science, philosophy, and theology, the term has long been deployed, along with its equivalents *ṭabīʿah* and *ṭābiʿ*, to refer to a mutable principle of motion and rest. Abu ʿAli Ibn Sīnā, or "Avicenna," a fourteenth-century neo-Aristotelian, deployed the term in his treatise on rarified heavenly bodies, and his theory was extended by other philosophers to certain "forms" *(ṣuwar)* and humors of the human body that mediate between corporeal substances and the soul.[15] Crucially, *ṭibāʿ* emerges for such philosophers not simply from a dialectic of the material and spiritual, the "evident" *(ẓāhir)* and "concealed" *(bāṭin)*, but also from a dialectic that becomes possible only through the interventions of the human intellect and soul.

Cassette poets are elaborating the dynamics of this principle through their own historical and technical dilemmas: the semantics of the term *ṭibāʿ* are employed with new effects by framing the duplicity of character in terms of inscription. This association has considerable historical depth. From the verb *ṭabaʿ*, meaning "to impress," "imprint," or simply "to print," *ṭibāʿ* conveys a sense of character that is figuratively marked as the second-order predicate of an original. In the Qurʾan, the authorial originator of such inscription is God, and most references to the root *ṭ-b-ʿ* refer to acts of unambiguous stamping or "sealing," as in "So God seals the hearts of the unbelievers" (*sūrah* 7:101). Poetry raises the specter of more questionable forms of authorial suasion, however. In the *Sūrah* of the Poets, the most famous excerpt of which is cited in the opening epigraph of this chapter, a verbal synonym meaning to follow, trace, or figuratively "characterize" *(yatabbiʿ)* signals the agency of "those who stray" *(al-ghāūn)* in company with the poets. In this case, poets and their doppelgangers are immediately rendered in graphic terms that are accessible to any viewer: "Do you not see how they aimlessly rove in every valley, / Preaching what they never practice." Where the moral intentions of these characterizing figures can be seen, a special empowerment is allotted to those who behold them, particularly those who behold their orally spoken words, true indices of their duplicitous inner being. Poets who remain pious and defend themselves well are given special reprieve from such characterization and, in the excerpt's final segment, are recognized to be allies of the righteous community.

In debates over temporal politics and moral authority in the Yemeni highlands, the potential duplicity of poets has been explored with similar graphic aesthetics, although a more elaborate set of scriptive terms has been introduced amid the contending claims of textual communities. Where literacy has historically been restricted, the most accessible medium of moral truth has been oral articulation, in keeping with the Qur'anic verse above. In poetry, loud speech that echoes from peak to peak indexes the vitality of social persons, and countless metaphors compare effective speech to thunder, storms, or raging floods—natural processes that express a poet's powerful locution. When the "imprint" of voice implies a separate replication, heightened attention is drawn to the mediation of language and to the problematic of this mediation for authors. Although literacy can offer more refined moral sentiments, its duplicated "characters" can also offer new kinds of moral agency to those who can reflect on the deceit of their graphic circulation, even if through the medium of writing.

In many poems I have collected, the term *ṭibāʿ*, as character, is introduced precisely at the point when the poet mentions writing or script. One afternoon, a young schoolteacher in Labʿūs produced a photocopy of an eighteenth-century poem that he had typed from an original handwritten copy. With the great care that is given to old documents, even if by association, the teacher handed me the photocopy, explaining that the *qaṣīdah* had been composed by a member of the al-Bakrī family, one of Yafiʿ's traditional houses of religious scholars *(faqīhs)*. Originally written as a "response" to a poet from the Ḥāshed tribe, with whom Yafiʿ was at war at the time, the poet refers to his receipt of a written "mark" in a section typically reserved for acknowledging a correspondent's "initiation" letter:

> The Ḥāshedī's mark arrived, and we have discovered 18
> That [his] tongue is layered with impressions *(ṭibāyyiʿ)*.
> Some have character *(ṭabʿ)*, while others have character stamped on them *(mutaṭṭabiʿ)*. 19
> Like stars fading in the west, verses rise in the east.
> There are desultory peoples amid [us] and tribes. 20
> You are the peoples, and the tribes are Yafiʿ.

In these verses, the arrival of the opponent's "mark," or *raqm*—from the verb "to write," *raqama*—is invoked by the semiotics of character, in all its problematic. His opponent's "tongue," "layered with impressions," confirms his "stamped" character. The Yafiʿi poet's own discovery of his correspondent's duplicitous script illuminates the integrity of his own character, which rises like a star. The assurance of the poet's own graphic character as well as that of his tribe is conveyed in a subsequent strophe that alludes to an original verse in the Qur'an: "Mankind! We created you from a male and female and made you into peoples and tribes so that you might come to know each other" (*sūrah* 49:13).

Among other early Yemeni poets, a slight variant of the verbal cognate *ṭ-b-ʿ* indexed more personal, inward agents that could be summoned forth by script. The term *ṭābiʿ* had long been used for an invisible, conjuring force that beckoned the poetic muse, although such a force is rarely mentioned by Yemenis anymore. Unlike the muses for Greek poets, the *ṭābiʿ* accompanied the poet's person and was not associated with genre or shared by all poets who composed in a particular genre.[16] In the opening verses of a *qaṣīdah* by Yahya ʿUmar, one of Yemen's most celebrated singers and poets who is reputed to have lived in the early eighteenth century, the *ṭābiʿ* seems to be invoked in no uncertain terms through script, although its accompanying spectral apparitions seem to provide no surer guidance to the poet:

Yahya ʿUmar said: By God, I didn't know
  That yearning could do this to me.
By God, had I known, I would not have grown mad.
  I would have been a brave poet. In confronting love
Out in the open, I would have cured my passion,
  Rising to become Yahya the Yafiʿi.
[Yet] late into the night, how I've sought and found nothing.
  I'll write out the script and set down my "*ṭābiʿ*."
How many labors I witnessed.
  They became like visions. Not a thing remained with me.

The poet imaginatively addresses his torturous yearning and inability to have acquired foreknowledge concerning the ways of courtship when he describes himself rising to self-authorization as "Yahya the Yafiʿi." But when he tries to commit his authorship to pen with the assistance of his *ṭābiʿ*, his efforts once again dissolve into graphic and objectual loss. Although the specter of the scriptive *ṭābiʿ* is a potential ally who might bring him great fame by circulating the poet's public testimonial of love, the poet defers to a popular sensibility that holds writing to be a form of alienation that can only bring loss. The apparent false promise of the muse-inspiring *ṭābiʿ* is performed through yet another layer of graphic marking by recent Yafiʿi editors who published this poem in a paperback volume of Yahya ʿUmar's verse, nearly three centuries after its composition: in an unusual editing decision seen nowhere else in the poem, the word *ṭābiʿ* is set between quotation marks.[17] Where quotation marks signal the voice of another agent who is not fully under the author's control, the abstracting demands of the *ṭābiʿ* force may yet exert their power.

The contrast in both these examples of early Yafiʿi poetry between essential, authentic oral articulation and false, alienating written script would be glossed by Jacques Derrida as an example of "logocentrism," the plague of much Western philosophy that he argues has held writing to articulate a fundamental alienation of the self from some unitary, oral other.[18] Although logocentrism does inform anxieties of mediation in the Arab world, the equivalences between communicative coding and subjectivity—between signs of orality or writing and notions of "original" selves—vary historically (as conditions of mediation change) and pragmatically (according to sociolinguistic contexts and communicative strategies). Poets are aware that the moral transparency of given media forms is continuously contested and seek moral and political credibility by locating the primary foundations of character in some forms rather than others.

In a twenty-first-century cassette industry in which poets and singers from across Yemen are collaborating toward the production of audio-textual material, duplicitous mediation remains a pivotal issue. As song and musical registers are being introduced to traditional poetry to generate sales, however, the problematic marks of character are being recast in a somewhat broader spectrum of communicative codes.

In responding to a poet who has challenged his stature, the famous cassette poet Shayef al-Khāledī "Bu Lōzah" begins his *qaṣīdah* in this way:

Bu Lōzah [said]: My place is stalwart, every red fire aflame. 1
Because a hunter sets his sight on me, though he shoots a hundred bullets,
Woe to al-Ṣunbaḥī [his opponent]! For he is in my wildfire, yet knows not
Where the [fiery] journey leads, [though] he dances to it with his double-reed flute.
Too bad he didn't show respect with his sayings or with a heroic dialect,
For he is a regular guy. It is not his custom to boast with his poetry.
His courage and reputation are as a poet from Ḥamrah, but he is no poet!
He told us this so he would appear clever so that one could know his share and price.
And now his tongue got long, opening ears to the charlatan, 5
So that he now attacks his uncle. [Sure,] he brought water [but] without the channel [to channel it].[19]

Although addressing in general terms the results of local elections and national politics, the narrative framework of the poem centers on character—the poet's own, his opponent's, and that of other cassette poets. In these verses, what perverts character is not written marks or inscriptions but rather metaphors of sound: a "tongue" that "opens ears to the charlatan," "sayings," a "heroic dialect," and a "double-reed flute." In an audio-recording industry in which political verse is being reproduced by a motley new chorus of aspiring poets, many of whom tailor their poems to the interests of pop-song artists *(fannāns),* the poet attends closely to the dangerously persuasive powers of wanton words and sounds. People can mischaracterize themselves, the poet suggests, as his opponent tried to do. Indeed, as a forewarning, the old discourse of shifty images initiates the first few verses: although the poet declares his own "place" to be fixed and "stalwart," his opponent, who is the supposedly watchful hunter, fails to recognize the poet's "red fire aflame." As in the martial eighteenth-century poem I mentioned earlier, specular faculties index oral faculties, and shiftiness in one domain can imply shiftiness in another. But the ground that separates sight from sound, good from evil, is all too human. It is only "four fingers" in the proverb previously mentioned and character in poetic terms—in both cases a difference of mediation. In the earlier poem, this mediated difference was made available for consideration by writing; the arrival of the written mark provided an occasion for considering characterological duplicity. In an increasing number of cassette poems, however, it is sound (the "double-reed flute") that becomes the mark of difference between images (with all their potential transience) and an ideal and now vehemently idealized oral primacy.

THE DIALECTIC TOWARD PRODUCTIVE SONG

Such transformations in character are helping Yemenis identify new demands on public authors as well as new means to react to these demands. As Derrida's logocentrism becomes particularly unsustainable as a guide to textual and moral practice, a better account is needed of how the cassette industry is providing conditions for a wider array of authorial responses.

The dialectic of the evident *(ẓāhir)* and the concealed *(bāṭin)*—the dialectic so central to the notion of character I have been discussing—has a long history in popular mystical practice in the Arab world and is richly elaborated in centuries of Islamic moral philosophy.[20] Most poets have ready access to such discourses (note the aforementioned verse "[The finest] incense exudes what it contains *(yiḥtawī)* and displays *(aẓhara)*"). I propose, however, that for poets who confront the circulation of their poems on the cassette-recording market, the discourse of the evident and concealed (in quotidian terms, the seen and unseen) becomes inflected by a trope of character whose ironic terms express certain problems that arise when epistolary correspondence is subject to forces of technological and industrial mediation.

As I have been explaining, a certain moral problematic of audio mediation is expressed by cassette poets. Such poets have concerns with the effects of the recording media on their work, and their concerns are expressed with equal urgency by singers as well as audiences, who, in numerous interviews I conducted, expressed keen interest in discussing the demands of new political, social, and economic forces on poetic form and practice. To be sure, new media technologies such as cassettes are seen to provide poets and singers with extraordinary access to public audiences and can bring political leverage, cultural influence, and fame. But the benefits of media are offset by their costs. Poets are sometimes accused of softening their political criticism to appease state or sectarian interests. No less serious to poets' integrities, as discussed in the previous chapter, are privatized concentrations of cultural and economic power. A commercial, metropolitan pop-song industry represents a constant threat to the political and moral loyalties of poets, particularly as tales circulate of immense profits being gained by singers and songwriters who have reached the limelight but who have sold their own local cultural traditions and audiences cheaply. For many, the temptations of fame are leading poets into alleyways of suspect intentions.[21] Scales of broadening circulation and publicity that are made available to folk poets and singers are of concern at more mundane levels, too. Some fans complained to me that in a radically decentralized and expansive cassette market, poet correspondents no longer know one another and have trouble pitching their verses to the actual social positions and habits of their addressees. More common are stories about unwarranted pretensions, outright charlatanry, and mistaken identities.

Rather than baldly denying the pressures of the market, cassette poets are leading the way in reconsidering their roles as authors in the marketplace. The more self-declaimed "political" poets decry those who openly take money or gifts for their verses: to barter poems for monetary return is to impugn one's credibility as an impartial political pundit. Nevertheless, as would-be exemplars of practical, everyday realism, poets acknowledge that words are by no means impervious to the influence of things precious or monetary. The verses by "Bu Lōzah" that I quoted, for example, spoke of an opponent's "tongue," which extends outward, threatening to get away from his control because he pursues a "share" and "price" for his words. In an increasing number of cassette poems since the late 1970s as the cassette industry reached full steam, metaphorical comparisons of speech to commerce have explored the alienation of words from authors—to effects more or less beneficial, depending on poets' strategies.[22]

Given that the recording industry is seen to have a powerful influence on the popularization and commercialization of verse, references to music, song (and dance), and the "double-reed flute"—quintessential registers of aural entertainment in Yemen—become iconic of buying and selling. In many poems, audiovisual media are represented explicitly as cheapening political poetry. Issued on the heels of the 1994 Yemeni war, for example, one cassette features a northern poet who sarcastically wonders how his opponent (in this case again "Abu Lōzah") can welcome the postwar outcome when he once sang and danced for communist ideologues:

After the solution was imposed by cannon and rifle, 26
Abu Lōzah the stern yielded, his character gave way.
What gained supremacy and changed its character and the arena?
Did you see him perform ablutions? Or was it only deceit by the deceiver?
Yesterday, Jubaīqah and Jaʿjaʿah [mythological tyrants] were in a ditch.
Today, [with] their total defeat, their sails have been hoisted!
How do I interpret your manner, when he was dancing,
His power amplified by the two importers of rumor [perhaps Marx and Lenin]?
How you sing of them and how your anthems supported them 30
In the pulpits and on television and radio.
Any interpretation was convincing, except one that was convincing. 31
May God destroy the world's greed and the gains of wheedling.[23]

The poet's oscillation here between second- and third-person pronouns underscores his opponent's shifty character. Such implications are confirmed by initial themes of specular uncertainty and elaborated as the poet tries to "interpret your manner" *(ufassir sulūkak)*.[24] Graphic cues slip toward unseen, inward intensions in subsequent verses as the power of "dancing" is amplified by "rumor" and then broadcast through song via classic instruments of state media: the pulpits (oral and visual), television (electronic audiovisual), and the radio (strictly aural). The commercial duplicity of character thus becomes underscored in terms of a difference of sonic mediation that abstracts potent oral articulation into registers of more passive reception.

In the efflorescence of recorded audio media that developed over the course of the 1970s and 1980s, character acquired a range of audio registers whose moral qualities become calibrated in proximity to the popular market and to "entertainment" *(salā)*. Such registers could be charted on a scale of declining moral authorship that maps the anxieties of poets on an axis of declining orality—from powerful oral articulation (often expressed in classic tribal genres and idioms), to oral news from more reliable sources, to rumor from less reliable sources, and finally to song with musical accompaniment. Such a taxonomy is at once (1) the historical and conditional response of a group of cassette poets who, engaged with the recording market, find themselves confronted with specific moral liabilities and challenges and (2) a response that is actively reflected on and queried as poets attempt to secure a more reliable ground of authorship that can translate their verse across conventional moral boundaries. Thus, poets compare their words with commerce and song and rework the moral implications of given audio registers by foregrounding, sidelining, or ironically flipping their conventional indices in the interests of gaining rhetorical advantage among growing popular audiences.

As cassette poets competitively characterize one another amid an array of aural registers whose instability is confirmed by shifting images and mobile things, some of the surest grounds of truth become, ironically, written. Where authorship through orality is especially liable to appropriation and transformation by an audiocassette market, writing becomes a comparatively more stable index of character, especially in its distance from market pressures. A rich semiotics of legitimate inscription emerges in many cassette poems as handwritten letters, legal documents, official stamps, reliable newspapers, and other media become cited by poets as evidence of moral rectitude. One northern cassette poet chastises a southern correspondent for praising socialist party leaders, accusing him of signing documents without legitimate authority:

There before you is ʿAli Sālem, Muhsen, and Salem, 16
  To whom you make melody with cassettes as if with films.
They won't pour you a drink if you are thirsty and starving.

> I have your complete news by pages and pens:
> Some officials like you didn't sign with the hand of a judge, 18
> And [their] affair[s] ended with prison, death, or execution.[25]

The problem here is sonic entertainment, which the poet evokes in the opening verse by referring to his opponent as a cassette-producing charlatan. His "melody," coded at the lower end of the taxonomy of virtue, is compared to "films." To underscore the severity of his opponent's moral shortcomings, the poet turns to references of writing in subsequent verses: although he writes truthfully with "pages and pens," his opponent fails to use writing responsibly, with potentially disastrous ends. In such poems, writing still proves to be dangerous because it circulates and can be used for nefarious purposes (hence a frequent ironic tenor in references to writing). Nevertheless, a semiotics of communicative stability is made available to cassette poets when, confronting the risks of a commercially driven recording market, they signal affiliation with long-standing institutions of literate authority. Such institutions are indexed by appropriate tokens of divine scripture and Islamic law and also of secular institutions, such as state bureaucratic offices (the courthouse, official thumbprints, and identity cards), state-managed print media (newspapers and journals), and formal and semiformal educational venues (diplomas and writing letters). By foregrounding tokens of writing (and practices of writing, as was shown in the last chapter), poets resort to more institutionally sanctioned codes of authorship that, as enfranchised literate agents, they can carry with them wherever they and their poems might travel.

Note here that such references to institutionalized literate authority are not solely concerned with Islamic precepts but are about civic virtue more generally. Cassette poets lack religious training, so they generally hedge their appeals to religious authorization and show far greater relish for signs of state and legal literate authority, such as bureaucratic stamps, driver's licenses, official documents, bank notes, and so forth. Indeed, these tokens of scriptive authority have had increasing relevance for Yemenis both at home and abroad in the decades after independence as literacy rates have climbed along with expanding bureaucracies and standardized forms personal documentation. Although poets borrow authorizing force from literate competences long associated with Islam, they are also translating these traditional competences into the conditions of everyday civic life and, in the process, creating new vocabularies of virtuous character.

PRESCRIBING TRUTHS

Cassette poets have been seeking marks of inscription to create a space for themselves in which authorship is more institutionally secure precisely for its distance from the treacherous playgrounds of spoken and heard sound. In contrast to a conventional axis of valuation, the public and visible presence of the inscribed word makes it morally secure. Poets return full circle to a state of original powerful oral articulation, this time with a crucial difference. How have they been able to reverse what, in a discourse of the seen and unseen, has been such a liability? The about-face would appear no small feat. For cassette poets ultimately have to confront the fact that inscription is fundamentally an imagistic medium that can be manipulated and distorted.

I would suggest that much of the secret to this puzzle lies in the fact that the signs of visual inscription that poets are employing are not actually visible. Recall that this strategy of returning to visual marks has emerged as a specific response to the dissemination of poetry on audiocassette in an industry in which authoritative, political words are mingling with the commercial production of song and music. Faced with such auditory perversion, cassette poets locate their own authorial integrity in an idiom of inscription, as I have shown. Inscription now becomes fixed, its textual power made immanent precisely in its removal from a visual world and its encompassment within a solely aural world. Poets do use signs of writing, but within the rhetorical fray in which moral grounds are being won and lost these signs are heard on audiocassette rather than seen. Poets depend on recorded sound for much of their authority, and identifying heard words with a fixed legitimacy—which is what such signs of inscription effectively do—helps them to reclaim an oral capacity that is effectively localized and genuine.

The discovery of an oral authorship made possible by unseen script is by no means unique in the Arab Islamic world. Since at least the seventh century, the Prophet Muhammad's oral message to humanity has been made safe against those who would mistakenly or willingly corrupt it by its permanent inscription in *the* "Book"—God's unseen book on high in which divine law and the fate of each individual are meticulously recorded. God's authority is crucially oral, and the Qur'an has long been memorized and passed on from generation to generation through recitation without any assistance of literacy. Nevertheless, God's authorship of hidden scripture ensures the wide circulation of his words and their translation in numerous dialects and languages so that rearticulation presents no threat to authorial integrity.

This discourse of hidden script and books is extremely persistent throughout the Arab world, as has been noted by other ethnographers.[26] I have encountered the discourse numerous times in Yemenis' narratives about history, genealogy, and important events, the true versions of which are said to be recorded in unique tomes that are never ultimately produced. Cassette poets are drawing from this logic of entextualization ("I have your complete news, by pages and pens"). Cassette poets' relation to the recording market puts them in a rather peculiar spot. For one thing, they are crafting persuasive verse in an industry that is investing audio texts with new kinds of authority. As tens of thousands of copies of poems are inscribed not onto pages but onto polyester recording tape, new discourses of authenticity are being produced. The notion of an "original copy" *(nuskhah aṣliyyah),* for example, has emerged in the Arab recording world. An original copy is a higher-priced, more-genuine cassette copy of a supposed original text. Forms of audio authority are also being newly created in a recording market that is radically decentralized and poorly regulated. Confronting the emergence of such new and questionable forms of authorship, cassette poets are keenly attuned to the ironies of original texts and original authors. The trope of character, I suggest, is precisely where the contradictions and possibilities of authorship for modern moral orators can be explored.[27]

Manfred Schneider considers in a suggestive recent account of early forms of religious mediation how the exchange of written letters in early Christendom facilitated new forms of authority and authorship.[28] He suggests that whereas early Judaic authority had bolstered the integrity of its predominantly oral transmission by investing sacred written texts with the power to transmit absolute original utterances, Paul and the apostles invested the image of the written word with the iconic immanence of spirit, which could be accessed by any faithful believer.[29] Although the interpretive competences of viewers would become more radically expressed in participatory acts of reading only after the Protestant print revolution in the sixteenth century, the scriptural image in early Christendom was on its way to becoming authorized through independent human interpretation as much as through hierarchies of orally codified divine authority. In the case at hand, the aural reproduction of audiocassettes ensures a scriptive durability that early Judeo, Christian, and Islamic believers did not have. The immanence of the image has a rough equivalent. Given the popular and vernacular production of cassette authors, however, the image has been subsumed within the authorial (original) if still iterable (disseminatable) vocal presence of sung cassette poetry. The spoken word is no longer the mouthpiece of a genuine presence of an author; rather, it has become chartable in degrees removed from a range of authorships.

CONCLUSION

The trope of *ṭibāʿ* that I discuss in this chapter accesses many of the same inscriptive dialectics that have distinguished the English word *character* (thus my translation of the term). As in the English term, the inscriptive and indeed iterative aspects of *ṭibāʿ* become especially salient in poets' metacommentaries on the problem of mediation. In Yemen, however, the tropic analogies of *ṭibāʿ* are articulated not in a literate culture of upper-bourgeois society but among vernacular poets who are using written correspondences and audiocassettes to convey sonorous recited and sung verse. In such conditions of textual production, authorship is expressed through aesthetic norms that are unlike those captured by the novel, which emphasizes the effects of subjectivity that are enabled by new forms of scriptive, particularly literary, circulation (including maps, calendars, newspapers, letters, and banknotes).

As I have suggested, a popular aesthetics of the seen and unseen remains the informing thread that stitches together poets' reflections on character. Where *ṭibāʿ* foregrounds script and what is seen, the trope allows reflection on what leads away from the viewer, away from more essential inner, unseen qualities that may promise a certain truth. Crucially, however, poets articulate this realm of unseen truth in different registers as transformations in media present them with different expressive challenges. Here I move from an aesthetics of first-order indexicality (embedded in the norms of communicative practice) to a kind of second-order aesthetics that is marked by a more pronounced, creative reflexivity.[30] This reflexivity is institutionally relative. In written epistolary practice especially before independence in Yemen when writing was mastered by only few, written script's mediated other was oral articulation, whose supposedly embodied, natural qualities complemented and secured authorship through writing. Under such conditions, authoritative knowledge was largely accessible through the vocal extension of true script or what one might call *scriptophonic* means.[31]

Over the last four decades in Yemen, the graphic and the seen have gradually shifted from writing (the marked medium of the recited epistolary tradition) to aurality (the uncertain medium of a prolific cassette industry). A shift in the "characterizing" of media has considerable moral entailments. As the standardization of literacy and print culture turned script into a resource for a wider array of citizen authors that was at once authoritative and also, given its accessibility and potential manipulation, problematic, authoritative knowledge withdrew toward *phonographic* competences—namely, seeing one's way to sounds of truth. In both cases, script and graphic aesthetics remain the principal indexes of knowledge, whether through visual apprehension or inquiry. Yet a switch in the nature of the knowing subject occurs from one whose authority rests principally in written media to one whose authority, although initiated in vision, gains steady influence through the media of an idealized speaker. The cacophony of double-reed flutes and audiocassettes invites listeners to consider the traditionally stable indexes of writing, recognize their fallen state, and move on toward unseen utterances that might still preserve the force of well-ordered origins.[32]

I have proposed that the trope of character privileges scriptive analogies. I would suggest, moreover, that further consideration of other scriptive or, more broadly, image-doubling tropes could provide significant leverage for understanding the cultural politics of authorship in other contexts.[33] As a mode of subjectivity that considers expressive capacity intimately linked to changes in discursive authority, authorship is best approached in political and historical terms as a form of power that advantages some performers over others and also in pragmatic terms as a position or "footing" that individuals achieve, maintain, and cultivate within specific contexts.[34] The function of such marks of difference in interrogating and in perpetuating power hierarchies may well be evident not only in the strategies of poets working in the stranger hinterlands of the recording industry but also in folk ideologies of authorship more generally.

I suggest that such scriptive reflexivity is likely to become more rather than less germane to studies of modernity as discourses of citizenship popularize neoliberal horizons of legality, as multinational corporations increasingly influence occupational and stylistic competences, as large numbers of young, educated men and women confront labor shortages with associational and affective adjustments, as faiths of scripture mobilize toward recruitment and political influence, and as media technologies continue to inform sign flow in all these domains. Crucially, however, authorship emerges in degrees both of proximity to and remove from such literate marks.[35] For Yemeni cassette poets and their fans, authorial characters become most convincing when rearticulated in the sounds and voices of those who are actively engaged in the moral claims of political life.

In the next chapter, I turn to the work of one particular poet, Shayef al-Khaledi, whose collaboration over several decades with the cassette singer Husain ʿAbd al-Nāṣer made him an exemplary if at times controversial spokesperson for Yemenis. Through his contributions to what would become Yemen's longest series of cassette poetry, Khaledi worked with other poets in developing a set of moral resources for addressing some of the country's largest political problems. Discussions, debates, and revelations about the nature of Khaledi's historical personality will help situate the scriptive aesthetics of authorship amid a broader set of concerns over the relations between national and global transformations and the integrity of local communities.

NOTES

A version of this chapter was published in *American Ethnologist* 32, no. 1 (2005): 82–99. Copyright © 2005 by the American Anthropological Association.

1. Michel Foucault, "What Is an Author?," in *Language, Counter-Memory, Practice* (Ithaca, N.Y.: Cornell University Press, 1977), 123.
2. The poem is by a southern Yafiʿi poet Yahya al-Sulaīmānī, an internal security official in the People's Democratic Republic of Yemen

who has a reputation for unflinching political satire. The respondent, ʿAbdallah "Abu Qaīs" al-ʿUlafī al-Ḥāshedī, a part-time migrant in Qatar, is of the Ḥāshed tribe of northern Yemen. Both ʿUlafi's poem and Sulaimani's response were released by Ḥusain ʿAbd al-Naser in 1986 on cassette 57. Sulaimani's poem begins with a meditation on the difference between the "good character muse" *(ṭābiʿ al-gaīd)* and the "coward" *(fasl)*. Notice in the following excerpt from ʿUlafi's response how the trope of circulating character is reiterated with a careful prelude that features a graphic display of charlatanry:

> [Sahhagi] has no steed, no truck, or even any engine.
> After nine years of commerce, his engine has gone kaput.
> He has become distracted, lost, obsessed with pleasing sights.
> By my account, he rides with no authority, carries no standard.
> His is nothing but a character who enjoys jesting and concealment.
> He wants to tickle a camel, but camels don't laugh when tickled.

3. In these verses, the southern poet's description of his northern correspondent's government as royalist and "reactionary" evokes a rhetorical framework that was commonly heard among southern socialists before the 1990s. Categorizations of Middle Eastern discourses into tribal and national frameworks have a voluminous literature. For Yemen, see Paul Dresch, *Tribes, Government, and History in Yemen* (New York: Oxford University Press, 1989); Dresch, "Imams and Tribes: The Writing and Acting of History in Upper Yemen," in *Tribes and State Formation in the Middle East,* ed. P. S. Khoury and J. Kostiner, 252–87 (Berkeley: University of California Press, 1990); Najwa Adra, "Tribal Dancing and Yemeni Nationalism: Steps to Unity," *Revue du Monde Musulman et de la Méditteranée* 67 (1994): 161–68; Steven Caton, *Peaks of Yemen I Summon: Poetry as Cultural Practice in a North Yemeni Tribe* (Berkeley: University of California Press, 1990); and W. Flagg Miller, "Public Words and Body Politics: Reflections on the Strategies of Women Poets in Rural Yemen," *Journal of Women's History* 14, no. 1 (2002): 94–122.
4. In his magnificent study of Muslim moral philosophy, ʿAziz al-ʿAzmeh states that notions of *ṭabʿ* are central to Muslim thought and suggests that they all converge "upon the sense of a continuous integrity of being, the identity of the origin and custodian of this continuity and its preserver notwithstanding." Aziz al-Azmeh,

Arabic Thought and Islamic Societies (London: Croom Helm, 1986), 11. The current emphasis on authorship suggests that while moral integrity remains central to the semantics of *ṭabʿ*, the notion also can invoke conflicting claims of origination and causality. Where poets draw nature into a moral economy in which some authors trump others, conventions of hierarchical authority can be overturned in the interests of "naturalizing" a more progressive moral agent.

5. *Taʾlīf,* the standard literary term for "authorship" in the Arab world, concisely expresses the moral stakes that I outline in this chapter (although the term is rarely mentioned by vernacular poets). From the verb that means "to join harmoniously, to unite" and "to compose through assemblage," *taʾlīf* foregrounds an unstable tension between compositional unity and multiplicity. Émile Benveniste and Jacques Derrida have explored the semantic elaborations of this dialectic in religious discourse by noting a distinction that has routinely cropped up in Western debates over religious inquiry since Cicero between religion as a practice of binding or uniting (from the Greek *ligare*) and religion as a practice of assembling or gathering (from the Greek *legare*). Jacques Derrida, "Faith and Knowledge: The Two Sources of 'Religion' at the Limits of Reason Alone," in *Religion,* ed. J. Derrida and G. Vattimo, 1–78 (Stanford: Stanford University Press, 1998). Setting aside the applicability of such distinctions to actual debates over religion in Europe or the United States, one can observe similar metaphysical antinomies at work in discourses of both authorship and religion. Unfortunately, authorship has come to be more frequently associated with individual and often secular identity (undoubtedly an association promoted by religious orthopraxy), and its substantial moral claims are underestimated.
6. Maurice Merleau-Ponty, *The Visible and the Invisible,* trans. I. Lingis (Evanston: Northwestern University Press, 1968 [1964]), 130.
7. Jane Hill, "Read My Article: Ideological Complexity and the Overdetermination of Promising in American Presidential Politics," in *Regimes of Language: Ideologies, Politics, and Identities,* ed. P. V. Kroskrity (Sante Fe: School of American Research Press, 2000), 262–63.
8. Ibid., 267.

9. Scholarship on *qaṣīdah* poetry has long focused on the relation between first-person narrational frameworks and a complex weave of second- and third-person verbal suffixes and pronominal markers that invest the authorial voice with rich social indexicality. Geert van Gelder, "The Abstracted Self in Arabic Poetry," *Journal of Arabic Literature* 14 (1983): 22–30; ʿAbd al-Wāsiʿ al-Hamīrī, *al-Dhāt al-Shāʿirah fī Shiʿr al-Ḥadāthah al-ʿArabiyyah* (Beirut: al-Muʾassasat al-Jāmaʿiyyah, 1999); and J. C. Lyons, *Identification and Identity in Classical Arabic Poetry* (Wiltshire, UK: Aris and Phillips, 1999), 38.
10. Brinkley Messick, *The Calligraphic State: Textual Domination and History in a Muslim Society* (Berkeley: University of California Press, 1993); Messick, "Indexing the Self: Intent and Expression in Islamic Legal Acts," *Islamic Law and Society* 8, no. 2 (2001): 151–78.
11. Lawrence Rosen, *Bargaining for Reality: The Construction of Social Relations in a Muslim Community* (Chicago: University of Chicago Press, 1984), 178–79.
12. William Beeman, *Language, Status, and Power in Iran* (Bloomington: Indiana University Press, 1986), 17–19, 202–03; Muhammad Arkoun, "Logocentrisme et verité réligieuse selon Abu al-Ḥasan al-ʿĀmirī," in *Essais sur la pensée islamique,* 2d ed (Paris: Maisonneuve & Larose, 1984 [1973]), 228.
13. Given historical linkages in the Arab world between poetry and networks of patronage and authority, the issue of plagiarism has been elaborated variously in a range of different discourses. Literary critics have outpaced all others in developing an extensive taxonomy of types of plagiarism, though many are acceptable variants of citation and allusion. Ibrāhīm ʿAwaḍaīn, *al-Muʿāraḍah fī-l-Adab al-ʿArabī* (Cairo: Maṭbaʿat al-Saʿādah, 1980), 8–59. Indeed among critics, plagiarism has traditionally been permitted as a necessary part of acknowledging that any articulation is always saturated with socially inhabited traces and that claims to innovative meanings *(maʿānī)* can be made only by God. Abdelfattah Kilito, *The Author and His Doubles: Essays on Classical Arabic Culture,* trans. M. Cooperson (Syracuse, N.Y.: Syracuse University Press, 2002), 9–23. Poets who vie for political leverage in more agonistic contexts tend to be less permissive. Alois Musil notes heated debates over correct attribution among Rwala Bedouin poets in

Saudi Arabia in the early twentieth century. Alois Musil, *The Manners and Customs of the Rwala Bedouins,* ed. J. K. Wright (New York: American Geographical Society, 1928), 283. Accusations of theft *(sarqah)* are frequently exchanged between Yemeni cassette poets, singers, and audiences.

14. Released in 1981 on ʿAbd al-Naser's cassette 10, this initiation *qaṣīdah* to Khaledi was written by Ahmad ʿAlī al-Qaīfī (from al-Qaīfah, an area formerly in North Yemen). Qaifi, who died in 1998, was one of the most celebrated of the cassette poets in the series. Along with Ahmad al-Sunbahi, he was one of the earliest poets to launch the debates between northern and southern poets that became the hallmark of the series. As usual, the response *qaṣīdah* is sung in succession on the remainder of side A of the cassette.
15. S. Nomanul Haq, "Ṭabīʿa," in *The Encyclopedia of Islam,* ed. T. Bianquis et al. (Leiden: E. J. Brill, 1998), 25.
16. Lucine Taminian, "Playing with Words: The Ethnography of Poetic Genres in Yemen," Doctoral dissertation, Department of Anthropology, University of Michigan, Ann Arbor, 2000, 99–100.
17. ʿAlī al-Ghulābī et al., eds., *Ghinā'iyyāt Yaḥyā ʿUmar* (Damascus: al-Kātib al-ʿArabī, 1993), 77.
18. Jacques Derrida, *Of Grammatology,* trans. G. Spivak (Baltimore: Johns Hopkins, 1974 [1967]).
19. The poem is a "response" to Ahmad al-Sunbahi from al-Baīḍā' (ʿAbd al-Naser cassette 61, 1987). As discussed in chapter 6, the exchanges between these two poets are the most famous on the ʿAbd al-Naser series, and some have reached hundreds of thousands of listeners (such as those on 99, released after the Yemeni War of 1994).
20. Distinctions between the manifest and outward *(ẓāhir)* and the nonmanifest and inward *(bāṭin)* have been elaborated extensively in traditions of Qur'anic exegesis. In popular metapoetic discourse in Yemen, the terms *ẓāhir* and *bāṭin* are frequently invoked when discussing the meanings of poems, and the category of esoteric poetry *(al-shiʿr al-bāṭanī)* is formally recognized as a genre. Most Yemenis define this genre more in terms of the use of localized symbols, indigenous knowledge, and moral conduct than in terms of religious mysticism.
21. Although ʿAbd al-Naser's cassettes cost approximately 130 YR

each in 2006 ($0.70 U.S.), almost all gross profits accrue to the cassette shop. As discussed in chapter 4, political cassette poets generally disdain suggestions that they take money for their verses, while singers are generally more prone to acknowledge professionalism.

22. W. Flagg Miller, "Metaphors of Commerce: Trans-valuing Tribalism in Yemeni Audiocassette Poetry," *International Journal of Middle East Studies* 34, no. 1 (2002): 29–57.
23. Composed by ʿAbdallah "Abu-Qaīs" al-ʿUlafi, this poem was released on ʿAbd al-Naser's record-breaking cassette 99 after the Yemeni War of 1994 and is discussed in chapter 6.
24. The verb "interpret" here invokes elaborated formal interpretation (as in Qur'anic interpretation *(tafsīr)*), whereas the verbal object "your manner" foregrounds the inward intensions of a single visible thread or line *(silk)*.
25. The poem, by Ahmad al-Qaifi, was sent to Shayef al-Khaledi (ʿAbd al-Naser cassette 64, 1988).
26. See Andrew Shryock, *Nationalism and the Genealogical Imagination: Oral History and Textual Authority in Tribal Jordan* (Berkeley: University of California Press, 1997), 213–21; Michael Gilsenan, "Sacred Words," in *The Diversity of the Muslim Community,* ed. Ahmed al-Shahi, 92–98 (London: Ithaca Press, 1987); Dale Eickelman, "The Art of Memory: Islamic Education and Its Social Reproduction," *Comparative Studies in Society and History* 20, no. 4 (1978): 485–516; and Brinkley Messick, "Media Muftis: Radio Fatwas in Yemen," in *Islamic Legal Interpretations: Muftis and Their Fatwas,* ed. M. K. Masud, B. Messick, and D. S. Powers, 311–20 (Cambridge, Mass.: Harvard University Press, 1996).
27. In his prescient essay on the growing impact of mass-marketed film on peoples' experience of authenticity, Walter Benjamin argued that mechanically reproduced images destroy the "aura" of objects by alienating viewers from their unique functions in historically situated contexts of usage. Walter Benjamin, "The Work of Art in the Age of Mechanical Reproduction," in *Illuminations,* 217–51 (New York: Schocken, 1968). I suggest that such an approach risks circumscribing "usage" into idealized stereotypes and that while perhaps helpful in studying ideology, it fails to account for the new functions that technological objects may acquire in contending historical regimes of truth and knowledge. In the case at hand, the au-

dible original copy may well contain an irony that confirms Benjamin's insights into consumers' sense of object alienation, but cassettes are gaining authority as media that help secure the integrity of previous moral utterances.

28. Manfred Schneider, "Luther with McLuhan," in *Religion and Media,* ed. H. d. Vries and S. Weber, 198–215 (Stanford: Stanford University Press, 2001).
29. Ibid., 202–03.
30. On first- and second-order indexicality, see Michael Silverstein, "Indexical Order and the Dialectics of Sociolinguistic Life," in *SALSA III: Proceedings of the Third Annual Symposium about Language and Society, April 1995,* 293–94 (Austin: University of Texas, 1996).
31. As I demonstrate in chapter 2, poets of *bidʿ wa jiwāb* verse routinely opened and closed their compositions with markedly written supplications to God and the Prophet Muhammad, although orally marked sections, whether stylized in religious or tribal idioms, ensured much of the contextual force of epistolary verse for audiences.
32. I have suggested elsewhere that the subjective index of poets' newfound vocal agency requires a project of what might be termed "phonogrammatology": a study of perceived sonic forms whose fixity is secured through possible differences in the scriptive double. W. Flagg Miller, "Of Songs and Signs: Audiocassette Poetry, Moral Character, and the Culture of Circulation in Yemen," *American Ethnologist* 32, no. 1 (2005): 94.
33. In Yemen, such scriptive tropes might include *(ḥikmah),* expressive dignity *(adab),* history *(tārīkh),* documentation *(tawthīq),* and public song *(fann).* As for image-doubling tropes, ethnomusicologist Jean Lambert has noted complaints from popular Yemeni singers and their audiences that televised images of performing artists now index a commercially devalued "character" *(his term),* even as such images have become instrumental to their success. Jean Lambert, "Du 'chanteur' à 'l'artiste': vers un nouveau statut du musicien," *Peuples Méditerranéans* 46 (1989): 71.
34. On "footing," see Erving Goffman, "Footing," in *Forms of Talk,* ed. I. Goffman (Philadelphia: University of Pennsylvania Press, 1981), 124–59.
35. Outlining the need for an anthropology of technology, Madeline

Akrich has argued that a study of the "description" of technical objects can help highlight the social objectifications that accompany given technologies and that become "inscribed" into the social fabric of local communities. Madeleine Akrich, "The De-Scription of Technical Objects," in *Shaping Technology / Building Society: Studies in Sociotechnical Change,* ed. W. Byker and J. Law, 205–24 (Cambridge, Mass.: MIT Press, 1992). This chapter illuminates how one group of producers has sought to "describe" relations of reproduction that are felt to have been imposed by a cassette industry—by deploying a historical semiotics of writing and orality to highlight a gap between newer demands of authorship being made by the cassette industry and older notions of oral authority that are discursively situated in highlands sociopolitical life. Such a reflexive approach provides an important cautionary to a persistent sociology that insists on distinguishing between the internal (technical) and external (contextual and historical) facets of given technologies. As poets' use of the trope of *ṭibāʿ* suggests, it is precisely by remooring the conventional boundaries of cassette recordings to notions of moral constitution, technical reproduction, and genre-relative authorship that the object of the cassette and the social relations it expresses become generative of new horizons of communal identity.

· SIX ·

The Significance of History's Personalities: The Legacy of the ʿAbd Al-Naser Series

As a people who prosper, move forward, and gaze upon the dawn, . . . one day, we will win control of our free will and of the right to govern our destiny! What is British history or the history of any free people but signs and lamps?

—*Communist party leader ʿAbdallah Bā Dhīb, "Greetings to the British Parliament," al-Nahḍah (newspaper), July 21, 1955*

I imagine myself as al-Khāledī. I can feel myself saying the same things. His words have such meaning for me! I enjoy putting myself in his position and watching what moves he makes, as if I were playing chess. What move will he make? And I?

—*Interview with ʿAli al-Ṭōlaqī, a fan of the ʿAbd al-Nāṣer cassette series, August 2, 1997*

On March 7, 1999, in the shadows of the vaporous smokestacks above the Ford Motor Company's Rouge River plant in Dearborn, the Yemeni-American Welfare Association received some two hundred Yemeni Americans and guests to mourn the natural death of the poet Shayef al-Khaledi. The memorial service was one of the largest commemorations ever held in the United States for a Yemeni patriot.[1] Khaledi's vernacular poems, couched in the expressive idioms of Yemenis of all socioeconomic backgrounds, had once again demonstrated their power to convene a discursive community. On this occasion, I found myself declaiming my own membership in this community. I spoke about my research in Yafiʿ, the Adeni cassette shop A Piece of My Land, and my last experiences with Khaledi as we watched the 1998 World Cup soccer finals together at his highlands home. Late into the night, in the final moments of a double-overtime shootout, we had both cheered France's victory over Brazil, a gold trophy snatched from the expected victor with help from French Algerian player Zain al-Din Zīdān.

Two months before the Dearborn memorial service, on January 6, 1999, thousands of Yafiʿis had gathered on the sun-drenched slopes of Yafiʿ's highest mountain for Khaledi's funeral. Friends and honored delegates from across Yemen followed one another in remembering Khaledi's life, initiating a series of eulogies and condolences that continued for over two weeks in Yemen's national newspapers and became formalized in the publication of a book about Khaledi's life and poetry.[2] But one speaker, the cassette singer Husain ʿAbd al-Naser, had a special message that reached Khaledi's cassette fans immediately after the funeral:

> My dear listener: Do you know, would you believe, that the esteemed and famous poet Shaikh Ahmad ʿAlī Tāher al-Qaīfī, "Abu Zaīd" Ahmad, died on the same date, at the same instant, of the same malady, and was buried in the very same tomb as Abu Lōzah [Khaledi]? This will apprise you of the ingenious devices, innovations, and tale of Abu Lozah. This is among the appendices to the biography *(sīrah)* of the life of Khaledi, which will last forever and ever. We accordingly ask everyone, including the appropriate Yemeni media, to give this personality *(shakhṣiyyah)* the full rights that he deserves to have recognized.[3]

Ahmad al-Qaifi, the most widely revered of Khaledi's cassette correspondents, had been the dialogic invention of Khaledi, an alter ego in a game of political debate that lasted over a decade. Qaifi had never been more than an imagined correspondent.

Or had he? What kind of doubling had occurred? Who had really been duped? ʿAbd al-Naser's narrative was related to me by a group of Yafiʿi Americans in Chicago on September 25, 2002, as the revelation of an incredible secret. Although I heard rumors of Khaledi's invented persona at the 1999 Dearborn memorial service, no one had ever offered such convincing evidence; nothing of this possibility had been remotely suggested to me during my fieldwork in Yemen. The Yafiʿi Americans with whom I marveled at Khaledi's craft were not only familiar with the latest news of the revelation, however, but were eager to participate in speculating about what kind of figure "Shaikh Ahmad al-Qaifi" was to those who recalled Khaledi's life.

"I heard this myself," said an elder man, "from a friend who attended Khaledi's funeral in Yafiʿ. It was all announced by Husain ʿAbd al-Naser, who told gatherers that Shayef al-Khaledi was not the only one to have died but that Ahmad al-Qaifi died with him. ʿAbd al-Naser added that he had been the sole privileged guardian of the secret *(sirr)* for many years, along with Khaledi's trusted neighbor."

As we sat chewing *qāt* and processing the news, another man confirmed that he had heard a similar account from trusted Yafiʿi colleagues while on a visit to Saudi Arabia in the previous year. Seeing my bewilderment, he added: "Recollect that when Khaledi was composing verse in the early 1980s, people couldn't speak as freely as they were able to in later years after the socialist administration grew more tolerant of political dissent. It was not easy to criticize the party openly. So Khaledi figured out a way to evade official censorship. When responding to Qaifi as the 'Poet of Riposte' *(shāʿir al-jiwāb),* Khaledi could defend his positions, even while [the foil of Qaifi allowed] venting criticisms of the party and its mismanagement of national affairs in the south."

I struggled to fathom the conditions under repressive state socialism that would have led Khaledi to risk his moral credibility with such an audacious bluff. Poets regularly created fictive dialogues with sentient animals, coffee trees, genies, and imaginary human interlocutors. Never, however, had I encountered such an elaborate attempt to sustain the fiction of an actual correspondent. But I also wondered about the political effects that Khaledi's ruse achieved among audiences. Recalling conversations that I had enjoyed with Yafiʿis about the Qaifi-Khaledi exchanges during my fieldwork, I remembered being struck by the immense respect that many audiences reserved not only for Khaledi but especially, in the context of poetic exchange, for Qaifi. Although I could find no one who had ever personally met with him, numerous fans of the series lauded Qaifi's superior political acumen. As one admiring poet had remarked, "He always attacks Khaledi for real flaws in the south, whereas Khaledi's defenses are always strained. Khaledi responds less by attacking real problems in the north than by making light of the flaws mentioned by Qaifi and even sometimes trying vainly to defend them." Even more prominent, however, were Qaifi's moral qualities, including his sincerity *(ṣidq),* his measured words and aversion to hyperbole *(mubālaghah),* and his ignorance of any knowledge of writing. Indeed, Qaifi's absolute illiteracy routinely cropped up among fans and led the same poet to assert that "his inability to read or write gives him the power to speak forcefully, straight from his muse *(hājis)* . . . in a different way than many literate poets after independence who have proclivities *(muyūl)* that compromise their integrity."[4] For these fans, Qaifi was Khaledi's purer, oral counterpart.

Sitting amid the Yafiʿi Americans, a young grocer spoke up. "No, no!" he exclaimed, rejecting the others' assertions that Qaifi had died with Khaledi. "Qaifi is a real human being! He is a tribal shaikh, and he lives in al-Qaīfah. But he's not just a fiction. He's real."

The elder man seemed to concede this possibility and replied: "Well, it's possible this shaikh is a real man, but he could not have been a poet. No, he must have entered into an agreement with Khaledi many years ago that the latter could pretend to write to him and could also attach his name to responses that he composed himself."

After a moment, he added: "After all, what kind of name is 'al-Qaifi,' given that al-Qaīfah is a huge region?"

"But al-Qaīfah is a single village," I said. I had once seen it labeled as such on a road map and hoped to elucidate matters.

"Well, it's really more of a wide valley between two mountains," he said, correcting me. "In fact, the valley was the site of a wild conflict between two tribes, each of which resided on one of the mountains. The conflict continued for a long time, until the imam [Yahya Ḥamīd al-Dīn] interceded in the early twentieth century by purchasing lands in the valley and establishing a protected enclave *(ḥawṭah)*. That helped settle the dispute for a while, although locals in the region grew resentful when tribal shaikhs from farther north, allies of the imam, later purchased tracts of land around the enclave and began settling there."

The valley's political history, the man seemed to suggest, provided a meeting ground for Yemenis from both northern and southern governorates. As a rallying point against injustices perpetrated by state-sponsored royalist landlords, al-Qaīfah was a natural site for populist resistance. Since the valley was located in the former Yemen Arab Republic, al-Qaīfah offered citizens of the former People's Democratic Republic of Yemen a valuable locale for considering moral commonalties between Yemenis that were transnational, extranational, and most important, given southern socialist interdictions at the time, tribal. The quest for a cassette poet's personal identity had found roots in history, and history had found new biographical moorings in the specter of Khaledi's penned correspondent. Where two men from different countries merged as one, history became deeply pan-Yemeni and nationalist at its core. But this was also history entwined with doubles, its narratives of poets and places inextricably linked to a version of tribalism that promised a tricky defiance against regimes of state authoritarianism. The *agent provocateur* of such tribalism, the real tribesman who was Qaifi, lingered behind a more playful figure that could circulate as a recognized "personality" *(shakhṣiyyah),* one whose sing-song success retained moral and political credibility only where the former's tongue was bound by a scriptive tether. In the end, the detailed narrative of al-Qaīfah's locality and history seemed to settle the issue for my Yemeni American colleagues, and our conversation turned to the Bears.

I focus in this chapter on poems released by the Yafiʿi singer Husain ʿAbd al-Naser, whose life and work I discuss in chapters 3 and 4. The more than five hundred *qaṣīdahs* that are featured on his series are an extraordinary archive of popular political discourse, representing over two decades of running commentary on everything from the cabinet shufflings of heads of state to the quality of blankets used for sleeping. My selection of excerpts from roughly a dozen poems reflects some of my own theoretical interests in this chapter, but I have sought to preserve objectivity by focusing on ten cassettes that were deemed by cassette-shop managers and audiences to have been the most popular releases in the series.[5] Much of this chapter foregrounds the series' principal poets, many of whom are part- or full-time migrants abroad.[6] At the time of my research, they were all living men rather than fictive *noms de plume,* a conclusion that I drew from my own encounters with them, from photographs, and from second-hand accounts of those who had actually met them (none of which I had acquired for al-Qaifi). Shayef al-Khaledi is the most celebrated of these poets, and so much of the chapter focuses on his work.

I want to ask two questions in particular, in this chapter: How did Khaledi's peculiarly clamorous, tribal "personality" become so important for fans of the ʿAbd al-Naser series? And during the pivotal decades of Yemeni nationalism, what do the contributions of the series poets' suggest about the popular reconfiguration of Yemeni political discourse, particularly in its southern governorates? In addressing these questions within a larger study of the moral resources of technological mediation, I devote special attention to the trope of history *(tārīkh),* nationalism's master sign.[7] As an expression of modern Yemeni culture and identity, few tropes prove as authoritative or as fertile. I approach history, moreover, as an ever-changing moral framework rather than as an objective narrative of past events. As an ontological index, history is a quality of being that links present individual experience with broader formations of enduring moral community. Most important, this long-term moral compass emerges in accounts of history by historiographers, literary specialists, manual laborers, and poets alike as a form of discourse whose ethical moorings are at once practical and ideal: potentially all citizens may write and speak history, but history is also a system of lettered truth and thus has an aesthetic of graphic and scriptive immanence that is more accessible for some than others. As in previous chapters, media forms and qualities help to emphasize history's predilections toward one ground or the other.

Yemenis find history's double voicing generative. Conflict between regimes of moral authority prevents such master signs from totalizing the human experience of modernity. This is no more the case than with Yemenis' moral assessments of nationalism. Although history provides one indexical framework for assessing the social and moral significance of various forms of media, its powerful state sponsorship constrains its vitality as a resource for political pluralism and renarration. History searches for translators, especially those in its own likeness. Toward this end, Khaledi's death and 'Abd al-Naser's subsequent revelations invite us to consider another equally powerful ontological trope that I call "personality" *(shakhṣiyyah)*.[8] At the end of his eulogy cassette for Khaledi, 'Abd al-Naser implores "everyone, including the appropriate Yemeni media, to give this personality the full rights that he deserves to have recognized." The plea to give Khaledi his "rights" is universally pitched to "everyone," although its specifically nationalist tenor is indicated through a special nod to "the appropriate Yemeni media." Much like history, personality invokes national recognition that is ideally due to all deserving citizens and is rendered even more graphically than history in qualities of visible ascendancy and future orientation (from *shakhaṣa* "to appear," "become lofty," "gaze upon," "stare"). Personality is a generalizing, circulatory force that draws and entrances the eyes of viewers. ʿAbd al-Naser's plea also implies that justice has not been adequately distributed. Rights have not been duly awarded, and the very need to recognize Khaledi's "personality" entails acknowledgment of deep imbalances in nationalism's higher aims. Even as a graphic trope, personality also involves jarring loss (*shakhaṣa* also means to "depart," "travel," "pass from one condition to another," "bray loudly"). Personality is adopted but must also perish. In this chapter, I explore how new personas or "personalities" that are elaborated by cassette poets on the ʿAbd al-Naser series work as somewhat glamorous reminders of history's toll on sentient being. By querying history's conventions of identity, such personalities help Yemenis turn history into a better resource for mobilizing political action toward more inclusive traditions of moral authority.

A TRANSNATIONAL MORAL CARTOGRAPHY: THE POETS OF THE ʿABD AL-NASER SERIES

Given the focus in this chapter on the poets of the ʿAbd al-Naser series, a brief survey of their backgrounds will be helpful. Migrants loom large among the poets who regularly contribute to the series, as discussed in chapters 3 and 4. Although only one quarter of the sixty-four contributing poets are full- or part-time migrants (most of them in Saudi Arabia and the Gulf states), approximately 95 percent of the cassettes in the series feature a migrant poet's composition, typically a *bidʿ wa jiwāb* exchange with a resident Yemeni poet (often Khaledi). A comparison of the categorical differences between "migrant" and "resident" poetry would be foolhardy, given how exceptions to the norm prove the rule. The status of migration does figure centrally, however, within *bidʿ wa jiwāb* debates in which metropolitan affiliations are portrayed negatively as signs of questionable circulation. Poets who reside abroad for long periods are often accused of losing touch with local issues, abandoning the revolution, or being softened by comfortable foreign standards of living, all of which implicate their nationalist loyalties. Migrant residence is rarely mentioned in poets' verses as a virtue.

In the early years of the series, most of the contributing poets were Yemeni colleagues who knew ʿAbd al-Naser from his residence in Doha. By the early 1980s, however, after ʿAbd al-Naser had begun numbering his cassettes and distributing them to Yemeni cassette shops, a wider community of poets began to be featured. Most of these poets sent ʿAbd al-Naser hand-written *qaṣīdahs* from residences in Yafiʿ, Aden, and other southern regions. But poets from northern Yemen also began sending him *qaṣīdahs,* attracted by his preference for outspoken political verse, his interest in poems that focused on rural life and traditional tribal discourses, and his fairly conservative musical tastes.

The poetic genre of preference on ʿAbd al-Naser's series reflects his orientation toward rural highlands political discourse: roughly 70 percent of the poems featured on the series are *bidʿ wa jiwāb qaṣīdahs,* an average well above the cassette recordings of most other contemporary popular singers in Yafiʿ. Accordingly, most contributing poets come from highland territories that are typically identified by anthropologists and Yemenis alike as home to the most prominent tribes in the country. They include Yafiʿis, who comprise 72 percent (forty-six poets) of the contributors and poets from the Shaʿībi, Quṭaībi, Ḥawshabi, and ʿAwdhali tribes of lower Yemen; from the Dharāhin, Ḥadā, and ʿAns tribes of lower and middle Yemen; and from the major confederations of Ḥāshed and Bakīl of upper Yemen. The potential critical leverage that such homelands offered to conventional nationalist ideology has been secured less by tribal affiliation than by the geographic location of most poets. With the exception of a few poets from Ibb, Sanaa, and Khawlān, the vast majority of poets herald from either side of the former boundary demarcation between the two Yemens.

The borderland residence of such poets has given their debates a different political tenor than is found in much official public rhetoric and has invested the series with a particular moral urgency. In the years when North and South Yemen were separated by contending nationalist ambitions, some of them driven by broader cold war alignments, the 'Abd al-Naser cassette series featured a genre of political poetry that was indigenous to Yemenis on both sides of the national border. While providing a forum for often heated debate over political and ideological differences, *bid' wa jiwāb* verse also underscored the common cultural heritage of Yemenis from the tribal highlands as well as farther afield, often through points of particular historical detail that revealed deep and ongoing continuities of interregional exchange. For southern audiences during the late 1970s and early 1980s, the tribal aspect of these debates was especially salient and would have differed markedly from the officially sponsored public discourse at the time, which held a dim view of references to tribal or regional particularism. Indeed, accusations of tribal resurgence were certainly matters of concern for the series' producers, particularly in the years before unification in 1990. Poets were occasionally thrown in jail by state authorities who tried to silence them, and 'Abd al-Naser himself also faced intimidation.[9] But the risks of sanctions from state mandarins of public discourse were offset by the support of a growing community of cassette listeners who valued a return to the politically charged, tribally inflected traditions of public dialogue that 'Abd al-Naser's innovative *bid' wa jiwāb* songs effectively reinvoked. When listening to the often brazen verses about dubious state appointments, corruption, disastrous fiscal policies, and popular demands for social justice, audiences on both sides of the border appreciated the series for invoking a public community whose moral loyalties were only partially determined by the radical demands of nations on their citizens.

Apart from regional and tribal origins, the borderland contributors to the series offered audiences another moral framework that discomfited nationalist ideology. This framework was religious. The series had grown popular among national audiences for featuring debates between Shafiʿi poets whose homelands were not isomorphic with older fault lines of Zaidi and Shafiʿi conflict that had been reaccentuated by contending programs of political culture over the twentieth century. As a result, the series gained moral credibility for some listeners across Yemen. One Sanaani fan remarked that he appreciated the series' debates precisely because they resisted displacing conflicts between the two Yemens onto irresolvable matters of religious difference. Although poets' could contest each another's respective piety, doctrinal variations were rarely at issue.

By requiring listeners to look elsewhere for points of contemporary political difference between the two Yemens, the series has provided Yemenis with a useful forum for considering how nationalist ideology can impose differences on subjects who might otherwise share deeper social commonalties. In exploring the poetic debates that unfold on the series, I attend to the graphic and especially scriptive aesthetic of history to substantiate this claim, while also considering how graphic registers of personality remind listeners of more complex strands of sociality. As is discussed below, poets' particular attention to the audio-recorded media of each other's letters helps them to consider history's abstractions as less than totalizing.

PERSONALITY *(SHAKHṢIYYAH)* THROUGH HISTORY

The distinct terms of moral inquiry on the ʿAbd al-Naser series emerge gradually in a sequence of verses, sung initiations and responses, and cassette releases. Indeed, much of the persuasive force and meaning of individual poems on the series derive from their relation to genealogies of poetic exchange that had developed over months, years, and sometimes decades, as is shown in chapter 1. Moving sequentially, then, through some of the hallmark releases on the series will clarify the uncertain historical authority of this emerging discourse.

Cassette 1, which reached audiences sometime between 1979

and 1980, was not the first of ʿAbd al-Naser's releases. Identified by shop owners as the seminal cassette of the series, however, "number 1" has come to overshadow other early releases, providing a certain memory whose archiving might remind audiences from whence the series had come.[10] Prominent on the cassette are two *qaṣīdahs* by Khaledi, and these are complemented by several poems about a "paint-cheeked maiden" that are exchanged, in the *bidʿ wa jiwāb* format, between two Yafiʿi poets.

Overall, the *qaṣīdahs* are wrought with a heavy symbolism that reflects poets' efforts to express political criticism while remaining attentive to the state's censorship of public discourse at the time.[11] Laden with symbolic figures of "daughters" and "fathers," "fruit pickers" and "guardians," rebellious "youths" and the ancient tyrant "Nimrod," poems evaluate a range of moral propensities while veiling precise political objectives. Nationalism provides some vocabulary for the poems, which speak of the party *(ḥizb)*, the people *(shaʿb)*, and marching ranks *(ṣufūf)* whose loyalties are Eastern *(sharqī)* or, less preferably, Western European *(gharbī ūrubbī)*. Tribalism is also briefly mentioned in one of Khaledi's *qaṣīdahs*, though only as the legacy of an overly protective old patriarch whose concerns for his daughter receives her rebuke: "You're an injurious tribesman *(qabīlī)* who declares death and war upon on me. My head, back, and spine complain to me of your cane." Exchanges remain decorous, in the traditional manner of much *bidʿ wa jiwāb* poetry, as well as jocular, and poets' own personalities are downplayed.

Released in the summer of 1980, cassette 2 sets a precedent for highlighting poets' own personalities, especially as cast on a nationalist stage. The national stakes of personality are emphasized both through a new interactional format of *bidʿ wa jiwāb* exchange and through a distinct set of poetic devices. In the former respect, the cassette features the first of many *bidʿ wa jiwāb* exchanges to follow between an initiating poet in North Yemen and a respondent in South Yemen. Side A contains a *qaṣīdah* initiation by Ahmad Muḥammad al-Ṣunbaḥī from al-Baīḍāʾ, the district facing Yafiʿ from just across the border, and the response poem from Shayef al-Khaledi continues from side A to side B. Their debates would become a signature of the series. Indeed, for many listeners, their names fell from the tongue as if they were a single poet *(Ṣunbaḥī-wa-l-Khāledī)* and would eventually feature on approximately a quarter of the series' cassettes. With the popular success of the release, other Yafiʿi poets took the cue. Within a few years, dozens of poets were writing *qaṣīdahs* to Sunbahi in hopes of a reply. By the mid-1990s, 37 percent of the cassettes on the ʿAbd al-Naser series (thirty-two cassettes) featured Sunbahi swapping verse with Yafiʿi poets.

The style, themes, and poetic devices featured on cassette 2 are equally innovative. The transnational origins of each poet allow the use of a more aggressive style of political satire *(hijāʾ)* that drew from earlier traditions of tribal sparring that had been zealously disparaged since independence and that lent a more agonistic tenor to the conventional protocol of *bidʿ wa jiwāb* poetry. Poets heightened the dramatic pitch of such debates, moreover, by making ample use of metonymy to associate collective nations with single individuals. As a result, moral assessments of countries, leaders, and poets became coimplicated, bringing praise or ignominy to all. Finally, both poets make creative use of metaphors that compare politics, moral sentiments, and each others' poetry to commerce traded on the market.[12] Where words, ideas, pens, cassettes, belongings, and other defining tools of the poetic craft were turned into commodities, the moral integrity of original poets and stentorian tribesmen, in particular, became jeopardized, even as cassette poets gained credibility as proponents of more contemporary forms of tribal identity.[13]

The nationalist stakes of the ʿAbd al-Naser series become more explicitly outlined in cassette 7/8, released six months later. This cassette, which links the integrity of poets to history and its textual authority,[14] is a benchmark of the series that is still enjoyed by listeners today. The cassette begins with an initiation *qaṣīdah* to Khaledi from the northern poet Ahmad al-

Qaifi, ostensibly from the governorate of Radāʿa (north of al-Baiḍāʾ) (see appendices for full text). Deploying aggressive tribalist idioms that had not been heard in southern media for years, Qaifi lambastes Khaledi and his region as a whole for failing to take revenge for the state's execution of several of its top leaders, most notably the People's Democratic Republic of Yemen's foreign minister Muhammad Ṣāleḥ "Mutīʿ" (the "possessor of curled horns" mentioned in line 10 below). Born in Khaledi's own district and raised in Aden, Mutiʿ had helped lead the National Liberation Front's "interior wing" toward more radical socialist commitments after independence in 1967, initiatives that fell hard on rural tribal authorities and that cost him popular support back at home.[15] In the wake of ʿAbd al-Fattah Ismāʿīl's forced exile in early 1980 and subsequent power struggles, Mutiʿ was arrested by the PDRY's president-elect ʿAli Nāṣer Muḥammad and executed without trial in February 1981.[16] After several other leading Yafiʿis were found hanged in their prison cells or disappeared, Qaifi's *qaṣīdah* fueled speculations that the state's new regional alignments were eroding Yafiʿ's traditional influence at national levels.

For many fans of the ʿAbd al-Naser series, the initial exchange between Qaifi and Khaledi is distinguished by its focus on history *(tārīkh)*. This framework is introduced in the opening greetings section of Qaifi's initiation *qaṣīdah* with the bold assertion that though he may lack the conventional authority or "right" to speak of "the country's conditions" and "past," he must nevertheless seize the opportunity as an obligation to "our current time and in what remains and the future":

O night traveler, may the Lord of heaven be with you. 1
  From Qaīfah, dispatch on the back of [your] horse.
Qaīfah is my land, the birthplace of my fathers, 2
  Whose star sits alight the towering mountains.
Carry to Abu Lozah a symbolic gift— 3
  Letters written in a script of red ink.
If he should ask you, tell him that the messenger of Ahmad ʿAli 4
  Has come to ask and interrogate you, O Bu Khulād.

Even if I don't have the right to ask, 5
  I will inquire about your circumstances and about conditions
    of the country *(bilād)*.
I will talk of the past and what has happened 6
  In our current time and in what remains and the future:
Regretfully for Yafiʿ, men of weapons, 7
  Their German rifles have been lost, and their Canadian guns.
The history of Yafiʿ is lost and its people astray, 8
  And now its history is marred with black.
Whoever said Yafiʿ is the bonfire of enemies has lied. 9
  Yafiʿ's bonfire has been extinguished and has become ash.
Gone is the mountain goat, possessor of curled horns, 10
  Yet you asked not why nor donned mourning clothes.

After beginning his poem in conventional form with a passing supplication to God, a messenger journey section, greetings, and a belated prelude (lines 1–6), Qaifi addresses the main message at hand: Yafiʿ has lost its tribal authority, symbolized by its dispossession of traditional firearms. Even more dire for its people, history has been lost, graphically stained or marred *(mulaṭṭakh)* with black (line 8). Like a bonfire that has become extinguished, history has become "ash," its radiance eliminated as a visible sign of its owners' honor (line 9). The permanence of such loss is definitive and extends not simply into the past but also into the present and future (lines 6–8). In the remaining ten verses of the *qaṣīdah,* Qaifi predicts that unification between the Yemens will not likely take place without the south's fundamental commitment to Shafiʿi Islam and its renunciation of communism. For southern listeners, Qaifi's challenge expressed unflinching defiance of state ideology that had developed in the People's Democratic Republic of Yemen for over a decade.

The graphic index of honor and shame is pursued vehemently in Khaledi's response *qaṣīdah*. In introductory verses, Khaledi paraphrases Qaifi's initiation in equivalent oral terms, greeting his "talk" with obligatory tribal generosity and declaring he will speak of the "past," despite Qaifi's attempts to obfuscate the truth. In line 5, however, Khaledi reminds audiences of Qaifi's accusation that "history is marred with black" and responds with equivalent authoritative imagery:

O you who began the talk, welcome to you and to it. 1
[To] him who has been generous to me, I will return his generosity in kind.
No sooner would I say I'll endure and take his injuries 2
Than I would see Qaifi with a keen knife.
He reminded me of the past, but I already know it well. 3
He will not fix anything like a covering over my eyes.
I have tested the heat and the cold, and Qaifi is ignorant. 4
He still barely discerns me from his bedroom and recumbence.
He who said that Yafiʿ is lost and its people astray, 5
That its history is marred with black,
His words are lies, or he who informed him lied. 6
The hand of Yafiʿ still rests on the trigger.
The history of Yafiʿ is a sun, white and honorable. 7
Its mighty hand strikes wherever it desires.

As in Qaifi's initiation poem, the opening theme of the response is tribal generosity, which is symbolized by the gift and countergift of "talk" *(qawl)* (line 1). Sarcasm quickly prevails, however. The potential moral affinities of a system of exchanged tribal discourse are undermined by Khaledi's strong disagreement with Qaifi: the "history" of Yafiʿ and its people is not forfeit by the execution of its "mountain goat." Rather, Yafiʿ preserves its history by virtue of a long legacy of honorable deeds, symbolized prominently by its possession of weapons (6–7). In subsequent verses, tribalism is depicted in hues of unadulterated violence, described as a record of "blood," "bile from the spleen," and "stabbing . . . in its streets and barren lots," as much as a legacy of "courage and fealty."[17] Much of Khaledi's narrative of bitter tribal honor is conveyed through a panorama of historical battles in which Yafiʿ achieves pyrrhic victory over neighboring regions and tribes, each of which witnesses visually *(yashhad)* and then attests orally to Yafiʿi "history." In noted respects, however, tribal conquest is framed as a bid for pan-Yemeni nationalism rather than dog-eat-dog particularism. This message is conveyed explicitly toward the end of the poem when Khaledi celebrates the revolution, or "mother," and demonstrates greater optimism about plans for a unifying "meeting" between the two Yemens. While Qaifi's question about history impels poets to declare tribal and regional prowess, history's "honor" *(sharaf)* can be achieved only on the field of a single, united Yemen, troubled though it may be. The compelling question that the poems raise, no more so than for southern listeners at the time, is not *if* national history can be narrated successfully by its tribes but rather how.

In approaching history as "talk" to be known, the poems offer two different hermeneutic principles, each dependent on similar graphic signs. As a principle of comprehension, the truth of history's story can be known and circulated as a single account of what really happened and, in this sense, becomes a subject of contest between those who would reveal its timeless dictates. Elaborated most explicitly in the initiation by Qaifi, this principle emphasizes history's inexorable claim on all subsequent action and forms of identity: "The history of Yafiʿ is lost and its people are astray, / And now its history is marred with blackness" (line 8).[18] Sometimes compared to an invisible "hand," this mode of knowing is readily accessible through visual apperception, as signs "marred with blackness" or else, in Khaledi's words, "white and honorable." A second mode of historical knowledge also exists, however, and it operates through what we might call the principle of insight. Here, the graphic signs of historical truth are less obvious and must be sought in the conveyance of their resonant messengers. This principle is elaborated in Khaledi's response, the second part of an exchange sequence that is most suited to reminding listeners of the "talk" that came before and of the personality who may have sponsored it. In place of monolithic signs, history becomes a matter of dialogue whose truth, still ideally graphic, must be discerned in the words and intentions of its narrators: "No sooner would I say I'll endure and take his injuries / Than I would see al-Qaifi with a keen knife. / He reminded me of the past, but I already know it well. / He will not fix anything like a covering over my eyes" (lines 2–3). Khaledi instructs his listeners to "see" the truth of historical narrative in the graphic signs of Qaifi himself and further assures his audience, invoking a contrast between himself and his vision-impaired opponent, of his authority in conveying a more accurate vision of history's accounts: "I have tested the heat and cold, and Qaifi is ignorant" (4). So too, however, must listeners begin by attending to the poets' own words. In subsequent verses, Khaledi depicts the truth of history in stirring graphic symbols of the "sun," "smoke," "forehead," "blood, and "fire," the moral significances of which can only be secured orally through the vocal affirmations of other regionalized personalities who confirm Khaledi's assertions. Central to this principle of history is a method of narration that is gradual, durative, and oral, even if aestheticized in graphic terms. History remains a potent sign, but personality becomes a metasign—what philosopher Charles Peirce would call an "indexical icon" that invites listeners to question history's reliability as a true account of a community's past.[19] Those best equipped to pose such questions are the poets, who promise insight into the hidden truths behind each others' outward appearances. They are the agents to whom Yemenis turn for lessons on national history.

HISTORY IN LETTERS OF FIRE, LIGHT, AND BLOOD

The many exchanges between Qaifi and Khaledi include some of the most popular poems among audiences and feature on approximately 17 percent of series cassettes. The question of the relation of tribal discourse and regional identity to larger nationalist trajectories would become generatively developed by later poets on the series. But Qaifi and Khaledi's bold deployment of "history" as a moral ledger for public identity was not theirs alone. They drew from a broader historiography, a discourse as well as an aesthetic of history, that had been developing in Yemen among scholarly elites, nationalist reformers, and political activists over much of the twentieth century, though few rural poets had redeployed its frameworks in such staunchly tribal idioms. Before continuing our analysis of other poems on the ʿAbd al-Naser series, let us consider the various strands of such historiography with the aim of assessing, even if in a cursory way, the nature of its authority.

Yemen's well-established institutions of learning and scholarship had produced an impressive range of regional histories by the first few decades of the twentieth century.[20] The project of assembling a consolidated history for the country, however, remained undeveloped until a series of bureaucratic reforms, commissioned by the imamate in northern Yemen, lent urgency to the production of a coherent account of peoplehood.[21] In 1937, the Committee for Writing the History of Yemen was first appointed by Imam Yahya Ḥamīd al-Dīn, and its mouthpiece was the flagship cultural journal *Yemeni Wisdom (al-Ḥikmah al-Yamaniyyah)*.[22] As a forum for launching one of the country's earliest modern Islamic reform movements, *al-Ḥikmah* held the faculties of reason and knowledge to be the cornerstones of a moral revitalization that might elucidate the shared "heritage" *(turāth)* of the Yemen people. Where colonialism had imposed difference on Yemenis, *al-Ḥikmah* would reach out to Yemenis from across the country to engage leading intellectuals in a common project of public education on matters of national history, culture, and society.

As suggested in the Committee's title, the drafting of history would license the editors of *al-Ḥikmah* to initiate a new kind of historical writing. Under sponsorship from the imam's brother, Prince ʿAbdullah Ḥamīd al-Dīn, and indebted to the scholarly establishment from which they had received formal training, the editors crafted an aesthetic of history that provided a single commonsense view of the past to Yemen's regionally various public. The editor principally commissioned with the task was Ahmad al-Muṭāʿ, a political activist and religious *sayyid* who eventually met his death in Yemen's rebellion against the imamate in 1948. In the first issues of the journal, Mutaʿ wrote a series of essays on the moral, religious, social, and cultural benefits of studying history. Urging his readers to cultivate a vigilance for history's graphic signposts, Mutaʿ wrote in 1940 that an interest in history is a sign of true human "character" *(ṭabʿ)*: "The character and inclination of human beings has indeed been to yearn for long-forgotten segments, to gaze back on beloved ruins, to pause before traces of antiquity, and to take pride in his traditions in all their past ages, glory, and history."[23] While Arabs had experienced a decline in recent centuries due to moral decay, political oppression, and the neglect of education, the "awakening" of human morals and character could occur through what Mutaʿ labels the "art of history" *(fann al-tārīkh)*. Mutaʿ's reformist ideas took cue from the essays of Rashid Riḍā, the Lebanese religious and literary thinker whose work had become foundational to Muslim modernist and nationalist movements throughout the Arab world.[24] Drawing from Rida's descriptions of historical inquiry as a mystical journey toward spiritual, moral, and physical revitalization, Mutaʿ instructs his readers that history provides "lights of guidance," "lights fires of sentiment in the heart," and "stokes the fires of zeal." As a broader political curative, moreover, history can illuminate from its "lofty peak" the nation's place among "the world's pageants, from East to West, as it seeks the knowledge of peoples and their progress, literatures, civilizations, morals, sciences, buildings, and beliefs."[25] History provides the "elevated observer" with nothing less than a window onto his own immanent nature.

The most important method for achieving such historical insight, according to Mutaʿ, is Arabic language reform. Through the study of Arabic and its cultural heritage, Yemenis could learn to practice the "art of history" for themselves. With a word of warning that reminds readers of his privileged role as public educator, Mutaʿ portrays history as a craft for virtuous reader spectators rather than for writers. Indeed, Mutaʿ cautions against the indiscriminate writing of events by unqualified or politically biased writers, a commonplace occurrence that had greatly hampered the quest for historical truth. Nevertheless, he asserts, history's technologies of literacy can also bring readers empowering and merciful access to gnostic insight. History's pages *(ṣaḥā'if)* and books *(asfār)* bathe readers with "suns of apperception," "tenderly refine their finest qualities," and conduct their spirit to "shelters of majesty." Through the retrospective of salubrious paintings *(al-rusūm al-'āfiyyah),* the hand *(yad)* of history's insight is fortified such that the authority of the Qur'an, moral custom *(sunnah),* Prophetic sayings *(ḥadīths),* and the treasures of "heritage" can become excavated by the virtuous reader without concern for dissipating history's singular truth. Much of the power of history's agentive media is conveyed through the revelation of its secrets, hidden things, and illusions. Yet in Muta''s reformist vision, no religious shaikh or collective assembly *(ḥalaqah)* is required to vouchsafe the readers' access to knowledge. As direct icons of a singular truth, history's media forms are themselves guides to self-discovery. Indeed, history's technologizing renders it potentially populist, assisting "the king in reforming his subjects, the politician in his tasks, the initiator in his goals, the social worker in his labor, the farmer in his life, as well as the judge, guide, educator, speaker, and others of all kinds and conditions."[26] Bearing a gift that allows individuals from vastly disparate social groups to experience the same underlying content—to speak the same "eternal tongue"—history asks only one thing in return: that it be aesthetically wrought in visible, shiny surfaces that are potentially accessible to every member of its community of readers.

For Yemen's diverse populace, however, a return in kind was, in many ways, too much to ask, especially when the hierarchical privileges of a "calligraphic state" were laid bare.[27] Alternative forms of scriptive mediation continuously plagued history's claims to immanent truth and took root in southern Yemen in such fields as the burgeoning song industry based in Aden, as well as in state-sponsored radical socialism during the 1950s. Among the most influential early representatives of southern nationalist song was a musician, historian, and prince of the Laheji sultanate, Ahmad Bin Faḍl al-ʿAbdalī (d. 1943) (see chapter 3). ʿAbdali pioneered efforts to put indigenous Yemeni song to sheet music and laid institutional groundwork for one of the country's first associations for nationalist song, The Musical Club of the South, which would produce a generation of influential artists. Try as he might to put oral tradition to pen, he was all too familiar with the pliancy of written script in the hands of popular singers and historians alike and suggested in one of Yemen's first books on regional history, *The Gift of the Age from the Chronicles of the Kings of Lahej and Aden,* that the problems of written texts would be reduced by print technologies. But even print was not infallible and needed monitoring through collective "comparison and correction," the results of which would call for a "second printing" *(al-ṭabʿah al-thāniyyah).*[28] Alert to new socialist discourses that were emerging out of Aden at the time, the prince averred that history's singular truth was not simply to be received by diligent readers but could be actively narrated by any "son of the lands" so long as they abided by a modern methodology in which history's authority would be subject to rounds of social consensus.[29]

Popular historiography was developed in new directions by a more aggressive generation of political revolutionaries in the 1950s and 1960s. The leader of Yemen's communist movement, ʿAbdallah Ba Dhib, wrote an article during his early years as a newspaper essayist and literary scholar in which he advocated an ostensibly more accessible methodology for narrating history. Entitled "In the Battle" and published by the League of the Sons of the South's weekly newspaper *The Awakening (al-Nahḍah),* Ba Dhib describes the formidable resources that counterrevolutionaries have at their disposal, employing an arsenal of punctuating devices to lend his narrative method an oratorical flair:

> We, the impoverished, who own nothing: What does one say? Yet we own everything. We own our consciences and our pens. We own our words and sensations. We own tomorrow and destiny!

> So we will write. We will write, as one of the heroes of the novel *The Mother* advises us. We will write "So that letters will have an outcry," as fire melts the ice of reactionaryism, and light detonates the gloom of treason.
>
> So that we prove to them that our new utterance, which has baffled them and has ripped the fabric of their piqued sensations, is not a matter of cloudy fanaticism, temporary agitation, or puerile stuttering but is rather a new conscience, a deepened scientific thinking, and a revolutionary capacity that cannot be exhausted.
>
> So that they will know that we don't play with fire or chase mere flies, that we mean every word we say, and that we say them fully aware of their every consequence and effect, and that we command responsibility. Though we are responsible solely to the people and to history.[30]

For Ba Dhib, writing provides the impoverished *(fuqarā')* with a critical weapon for moral and political transformation. Its letters of "fire" and "light," symbols frequently invoked in his essays, promise the kind of explosive and even messianic retribution that Karl Marx evoked in describing the overthrow of the capitalist system.[31] Where such writing could serve ideological ends, mobilizing "our consciences and our pens," Yemenis whose thoughts of liberation had been suppressed by British colonial rule could reclaim their words, sensations, and destinies. Embedded in Ba Dhib's new historiography is an ambition to convert script into the currency of everyday oral discourse and bodily action. Written letters will have an "outcry" and express "our new utterance." Although calculated to engage Yemenis' sense of "responsibility" *(mas'ūliyyah),* Ba Dhib's populism is nevertheless qualified as a horizon to be enjoyed largely by restricted cadres of aesthetes. His true heroes are those who might draw inspiration from novels, a literary form familiar to few Yemenis at the time, or who might command the "deepened scientific thinking" of committed party members. For most Yemenis, Ba Dhib's activist method was a performance of populist historiography as much as an actual resource that could be used.

By the 1970s in South Yemen, some of the most progressive literacy campaigns in the Arab world had begun to change this situation.[32] The success of such campaigns is remarkable by any standards. By 1973, an estimated 53.8 percent of the People's Democratic Republic of Yemen's populace had received some kind of formal literacy training through "cultural centers" that were established in every district. A decade later, through a nationwide campaign conducted in 1983 and 1984, this proportion appears to have climbed to 81.4 percent.[33] Fueling such transformations was a state-managed print industry that supplied readers with pamphlets, cultural magazines, youth magazines, literary journals, state-run newspapers, and paperback novels. Along with gains in popular literacy and education, came inevitable delineations of intellectual and cultural competence. Reading produced readership, and pens penmanship, but could both produce authors, and if so, were all authors equal? The friction between actual and ideal competences was highlighted in debates over civil justice and the fruits of nationalism.

Other registers of nationalist historiography thus provided Yemenis with fertile sources for reconsidering, extending, and qualifying ideals of citizenship and cultural competence. Together with the expansion of literacy in Yemen during the 1970s and 1980s, Yemen's audiocassette industry emerged with its own panoply of artists, authors, and heroes. Their nationalist credentials were secured in many ways through the same institutions of state culture that were accessed by authors of written and printed material. Indeed, where pop-song audiocassettes were vital conduits of nationalist ideology, the state redoubled its efforts to centralize the cassette industry and recruit its producers.[34] Even as cassette producers gained new influence as nationalist luminaries, however, the ongoing decentralization of the industry and its regional audiences ensured a fertile tension with nationalist norms. The revolutionary "outcry" of written and printed letters was ensured by the twin emergence of print and audiocassette technologies during pivotal years of Yemeni nation-state development and by the dissonance of authority that cassettes could credibly evoke. For producers and consumers attuned to the value of political pluralism for nationhood, such dissonance could be explored fruitfully through the relation between history and the personalities who continued to shape it.

When I raised the topic of history with Yafiʿi poets and their fans, I frequently felt that those who knew most about it also seemed least willing to acknowledge competence in narrating it. The widespread campaigns for literacy and cultural education in the former PDRY led almost every remote rural village to have men, usually of a range of ages, who had an avid interest in reading Yemen's history, especially accounts of the generation who had grown up just before the 1962 and 1967 independences. Some informants knew a great deal about world history, too. One afternoon, as I was chewing *qāt* in the crowded guest room of a friend's house, a middle-aged villager indulged me with a detailed description of European relations during the course of World War II and their consequences for the Middle East. Noting the obvious signs of an avid historian, I remarked: "It's great you have such an interest in history *(tārīkh)*." He corrected me: "Not history really, but events *(ḥawādith)*." When I asked him about the difference, he thought for a moment, and then proposed that history concerned "the profound and total origins of a given people *(qawm)*," a project to which he felt he could not lay claim. On other occasions, discussions of "history" occasioned similar qualifications by informants and frequently involved delicate negotiations between interlocutors over who should speak first, who should be addressed, which settings are suitable for narrating history, what the relation of such narratives is to other conversational topics, and so forth. Widespread gains in literacy and education had certainly made "the profound and total origins of a given people" a popular subject of interest among Yemenis. The narration of history, however, remained highly contentious and was subject to delicate negotiations of social competence and authority. History seemed widely known but difficult to vocalize publicly.

There was one kind of historical oration, however, that was appreciated by a wide range of Yemenis and that could be heard in both private and public settings. Resonant of other times and places, the mellifluous descriptions of history by the region's leading cassette poets commanded widespread respect among audiences, however controversial their politics or stylistic adaptations. "Something about history!" customers would sometimes ask when entering a cassette shop devoted to Yafiʿi songs. For many fans, even those not from Yafiʿ, the credibility of historical claims made by cassette poets inhered in a register of political dissent that was at once populist and selective, nationalist and expressive of a subnational community of capable media producers. "These cassettes are really something!" I recall hearing from a listener in Sanaa who was spending an afternoon with Yafiʿi colleagues. "You guys in Yafiʿ are effectively the party of opposition *(ḥizb al-muʿāraḍah)*! Every individual speaks up, taking responsibility *(mas'ūliyyah)* and representing his countrymen—without education, necessarily, but more by instinct. Your history gives you all the right to speak, and your words descend to everyone on the streets." The listener's comments sparked a conversation about the latest exchanges of the ʿAbd al-Naser series poets, whose verses had launched new debates about the finance minister's role in the country's latest corruption scandal, this time involving the misappropriation of oil revenues. For these fans, cassette poets' narratives of history were valid because they represented a vein of public opinion that contrasted with that typically represented by the state. Like an "opposition party," cassette producers offered an alternative nationalist vision whose moral vitality lay in its simultaneous coproduction as the expression of every individual *(kull wāḥid)* and yet also of specific delegates, especially cassette poets whose "words descend to everyone on the streets." Oral discourse was the medium for such interpersonal utterances, even more than education, with its conventions of reading, writing, and state-sponsored knowledge. The moral foundation of poets' expressions was instinct *(fiṭrah)*, asserted the listener. But the seal that bound the diversity of instinctive expressions into one collective will was history: "Your history gives you all the right to speak, and your words descend to everyone on the streets." History provided the ledger for fixing and securing the collective value of oral narrative, quite aside from institutions of literate authority. Indeed, for the listener, as for other fans of Yafiʿi political poetry, history's power of oral inscription worked through another technology altogether: the audiocassette. Where cassettes could imaginably abstract spoken words from the questionable moral tempests of "education" and mainstream state politics, history was provided with a true messenger, particularly when deployed through "instinct" by competent individuals.

Few demonstrated as much respect for cassette poets' authority in conveying communal history than other poets who felt history too formidable a topic to address. Some of these poets had grown up in the region, exchanged *bidʿ wa jiwāb* poems with others across Yemen, but preferred to focus on spiritual life and human nature. "What do I know of history?" responded one such poet when I asked him why he hadn't distributed his wonderful verse on cassette: "No, there are others who can speak about that subject better than I." On another occasion, a different response was given by one of Yafiʿ's most celebrated published poets, who also served as the director of culture and tourism in Yafiʿ. When exchanging talk and poems with other Yemenis during a trip to the governorate of Hadramawt, the poet recited several *qaṣīdahs* about recent political events, including a visit to Yafiʿ by one of the country's most powerful leaders, the parliamentary speaker and tribal shaikh ʿAbdallah Bin Ḥusaīn al-Aḥmar, and then received the request: "Do you have any poems about history?" The poet responded: "Well, the issue is this. I put myself in Shaikh al-Ahmar's position, and I think: 'What would I want to hear from these people?' I think that he'd want to hear about local conditions. So I reflect on that and speak mostly for those who are suffering. I can't speak for everybody from Mt. Nuqum to Mt. Shamsān [above Sanaa and Aden, respectively]. I can speak only about our local issues: a school that needs repairing or a local water project. What is most important to me is equality between al-Ahmar and myself." Sensing the audience's cool response, he then added: "But I hope to come back to Hadramawt a second time with Khaledi." In actual fact, few colleagues of mine knew history better than the poet, and I had seen him regale audiences back in his village with great authority on historical details both near and far. On this occasion, however, he was reciting formal *qaṣīdahs,* and perhaps as a result of speaking to strangers in another part of the country, the poet felt obliged to defer to the authority of the absent cassette poet and to Khaledi in particular.

Cassette poets, then, hold a special moral license to narrate history. For many Yemeni fans of political poetry, the credibility of cassette poets' views on history derives from their authority less as state men, literati, or schooled essayists than as traditional, dyed-in-the-wool orators. Yet like Qaifi, who had never been met, or Khaledi who might return to Hadramawt with my colleague a second time, these orators preserve their power by remaining once removed from the fray of everyday live performance. The curious abstraction of such orators may suggest that Yemenis find live oral narratives of history somehow fraught, when compared to the authority of histories written in manuscripts or printed in books. Cassette poets' verse may be enjoyed because it conveys a certain irony in Yemenis' modern experience with oral history, no longer quite the stuff of cultural authenticity that it would seem. However, cassette poets have also discovered ways to acknowledge such conflicting sentiments and have thus created persuasive insights on the nature of discursive authority and its exemplars. In the unfolding set of debates featured on the ʿAbd al-Naser series, the trope of personality offers listeners a new mode of historical being. On one occasion, when I was conversing about Khaledi with Yafiʿi American colleagues several years after his death, one young man intoned, "Khaledi *is* our history." For such fans, history became more accessible through the experience of a famous cassette poet partly through shared regional and genealogical backgrounds that might link the listener to the poet's own experience of broader historical events and contexts. As this review of cassette poetry debates suggests, however, history also became more accessible in being mediated afresh, through the intervention of a personality whose words could resolve conflicts between renditions of historical truth that were heard, spoken, and especially seen.

NEWS, RUMORS, SECRETS, AND AUDIOCASSETTE LISTENERS

After the release of the exchange between Qaifi and Khaledi on cassette 7/8, debates between northern poets and their Yafi'i counterparts came to fill the vast majority of subsequent cassettes. Challengers from the north included a poet of the Ḥāshed confederation, four more poets from the al-Baīḍā' region, and poets from Rūs (just south of Sanaa), Ibb, and Damt. Several other southern poets from Juban and the 'Awdhali territories in Abyan also joined the fray. Many of the cassette exchanges were heated, given strained relations between North and South Yemen at the time. Northern poets typically assailed the south and especially Yafi'i poets for communist orientations and lax piety, while Yafi'is responded with criticism of North Yemen's conservative Islamism, tribalism, and dependence on Saudi Arabia. Amid the shortcomings of respective nationalist projects, older regional identities supplied poets with comparatively local grounds of social affiliation. So, too, however, did the series' poems invite listeners to consider a wider range of nationalist commitments. This was especially the case since legislation in the early 1980s facilitated administrative and cultural decentralization in the People's Democratic Republic of Yemen thereby promoting a greater plurality of regional and social narratives.[35]

Amid the flurry of cassette exchanges, poets devoted increasing attention to the circulation of oral discourse that mediated their exchange and to the moral fiber of the agents that sponsored them. In the following year, another exchange between Sunbahi and Khaledi on cassette 25 found large audiences. At the outset of his "initiation" *qaṣīdah,* Sunbahi declares that he will use a "pen" and an "urgent letter" to help elucidate true "history" that has become obscured by "news," "useless advice," "insults" and meddling "laughter":

Sunbahi [said]: I have your injunction, so give me a pen this night. 1
I'll write an urgent letter to our noble brothers.
Khaledi and Qaifi are people of knowledge and dignity, 2
[Yet] they ignited everything and brought divisions between brethren.
From the circulated news, I see the accused. 3
God only knows if it's camaraderie or rivalry between them.
Khaledi, you are not obliged to pursue malignant talk. 4
If there is malice between you two, stabbing the corpse is forbidden.
I won't continue to insult you, for he has already laughed and smiled at you, 5
Meddling in your situation, politics, and administration.
The Yafi'i is [already] famous, so we won't praise him heaps and heaps. 6
His ancestor wrote his history, and it was renewed over a year ago.
No one [can] say anything today. Truth dwells with those who are venerated. 7
Whoever said anything about the Yafi'i, see how they become confounded and capitulate.

At the outset of his poem, Sunbahi describes Khaledi and Qaifi as ideal tribesmen who are "noble" and have "knowledge and dignity" (line 2). Their exemplary qualities, however, have been perverted by their own destructive "igniting" of serious "divisions between brethren" (2), the discursive tenor of which is elaborated in the following two verses. Although circulated news *(akhbar shāʿah)* of their exchange would seem to offer clarification (3), the sincerity of their fracas is unclear, and "malignant talk" or counsel *(shōr al-ʿadam)* from Qaifi is compared to a "corpse" that is best left alone (4).

Sunbahi subsequently extracts himself from the oral persiflage, setting a course for other exemplary poets, by declaring his own reticence to sling further insults or excessive praise (lines 5–6). Seeking a quieter and more dignified discourse, Sunbahi declares that the sheer fame of "the Yafiʿi", fixed by written "history," preserves the truth against anyone who might "say anything today." The silent record of the historical "Yafiʿi", moreover, is not divorced from all human agency but, on the contrary, secured by "his ancestor," a more propitious kind of deceased narrator (6). Although the truth of history remains preserved by its remove from present vocal clamor, history is also endowed with a genealogical substance that befits the ongoing contributions of tribal cassette poets, especially those who are famous.

The impulse to locate agency in a historical personality whose moral claims could rise above discursive dissonance was further elaborated through poets' attention to another sensory register, that of hearing. In his response to Sunbahi on cassette 25, Khaledi reassures his poetic muse *(ḥājis)* that the sound of *bāl* poetry *(ṣawt al-bāl)* will overcome "empty chatter" and "talk" of the cassette market, especially when backed by himself, along with a hot poker wielded against "the enemy." As the series progressed, poets' increasing attention to the clamor of the cassette market helped provide a context for reasserting the ability to hear a few stable bass notes amid the acoustic din. On cassette 37, when writing to correct Khaledi's narrative of historical feuding on cassette 7/8, one northern poet asserts, "I heard that a stone fight [has broken out] between you and Ahmad ʿAli (al-Qaifi)," but he admits that the "claims" fielded by "your first senseless *qaṣīdah* to Abu Zaid (al-Qaifi)" are anything but clear. Appointing Khaledi and himself with the authority to rectify matters, the poet instructs his imaginary messenger to "Tell the Father of Lozah to speak, and I [too will] speak. / If you seek honesty, then we'll set out decisive news." Khaledi's own response avers similar authority in newsworthy oral pontification, a position elaborated more fully on cassette 39 several months later, in his response to a Yafiʿi correspondent. Initiating his poem by comparing his own greetings to perfumes "purchased with cash, all due apologies," Khaledi wryly intimates that his speech has become quantifiable commerce. Subsequently, however, when addressing recent administrative appointments and the "news that you said is circulating," Khaledi suggests that his own banter might be more reliable than that of others', even despite his penchant for the sporty gab of a news anchor:

If you heard the summary of my broadcast, in short, 19
  Perhaps you wouldn't accept what expressions have been spread.
As for other news, take it and put it to song! 20
  How much distorted news there is, lacking all value.
How much rumor is spread, and how much claptrap. 21
  One hears its news in every street and quarter.
That one's a rightist, they say to you, and that one's leftist. 22
  Each one fills a page. One's savvy is one's fruit.
Their aim is to present you with a gift of prattle, 23
  Passing on to you pimped pictures.
Really, you must read from the book of al-Bukhārī. 24
  With luck, you'll acquire news before it spreads.
That's one part about the news that you said is circulating. 25
  As for the situation, I'll explain to you its outline. . . .
It didn't happen as you said. We measured it out with our forearms, 28
  [Though] one might be "Mr. Broadcast" and one keep his secrets.

In these verses, Khaledi instructs his correspondent of the advantages of hearing "my broadcast" rather than that of an anonymous "Mr. Broadcast" *(Bū Iʿlān)* whose authority is questionable (lines 19 and 28). Indeed, he proceeds to enumerate a range of unreliable sources of information. This includes oral discourse that is heard, such as playful "song" *(bāl),* "rumor," "claptrap," "prattle," and "news in every street and quarter." This also includes more visible sources that should usually serve as trusty signposts: a "page," "pictures," and the ninth-century compendium of Muhammad al-Bukhārī, considered to be one of the most reliable collections of the Prophet Muhammad's words and deeds, which can promise accurate news only "with luck" (24). As discussed in the last chapter, written documents could sometimes be invoked by poets in the series with considerable authority to underscore poets' own larger public competences. Such scriptive signposts could be tumultuously undermined, however, in hypermediated commercial markets that are frequented by cassette-poet personalities.[36] In such settings, the moral purchase of hearing becomes even more important than seeing. Amid the traffic of mediated texts, cassette poets' oral utterances frequently emerge as the most reliable sources for truth, particularly when guaranteed by poets' own assurances that they have mastered and set aside the practical business of the media industry.

During the mid- to late 1980s, as cassette series numbers climb from the 40s to the 60s, the authority of oratorical personalities hinges increasingly on "news" and extended treatments of news focus on the motivations of poets and their allies in preserving or corrupting Yemen's noble history. The term for "news" *(akhbār)* has a venerable history in the Muslim world as a genre of self-contained oral histories. In Yemen, especially before the expansion of electronic and print technologies in the mid-twentieth-century, chronicles of *akhbār* typically focused on tribes and lacked the defining chronological sequences that defined written state historiography.[37] In keeping with this older tradition, the ʿAbd al-Naser series poets continued to associate *akhbār* with oral discourse on social life in the country's peripheries. After several decades of experience with modern radio, newspaper, and television news, however, as well as with nationalist history, poets also preserved a critical perspective toward *akhbār,* drawing attention to its inherent disorganization, ambiguity, and potentially disruption of traditions of moral knowledge. In exchanges between poets, oral *akhbār* is often first introduced as indirect and reported hearsay rather than as direct discourse from authoritative spokespersons. Indeed, such hearsay typically recurs to reports of written and visual media, attributing to "news" a graphic aesthetic that while ostensibly coherent and sequential is also fundamentally problematic.

Khaledi's own election in 1983 to a position of leadership in Yafiʿ's regional administrative body, the Local People's Council, helped him emerge as a prominent middleman for accessing, disseminating, and guarding "news." After Qaifi addresses Khaledi, on cassette 46, by asking how such a rube could have won regional elections without bribery, Khaledi warns Qaifi away from "news" spread by his enemies:

News came to you randomly and fleeting. 14
  Cross it out, in all of its lines.
Don't consider it news from [direct] sources. 15
  See it as rumor from a bunch of individuals,
Disseminated by a despicable mob, most treacherous, 16
  And [by] clever people who lack all counsel—
Those who are rejected and mocked by our nation's people 17
  And whose injustice and harms have been repudiated.
They import news by mule trains 18
  And from foxes who remain determined in their dens.
Against the citizens, they appear as ʿAntar [Bin Shaddād]. 19
  In the name of the revolution, they are honored as revolutionaries.
Each is with the revolution, saying, "I'm a revolutionary," 20
  While they leave no trace or trackings on it.
You encounter them only in [influential] circles 21
  In clever and cunning sinecures.
I am not among their supporters, Ahmad ʿAli, 22
  Saying that they are good and beneficial men.
[I am] their enemy. See me with my uncovered face. 23
  I remain against them, by night and by day.
I told you about them earlier, if you remember. 24
  I revealed to you their secrets in full.

Warning Qaifi not to trust the news he "sees," Khaledi urges him to place confidence in his previous oral admonitions, "I told you about them earlier" (line 24). Although news suggests the possibility of a clear vision of recent electoral events in Yafiʿ and its unfolding social history, its narratives are undermined by malicious and ignorant "rumor" (15). In the context of such dissonant news script, truth can be salvaged only through the more authoritative oral accounts of Khaledi's person, itself equipped with the graphic arsenal of the media industry: "[I am] their enemy. See me with my uncovered face" (23). In this case, Khaledi's "enemy" is the coterie of corrupt government officials, those in high state "circles" *(dawāʾir)* whose honor rests merely on oral tales that they relate of such legendary pre-Islamic heroes such as ʿAntar Bin Shaddād rather than on more durable moral "trackings" *(āthār)* (20–21). On cassettes released in the late 1980s and 1990s, Khaledi's comparatively more reliable authority as a homegrown crusader with no small degree of media savvy would be underscored to great acclaim by a set of contributions from a Ḥāshedi poet from the largest tribe of northern Yemen, whose membership included President ʿAli ʿAbdallah Ṣāleḥ. On cassette 52, ʿAbdallah "Abu Qaīs" al-ʿUlafī sets the tone for his correspondences with a tribute to Khaledi at the outset of his poem:

The young Abu Qais [says]: I'll broadcast my word with being shy. 1
Whoever said Shayef is a pushover is a liar who has shaved his mustache.
By God, he is a mountain, and what mountain like him can be compared? 2
Aged with wide experience, a poet whose steadfastness has no likeness. . . .
Whomever has tested and then rejected him, cannot, in my mind, be a true tribesman. 5

Aside from Khaledi's own growing reputation as a political leader, other events in South Yemen during the mid-1980s set the tone for greater attention to the substance and secrets of prominent media personalities. On January 13, 1986, Aden exploded in violence between two rival factions, one led by President ʿAli Nasir Muhammad with its support networks in the Abyan and Shabwah governorates, and the other an amalgam of state authorities from Lahej, Hadramawt, and Aden. After the assassination of a large part of the Politburo, followed by ten days of lawless violence in the streets of Aden that left thousands dead and many more homeless, the president fled the country. In the flurry of analyses to explicate modern Yemen's worst atrocity, speculations abounded across the country about the role of the media in misrepresenting what had occurred and about the duplicitous personalities who had helped orchestrate the catastrophe.[38]

When fans of the ʿAbd al-Naser series recollected trends in poetic exchanges during these years, distinctions between socially relevant or topical poetry *(al-shiʿr al-mawḍūʿī),* and self poetry (*al-shiʿr al-ānī* or *shiʿr al-dhāt*) were frequently invoked. Some listeners evoked a contrast between these two genres and suggested that after the collective moorings of national identity and history had been dislodged by the events of January 13, poets retreated from more germane public issues to more introspective verse, not all of which was helpful. When discussing the ʿAbd al-Naser series, one poet who was well known for modern sentimental verse contrasted Khaledi's response to Qaifi on cassette 7/8 to later exchanges after January 13, 1986 in the following way:

> Khaledi's response set forth the truth about affairs that people had been afraid to express at the time. The vigor of his response was partly justified, given that he was defending himself from a bitter initiation from Qaifi, and by speaking with such ésprit *(nafas),* he was able to address topical *(mawḍūʿī)* affairs that had real social relevance. That's why Khaledi's poem was so refreshing for audiences. Later poems, however, have grown murky *(ghāmiḍ)*. Poems by Sunbahi and others tend to ask questions rather than provide responses, and in cloaking affairs with [unrevealed] secrets, they fill listeners with uncertainty and fear.

Elaborating on his perspective on another occasion, the listener commented further on recent trends in Yafiʿi cassettes poetry:

> The problem with poetry today, especially on cassettes, is its lack of wisdom. Such poetry deals with daily problems and events but is often unable to step back from the toss and tumble and present a meaningful portrait *(ṣūrah)* of the connections between daily experience and the realm of the spirit *(rūḥ)*. Such poetry is not able to link experience back to basic morals *(akhlāq)* in a way that could make such verse endure as a perspective that is more than just temporary. Only in this way can verse really be relevant *(mawḍūʿī)*.

By contrast, he added, poems that focus primarily on temporary events *(ḥawādith)* and personalities *(shakhṣiyyāt)* can be categorized as self poetry *(al-shiʿr al-ānī)*.

Other listeners held the eventful engagements of cassette-poet personalities in higher esteem, despite controversy over poets' abilities to convey enduring moral perspectives. These fans often spoke to me in detail of what they had learned from cassettes about each poet's backgrounds and commitments and enjoyed comparing the perspectives of cassette poets with their own. One rural enthusiast confided to me, "I imagine myself as Khaledi. I can feel myself saying the same things. His words have such meaning for me! I enjoy putting myself in his position and watching what moves he makes, as if I were playing chess. What move will he make? And I?"[39] Khaledi's verse captured this listener's imagination partly through the poet's own "position" *(makān)*, which the listener could momentarily occupy, as if he too was engaged in the heat of cassette poetry debate. The poet's significance as a figure to be emulated was conveyed visually through the metaphor of a chess game whose neat representational matrix could bind players within a single, dynamic moral universe: "What move will he make? And I?" Like the former listener who spoke of the need for a "portrait" and "perspective," visual idioms expressed the more durable, foundational tenor of poetry. For this listener, however, cassettes didn't diminish poets' credibility as moral wordsmiths. Indeed, the "meaning" of Khaledi's exemplary person was conveyed foremost for this listener through an especially emotional form of oral discourse: the *feeling* of talking like Khaledi. While Khaledi's "position" could circulate as a graphic icon to be emulated, his verse also resonated as a deeply personal, if silent, mode of shared oral discourse. Much in keeping with folk singer Muhammad Naji's discourse model of song, cited in the introduction to this book, the power of vernacular poetry to build community derived from a visual response to it that was keenly sensed.

In the cassette exchanges during the late 1980s and into the 1990s, poets' personalities became increasingly elaborated on the series, even as history continued to provided a central anchor in many debates. Where historical benchmarks routinely underscored national and subnational claims, typically in scriptive aesthetics, debates over the authority of cassette-mediated personalities introduced a more pliable set of scriptive tokens, many of them inflected with clamorous vocality. Humorous and often irreverent details of poets' own habits of dress, behavior, occupation, and lifestyle offered listeners insight into the unfolding contingencies of history, a perspective that could be emphasized in varying degrees, depending on poets' and singers' aims in any given debate.[40] Along with poets' capacities to reauthorize history in new registers of oral declamation, moreover, comes an increasing attention to secrets. In the uncertainty of contending claims to news, secrets could indicate the truths of poets' intimate knowledge of history and of the personalities who guarded them.[41]

On cassette 61, Sunbahi sends an initiation *qaṣīdah* to Khaledi to inquire about his failed reelection to the Local People's Council in 1986. After an opening prelude in which he commands his own musing "head" to destroy the illusion *(wahm)* of Khaledi's prowess, Sunbahi summons the authority of written history to help him with his task:

It is my obligation to record in history a venerable page 6
To the coming generation ahead, so that they know about our time and its secrets.
And you, my messenger, translate to the illiterate and the learned. 7
Tell Khaledi to yield and not to fall victim to his own ideas.

While history's "venerable page" suggests the conveyance of firm moral guidance to a younger generation, the author of the historical record and revealer of "secrets" is the poet himself. The possession of history's secrets by specific persons is further underscored in the following verse: the imaginary messenger, whom the poet addresses "And you," also possesses valued knowledge about Khaledi's hubris and is charged with "translating" details of Khaledi's perspectives to public audiences. Foremost among the messenger's recipients is the illiterate *(ummī)*, even more than the learned *(mutaʿallim)*, a contrast that emphasizes the relevance of history's truths to hearers and also suggests, with subtle humor, that "learning" through sound alone may be futile.

In much of the remainder of the poem, Sunbahi offers listeners an extended exposé of Khaledi's alleged personality. Through a verbal roast that blends fact and fiction, Sunbahi details rumors of Khaledi's one-time job guarding the door of an Adeni night club, his smuggling of "mustard seed," his "gray hair," and other personal matters, many of them visually evocative. Preparing listeners for his own claims to true news, Sunbahi also belittles the personal authority of other cassette poets on the series, notably the Ḥāshed poet ʿAbdallah al-ʿUlafi, who had tried to sow dissension between Sunbahi and Khaledi on a previous cassette:

No one commissioned him to talk or compose [poetry] from the lofty peak. 33
Baīḍā', Ḥāshed, and Adḥam acknowledged that his position was destroyed.
He's from neither Naʿwah or Ḥāshed. All his life he has submitted kneeling. 34

> He ingratiates himself to us and attests. [Yet] his weapon has no trigger.
>
> Ask the tribes of Tanham about his origins and what he produced. 35
> His identity is forgotten. Understand, and don't let a thing from his poetry deceive you.
>
> See where he lives, in Naʿwah. With his turbans, he pours coffee. 36
> If you ask, he has no honor [or] dignity, and his traces have been cut short.
>
> Whatever the inciter ʿAbdallah [al-ʿUlafi] said to you, I have his answer with me. 37
> And yet my hand is unwilling, and the nib of my pen is flustered.
>
> Leave things in their place. I will not reveal all of his secret. 38
> He is in its shadow, not the shadow [itself], and I am the keeper of his secrets.

According to Sunbahi, ʿUlafi's widely disseminated "talk" and "poetry" has won him a renown that is altogether incommensurate with his unremarkable tribal status, depicted in idioms of lowly descent, courage, and occupation (lines 34–36). The visual aesthetics of history—here ʿUlafi's personal history—are reinvoked with the command to "See where he lives" and the subsequent claim that "his traces *(athār)* have been cut short" (36). Rather than engage in further attempts to clarify the truth of ʿUlafi's "answer" through writing, however, Sunbahi announces that he will cease writing altogether: "my hand is unwilling. The nib of my pen is flustered" (37). Ostensibly in deference to epistolary relations in a social world made fragile by rumor, lies, and charades, Sunbahi promises that he will remain a "keeper of his secrets" (38). The moral register of history remains written inscription, but where history has become a matter of voluble, personal, and mercurial temperament, its marks withdraw inward. History's revelation becomes the prerogative of authorial discretion and is no longer fixed eternally for all to view.

In earlier poems, the truth of history was secured through a similar retraction from oral clamor (recall Sunbahi's assertion on cassette 25 that regarding history, "No one [can] say anything today. Truth dwells with those who are venerated"). The repository of moral truth in a more proximate and less industrious economy of signs, frequently conveyed through the graphic aesthetics of a unified circuit, is a trend that we have explored in earlier chapters in tropes of region and character. As the ʿAbd al-Naser series gains popularity through the late 1980s and 1990s, however, the authority to quell verbal clamor and news with more reliable assertions of social truth becomes the prerogative not solely of history itself or deceased ancestors but also of ebullient personalities and those who engage acoustically with their discourse.

On cassette 52, Sunbahi seizes on Khaledi's recent return from a pilgrimage to Mecca to speculate about the true extent of his piety. "News" again supplies the topic of the poem, and its delivery is entrusted to the poet's messenger who will carry it by horseback to listeners of various temperaments:

> Abu Saqr [Sunbahi] says: The news has been wrapped up, acquired from the traveler of the world. 1
> O rider of the bridled steed, deliver to the defiant and submissive.
> Tell them that Bu Lozah has submitted, discovering what he is allowed and forbidden. 2
> They said he drank from the [holy] reservoir of Zamzam and embraced the right-most pillar [of the Kaʿbah]. 3

The irony that world news is, in fact, about Khaledi himself is elaborated in subsequent verses through a long narrative of Khaledi's efforts to secure a personality by acquiring a desultory supply of flashy signs of modern identity, from new clothes and a pair of dentures, to scriptive documents including V.I.P. cards, Yemeni banknotes, checks, wax seals, thumbprints, and official documents giving him permission for a "hideout." In a final section of the poem, when addressing the two Yemens' unity and shared history, Sunbahi admonishes his colleague to stop writing poetry altogether and instead to return to a more deferential mode of authoritative tribal "speaking":

> Between you and me is a guaranteed contract to repair the damaged house, 26
> And if you reply, "No, it has been divided," then I don't want [the company] of those who spurn me.
> If you continue to mention the house of Tanḥam or the friends of Naʿwah or Muraddam, 27
> Even as your kneeling mount is bridled by those with trusted weapons,
> Stop your pen, and beware of speaking against the tribes. Show deference, 28
> Or else annihilation in this world is assured. I must respond to whomever summons me.
> By the creative power of Jesus, son of Mary, I will not submit or listen to you strike forth 29
> Or mention my friends with insults, those who have dignity in this life.

Proclaiming his own readiness in riposte, as well as his aural vigilance against any further slights, Sunbahi then initiates an oral riddle in subsequent verses in which he sets out the terms for a new register of authoritative speech. At the outset of the riddle, he gives the answer to Khaledi's own riddle, posed to him on an earlier cassette: "Fingernails" whose tips are carelessly "scratched." He then presents the puzzle of a rather different scriptive instrument:

> The riddle that came to me is numbered, its explanation and interpretation are well-calculated: 30
> Fingernails whose tips are scratched, surmounting the ends of the fingers.
> Now you guess: A mute camel that writes, reads, and even understands, 31
> Its chest is like a garden and softer. An artist, with a brownish hue.
> 'Cross East and West, it is turbaned. It prattles and speaks through a muzzle. 32

It has become a medium for the children of Adam, for preserving and publishing declarations.
33 This pronouncement from me is complete. I conclude with the exalted Lord of Creation
And with Muhammad, who expels all anguish, and who ascended straight to the throne.

Revisiting the image of the bridled and globe-trotting "steed" introduced at the outset of the poem, the answer to the riddle (immediately guessed correctly by listeners with whom I first heard this poem) is a fax machine. The device is evoked in scriptive terms, as something that "writes, reads, and even understands" (line 31). First and last, however, the machine is personified orally as a "camel" that is "mute" (31) and yet that also "prattles and speaks through a muzzle" (32). The creature is indeed graced with a certain global Arab finesse, being "turbaned" and "brownish" from "East to West," but so too is it cast in the mold of the vernacular Yemeni cassette poet, a clever "artist" *(fannān)* who, although muzzled, can still prattle and deliver a clarifying "declaration" *(bayān)* to the "the children of Adam" (32). Here then is the poet's solution to the circulatory and especially scriptive deceit that is featured in the main section of the *qaṣīdah*. The moral veracity of Yemen's social history is ensured not by scratch-marked fingernails but by a modern instrument of oral inscription that remains aloof of the corrupting media of political hubbub.

As plans for unification solidified in the late 1980s and optimism spread across the country, poets found recourse to scriptive orality somewhat less necessary. Where consensus over national history was best obtained by emphasizing shared cultural and political objectives, differences of contending oral narratives, scandalous news, alternative economies of script, and transient personalities were more often deferred with diplomacy. On cassette 73, released shortly before the official announcement of unity in 1990, Qaifi sends his last letter to Khaledi. Befitting the occasion, both poets foreground the epistolary ceremony of traditional *bidʿ wa jiwāb* verse, devoting special attention to extended messenger sections that detail the fragrant journey of each poet's written *qaṣīdah* to the house of the recipient, followed by bounteous greetings and good wishes. Henceforth, whatever turmoil ensued in the country, whatever conflict southern inhabitants experienced when tribalism returned to become an official mode of state governance, whatever personalities arose to grapple with new transregional tensions, Qaifi's voice would never again surface.

The moral value of an imagined oral tribesmen who could redeem history with scriptive and graphic finesse, however, would continue to find expression in successors. By 1992, relations soured between officials in the still young united republic, and two years later, a war broke out between secessionists among the Yemeni Socialist Party in the south and the supporters of existing President ʿAli ʿAbdallah Saleh. After two months of fighting culminated in the grueling siege of Aden, followed by its capture, a new round of barbed exchanges ensued between cassette poets, along with hard questions about Yemen's history, personalities, secrets, and truths. Tribalism provided a salient context for embellishing poets' verse with qualities of orality, face-to-face dialogue, rural authenticity, and potential violence. Poets' crafted attention to tribal sentiments provided listeners with especially apt commentary on the state's controversial reinstitution of regional tribal counsels, much of which was designed to slow the deterioration of security and due legal process in the countryside and to address popular interest in administrative decentralization through a register familiar to northern Yemenis. In a host of cassette poems released by ʿAbd al-Naser as well as other younger Yafiʿi cassette singers, the mouthpiece for such tribally inflected epistolary exchange was the Ḥāshedi poet ʿAbdallah "Abu Qais" al-ʿUlafi. A brilliant and witty polemicist, ʿUlafi routinely invoked the hazardous circulation of false news and reports, frequently recurring to the modern virtues of listening and speaking tribesmen as prophylactics.

One of ʿUlafi's most famous poems was delivered to Khaledi

in the wake of the 1994 Yemeni War and was released on the series' top-selling cassette 99 that would reach hundreds of thousands of listeners.[42] Focusing on Khaledi's questionable personality and role in southern secessionism, the poem offers tribute in its opening section to the paramount shaikh of the Ḥāshed tribe and a chief leader of armed forces at the time, ʿAbdallah Bin Husain al-Ahmar, as well as to President Saleh and the troops for their prominent roles in recording "history":

Just as we commission him paramount shaikh and higher, 12
  Just as those who recorded their valiant history,
His mettle, as time passes, only gets brighter. 13
  Their deeds are attested to by a hand of protection and combat.
What would have happened if "Mr. True" [Ahmar] had been absent or hadn't said no? 14
  Maybe the jackals in the forest would have eaten the lions
That have been accustomed to excellence and sated by it. 15
  It is inconceivable to me the scale of sacrifice in defense.
Our shaikh had confidence that we'd follow in your [Ahmar's] path
  As long as you are our overseer in all the regions.

The integrity of Ahmar's appointment, like that of the troops who "recorded their valiant history," is ensured graphically by the bright "mettle" of his person, labeled Mr. True *(Abū Ṣādiq)*, as well as by his "hand of protection and combat" (lines 13–14). So too does Ahmar's authority as "our overseer" *(mushrifunā)* unite the diversity of Yemen's regional historians on a single "path" *(darb)* (16). At the conclusion to his poem, however, ʿUlafi turns to more populist aural and oral media to deliver his prescription for the country's political and material wellbeing. Describing the impression of his voice on the inner-ear membrane, or tympanum, of the listener, he concludes:

That's my speech, and what remains in my heart takes cue. 42
  My pearl will emerge from the sea whose depths are wavy.

Honored is he who reads my speech and responds in rhyme 43
With the tympanum of the listener, for the finest hearing.
If the family repairs our people, [then] they will not split asunder. 44
Let a hole deteriorate, and it may cause loss.
We are in a battle, [and] the state of our economy is fragile. 45
We must still recognize this and improve its foundations,
[For] a murderer behind its walls is still rapping, 46
Waiting for the day of Yemen's division and swallowing.
He will not flag or tire, ever, and lo that he should be satisfied. 47
His gluttony will attain the bounds of the hideous.
His power lies in our unraveling and our collective weakness, 48
Such that we could say our endeavors were dashed.
[Yet] he will continue to wait, for Yemen will not shake, 49
Though summon what he may, hour by hour.
The past makes no vows to anyone, so no right is lost. 50
As long as one has claims, they will be secured.
Here, I'll conclude my verses by mentioning the savior. 51
Who do we have except Abu Qasem on the day of salvation?

In summing up his *qaṣīdah,* the poet likens his verse to a "speech" whose heart-felt truth emerges from the poetic unconscious, or "sea," like a lustrous pearl (line 42). The poet also imagines an honorable listener who will receive his good words not as unmediated oral utterances but through an act of sonorous exchange with a listener who possesses keen scriptive discrimination—who first "reads" his speech and then responds with a peculiar sensibility, described as the impression of oral words onto the tympanum *(ghalālij)* of the ear (43). True communication must occur, in other words, through dialogue with an ideal audio recorder.

In subsequent verses, the poet considers Yemen's moral integrity and loss by developing the initial tympanal imagery with a broader array of graphic membrane metaphors. The poet first suggests that a "family" *(ahl)* of responsible citizens can improve the country's economic conditions by securing the national fabric of its people from a "split" or "hole" (44–45). He then invokes the specter of a "murderer" whose incessant "rapping" and gluttony threatens the "walls" of the community and whose threat lurks in reaching if not transcending the "bounds *(ḥudūd)* of the hideous" (46–47). Amid such demotic visual signposts, careful audio inscription becomes a form of ethical action on behalf of the nation and its people, just as communal vitality itself rests on the proper reception of the poet's measured oral verse. After warning of the community's fibrous "unraveling" in the next strophe (48), the poet prophesies a long period of communal vitality: "he will continue to wait," he says of the murderer, but "Yemen will not shake, / Though summon what he may, hour by hour" (49). At this juncture, the poet returns to the aesthetic of history to redeem the country's moral fiber from the threat of the imagined murderer. The "rights" and "claims" of Yemen will remain as durable as a steadfast mountain (50). But the poet speaks of the "past" *(zaman)* rather than invoking the poem's earlier framework of "history" and in so doing suggests a moral path that could be secured beyond the vision of script. Instead of an immanence of bygone "generations" and their "ages" that is vouchsafed by written marks, the past evoked by the poet favors a register of discourse that is ostensibly more democratic. Progressing "hour by hour," the nature of such discourse permeates the entire final section of the poem as a form of secure orality that is scriptive while not scriptural or stately, immanent while not unchanging. The poet's signs of history seem to be secured finally through a generalized hearing personality whose moral foundation rests in an ethics not only of seeing but of reproducing true sound. Like the figure of Qaifi, though now more generalized and a better listener, an oral tribesman is imagined whose moral life is secured scriptively, albeit at a critical difference from the indelible marks of writing. The blood of such a tribesman certainly flows, and like history it pulses steadily through time. The idea of such a life force coheres, however, just beyond the visible world in a vein of sonorous public verse that is best circulated on cassette.

CONCLUSION

On October 10, 1997, twenty-five tribal shaikhs and state officials from both Yafiʿ and northern Yemen, accompanied by hundreds of other delegates, convened in the principal village in Quʿaīṭi, Khaledi's own natal district, to sign a contract of tribal law. Five years earlier, a murder had claimed the lives of four villagers, and the state court system had still not brought the perpetrators of the killing to justice. The settlement of such a major dispute by tribal law had not occurred in Yafiʿ since South Yemen's independence in 1967. The exceptional terms of the settlement became national news, as journalists flocked to the village and released headlines such as "Resolution by the Sons of al-Quʿaīṭi a Harbinger Deserving Respect and Appreciation." With revenge killings on the rise throughout the south, the result of a deterioration of state authority that followed the Yemeni War of 1994, tribal law was declared to be the necessary palliative. As one shaikh concluded at the end of the conference: "I hope that our slogan 'No to revenge killing!' will be applied by word and deed, so that we can close the black pages of our history, a history that should be glorious and a source of pride for all those from Yafiʿ, with its ancient lineage, fame, and authenticity."[43]

Tribalism was not what it had been, and as the shaikh's comment suggests, the actions taken in al-Quʿaīṭi looked forward to the application of new, more voluble "slogans" against the "black pages" of history, as much as they looked backward to genealogy and authentic culture. History is best inscribed by new agents, through new kinds of media. Indeed within days, photocopies of poems began circulating, the most impressive of which was an eleven-page commemorative pamphlet featuring over sixty tribal *zāmil* poems that had been chanted heartily in chorus by participants at the celebration, along with celebratory *qaṣīdahs* in the pamphlet's final pages. Centrally positioned on the cover of this document was a ribbon-festooned medal, an adornment uncommon in highland Yemen and instead suggestive of a more global form of recognition by other peoples and empires. Although designed with desktop publishing software, the medal held three handwritten words at its center, each set down with two separate scripts whose marks incompletely shadowed the other: "Shayef Muhammad al-Khaledi." Several verses from one of Khaledi's poems arched above the composition:

> The Quʿaīṭi said: I take aim with my gun,
> [For although] the gun's aim is singular, its wound infects all.
> I cured my self, and God gave me health,
> And an illness that tormented my heartmind was banished.[44]

The commemorative pamphlet was disseminated far more widely than the official legal document, and for audiences with whom I discussed the event, it served as a primer for recalling the importance of the event, even if they had been absent at the time. The medal on the pamphlet's cover suggested that some final solace was provided by Khaledi's image of an armed tribesman who could defend himself and his community through independent action, especially if channeled through sounds of poetry inscribed awkwardly onto a global badge of honor.[45]

Throughout this chapter, we have considered the function of a mass-mediated "personality" in helping Yemenis to consider their own moral relations to collective nationalist demands, especially those harnessed to the concept of history. My interest in a generalized personality partly reflects approaches developed in studies of the "public sphere" that have explored how subjects of durable, rational discrimination emerge amidst the fray of discursive and textual disjunctions that occur in communicative practice.[46] Where conventions of public discourse and representation are challenged, new agents are needed to secure interactional standards, and such studies have helpfully suggested that a dialectic exists between expanding parameters of social engagement and authority and virtues of personal integrity. In reviewing the exchanges of the ʿAbd al-Naser series and the accompanying personalities who contributed to its popularity, however, we have gained insights into the hierarchical privileges that accompany public culture when it is circulated through overly regimented notions of national history. Poets living along the borders of the two former Yemens found state narratives of history too confining to address the needs of their communities and too repressive of overt political expression. To promote alternative versions of history that could better accommodate their inclusion as public spokespersons, poets sought to invest history with a different ontological premise. Where history's truths could be founded in their unfolding oral narration, the identity of its denizens would be inseparably conjoined to ongoing exchange and dialogue. In this way, the virtues of personal integrity, responsibility, public knowledge, and moral leadership could all be conditioned by the competences of those best equipped to broker more accessible forms of public orality.

The prominent brokers of such oral history relied on sung *bidʿ wa jiwāb* poetry and knew how to guard their words as much as disseminate them. Where orality is an aesthetic of mediated identity as much as a communicative register, its power could derive from knowing how to control one's tongue or at least how to craft it with more rarified tones. Religious scholar Michelle Gendreau-Massaloux has suggested that in a context of global media in which television networks favor Western European and Christian producers, secrets may hold renewed moral relevance for those least advantaged by its screens.[47] She suggests that where television disseminates information through salient visual icons, an aesthetic resource perfectly familiar to Catholic communities as well as to proponents of direct democracy, Muslims and Jews, in particular, may find a valuable sanctuary in secrets. Aside from the offering possible access to the presence of spoken orality, secrets might also stake out a mediated difference from the resolute iconicity of ostensibly transcendent authority. Interreligious differences aside, I find her observations corresponding with my own, though for a different set of media concerns. The particular terms of orality developed by cassette poets may advantage them unfairly over other

Yemenis (notably women, those from less prominent tribal regions, and composers of modern verse), but so too do poets tailor the ontological foundations of public discourse toward greater inclusiveness. As I have suggested, poets place tremendous faith in the resource of orality, though not solely as an embodied, authoritative "presence" that might be commanded by the speaker. In the audiovisual marketplace of news and rumor, orality is vital precisely because it is mediated and thus masks foundational iteration. Through incessant stylization and double meanings, oral articulation forestalls definitive knowledge that might be circulated in endless repetition, if only for the moment. Only under such conditions do poets withdraw toward quieter secrets that might yet preserve a moral center, a single known history. And yet secrets retain their power for audiences only insofar as the possibility of their revelation continues to be spoken.

Personality, the locus of secrets told, becomes a resonant "metasign" of history's motivation, a dense passage through which the fraudulent logic of history's comprehensive sign is exposed. The ironies of such a disturbing public figure are potentially rich, given the different Arab media industries that inform the aesthetics of both personality and history, the former wed to modern twentieth-century audiovisual media, the latter inextricably linked to writing and print, whether nationalist or earlier. Nevertheless, personality ceases being ironic where it carries its own immediate force of persuasion and authority. Part of its appeal lies in conveying history's alterior and more contingent qualities: even as history is socially generalized, durable over time and space, so too is history intimate, malleable, playful, sonorous, and transformative. History is also more scriptive, at least in practice, than are the usual graphemes of personality and thus can be a valuable resource for those who seek to etch their way back into dominant nationalist representations. As a metasign, however, personality also gains force as a signal of history's dangerous denial of its own popular accessibility. History's letters, we are reminded, can all too easily turn hegemonic when its conventions of representation become tools of silence rather than of dialogue. History is typically depicted by poets as written on durable mountains or stones in letters of immanent light, whereas the aesthetics of personality privilege images that resist permanent fixation, such as flashy paraphernalia and sartorial fashion, blood and flesh. When speaking of Khaledi's poetic responses, admirers frequently compared the poet to a boxer who could deliver knockout blows, suggesting that he too could leave lasting physical marks displaced onto the human body. One fan qualified his sense of Khaledi's forceful impressions, describing them as delivered from the inside out: "He pinches from beneath the skin! He pinches so cleverly that it doesn't seem like he's pinching at all, but it's all the more dangerous since it's from within." The elegance of such deft attacks left his opponents with dignity, the fan marveled, ensuring further rounds of exchange.

Rather than succeeding each other chronologically as dictated by shifts in media culture, the tropes of history and personality also dance back and forth, their relations of complementarity and opposition continuously defined through struggles over place, event, responsibility, and collective memory as illustrated through the life and work of Khaledi. When Khaledi or other poets invoked the aesthetics of history or personality, they didn't oscillate between "public" or "counterpublic" forms of identity but rather invoked coexisting models of public engagement, each of which could be asserted or upturned strategically in conjunction with the symbolic resources afforded by a specific expanding media industry. At one glance, the graphic or scriptive aesthetics of history or personality could translate local concerns into the general presuppositions of nationalist and transnational debates. At another glance, prominent images and letters dissipated into vociferous regional and tribal particulars. In either case, the full dimensions of poets' authority emerged in the knowledge shared among fans that any single facet accessible on cassette was only part of an immeasurably vast repertoire, the best part of which remained latent.

NOTES

1. Khaledi died on December 13, 1998. The deaths of two of Yemen's preeminent poet laureates, ʿAbdallah al-Baraddūnī in 1999 and Husain Abu Bakr al-Miḥḍār in 2000, were met with greater national grievance in Yemen than in the United States.
2. The book was assembled by the editors of southern Yemen's most creative satire magazine, *Sum Bum,* and is entitled *The Heritage of My Eternal (Khālid) People: Shayef al-Khaledi (Turāth Shaʿbī Khālid: Shāʾif al-Khāledī)* (Aden: University of Aden, 1999). The book was not the first devoted to Khaledi's life and work; see Ṣāleḥ Ḥulaīs, *Yāfiʿ fī ʿUyūn al-Shiʿr wa Dumūʿ al-Qalam* (Riadh: Maktabat al-Mūʾayyid lil-Nashr wa-l-Tawzīʿ, 1993).
3. This message concludes the end of ʿAbd al-Naser's first cassette of eulogy *qaṣīdahs,* released on January 20, 1999. The statement is followed only by ʿAbd al-Naser mentioning his own name.
4. Interview, January 27, 1996.
5. These ten cassettes numbers are 1, 7/8, 25, 39, 54, 61, 73, 83, 99, and 103. These cassettes were prioritized for analysis in the first year of fieldwork before I decided to focus on discourses of circulation and the aesthetics of media. About half of these cassettes follow major regional and national events and continue to sell well today. Since cassettes 83 and 103 are devoted exclusively to rereleases of preindependence poems, I do not discuss them directly.
6. The cassette poets who spend much of their time abroad include Ahmad al-Sunbahi, ʿAbdallah al-ʿUlafi, and Ahmad Ḥusaīn Bin ʿAskar, who are featured on over 45 percent of the reviewed ʿAbd al-Naser cassettes, as well as "Abu Raʿd" al-Ḥajjājī, and Husain ʿAbd al-Naser himself, an occasional poet.
7. Nicholas B. Dirks, "History as a Sign of the Modern," *Public Culture* 2, no. 2 (1990): 25–32.
8. Early Muslim scholars such as the celebrated fourteenth-century social historian ʿAbd al-Rahman Ibn Khaldūn used the concept of "history" *(tāʾrīkh)* as proof of sociotemporal fixity against the duplicity of persons, documents, and words. A. Chejne, "The Concept of History in the Modern Arab World," *Studies in Islam* 4 (1967): 14. The utility of history in securing firm knowledge from the quiddity of persons, documents, and words continues to avail

contemporary cassette poets. As the present study suggests, however, the moral value of history can also emerge through greater interactive relations with its principal media forms.

9. Khaledi was imprisoned seven times between 1971 and 1985, each time for several weeks, and some cassettes (46 and 47) feature *qaṣīdahs* that were written during his confinement. ʿAbd al-Naser has faced less punitive attempts to manage his work, largely through interventions from Yemeni authorities based in the embassy in Qatar. On occasion, the embassy has obtained copies of poems to be released on cassette before ʿAbd al-Naser has recorded them and has demanded that he modify selected verses.
10. The serial numbering of cassettes was standardized after cassette 7/8, when singers began announcing volume numbers at the start of each cassette. Since the 1980s, numbered series have been typical for acclaimed recording artists. At the start of cassettes, the names of singers, musicians, and sponsoring studios are mentioned, and then the volume number is generally announced. On folk-poetry cassettes, the names of poets are also mentioned, along with occasional comments about key issues and events.
11. At the start of the 1980s, the socialist party had begun to adopt more liberal policies toward expressions of regional identity. In March 1980, the boundaries of the People's Democratic Republic of Yemen's six governorates were modified to take better account of regional territorial claims and were given local names in lieu of previously assigned numbers ranging 1 through 6. Nevertheless, nationalist discourses of the 1960s and 1970s continued to influence public associations of both "tribalism" *(qabaliyyah)* and "regionalism" *(minātiqiyyah)* with evidence of counterrevolutionary "reactionaryism" *(ragʿiyyah)* and "sectarianism" *(iqṭāʿiyyah)*. A measure of Yafiʿis' self-censorship at the time and of the state's changing attitudes was conveyed in comments by the former PDRY foreign minister, Muhammad Mutiʿ, who complained during a celebration in Yafiʿ in 1980 that only nationalist anthems *(nashīds)* had been sung and that no tribal *zāmils* had been featured (interview with a Yafiʿi informant, May 2, 1998).
12. I include below the verses of Sunbahi's first *qaṣīdah* to illustrate the interlinking themes of poetic composition, politics, and commerce. ʿAbd al-Naser sings the poem to a quick 4/4 beat melody that carries the *qaṣīdah* along with rakish pluck. Note that the term "sea"

(bahr) is a conventional metaphor for the poet's subconscious and is also a term for poetic "meter." Several informants explained that the intended target of Sunbahi's ridicule may have been a former PDRY president, ʿAbd al-Fattah Ismaʿil, who had been forced into exile just a few months before the cassette's release:

Sunbahi [said]: The ring fell into the sea and its depths. 1
Its owner for the day slipped away. What will follow in his place?
A proprietor of paltry reason! Tell me, what drove him to slip off. 2
Instead of putting [the ring] on his finger or returning it to its case?
The wave of the sea is mighty and carries off its flotsam 3
[So that] it won't return, to follow whomever found his shrine.
The darkness of his spleen defrauded [the shrine], so he won't get the rewards of his appointment. 4
Eastward and westward, its slippage is not a great infraction,
[For] it was not on my hand. If it dropped, Lord knows I won't forget its pain. 5
See how the nitwit set off, fleeing his countrymen?
What he had was a fake ring. Its loss was cheap. 6
He [would have] lost it or broken it, if he didn't sell it first.
It's of no concern. The merchant could not guarantee its price in the market. 7
He who brought along a sordid thing: it is his reputation that is sordid.

13. See W. Flagg Miller, "Metaphors of Commerce: Trans-valuing Tribalism in Yemeni Audiocassette Poetry," *International Journal of Middle East Studies* 34, no. 1 (2002): 29–57.
14. This cassette was catalogued 7/8 by Thamūd Exhibition and is the only cassette in the series to be catalogued by two numbers. Store managers explained the serial lapse to me by asserting that the cassette fell between numbers 6 and 9. The cassette is labeled "17" by ʿAbd al-Naser himself, who was likely counting earlier releases distributed in more informal networks. This number provides the benchmark for the archival standardization of his subsequent cassettes in shops. The mystery of cassette's double digitization remains unsolved. Listeners cited either number, although not both.
15. For a fine account of Yemeni Socialist Party initiatives in the early years of the People's Democratic Republic of Yemen, see

Zaid Mahmud Abu-Amr, "The People's Democratic Republic of Yemen: The Transformation of Society," Doctoral thesis, Georgetown University, Washington, D.C., 1986.

16. In his later years as foreign minister (1973–79), Mutiʿ regained the confidence of more moderate socialists by championing liberal economic reforms favoring small-business owners and migrant entrepreneurs. It was likely his growing influence among mercantile elites and foreign state officials that led ʿAli Naser to consider him a threat. Qaifi's homage to Mutiʿ's leadership would thus have been appreciated by listeners who resented the PDRY's ideological conservatism. By contrast, Khaledi's own response put him into the extraordinary position of supporting tribalism even as he commends the state's more conservative socialist ideals.
17. A tradition of reflecting on the ignoble sides of tribalism is conveyed in a Yafiʿi proverb: "Yafiʿ of the sword, Yafiʿ of the guest, and Yafiʿ of the dog" *(Yāfiʿ as-sēf, Yāfiʿ aḍ-ḍēf, wa Yāfiʿ al-kalb).*
18. In lines 8 to 11 of Qaifi's poem, the juxtaposition of history's past-perfect events with present entailments is developed in contrastive strophes that separately emphasize each aspect.
19. Although an indexical icon, the trope of personality also unfolds in stages over time, conveying as much a sense of its own possibility (a "rheme," in Peirce's terms) as its actuality. If history is taken to be an ideal expression of a given community's temporal existence or an "ultimate logical interpretant," then personality is its "dynamical object," a signal that shows how history's presumed stable qualities are motivated by selective forms of social interpretation. In the case at hand, the nature of history, expressed in scriptive and graphic immanence, can never be fully known but can only approximated through the collateral experience of graphic transience, of talk about history, and of history's emergence from the course of bloody events. An introduction to Peirce's writings can be found in Justus Buchler, ed., *Philosophical Writings of Peirce* (New York: Dover, 1955 [1940]).
20. For a review of such regional histories, see Brinkley Messick, *The Calligraphic State: Textual Domination and History in a Muslim Society* (Berkeley: University of California Press, 1993), 123–31; and ʿAbdallah al-Baraddūnī, *al-Thaqāfah wa-l-Thawrah fī-l-Yaman,* 4th ed. (Damascus: Dār al-Fikr, 1998), 231–32. On contending discourses of state and tribal history, see Paul Dresch,

"Imams and Tribes: The Writing and Acting of History in Upper Yemen," in *Tribes and State Formation in the Middle East,* ed. P. S. Khoury and J. Kostiner (Berkeley: University of California Press, 1990).

21. Messick, *The Calligraphic State,* 124–27.
22. *Al-Ḥikmah's* first editors were Ahmad Bin ʿAbd al-Wahhāb al-Warīth and Ahmad al-Mutaʿ, both of whom were members of the Committee for Writing the History of Yemen, as well as ʿAbdallah al-ʿAzab. The journal was suspended after twenty-eight issues in 1941 by Imam Yahya, who viewed its calls for reforms as subversive, but it was reinaugurated in 1973. Muṣṭafā Sālem and ʿAlī Abū al-Rijāl, eds., *Majallat al-Ḥikmat al-Yamaniyyah: Wa Ḥarakat al-Iṣlāḥ fī-l-Yaman (1938–1941),* 2d ed. (Sanaa: Markaz al-Buḥūth wa-l-Dirāsāt al-Yamanī, 1988), 4:18. For the importance of Islamic heritage *(turāth)* for this committee, see Thurayyā Manqūsh, *Qaḍāyā Taʾrīkhiyyah wa Fikriyyah min al-Yaman* (Beirut: Maṭbaʿat al-Karmil, 1979), 113.
23. Sālem and al-Rijāl, *Majallat al-Ḥikmat,* 322.
24. Manqūsh, *Qaḍāyā Taʾrīkhiyyah,* 186.
25. Aḥmad al-Muṭāʿ, "Fī-l-Taʾrīkh al-Yamanī," *al-Ḥikmah* 6 (1940): 318–19.
26. Ibid., 325.
27. On North Yemen's manuscript culture and legal reform, see Messick, *The Calligraphic State;* and Messick, "Kissing Hands and Knees: Hegemony and Hierarchy in Sharīʿa Discourse," *Law and Society Review* 22 (1988): 637–59.
28. Aḥmad Faḍl al-ʿAbdalī, *Hadiyyat al-Zaman fī Akhbār Mulūk Laḥaj wa ʿAdan* (Beirut: Dār al-ʿAwdah, 1980 [1930]), 3.
29. *The Gift of the Age* was written as a response to an influential history of *Greater Yemen (al-Yaman al-Kubrā),* published three years earlier by ʿAbd al-Wasiʿ al-Wāsiʿī, which surveys the thousand-year history of the Zaidi imamate. Paul Dresch, *A History of Modern Yemen* (Cambridge: Cambridge University Press, 2000), 49–50. After independence in 1967, ʿAbdali's writings and songs were cited in state documents as precursors of Yemen's distinct "scientific socialism." See, for example, *al-Muʾtamar al-ʿĀm al-Awwal li-l-Adab wa-l-Turāth al-Shaʿbī fī-l-Muḥāfaẓah al-Thāniyyah* (Lahej: Maṭābiʿ al-Falāḥ, 1974), 85–86. The introduction to *The Gift of the Age* conveys a sense of what socialists might

have found progressive in his work. Disdaining the penchant for rhymed prose *(saj')* that had long been a hallmark of historical writing, the prince addresses the problem of writing in a relatively simple register: "Given that I am a son of the lands of Lahej, I saw that what authors had written about our lands was replete with hidden and obvious errors. Thus, I consulted books, gathered narratives, commissioned oral chronicles from the young and old, all the while alert to delusions and lies, for as the proverb goes, 'The Meccans know their own people.' We encountered troubles, however, in gathering some of the penned Yemeni histories, whose manuscripts were difficult to read, either because they were old or because they lacked dotting or articulation marks *(ghayr manqūṭah wa lā mashkūlah),* a subject of complaint by many who read manuscripts of Yemeni history. We have, thus, decided to produce a [printed] copy, a task all too rarely performed by others, in the interests of comparison and correction . . . and if God grants us time and informs us of additional useful material, we will append it to this book in a second printing, God willing." al-ʿAbdalī, *Hadiyyat al-Zaman,* 3.

30. ʿAbdallah Bā Dhīb, "In the Battle," *al-Nahḍah,* August 25, 1955.
31. According to one informant, Karl Marx's dictum "The history of . . . their expropriation is written in the annals of mankind in letters of blood and fire" was being popularized in southern Yemen through translated excerpts of his work during the 1950s. I found this excerpt in Karl Marx, *Capital: A Critique of Political Economy* (New York: Charles H. Kerr, 1906 [1867]), 1:786.
32. Such campaigns were modeled on Mao Zedong's own, which were being implemented at the same time in China. South Yemen's relations with China were greatly consolidated under the administration President Salem Rubaīʿ ʿAlī, though in the later 1970s the People's Democratic Republic of Yemen moved closer to Moscow. The literacy campaigns in both countries were committed to Lenin's assertion that it is "impossible to build socialism in a country congested with illiterates." Glen Peterson, *The Power of Words: Literacy and Revolution in South China, 1949–95* (Vancouver: University of British Columbia Press, 1997), 149.
33. Karāma Sulaīmān, *al-Tarbiyyah wa-l-Taʿlīm fī al-Shaṭr al-Janūbī min al-Yaman* (Sanaa: Markaz li-l-Dirāsāt wa-l-Buḥūh al-Yamanī, 1994), 1:76–77, 225.

34. In South Yemen, the Ministry of Culture imposed tight regulations on a number of privately owned cassette shops after independence and sponsored artists who recorded primarily for state-run radio and television. A Union of Democratic Yemeni Artists was also established in the 1970s to assist artistic endeavors not directly funded by the ministry. All cassette shops were licensed by the ministry, and censorship was tight until the 1980s, when constraints on political expression began to be somewhat alleviated. North Yemen cassette shops enjoyed more freedom after independence, contributing to a comparatively more decentralized song culture for many years. One of the first state-licensed recording studios was Stereo al-Maṭarī in Sanaa, although a host of licensed cassette studios followed suit in the 1980s and 1990s. Outside of Sanaa, Stereo al-Kawmānī in Dhamār, founded in 1976, has become one of the state's most reliable suppliers, especially for rousing anthems *(nashīds)* based on traditional songs.
35. See note 11.
36. Much of this thematic of dubious script focuses on the paraphernalia that define the everyday identities of citizens, including letters, documents, books, engravings, licenses, diplomas, and so forth. When the topic of debate is piety, poets are especially likely to invoke authority in deciphering scriptive truth from falsity by likening themselves to *qāḍīs* of Islamic courts or state-court judges *(ḥākims)* and in condemning others for failing to adhere to Islamic law *(sharī'ah)*. More often, however, poets spar over relative degrees of authority in terms of bureaucratic and secular inscriptive practices engaged in by average citizens, those whose communicative competencies, as I argue in this chapter, lie very much at the forefront of history making.
37. Paul Dresch, "Imams and Tribes: The Writing and Acting of History in Upper Yemen," in *Tribes and State Formation in the Middle East,* ed. P. S. Khoury and J. Kostiner (Berkeley: University of California Press, 1990), 272.
38. The Ministry of Culture and Information's official report, published in both Arabic and English in April of the same year, illustrates the tenor of narratives about the role of the media and personalities that would become central to narratives of the conflict. The first-page "Prelude" begins with a paragraph steeped in the

language of a spy thriller: "0720 hours GMT (10:20 A.M. Aden time), Monday, January 13, 1986: Hassan [sic], a stocky, well-built personal bodyguard of the president, rushes into the Politburo meetings hall, points his Scorpion mini-machine gun at the vice president, and shoots him in the back." The next four paragraphs each focus on different media networks' reportage of the event, including (in sequence) Aden Radio and TV broadcast, BBC Arabic service, world wire services, and finally, again, Aden Radio and TV. The prelude ends with the following indictment: "What happened in Aden and why is the theme of this publication. It seeks to shatter the wall of silence that engulfed Aden once it became known in the West that the coup had failed and the 'moderate president' had fled the country. Western media did everything possible to bury the truth and continue to do so. AND HERE IS THE 'TRUTH'." *Aden's Bloody Monday* (Aden: Ministry of Culture and Information, 1986), 2–3.

39. Interview, August 2, 1997.
40. Cassette 54 (one of the ten cassettes originally designated for analysis) illustrates how singers could selectively arrange poems to foreground poet's vocal personalities without compromising attention to the aesthetics of national history. Of five *qaṣīdahs,* the first pair features a *bidʿ wa jiwāb* exchange between Qaifi and Khaledi that elaborates their respective oral responses to the bloodshed of January 13, 1986; the second pair features an exchange between two Yafiʿi poets that situates the events in Aden historically in relation to calendrical time and the written assurances of state law; and the final poem concludes the cassette with a love poem whose themes of personal lament and nostalgia are expressed in sonorous rhymed couplets that end *aḥ/-āḥ*. History's script is framed on both ends by registers of orality, the latter especially resonant.
41. Jean and John Comaroff have argued similarly that the power of personhood among the Southern Tswana in Africa lies precisely in a capacity to conceal. John Comaroff and Jean Comaroff, "On Personhood: An Anthropological Perspective from Africa," *Social Identities* 7, no. 2 (2001): 267–83. As the authors suggest, a certain freedom of action and social position is granted where personic goals, possessions, orientations, practices, and even more subtly, concealment itself can be concealed.

42. Multiple listeners urged me to study this poem for its rhetorical elegance. On one occasion, I witnessed a fan elaborate to Khaledi exactly why he felt the poem had presented such a challenge and why Khaledi's response had been crafted with extraordinary "diplomacy." For the listener, ʿUlafi's initiation was "dangerous" because, among other things, it isolated Khaledi's person from the entirety of Yafiʿ, which ʿUlafi made sure to praise, and then assailed Khaledi's tribal identity in a way that incriminated the region and the entire south indirectly. The listener further explained that Khaledi's response had been equally brilliant precisely because it countered ʿUlafi's charges in like terms of tribal standing while never once directly claiming the identity of "tribesman" *(qabīlī).* Such a response underscores listeners' appreciation for the functions that personic representations have in underscoring or undermining regional identity. More generally, the response indicates the nuance with which Khaledi helped listeners substantiate the moral foundations of tribal identity while sidelining its problematic touchpoints in southern political rhetoric.
43. Both citations in this paragraph are taken from Mushtaq ʿAbd al-Razzāq "al-Qaḍāʾ ʿalā al-Thār Wājib Yamlīhi ʿalayhi Dīnunā al-Ḥanīf," *Al-Ayyām,* November 9, 1997, 3.
44. qāl al-Quʿaīṭī ṣōbatī min bunduqī — wa-ṣ-ṣōb wāḥid wa-l-alam ṣāb al-gamīʿ
ʿālajat nafsī wa-sh-shifāʾ min khāliqī — w-inhēt ʿillah min-hā al-khātir wagīʿ
45. The pairing of Khaledi's stylized tribal personality with a self-reflexive global medium is replicated on the paperback cover of a commemorative biography of Khaledi's life and poetry that was released after his death. The front cover features a watercolor sketch of Khaledi in his later years, dressed with a Palestinian *kufiyyah,* a tribal dagger at his waist, and a pen in its sheath. On the back cover is a cartoon that portrays a comic caricature of Khaledi riding a pudgy stallion with his spear and shield in hand.
46. Concepts of public personality are explored fruitfully by Jürgen Habermas, *The Theory of Communicative Action* (Boston: Beacon Press, 1985); Seyla Benhabib, "Models of Public Space: Hannah Arendt, the Liberal Tradition, and Jürgen Habermas," In *Habermas and the Public Sphere,* ed. C. Calhoun (Cambridge,

Mass.: MIT Press, 1992 [1997]), 85–86; Norbert Elias, *The Civilizing Process* (New York: Urizon Books, 1978), 245–63.

47. Cited in Jacques Derrida, "Above All, No Journalists!," in *Religion and Media* (Stanford: Stanford University Press, 2001), 83.

Conclusion

The importance of poetry to studies of verbal culture is readily apparent to many Arabic speakers by virtue of the historical legacy of Islam. After the Prophet Muhammad had finished delivering the last of the Qur'anic revelations in A.D. 632, subsequent generations of Muslims became acutely aware of the need for a more expansive set of guidelines for interpreting scripture and understanding its significance for a growing diversity of Muslims. While some scholars devoted their efforts to archiving the words and deeds of the Prophet and his companions, others set about codifying the basic structures of Arabic grammar and linguistic usage in the interests of better understanding, extending, and teaching Islam's message. These latter grammarians identified source material from which Arabic could be formalized and gave special attention to the speech of the pastoral nomads from the central plains of Arabia who were closest to Muhammad's own tribe of Quraīsh. The poetry of such regions was felt to provide the finest gloss of the sublime diction recorded in the Qur'an. Exchanged among itinerant herders, craftsmen, merchants, soldiers, and town-based administrators, poetry provided the cultural flesh for an inimitable ideal and has been appreciated ever since by generations of influential Muslim thinkers.[1]

A half century ago, the value of poetry to studies of language and culture was underscored for Westerners by linguist Roman Jakobson, who reminded his audience of the pitfalls of overly formalist conceptions of verbal practice.[2] Poetry shows not merely how the transmitted aspects of "ideation" in language are inflected and sometimes overwhelmed by "emotive" aspects.[3] Poetry also reminds us that language is a powerful source of self-discovery. By employing ambiguity to query norms of behavior, action, and feeling, poetry creates a "double-sensed message" that is expressed "in a split addresser, in a split addressee, and . . . in a split reference."[4] The specific instrument for such multiplication of poetic agents and referents is acoustic equivalence—syllables, stress, meter, rhyme, and grammatical parallelism—whereby a single unit of meaning, including its implications for language users, is conjoined with others.[5] The result, Jakobson suggests, is a host of co-occurring possible meanings within a single utterance. Rather than destabilizing language, such polysemy ultimately enriches it by imposing an extraordinary requirement on interlocutors: the obligation to reiterate.[6] By having to clarify what has been said in new terms, language users continuously unveil latent understandings about the world and its orders, discovering new relations between "addressers," "addressees," and "references." In the process of reiteration, things felt to be essential and yet absent become more public, encoded, and potentially circulated in new patterns of verbal usage and recognition. Jakobson's attention to the reflexive value of poetry in language and the dynamic role of associative sounds in expressive life highlighted new opportunities for studying the cultural foundations of human communication.[7]

My focus on media technologies and specifically on audiocassettes has been directed toward exploring poetry's iterative role in expressive culture through a range of social and historical variables. Poetry has long been a "public register of the Arab people" *(dīwān al-ʿArab),* as noted by early Arab grammarian Ahmad Ibn Fāris. However, this "register" has also been a matter of techniques, competences, and material resources that have been unevenly distributed over time. To a large extent, as I have suggested throughout this book, Yemenis find poetry ethically compelling because it calls attention to contending economies of textual iteration and multiple conceptions of moral authority, even as it provides a structure that would seem to resolve such tensions. I have argued that the groundwork for such ethical discernment begins with attention to the sensory qualities of media, especially its visual and sonic aspects, which for the purposes of this monograph I have correlated with "circulating" *(sayyār)* and "resonant" *(muʿabbir)* aesthetics, respectively. Where verbal life is mediated visually by light or darkness, delicacy or crudity, or quickness or gradualism, attention is drawn to potentially common values that can circulate in the world and be reproduced. Conversely, where communicative channels become loud, quiescent, noisy, melodious, murmuring, or even orally liquidous, they are felt to signal more localized, embodied, and irreducible engagements. The obvious links between these two rather different aesthetics and their implications for selfhood invite us to consider how they work relationally with each other and are prioritized variably according to communicative aims, participant structures, historical periods, and so forth. Such binary aesthetics also invite broader comparisons with notions of the seen and heard in other cultural settings, as I have suggested throughout the book with observations on comparable notions of scripture, metropolitanism, character, personality, and national history in other, non-Yemeni contexts.

By attending to the construction and composition of texts, however, and especially to the physical and metaphysical qualities of script, I have also argued that the ethics of such sensory antinomies can be approached only through an ethnographic study of ways of knowing as evidenced in the work and lives of specific individuals. My enquiry into such ethical attunements has considered some of the problems with arguments that posit determining influences of literacy or audiovisual media on traditional societies. By showing how Yemenis routinely employ a repertoire of textual competences in assessing communal authority and ethical norms, I have deferred making oversimplistic equations between literacy acquisition and a host of liberal political commitments, from state-managed civil society to rationality. Here I review several of the elements in this argument before summarizing my prescription for a better method of studying the moral authority of media. This prescription, as I outline in this book, is to explore media culture through commonly used figures of speech, or tropes, that call attention to the social and cultural moorings of a wider set of progressive public selves.

Much of the comparative leverage that this book offers to studies of verbal interaction, media, religion, and other domains of expressive life draws from a set of claims about the function of discrete communicative codes in people's value systems, especially in conceptions of moral authority. The most prominent of these codes is writing, access to which was historically the privilege of members of notable houses—mercantile, religious, and administrative—in ways that find ready parallels in a variety of settings throughout the world. In the highlands of southwestern Arabia, where seasonal rains ensured greater population densities and more concentrated forms of state organization than anywhere else on the peninsula, indigenous systems of writing matured within a particular set of cultural ecologies. After pre-Islamic dynasties had institutionalized scribal officiates to help with administrative and commemorative tasks, Yemen's reputation for scholarly and moral authority grew further with the efflorescence of rural schools for Qur'anic learning and jurisprudence after the seventh century. The development of an increasingly managerial Zaidi (Shi'ite) state after the sixteenth century invested scribal writ with a more elaborated set of legal and symbolic associations, elements of which matured in a sophisticated culture of literary production and song that centered in Sanaa and its environs. During the twentieth century, the spread of state education and literacy campaigns allowed unprecedented numbers of people to gain skills in reading and writing, especially in South Yemen, although new hierarchies of literate competence also emerged amid the politics of intellectual and cultural prestige. Throughout the book, I explore the implications of such transformations for poets, singers, and their audiences, especially those who have sought to take advantage of a burgeoning audio-recording industry that developed in Aden after the 1940s.

My argument about the moral value of *qaṣīdah* poetry is premised centrally on the legacy of such economies of script in Yemenis' perceptions of authoritative verse. In considering epistolary "initiation and response" *(bidʿ wa jiwāb)* poetry in chapter 2, I suggest that Yemenis have long distinguished a written from an oral textual style through a set of formal compositional features, including overall synthetic unity and length, a scarcity of verbal formulas to assist memorization and recitation by rote, a seven-part thematic sequence that foregrounds explicit references to writing and to traditions of literate Muslim eloquence, and dense intertextuality in the response poem. I additionally suggest, both in this chapter and elsewhere, that where technologies of writing and inscription (including audio inscription) facilitate recording, storage, documentation, archiving, and accumulation, they can become resources for users as they consider the power of historically specific social and economic forces to inform expressive lifeworlds, for the better and for the worse. These observations accord, in part, with studies that examine the effect of writing systems on oral communication and associated patterns of thought, especially with their assertions about the referential, abstractive functions of such systems.[8] I differ from such studies by beginning with questions of aesthetics, approaching functions of literate discourse as registers of moral sensibility that are continuously reordered and rearticulated in practice rather than as technologically determined semiotic modes.

In presenting his brilliant formula for critical political action, or "praxis," Antonio Gramsci begins with what he calls "spontaneous philosophy," a competence available not solely to specialists or professionals but to everyone.[9] This philosophy is expressed through three primary means: "1) Language itself, which is a totality of determined notions and concepts and not just of words grammatically devoid of content; 2) 'common sense' and 'good sense'; 3) popular religion and, therefore, also . . . the entire system of beliefs, superstitions, opinions, ways of seeing things and of acting, which are collectively bundled together under the name of 'folklore.'"[10] My interest in locating the political agency of Yemenis at the intersections of language ideology, ethical sensibilities, and spiritual "ways of seeing things and of acting" parallels Gramsci's own, although my attempts to theorize sociopolitical change have concentrated on a more restricted cultural setting. To foreground Yemenis' own critical resources, I have continually revisited a popular belief that, among sensory faculties, vision provides the surest access to commonsense truth. Things that are plainly visible for all to see can provide an anchor for potential consensus when other things in the world remain obscured. Nevertheless, Yemenis also recognize subtler forms of sensory apperception, registers of "good sense" that access keener truths, and for this reason I have urged attention to distinctions between "visual" and "graphic" aesthetics. Where graphic orders are signs of what is seen rather than actual visual cues and where these signs can be communicated in nonvisual ways, such as through song lyrics, vast new opportunities are created for exploring the emergence of alternative or subaltern forms of ethical discrimination, knowledge, authority, and distinction as potentially public resources. This book focuses on the political deployment of such graphic claims by a host of largely rural poets, singers, and audiences who work to address their communities' needs for security, justice, and unity in an era of radical social transformation.

My attention to a process of ethical attunement in which more extensive and "circulated" forms of knowledge are considered alongside more intensive, "resonant" insights readily lends itself to studies of the way selfhood is recognized and performed. Wary of attempts to demystify identity through recourse to a single set of underlying psychological or cultural motivations, however, my analysis reflects Gramsci's interests in exploring the ways in which contending discourses of moral authority are situated historically and the legacies of such discourses for peoples' efforts to alleviate modern social ills. Such phenomena as vision and orality are significant for users, as noted by media theorist Régis Debray, through ecologies of technical, symbolic, and generic practice that are variously elaborated over time.[11] I have approached this "mediology," as Debray terms it, through acts of text making that constitute two domains of Yemeni noetic culture—*bid' wa jiwāb* poetry and the audio-recording industry.

My interest in a specific genre of poetic texts enabled a study of a centuries-old Muslim epistolary practice that has provided an extraordinarily interpersonal forum for exploring the public concerns of multiple discursive communities. Much of my argument has been designed to highlight the continuing vitality of orally performed verse for Yemenis as they link generalized frameworks of identity and moral authority to indigenous ethical practice. If "locality" is continuously rearticulated in relation to wider, translocal contexts and is not simply a spatial constant,[12] then this study has shown how a poetics of orality provides a certain recuperative agency for Yemenis as they organize communal responses to specific events. Within the ideological purview of written *bid' wa jiwāb* poems that were exchanged between literate rural notables and performed for larger nonliterate audiences, vernacular orality had long been associated with the everyday habits of unpolished rural inhabitants. When oral utterances invoked sentiments of honor with such values as courage, generosity, or a capacity for violence, they acquired especially tribal inflections. Some of the most socially nuanced aesthetics of orality were elaborated in the seven-part thematic sequence of *bid' wa jiwāb* poems, especially in a "prelude" section in which the poet announces an authorial epithet, a "messenger-journey" section that draws attention to the oral medium of the poet's message but also to its vulnerability in travel and its need for the more durable mediation of writing, a "greetings" section in which praise and social intimacy are lavished on the correspondent to whom the poem is addressed, and finally a "riddle" section in which orality provides pleasurable entertainment through a test of wits. Through texts of epistolary verse, orality was defined as an ethical practice whose merits and constraints emerged in contrast with norms of written composition. The ethical content of a written style also emerged in sharper relief: written media were more suitable for general moral pronouncements, more durable in travel, and more removed from presumptions of social autochthony. Above all, however, I have argued that the ethics of both oral and written styles and their respective discursive communities have been inseparably linked. The coimplication of both forms of communicative media has allowed us to revisit older arguments about tribes and states with better insights into the cultural pragmatics of moral authority. In broader terms, such an approach has highlighted the sociohistorical variables that enable Yemenis to reiterate what has been said in several registers.

The recourse of poets and singers to an innovative audio-recording industry, once the second largest in the Arab world, enabled me to explore the relationship of such mediated moral claims to a host of new social imaginaries. Orality continues to provide an important moral counterweight to assertions of scribal authority. As literacy and writing skills became more accessible to Yemenis through the 1950s and 1960s, however, oral pronouncements gained credibility in relation to the rarefied virtues of new inscriptive media, as originary impulses of recording stars whose competences, if beyond the reach of the vast majority of Yemenis, were still to be emulated. Chapters 3 to 6 explore the advantages enjoyed by poets as they collaborate with singers and other recording industry agents, as well as the problems associated with relinquishing control of one's verse. The most important discourse of political allegiance shaping all these chapters is nationalism, whose hallmark steps toward popular liberation from 1948 to 1967 occurred precisely during the years that audio-recording media such as the radio, records, and early audio-tape technologies were reaching unprecedented audiences. Even as citizens' expressive powers were assessed in registers of patriotism *(waṭaniyyah),* progressivism *(taqaddumiyyah),* cultural heritage *(turāth),* artistry *(fann),* the intellectual *(al-adīb),* and history *(tārīkh),* so too did the aesthetics of the human voice become conditioned by the reproductive capacities of mass media. In assessing Yemenis' views of such shifts in public oration, I have drawn special attention to the critical resources of the standard Philips audiocassette. As in many Arab countries, the cassette utility as a technology for political and moral reform was due partly to its uptake by popular audiences at a specific historical period. Accessible in popular markets by the late 1960s and early 1970s, the cassette proved instrumental to Yemenis after independence had already been achieved, during shaky years of state consolidation in which public culture was tightly monitored and censorship often vigorous.[13] The cassette's user-friendly recording capacity offered citizens special leverage in assessing the nation's highest ideals in light of everyday practice.

The social and ethical terrain for such mediology has been Yafiʿ, a region of cassette poets, highland tribal chanting, and venerable traditions of love song whose phonic associations for Yemenis are intimately linked with its contributions to Yemen's political life. A renowned early exporter of frankincense, myrrh, and later coffee, Yafiʿ proved home to mercantile and religious houses with extensive transregional networks and by the fifteenth century had developed a centralized administrative apparatus that committed the region's inhabitants to norms of statecraft. Yafiʿ also was known for its precipitous peaks, canyons that provided sanctuary to renegades, maverick warriors, fiery religious reformers, and imperious disdain for the yoke of outside rule. These two aspects of the region, one civil and the other unruly, became narrated alongside each other because Yafiʿ occupied an ecological borderlands and because two different sets of ethical standards had been joined into a single fraught compass by those dedicated to a vision of community.

The development of this ethnographic register of "spontaneous philosophy" through the audiocassette medium has enabled me to study this community's role in contemporary expressive culture. As Yafiʿi identity is conscripted into debates over nationalism, emerging commodity markets, civil society, and transnational labor flows, the cassette provides producers and consumers with a means to assess changes in moral authority through a new range of textual practices. With growing collaboration among *bidʿ wa jiwāb* poets, urbanized singers, and cassette-shop managers, the ethical costs and benefits of using cassettes are considered in relation to various horizons of sociality, especially metropolitanism and tribalism.

Comparisons between cities and rural life, on the one hand, invite reflection on territories of accumulation and related habits of embodiment. When channeled through nationalist discourses, metropolitanism becomes a horizon of access to the goods, services, and symbolic repertoires of global citizens whose ecumenical habits are expressed in acculturated civility. Ruralism, in turn, becomes the spatiotemporal antecedent to metropolitanism, a set of values and dispositions that are coded by nationalists in more ambivalent terms but that become critical resources for rural inhabitants themselves who rework its illiberal associations toward more general ethical claims. Chapters 2 to 4 focus on the deployment of metropolitan and rural associations in specific contexts of communicative action as participants build consensus about discursive community.

Tribalism emphasizes a distinct ethical register by foregrounding the management of communal obligations. Its nuanced vocabulary of compliance and autonomy finds ready uptake in a range of political discourses in Yemen. Broader trends in the Arab world toward urbanization, education, travel, and migration suggest that tribalism holds little appeal for most Arab communities. My analysis of the relevance of tribalism for some twenty-first-century activists, however, suggests how idioms of honor, descent, courage, generosity, manliness, direct interpersonal engagement, and potential violence may continue to provide ethical leverage, whether as a set of symbols that draws attention to the dangers of neglecting civil society or as a resource for political mobilization in periods of duress. The work and lives of the folk poet Shayef al-Khāledī and the singers Husain ʿAbd al-Nāṣer and ʿAli Ṣāleḥ, have provided much of this book's central insights into the versatility of tribalism for Yemenis. Set within national and transnational contexts in chapters 1, 4, 5, and 6, their contributions show how tribalism foregrounds an indigenous demand for accountability from regimes of commerce, accumulation, and associated forms of metropolitan and rural identity. As an ideological charter for securing justice among society's members, tribalism survives not as an independent moral code but rather as a relational ethics that, as narratives of Yafiʿi identity suggest, is continuously modified over time in tension with other moral discourses. In a global media industry that overwhelms the contributions of most small-scale producers, audiocassettes supply one of the latest means to explore the values that tribalism might hold for addressing urgent inequalities in public discourses of law and order. When cassette-recorded performances of tribal identity are held to domesticate alienated voices, persons, and places in the lifeways of local communities, audiences are invited to appreciate the talents of rural inhabitants in confronting modern forms of disempowerment. In the same vein, audiences grant rural cassette producers special credibility in tailoring older norms of honor and shame to more universal ethical principles. The cassette provides an outstanding resource for enabling both "inward" and "outward" attunements as a device for recording, disseminating, and aestheticizing particular ecologies of human sound.

Political liberalism is broadly understood as a particular condition of modernity in which, through reasoned dialogue, people agree to respect each others' opinions in public debates about the foundations of political order and participation. Much of this book highlights the moral resources employed by rural poets, singers, and their fans as they seek to expand Yemen's horizons of political participation with a more inclusive range of regionally and ethnically marked expressive registers. Studies of the "public sphere" have supplied general guidance throughout, especially insofar as they link social and economic transformations to specific discursive strategies. My analysis of a vernacular tradition of epistolary poetry thus shows how individuals seek to hold their public representatives accountable by engaging in reasoned debates that are ostensibly open to everyone and that find ethical purchase through credible detachment from the corrupting influences of markets and states. I have examined many of the techniques employed in such public efforts by attending to the ways Yemenis circulate and publicize letter poems using a variety of communicative strategies, including linguistic register, norms of audience address, poetic themes, intertextuality, and regional frameworks. As I discuss further below, I have given special attention to tropes of public selfhood, notably the generalized tribesman (chapter 4), character *(ṭibāʿah)* (chapter 5), and personality *(shakhṣiyyah)* (chapter 6). All such strategies signal a commitment to institutions of writing, recording, and formal education that are held to provide important moral foundations to the public sphere.

The intertwining of oral and written practices in Islam and generative debates about reason, embodiment, and the metaphysics of material exchange in Muslim communities provide valuable opportunities to study the cultural mooring of public spheres. Scholars conducting work in Muslim societies have helped develop such studies by exploring the role of legal and educational reforms in fostering more participatory forms of civil society. With special attention to the rise of Islamism, many studies have examined how the development of newspapers and literary venues, formal schooling programs, administrative systems, and new media technologies have helped codify Islam.[14] By becoming a more "objectified" body of thought and doctrine, Islam becomes a more accessible system of knowledge that can be referenced and evaluated by people of a wider range of backgrounds, training, and orientation. Such processes have enabled healthy foundations for Muslim pluralism, since diverse ideas can be considered and discussed without being seen to compromise the central precepts of a single faith.[15]

With the aim of contributing to our understanding of the diversity of Muslim moral discourses and their relation to textual practice, I have employed a language-centered approach to modern self-reflexivity that enables more refined considerations of public culture. Rather than approaching moral authority through Islamism or through the institutional conventions of state actors, I privilege poetry to explore how registers of sensibility, comportment, and responsibility are evaluated according to various discursive communities that each offers a different engagement with traditions of moral knowledge and action. As Yemenis craft texts and debate about their potential social effects, media forms and qualities become significant in helping to identify the expressive currency of given communities. I share the goals of many public sphere and media theorists of linking modes of social subjectivity to historical shifts in media practice. However, my attention to the complex ethical engagements of individuals in a specific ethnographic setting places greater emphasis on the imagination as it is used to flesh out norms of public interaction through culturally informed patterns of knowledge, perception, and emotion. Claims to public identity become ethically compelling when leveraged against generic habits of common sense that are revealed, if only by wordsmiths, to be collectively inhibiting. The imagination can play an important role in steering public life toward more enabling forms of cultural iteration.

I have advanced my argument about the role of the imagination in public life and in traditions of Muslim knowledge by developing a semiotics of media apperception that hinges on authorship and graphic tropes. Authorship is partly a function of institutional recognition, especially through public accreditations of literacy, education, and intellectual entitlement. But authorship can also be an ethical discourse about the conditions of one's credibility as a public spokesperson. If authorship is evaluated primarily on the basis of creativity, as many modern critics, Yemenis among them, might assert, the author's work becomes subject to the terms of public-sphere rationality insofar as artistic genius is held to lie beyond the market in the craft of a moral innovator who reworks a system of consensually recognized values. However, authorship can also be more exploratory than intentional and more collaborative than independent. For the Yemenis who are the focus of this book, authorship is less a matter of creativity and authenticity, distinctions they leave to metropolitan elites, than it is of responsibility *(mas'ūliyyah)*.[16] When assembling or evaluating poems, a composer begins by considering his or her responsibility to others as refracted through specific events, news, or community concerns. The entailments of responsibility are subsequently explored in imaginative dialogue with addressees, including social groups, specific correspondents, and even personified issues or texts. When asked about the goals of their work, such artists typically decline self-aggrandizement, emphasizing the needs of their community and its rights *(ḥuqūq)* as determined by its members' roles on the larger stage of history. Responsibility is a collective ethics keenly attuned to modern aspirations.

Poets and singers who use cassettes have found the medium useful for disseminating their views of responsibility and also for expanding the significance of their contributions for wider groups of Yemenis. I have argued, in chapters 4 to 6, that cassette producers pitch their work to wider audiences by developing new models of authorship that foreground deep asymmetries in public norms of authority. Insofar as they seek to establish alternative, more inclusive forms of political identity, their efforts might seem to constitute a "counterpublic," especially when they engage in the performative flaunting of civil norms with marked colloquialism, chattiness, irreverent humor, peripheral topicality, and other signs of estrangement from rational political discourse.[17] However, their attention to the material conditioning of civil norms and counternorms urges audiences to move beyond the logic of the identity as defined by liberal and counter-liberal publics. An emphasis on the circulation and resonance of media reminds Yemenis of the contentious sociality of communicative life and the ongoing process of community formation in which multiple voices struggle to be heard.

Graphic tropes provide the critical hermeneutic resource in this ethics of authorship. Figures of regional identity *(lawn),* character *(ṭibāʿah),* personality *(shakhṣiyyah),* news *(akhbār),* and history *(tārīkh)* are morally compelling to Yemenis by virtue of their associations with emerging public sensibilities and with traditions of Muslim apperception that have long addressed complex matters of origination and causality. Tropes work by making a single concept into a function of at least two denotational orders, each of which correlates with the other to indicate how the concept can truly be known.[18] While one order takes a position of greater salience, identifying the concept by more commonly recognized features, another order cues interpreters to a subtler logic whose features are informed by forces of entextualization that can be appreciated only with more refined ways of knowing. This latter, more resonant moral authority winks at the interpreter, signaling that the priorities of normative ordering are decoys. Critically, the power of tropes derives not from a consensus on norms of denotation but from their construal in social action. As assignations of responsibility, competence, and redress are sought in the heat of an unfolding event, participants use graphic tropes to signal their skill in identifying the kind of readily circulated values that might address the needs of the moment and to draw attention to their own agency as iterative hosts who might be trusted, in future events, to see the falsities of the world for what they are. Tropes are intriguing because their moral prescriptions always emerge in the process of telling, even if managed through audiocassettes.

Throughout the book, Yemenis are shown exploring the ordering of tropes through the graphic qualities of script. Technologies of verbal inscription and duplication help structure people's expectations of tropic orders partly by their ecological and social reticulation among diverse traditions of knowledge and partly by their historical and ongoing usefulness in reauthorizing texts with imaginative insight. Indeed, "scriptographic" tropes provide critical leverage because they invoke concepts of responsibility, personhood, community, and place that are linked to a wide range of ethical practices that exist quite apart from regimes of inscription. When hitched to script, tropes draw these guiding concepts into communicative economies whose totalizing claims are necessarily compromised. Such a strategy stacks the deck in favor of the *agent provacateur* and increases the likelihood that the poet will gain control over the world's recognized entextualizing orders. In this setting, performances of tribalism, in their hallmark voluble clamor, can lend collective support to bids for progressive change.

The substance of such new and reiterable claims depends on how graphic tropes are developed in league with other tropes that guide the imagination toward establishing ethical norms. Although graphic tropes appear to rely on themselves, largely because they engage fundamental feelings and experiences, the bulk of their force derives from their relation to figures of thematic mood, expressive form and function, spatial and temporal orientation, and social similitude.[19] I have focused on a host of graphic tropes that are central to Yemeni political discourse to situate their resourcefulness within the fuller contexts of human experience. If culture lies in transmitted ways of knowing how to clothe society's needs in imaginative form, this monograph shows how a specific community of poetry fans turns culture toward ethical ends. Such a project underscores the centrality of anthropology and the humanities to studies of liberal political formations. The individuals who are discussed in this book understand the importance of public ideals of reason, civil debate, and inclusiveness in managing communal solidarity. As their attention to the aesthetics of media suggests, however, they also seek forms of public activism that better address systemic inequalities in public norms of verbal communication, feeling, and behaving. Their "weapon" for achieving such critical discourse, as suggested by Yemeni singer Muhammad Nājī, is folk poetry, an expressive tradition whose power to catalyze new horizons of imagination and action can be appreciated only as an historically situated literary experience.[20] The *qaṣīdah,* in particular, is one such cultural tool, an assembly of verses stitched together, as events would require, with special elegance. Where audiences can witness a collective heritage being freshly mobilized, they can sense the majesty as well as contingency of received authority. Such an experience certainly transcends the cassette poem, as Naji suggested in evoking a magical graphic "portrait" of circulating song. But the cassette poem provides a way in.

NOTES

1. Contrary to popular opinion, Arab *qaṣīdah* poetry, like Islam itself, has never been solely a desert phenomenon but developed historically in contact zones between settled and rural areas. *Qaṣīdah* poetry has arguably had a special relation to memory and nostalgia, in particular, and its correspondence with Islam's emphasis on "remembering" *(dhikr)* has been noted by other scholars; see, for example, Michael Sells, *Approaching the Qur'án: The Early Revelations* (Ashland, Ore.: White Cloud Press, 2002), 9–10. My observations on emerging forms of metropolitanism and their rural antecedents have provided insights into the sociospatial and ethnic qualities of memory. I have attended to how such qualities are invoked by Yemenis in a practical ethics of social justice.
2. Roman Jakobson, "Concluding Statement: Linguistics and Poetics," in *Style in Language,* ed. T. A. Sebeok, 350–73 (Cambridge, Mass.: MIT Press, 1960).
3. Ibid., 353.
4. Ibid., 371.
5. Attentive to the structuring principles of verbal selection and combination that are familiar to linguists, Jakobson defines the unique function of poetry in this way: "The poetic function projects the principle of equivalence from the axis of selection into the axis of combination. Equivalence is promoted to the constitutive device of the sequence" (ibid., 358).
6. Ibid., 371.
7. Unfortunately, studies of the roles of sound and aesthetics in lan-

guage were overshadowed in subsequent years by structuralist trends in linguistics that drew attention to Jakobson's cognitive insights. Countering this trend, Prague School linguist Jan Mukarovsky's work deserves special mention. His analysis of the "structured" and "unstructured" aesthetics of language—the former more general, supraindividual, and stable and the latter tending toward uniqueness and pragmatic specificity—provides an exceptionally elegant formal elaboration of my own contrast between the aesthetics of "circulation" and "resonance." Jan Mukarovsky, "The Esthetics of Language," in *Prague School Reader on Esthetics, Literary Structure, and Style,* ed. P. L. Garvin, 31–69 (Washington, D.C.: Georgetown University Press, 1964 [1948]).

8. Strong arguments for such a perspective have been developed by Jack Goody and Ian Watt, "The Consequences of Literacy," *Comparative Studies in Society and History* 5, no. 3 (1963): 304–05; Deborah Tannen, "The Oral/Literate Continuum in Discourse," in *Spoken and Written Language: Exploring Orality and Literacy,* ed. D. Tannen, 1–16 (Norwood, N.J.: Ablex, 1982); and Helen Leckie-Tarry, *Language and Context: A Functional Linguistic Theory of Register* (New York: Pinter, 1995). Walter Ong's work has been especially influential. Walter Ong, *Orality and Literacy: The Technologizing of the Word* (New York: Routledge, 1993 [1982]). In my view, Ong's greatest lapse is his failure to recognize such concepts as abstraction, storage, accumulation, and linear thinking as ideologies that reflect the investments of centralized systems of authority. Media culture does not spring from centralizing forces alone.
9. A. Gramsci, *Selections from the Prison Notebooks,* trans. Q. Hoare and G. N. Smith (New York: International, 2003 [1971]).
10. Ibid., 322.
11. Regis Debray, *Media Manifestos: On the Technological Transmission of Cultural Forms* trans. E. Ruth (New York: Verso, 1996), 133–56.
12. For this generative approach to locality, see Arjun Appadurai, *Modernity at Large: Cultural Dimensions of Globalization* (Minneapolis: University of Minnesota Press, 1996), 178.
13. Throughout the Arab world, audio technologies that preceded the cassette, such as the record and radio broadcasting, emerged with

nationalist movements that gained momentum from the 1940s to 1960s. During these two decades, most Arab states achieved independence from colonial powers (six countries in the 1950s and another six in the 1960s). The Philips audiocassette thus came to full force five to fifteen years after Arab nationalists' benchmark achievements.

14. John R. Bowen, "Legal Reasoning and Public Discourse in Indonesian Islam," in *New Media in the Muslim World* (Bloomington: Indiana University Press, 1999); Dale Eickelman and Jon Anderson, "Defining Muslim Publics," in *New Media in the Muslim World,* ed. D. E. a. J. Anderson, 80–105 (Bloomington: Indiana University Press, 1999); Nilüfer Göle, "The Gendered Nature of the Public Sphere," *Public Culture* 10, no. 1 (1997): 61–81; Armando Salvatore, *Islam and the Political Discourse of Modernity* (Ithaca, N.Y.: Ithaca Press, 1997); and Gregory Starrett, *Putting Islam to Work: Education, Politics, and Religious Transformation in Egypt* (Berkeley: University of California Press, 1998).
15. Dale Eickelman, "The Art of Memory: Islamic Education and Its Social Reproduction," *Comparative Studies in Society and History* 20, no. 4 (1978): 510–12; and Dale Eickelman, "Inside the Islamic Revolution," in *Revolutionaries and Reformers,* ed. B. Rubin, 203–06 (Buffalo: State University of New York Press, 2003).
16. The ethics of authorial creativity and responsibility are discussed with much insight by Mario Biagioli in his study of the liberal foundations of a Euro-American biomedical industry. Mario Biagioli, "Aporias of Scientific Authorship: Credit and Responsibility in Contemporary Biomedicine," in *The Science Studies Reader,* ed. M. Biagioli and P. Galison, 12–30 (New York: Routledge, 1999). While Yemenis' sense of responsibility is similarly attuned to liberal public obligations, the concept also gains purchase from broader contexts of credibility and responsiveness.
17. Michael Warner, "Publics and Counterpublics," *Public Culture* 14, no. 1 (2002): 81–89.
18. Asif Agha, "Tropic Aggression in the Clinton-Dole Presidential Debate," *Pragmatics* 7, no. 4 (1997): 461–97.
19. Paul Friedrich has argued brilliantly for the importance of image tropes and for their interconnections with four other types of tropes that he identifies as imagistic, modal, formal, contiguous,

and analogical. Paul Friedrich, "Polytropy," in *Beyond Metaphor: The Theory of Tropes in Anthropology*, ed. J. Fernandez (Stanford: Stanford University Press, 1991), 26–39. My own categorizations here reflect his work.

20. Muḥammad Nājī, *Aghānīnā al-Shaʿbiyyah* (Aden: Dār al-Jamāhīr, 1959), 140. The fuller citation is discussed in the introduction.

Appendix A
Transliteration of qaṣīdahs by Husain ʿUbaīd al-Ḥaddād and Shaikh Rageh Haīthem Bin Sabʿah

"INITIATION" *QAṢĪDAH*
BY HUSAIN ʿUBAID AL-HADDAD

wa b-ism-illāh ataʿwadht[-] min rabb[i] dhī l-falaq [meter rough] 1
bi-kalmāt[i] min ṣumm il-ḥigārah tafallaqah
wa min kull[i] mā yakrah wa min sharr[i] mā khalaq 2
bi-qawlah mukhallaqah wa ghēr[a] mukhallaqah
wa subḥān[i] dhī kawwan min il-kawn[i] dhī dafaq 3
ṣuwar marḍiyyah min ṣulb[i] li-t-turāb[a] dāfaqah [meter rough]
wa ṣullū ʿalā min nūruh awwal bi-hā fataq 4
wa min qabl Ādam zahrat in-nūr[a] fattaqah
khalaq min-[a]-hā dhī ṭāf bi-s-sabʿah aṭ-ṭabaq 5
wa ṭāfah bi-hā l-malāk[a] w-aqṣū muṭābiqah
muḥabbēn[a] ḥabbū nūr[a] l-anwār[i] dhī sharaq 6
wa tālī nabbī l-anwār[a] min khadduh ashraqah
wa tarḍā ʿan aṣḥābuh Abā Bakr[i] dhī ṣadaq 7
wa āluh wa ṣaḥbuh dhī ʿalā ad-dīn[i] ṣādaqah
wa tarḍā ʿAlī dhī bi-yaduh as-sēf[a] buh maḥaq 8
wa dammar guyūsh il-kufr[i] lammā tamalḥaqah

wa kharrab masākinhum wa ḥaraq bi-hā wa daqq 9
wa l-aṣnām[a] kasarhā baqiyyah mudaqdaqah
yaqūl al-fatā khū Hādī an-nās[a] bi-ḍ-ḍayyiq 10
min il-qahr[i] w-aḥkām al-ḥukūmah taḍayyaqah
wa dha-l-ḥēn[a] yā sayyār[a] min ṭarraf il-ʿayiq 11
min awkār[i] haymā ḥēth[a] mā aṭ-ṭayr[a] ʿayyaqa
tawakkul bi-khāṭṭī qabl[a] lā yaṭlaʿ ash-shafaq 12
waṣal lā rubāṭ ish-shēkh[a] niyyātuh ashfaquh
wa suw fātiḥah ʿind al-walī gadd[a] man ḥadhaq 13
wa bēt is-siyāsah wa-l-baṣar wa muḥādhiqah [meter rough]
wa khamsah makātib shawr[a] wāḥid ʿalā al-ḥanaq 14
wa lēlah yasī lēlah qubl ʿalā al-muḥānaqah
ṭarīqik Yihar w-inhī sabā ṣalaḥū ḥalaq 15
wa ʿādāt[a]hum kāna bi-tghazzī wa ḥallaqah
waṣal lā Ḥamūmah yōm[a] khudh lak bi-hā rashaq 16
ʿalā ash-shādhiliyyah wa l-ḥuṣūn il-murashshaqqah
wa mā'wāk[a] dār al-maʿqilah ʿahd[a]hum wathaq 17
maʿ ash-shēkh[a] Rāgaḥ dhī ʿuhūduh muwaththaqah
salāmī li-Bin Haīthem wa min ʿinduh ittafaq 18
min akhuh wa-awlāduh wa l-aṣḥāb[a] wāfaqah
bi-mā ward[a] dhī aṣluh min il-Ḥāshemī ʿaraq 19
wa bi-l-ʿiṭr[i] dhī ygī bi-z-zugāg il-musandaqah
wa la-tkhabbarak lā tudhkur al-ḥuwb[a] wa l-ʿalaq 20
min akhbār[a] Yāfiʿ wa-l-fitan wa-l-maʿālaqah
lahum yōm[a] yadaʿīhum ʿalā ash-shiḥ[i] wa-r-rawaq 21
yabūn al-fitan wa lā yabūn al-murāwaqah
wa qul luh raʿ al-maqṣūd[a] min ḥēth[a] mā zaʿaq 22
daraywāl[a] bi-l-bābūr[i] daqqū ṭarāyyaquh
wa ʿāduh b-arḍ Abyan[a] waqaʿ ams buh ḥanaq [meter rough] 23
wa dhā l-yōm[a] li-s-sirkāl[i] mā buh muḥānaqah
saraq Bin ʿAṭiyyah bi-l-biyas wa Abyan istaraq 24
wa arḍ al-Quʿaīṭī ḥāl[a]hā yā musāraqah
kibārāt[a] Yāfiʿ qatalūhum min is-samaq 25
qafā l-arbaʿah dhī bi-l-ḥukūmah tasammaqah
lamah dōlat al-Qārah mugannad[a] maʿ Baraq 26
ʿalā Abyan sakat dhī kān luh taḥt bēraquh
thalāthah yamurrēnak fa-lā hun ṭarīq[a] ḥaqq 27
wa lā tabqā ad-dunyā ramādan wa mashaqah

fa-lā naqbil ash-shaklah wa samrah ṭaraf salaq 28
  wa ṭarḥ al-ganābī wa l-khazēn al-murannaqah
wa lā salṭanū Rāgaḥ lanā budd[a] bi-r-rawaq 29
  wa yasta'āhl al-ma'shār[a] dasmāl[a] mafraqah
kam-min-uh 'aqīd al-qawm[i] lā ḥēth[a] mā sabaq 30
  bi-nāruh wa lā gannah bi-ridhluh wa zandaqah
wa Yāfi' makātib bayyanuh qasamū firaq 31
  riḥm dhī tiḥzir ḥill[a] mā an-nās[a] farraqa [meter rough]
li-qaṭ min Bannā lā 'Aqwar ash'āb[a]hā ḥazaq 32
  wa 'awgā 'agiyyah wa-sh-shawāmikh muḥazliqah
'agiyyah wa ṭurūqhā mushaqqah 'alā aṭ-ṭuruq 33
  kinān ahl[i]hā wa-l-lēl[a] hum min ṭawāraqah
gazīrah fa-lā yalqūn[a] marsā bi-hā ṭalaq 34
  wa lā mashū l-bābūr[a] luh arḍ[a] maṭlaqah [meter rough]
wa yā shēkh[a] sāmaḥnī min il-ḥarf[i] lā zahaq 35
  wa nistaghfur Allāh min kalām il-muzāhaqah
wa b-aḥzīk[a] min bāzil[i] ma' bāzil ittafaq 36
  ma' bāzilēn ithnēn[i] ḥayawān[a] wāfiq[ah] [meter rough]
ṭalab minhum bakrah wa kullan bi-hā naṭaq 37
  wa kalimāt[a] bi-l-Qur'ān[i] mashrūḥ[a] manṭiqah
wa ṣullū 'alā man nūruh awwal bi-hā fataq 38
  wa min qabl Ādam zahrat in-nūr[a] fattaqah

"RESPONSE" *QAṢĪDAH* BY SHAIKH RAGEH HAITHEM B. SAB'AH

tawakalt[a] bik yā-Allāh[i] yā muṭlaq al-ghalaq 1
  tasūq al-mikyalah w-aṭlaq abwāb[a] mughlaqah [meter rough]
wa yā ḥāfiẓ iḥfaẓ kull[a] muslim min il-gharaq 2
  wa zilzil 'adūw Allāh[i] fī l-baḥr[i] w-ighraquh
wa nagētanā min mihrat il-kēd[a] wa-n-nafaq 3
  wa min mihrat ash-shaīṭān[a] w-ahl il-munāfaqah
wa b-adhkur Muḥammad dhī sharaḥ ṣadruh wa shaqq [meter rough] 4
  wa fakk al-gamal dhī kān[a] li-dh-dhabḥ wa a'taquh
wa qāl Ibn[a] Haīthem man banā ḥakam aṭ-ṭawaq 5
  wa lā shay ḥagar 'awgā kasarhā bi-miṭraqah

wa dhī mā yuqāyis ʿaṭal ad-dār[a] w-iltawaq 6
wa l-arkān ba-tagī shayyiz ʿawgā mulawwaqah
wa lī ganb[a] gāsir min qūwah sāʿiduh dalaq 7
wa baʿdī Yihar ḥill il-ḥawā li-l-mudālaqah
wa lā ṭālat al-fitnah fa-lā min[a]-hā ʿathaq 8
wa ḥattā wa lā ḥad bi-l-makātib taʿathaqqa
wa bā-aqūl[a] ḥayyā kullamā arkhā wa mā adaq 9
wa mā thawwar al-gāhim wa l-amzān[a] adaqqah
waṣal qawl[a] min dhī yaʿrif al-ḥaqq[a] wa-l-ḥanaq 10
wa yaʿrif ṭarīq al-ʿīs[i] kam-min masawwiqah
Akhū Hādī dhī l-mashhūr[a] fī maḥrāh[i] nasaq 11
wa sāʿah ba-yughruq fī l-buḥūr al-muʾawwaqah
wa baʿḍ al-ʿarab ʿattāt ba-yagurr[a] naḥwa shaqq 12
wa qaṭaʿ zalām al-bīr[i] wa-d-dalw bazaquh
wa man ḥamal[a] b-yizkin ʿalā l-ḥaml[i] wa-l-wasaq 13
wa la-tqāṣiruh l-aṭrāf[a] wāsiq muwāsaqah
wa lā mayyal al-ḥamāl[a] mā wasaṭ il-ḥalaq 14
wa lā yidrī illā wa-l-ḥumūlah munadhdhaqah
wa dhī huw ṣadīruh yuʾaddī l-mēl[a] mā nadhaq 15
wa lākin ṭaraḥ ḥamluh wa dhalaḥ shaqāshaqah
wa Yāfiʿ bilād agbār[a] min ḥēthamā baraq 16
wa lā qaṭ qālū Yāfiʿī ḥaṭṭ[a] bunduquh [meter rough]
kam-min il-ḥanash lā qad lasaʿ bi-l-ḥummah zaraq 17
wa ʿizz il-qabāyil bi-n-naṣīl al-mudhallaqah
wa man qārab al-makrīb[a] min nāruh iḥtaraq 18
wa Yāfiʿ gahannam man tuhawwin buh aḥraqa
wa rās ar-radā man yakbar al-luqmah ikhtanaq 19
taʿībuh bi-sarṭathā wa mā baʿ tawaddaqa
wa dhī ḥaram al-wālid b-yishrab min il-maraq 20
wa man kul ʿashā ahl il-bēt[a] baʿduh muḥānaqah
wa lā b-yigzaʿ aḍ-ḍūḥah wa lā b-yaqrab al-wahaq 21
wa man hū shaqīq al-ganb mā ḥad yuwahhaquh
w-anā qad katab lī razq[a] min ḥēthamā razaq 22
wa ṣābir wa mutqannaʿ ʿalā Allāh wa murzaquh
wa Bū Hāshem atawakkul wa bi-l-ganbiyyah ṭaraq 23
wa ṣāfaḥ bi-hā Sēgar wa qaṭaʿ ʿawātiquh
wa Dēfī taqārab w-in[a] dhā bū khashab zaʿaq 24
wa qāl Ibn[a] ʿAwās intawal min zawāʿaquh

wa lā bēn[a] dhī raqaʿ wa lā bēn[a] dhī bazaq 25
  wa l-aṭrāf[a] sīruh wa-l-maḥāzim tabazzaqah
wa min-nik ʿasal marwī wa min-nī ʿasal ʿasaq 26
  wa lā ḍēʿ al-makhlaṣ bi-ḥēlah wa ṭarbaqah
wa min ʿaṣr[a] sayyidnā Sulaīmān[a] dhī sabaq 27
  takhabbar ʿalā Bilqīs[a] waqt il-maʿāshiqah
wa qāl alladhī ʿinduh min il-ʿilm[i] wa-dh-dhalaq 28
  naʾtī bi-hā dha-l-ḥēn[a] tabdī muzahlaqah [meter rough]
wa gāwab bi-hā l-ʿifrīt[a] min qabl[a] mā ramaq 29
  wa yartad[a] ṭarf il-ʿēn[a] ḥāgib ḥawādaquh
wa b-adhkur Muḥammad dhī sharaḥ ṣadruh wa shaqq [meter rough] 30
  wa fakk al-gamal dhī kān[a] li-dh-dhabḥ wa aʿtaqah

Appendix B
Translation of qaṣīdahs by Ahmad ʿAlī al-Qaifī and Shayef al-Khāledī on Husain ʿAbd al-Nāṣer Cassette 7/8

"INITIATION" *QAṢĪDAH* BY AHMAD ʿALI AL-QAIFI

O night traveler, may the Lord of heaven be with you 1
From Qaifah dispatch on the back of [your] horse
Qaifah is my land, the birthplace of my fathers 2
Whose star sits alight the towering mountains
Carry to Abu Lōzah a symbolic gift 3
Letters written in a script of red ink
If he should ask you, tell him that the messenger of Ahmad ʿAli 4
Has come to ask and interrogate you, O Bu Khulād
Even if I don't have the right to ask 5
I will inquire about your circumstances and about conditions of the country
I will talk of the past, and what has happened 6
In our current time, and in what remains and the future:
Regretfully for Yafiʿ, men of weapons 7
Their German rifles have been lost, and their Canadian guns
The history of Yafiʿ is lost and its people astray 8
And now its history is marred with black

Whoever said Yafiʿ is the bonfire of enemies has lied 9
  Yafiʿ's bonfire has been extinguished and has become ash
Gone is the mountain goat, possessor of curled horns 10
  Yet you asked not why, nor donned mourning clothes
Your chosen shepherd took its [Yemen's] fat, 11
  And [now] a wolf has eaten him in the wilderness and wastes
I swear that those like you and your sorts 12
  Are nothing but a ram to the people, to be had by whomever hunts
We now count thirteen years for you 13
  And [still] you have not discovered the way to sensible routes
You debauched the daughter, and [now] you want her mother 14
  To follow her into suffering and corruption
You want the two spouses to agree once-and-for-all 15
  By God, acceptance and settlement will not take place
What is found [in the North] is pure, while that robe is soiled 16
  And we are supposed to pray in one line, together!
We won't accept Communism as Shafiʿi religion 17
  Without [your saying] the *shahādah* or [your] being converted through holy war
If you [want to] remain brothers, from one mother and father 18
  It is your obligation to recognize the God of submission
Else heaven is for us, while for you 19
  [Is only] the fire of scorching hell, come the day of reckoning
We will not have pity on you: 20
  You are its firewood, and its best the fires be kept stoked.

"RESPONSE" *QAṢĪDAH* FROM SHAYEF AL-KHALEDI

O you who began the talk welcome to you and to it 1
  [To] he who has been generous to me, I will return his generosity in kind
No sooner would I say I'll endure and take his injuries 2
  Than I would see Qaifi with a keen knife
He reminded me of the past, but I already know it well 3
  He will not fix anything like a covering over my eyes
I have tested the heat and the cold, and Qaifi is ignorant 4

He still barely discerns me from his bedroom and recumbence
He who said that Yafiʿ is lost and its people astray 5
That its history is marred with black
His words are lies or he who informed him lied 6
The hand of Yafiʿ still rests on the trigger
The history of Yafiʿ is a sun, white and honorable 7
Its mighty hand strikes wherever it desires
Ask Naʿwah, for it will attest to us 8
And Qaīfah will attest, as will Murād
At night we raided it by the smoke of the rifle 9
We took away its forces and munitions
Its streets remained hennaed with blood 10
Dyed red like the forehead of Suʿād
Its flames of fire continued to leap around it 11
And stabbing continued in its streets and barren lots
The weak-one surrendered voluntarily, submitted assenting, 12
While for the resistor we poured bile from the spleen
Or ask al-Baīḍā', the impregnable metropolis 13
About the army of Yafiʿ and how many it mowed down and annihilated
We took the district of al-Baīḍā' and scattered afterward 14
[Back] along the Dhī Nāʿim trail and that facing Kassād
The charlatan of Sanaa will also attest, [he] who reigned 15
Over the people of Yemen spreading its injustice and worse
[He] who had confiscated their surpluses 16
While our prosperous people were under oppression
He will confirm that Yafiʿ is of courage and fealty 17
We are truthfully those who can be depended on.
In the past, we were vanguards of the tribe 18
When we stamped as a raider or took control of the country
We were neither a protectorate with Britain 19
Nor did we ever recognize the authority of the Federation
And now, for the revolution we have exerted our spirits 20
We are with the revolution, with intention and with conviction
We are protectors of the revolution and we defend its adherents 21
There is no reactionaryism amongst us nor any counter-revolution
From the first day, we said we would follow it 22

In one line; we do not want distancing.
You mentioned the possessor of the curled horns: 23
If he went, I warned him on the first of *Jumād* (an Islamic month)
The mother commissioned him, she who weaned him with [her] milk 24
It is her right if she punishes him severely.
The loss of one individual among his brothers is not a great one 25
If he struck out on his own and sought isolation
The camel will still bring whatever follows 26
God knows, some clever ones will lose and [some] gain
She lost one son, [but] another son will come 27
The radiant sun does not eclipse over Hyderabad
I am not with the crooked nor am his friend 28
Whoever is not straight, I will straighten him out [like a] cane
The truant has been eaten by he who stalked 29
Neither you nor I have had a goat who has led and brought benefit.
And furthermore Ahmad Ali, regarding what you told me 30
[That] we will cause the dear mother to enter into corruption
Your erred in your words, your expression is flawed 31
None of us are cowardly or have enmity for her
We have seen her as mother, and we as her children 32
And the daughter, too, is the daughter of glorious heroes
We will not demolish her or undermine her majesty 33
When we have raised her flags atop poles
In a period of thirteen years, as you mentioned 34
We have accomplished much and have put forth exertion
We have our carried out our duty and the duty of our daughter 35
We protect her gains and build her economy
And our work still remains continuous 36
Thanks to what our strong forearms have achieved
There is no comparison to what we have accomplished from work 37
We reap what we sew in the season of harvest.
As for you (pl.), you have worked even harder than us 38
And still we see not one of you profiting or benefiting
If the law-abiding man sews and others reap the harvest 39
What remains of his crop will be eaten by locusts

As for you (sing.), I see that today your opinion differs [from mine] 40
Since you forwarded several criticisms
According to your words, the meeting [between the two Yemens] is far away 41
And you swore to me that agreement and settlement will not occur
Even if I looked around for you, you wouldn't be found 42
What caused you to flee already, seeking distance?
Your property lies with those who devoured your rights and expelled you 43
I don't contest you regarding what you shouted with vigor
If we haven't agreed now, it is not a problem: 44
We have never agreed, from the age of Tubaʿ and ʿĀd
[And] since colonialism divided us 45
Zaīd has still not gotten to know Bu Ziyād
We were the South, at first, and you were 'Abu Yaman' 46
Sheep without a shepherd, abandoned in every wadi
And now, why you have everything you need! 47
If road-kill came to you, you'd smell it as the sweetest salve
It is wrong to pray together after destroying the aim [of unity] 48
Even if you have arranged mats and cushions for me
How can a pig be cleansed of the scum of pestilence? 49
Its smell is putrescence, even if it is in a ditch
If you have anything with you, Ahmed, [like] rotten goods 50
It would definitely be better to bottle them up tight!
Where are you to heaven when I am its gatekeeper? 51
You who want it for yourself, and yet who has no heart
Whoever lives in this world a tormenter and oppressor 52
Does not get to heaven or reach his goal
I conclude my prayers as many times as the reader recites 53
The Ṭāhā and the *sūrah* of K-H-Y-ʿ-Ṣ

Bibliography

ʿAbd al-Razzāq, Kamāl al-Dīn. *Kitāb al-Istilāḥāt al-Ṣūfiyyah.* 2d ed. Edited by A. Sprenger. Lahore: al-Irshād, 1974 [1845].

ʿAbd al-Razzāq, Mushtāq. "al-Qaḍāʾ ʿalā al-Thār Wājib Yamlīhi ʿalayhi Dīnunā al-Ḥanīf," *Al-Ayyām,* November 9, 1997, 3.

ʿAbd Rabbuh, Sālem, and Mundaʿī Dayyān. *Jabhat al-Iṣlāḥ al-Yāfiʿiyyah.* Aden: Muʾassasat 14 Uktūbir, 1990.

āl-ʿAbdalī, Aḥmad Bin Faḍl. *Hadiyyat al-Zaman fī Akhbār Mulūk Laḥaj wa ʿAdan.* Beirut: Dār al-ʿAwdah, 1980 [1930].

Abu-Amr, Zaid Mahmud. "The People's Democratic Republic of Yemen: The Transformation of Society." Doctoral thesis, Georgetown University, Washington, D.C., 1986.

Abu-Deeb, Kemal. "Towards a Structural Analysis of Pre-Islamic Poetry." *International Journal of Middle Eastern Studies* 6 (1975): 148–84.

Abu-Lughod, Janet. "The Islamic City: Historic Myth, Islamic Essence and Contemporary Relevance." *International Journal of Middle East Studies* 19 (1987): 155–76.

Abu-Lughod, Lila. *Veiled Sentiments: Honor and Poetry in a Bedouin Society.* Berkeley: University of California Press, 1986.

Abu-Nasr, Donna. "Islamic Groups Benefitted from Loyalty in Civil War." *Associated Press,* October 28, 2000.

Aden's Bloody Monday. Aden: Ministry of Culture and Information, 1986.

Adra, Najwa. "Dance and Glance: Visualizing Tribal Identity in Highland Yemen." *Visual Anthropology* 11 (1998): 55–102.

———. "Qabyala: The Tribal Concept in the Central Highlands, the Yemen Arab Republic." Doctoral thesis, Temple University, Philadelphia, 1982.

———. "Tribal Dancing and Yemeni Nationalism: Steps to Unity." *Revue du Monde Musulman et de la Méditteranée* 67 (1994): 161–68.

Agha, Asif. "Tropic Aggression in the Clinton-Dole Presidential Debate." *Pragmatics* 7, no. 4 (1997): 461–97.

Akrich, Madeleine. "The De-Scription of Technical Objects." In *Shaping Technology/Building Society: Studies in Sociotechnical Change,* edited by W. Byker and J. Law, 205–24. Cambridge, Mass.: MIT Press, 1992.

Ali, Mohamed M. Yunis. *Medieval Islamic Pragmatics: Sunni Legal Theorists' Models of Textual Communication.* Richmond, Eng.: Curzon Press, 2000.

Anderson, Benedict. *Imagined Communities: Reflections on the Origin and Spread of Nationalism.* New York: Verso, 1983.

Appadurai, Arjun. *Modernity at Large: Cultural Dimensions of Globalization.* Minneapolis: University of Minnesota Press, 1996.

Arkoun, Mohammed. "The Concept of Authority in Islamic Thought." In *Islam: State and Society.* Edited by K. Ferdinand and M. Mozaffari, 53–73. London: Curzon Press, 1988.

———. "Logocentrisme et verité réligieuse selon Abu al-Ḥasan al-ʿĀmirī." In *Essais sur la pensée islamique,* 2d ed. Paris: Maisonneuve & Larose, 1984 [1973].

el-Aswad, el-Sayed. *Religion and Folk Cosmology: Scenarios of the Visible and Invisible in Egypt.* New York: Praeger, 2002.

ʿAwaḍaīn, Ibrāhīm. *al-Muʿāraḍah fī-l-Adab al-ʿArabī.* Cairo: Maṭbaʿat al-Saʿādah, 1980.

al-Azmeh, Aziz. *Arabic Thought and Islamic Societies.* London: Croom Helm, 1986.

Bā Dhīb, ʿAbdallah. *ʿAbdallah Bā Dhīb: Kitābāt Mukhtārah.* Vol. 1. Beirut: Dār al-Farābī, 1978.

Bā Salīm, Ḥusaīn. *Idhāʿat ʿAdan: 42 ʿĀman fī Khidmat al-Mustamiʿ.* Aden: 14 Uktūbir, 1996.

Badran, Margot. "Unifying Women: Feminist Pasts and Presents in Yemen." *Gender and History* 10, no. 3 (1998): 498–518.

Bailey, Clinton. *Bedouin Poetry from Sinai and the Negev: Mirror of a Culture.* Oxford: Clarendon Press, 1991.

Bakhtin, M. M. *The Dialogic Imagination.* Austin: University of Texas Press, 1994 [1975].

———. "The Problem of the Text in Linguistics, Philology, and the Human Sciences: An Experiment in Philosophical Analysis." In *Speech Genres and Other Essays,* 103–31. Austin: University of Texas Press, 1986.

al-Bakrī, Ṣalāḥ. *Fī Sharq al-Yaman.* Beirut, 1955.

Banerjee, Sumanta. *Audio Cassettes: The User Medium.* Paris: UNESCO, 1977.

Banfield, Ann. "Where Epistemology, Style, and Grammar Meet Literary History: The Development of Represented Speech and Thought." In *Reflexive Language: Reported Speech and Metapragmatics,* edited by J. Lucy, 341–64. Cambridge: Cambridge University Press, 1993.

al-Baraddūnī, ʿAbdallah. *Riḥlat fī-l-Shiʿr al-Yamanī Qadīmihi wa Ḥadīthihi.* 5th ed. Damascus: Dār al-Fikr, 1995 [1972].

———. *al-Thaqāfah wa-l-Thawrah fī-l-Yaman.* 4th ed. Damascus: Dār al-Fikr, 1998.

Barthes, Roland. "The Death of the Author." In *Image-Music-Text,* 142–48. New York: Hill and Wang, 1977.

Bateson, Gregory. "A Theory of Fantasy and Play." In *Steps to an Ecology of the Mind,* 177–93. San Francisco: Chandler, 1972.

Bauman, Richard. "Contextualization, Tradition and the Dialogue of Genres: Icelandic Legends of the Kraftaskáld." In *Rethinking Context,* edited by C. Goodwin and A. Duranti, 125–45. Cambridge: Cambridge University Press, 1992.

Bauman, Richard, and Charles L. Briggs. "Poetics and Performance as Critical Perspectives on Language and Social Life." *Annual Reviews of Anthropology* 19 (1990): 59–88.

Becker, Alton L. *Beyond Translation: Essays toward a Modern Philology.* Ann Arbor: University of Michigan Press, 1995.

Beeman, William. *Language, Status, and Power in Iran.* Bloomington: Indiana University Press, 1986.

Benhabib, Seyla. "Models of Public Space: Hannah Arendt, the Liberal Tradition, and Jürgen Habermas." In *Habermas and the Public Sphere,* edited by C. Calhoun, 73–98. Cambridge, Mass.: MIT Press, 1992 [1997].

Benjamin, Walter. "The Work of Art in the Age of Mechanical Reproduction." In *Illuminations,* 217–51. New York: Schocken, 1968.

Bernstein, Basil. "Classes, Modalities, and the Process of Cultural Reproduction: A Model." *Language in Society* 10 (1981): 327–63.

Besnier, Niko. "The Linguistic Relationships of Spoken and Written Nukulaelae Registers." *Language* 64, no. 4 (1988): 707–36.

Bhabha, Homi. "Dessimi-Nation: Time, Narrative, and the Margins of the Modern Nation." In *Nations and Narration,* 291–322. New York: Routledge, 1990.

Biagioli, Mario. "Aporias of Scientific Authorship: Credit and Responsibility in Contemporary Biomedicine." In *The Science Studies Reader,* edited by M. Biagioli and P. Galison, 12–30. New York: Routledge, 1999.

Blommaert, Jan. *Discourse: A Critical Introduction.* Cambridge: Cambridge University Press, 2005.

Blumi, Isa. "Looking beyond the Tribe: Abandoning Paradigms to Write Social History in Yemen during World War I." *New Perspectives on Turkey* 22 (2000): 117–43.

Boas, Franz. "The Stylistic Aspects of Primitive Literature." *Journal of American Folklore* 38, no. 149 (1925): 329–39.

Bourdieu, Pierre. *Algeria, 1960: The Disenchantment of the World.* New York: Cambridge University Press, 1960 [1963].

———. *Distinction: A Social Critique of the Judgment of Taste.* Cambridge, Mass.: Harvard University Press, 1984.

———. "The Economics of Linguistic Exchanges." *Social Science Information* 16, no. 6 (1977): 645–68.

———. *The Field of Cultural Production.* New York: Columbia University Press, 1993.

———. *Language and Symbolic Power.* 3d ed. Cambridge, Mass.: Harvard University Press, 1994 [1982].

Bowen, John R. "Legal Reasoning and Public Discourse in Indonesian Islam." In *New Media in the Muslim World,* edited by D. E. a. J. Anderson, 80–105. Bloomington: Indiana University Press, 1999.

———. "On Scriptural Essentialism and Ritual Variation: Muslim Sacrifice in Sumatra and Morocco." *American Ethnologist* 19, no. 4 (1992): 656–71.

Boyd, Douglas A. *Egyptian Radio: Tool of Political and National Development.* Lexington, Ky.: Association for Education in Journalism, 1977.

Buchan, D. *The Ballad and the Folk.* London: Routledge and Kegan Paul, 1972.

Buchler, Justus, ed. *Philosophical Writings of Peirce.* New York: Dover Publications, 1955 [1940].

Bujra, Abdallah S. "Political Conflict and Stratification in Hadramaut." *Middle Eastern Studies* 3–4 (1966–67): 355–75.

———. "Urban Elites and Colonialism: The Nationalist Elites of Aden and South Arabia." *Middle East Studies* 6, no. 2 (1970): 189–212.

al-Būnī, Aḥmad Bin ʿAlī. *Shams al-Maʿārif al-Kubrā wa Laṭāʾif al-Maʿārif (The Sun of Grand Insights and the Subtleties of Insights).* Cairo: Muḥammad ʿAlī Ṣubayḥ wa-Awlādih, n.d.

Bunzl, Matti. "Boas, Foucault, and the 'Native Anthropologist': Notes toward a Neo-Boasian Anthropology." *American Anthropologist* 106, no. 3 (2004): 435–42.

Butler, Judith. *Gender Trouble: Feminism and the Subversion of Identity.* New York: Routledge, 2000.

Caton, Steven C. "Diglossia in North Yemen: A Case of Competing Linguistic Communities." *Southwestern Journal of Linguistics* 10, no. 1 (1991): 214–34.

———. "Icons of the Person: Lacan's 'Imago' in the Yemeni Male's Tribal Wedding." *Asian Folklore Studies* 52 (1993): 359–81.

———. *Peaks of Yemen I Summon: Poetry as Cultural Practice in a North Yemeni Tribe.* Berkeley: University of California Press, 1990.

———. "Salām Taḥīya: Greetings from Highland Yemen." *American Ethnologist* 13 (1986): 290–308.

———. *Yemen Chronicle: An Anthropology of War and Mediation.* New York: Hill and Wang, 2005.

Certeau, Michel de. *The Writing of History.* Translated by T. Conley. New York: Columbia University Press, 1988.

Chejne, A. "The Concept of History in the Modern Arab World." *Studies in Islam* 4 (1967): 1–31.

Comaroff, John, and Jean Comaroff. "On Personhood: An Anthropological Perspective from Africa." *Social Identities* 7, no. 2 (2001): 267–83.

Communists since the Year 1000. Edited by Gordian Troeller and Claude Deffarge. New York, N.Y.: First Run/Icarus Films, 1973.

Cutler, Chris. "Necessity and Choice in Musical Forms: Concerning Musical and Technical Means and Political Needs." In *Cassette Mythos,* edited by R. James, 160–64. Brooklyn: Autonomedia, 1992.

Ḍafārī, Ja'far S. "Humaini Poetry in South Arabia." Doctoral thesis, University of London, 1966.

Daiber, H. "Masā'il wa Adjwiba." In *Encyclopedia of Islam,* 636–39. Leiden: E. J. Brill, 1954.

Dayyān, Muḥsen. *Yāfi': Bayn al-Aṣālah wa-l-Mu'āṣirah al-Yamaniyyah.* Damascus: al-Kātib al-'Arabī, 1995.

Debray, Regis. *Media Manifestos: On the Technological Transmission of Cultural Forms.* Translated by E. Rauth. New York: Verso, 1996.

Derrida, Jacques. "Above All, No Journalists!" In *Religion and Media,* edited by H. d. Vries and S. Weber, 56–93. Stanford: California University Press, 2001.

———. "The Double Session." In *A Derrida Reader: Between the Blinds,* edited by P. Kamuf, 171–99. New York: Columbia University Press, 1991 [1972].

———. "Faith and Knowledge: The Two Sources of 'Religion' at the Limits of Reason Alone." In *Religion,* edited by J. Derrida and G. Vattimo, 1–78. Stanford: California University Press, 1998.

———. *Of Grammatology.* Translated by G. Spivak. Baltimore: Johns Hopkins, 1974 [1967].

Desjarlais, Robert. *Sensory Biographies: Lives and Deaths among Nepal's Yolmo Buddhists.* Berkeley: University of California Press, 2003.

Dirks, Nicholas B. "History as a Sign of the Modern." *Public Culture* 2, no. 2 (1990): 25–32.

Dresch, Paul. *A History of Modern Yemen.* Cambridge: Cambridge University Press, 2000.

———. "Imams and Tribes: The Writing and Acting of History in Upper Yemen." In *Tribes and State Formation in the Middle East,* edited by P. S. Khoury and J. Kostiner, 252–87. Berkeley: University of California Press, 1990.

———. "The Position of Shaykhs among the Northern Tribes of Yemen." *Man* 19, no. 1 (1984): 31–49.

———. "The Tribal Factor in the Yemeni Crisis." In *The Yemeni War of 1994: Causes and Consequences,* edited by J. S. al-Suwaidi and M. C. Hudson, 33–55. London: Saqi Books, 1995.

———. "Tribal Relations and Political History in Upper Yemen." In *Contemporary Yemen: Politics and Historical Background,* edited by B. R. Pridham, 154–74. London: Croom Helm, 1984.

———. *Tribes, Government, and History in Yemen.* New York: Oxford University Press, 1989.

Dresch, Paul, and Bernard Haykel. "Islamists and Tribesfolk in Yemen: A Study of Styles and Stereotypes." *International Journal of Middle East Studies* 27 (1995): 405–31.

Eickelman, Dale F. "The Art of Memory: Islamic Education and Its Social Reproduction." *Comparative Studies in Society and History* 20, no. 4 (1978): 485–516.

———. "Inside the Islamic Revolution." In *Revolutionaries and Reformers,* edited by B. Rubin, 203–06. Buffalo: State University of New York Press, 2003.

———. *The Middle East: An Anthropological Approach.* Englewood Cliffs, N.J.: Prentice-Hall, 1981.

Elias, Norbert. *The Civilizing Process.* Translated by E. Jephcott. New York: Urizon Books, 1978.

Far'a, Taha. *Lamaḥāt min Ta'rīkh al-Ughniyyah al-Yamaniyyah al-Ḥadīthah.* Aden: Dār al-Hamdānī, 1985.

Fathi, Asghar. "The Role of the Islamic Pulpit." *Journal of Communication* 29, no. 3 (1979): 102–06.

Ferguson, Charles. "The Arabic Koiné." *Language: The Linguistic Society of America* 35 (1959): 616–30.

———. "Diglossia." *Word* 15 (1959): 325–40.

Finnegan, Ruth. *Oral Poetry: Its Nature, Significance and Social Context.* Bloomington: Indiana University Press, 1992.

Flew, Terry. *New Media: An Introduction.* Oxford: Oxford University Press, 2002.

Foucault, Michel. *The Archaeology of Knowledge and the Discourse on Language.* Translated by A. Smith. New York: Pantheon Books, 1972.

———. *Discipline and Punish.* New York: Vintage Books, 1979 [1975].

———. *Madness and Civilization: A History of Insanity in the Age of Reason.* Tavistock: London, 1967.

———. "What Is an Author?" In *Language, Counter-Memory, Practice,* edited by D. F. Bouchard, 113–38. Ithaca, N.Y.: Cornell University Press, 1977.

Friedrich, Paul. "Poetic Language and the Imagination: A Reformulation of the Sapir-Whorf Hypothesis." In *Language, Context, and the Imagination,* 441–512. Stanford: California University Press, 1979.

———. "Polytropy." In *Beyond Metaphor: The Theory of Tropes in Anthropology,* edited by J. Fernandez, 17–55. Stanford: California University Press, 1991.

Gavin, R. J. *Aden under British Rule, 1839–1967.* New York: Barnes & Noble Books, 1975.

Geertz, Clifford. "Religion as a Cultural System." In *The Interpretation of Cultures,* 87–125. New York: Basic Books, 1973.

Gelder, Geert van. "The Abstracted Self in Arabic Poetry." *Journal of Arabic Literature* 14 (1983): 22–30.

Gerholm, Tomas. *Market, Mosque, and Mafraj: Social Inequality in a Yemeni Town.* Stockholm: Stockholm University Press, 1977.

Ghānem, Muḥammad ʿAbduh. *Shiʿr al-Ghināʾ al-Sanʿānī.* Damascus: Dār al-ʿAwdah, 1987.

al-Ghulābī, ʿAlī, Aḥmad Raḥīm Bū Maḥdī, Muḥsen Dayyān, and Muthannā Qāsem, eds. *Ghināʾiyyāt Yaḥyā ʿUmar.* Damascus: al-Kātib al-ʿArabī, 1993.

Gilsenan, Michael. *Recognizing Islam: Religion and Society in the Modern Arab World*. London: Tauris, 1990 [1982].

———. "Sacred Words." In *The Diversity of the Muslim Community*, edited by Ahmed al-Shahi, 92–98. London: Ithaca Press, 1987.

Goffman, Erving. "Footing." In *Forms of Talk*, edited by I. Goffman, 124–59. Philadelphia: University of Pennsylvania Press, 1981.

———. *Frame Analysis: An Essay on the Organization of Experience*. New York: Harper & Row, 1974.

Göle, Nilüfer. "The Gendered Nature of the Public Sphere." *Public Culture* 10, no. 1 (1997): 61–81.

Goody, Jack. "Alternative Paths to Knowledge in Oral and Literate Cultures." In *Spoken and Written Language: Exploring Orality and Literacy*, edited by D. Tannen, 201–15. Norwood, N.J.: Ablex, 1982.

———. "Introduction." In *Literacy in Traditional Societies*, edited by Jack Goody, 1–26. New York: Cambridge University Press, 1968.

———. "Restricted Literacy in Northern Ghana." In *Literacy in Traditional Societies*, edited by J. Goody, 198–264. New York: Cambridge University Press, 1968.

Goody, Jack, and Ian Watt. "The Consequences of Literacy." *Comparative Studies in Society and History* 5, no. 3 (1963): 304–45.

Graeber, David. *Toward an Anthropological Theory of Value: The False Coin of Our Own Dreams*. New York: Palgrave, 2001.

Graham, William A. *Beyond the Written Word: Oral Aspects of Scripture in the History of Religion*. Cambridge: Cambridge University Press, 1987.

Gramsci, A. *Selections from the Prison Notebooks*. Translated by Q. Hoare and G. N. Smith. New York: International, 2003 [1971].

Gumperz, John. "The Speech Community." In *Language and Social Context*, edited by P. P. Giglioli, 219–31. Baltimore: Penguin Books, 1972 [1968].

Gumperz, John, and Dell Hymes. *The Ethnography of Communication*. Washington, D.C.: American Anthropological Association, 1964.

Habermas, Jürgen. *The Structural Transformation of the Public Sphere*. Translated by T. Burger. Oxford: Polity Press, 1992 [1962].

———. *The Theory of Communicative Action*. Translated by T. A. McCarthy. Boston: Beacon Press, 1985.

al-Ḥibshī, ʿAbdallah Muḥammad. *Ḥayāt al-Adab al-Yamanī fī ʿAṣr Banī Rasūl*. 2d ed. Sanaa: Ministry of Information and Culture, 1980.

al-Ḥakamī, ʿUmārah Bin ʿAlī. *Taʾrīkh al-Yaman*. Cairo, 1957.

Halliday, Fred. *Arabia without Sultans: A Political Survey of Instability in the Arab World*. New York: Penguin, 1975.

al-Hamdānī, al-Ḥasan Bin Aḥmad. *Kitāb Ṣifah Jazīrat al-ʿArab*. Edited by M. al-Najdī. Cairo: Maṭbaʿat al-Saʿādah, 1953.

al-Hamīrī, ʿAbd al-Wāsiʿ. *al-Dhāt al-Shāʿirah fī Shiʿr al-Ḥadāthah al-ʿArabiyyah*. Beirut: al-Muʾassasat al-Jāmaʿiyyah, 1999.

Hanbalah, Idrīs. *Al-Majmūʿat al-Kāmilah*. Aden: Muʾassasat 14 Uktūbir, n.d.

Hanks, William F. *Language and Communicative Practices*. Chicago: Westview Press, 1996.

Haq, S. Nomanul. "Ṭabīʿa." In *The Encyclopedia of Islam*, edited by T. Bianquis, C. E. Bosworth, E. v. Donzel, and W. P. Heinrichs, 25–28. Leiden: E. J. Brill, 1998.

Harharah, ʿAbd al-Qāder ʿĀṭaf. *Taʾrīkh al-Usrah al-Harharah*. Dearborn, Mich.: Discovery Marketing, 1998.

Ḥārethī, Ṣāleḥ. *al-Zāmil fī al-Ḥarb w-al-Munāsabāt*. Damascus: al-Kātib al-ʿArabī, 1990.

Haykel, Bernard. *Revival and Reform in Islam: The Legacy of Muhammad al-Shawkani*. Cambridge: Cambridge University Press, 2003.

Hebdige, Dick. *Subculture: The Meaning of Style*. New York: Methuen, 1979.

Hegel, Georg Wilhelm. *Hegel's Philosophy of Nature*. Vol. 2. Translated by M. J. Petry. New York: Allen and Unwin, 1970.

Hertz, Robert. "The Pre-eminence of the Right Hand: A Study in Religious Polarity." In *Death and the Right Hand*, 89–113. Glencoe, Ill.: Free Press, 1960 [1909].

Hill, Jane. "Read My Article: Ideological Complexity and the Overdetermination of Promising in American Presidential Politics." In *Regimes of Language: Ideologies, Politics, and Identities*, edited by

P. V. Kroskrity, 259–91. Sante Fe: School of American Research Press, 2000.

Hirschkind, Charles. *The Ethical Soundscape: Cassette Sermons and Islamic Counterpublics.* New York: Columbia University Press, 2006.

The Holy Qur'an. Translated by A. Y. ʿAlī. 6th ed. Lahore: Muslim Converts' Association of Singapore, 2004 [1946].

Al-Hubaishi, Hassan A. *Legal System and Basic Law in Yemen.* Worcester, UK: Billing and Sons, 1988.

Ḥulaīs, Ṣāleḥ. *Yāfiʿ fī ʿUyūn al-Shiʿr wa Dumūʿ al-Qalam.* Riadh: Maktabat al-Mūʾayyid lil-Nashr wa-l-Tawzīʿ, 1993.

Hunā ʿAdan. Aden: South Arabian Broadcasting Service, May 1961.

Hymes, Dell. "The Ethnography of Speaking." In *Anthropology and Human Behavior,* edited by T. Gladwin and W. C. Sturtevant, 13–53. Washington, D.C.: Anthropological Society of Washington, 1962.

———. "Phonological Aspects of Style: Some English Sonnets." In *Style in Language,* edited by T. Sebeok, 109–31. Cambridge, Mass.: MIT Press, 1960.

———. "Toward Ethnographies of Communication: The Analysis of Communicative Events." In *Language and Social Context,* edited by P. P. Giglioli, 21–44. Baltimore: Penguin Books, 1972 [1964].

Ingrams, Doreen. *Records of Yemen.* Vol. 15. Chippenham: Archive Editions, 1993.

Jacobi, Renate. "The Origins of the Qasidah Form." In *Qasida Poetry in Islamic Asia and Africa,* edited by S. Sperl and C. Shackle, 22–34. New York: E. J. Brill, 1996.

Jakobson, Roman. "Concluding Statement: Linguistics and Poetics." In *Style in Language,* edited by T. A. Sebeok, 350–73. Cambridge, Mass.: MIT Press, 1960.

Jamous, Raymond. *Honneur et Baraka: Les structures sociales traditionelles dans le Rif.* New York: Cambridge University Press, 1981.

al-Jāwī, ʿUmar. "Kayfa Nafham al-Shiʿr al-Shaʿbī?" *al-Turāth* no. 4 (1992): 70–79.

Al-Khāledī, Shāyef. *Waḥdah wa Min Qarḥin Yaqraḥ*. Aden: Dā'irat al-Ṣaḥāfah wa-l-Ṭibā'ah wa-l-Nashr, 1990.

Khaldūn, 'Abd al-Raḥman Ibn. *Les Prolégomènes d'Ibn Khaldoun*. Vol. 3. Translated by M. d. Slane. Paris: Imprimerie Impériale, 1868.

Kilito, Abdelfattah. *The Author and His Doubles: Essays on Classical Arabic Culture*. Translated by M. Cooperson. Syracuse, N.Y.: Syracuse University Press, 2002.

Lackner, Helen. *P.D.R. Yemen: Outpost of Socialist Development in Arabia*. London: Ithaca Press, 1985.

Lambek, Michael. *Knowledge and Practice in Mayotte: Local Discourses of Islam, Sorcery, and Spirit Possession*. Toronto: University of Toronto Press, 1993.

Lambert, Jean. "Aspects de la poésie dialectale au Yémen." Master's thesis, University of Paris, 1982.

———. "Du 'chanteur' à 'l'artiste': vers un nouveau statut du musicien." *Peuples Méditerranéans* 46 (1989): 57–76.

———. *La médecine de l'âme: Le chant de Sanaa dans la société yéménite*. Nanterre: Société d'Ethnologie, 1997.

———. "Musiques régionales et identité nationale." *Révue du Monde Musulman et de la Méditerranée* 67 (1993): 171–86.

Landberg, Carlo de. *Études sur les dialectes de l'Arabie méridionale: Daṭînah*. Vol. 1. Leiden: E. J. Brill, 1905.

———. *Études sur les dialectes de l'Arabie méridionale: Haḍramoût*. Vol. 1. Leiden: E. J. Brill, 1901.

———. *Glossaire datînois*. Leiden: E. J. Brill, 1920.

———. *La langue arabe et ses dialectes. Communication faite au XIVe Congrès international des orientalistes à Alger*. Leiden: E. J. Brill, 1905.

"Leader of Armed Gang Sentenced to Death, Other Members Jailed." Republic of Yemen Television, via *BBC Summary of World Broadcasts*, October 23, 1998.

Leckie-Tarry, Helen. *Language and Context: A Functional Linguistic Theory of Register*. New York: Pinter, 1995.

Lee, Benjamin. "Textuality, Mediation, and Public Discourse." In *Habermas and the Public Sphere*, edited by Craig Calhoun, 402–18. Cambridge, Mass.: MIT Press, 1992.

Lord, Albert. *The Singer of Tales*. 4th ed. Cambridge, Mass.: Harvard University Press, 1960.

Lunt, James D. *The Barren Rocks of Aden*. London: Jenkins, 1966.

Luqmān, Ḥamzah ʻAlī. *Taʼrīkh al-Qabāʼil al-Yamaniyyah*. Sanaa: Dār al-Kalimah, 1985.

Lyons, J. C. *Identification and Identity in Classical Arabic Poetry*. Wiltshire, UK: Aris and Phillips, 1999.

Madigan, Daniel. *The Qur'an's Self-Image: Writing and Authority in Islam's Scripture*. Princeton: Princeton University Press, 2001.

Manqūsh, Thurayyā. *Qaḍāyā Taʼrīkhiyyah wa Fikriyyah min al-Yaman*. Beirut: Maṭbaʻat al-Karmil, 1979.

Manuel, Peter. *Cassette-Culture: Popular Music and Technology in North India*. Chicago: University of Chicago Press, 1993.

al-Maqāleḥ, ʻAbd al-ʻAzīz. *Shiʻr al-ʻAmiyyah fī-l-Yaman*. Beirut: Dār al-ʻAwdah, 1978.

Marx, Karl. *Capital: A Critique of Political Economy*. Translated by S. Moore. New York: Charles H. Kerr, 1906 [1867].

McDonald, M. V. "Orally Transmitted Poetry in Pre-Islamic Arabia and Other Pre-Literate Societies." *Journal of Arabic Literature* 9 (1978): 14–31.

McLuhan, Marshall. *Understanding Media: The Extensions of Man*. New York: McGraw Hill, 1964.

McLuhan, Marshall, and Eric McLuhan. *Laws of Media: The New Science*. Toronto: University of Toronto Press, 1988.

Meeker, Michael E. *Literature and Violence in North Arabia*. Cambridge: Cambridge University Press, 1979.

Merleau-Ponty, Maurice. *The Visible and the Invisible*. Translated by I. Lingis. Evanston: Northwestern University Press, 1968 [1964].

Messick, Brinkley. *The Calligraphic State: Textual Domination and History in a Muslim Society*. Berkeley: University of California Press, 1993.

———. "Indexing the Self: Intent and Expression in Islamic Legal Acts." *Islamic Law and Society* 8, no. 2 (2001): 151–78.

———. "Just Writing: Paradox and Political Economy in Yemeni Legal Discourse." *Cultural Anthropology* 4, no. 1 (1989): 26–50.

———. "Kissing Hands and Knees: Hegemony and Hierarchy in Sharīʿa Discourse." *Law and Society Review* 22 (1988): 637–59.

———. "Legal Documents and the Concept of Restricted Literacy." *International Journal of the Sociology of Language* 42 (1983): 41–52.

———. "Media Muftis: Radio Fatwas in Yemen." In *Islamic Legal Interpretations: Muftis and Their Fatwas,* edited by M. K. Masud, B. Messick and D. S. Powers, 311–20. Cambridge, Mass.: Harvard University Press, 1996.

Miller, W. Flagg. "Invention (Ibtidāʿ) or Convention (Ittibāʿ)? Islamist Audiocassettes and Tradition in Yemen." Paper delivered at the American Anthropological Association Meeting, San Francisco, November 2000.

———. "Metaphors of Commerce: Trans-valuing Tribalism in Yemeni Audiocassette Poetry." *International Journal of Middle East Studies* 34, no. 1 (2002): 29–57.

———. "Public Words and Body Politics: Reflections on the Strategies of Women Poets in Rural Yemen." *Journal of Women's History* 14, no. 1 (2002): 94–122.

———. "Of Songs and Signs: Audiocassette Poetry, Moral Character, and the Culture of Circulation in Yemen." *American Ethnologist* 32, no. 1 (2005): 82–99.

———. "Yafiʿ Has Only One Name: Shared Histories and Cultural Linkages between Yafiʿ and Hadramawt." In *Cultural Anthropology of Southern Arabia: Hadramawt Revisited,* edited by M. N. Souvorov and M. A. Rodionov, 63–77. St. Petersburg: Museum of Anthropology and Ethnography (Kunstkamera), 1999.

Miller, W. Flagg, and Ulrike Freitag. "Three Poems on British Involvement in Yemen, from the Yemeni Press 1937." In *The Modern Middle East: A Sourcebook for History,* edited by C. M. Amin, B. C. Fortna, and E. Frierson, 492–500. Oxford: Oxford University Press, 2005.

Mitchell, Timothy. *Colonizing Egypt.* Berkeley: University of California Press, 1988.

Monroe, James. "Oral Composition in Pre-Islamic Poetry." *Journal of Arabic Literature* 3 (1972): 1–53.

Mubannan, ʿAlī. "al-Sīnamāʾ fī-l-Yaman: Rūʾiyyah Mustaqbiliyyah."

In *al-Thaqāfat al-Yamaniyyah: Rū'iyyah Mustaqbiliyyah,* 261. Sanaa: Ministry of Culture and Tourism, 1991.

Mukarovsky, Jan. "The Esthetics of Language." In *Prague School Reader on Esthetics, Literary Structure, and Style,* edited by P. L. Garvin, 31–69. Washington, D.C.: Georgetown University Press, 1964 [1948].

———. "The Sound Aspect of Poetic Language." In *On Poetic Language,* edited by J. Burbank and P. Steiner, 23–37. Lisse: Peter de Ridder Press, 1976.

Mundy, Martha. *Domestic Government: Kinship, Community, and Polity in North Yemen.* London: I. B. Tauris, 1995.

Munjad fī-l-Lughah wa-l-ʿAlām. 35th ed. Dimashq: Dār al-Mashraq, 1986.

Munn, Nancy. "Gawan Kula: Spatiotemporal Control and the Symbolism of Influence." In *The Kula: New Perspectives on Massim Exchange,* edited by J. Leach and E. Leach, 277–308. Cambridge: Cambridge University Press, 1983.

Musil, Alois. *The Manners and Customs of the Rwala Bedouins.* Edited by J. K. Wright. New York: American Geographical Society, 1928.

al-Muṭāʿ, Aḥmad Bin Aḥmad. "Fī-l-Ta'rīkh al-Yamanī." *al-Ḥikmah* 6 (1940): 171–75.

al-Mu'tamar al-ʿĀm al-Awwal li-l-Adab wa-l-Turāth al-Shaʿbī fī-l-Muḥāfaẓah al-Thāniyyah. Lahej: Maṭābiʿ al-Falāḥ, 1974.

Nahj al-Balāghah (Peak of Eloquence). 2d ed. Bombay: Islamic Seminary for World Shia Muslim Organisation, 1978.

Nājī, Muḥammad Murshed. *Aghānīnā al-Shaʿbiyyah.* Aden: Dār al-Jamāhīr, 1959.

———. "Fann al-Ghinā' wa-l-Mūsīqā fī al-Yaman." In *al-Thaqāfat al-Yamaniyyah: Rū'iyyah Mustaqbaliyyah,* 199–219. Sanaa: Ministry of Culture and Tourism, 1991.

———. *al-Ghinā' al-Yamanī al-Qadīm wa Mashāhīruh.* Kuwait: al-Ṭalīʿah, 1983.

al-Natā'ij al-Nihā'iyyah li-Muḥāfiẓah Laḥaj: al-Taqrīr al-Thānī, 1994. Sanaa: Ministry of Planning and Development, 1996.

Nietzche, Friedrich. *On the Genealogy of Morals.* Translated by D. Smith. New York: Oxford University Press, 1996.

Ohnuki-Tierney, Emiko. "The Monkey as Self in Japanese Culture." In *Culture through Time: Anthropological Approaches,* edited by E. Ohnuki-Tierney, 128–53. Stanford: California University Press, 1990.

Ong, Walter. *Orality and Literacy: The Technologizing of the Word.* New York: Routledge, 1993 [1982].

Pellat, Charles. "Hidjā'." In *Encyclopedia of Islam.* Vol. 3, 352–55. Leiden: E. J. Brill, 1971.

Peterson, Glen. *The Power of Words: Literacy and Revolution in South China, 1949–95.* Vancouver: University of British Columbia Press, 1997

Phillips, Catherine. *Gerard Manly Hopkins: The Major Works.* Oxford: Oxford University Press, 2002.

Piamenta, Moshe. *Dictionary of Post-classical Yemeni Arabic.* Vol. 1. New York: Brill, 1990.

Putnam, Hilary. "The Meaning of 'Meaning'." In *Mind, Language and Reality.* Cambridge: Cambridge University Press, 1975.

al-Qāsemī, Khāled. *al-Awāṣir al-Ghinā'iyyah: Bayn al-Yaman wa-l-Khalīj.* al-Sharqah: Dār al-Thaqāfah al-ʿArabiyyah, 1988.

al-Qāsemī, Khāled, and Nazār Ghānem. *Judhūr al-Ughniyyah al-Yamaniyyah fī Iʿmāq al-Khalīj.* 2d ed. Beirut: Dār al-Ḥadāthah, 1993.

———. *al-Ughniyyah al-Yamaniyyah al-Khalījiyyah.* al-Sharqah: Dār al-Thaqāfah al-ʿArabiyyah, 1993.

al-Qaṣīr, Aḥmad. *al-Yaman: al-Hijrah wa-l-Tanmiyyah.* Cairo: Dār al-Thaqāfah al-Jadīdah, 1985.

Rābiḍah, Aḥmad Ṣāleḥ. "Shuʿarā' ʿAdan fī ʿAṣr Banī Zurayʿ." *al-Turāth,* no. 4 (1992): 49–69.

Racy, Ali Jihad. "Record Industry and Egyptian Traditional Music: 1904–1932." *Ethnomusicology* 20, no. 1 (1976): 23–49.

Reckert, Stephen. *Beyond Chrysanthemums: Perspectives on Poetry East and West.* Oxford: Clarendon Press, 1993.

Reynolds, Dwight Fletcher. *Heroic Poets, Poetic Heroes: The Ethnog-*

raphy of Performance in an Arabic Oral Epic Tradition. Ithaca, N.Y.: Cornell University Press, 1995.

Rodionov, Mikhail. *Poetry and Power in Hadramawt.* St. Petersburg: St. Petersburg University Press, 1992.

———. "Poetry and Power in Hadramawt." *New Arabian Studies* 3 (1996): 118–33.

Rosen, Lawrence. *Bargaining for Reality: The Construction of Social Relations in a Muslim Community.* Chicago: University of Chicago Press, 1984.

Rossi-Landi, Ferruccio. *Language as Work and Trade: A Semiotic Homology for Linguistics and Economics.* South Hadley, Mass.: Bergin and Garvey, 1983.

Sab'ah, Naṣer S. *Min Yanābī' Ta'rīkhinā al-Yamanī.* Damascus: al-Kātib al-'Arabī, 1994.

Sālem, Muṣṭafā, and 'Alī Aḥmad Abū al-Rijāl, eds. *Majallat al-Ḥikmat al-Yamaniyyah: Wa Ḥarakat al-Iṣlāḥ fī-l-Yaman (1938–1941).* 2d ed. Vol. 4. Sanaa: Markaz al-Buḥūth wa-l-Dirāsāt al-Yamanī, 1988.

Salvatore, Armando. *Islam and the Political Discourse of Modernity.* Reading, UK: Ithaca Press, 1997.

Saqqaf, Abu Bakr. "Problèmes de L'Unité Yéménite." *La Révue du Monde Musulman et de la Méditerranée* 67 (1993): 95–108.

al-Sayyādī, Anwar. "Yemen Comes to Grips with Intellectual Rights." Pts. 1–2. *Yemen Times,* April 14–20, 21–27, 1997.

Schippmann, Klaus. *Ancient South Arabia: From the Queen of Sheba to the Advent of Islam.* Princeton, N.J.: Markus Wiener, 2001.

Schneider, Manfred. "Luther with McLuhan." In *Religion and Media,* edited by H. d. Vries and S. Weber, 198–215. Stanford: Stanford University Press, 2001.

Schuyler, Philip. "Music and Tradition in Yemen." *Asian Music* 22, no. 1 (1990–91): 51–71.

Sells, Michael. *Approaching the Qur'án: The Early Revelations.* Ashland, Ore.: White Cloud Press, 2002.

———. "The Qasidah and the West: Self-Reflective Stereotype and Critical Encounter." *Al-Arabiyyah* 20 (1987): 307–57.

Serjeant, Robert. *Prose and Poetry from Hadhramawt.* London: Taylor's Foreign Press, 1951.

———. "Société et gouvernement en Arabie du Sud." *Arabica* 14, no. 3 (1967): 284–97.

———. "Yāfiʿ, the Zaidīs, Āl-Bū Bakr b. Sālim and Others: Tribes and Sayyids." In *On Both Sides of the al-Mandab: Ethiopian, South-Arabic and Islamic Studies Presented to Oscar Lofgren,* 83–105. Stockholm: Svenska Forskningsinstituteti Istanbul, 1989.

———. "The Yemeni Poet al-Zubayri and His Polemic against the Zaydi imams." *Arabian Studies* 5 (1979): 87–130.

Shāmī, H. E. Aḥmad. "Yemeni Literature in Ḥajjah Prisons." *Arabian Studies* 2 (1975): 43–60.

Shannon, Jonathan H. "Emotion, Performance, and Temporality in Arab Music: Reflections on *Tarab.*" *Cultural Anthropology* 18, no. 1 (2003): 72–98.

El-Shawan, Salwa C. "Some Aspects of the Cassette Industry in Egypt." *The World of Music* 24, no. 2 (1987): 32–45.

al-Shawkānī, Muḥammad Bin ʿAlī. *Adab al-Ṭalab wa Mashhā al-Adab.* Edited by A. Y. al-Surayhi. Sanaa: Maktabat al-Irshād, 1998 [1834].

Sherzer, Joel. *Verbal Art in San Blas.* New York: Cambridge University Press, 1990.

Shryock, Andrew. *Nationalism and the Genealogical Imagination: Oral History and Textual Authority in Tribal Jordan.* Berkeley: University of California Press, 1997.

Silverstein, Michael. "Indexical Order and the Dialectics of Sociolinguistic Life." In *SALSA III: Proceedings of the Third Annual Symposium about Language and Society, April 1995,* 293–94 (Austin: University of Texas, 1996).

Silverstein, Michael, and Greg Urban. *Natural Histories of Discourse.* Chicago: University of Chicago Press, 1996.

Socin, Albert. *Diwan aus Centralarabien.* Leipzig: B. G. Teubner, 1901.

Somekh, Sasson. "The Neo-Classical Arabic Poets." In *Modern Arabic Literature: The Cambridge History of Literature,* edited by M. M. Badawi, 36–81. Cambridge: Cambridge University Press, 1992.

Sowayan, Saad Abdullah. *Nabati Poetry: The Oral Poetry of Arabia.* Berkeley: University of California Press, 1985.

Sperl, Stefan, and Christopher Shackle. "Introduction." In *Qasida Po-*

etry in Islamic Asia and Africa, edited by S. Sperl and C. Shackle, 1–62. New York: E. J. Brill, 1996.

Spitulnik, Debra. "The Social Circulation of Media Discourse and the Mediation of Communities." *Journal of Linguistic Anthropology* 6, no. 2 (1996): 161–87.

Sreberny-Mohammadi, Annabelle, and Ali Mohammadi. *Small Media, Big Revolution: Communication, Culture, and the Iranian Revolution.* Minneapolis: University of Minnesota Press, 1994.

Starrett, Gregory. *Putting Islam to Work: Education, Politics, and Religious Transformation in Egypt.* Berkeley: University of California Press, 1998

———. "Violence and the Rhetoric of Images." *Cultural Anthropology* 18, no. 3 (2003): 398–428.

Stetkevych, Jaroslav. "The Arabic Lyrical Phenomenon in Context." *Journal of Arabic Literature* 6 (1975): 57–77.

Stetkevych, Suzanne Pinckney. *The Mute Immortals Speak: Pre-Islamic Poetry and the Poetics of Ritual, Myth and Poetics.* Ithaca, N.Y.: Cornell University Press, 1993.

———. "Structuralist Interpretations of Pre-Islamic Poetry: Critique and New Directions." *Journal of Near Eastern Studies* 42 (1983): 85–107.

Stookey, Robert W. *South Yemen: A Marxist Republic in Arabia.* Boulder: Westview Press, 1982.

Sulaīmān, Karāma Muḥammad. *al-Tarbiyyah wa-l-Taʿlīm fī al-Shaṭr al-Janūbī min al-Yaman.* 2 vols. Sanaa: Markaz li-l-Dirāsāt wa-l-Buḥūh al-Yamanī, 1994.

Ṣūrī, Khāled. *Khalīl Muḥammad Khalīl.* Aden: Dār al-Hamdānī, 1984.

Suyūṭī, ʿAbd al-Raḥman. *al-Muzhir fī ʿUlūm al-Lughah w-Anwāʿihī.* Cairo: Dār Iḥyāʾ al-Kutub al-ʿArabiyyah, 1971.

Taminian, Lucine. "Persuading the Monarchs: Poetry and Politics in Yemen, 1920–1950." In *Le Yémen Contemporain,* edited by R. Leveau, F. Mermier, and U. Steinbach, 203–19. Paris: Éditions Karthala, 1999.

———. "Playing with Words: The Ethnography of Poetic Genres in Yemen." Doctoral dissertation, Department of Anthropology, University of Michigan, Ann Arbor, 2000.

Tannen, Deborah. "The Oral/Literate Continuum in Discourse." In *Spoken and Written Language: Exploring Orality and Literacy,* edited by D. Tannen, 1–16. Norwood, N.J.: Ablex, 1982.

al-Thaʿlabī, Aḥmad Bin Muḥammad. *ʿArāʾis al-Majālis.* Beirut, n.d.

Turāth Shaʿbī Khālid: Shāʾif al-Khāledī. Edited by the staff of *Ṣum Bum* magazine. Aden: University of Aden, 1999.

Tyler, Stephen. *The Unspeakable: Discourse, Dialogue and Rhetoric in the Postmodern World.* Madison: University of Wisconsin Press, 1987.

Urban, Greg. *Metaphysical Community: The Interplay of the Senses and the Intellect.* Austin: University of Texas Press, 1996.

Vanhove, Martine. "Notes on the Arabic Dialectal Area of Yafiʿ, (Yemen)." *Proceedings of the Seminar for Arabian Studies* 25 (1995): 141–52.

Wagner, E. "Munāẓara." In *Encyclopedia of Islam.* Vol. 7, pp. 565–68. Leiden: E. J. Brill, 1993 [1954].

Warner, Michael. *The Letters of the Republic: Publication and the Public Sphere in Eighteenth-Century America.* Cambridge, Mass.: Harvard University Press, 1990.

———. "Publics and Counterpublics." *Public Culture* 14, no. 1 (2002): 49–90.

al-Wāsiʿī, ʿAbd al-Wāsiʿ Bin Yahyā. *Taʾrīkh al-Yaman.* Cairo: al-Maṭbaʿah Salafiyyah wa Maktabatuhā, 1927.

Weir, Shelagh. *A Tribal Order: Politics and Law in the Mountains of Yemen.* Austin: Texas University Press, 2006.

Whallon, W. *Formula, Character, and Context: Studies in Homeric, Old English, and Old Testament Poetry.* Cambridge, Mass.: Harvard University Press, 1969.

Whorf, Benjamin. "The Relation of Habitual Thought and Behavior to Language." In *High Points in Anthropology,* edited by P. Bohannan and M. Glazer, 149–71. New York: Knopf, 1988 [1939].

Williams, Raymond. *Marxism and Literature.* Oxford: Oxford University Press, 1977.

Yammine, H. "Correspondence entre la musique tribale et la musique citadine (Sanaʿa) dans la région des hauts plateaux yéménites." In

Le chant arabo-andalou, edited by N. Marouf, 119–28. Paris: L'Harmattan, 1995.

"Yemeni President Confers with Opposition as It Steps Up Campaign against Detention of Activists." *Mideast Mirror*, August 19, 1997.

Zayd, Nāṣer Ḥāmid Abū. *Mafhūm al-Naṣṣ: Dirāsah fī 'Ulūm al-Qur'ān*. Cairo: al-Hay'at al-Miṣriyyat al-'Āmah li-l-Kitāb, 1990.

Zwettler, Michael. *The Oral Tradition of Classical Arabic Poetry: Its Character and Implications*. Columbus: Ohio State University Press, 1978.

Index

Note: Italicized numbers refer to illustrations.

'Abdalī, Aḥmad Bin Faḍl ("al-Qumandān"), 196n13, 200, 232, 270n5, 401, 436n28
'Abd al-Nāṣer, Gamāl, 82, 252
'Abd al-Nāṣer, Ḥusaīn, 253, 432n6; adaptations made by, 317–318, 320; biographical sketch of, 241–245, 388; cassette jackets featuring, 258, 309–314, *310,* 333; cassette 1 of series of, 390–391; cassette 2 of series of, 391–392; cassette 7/8 of series of, 392–397, 408, 410, 415, 434n14, 468–472; cassette 25 of series of, 408–410, 420; cassette 37 of series of, 174, 410; cassette 39 of series of, 410–411; cassette 46 of series of, 413; cassette 52 of series of, 414, 420–422; cassette 54 of series of, 439n40; cassette 61 of series of, 417–419; cassette 73 of series of, 422–423; cassette 99 of series of, 318, 376n19, 377n23, 424, 432n5; cassette series sung by, 174, 241, 244, 245, 259–60, 265–266, 342n37, 373n2, 376n14, 385, 387–390, 405, 407, 420, 428, 432n6; as disdaining profits from sale of his cassettes, 377n21; Khāledī's collaborations with, 55, 71–72, 265–66, 287, 372; meeting of poets associated with, with government leaders, 130n45; number of cassettes produced by, 244; number of poets on cassette series of, 51, 55, 244; political significance of folk songs of, 245, 388–389, 452; on Qaīfī's identity, 381–382, 386–387; style used by, 307; Ṣunbaḥī's collaborations with, 71, 265, 391–392
Abū 'Alī Ibn Sīnā, 356
Abu Dhabi (place), 244, 277n50
Abū Ḥāfeẓ. *See* Sulaīmānī, Yahyā 'Alī al-
Abu-Lughod, Janet, 205n64
Abu-Lughod, Lila, 339n15
Abū Lōzah. *See* Khāledī, Shāyef Muḥammad al-
Abū Qaīs. *See* 'Ulafī, 'Abdallah "Abū Qaīs" al- (al-Ḥāshedī)
Abū Saqr. *See* Ṣunbaḥī, Aḥmad Muḥammad al-
Abū Zaīd. *See* Qaīfī, Aḥmad al-

HARVARD MIDDLE EASTERN MONOGRAPHS

1. *Syria: Development and Monetary Policy,* by Edmund Y. Asfour. 1959.
2. *The History of Modern Iran: An Interpretation,* by Joseph M. Upton. 1960.
3. *Contributions to Arabic Linguistics,* Charles A. Ferguson, Editor. 1960.
4. *Pan-Arabism and Labor,* by Willard A. Beling. 1960.
5. *The Industrialization of Iraq,* by Kathleen M. Langley. 1961.
6. *Buarij: Portrait of a Lebanese Muslim Village,* by Anne H. Fuller. 1961.
7. *Ottoman Egypt in the Eighteenth Century,* Stanford J. Shaw, Editor and Translator. 1962.
8. *Child Rearing in Lebanon,* by Edwin Terry Prothro. 1961.
9. *North Africa's French Legacy: 1954-1962,* by David C. Gordon. 1962.
10. *Communal Dialects in Baghdad,* by Haim Blanc. 1964.
11. *Ottoman Egypt in the Age of the French Revolution,* Translated with Introduction and Notes by Stanford J. Shaw. 1964.
12. *The Economy of Morocco: 1912-1962,* by Charles F. Stewart. 1964.
13. *The Economy of the Israeli Kibbutz,* by Eliyahu Kanovsky. 1966.
14. *The Syrian Social Nationalist Party: An Ideological Analysis,* by Labib Zuwiyya Yamak. 1966.
15. *The Practical Visions of Ya'qub Sanu',* by Irene L. Gendizier. 1966.
16. *The Surest Path: The Political Treatise of a Nineteenth-Century Muslim Statesman,* by Leon Carl Brown. 1967.
17. *High-Level Manpower in Economic Development: The Turkish Case,* by Richard D. Robinson. 1967.
18. *Rebirth of a Nation: The Origins and Rise of Moroccan Nationalism, 1912-1944,* by John P. Halsted. 1967.
19. *Women of Algeria: An Essay on Change,* by David C. Gordon. 1968.